ADVANCING SOCIAL RIGHTS IN CANADA

ADVANCING SOCIAL RIGHTS IN CANADA

edited by
MARTHA JACKMAN & BRUCE PORTER

IRWIN LAW

Advancing Social Rights in Canada

Published in 2014 by

Irwin Law Inc.
14 Duncan Street
Suite 206
Toronto, ON
M5H 3G8

www.irwinlaw.com

ISBN: 978-1-55221-374-2
e-book ISBN: 978-1-55221-375-9

Library and Archives Canada Cataloguing in Publication

Advancing social rights in Canada / edited by Martha Jackman, Bruce Porter.

Includes bibliographical references.
Issued in print and electronic formats.

ISBN 978-1-55221-374-2 (pbk.).—ISBN 978-1-55221-375-9 (pdf)

1. Human rights—Canada. 2. Social rights—Canada. I. Jackman, Martha, editor II. Porter, Bruce, 1952–, editor

KE4381.5.A77 2014	342.7108'5	C2014-904162-4
KF4483.C5A38 2014		C2014-904163-2

The publisher acknowledges the financial support of the Government of Canada through the Canada Book Fund for its publishing activities.

We acknowledge the assistance of the OMDC Book Fund, an initiative of Ontario Media Development Corporation.

Printed and bound by CPI Group (UK) Ltd, Croydon, CR0 4YY

1 2 3 4 5 18 17 16 15 14

TABLE OF CONTENTS

INTRODUCTION
ADVANCING SOCIAL RIGHTS IN CANADA*

BRUCE PORTER† AND MARTHA JACKMAN‡

A. THE HUMAN RIGHTS CRISIS IN CANADA

A book that purports to discuss advancing social rights in Canada in 2014 may be viewed by some as an exercise in denial. Thirty years into Canada's post-*Charter* democracy, growing economic inequality and violations of social rights, disproportionately experienced by Aboriginal people, sole-support mothers and their children, people with disabilities, racialized groups and newcomers, represent egregious human rights failures that call into question our collective commitment to what have long been understood as definitional values. As former NDP leader Jack Layton observed:

> Canadians, overwhelmingly, believe in justice and equality. These are values we trust, and we want to bring them to life in our communities.

* We wish to acknowledge and thank the Social Sciences and Humanities Research Council of Canada (SSHRC) Community-University Research Alliance (CURA) Program for its generous funding support, Andrei Ilas for his invaluable editorial assistance, the many student research assistants from the participating universities for their important contributions, and the University of Ottawa Faculty of Law for its ongoing support for the CURA project and for hosting the symposium which led to this book.

† Bruce Porter, Executive Director, Social Rights Advocacy Centre and Co-Director (Community) of the SSHRC-CURA Research Project "Reconceiving Human Rights Practice," online: www.socialrightscura.ca.

‡ Martha Jackman, Professor, Faculty of Law, French Common Law Program, University of Ottawa and Co-Director (Academic) of the SSHRC-CURA Research Project "Reconceiving Human Rights Practice," online: www.socialrightscura.ca.

> Our vision of the just society forms the core of our sense of identity *as Canadians*. But rejecting poverty in our national heart hasn't stopped poverty from festering. Our society enters this new millennium with open wounds and a poverty rate that stands among the worst in the developed world.[1]

In recent years, civil society and Aboriginal organizations in Canada have consistently identified poverty, food insecurity, inadequate housing, and lack of access to health care, education, and decent work as fundamental violations of human rights.[2] UN human rights bodies have also expressed "grave concern" about the extent and systemic impact of homelessness, hunger, and poverty in Canada and have called for immediate and concerted federal and provincial/territorial government action to address these issues.[3] It is not, as the Canadian government likes to suggest, that the UN mistakenly believes that hunger and homelessness are more extreme in Canada than in struggling economies in Africa or Asia.[4] These harms are seen as a human rights crisis in Canada because they are completely

---

1 Jack Layton, "Foreword to the First Edition" in Dennis Raphael, *Poverty in Canada*, 2d ed (Toronto: Canadian Scholars' Press, 2011) at xii.

2 See, for example, Ligue des droits et libertés, *Rapport sur l'état des droits humains au Québec et au Canada* (2013), online: LDL http://liguedesdroits.ca; Bruce Porter & Leilani Farha, "Reaffirming Canada's Commitments to Human Rights" in *Poverty and Parliament* (Spring 2009), online: Social Rights in Canada CURA www.socialrightscura.ca; Leilani Farha, Alex Neve, & Bruce Porter, "The Universal Periodic Review of Canada: February 2009: An Overview of a Select Number of Canadian NGO Concerns and Recommendations" (January 2009), online: Social Rights in Canada CURA www.socialrightscura.ca; Assembly of First Nations, *Submission to the United Nations Human Rights Council Universal Periodic Review of Canada's Human Rights Obligations* (October 2012), online: Universal Periodic Review www.upr-info.org; Senate, Subcommittee on Cities of the Standing Senate Committee on Social Affairs, Science and Technology, *In from the Margins: A Call to Action on Poverty, Housing and Homelessness* (December 2009) (Chair: Hon Art Eggleton, PC at 15: "[w]hether the subject was poverty, housing or homelessness, many witnesses described the problems in terms of rights denied"); Canadian Human Rights Act Review Panel, *Promoting Equality: A New Vision* (Ottawa: Department of Justice, 2000) (Chair: Hon GV LaForest at 106: "[d]uring our consultations we heard more about poverty than any other single issue."

3 Bruce Porter & Martha Jackman, *International Human Rights and Strategies to Address Homelessness and Poverty in Canada: Making the Connection*, Ottawa Faculty of Law Working Paper No 2013-09, online: CURA http://socialrightscura.ca at 47–54. See also Bruce Porter's discussion in Chapter 1.

4 *House of Commons Debates*, 41st Parl, 1st Sess, No 127 (18 May 2012) at 1155 (Deepak Obhrai).

unnecessary in a country experiencing unprecedented affluence and economic prosperity. Rather they are the result of governmental choice and symptomatic of a serious retrogression from the respect for social rights norms that the UN had come to expect of postwar Canada.[5]

At one time ranked by the international community as a leading voice for human rights and a model for emerging constitutional democracies, Canada is now more often viewed as shamelessly pursuing environmentally unsustainable development within and beyond its own borders in ways that primarily benefit the most affluent, exploit vulnerable groups, damage ecologies, disinherit Indigenous communities, and exacerbate global and domestic inequality.[6] In response to increasing criticism of Canada's human rights and environmental record at home and abroad, the Canadian government has staged a dramatic retreat from Canada's earlier engagement with international human rights norms and accountability mechanisms.[7] Instead of being an active proponent of advances in international human rights at the UN, as it had been in earlier years, Canada has resisted recent progressive reforms in the field of social rights. In particular, Canada has failed to support the development of, and then refused to ratify, new complaints procedures that would empower those whose social rights have been violated in Canada to seek international adjudication of their claims.[8]

---

5 United Nations Human Rights Council, *Report of the Special Rapporteur on the Right to Food, Olivier De Schutter, Addendum, Mission to Canada*, UNHRCOR, 22nd Sess, A/HRC/22/50/Add.1, (2012), online: OHCHR www.ohchr.org [*Report of the Special Rapporteur on the Right to Food*].

6 "International Human Rights: Canada's Role Dwindling" *The Toronto Star* (4 April 2011); Les Whittington, "Canadian Mining Firms Worst for Environment, Rights: Report" *The Toronto Star* (19 October 2010); House of Commons, Standing Committee on Foreign Affairs and International Trade, *Mining in Developing Countries and Corporate Responsibility* (2005) (Chair: Bernard Patry), online: Parliament of Canada www.parl.gc.ca; Alain Deneault & William Sacher, *Imperial Canada Inc: Legal Haven of Choice for the World's Mining Industries* (Vancouver: Talonbooks, 2012).

7 Alex Neve & Béatrice Vaugrante, "Op-Ed: Time for a Human-Rights Reboot" *Ottawa Citizen* (29 December 2013); John E Trent, "The United Nations and Canada: What Canada Has Done and Should Be Doing at the UN" (2013), online: Academic Council on the United Nations System http://acuns.org.

8 Canada has refused to ratify any of the three complaints procedures that include social rights: *Optional Protocol to the International Covenant on Economic, Social and Cultural Rights*, GA Res 63/117, UNGAOR, 63d Sess, Supp No 49, UN Doc A/RES/63/117, (2008) [*OP-ICESCR*]; *Optional Protocol to the Convention on the Rights of Persons with Disabilities*, GA Res 61/106, UNGAOR, 61st Sess, UN Doc A/RES/61/106, (2006); and *Optional Protocol to the Convention on the Rights of the Child on a Communications Procedure*, UNHRCOR, 17th Sess, UN Doc A/HRC/RES/17/18, (2011). On Canada's

As the current Canadian government would have it, serious human rights violations only occur in other countries, and Canada needs no lessons from the UN in this sphere.[9]

When UN human rights bodies have pointed to the estimated 150,000–300,000 people who are homeless across Canada[10] and the close to a million adults and children relying on food banks to provide necessary supplements to inadequate diets[11] — phenomena which would have been unimaginable when Canada ratified the *International Covenant on Economic, Social and Cultural Rights*[12] along with the *International Covenant on Civil and Political Rights*[13] in 1976[14] — the federal government has insisted that such concerns are both misplaced and politically biased.[15] When the UN Special Rapporteur on the Right to Food conducted a mission to Canada in 2013, voicing distress about the extent of hunger in so affluent a country and questioning the absence of a national food security strategy or legal protection for the right to food, Canada's response was to launch a personal

---

role in opposing development of a complaints procedure for social rights, see Bruce Porter, "The Reasonableness of Article 8(4): Adjudicating Claims from the Margins" (2009) 27:1 Nordic Journal of Human Rights 39 at 44–47.

9 Laura Payton, "UN Official Sparks Debate over Canadian Food Security" *CBC News* (16 May 2012), online: CBC News www.cbc.ca.

10 United Nations Human Rights Council, *Report of the Special Rapporteur on Adequate Housing as a Component of the Right to an Adequate Standard of Living, and on the Right to Non-discrimination in This Context, Miloon Kothari — Addendum — Mission to Canada* (October 2007), UNHRCOR, 10th Sess, UN Doc A/HRC/10/7/Add.3, (2009) at para 54, online: OHCHR www2.ohchr.org. Current estimates suggest that there are 150,000 individuals using shelters in Canada annually and that there are three times as many "hidden homeless" as the number living in shelters or unsheltered. Stephen Gaetz et al, *The State of Homelessness in Canada 2013* (Toronto: Canadian Homelessness Research Network, 2013) at 21–24.

11 *Report to the Special Rapporteur on the Right to Food*, above note 5 at para 7.

12 *International Covenant on Economic, Social and Cultural Rights*, 16 December 1966, 993 UNTS 3, Can TS 1976 No 46 (entered into force 3 January 1976, accession by Canada 19 May 1976) [*ICESCR*].

13 *International Covenant on Civil and Political Rights*, 19 December 1966, 999 UNTS 171, Can TS 1976 No 47 (entered into force 23 March 1976, accession by Canada 19 May 1976) [*ICCPR*].

14 Bruce Porter, "ReWriting the *Charter* at 20 or Reading It Right: The Challenge of Poverty and Homelessness in Canada" in Wesley Cragg & Christine Koggel, eds, *Contemporary Moral Issues*, 5th ed (Toronto: McGraw-Hill Ryerson, 2005) 373.

15 Government of Canada, *Interactive Dialogue with the Special Rapporteur on the Right to Adequate Housing, UN Human Rights Council OR, 10th Sess, Response to the Addendum Report on Canada* (9 March 2009) online: Social Rights in Canada CURA http://socialrightscura.ca.

and very undiplomatic attack. Leading members of the government characterized the special rapporteur as a meddling academic who was wasting UN funds by investigating Canada when he could have been somewhere with real hunger and food issues.[16] When the UN Committee on the Rights of the Child commented negatively on Canada's human rights performance with respect to growing poverty among Aboriginal, immigrant, and disabled children, the Canadian government dismissed these concerns as politically motivated. The justification in that case: one of the committee experts was of Syrian origin, a country with its own record of serious human rights violations.[17] This approach, accurately described by the special rapporteur as a new Canadian self-righteousness,[18] is deeply disturbing, not least because it undermines Canada's adherence to human rights and sustainable development as important and viable objects of international co-operation and respect.

B. LOOKING BACK: THE HISTORIC SOCIAL RIGHTS PARADIGM IN CANADA

Those seeking to advance social rights in Canada today must not only remind people of what has been lost but also support a human rights paradigm that is larger than one particular government or decade of Canadian political history. The problems associated with growing economic inequality in an era of neo-liberalism are not unique to Canada. However, the unwillingness of Canadian governments and courts to address the resulting violations of social rights is surprising, at least to international observers, in light of Canada's postwar image and self-identity. Unlike its neighbour to the south, by ratifying the *ICESCR* in 1976, Canada formally acknowledged that adequate food, housing, health care, education, social security, and just and favourable conditions of work were not simply laudable goals of social policy. These were recognized as fundamental human rights, requiring progressive implementation to the maximum of available resources by all

16 Open Letter from human rights organizations and allied individuals to Prime Minister Stephen Harper concerning the Government of Canada's treatment of the United Nations human rights Special Rapporteur on the right to food (30 May 2012), online: Social Rights Advocacy Centre www.socialrights.ca.

17 *House of Commons Debates*, 41st Parl, 1st Sess, No 178 (27 September 2012) at 1500 (Bob Dechert).

18 Sarah Schmidt, "UN Envoy Blasts Canada for 'Self-Righteous' Attitude over Hunger, Poverty" *Postmedia News* (15 May 2012).

appropriate means and demanding access to justice and effective remedies for rights claimants when governments fail to meet their obligations.[19]

While social rights in the 1970s were not always implemented in legislation or programs, what is striking in retrospect is the degree to which they were referred to as core "Canadian values." In a period when Canada defined itself largely in relation to the US, Canada's ratification of the *ICESCR* and its recognition of the positive role governments must play in protecting rights was seen as part of Canada's national identity. Former prime minister Pierre Trudeau had, for instance, written of the importance of economic and social rights as a young academic,[20] and his campaign for the "just society" capitalized on widespread public acceptance of social justice as a central component of Canadians' self-identity. As Trudeau reaffirmed as prime minister in June of 1968, "[M]ost people take it for granted that every Canadian is assured a reasonable standard of living. Unfortunately, that is not the case . . . . The Just Society will be one in which all of our people will have the means and the motivation to participate."[21]

Parallel to, and nurtured by, Canada's engagement with international human rights, the 1970s saw the emergence of vibrant domestic human rights movements.[22] Though influenced by the American civil rights campaign, they were grounded in a different rights paradigm than the one that predominated in the US. In both Quebec and the rest of Canada, domestic human rights protections were linked to a commitment to internationalism and to a more comprehensive conception of human rights. Cold war dichotomies, including the rigid distinction drawn between social and economic *versus* civil and political rights, were less firmly entrenched in 1970s Canada than in the US.[23] Social rights were particularly important in Quebec. With the adoption of its new *Charter of Human Rights and Freedoms*[24] in 1976, Quebec provided explicit legal recognition for social rights, including

19 *ICESCR*, above note 12.

20 Pierre Trudeau, "Economic Rights" (1961) 8 McGill LJ 122 at 125.

21 Cited in Ron Graham, ed, *The Essential Trudeau* (Toronto: McLelland & Stewart, 1998) at 16–20.

22 Dominique Clément, Will Silver, & Daniel Trottier, *The Evolution of Human Rights in Canada* (2012), online: Canadian Human Rights Commission www.chrc-ccdp.ca [*The Evolution of Human Rights in Canada*].

23 *Ibid* at 5 and 17; Chaviva Hosek, "Women and Constitutional Process" in Keith Banting & Richard Simeon, eds, *And No One Cheered: Federalism, Democracy & the Constitution Act* (Toronto: Methuen Publications, 1983) 280; Cynthia Soohoo, Catherine Albisa, & Martha F Davis, *Bringing Human Rights Home: A History of Human Rights in the United States* (Westport, CT: Praeger, 2008).

24 *Charter of Human Rights and Freedoms*, RSQ, c C-12 [Quebec *Charter*].

to free public education, an "acceptable standard of living," and a healthful environment in which biodiversity is preserved. The Quebec *Charter* was, as Pierre Bosset and Lucie Lamarche point out, strongly influenced by the international human rights context: "Le Québec, qui connaît sa révolution tranquille et développe l'État social, tient alors à s'inscrire dans la mouvance d'un droit international qui, officiellement, reconnait ces droits . . . ."[25]

New social movements across Canada increasingly articulated struggles for justice and equality as human rights struggles. In 1981, people with disabilities mobilized around the International Year of Persons with Disabilities and the celebrated "Obstacles" report,[26] issued by an all-party House of Commons Committee — an early expression of the "social model of disability" that was adopted more than two decades later in the UN *Convention on the Rights of Persons with Disabilities*.[27] Emerging rights-based approaches to social justice fed directly into debates about the wording and content of rights in the proposed new *Canadian Charter of Rights and Freedoms*.[28] Disability rights organizations insisted that mental and physical disabilities be added to the list of prohibited grounds of discrimination in section 15 of the new *Charter*.[29] Aboriginal organizations demanded that the constitutional debates not ignore the desperate conditions on reserves and called for positive recognition of treaty rights, the right to self-determination, and control over resources and development.[30] For their part, women's organizations orchestrated a historic cross-country campaign for changes to the heading

25 Pierre Bosset & Lucie Lamarche, "Introduction: Donner droit de cité aux droits économiques, sociaux et culturels" in Pierre Bosset & Lucie Lamarche, eds, *Droit de cité pour les droits économiques, sociaux et culturels : La Charte québécoise en chantier* (Cowansville: Éditions Yvon Blais, 2011) 1 at 3.

26 House of Commons, Special Parliamentary Committee on the Disabled and the Handicapped, *Obstacles*, 32nd Parl, 1st Sess (February 1981).

27 *Convention on the Rights of Persons with Disabilities*, GA Res 61/106, UNGAOR, 61st Sess, Supp No 49, UN Doc A/61/611, (2007) [*CRPD*].

28 Gwen Brodsky & Shelagh Day, *Canadian Charter Equality Rights for Women: One Step Forward or Two Steps Back* (Ottawa: Canadian Advisory Council on the Status of Women, 1989) at 15–17; Part I of the *Constitution Act, 1982*, being Schedule B to the *Canada Act 1982* (UK), 1982, c 11 [*Charter*].

29 Yvonne Peters, "From Charity to Equality: Canadians with Disabilities Take Their Rightful Place in Canada's Constitution" in Deborah Stienstra & Aileen Wight-Felske, eds, *Making Equality: History of Advocacy and Persons with Disabilities in Canada* (Concord, ON: Captus Press, 2003) 119 [*Making Equality*].

30 *The Evolution of Human Rights in Canada*, above note 22 at 31; Douglas E Saunders, "The Indian Lobby" in Banting & Simeon, eds, *And No One Cheered*, above note 23, 301.

and wording of section 15,[31] in order to put an end to the formal, negative rights equality paradigm that had been adopted by the courts under the *Canadian Bill of Rights*.[32] Demanding the inclusion of a right to the "equal protection and equal benefit of the law" in section 15, they sought to ensure that the *Charter* would directly engage with government obligations to institute programs and benefits to address historic patterns of exclusion and disadvantage.[33]

Social movements adopting new rights-based approaches were ultimately successful in transforming the architecture of equality under the new *Charter*. Then Justice Minister Jean Chrétien succumbed to the pressure from women's groups and endorsed the proposed changes to section 15, as he put it, "to stress the positive nature of this important part of the *Charter*."[34] Moreover, Canada became the first democracy to include disability as a constitutionally prohibited ground of discrimination. This advance was critical from a social rights perspective because a negative rights framework is so clearly inadequate in relation to disability discrimination, which frequently results from failures of law and policy to address unique circumstances, needs, and capabilities and which often requires positive measures to ensure real, instead of merely formal, equality.[35] Yvonne Peters, one of the contributors to this book and a key advocate for disability rights at the time, has observed that the constitutional recognition of disability was

> a watershed event that occurred at a time when people with disabilities were just beginning to construct a new vision and analysis of the disabil-

---

31 Penny Kome, *The Taking of Twenty-Eight: Women Challenge the Constitution* (Toronto: Women's Press, 1983) at 34–36; Hosek, "Women and Constitutional Process," above note 23.

32 *Canadian Bill of Rights*, SC 1960, c 44.

33 Mary Eberts, "The Equality Provision of the *Canadian Charter of Rights and Freedoms* and Government Institutions" in Claire Beckton & A Wayne MacKay, Research Coordinators, *The Courts and the* Charter (Ottawa: Minister of Supply and Services Canada, 1985) 133; Francine Fournier, "Égalité et droits à l'égalité" in Lynn Smith et al, eds, *Righting the Balance: Canada's New Equality Rights* (Saskatoon: Canadian Human Rights Reporter, 1986) 25; Bruce Porter, "Expectations of Equality" (2006) 33 Sup Ct L Rev (2d) 23 [Porter, "Expectations of Equality"].

34 Statement by the Honourable Jean Chrétien, Minister of Justice, to the Special Joint Committee on the Constitution (12 January 1981) (Government of Manitoba Archives).

35 Yvonne Peters, *Twenty Years of Litigating for Disability Equality Rights: Has It Made a Difference?* (Winnipeg: Council of Canadians with Disabilities, 2004); Dianne Pothier, "Legal Development in the Supreme Court of Canada Regarding Disability" in Dianne Pothier & Richard Devlin, eds, *Critical Disability Theory: Essays in Philosophy, Politics, Policy and Law* (Vancouver: UBC Press, 2006) 304. See the discussion in Chapter 7.

> ity experience . . . . The disability rights movement rejected the medical model of disability, and argued that it was social barriers and prejudices that created disabilities . . . . This shift to a rights-based analysis therefore represents a profound and decisive turning point in the history of people with disabilities.[36]

Substantive equality, as articulated by women's organizations, the disability rights movement, and other equality-seeking groups in Canada, was and remains a social rights paradigm. It emphasizes positive rights, social inclusion, a hybrid of group/individual rights, and the necessity of structural change and historical transformation to achieve the realization of rights over time. The equality/social rights paradigm is remedial in its focus — defined by the broad purposes of human rights, rather than by restorative or compensatory justice in relation to a single individual.[37] From the outset, it was nurtured by jurisprudence developed under provincial and federal human rights legislation and by the work of newly created national and provincial human rights institutions across the country.[38] In landmark cases, such as *Action Travail des femmes v CNR*,[39] equality advocates insisted upon, and Canadian courts and tribunals recognized, the necessity of placing obligations on both governments and private actors to address systemic inequality through positive action, including social programs, measures to address the needs of people with disabilities, and "employment equity" to combat systemic inequality in the workplace. Building on this social rights paradigm, the *Charter* was expected to ensure that access to housing, health care, nutrition, jobs, child care, and social assistance for those in need would be accorded as much importance as negative guarantees of freedom from unreasonable government interference.[40]

Equality-seeking groups mobilized and won support for an approach to constitutional rights centred on a commitment to substantive equality as a framework for proactively addressing what were seen as the critical

---

36 Yvonne Peters, "From Charity to Equality: Canadians with Disabilities Take Their Rightful Place in Canada's Constitution" in *Making Equality*, above note 29, 122.

37 Colleen Sheppard, "Recognition of the Disadvantaging of Women: The Promise of *Andrews v. Law Society of British Columbia*" (1989) 35 McGill LJ 207; *Andrews v Law Society of British Columbia*, [1989] 1 SCR 143; Mary Eberts, "Section 15 Remedies for Systemic Inequality: You Can't Get There from Here" in Sheila McIntyre & Sanda Rogers, *Diminishing Returns: Inequality and the Canadian Charter of Rights and Freedoms* (Markham, ON: LexisNexis Butterworths, 2006) 389 [*Diminishing Returns*].

38 *The Evolution of Human Rights in Canada*, above note 22.

39 *CN v Canada (Canadian Human Rights Commission)*, [1987] 1 SCR 1114.

40 Porter, "Expectations of Equality," above note 33.

sources of inequality and exclusion in Canadian society: poverty, lack of access to appropriate housing, employment, education, and social programs. Barbara Cameron, another contributor to this book, accurately predicted in 1984 that the neo-liberal version of equality of opportunity would only mean that "equalization is downwards."[41] She emphasized that ensuring the "just and favourable conditions of work," to which Canada was committed under the *ICESCR*, required active government engagement in labour markets, through employment equity, affirmative action, and other positive measures.[42] Appearing before the Subcommittee on Equality Rights of the Standing Committee on Justice and Legal Affairs in 1985, two other contributors to this book, Gwen Brodsky and Shelagh Day, argued that the new constitutional right to equality demanded positive measures to protect social rights. Gwen Brodsky stated on behalf of the National Association of Women and the Law that "[u]nless the Government implements positive programs to remove barriers to equality it will be signaling tolerance of discrimination and indifference to the expectations of Canadian women."[43] Speaking for the Women's Legal Education and Action Fund (LEAF), Shelagh Day affirmed that the right to equality embodies "a fresh beginning" and a rejection of "[n]arrow interpretations or technical pathways that lead us away from what is really happening to the lives of Canadians and to the lives of Canadian women . . . ."[44]

Social rights were not seen as relying solely on *Charter* rights, however. They were supported by legislative and programmatic commitments in the areas of health care, education, housing, social security, and financial assistance for those in need, particularly through the mechanism of joint federal-provincial/territorial cost sharing agreements such as the *Canada Health Act*[45] and the *Canada Assistance Plan Act*.[46] The *CAP*, for example, created an entitlement to an adequate level of financial assistance for anyone in need, regardless of cause, in exchange for shared federal funding of provincial social assistance costs. The *CAP* requirement to provide an adequate level of social assistance was subject to judicial review for reason-

41 Barbara Cameron, "Labour Market Discrimination and Affirmative Action" in Jill McCalla Vickers, ed, *Taking Sex into Account: The Policy Consequences of Sexist Research* (Ottawa: Carleton University Press, 1984) 135.

42 *Ibid*.

43 House of Commons, Subcommittee on Equality Rights of the Standing Committee on Justice and Legal Affairs, *Minutes of Proceedings*, 33rd Parl 1st Sess, Vol 3 (17 April 1985) at 3:9, cited in Porter, "Expectations of Equality," above note 33 at 30–31.

44 *Ibid*.

45 *Canada Health Act*, RSC 1985, c C-6 [*CHA*].

46 *Canada Assistance Plan*, SC 1966-67, c 45 [*CAP*].

able compliance and to systemic (though not individual) remedy by courts.[47] Similarly, the *CHA* implemented five legally binding principles: public administration, comprehensiveness, universality, portability, and accessibility. These *CHA* conditions were understood and embraced as social rights principles, designed to guarantee access to health care based on need, rather than ability to pay, as a fundamental human right.[48] The commitment to implementing social rights through programmatic entitlements such as these was given concrete expression in section 36 of the *Constitution Act, 1982*, which entrenches an explicit undertaking by governments in Canada to "promote the well-being of Canadians and to provide essential public services of reasonable quality to all Canadians."[49] In its submissions to UN treaty monitoring bodies, the Canadian government has described the constitutional commitment in section 36 as a core element in the implementation of Canada's social rights obligations under international human rights law.[50]

Canada of the 1970s and 1980s was not a Camelot for social rights. While food banks and homelessness did not exist to the extent and in the same way as they do now, there were nevertheless serious violations of social rights during this period, particularly among Aboriginal communities, racialized groups, women, and LGBT communities. Still, what is striking, looking back, is the extent to which social rights values were accepted as definitional during that period. Commitments to social rights, under both international and domestic law, created the foundation for a distinctive

---

47 In *Finlay v Canada (Minister of Finance)*, [1986] 2 SCR 607, the Supreme Court determined that an affected individual had public interest standing to challenge provincial non-compliance with the adequacy requirements of *CAP*. Subsequently, in *Finlay v Canada (Minister of Finance)*, [1993] 1 SCR 1080 at para 81, the Court found that *CAP* "requires assistance to be provided in an amount that is compatible, or consistent, with an individual's basic requirements" but provides for some flexibility and for the recovery of overpayments.

48 Marie-Claude Prémont, *The Canada Health Act and the Future of Health Care Systems in Canada Discussion Paper No 4* (Saskatoon: Commission on the Future of Health Care in Canada, 2002); Martha Jackman, "Law as a Tool for Addressing Social Determinants of Health" in Nola Ries, Tracey Bailey, & Timothy Caulfield, eds, *Public Health Law and Policy in Canada*, 3d ed (Markham, ON: LexisNexis Canada, 2013) 91.

49 *Constitution Act, 1982*, being Schedule B to the *Canada Act 1982* (UK), 1982, c 11, s 36; See, generally, Martha Jackman & Bruce Porter, "Rights-Based Strategies to Address Homelessness and Poverty in Canada: The Constitutional Framework," Ottawa Faculty of Law Working Paper No 2013-10, online: CURA www.socialrightscura.ca.

50 Canadian Heritage, *Core Document Forming Part of the Reports of States Parties: Canada* (October 1997), online: Canadian Heritage www.pch.gc.ca. The document was submitted by Canada pursuant to HRI/CORE/1 sent to States parties by note verbale of the Secretary General, G/SO 221 (1) of 26 April 1991.

social rights paradigm to take root and flourish in post-*Charter* Canada. Today, commitments to a distinctive idea of substantive equality, linked to social rights and international human rights law, are still strong, or stronger at the community level, where disability rights, anti-poverty, food security, women's, and other groups in all parts of the country continue to embrace both social rights and the international nature of the human rights project.[51] Beyond that, however, there is far less evidence of any meaningful commitment to the distinctive Canadian social rights paradigm that was widely affirmed in the period leading up to, and immediately following, the adoption of the *Charter*. As Layton accurately described, widespread poverty, homelessness, and hunger amidst affluence have created an open wound in the Canadian body politic.[52]

C. THE *CHARTER* CRITICS AND THE JUSTICIABILITY OF SOCIAL RIGHTS

There was some indication in early *Charter* jurisprudence that a distinctive Canadian human rights paradigm inclusive of social rights might take root in the courts. In his 1986 decision in *R v Oakes*, Dickson CJ spoke eloquently of the values and principles that must guide *Charter* interpretation, including "respect for the inherent dignity of the human person, commitment to social justice and equality, accommodation of a wide variety of beliefs, respect for cultural and group identity, and faith in social and political institutions which enhance the participation of individuals and groups in society."[53] In 1989, in *Irwin Toy Ltd v Quebec (AG)*[54] the Supreme Court rejected a corporate challenge to a ban on children's advertising, emphasizing that the protection of vulnerable groups is a core value that must guide the interpretation of *Charter* rights, as well as the assessment of reasonable limits under section 1. The Court concluded in *Irwin Toy* that corporate-commercial economic rights were not included in section 7.[55] However, Dickson CJ was careful to distinguish these private property-related rights from the social

---

51 *Empty Words and Double Standards: Canada's Failure to Respect and Uphold International Human Rights. Joint Submission to the United Nations Human Rights Council in Relation to the May 2013 Universal Periodic Review of Canada* (Ottawa, October 2012), online: Social Rights in Canada CURA http://socialrightscura.ca; Bruce Porter, "Claiming Adjudicative Space: Social Rights, Equality and Citizenship" in Margot Young et al, eds, *Poverty: Rights, Social Citizenship, and Legal Activism* (Vancouver: UBC Press, 2007) 77.

52 Above note 1.

53 *R v Oakes*, [1986] 1 SCR 103 at 136.

54 [1989] 1 SCR 927 [*Irwin Toy*].

55 *Ibid* at 1003.

and economic rights "included in various international covenants, as rights to social security, equal pay for equal work, adequate food, clothing and shelter . . . ."[56] This latter category of rights, the Court cautioned, should not be excluded from the scope of section 7 at such an early stage of the *Charter*'s development.[57]

In retrospect we can also see the serious challenges facing the emergent social rights paradigm in Canada. While attracting a very high level of public support in all parts of the country, the enactment of the *Charter* was met with significant ambivalence and skepticism within some political, academic, and judicial circles. Many remained loyal to the Westminster tradition of parliamentary supremacy and were concerned about expanding the role of the courts.[58] When it came time to reconcile the two traditions of parliamentary sovereignty and constitutional supremacy, the traditional distinctions between civil and political rights on the one hand and social rights on the other provided a convenient, though misguided, way of limiting constitutional supremacy. Traditional civil and political rights, conceived as negative rights, were ascribed to the courts while social rights, conceived as positive rights, were deemed to fall within the exclusive purview of legislatures, engaging matters beyond the institutional legitimacy and competence of the courts.[59] Quoting from Oliver Wendell Holmes, for example, constitutional scholar Peter Hogg characterized social rights as "issues upon which elections are won and lost"[60] — an oft-repeated statement in Canadian social rights jurisprudence.

---

56 *Ibid.*

57 *Ibid.*

58 See, for example, Ronald I Cheffins & Patricia A Johnson, *The Revised Canadian Constitution: Politics as Law* (Toronto: McGraw-Hill Ryerson, 1986).

59 See, generally, David Robitaille, *Normativité, interprétation et justifications des droits économiques et sociaux : Les cas Québécois et Sud-Africain* (Brussels: Éditions Bruylant, 2011); Martha Jackman, "The Protection of Welfare Rights under the *Charter*" (1988) 20 Ottawa L Rev 257 at 330–37.

60 As Hogg expressed it:

> It has been suggested that 'security of the person' incudes the economic capacity to satisfy basic human needs . . . . The trouble with this argument is that it . . . involves a massive expansion of judicial review, since it would bring under judicial scrutiny all of the elements of the modern welfare state, including . . . of course, the level of public expenditures on social programmes. As Oliver Wendell Holmes would have pointed out, these are the issues upon which elections are won and lost; the judges need a clear mandate to enter that arena and s. 7 does not provide that clear mandate.

Peter Hogg, *Constitutional Law of Canada*, 4th ed (Scarborough, ON: Carswell, 1997) at 1073.

The problematic and now widely discredited distinction between justiciable civil and political rights and non-justiciable social rights has a number of adverse consequences for *Charter* interpretation, however. When they are conceived solely as negative rights, broadly framed guarantees, such as rights to life and security of the person, are whittled down to freedom from government interference and stripped of their social rights content. The effect is to disenfranchise disadvantaged groups from the protection of section 7 since, as the Supreme Court noted in *Irwin Toy*, "Vulnerable groups will claim the need for protection by the government whereas other groups and individuals will assert that the government should not intrude."[61] Moreover, a negative rights framework reduces section 15 — the very *Charter* section that was drafted to ensure substantive rather than formal equality for disadvantaged groups — to a guarantee of freedom simply from direct discrimination.[62] Finally, the remedial promise of section 24 is rendered illusory in relation to social rights if claims requiring positive action are deemed to be non-justiciable.

The bifurcation of positive and negative rights as a simplistic solution to the separation of powers has thus seriously undermined the inclusive paradigm of social rights for which women, people with disabilities, and other stakeholders fought. This approach has also been profoundly out of step with the growing international recognition of the interconnectedness and interdependence of all human rights.[63] When characterized as

---

61 *Irwin Toy*, above note 54 at 993. See, generally, Cara Wilkie & Meryl Zisman Gary, "Positive and Negative Rights under the *Charter*: Closing the Divide to Advance Equality" (2011) 30 Windsor Rev Legal Soc Issues 37; David Wiseman, "Taking Competence Seriously" in Young et al, eds, above note 51, 263; David Wiseman, "The *Charter* and Poverty: Beyond Injusticiability" (2001) 51 UTLJ 425.

62 Margot Young, "Blissed Out: Section 15 at Twenty" in *Diminishing Returns*, above note 37, 45; Fay Faraday, Margaret Denike, & M Kate Stephenson, eds, *Making Equality Rights Real: Securing Substantive Equality under the Charter* (Toronto: Irwin Law, 2006); Sharon Donna McIvor, "Aboriginal Women Unmasked: Using Equality Litigation to Advance Women's Rights" (2004) 16 CJWL 106 at 111; Gwen Brodsky & Shelagh Day, "Beyond the Social and Economic Rights Debate: Substantive Equality Speaks to Poverty (2002) 14 CJWL 185.

63 On interdependence of social rights and women's equality rights, see, for example, Leilani Farha, "Committee on the Elimination of Discrimination against Women: Women Claiming Economic, Social and Cultural Rights — The CEDAW Potential" in Malcolm Langford, ed, *Social Rights Jurisprudence: Emerging Trends in International and Comparative Law* (New York: Cambridge University Press, 2008) 553; Leilani Farha, Shelagh Day, & Marianne Mollman, "The Montreal Principles: Needed Clarity on Women's Right to Equal Enjoyment of Economic, Social and Cultural Rights" (2004) 22:3 Nordic Journal of Human Rights 345.

non-justiciable, and as matters to be relegated to legislatures and "resolved" by elections, social rights lose their legitimacy as rights claims and become no more than competing policy positions advocated by "interest groups" lacking in political power. The result, intentional or not, has too often been to banish those living in poverty and homelessness from access to justice and the equal protection and benefit of the *Charter.*

Unfortunately, the argument that courts should not engage with issues of social policy in response to *Charter* claims was made not only by the conservative right. It also found support in a parallel critique of rights discourse put forward by prominent voices within the social democratic left.[64] Among the leftist *Charter* critics, the concern was about vesting privileged and unelected judges with the power to review social policy and programs adopted by democratically elected and accountable legislatures. Like their conservative counterparts, these critics accepted that the dominant legal paradigm under the *Charter* would be individualistic and negative-rights oriented. On that basis they insisted that the pursuit of social justice through the courts would prove illusory and would distract social justice movements from more fruitful political avenues for seeking progressive change. Rather than insisting that the judicial system be reformed or transformed to realize the expectations inherent in the social rights paradigm put forward by women's and other equality-seeking groups, *Charter* critics tended to accept the *status quo*, pointing to negative legal outcomes in social rights cases as proof that rights-based approaches were misguided.

While the Canadian courts have been accused by some of undue *Charter* activism, nothing could be further from the truth insofar as the socio-economic rights claims of the poor and other disadvantaged groups are concerned. In response to the challenge of reconciling constitutional supremacy with parliamentary democracy, judicial culture in Canada has made a virtue out of deference to legislatures and Parliament on matters of social policy. There has been a widespread failure to acknowledge that, in many cases, such deference can amount to an abdication of judicial responsibility to ensure that the *Charter* provides adequate safeguards for the rights and interests of the most marginalized groups in Canadian society. Those attempting to litigate social rights claims have been subject to criticism for risking negative jurisprudence, or for misleading rights claimants

---

64 See, for example, Harry J Glasbeek & Michael Mandel, "The Legalization of Politics in Advanced Capitalism: The *Canadian Charter of Rights and Freedoms*" (1984) 2 Socialist Studies 84; Andrew Petter, "The Politics of the *Charter*" (1986) 8 Sup Ct L Rev 473; Allan C Hutchinson & Andrew Petter, "Private Rights/Public Wrongs: The Liberal Lie of the *Charter*" (1988) 38 UTLJ 278.

into thinking that rights could actually be realized through the courts. Thus Louise Arbour has noted that "the first two decades of *Charter* litigation testify to a certain timidity — both on the part of litigants and the courts — to tackle head on the claims emerging from the right to be free from want."[65] But the less Canadian courts have been asked, or have been willing, to determine social rights claims, the more the negative rights paradigm appears to have settled in, almost by default.[66]

What is remarkable about the first thirty years of *Charter* jurisprudence in relation to social rights claims is not any observable trend of having been successful or unsuccessful — there are examples of both.[67] Rather, it is the relative absence of cases addressing what were seen at the outset of the *Charter* as the critical human rights issues of poverty and systemic inequality. Social rights have, with limited exceptions, remained largely unclaimed. Those few cases with significant social rights potential that have been brought before the courts have, as often as not, been unheard: victims of motions to strike or of lower court losses, with leave to appeal usually denied by appellate and the Supreme Court.[68] As a consequence, more than three decades after the enactment of the *Charter*, the critical question of the extent to which the *Charter* protects rights to life, security of the person, and equality, including social rights guaranteed under international human rights law, remains unanswered by the Canadian courts.

In *Gosselin v Quebec (AG)*,[69] the only Supreme Court case to directly address the issue of whether social rights guaranteed under international human rights law ought to be included in the interpretation of section 7, since the question was left open in *Irwin Toy*, the scope of the *Charter*'s protection for social rights was again left unresolved. However, Canadian lower courts appear to be taking the Supreme Court's silence and continued denials of

---

65 Louise Arbour, "'Freedom from Want' — From Charity to Entitlement," LaFontaine-Baldwin Lecture, Quebec City (2005) 7; Margot Young, "Why Rights Now? Law and Desperation" in Young et al, eds, above note 51, 317; Barbara Billingsley & Peter Carver, "Sections 7 and 15(1) of the *Charter* and Access to the Public Purse: Evolution in the Law?" (2007) 36 Sup Ct L Rev (2d) 223.

66 Martha Jackman, "*Charter* Remedies for Socio-economic Rights Violations: Sleeping under a Box?" in Robert J Sharpe & Kent Roach, eds, *Taking Remedies Seriously* (Montreal: Canadian Institute for the Administration of Justice, 2010) 279.

67 Martha Jackman & Bruce Porter, "Socio-economic Rights under the Canadian *Charter*" in Malcolm Langford, ed, above note 63, 209.

68 Sanda Rodgers, "Getting Heard: Leave to Appeal, Interveners and Procedural Barriers to Social Justice in the Supreme Court of Canada" (2010) 50 Sup Ct L Rev (2d) 1 at 40. See also the review in Chapter 2.

69 2002 SCC 84.

leave to appeal in poverty-related cases as a licence to treat the matter as closed, preventing poor people from even getting a hearing into denials of civil legal aid, access to housing, or other critical social rights challenges.[70] Perhaps the overriding lesson of the last decade, then, is less about the track record of social rights claims under the *Charter* and more about the failure of political solutions that social rights claimants were advised by the *Charter* critics to rely upon. There has been little diversion of attention or resources to legal cases addressing social rights claims in Canada. The failure of Canadian democracy to address poverty and homelessness and the denial of meaningful access to democratic procedures for those affected by social rights violations is a much bigger story than that.

D. SOCIAL RIGHTS BEYOND THE COURTS

The federalist dimensions of the social rights paradigm of 1980s Canada also proved to be fragile. The worldwide pressure for structural adjustment in the early 1990s resulted in the Canadian government relinquishing social rights standards embedded in cost-sharing agreements with the provinces.[71] In particular, the *Canada Assistance Plan*[72] was abandoned in 1995, and with it any political commitment to implementing and protecting the right to adequate social assistance through such conditional shared-cost programs.[73] Non-binding principles, sometimes not even put in writing, have come to replace social entitlements embedded in legislation. Provinces have further downloaded key programs in housing, social assistance, and health care to municipalities and local service providers. The "reinventing government" movement has brought about widespread privatization of publicly delivered services and the replacement of social rights–based standards with market criteria to assess public services.[74]

---

70 See, for example, *Tanudjaja v Canada (AG)*, 2013 ONSC 5410; *Canadian Bar Assn v British Columbia*, 2008 BCCA 92; Martha Jackman, "Constitutional Castaways: Poverty and the McLachlin Court" (2010) 50 Sup Ct L Rev (2d) 297.

71 International Monetary Fund, *Canada: Article IV Consultation Discussions Statement by the Fund Mission to the Minister of Finance* (Ottawa, 7 December 1995), online: The Halifax Initiative www.halifaxinitiative.org.

72 *CAP*, above note 46.

73 Martha Jackman, "Women and the Canada Health and Social Transfer: Ensuring Gender Equality in Federal Welfare Reform" (1995) 8 CJWL 371; Shelagh Day & Gwen Brodsky, *Women and the Equality Deficit: The Impact of Restructuring Canada's Social Programs* (Ottawa: Status of Women Canada, 1998).

74 Barbara Cameron, "Accounting for Rights and Money in the Canadian Social Union" in Young et al, eds, above note 51, 162; Lucie Lamarche, "The 'Made in Québec' Act to

Over the past decade, the capacity of civil society organizations to pursue social rights claims, either in court or through social mobilization, has also been seriously eroded. Since the 1970s, the human rights movement in Canada has depended heavily on government recognition of, and financial support for, the independent role of civil society organizations as a means of giving voice to concerns of groups that would otherwise lack the resources or ability to participate in democratic processes. Unlike their counterparts in other countries, where charitable or development funding is more available, human rights groups in Canada have relied primarily on public rather than private funding. This was seen as the hallmark of a social democracy, mitigating the need to cater to charity and charitable models of addressing social rights violations linked to poverty and inequality.[75] With the election in 2004 of a federal party whose leader had been steadfastly hostile to human rights "interest groups," the fragility of this commitment became clear.

The systematic exclusion of human rights and equality-seeking groups from the federal programs that remain in existence and the outright cancellation of funding for the Court Challenges Program of Canada, Status of Women Canada's Policy Research Program, the Law Commission of Canada, the National Council on Welfare, Aboriginal health programs, and many other organizations and institutions promoting human rights accountability have had profound effects on the capacity of civil society organizations to advocate for social rights in Canada.[76] Moreover, in response to the increased reliance of human rights and environmental organizations on charitable donations, the federal minister of finance has allocated 8 million dollars of special funding to the Canada Revenue Agency to conduct audits of organizations suspected of expending more than 10 percent of their resources on any form of advocacy, including public education, research, meetings, or other activities, that might promote change to or retention of existing programs, policies, or laws. This has had a significant chilling effect across the

---

Combat Poverty and Social Exclusion: The Complex Relationship between Poverty and Human Rights" in Young et al, eds, *ibid*, 139. See the discussion in Chapter 4.

75 Voices-voix, *Submission to the United Nations Human Rights Council. Universal Periodic Review of Canada's Human Rights Obligations* (October 2012), online: OHCHR http://lib.ohchr.org [Voices-voix, *Canada's Human Rights Obligations*].

76 Maria Gergin, *Silencing Dissent: The Conservative Record* (Ottawa: Canadian Centre for Policy Alternatives, 2011), online: Canadian Centre for Policy Alternatives www.policyalternatives.ca; Kathleen Rodgers & Melanie Knight, "'You Just Felt the Collective Wind Knocked Out of Us': The Deinstitutionalization of Feminism and the Survival of Women's Organizing in Canada" (2011) 34 Women's Studies International Forum 570.

country, creating a fear that charitable status could be lost by speaking out about violations of human rights where remedies require changes to policy or legislation.[77]

E. ONGOING ENGAGEMENT WITH SOCIAL RIGHTS

A major strength of the social rights paradigm in Canada is its grounding in evolving international human rights procedures, frameworks, and norms. Notwithstanding a hostile domestic climate, Canadian NGOs have continued to engage with all aspects of UN human rights review, adjudication, and norm-setting procedures. These have included periodic reviews of Canada undertaken by various UN treaty monitoring bodies, the Universal Periodic Review before the UN Human Rights Council, missions by special rapporteurs to Canada, petitions under optional complaints procedures, and investigations into rights violations in Canada conducted by international and regional bodies.[78] Beyond engaging in these existing mechanisms related to Canada's compliance with international and regional human rights instruments, social rights advocates in Canada have also participated in new international developments in the field of social rights. The dynamic evolution of social rights practices, in other countries and at the international level, has provided a framework for advancing social rights at home, despite the comparative inertia of Canadian courts and legislators.

For example, disability rights groups in Canada were actively involved in the negotiation of the text of the new *Convention on the Rights of Persons with Disabilities* and its *Optional Protocol*.[79] The *CRPD* provides for self-standing rights to housing, education, health care, work, social security, an adequate standard of living, social protection, and the right to live independently in the community. It acts as a key reference point for domestic advocacy groups, such as the Council of Canadians with Disabilities, working to advance the rights of people with disabilities in Canada.[80] Aboriginal

77 Voices-voix, *Canada's Human Rights Obligations*, above note 75.

78 Civil society and Indigenous initiatives in Canada in relation to these procedures are outlined at CURA, "International and Regional Accountability Initiatives" (2013), online: Social Rights in Canada CURA http://socialrightscura.ca.

79 Council of Canadians with Disabilities, "Canada and the CRPD Archives" (2013), online: Council of Canadians with Disabilities www.ccdonline.ca/en/international/un/canada/archives; *CRPD*, above note 27.

80 Council of Canadians with Disabilities, online: Council of Canadians with Disabilities www.ccdonline.ca.

representatives from Canada also participated actively in the drafting of the UN *Declaration on the Rights of Indigenous Peoples* (*UNDRIP*), which addresses many social rights issues in the context of Indigenous and treaty rights, colonization, and dispossession of Indigenous lands and resources.[81] While Canada was one of the few States refusing to support it when it was adopted by the UN Human Rights Council and the UN General Assembly, the *UNDRIP* has been central to social rights advocacy undertaken by Indigenous organizations in Canada. The federal government eventually reversed its position and agreed to endorse the *UNDRIP*.[82]

Advocates from Canada were also actively engaged in the ongoing debate over the justiciability of economic, social, and cultural rights, including at the Open Ended Working Group mandated by the UN Human Rights Council to consider an *Optional Protocol* to the *ICESCR*[83] to establish a complaints procedure for victims of violations of economic and social rights. The adoption on 10 December 2008, and entry into force on 5 May 2013, of the *OP-ICESCR* marked the international community's formal acceptance of the fact that access to adjudication and remedy for rights violations is as fundamental for social rights as it is for civil and political rights claimants. The government of Canada has continued to oppose recognition of the justiciability of social rights and, as noted above, has refused to support, sign, or ratify the *OP-ICESCR*.[84] Whatever position governments may take regarding the justiciability of social rights, either internationally or before Canadian courts, however, social rights advocates now operate firmly within this new internationally recognized social rights paradigm. That paradigm directly informs not only legal but also political social rights advocacy in Canada.[85]

---

81 Jackie Hartley, Paul Joffe, & Jennifer Preston, eds, *Realizing the UN Declaration on the Rights of Indigenous Peoples: Triumph, Hope, and Action* (Saskatoon: Purich Publishing, 2010); UNGAOR, 61st Sess, UN Doc A/61/L.67, (2007) [*UNDRIP*].

82 Foreign Affairs, Trade and Development Canada, News Release, No 361, "Canada Endorses the United Nations Declarations on the Rights of Indigenous Peoples" (12 November 2010), online: Foreign Affairs, Trade and Development Canada www.international.gc.ca.

83 Activities in support of the development of the *OP-ICESCR* are outlined at CURA, "Promoting a Complaints Adjudication Procedure for Social Rights at the International Level: The Optional Protocol to the International Covenant on Economic, Social and Cultural Rights" (2013), online: Social Rights in Canada CURA http://socialrightscura.ca.

84 Above note 8.

85 The claim in *Tanudjaja v Canada (AG)*, above note 70, is an example of legal advocacy informed by the international human rights paradigm. An example of a political

While it is undeniable that resources and capacity have been severely reduced by the Harper government's attacks on human rights and programs that support them, at the same time many new spaces are opening up, and many new actors are becoming involved in social rights advocacy at the domestic level. Current developments in the field of law and in social policy suggest that social rights practice will be more diversified in the future than may have been imagined in the past. On the social policy side, the new federalism and the contracted-out State make it difficult to envisage any comprehensive protection of social rights that does not include multiple actors and a number of different policy areas. In the future, social rights strategies may need to encompass a variety of formal and informal instruments and processes. As the Special Rapporteur on the Right to Food made clear in his recommendations to Canada following his 2013 mission, an effective food security strategy, for example, will need to engage with a range of policies, programs, and instruments, including income security, minimum wage, Indigenous rights to land and resources, social security, affordable housing programs, support for alternative food production, landholding regulation, and new supply management and distribution systems.[86]

As for the legal context for advancing social rights in Canada, the Supreme Court has increasingly moved to diversify the space for rights claims to be heard and enforced. The Court has recognized that a broad array of administrative decision makers and tribunals must actively engage with human rights norms.[87] This means that rights must be protected at the level where decisions affecting rights are made: both where they are put at risk and where decision making can play a constructive role in realizing rights. In two of its most important *Charter* cases in the social rights area, *Eldridge v British Columbia (AG)*[88] and *Canada (AG) v PHS Community Services Society (Insite)*,[89] the Supreme Court has drawn attention to the fact that substantive rights, such as access to health care for vulnerable groups, may

---

initiative informed by recent developments internationally is Bill C-400, *An Act to Ensure Secure, Adequate, Accessible and Affordable Housing for Canadians*, 1st Sess, 42nd Parl, 2012 (first reading 16 February 2012). See, generally, the discussion in Chapter 1 in this book.

86 *Report of the Special Rapporteur on the Right to Food*, above note 5.

87 See the discussion of the dissemination of rights adjudication to a wide range of administrative tribunals in Chapter 11.

88 [1997] 3 SCR 624.

89 2011 SCC 44 [*Insite*]; Matthew Rottier Voell, "*PHS Community Services Society v Canada (Attorney General)*: Positive Health Rights, Health Care Policy, and Section 7 of the *Charter*" (2011) 31 Windsor Rev Legal Soc Issues 41. These cases are discussed in Chapters 2 and 14.

often depend more on the quality of delegated decision making than on the precise wording or explicit provisions of any applicable legislation. By articulating a standard of reasonable decision making, consistent with the *Charter* and international human rights, the Court has opened up an expanded field of government decision making to review for compliance with domestic and international social rights norms.[90] The scope of protection for social rights in Canadian law is unlikely to be resolved by a single administrative or *Charter* decision answering for all time the question, left open in the *Irwin Toy* case, of the status of social and economic rights under the *Charter*. Rather, the answer will evolve as a number of administrative and judicial bodies confront the questions that have been put before them as a result of the Supreme Court's opening up of new spaces in which social rights–related claims can be advanced.

F. MOVING FORWARD: NEW AVENUES FOR SOCIAL RIGHTS PRACTICE

What is required, then, to advance social rights in Canada? On the one hand, it will be important to maintain a commitment to international human rights and to equality-seeking social movements — the twin foundations of social rights in Canada. As described above, the human rights paradigm that has emerged internationally has strong resonance with the ideal of substantive equality as it has been articulated and pursued by women's, disability, and other equality-seeking groups in Canada over the past four decades. The critical links between domestic and international human rights have been under assault from recent governments in Canada, but they continue to be solid at the civil society level. On the other hand, it will be necessary to diversify social rights practice: to take advantage of the variety of fora that are now available for advancing social rights claims in Canada, to address the challenges of the contracted-out State and downloading of social service delivery, and to engage more constructively with new models of federalism. It will also be important to ensure that the new social rights paradigm is inclusive of experiences of Aboriginal communities, people with disabilities, racialized groups, migrants, and others who have been marginalized, not only from mainstream politics but, all too often, from the human rights movement itself.

This book emerged from a Social Sciences and Humanities Research Council of Canada (SSHRC) Community-University Research Alliance

---

90 See the analysis in Chapter 11.

(CURA) project entitled "Reconceiving Human Rights for the New Social Rights Paradigm." The SSHRC's CURA program and the CURA research project we co-directed provided unique opportunities to link innovative academic research in domestic and international social rights law and policy to community-based social rights initiatives in a wide range of fields of human rights practice. The CURA grant enabled us to bring a number of Quebec and Canadian academics and activists together for a symposium on emerging approaches to social rights practice, leading to the publication of this edited collection, which includes contributions by many of the CURA researchers and collaborators. The book provides examples of just some of the wide range of new spaces, approaches, and opportunities for advancing social rights in Canada. It is hoped that the underlying methodology and commitment evidenced by the authors in the book, including both academics and community-based social rights advocates, will act as a catalyst for ongoing work and networking in this critical area of research.

In Chapter 1, Bruce Porter explores how proposals for rights-based housing and anti-poverty strategies in Canada have opened an important new space for advancing social rights. He considers how the new paradigm of social rights, as claimable rights under international law, can provide a framework for such domestic strategies. Porter proposes a more robust integration of rights and social policy, to engage directly with Canada's international human rights law obligation to progressively realize social rights to the maximum of available resources. He suggests how the standard of "reasonableness" that has been adopted under the new *OP-ICESCR*[91] offers a normative framework for housing and anti-poverty strategies in Canada. And he explains how such strategies must entail coherent and coordinated initiatives engaging multiple levels of government, Aboriginal peoples, and other stakeholders; incorporating goals and timelines; and providing effective claiming, adjudication, and monitoring procedures.

In Chapter 2, Martha Jackman and Bruce Porter consider the implications of evolving domestic constitutional and human rights jurisprudence for the protection of social rights to housing, food, and an adequate standard of living, in order to assess whether a rights-based framework for housing and anti-poverty strategies can also be found in the Canadian *Charter*. Examining recent Supreme Court caselaw on the right to life and security of the person under section 7 and the Court's professed return to a substantive approach to equality under section 15, the authors contend that there is ample room for the courts to address Canadian governments' failure to combat widespread homelessness, hunger, and poverty, as violations

91 *OP-ICESCR*, above note 8.

of the *Charter*. They further argue that the reasonableness of government action and inaction in relation to poverty and homelessness can be effectively assessed under section 1 of the *Charter*. Beyond judicial recognition of social rights claims, however, the authors suggest that rights-based federal, provincial/territorial, and municipal anti-poverty and housing strategies are urgently required.

In Chapter 3, Vincent Greason provides a critical assessment of existing anti-poverty strategies both in Quebec and in other Canadian provinces. Greason finds that anti-poverty strategies have been shaped by the context in which they were created: one of neo-liberal consolidation, reduced taxation, and offloading of State responsibilities to non-State entities. He identifies five common themes in provincial anti-poverty initiatives: (1) the repackaging of poverty as a social rather than material deprivation, (2) a focus on poverty measurement rather than poverty elimination, (3) emphasis on individual responsibility, (4) integrating philanthropic organizations as key actors, and (5) reframing social services to address a range of social needs rather than addressing economic deprivation. Greason notes that two themes have been markedly absent from anti-poverty strategies: attention to growing income disparities and the incorporation of a human rights framework for fighting poverty. Greason calls for a reorientation of anti-poverty strategies in Quebec and Canada around a framework of social rights and redistributive justice.

In Chapter 4, Barbara Cameron provides an updated analysis of the federal spending power as an instrument for advancing social rights in Canada. She argues that there are three distinct accountability relationships implicated in federal transfers to fund provincial social programs: the social rights relationship (legislature to citizen), the federal relationship (federal to provincial executive), and the responsible government relationship (executive to legislature). By distinguishing these three sets of accountability relationships, Cameron is able to identify three corresponding accountability regimes that have governed federal social transfers in Canada: the administrative accountability regime, seen in the *Canada Assistance Plan*;[92] the political accountability regime, evident in the *Canada Health Act*;[93] and the public reporting accountability regime, associated with the Social Union Framework agreements. Cameron finds that none of these is entirely satisfactory, and she proposes an alternative accountability regime that would affirm the expansion of the social citizenship rights of members of Canadian society as the primary purpose of federal social transfers.

---

92 *CAP*, above note 46.

93 *CHA*, above note 45.

In Chapter 5, Marie-Eve Sylvestre and Céline Bellot develop a critical understanding of homelessness as a human rights issue by documenting and assessing discriminatory and punitive responses to homelessness in Canada. The authors argue that an analysis of the discriminatory discourses that prevail in relation to homeless people strongly supports the recognition of homelessness as an analogous ground of discrimination, as well as supporting housing rights claims under sections 7 and 15 of the *Charter*. The authors contend that the courts must consider the complexity of embedded social structures and interactions at play in this area, understanding homelessness as a social construct and characteristic that is difficult for affected individuals to change. Recognizing the discriminatory underpinnings of, and responses to, homelessness should also lead, in Sylvestre and Bellot's view, to a reorientation of social programs to address the structural causes of homelessness and the reversal of cuts to income support, housing, and employment programs that have been part of the punitive responses to homelessness in Canada in recent years.

In Chapter 6, Kerri Froc explores the interdependence of equality and social rights, analyzing how Canadian courts have dealt with discrimination linked to socio-economic status and women's right to just conditions of work in section 15 *Charter* cases. She finds that in cases involving women at work, the test for analogous grounds, initially sensitive to social and historical context and power relations, has been increasingly applied as a hard status/conduct binary. The formerly contextualized concept of "discrete and insular minorities" has, in Froc's view, been fused with a static notion of immutability, undermining women's legitimate claims to equality and denying discrimination in cases of mutable, gendered conduct that is fundamentally linked to women's socio-economic inequality. Froc argues that recognizing the gendered nature of women's work would shift the focus of discrimination analysis from considerations of immutability to how systems of economic and gender subordination operate in fact to construct women's work.

In Chapter 7, Shelagh Day, Gwen Brodsky, and Yvonne Peters analyze the current legal landscape for litigating the substantive equality rights of people with disabilities. While the Supreme Court's decisions in *British Columbia (Public Service Employee Relations Comm) v BCGEU* (*Meiorin*)[94] and *British Columbia (Superintendent of Motor Vehicles) v British Columbia (Council of Human Rights)* (*Grismer*)[95] were cause for optimism that the courts would take adverse effects discrimination seriously and apply the duty to

94 [1999] 3 SCR 3.

95 [1999] 3 SCR 868.

accommodate so as to engage with systemic obstacles to equality, the authors describe how subsequent human rights caselaw has regressed toward a minimalist version of accommodation. The authors note, however, that in the recent *Moore v British Columbia (Education)*[96] decision, the Supreme Court rejected the formalistic use of a comparator group and rejected a narrow conception of services available to the public. They explain that this positive development comes at a time when Canada's ratification of the UN *Convention on the Rights of Persons with Disabilities*[97] should also provide domestic tribunals and courts with motivation for fusing social rights with substantive equality analysis and recommitting to the promise of social transformation and inclusion of persons with disabilities that is at the core of the section 15 equality guarantee.

In Chapter 8, Vince Calderhead and Claire McNeil reflect on their experience representing low-income consumers of electricity in Nova Scotia, in the *Boulter v Nova Scotia Power Incorporated*[98] case, challenging a legislative provision prohibiting utilities monopolies from adjusting rates based on ability to pay. The authors explain that, while most social rights equality litigation has addressed unequal access to government services or benefits, the *Boulter* case raised the important issue of inequalities in accessing essential services provided by private actors, the regulatory responsibilities of governments to ensure access by all who are in need, and the expense rather than the income side of household finances. The authors point out that what the courts found particularly challenging in *Boulter* was the idea of applying constitutional equality rights to market pricing. While the litigation was ultimately unsuccessful, the issues raised in the case were critical for those living in poverty, and the authors suggest that the basis for the *Boulter* decision may ultimately be revisited in light of more recent Supreme Court jurisprudence rejecting formal comparator group analysis.

In Chapter 9, Constance MacIntosh assesses the viability of new approaches to litigating Aboriginal claims to the right to water in Canada, focusing on whether fiduciary law creates an actionable right to safe drinking water for Aboriginal peoples living on reserves. Reviewing the shocking state of water safety on reserves, the author points out that the Crown has not only offloaded to First Nations governments the responsibility to meet water quality standards which the Crown had previously failed to meet, it has also failed to provide First Nations with the facilities or resources that would enable them to achieve these basic standards. Such policies do not,

96 [2012] 3 SCR 360.

97 Above note 27.

98 2009 NSCA 17 [*Boulter*].

MacIntosh argues, comply with standards of reasonableness and due diligence under fiduciary law. While the author notes that Canada has resisted recognizing the right to water under international human rights law, that right is now firmly established internationally as a component of treaties ratified by Canada and provides reinforcement for a rigorous standard of review of whether the Crown has met its fiduciary duties towards First Nations.

In Chapter 10, Alana Klein considers new avenues for advancing the right to health in Canada, focusing on the challenging issue of human rights scrutiny of health resources distribution. Reviewing the current state of *Charter* jurisprudence on the issue of health care equity, Klein observes a judicial reticence to engage with critical issues of resource distribution and considers what benefits judicial review of health care decisions may offer. Since Canadian provinces have come to rely on participation and accountability to drive more responsive resource allocation, Klein suggests that promoting participatory and accountable governance at the provincial and local levels may be an avenue for activism in support of the right to health in Canada. The existence of accountability and participation requirements at the local level might then serve to enhance judicial confidence in addressing human rights claims and enable health policy decision making to be more responsive to rights-based claims and adjudication. Klein suggests that international actors may also play an important role in monitoring the outcome of participatory governance in Canadian health care.

In Chapter 11, Lorne Sossin and Andrea Hill consider the possibilities for advancing social rights in the crucial area of administrative decision making. As the focus of social rights compliance has turned toward government plans and policies, the authors contend that the role of agencies, boards, and commissions charged with implementing those plans and policies must be better recognized as a critical area of social rights compliance and implementation. In particular, they argue that such bodies should create a meaningful and accessible system of establishing and protecting social rights by firmly rooting adjudication in constitutional and international human rights commitments, in the practical realities of the administrative justice system, and in the lived experiences of the parties who come before them. While the Supreme Court's recent decision to adopt a new robust standard of administrative law reasonableness, in *Doré v Barreau du Québec*,[99] offers significant potential for protection of social rights in day-to-day administrative decision making, the authors raise the concern that

99 [2012] 1 SCR 395.

without adequate resources, administrative tribunals will not be able to fulfill the critical role that has now been assigned to them.

In Chapter 12, Sylvie Paquerot examines the practical application of the principle of the interdependence of environmental and human rights in the work of the Ligue des droits et libertés du Québec (Ligue). She explains that the Ligue first focused on the connection between procedural rights and environmental protection: advocating against strategic lawsuits against public participation (SLAPPs) used by corporations in an attempt to silence environmental challenges. Later the Ligue advocated more substantively for rights to water, health, and self-determination, in its opposition to fracking for shale gas in Quebec. The author suggests that situating environmental issues within a human rights framework allowed the Ligue to reinforce principles of environmental responsibility, both politically and judicially. She advocates further alliances between human rights and environmental groups, proposing a transformation of sector-specific advocacy into a more comprehensive and inclusive affirmation of the right to public participation in social and environmental decisions, mobilizing around the right to "say no" to development that would undermine social and environmental rights.

In Chapter 13, Graham Mayeda engages with another critical question for social rights advocacy: the relationship between courts and social protest movements. Mayeda analyzes how courts in Canada have traditionally considered the right to protest in terms of competing rights or claims to public space, pitting protestors' right to freedom of expression against the rights of residents to walk their dogs or use parks for recreational purposes, and linking the rights of dog-walkers, rather than the rights of protestors, to the public interest. In opposition to the competing rights paradigm, Mayeda outlines a social rights approach that would promote legal rules that facilitate rather than silence protest. Drawing on the transformative dimension of social rights emphasized in South African commentary and jurisprudence, Mayeda proposes that a social rights approach recognize and support the transformative role of public protest and social conflict in a democratic State. He further urges the courts to recognize deliberative democracy as a core public interest and acknowledge and facilitate claims made by the public against the "justice" of the existing social order.

In the final chapter, Margot Young reflects on judicial responses to neo-liberalism and widening socio-economic inequality in Canada in the adjudication of recent claims under sections 7 and 15 of the *Charter*. Focusing on the *Adams*[100] and *Insite*[101] cases, she argues that the rights claims must

100 *Victoria (City) v Adams*, 2009 BCCA 563.

101 *Insite*, above note 89.

be contextualized in the spatial aspect of struggles for equality and justice. The author suggests that in both of these cases, consideration of the social context of poverty and homelessness is critical, but that context also has a geographical and spatial dimension. She points out that rights claims advanced in these cases demanded a reshaping of city space around the realization of a social right. Young finds that the legal victories in *Adams* and *Insite* are localized, however, leaving the systemic barriers to realizing social rights largely intact. Effective challenges to neo-liberal inequality within urban landscapes will, according to Young, require a broader re-ordering and re-allocation, and, thus, a reproduction, of spaces and civic geography.

G. CONCLUSION

The contributors to this book hope to advance social rights in Canada by outlining opportunities and challenges in a wide range of fields. Provincial and national housing and anti-poverty strategies may be transformed by a revitalized social rights paradigm; so too may new and existing accountability regimes within Canadian federalism. Substantive equality can be reconceived and updated by addressing discriminatory and punitive responses to homelessness, by relinquishing the judicial obsession with immutability as a marker of disadvantage, by reconceptualizing reasonable accommodation of disability, and by engaging with governments' obligations to regulate private actors. Relationships between Aboriginal communities and the Crown may be recontoured through recognition and enforcement of Aboriginal and treaty-related social rights claims. Health care adjudication and administrative decision making can become new spaces for the pursuit of social rights claims. Incorporating environmental rights, social protest, and the struggles of marginalized communities in Canadian inner cities may give rise to a more inclusive, comprehensive, and creative human rights practice. All of these advances would engage social rights claimants in a revitalized, more inclusive human rights movement in Canada.

The central role of social rights as a response and corrective to inequality and exclusion within Canada's constitutional democracy may be profoundly threatened — but not lost. The social rights paradigm that emerged in Canada in the pre-*Charter* period continues to be embraced by an increasingly wide range of constituencies. The reasons are clear. Social rights are interdependent with, and indivisible from, civil and political rights. They speak in a more direct way to aspects of material well-being that are necessary conditions for full and effective participation in social, economic, and political life. Social rights are founded upon a more holistic understanding of both government and citizenship. They do not simply restrain governments. They reflect and reinforce the indispensable role of governments in ensuring the well-being of individuals, households, and communities. They engage with the need for ongoing social transformation and structural change that flows from providing fair hearings to previously silenced voices and unheard claims. Social rights remain fundamental to recognizing the unique circumstances and needs of equality-seeking and marginalized groups and to "giving real effect to equality."[102]

As Cory J observed in his concurring judgment for the majority of the Supreme Court in *Vriend v Alberta*, the notions of equality and the "just society" as core values require more than rhetorical affirmation if they are to continue to define our collective identity:

> The rights enshrined in s. 15(1) of the *Charter* are fundamental to Canada. They reflect the fondest dreams, the highest hopes and finest aspirations of Canadian society . . . . It is easy to praise these concepts as providing the foundation for a just society which permits every individual to live in dignity and in harmony with all. The difficulty lies in giving real effect to equality. Difficult as the goal of equality may be it is worth the arduous struggle to attain.[103]

The gap between our national self-image and the reality of rights violations perpetrated by Canadian governments at home and abroad can no longer be filled with reassuring affirmations of shared values of equality and the just society. If we are to engage in the "arduous struggle" that is at the heart of the social rights/equality paradigm, poverty, homelessness, hunger, and Aboriginal dispossession in the midst of affluence and unsustainable development must be understood first and foremost as human rights violations demanding urgent and concerted attention. Canada is at a crossroads. Social justice, equality, and inclusiveness require a broad re-engagement with the international human rights project and a recommitment to the transformational goals that were embraced by equality-seeking groups and others in the early years of Canada's constitutional democracy.

Social rights practice in Canada need not start from scratch. It is not a matter of renegotiating the content of constitutional rights in Canada but rather of retrieving and building on the existing domestic and international human rights foundation. Key questions about the scope and meaning of relevant *Charter* provisions remain open. Evolving international human rights norms continue to be accepted by courts, at least in theory, as rel-

---

102 *Vriend v Alberta*, [1998] 1 SCR 493 at para 68.

103 *Ibid.*

evant and persuasive in interpreting and applying domestic law. Canada remains a State party to UN treaties guaranteeing social rights. There is a lot to work with. However, the time has come for us to choose the kind of country we want to live in. The contributors to this book have sketched the beginnings of a blueprint for reconceiving and retrieving social rights in a range of spheres of human rights practice, both political and legal. Meaningful advances in social rights in Canada will, however, depend on a broader commitment to renew and update the struggle to realize social rights and equality, among legislators and policy makers, administrative decision makers and tribunals, Canadian courts at all levels, and within civil society itself. This book can only offer direction: the choice to commit to social rights is one we must all make.

CHAPTER 1

INTERNATIONAL HUMAN RIGHTS IN ANTI-POVERTY AND HOUSING STRATEGIES

MAKING THE CONNECTION*

BRUCE PORTER†

A. INTRODUCTION

Since the adoption of the *Universal Declaration of Human Rights* (*UDHR*) in 1948, poverty and homelessness, and the adverse health consequences that flow from them, have been understood not only as issues of economic and social deprivation but also as matters of basic human rights. In recent years, calls for a "rights-based" approach to addressing poverty and homelessness have become commonplace, particularly within the UN human rights system.[1] Since the mid-1990s UN human rights bodies have urged Canadian governments to adopt and implement strategies to address the crisis of increasing poverty and homelessness within a human rights framework, based on the recognition of the right to an adequate standard of living and the right to adequate housing as guaranteed in international human rights law ratified by Canada.[2] These recommendations have been

---

* This paper has been developed from the author's contribution to a longer paper which was jointly written with Martha Jackman. The author gratefully acknowledges the University of Ottawa Institute for Population Health, the Social Sciences and Humanities Research Council Community-University Research Alliance (SSHRC-CURA) program, and the Law Foundation of Ontario for their support.

† Executive Director, Social Rights Advocacy Centre and Co-Director (Community) of the SSHRC-CURA Research Project "Reconceiving Human Rights Practice," online: www.socialrightscura.ca.

1 These are described in Section B, below in this chapter.

2 See Section D, below in this chapter.

echoed by Senate and House of Commons committees, a wide range of civil society organizations, and many human rights, legal, and policy experts.[3]

What is meant by a rights-based approach, however, is not always clear. Is the point of affirming housing and freedom from poverty as fundamental rights in the context of housing and anti-poverty strategies simply to create a moral imperative on governments to act to improve housing and income support programs? Does a rights-based strategy rely on accepting these rights as justiciable and allocating a central role to courts? Does it affect the design and content of housing and anti-poverty strategies or merely describe their goal?

In this chapter, calls for rights-based approaches to housing and anti-poverty strategies will be situated within the context of new understandings of social rights that have emerged internationally. In earlier years, socio-economic rights such as the right to housing and an adequate standard of living were relegated to a "second generation" of human rights, conceptualized as worthy goals or future aspirations of government policy rather than as enforceable rights. Socio-economic rights are now generally understood within the UN system as equal in status to civil and political rights not just in conceptual terms (as being equally important), but equal in terms of human rights practice. They are understood to be claimable by rights holders and subject to effective remedies. They are also seen as a site for a revitalized human rights practice, centred on rights claimants and parallel to more traditional civil and political human rights practice. This sea change in the understanding of human rights as a unified framework for human rights practice has occurred gradually over the course of a generation, but it was firmly entrenched at an institutional level when, on 10 December 2008, the UN General Assembly adopted the *Optional Protocol to the ICESCR* and, on 5 May 2013, when the *Optional Protocol* came into force.[4] The *Optional Protocol* permits the Committee on Economic, Social

---

3 Martha Jackman & Bruce Porter, *International Human Rights, Health and Strategies to Address Homelessness and Poverty in Ontario: Making the Connection*, Exchange Working Paper Series, PHIRN, 3(3): 2012 at 40–46, online: RRASP/PHIRN www.rrasp-phirn.

4 The Protocol entered into force three months after the tenth ratification, see *Optional Protocol to the International Covenant on Economic, Social and Cultural Rights*, 10 December 2008, GA Res A/RES/63/117 (entered into force 5 May 2013) at art 18(1) [*Optional Protocol*]. For updates on signatures and ratifications, see United Nations Treaty Collection, online: http://treaties.un.org. The Government of Canada has indicated that it does not intend to ratify the *Optional Protocol*, see United Nations Human Rights Council, *Report of the Working Group on the Universal Periodic Review: Canada, Addendum, Views on Conclusions and/or Recommendations, Voluntary*

and Cultural Rights (CESCR) to adjudicate petitions alleging violations of *ICESCR* rights in the same manner as petitions have been considered in relation to civil and political rights for forty years. This institutional accomplishment was appropriately heralded by Louise Arbour, then UN High Commissioner on Human Rights, as "human rights made whole."[5]

If governments are to be held accountable for failures to meet their obligations with respect to economic and social rights, institutional mechanisms must be in place to enable rights holders to claim their rights. Conceiving of socio-economic rights primarily in relation to governments and their commitments rather than in relation to rights holders and their claims — as rights without claimants — reinforced patterns of exclusion of the most powerless and marginalized groups that human rights are supposed to remedy.[6] The new unified approach, by contrast, recognizes that all human rights must be subject to the rule of law and the overarching principle that individuals must have access to effective remedies if their rights are violated.

The modern conception of social rights opens up possibilities for a new understanding of the interplay between human rights and socio-economic policy. Social rights claims are now seen as transformative in nature, as tools for challenging structural disadvantage, social exclusion and political powerlessness, and for addressing poverty and homelessness as denials not only of basic needs but also of equal citizenship, dignity, and rights. While rights claims in the more traditional civil and political rights framework tend to focus on remedies that can be immediately granted by courts, establishing operational rules for government programs subject to immediate enforceability, the new paradigm of social rights brings broader strategic aspects of policy and program development that are not subject to immediate remedies into the field of human rights practice. It thus

---

Commitments and Replies Presented by the State under Review, UNHRCOR, 11th Sess, UN Doc A/HRC/11/17/Add.1, (2009) at paras 9 and 11 [Response to *UPR*].

5 Louise Arbour, "Human Rights Made Whole" *Project Syndicate* (26 June 2008), online: Project Syndicate www.project-syndicate.org.

6 Philip Alston, "No Right to Complain about Being Poor: The Need for an Optional Protocol to the Economic Rights Covenant" in Asbjørn Eide & Jan Helgesen, eds, *The Future of Human Rights Protection in a Changing World: Fifty Years since the Four Freedoms Address. Essays in Honour of Torkel Opsahl* (Oslo: Norwegian University Press, 1991) 79; Bruce Porter, "The Right to Be Heard: The Optional Protocol to the International Covenant on Economic, Social and Cultural Rights: What's at Stake?" (2005) 11:3 Hum Rts Trib 1; Bruce Porter, "Claiming Adjudicative Space: Social Rights, Equality and Citizenship" in Margot Young et al, eds, *Poverty: Rights, Social Citizenship, and Legal Activism* (Vancouver: UBC Press, 2007) 77 [Porter, "Claiming"].

demands a reconceptualization of claims, adjudication, and remedy so as to implement strategies to address structural causes of poverty and homelessness, creating the foundations for a more principled and strategic approach to rights-based policy development.

The interplay between human rights and future-oriented plans and strategies to implement and realize rights within a reasonable period of time has thus become a critical issue in the emerging field of social rights practice, arising in both legal and social policy domains. In the legal sphere, with the adjudication of more complex structural social rights claims, advocates and judges are called upon to devise new approaches to judicial remedies and enforcement. Here, the challenges relate to developing effective programmatic remedies that extend into the future: to ensure the development and implementation of necessary legislation, programs, and strategies within a reasonable period of time; to facilitate meaningful participation of rights claimants in the design and implementation of programs; to guarantee ongoing accountability of governments; and to monitor outcomes against projected timelines and appropriate indicators.[7]

Beyond the judicial sphere, and extending into the social policy domain, the new understanding of social rights has also inspired the emergence of innovative programmatic approaches to addressing poverty and homelessness in a rights-based framework, drawing on some of the same principles that have been developed in the legal context. The new conception of social rights obliges governments to facilitate the design of strategies and programs to realize rights within identified time-frames and with measurable goals and targets; to recognize the central role that must be played by rights claimants; and to strengthen governmental accountability through complaints procedures, monitoring, and evaluation. Claimable rights are not restricted to justiciability in the narrow sense. Governments are obliged to take appropriate measures to realize rights over time and to consider how their programs and strategies can incorporate mechanisms to ensure ongoing accountability to rights holders through administrative procedures with recourse to courts when necessary.

---

7 See, for example, John Squires, Malcolm Langford, & Bret Thiele, eds, *The Road to Remedy: Current Issues in the Litigation of Economic, Social and Cultural Rights* (Sydney: Australian Human Rights Centre, 2005). See also papers prepared for the "Project on Enforcement of ESCR Judgments" (International Symposium, Bogota, Colombia, 6–7 May 2010), online: ESCR-Net www.escr-net.org.

B. THE INTERNATIONAL "COMMON UNDERSTANDING" OF RIGHTS-BASED APPROACHES

The UN Population Fund (UNFPA) describes the conceptual shift to a "rights-based" approach within UN agencies as follows:

> Before 1997, most UN development agencies pursued a "basic needs" approach: they identified basic requirements of beneficiaries and either supported initiatives to improve service delivery or advocated for their fulfilment.
>
> UNFPA and its UN partners now work to fulfil the rights of people, rather than the needs of beneficiaries. There is a critical distinction: a need not fulfilled leads to dissatisfaction. In contrast, a right that is not respected leads to a violation, and its redress or reparation can be legally and legitimately claimed.
>
> . . . A rights-based approach strives to secure the freedom, well-being and dignity of all people everywhere, within the framework of essential standards and principles, duties and obligations. The rights-based approach supports mechanisms to ensure that entitlements are attained and safeguarded.[8]

During the 1990s the Committee on Economic, Social and Cultural Rights had wrestled, in the context of periodic reviews of State parties to the Covenant, with growing poverty and widening inequality in both developed and developing countries. The committee identified a critical need for a better understanding of the role of human rights in poverty reduction strategies and, in 2001, asked the UN Office of the High Commissioner for Human Rights (OHCHR) to develop guidelines for the integration of human rights into poverty reduction strategies. In response to this request, Mary Robinson, the UN high commissioner, asked three experts — professors Paul Hunt, Manfred Nowak, and Siddiq Osmani — to consult with national officials, civil society, and international development agencies and to prepare draft guidelines.[9] This resulted in the OHCHR's publication in 2002 of the *Draft Guidelines: A Human Rights Approach to Poverty Reduction Strategies.*[10]

---

8 United Nations Population Fund, *The Human Rights-Based Approach*, online: United Nations Population Fund www.unfpa.org.

9 United Nations Office of the High Commissioner for Human Rights, *Draft Guidelines: A Human Rights Approach to Poverty Reduction Strategies* (Geneva: OHCHR, 2002) at preface.

10 *Ibid.*

A "common understanding of a rights-based approach" outlined in *The Human Rights Based Approach to Development Cooperation: Towards a Common Understanding among the UN Agencies*[11] was then adopted by UN development agencies in 2003. Four key ingredients of rights-based programming were identified in the *Common Understanding*:

- Identifying the central human rights claims of rights holders and the corresponding duties of "duty bearers," and identifying the structural causes of the non-realization of rights.
- Assessing the capacity of rights holders to claim their rights and of duty bearers to fulfill their obligations and develop strategies to build these capacities.
- Monitoring and evaluating both outcomes and processes, guided by human rights standards and principles.
- Ensuring that programming is informed by the recommendations of international human rights bodies and mechanisms.[12]

The *Common Understanding* affirmed that "the application of 'good programming practices' does not by itself constitute a human rights-based approach, and requires additional elements."[13] It called for a dynamic interdependence of social policy, human rights principles, and legal entitlements. It also required that strategies and programs ensure meaningful engagement with, and participation of, those living in poverty as rights claimants, with access to effective remedies.[14] Rights-based programming, the UN agencies affirmed, recognizes stakeholders as "key actors" and participation as both a means and a goal — empowering marginalized and disadvantaged groups, promoting local initiatives, adopting measureable goals and targets, developing "strategic partnerships," and supporting "accountability to all stakeholders."[15] The *Common Understanding* emphasized that rights-based strategies and programs should also:

---

11 United Nations Development Group, *The Human Rights Based Approach to Development Cooperation: Towards a Common Understanding among the UN Agencies* (2003), online: HRBA Portal http://hrbaportal.org [*Common Understanding*].

12 *Ibid.*

13 *Ibid* at 3.

14 *Ibid* at 2.

15 *Ibid* at 3.

- Monitor and assess budgetary allocations.
- Build awareness of rights among rights holders.
- Ensure effective participation by stakeholders in the design, implementation, monitoring, and evaluation of programs.
- Develop appropriate indicators and data collection disaggregated by gender and other characteristics.
- Integrate international, national, sub-national, and local initiatives and strategies.
- Address critical emerging issues, such as migration, urbanization, and demographic changes.
- Integrate equality and non-discrimination principles into strategies.
- Address forms of social exclusion affecting those living in poverty.
- Integrate recommendations of UN treaty bodies and the UN Human Rights Council (HRC).[16]

The 2006 publication *Principles and Guidelines for a Human Rights Approach to Poverty Reduction Strategies*[17] affirmed that "the adoption of a poverty reduction strategy is not just desirable but obligatory for States which have ratified international human rights instruments."[18] The *Guidelines* explain the human rights approach as follows:

> The human rights approach offers an explicit normative framework — that of international human rights. Underpinned by universally recognized moral values and reinforced by legal obligations, international human rights provide a compelling normative framework for the formulation of national and international policies, including poverty reduction strategies.[19]

The *Guidelines* recommend that poverty reduction strategies include four categories of accountability mechanisms: judicial, quasi-judicial, administrative, and political[20] and that "[t]hose responsible for formulating and implementing the poverty reduction strategy receive basic human rights training so that they are familiar with the State's human rights commitments and their implications."[21] The *Guidelines* recommend that civil

---

16 *Ibid* at 2.

17 United Nations Office of the High Commissioner for Human Rights, *Principles and Guidelines for a Human Rights Approach to Poverty Reduction Strategies*, UN Doc HR/PUB/06/12 (Geneva: OHCHR, 2006) [*Guidelines*].

18 *Ibid* at para 19.

19 *Ibid* at para 16.

20 *Ibid* at para 77.

21 *Ibid* at para 40.

society organizations and other rights holders should also have a role in monitoring poverty and housing strategies to ensure that governments are held to account for failures (or successes) and to best identify areas that may need increased attention and resources.[22] No singular mechanism should be relied upon for effective accountability and remedies, however. As the WHO and the OHCHR's joint report on health and poverty reduction puts it:

> Some processes of accountability are specific to human rights, for example inquiries by national human rights institutions and reporting to the UN human rights treaty-monitoring bodies. Others are general, including administrative systems for monitoring service provision, fair elections, a free press, parliamentary commissions and civil society monitoring. The principle of accountability requires that PRS [Poverty Reduction Strategy] processes of design, implementation and monitoring should be transparent and decision makers should answer for policy process and choices. In order to achieve this, the PRS should build on, and strengthen links to, those institutions and processes that enable people who are excluded to hold policymakers to account.[23]

The shift from needs-based to rights-based approaches is linked to a fundamental reconceptualization of poverty and homelessness. No longer considered solely in terms of economic deprivation, poverty and homelessness are now seen as deprivations of rights and capacity — symptomatic of failures not just of social and economic programs and policies but also of legal and administrative regimes, justice systems, human rights institutions, and other participatory mechanisms through which governments can be held accountable to human rights and rights-holders can become active citizens. Among other sources, the new approach has drawn inspiration from the work of Nobel Prize–winning economist Amartya Sen. In his early groundbreaking research, Sen showed that poverty and famine were not generally caused by a scarcity of goods or discrete failures of programs but rather involved broader "entitlement system failures" that arose in large part from a devaluing of the basic rights claims of the most vulnerable members of society.[24] This led to Sen's later understanding of poverty as a depriv-

22 *Ibid* at paras 75 and 86.

23 United Nations Office of the High Commissioner for Human Rights & World Health Organization, *Human Rights, Health and Poverty Reduction Strategies*, UN Doc HR/PUB/08/0 (Geneva: OHCHR, WHO, 2008) at 8 [OHCHR & WHO].

24 Amartya Sen, "Property and Hunger" (1988) 4:1 Economics and Philosophy 57, reprinted in Wesley Cragg & Christine Koggel, eds, *Contemporary Moral Issues*, 5th ed

ation of capabilities that is tied, but not reducible, to low income levels.[25] Eliminating poverty and homelessness is now seen not only as attending to unmet economic needs but also as re-valuing the rights claims of those living in poverty, empowering them as rights holders; identifying the entitlement system failures that lie behind poverty, hunger, and homelessness; challenging systemic barriers to equality that confront marginalized and disadvantaged groups; redressing failures of governmental accountability towards them; and remedying the forms of discrimination and social exclusion they experience.

Designing and implementing such rights-based strategies requires considering what specific rights need to be protected, where and how they are to be claimed, what institutional competency is available for hearing and adjudicating them, what remedies ought to be available, how outcomes are to be evaluated and monitored, and what corrective mechanisms will be in place where desired outcomes are not forthcoming. The role of courts, human rights institutions, civil society, and local organizations must be assessed in the context of designing and implementing programs and legislation, so as to ensure that program beneficiaries are made rights claimants with access to participatory processes through which claims can be collaboratively given voice, provided with hearings, and made subject to effective and responsive remedies.

C. INTERNATIONAL HUMAN RIGHTS NORMS RELEVANT TO ANTI-POVERTY AND HOUSING STRATEGIES IN CANADA

1) The Right to Effective Remedies for Rights Violations

Despite the fact that international human rights are not directly enforceable in Canada except through domestic law, they still provide the normative framework for the rights-based approach that has emerged internationally. International human rights are an important source of both substantive and procedural rights protections for those who are living in poverty or who are denied adequate housing in Canada. As noted by the Senate Subcommittee on Cities in its seminal report, *In from the Margins: A Call to Action on Poverty, Housing and Homelessness*, international human rights are a persuasive source for the interpretation of the *Charter* and other domestic law and may be given effect by being incorporated into domestic

---

(Toronto: McGraw-Hill Ryerson, 2005) 402.

25 See Amartya Sen, *Inequality Reexamined* (New York: Russell Sage Foundation, 1992); Amartya Sen, *Development as Freedom* (New York: Anchor Books, 2000).

legislation.[26] Moreover, remedies for international human rights violations may be sought through periodic review procedures before UN treaty bodies, at the Universal Periodic Review before the UN Human Rights Council, through optional complaints procedures before human rights treaty bodies, or by way of fact-finding missions and recommendations from "mandate holders" such as the UN Special Rapporteur on Adequate Housing. While governments in Canada have paid far too little attention to these procedures and the remedial recommendations that have emerged from them, those affected by poverty and homelessness in Canada have increasingly turned to them both for the normative framework for anti-poverty and housing programs and for access to procedures through which claims that are not being heard by Canadian courts can receive a fair hearing.

International procedures cannot, however, suffice in themselves. An overriding obligation under international law, and one implicit in the principle of the rule of law, is to provide effective domestic remedies for violations of human rights. This obligation applies equally to economic and social rights as to civil and political rights.[27] While emphasizing the important role that courts must play, the CESCR has acknowledged the need for some flexibility as to how effective remedies are provided. Where judicial remedies are not available, alternative, effective remedies for violations of the right to adequate housing and an adequate standard of living must be implemented, outside of courts.[28] For example, human rights commissions have broad authority to review legislation, to hold inquires, and to develop policy statements, and thus can play an important remedial role. Many other administrative bodies involved in housing or income assistance could likewise provide new venues through which rights claimants can obtain a hearing and secure effective remedies.

Access to judicial review is critical, but equally important to a rights-based approach is the implementation of other accessible, affordable, and timely procedures to ensure effective remedies without always relying on courts. The new rights-based approaches call for a more thorough integration of law and policy, framed by the notion of social rights as claimable.

---

26 Senate, Subcommittee on Cities of the Standing Senate Committee on Social Affairs, Science, and Technology, *In from the Margins: A Call to Action on Poverty, Housing and Homelessness* (December 2009) (Chair: Hon Art Eggleton, PC) at 69–72, online: Parliament of Canada www.parl.gc.ca [Senate, *In from the Margins*].

27 United Nations Committee on Economic, Social and Cultural Rights, *General Comment 9: The Domestic Application of the Covenant*, UNCESCROR, 19th Sess, UN Doc E/C.12/1998/24, (1998) [*General Comment 9*].

28 *Ibid.*

Judicial and quasi-judicial mechanisms should thus be integrated with effective informal and administrative procedures for claiming and enforcing social rights under legislated housing and poverty reduction strategies.

There are multiple fora in which rights to housing and an adequate standard of living can be claimed, defined, and applied, and many ways in which rights can and should affect policies and programs, short of court orders. The Supreme Court of Canada has yet to decide to what degree programs to remedy poverty or homelessness are constitutionally mandated, but it has affirmed that such measures are constitutionally "encouraged" by *Charter* values.[29] Chief Justice McLachlin has observed that the *Charter* does not belong to the courts but "to the people."[30] Rights-based strategies for the elimination of poverty and homelessness may serve as one way to reclaim rights and to provide access to new types of adjudication and remedies that are too often denied within the judicial system as it currently operates.

2) "Progressive Realization" and the Obligation to Implement Strategies

Under both domestic and international law, key components of economic and social rights are subject to "progressive realization." Obligations are assessed relative to the available resources and to the stage of development of institutions and programs within the State party.[31] Article 2(1) of the *ICESCR* requires the government of a State party "to take steps . . . to the maximum of its available resources, with a view to achieving progressively the full realization of the rights recognized in the present Covenant by all appropriate means, including particularly the adoption of legislative measures."[32]

Where violations of the right to housing or to an adequate standard of living result from a denial of an immediate, minimal entitlement that is within the government's means to provide, the remedy is straightforward: the government must immediately provide the benefit. The progressive realization standard, however, also creates additional future-oriented obli-

29 *Schachter v Canada*, [1992] 2 SCR 679.

30 *Cooper v Canada (Human Rights Commission)*, [1996] 3 SCR 854 at para 70, McLachlin J (as she then was), dissenting.

31 *International Covenant on Economic, Social and Cultural Rights*, 16 December 1966, 993 UNTS 3, Can TS 1976 No 46 (entered into force 3 January 1976, accession by Canada 19 May 1976) at art 2 [*ICESCR*].

32 *Ibid*.

gations to fulfill the right to adequate income or housing within a reasonable time and, at the same time, to address broader structural patterns of disadvantage and exclusion which take time to remedy. The rights can only be fulfilled in the future, but the requirement to design and implement appropriate strategies through legislation and programs is an immediate obligation. The CESCR has consistently emphasized, from its first general comment on, that even if the full implementation of *ICESCR* rights cannot be achieved immediately, there is still an overriding obligation to develop "clearly stated and carefully targeted policies, including the establishment of priorities which reflect the provisions of the Covenant."[33] There is a specific obligation "to work out and adopt a detailed plan of action for the progressive implementation" of each of the rights contained in the Covenant.[34] In *General Comment No 3, on the Nature of States Parties' Obligations*, the CESCR noted that while *ICESCR* rights are subject to progressive realization, there are two overriding obligations which are of immediate effect: the obligation to ensure non-discrimination and the obligation "to take steps."[35] The steps taken "should be deliberate, concrete and targeted as clearly as possible towards meeting the obligations recognized in the Covenant."[36] "Moreover, the obligations to monitor the extent of the realization, or more especially of the non-realization, of economic, social and cultural rights, and to devise strategies and programmes for their promotion, are not in any way eliminated as a result of resource constraints."[37]

Legislative measures are almost always desirable and in some cases indispensable. The CESCR notes that a critical concern is whether legislative measures "create any right of action on behalf of individuals or groups who feel that their rights are not being fully realized."[38] In *General Comment No 4* on the right to adequate housing,[39] the CESCR noted that the *ICESCR* "clearly requires that each State party take whatever steps are necessary" for

---

33 United Nations Committee on Economic, Social and Cultural Rights, *General Comment 1: Report by States Parties*, UNCESCROR, 3d Sess, UN Doc E/1989/22, (1989) at para 4.

34 *Ibid.*

35 United Nations Committee on Economic, Social and Cultural Rights, *General Comment 3: The Nature of States Parties Obligations (art. 2, para. 1 of the Covenant)*, UNCESCROR, 5th Sess, UN Doc E/1991/23, (1990) [*General Comment 3*].

36 *Ibid* at para 2.

37 *Ibid* at para 11.

38 *Ibid* at para 6.

39 United Nations Committee on Economic, Social and Cultural Rights, *General Comment 4: The Right to Adequate Housing (art 11(1) of the Covenant)*, UNCESCROR, 6th Sess, UN Doc E/1992/23, (1991) [*General Comment 4*].

fulfilling the right to adequate housing and that this "will almost invariably require the adoption of a national housing strategy."[40] Legal remedies must be available to groups facing evictions, inadequate housing conditions, or discrimination in access to housing.[41] The CESCR has affirmed similar obligations in other general comments such as those relating to the right to adequate food,[42] the right to social security,[43] the right to work,[44] the right to health,[45] and the right to water[46] calling on States to create targeted national strategies based on human rights principles to ensure that each of these rights is fulfilled.

3) The Reasonableness Standard

The standard to be applied in assessing whether strategies or programs comply with the "progressive realization" standard under article 2(1) of the *ICESCR* was the object of intense debate during the drafting of the optional complaints procedure to the *ICESCR*. Skeptical States, such as Canada, the United States, and Australia, argued that the *Optional Protocol* should prescribe a deferential standard of review, encouraging the CESCR to apply a "broad margin of discretion" or to require a finding of "unreasonableness" before a finding of a violation could be made.[47] Other States argued that

---

40 *Ibid* at para 12.

41 *Ibid* at para 17.

42 United Nations Committee on Economic, Social and Cultural Rights, *General Comment 12: The Right to Adequate Food (art 11)*, UNCESCROR, 20th Sess, UN Doc E/C.12/1999/5, (1999) at paras 4 and 21 [*General Comment 12*].

43 United Nations Committee on Economic, Social and Cultural Rights, *General Comment 19: The Right to Social Security (art 9)*, UNCESCROR, 39th Sess, UN Doc E/C.12/GC/19, (2007) at paras 41, 48, and 67 [*General Comment 19*].

44 United Nations Committee on Economic, Social and Cultural Rights, *General Comment 18: The Right to Work (art 6)*, UNCESCROR, 35th Sess, UN Doc E/C.12/GC/18, (2006) at para 31 [*General Comment 18*].

45 United Nations Committee on Economic, Social and Cultural Rights, *General Comment 14: The Right to the Highest Attainable Standard of Health (art 12)*, UNCESCROR, 22d Sess, UN Doc E/C.12/2000/4, (2000) at para 43(f) [*General Comment 14*].

46 United Nations Committee on Economic, Social and Cultural Rights, *General Comment No. 15: The Right to Water (arts. 11 and 12)* E/C.12/2002/11, (2002) at paras 28 and 31 [*General Comment 15*].

47 United Nations Committee on Economic, Social and Cultural Rights, *Report of the Open-Ended Working Group to Consider Options Regarding the Elaboration of an Optional Protocol to the International Covenant on Economic, Social and Cultural Rights on its Third Session*, UN Commission on Human Rights, 62d Sess, UN Doc E/CN.4/2006/47, (2006) at para 92.

such a deferential standard would defeat the very purpose of the *Optional Protocol* by undermining any meaningful accountability of States in relation to the *ICESCR*'s key substantive programmatic obligations.[48] In the end, proposals for a deferential standard of review were not accepted, and references to a margin of discretion were omitted. The final text of the *Optional Protocol* prescribes a standard of "reasonableness" in assessing steps taken to achieve progressive realization of *ICESCR* rights, requiring compliance with the substantive guarantees in Part II of the *ICESCR* while recognizing there may be a variety of ways for governments to achieve the results necessary for compliance:

> When examining communications under the present Protocol, the Committee shall consider the reasonableness of the steps taken by the State Party in accordance with Part II of the Covenant. In doing so, the Committee shall bear in mind that the State Party may adopt a range of possible policy measures for the implementation of the rights.[49]

The specific wording used in the *Optional Protocol* was taken from a paragraph of the now famous *Grootboom*[50] decision on the right to adequate housing in South Africa, in which the South African Constitutional Court first developed its reasonableness standard for review of compliance with the justiciable economic and social rights in the South African Constitution.[51] In adopting this formulation, the Open Ended Working Group mandated to draft the *Optional Protocol* was also guided by a statement prepared by the CESCR: *An Evaluation of the Obligation to Take Steps to the "Maximum of Available Resources" under an Optional Protocol to the Covenant*, in which the committee suggested for the first time that in evaluating compliance with article 2(1) of the *ICESCR*, it would assess the "reasonableness" of steps taken.[52] In its statement, the CESCR identified a number of pos-

---

48 See Bruce Porter, "The Reasonableness of Article 8(4): Adjudicating Claims from the Margins" (2009) 27:1 Nordic Journal of Human Rights 39 [Porter, "Reasonableness"]; Brian Griffey, "The 'Reasonableness' Test: Assessing Violations of State Obligations under the Optional Protocol to the International Covenant on Economic, Social and Cultural Rights" (2011) 11 HRL Rev 275 at 290. Porter and Griffey provide descriptions of the debates on the reasonableness standard.

49 *Optional Protocol*, above note 4.

50 *Government of the Republic of South Africa v Grootboom*, [2000] ZACC 19 (SAFLII) (S Afr Const Ct).

51 Porter, "Reasonableness," above note 48.

52 United Nations Committee on Economic, Social and Cultural Rights, *An Evaluation of the Obligation to Take Steps to the "Maximum of Available Resources" under an Optional Protocol to the Covenant*, UNCESCROR, 38th Sess, UN Doc E/C.12/2007/1,

sible factors to be considered in determining whether steps taken by a State party meet the reasonableness standard, including

- the extent to which the measures taken were deliberate, concrete, and targeted towards the fulfilment of economic, social, and cultural rights;
- whether discretion was exercised in a non-discriminatory and non-arbitrary manner;
- whether resource allocation is in accordance with international human rights standards;
- whether the State party adopts the option that least restricts *ICESCR* rights;
- whether the steps were taken within a reasonable timeframe;
- whether the precarious situation of disadvantaged and marginalized individuals or groups has been addressed;
- whether policies have prioritized grave situations or situations of risk; and
- whether decision making is transparent and participatory.[53]

Beyond the CESCR's commentary on the reasonableness standard under the *Optional Protocol*, there is extensive jurisprudence in CESCR's general comments and in its concluding observations on periodic reviews of State parties that provides further clarification as to the requirements of policies and strategies for compliance with article 2(1) of the *ICESCR*. Comprehensive and purposive legislative measures are almost always required,[54] and strategies must be informed by an equality framework, prioritizing the needs of disadvantaged groups and ensuring protection from discrimination.[55]

(2007) [CESCR, "Maximum Available Resources"]; Malcolm Langford, "Closing the Gap? — An Introduction to the Optional Protocol to the International Covenant on Economic, Social and Cultural Rights" (2009) 27:1 Nordic Journal of Human Rights 1.

53 *Ibid.*

54 *General Comment 3*, above note 35.

55 United Nations Committee on Economic, Social and Cultural Rights, *General Comment 20: Non-discrimination in Economic, Social and Cultural Rights (art 2 para 2)*, UNCESCROR, 42d Sess, UN Doc E/C.12/GC/20, (2009) at para 9 [*General Comment 20*]. See also UN Commission on Human Rights, *Note Verbale Dated 86/12/05 from the Permanent Mission of the Netherlands to the United Nations Office at Geneva Addressed to the Centre for Human Rights ("Limburg Principles")*, UN Doc E/CN.4/1987/17, (1987) at para 39: "Special measures taken for the sole purpose of securing adequate advancement of certain groups or individuals requiring such protection as may be necessary in order to ensure to such groups or individuals equal enjoyment of economic, social, and cultural rights shall not be deemed discrimination."

Strategies must specifically address issues of systemic discrimination and the barriers faced by individuals who have suffered historic discrimination or prejudice and should include "efforts to overcome negative stereotyped images."[56] They should rely on effective "coordination between the national ministries, regional and local authorities."[57] Human rights institutions may scrutinize existing laws, identify appropriate goals and benchmarks, provide research, monitor compliance, examine complaints of alleged infringements, and disseminate educational materials.[58]

The CESCR has emphasized that monitoring and redress should also include assessment of budgetary measures.[59] The reasonableness of budgetary allotment can be assessed based on information about the percentage of the budget allocated to specific rights under the *ICESCR* and may be compared to that of other States with similar levels of development.[60]

As Brian Griffey notes, "questions remain as to how the 'reasonableness' test will be applied, but the answer must be consistent with *ICESCR* obligations and the object and purpose of the *Optional Protocol*."[61] Reasonable strategies will be based on a commitment to ensuring access to adequate housing and freedom from poverty as fundamental human rights that can be effectively claimed and enforced.

---

56 *Ibid* at para 41.

57 United Nations Committee on Economic, Social and Cultural Rights, *General Comment 15: The Right to Water (art 11 & 12)*, UNCESCROR, 29th Sess, UN Doc E/C.12/2002/1, (2002) at para 51 [*General Comment 15*].

58 United Nations Committee on Economic, Social and Cultural Rights, *General Comment 10: The Role of National Human Rights Institutions in the Protection of Economic, Social and Cultural Rights*, UNCESCROR, 19th Sess, UN Doc E/C.12/1998/25, (1998) at para 3.

59 *General Comment 3*, above note 35 at para 11.

60 Manisuli Ssenyonjo, "Reflections on State Obligations with respect to Economic, Social and Cultural Rights in International Human Rights Law" (2011) 15:6 Int'l JHR 969 at 980–81. See, for example, United Nations Committee on Economic, Social and Cultural Rights, *Consideration of Reports Submitted by States Parties under Articles 16 and 17 of the Covenant: Concluding Observations of the Committee on Economic, Social and Cultural Rights: Democratic Republic of Congo*, UNCESCROR, 43d Sess, UN Doc E/C.12/COD/CO/4, (2009) at para 16, where the committee found that the State's decreased allocation of resources to social sector development combined with increased levels of military spending resulted in a violation of its Covenant obligations; Brian Griffey, "The 'Reasonableness' Test: Assessing Violations of State Obligations under the Optional Protocol to the International Covenant on Economic, Social and Cultural Rights" (2011) 11 HRL Rev 275 at 290 [Griffey, "The Reasonableness Test"].

61 Griffey, "The Reasonableness Test," *ibid* at 304.

As Sandra Liebenberg and Geo Quinot have argued in relation to the reasonableness standard in South African jurisprudence, the requirement of "reasonableness" itself demands a rights-conscious strategy, commensurate with the special status of "rights" in comparison to other legitimate policy objectives:

> It is not enough that the objectives which the State sets itself fall within the broad range of what are regarded as "legitimate" State objectives. These objectives must be consistent with the normative purposes of the rights. This implies a rights-conscious social policy, planning and budgeting process. It is noteworthy in this context that one of the core obligations identified by the UN Committee on Economic, Social and Cultural Rights in relation to the rights protected in the International Covenant on Economic, Social and Cultural Rights (1966) is the adoption of a national strategy and plan of action aimed at the realisation of the relevant rights. Such a national plan must be participatory and transparent and set clear goals as well as indicators and benchmarks by which progress can be monitored. Particular attention must be given in the plan to vulnerable or marginalised groups.[62]

An important avenue for the integration of international human rights norms into housing and anti-poverty strategy in Canada, as in South Africa, will be through the development of domestic standards of reasonableness under both administrative and constitutional law.[63] Reasonable decision making in domestic law in Canada, as was affirmed by the Supreme Court of Canada in *Baker*, requires conformity with both international human rights values and with the *Charter*.[64] In *Eldridge*, the Supreme Court found that the duty to take reasonable positive measures to accommodate disability is a component of section 1 of the *Charter*.[65] In the recent decision of *Doré v Barreau du Québec*,[66] the Court departed from some of its earlier jurisprudence[67] by proposing that in cases where administrative decision

62 Geo Quinot & Sandra Liebenberg, "Narrowing the Band: Reasonableness Review in Administrative Justice and Socio-economic Rights Jurisprudence in South Africa" (Paper delivered at the Law and Poverty Colloquium, Stellanbosch University, South Africa, 29–31 May 2011), [unpublished, on file with authors].

63 United Nations Committee on Economic, Social and Cultural Rights, *General Comment 1: Report by States Parties*, UNCESCROR, 3d Sess, UN Doc E/1989/22, (1989).

64 *Baker v Canada (Minister of Citizenship and Immigration)*, [1999] 2 SCR 817 at paras 69–71 [*Baker*].

65 *Eldridge v British Columbia (AG)*, [1997] 3 SCR 624 at para 79 [*Eldridge*].

66 *Doré v Barreau du Québec*, 2012 SCC 12 [*Doré*].

67 *Multani v Commission scolaire Marguerite-Bourgeoys*, 2006 SCC 6.

making under statutory authority is alleged to have been exercised in a manner that is contrary to the *Charter*, judicial review of such decisions may be conducted under a "robust" administrative law test of reasonableness, nurtured by the *Charter*, which can provide essentially the same level of protection of *Charter* rights as does a section 1 analysis.[68] In its more recent decision in the *Insite* case (*PHS Community Services Society*[69]), the Supreme Court found that where decisions impact on the rights to life and security of the person, discretion must be exercised also in conformity with principles of fundamental justice. Principles of fundamental justice must include international human rights norms.[70] Drawing on this jurisprudence, there is ample room to apply both domestic and international standards of reasonableness as a legal requirement of strategies and programs to address poverty and homelessness.

D. RECOMMENDATIONS OF INTERNATIONAL HUMAN RIGHTS BODIES FOR HOUSING AND ANTI-POVERTY STRATEGIES IN CANADA

Concerns among international human rights bodies about the growing crisis of poverty and homelessness in Canada, one of the most affluent countries to have ratified the *ICESCR*, have reached unprecedented levels in recent years. The centrepiece of the CESCR's recommendations with respect to poverty and homelessness in Canada has been a strategy for the reduction of homelessness and poverty that integrates economic, social, and cultural rights.[71] The CESCR has emphasized that a strategy in Canada should include "measurable goals and timetables, consultation and collaboration with affected communities, complaints procedures, and trans-

---

68 *Doré*, above note 66 at para 29. For a discussion of the implications of the evolving jurisprudence on reasonableness in administrative law, see Chapter 11.

69 *Canada (AG) v PHS Community Services Society*, 2011 SCC 44 [*PHS Community Services Society*].

70 *Suresh v Canada (Minister of Citizenship and Immigration)*, 2002 SCC 1.

71 United Nations Committee on Economic, Social and Cultural Rights, *Consideration of Reports Submitted by States Parties under Articles 16 and 17 of the Covenant: Concluding Observations of the Committee on Economic, Social and Cultural Rights: Canada*, UNCESCROR, 19th Sess, UN Doc E/C.12/1/Add.31, (1998) at para 46 [*Concluding Observations* 1998]. See also United Nations Committee on Economic, Social and Cultural Rights, *Consideration of Reports Submitted by States Parties under Articles 16 and 17 of the Covenant: Concluding Observations of the Committee on Economic, Social and Cultural Rights: Canada*, UNCESCROR, 36th Sess, UN Doc E/C.12/CAN/CO/4 & E/C.12/CAN/CO/5, (2006) at para 60 [*Concluding Observations* 2006].

parent accountability mechanisms, in keeping with Covenant standards."[72] The CESCR has referred Canada to its statement, *Poverty and the International Covenant on Economic, Social and Cultural Rights*, which is aimed at "encouraging the integration of human rights into poverty eradication policies by outlining how human rights generally, and the *ICESCR* in particular, can empower the poor and enhance anti-poverty strategies."[73] The CESCR has emphasized that "anti-poverty policies are more likely to be effective, sustainable, inclusive, equitable and meaningful to those living in poverty if they are based upon international human rights."[74]

The CESCR's recommendations were reinforced during the 2007 visit to Canada of the UN Special Rapporteur on Adequate Housing Miloon Kothari. A key recommendation in Kothari's Mission Report on Canada was for "a comprehensive and coordinated national housing policy based on indivisibility of human rights and the protection of the most vulnerable."[75] Kothari reiterated the recommendations of the CESCR that the strategy should include measurable goals and timetables, complaints procedures, and transparent accountability mechanisms.[76] He recommended that federal and provincial governments work in close collaboration and coordination and "commit stable and long-term funding to a comprehensive national housing strategy."[77] The special rapporteur also strongly advocated for the improvement of legal remedies for poverty and homelessness, recommending that the "right to adequate housing be recognized in federal and provincial legislation as an inherent part of the Canadian legal system."[78]

The UN Human Rights Council's two reviews of Canada under the new Universal Periodic Review (UPR) procedure have also highlighted the need for anti-poverty and housing strategies based on human rights. Prior

---

72 *Concluding Observations* 1998, *ibid* at para 62.

73 United Nations Committee on Economic, Social and Cultural Rights, *Substantive Issues Arising in the Implementation of the International Covenant on Economic, Social and Cultural Rights: Poverty and the International Covenant on Economic, Social and Cultural Rights*, UNCESCROR, 25th Sess, UN Doc E/C.12/2001/1, (2001) at para 3 [*Poverty and the ICESCR*].

74 *Ibid* at para 13.

75 United Nations Human Rights Council, *Report of the Special Rapporteur on Adequate Housing as a Component of the Right to an Adequate Standard of Living, and on the Right to Non-discrimination in This Context, Miloon Kothari — Addendum — Mission to Canada (9–22 October 2007)*, UNHRCOR, 10th Sess, UN Doc A/HRC/10/7/Add.3, (2009) at para 90 [*SR Mission to Canada*].

76 *Ibid.*

77 *Ibid* at para 92.

78 *Ibid* at para 88.

to Canada's appearance for its UPR before the UN Human Rights Council in 2009, an NGO Steering Committee coordinated six meetings in cities across the country with over 200 civil society and Aboriginal organizations as well as representatives from the federal and provincial governments. Drawing on these meetings, a briefing document outlining major human rights concerns was prepared and provided to members of the Human Rights Council in informal meetings in Geneva in the days leading up to Canada's review.[79] The briefing document highlighted poverty and homelessness as the issues of greatest concern to all NGOs, Aboriginal communities, and stakeholders, and strongly recommended the development of human rights–based strategies to address both.[80]

Recommendations considered under the UPR come from other States participating in the UPR process and may be either formally accepted or rejected by the State under review. Among the recommendations in Canada's 2009 *UPR* were that Canada develop "a national strategy to eliminate poverty" and "consider taking on board the recommendation of the Special Rapporteur on adequate housing, specifically to extend and enhance the national homelessness programme."[81] Further to this, it was recommended that Canada "intensify the efforts already undertaken to better ensure the right to adequate housing, especially for vulnerable groups and low-income families."[82]

The recommendation to adopt a national strategy to address poverty was not accepted by Canada in its response to the 2009 *UPR*. The federal government expressed support for the provincial strategies but refused to commit to implementing the recommended federal plan.[83] Canada did, however, formally accept the recommendations with respect to the right to adequate housing, and partially accepted a recommendation to "integrate economic social and cultural rights in its poverty reduction strategies in a way that

79 *The Universal Periodic Review of Canada: February 2009: An Overview of a Select Number of Canadian NGO Concerns and Recommendations* (31 January 2009), online: Social Rights CURA www.socialrightscura.ca.

80 *Ibid.*

81 United Nations Human Rights Council, *Report of the Working Group on the Universal Periodic Review: Canada*, UN Human Rights Council OR, 11th Sess, UN Doc A/HRC/11/17, (2009) at paras 45, 72, and 75 [2009 *UPR*].

82 *Ibid* at para 72.

83 United Nations Human Rights Council, *Report of the Working Group on the Universal Periodic Review: Canada, Addendum, Views on Conclusions and/or Recommendations, Voluntary Commitments and Replies Presented by the State under Review*, UNHRCOR, 11th Sess, UN Doc A/HRC/11/17/Add.1, (2009) at paras 9, 11, and 27 [Response to 2009 *UPR*].

can benefit the most vulnerable groups in society."[84] Recommendations for strategies to address homelessness and poverty were made again in Canada's 2013 *UPR*, supplemented by further recommendations for strategies to ensure food security and the rights to water and sanitation.[85] Canada again refused to accept any of the recommended strategies to reduce and eliminate hunger, poverty, or homelessness and thus continues to resist sustained and growing pressure from UN human rights bodies to address these crises within a human rights framework.[86]

E. CALLS FOR NATIONAL RIGHTS-BASED HOUSING AND ANTI-POVERTY STRATEGIES IN CANADA

In 2008, the Subcommittee on Cities of the Standing Senate Committee on Social Affairs, Science, and Technology held a national consultation on housing and homelessness, soliciting feedback from numerous experts and civil society representatives. In its report, *In from the Margins: A Call to Action on Poverty, Housing and Homelessness*, the subcommittee noted that

> [w]hether the subject was poverty, housing or homelessness, many witnesses described the problems in terms of rights denied. Pointing to both domestic human rights legislation and international commitments made by Canada to United Nations declarations and conventions, these witnesses identified the failure of governments to live up to these obligations, and the importance of providing access for individuals to hold governments accountable and to claim rights in appropriate courts and tribunals.[87]

The subcommittee's report went on to cite then UN High Commissioner on Human Rights Louise Arbour's statement that poverty "describes a complex of interrelated and mutually reinforcing deprivations, which impact on people's ability to claim and access their civil, cultural, economic,

---

84 2009 *UPR*, above note 81 at para 45; Response to 2009 *UPR*, above note 83 at paras 26 and 28.

85 United Nations Human Rights Council, *Report of the Working Group on the Universal Periodic Review: Canada*, UNHRCOR, 24th Sess, UN Doc A/HRC/24/11, (2013) at paras 128.124–128.126 and 128.30–128.133.

86 United Nations Human Rights Council, *Report of the Working Group on the Universal Periodic Review: Canada, Addendum, Views on Conclusions and/or Recommendations, Voluntary Commitments and Replies Presented by the State under Review*, UNHRCOR, 24th Sess, UN Doc A/HRC/24/11/Add.1, (2013) at para 30.

87 Senate, *In from the Margins*, above note 26 at 15.

political, and social rights. In a fundamental way, therefore, the denial of human rights forms part of the very definition of what it is to be poor."[88]

The senate subcommittee called for a national housing and homelessness strategy to complement similar initiatives being launched at the provincial/territorial level.[89] In support of a rights-based approach, the report identified three main sources of legal rights relevant to poverty and homelessness: (1) international law that has been ratified by Canada, (2) the *Canadian Charter of Rights and Freedoms*, and (3) provincial and federal human rights legislation.[90] The subcommittee recommended measures to enhance the ability of people living in poverty to claim their rights, including legal representation in "law reform cases with respect to their human rights."[91] In order to strengthen the status of international human rights law in relation to the treatment of poverty and homelessness in Canada, the subcommittee recommended that the federal government "explicitly cite international obligations ratified by Canada in any new federal legislation or legislative amendments relevant to poverty, housing and homelessness."[92]

In 2010, following up on the recommendations by the senate subcommittee, the House of Commons Standing Committee on Human Resources, Skills and Social Development and the Status of Persons with Disabilities (HUMA Committee) held hearings and issued a report on a federal poverty reduction plan.[93] The committee reported that

> [t]he Committee was told that we also need a shift in perspective if we are to significantly reduce poverty in Canada. Poverty reduction measures must not be seen only as charity work or only be guided by moral principles, but must be set within a human rights framework, specifically the recognition that governments have a duty to enforce socio-economic and civil rights. Adopting a human rights framework also limits the stigmatization of people living in poverty. The Committee fully endorses such a framework in this report.[94]

---

88 *Ibid* at 71.

89 *Ibid* at 104.

90 *Ibid* at 69–72.

91 *Ibid* at 16.

92 *Ibid.*

93 House of Commons, Standing Committee on Human Resources, Skills and Social Development and the Status of Persons with Disabilities (Chair: Candice Hoeppner), *Federal Poverty Reduction Plan: Working in Partnership Towards Reducing Poverty in Canada* (November 2010), online: Parliament of Canada www.parl.gc.ca [HUMA Committee].

94 *Ibid* at 2.

The HUMA Committee referred to the development of a new human rights paradigm for poverty reduction at the international level, quoting from a 2004 publication of the Office of the High Commissioner for Human Rights, which led to the adoption of the 2006 OHCHR *Guidelines*:

> The recognition that the way poor people are forced to live often violates their human rights — or that promoting human rights could alleviate poverty — was a long time in coming. Now a human rights approach to poverty reduction is increasingly being recognized internationally and is gradually being implemented.[95]

The HUMA Committee noted the importance of Canada's international obligations, both under the *UDHR* and in ratified human rights treaties, to ensure an adequate standard of living, including adequate housing.[96] It recommended the federal government "endorse the *United Nations Declaration on the Rights of Indigenous Peoples* and implement the standards set out in this document."[97] The committee also emphasized the importance of ensuring that measures to reduce poverty among people with disabilities are linked to human rights protections, including the recently ratified *Convention on the Rights of Persons with Disabilities*.[98]

The central recommendation of the HUMA Committee was for a rights-based federal action plan for the reduction of poverty. In the committee's view:

> This action plan should incorporate a human rights framework and provide for consultations with the provincial and territorial governments, Aboriginal governments and organizations, the public and private sector, and people living in poverty, as needed, to ensure an improvement in lives of impoverished people.[99]

An important initiative to incorporate international human rights within federal legislation along the lines suggested by the HUMA Committee was found in Bill C-304, *An Act to Ensure Secure, Adequate, Accessible and*

95 *Ibid* at 92, citing United Nations Office of the High Commissioner for Human Rights, *Human Rights and Poverty Reduction: A Conceptual Framework*, UN Doc HR/PUB/04/1, 2004 at iii [OHCHR, *Conceptual*].

96 HUMA Committee, above note 93 at 53.

97 *Ibid* at 164.

98 *Ibid* at 134.

99 *Ibid* at 96.

Affordable Housing for Canadians.[100] Originally introduced as a private member's bill by New Democratic Party (NDP) MP Libby Davies and receiving widespread support from civil society organizations across Canada,[101] the bill was substantially amended after second reading to include a more robust human rights framework, in line with recommendations from UN treaty bodies.

The amendments to Bill C-304 required the implementation of "a national housing strategy designed to respect, protect, promote and fulfil the right to adequate housing as guaranteed under international human rights treaties ratified by Canada."[102] The bill called for the national housing strategy to include

- targets and timelines for the elimination of homelessness;
- an independent process for bringing, reviewing, and reporting on complaints about possible violations of the right to adequate housing;
- a process for reviewing and following up on any concerns or recommendations from UN human rights bodies with respect to the right to adequate housing;
- a focus on the needs of those who are homeless, groups facing discrimination, people with disabilities, and Aboriginal communities;
- a key role for civil society organizations, including those representing groups in need of housing and Aboriginal communities, in designing the delivery, monitoring, and evaluation of programs required to implement the right to adequate housing; and
- a provision recognizing Quebec's unique commitment to the rights in the *ICESCR*.[103]

---

100 Bill C-304, *An Act to Ensure Secure, Adequate, Accessible and Affordable Housing for Canadians*, 3d Sess, 40th Parl, 2011 (Committee report presented in House of Commons 21 March 2011) [Bill C-304].

101 Rob Rainer, "The Right to Housing: The Red Tent Campaign and Bill C-304" *Canada without Poverty Advocacy Network* (14 July 2010), online: Social Policy in Ontario http://spon.ca.

102 Bill C-304, above note 100, s 3(1).

103 *Ibid*, s 3.1. The French version of the provision reads, "Le Québec peut, ayant adhéré au *Pacte international relatif aux droits économiques, sociaux et culturels*, utiliser les avantages découlant de la présente loi dans le cadre de ses propres choix, de ses propres programmes et de sa propre stratégie en matière d'habitation sur son territoire." This provision was incorrectly translated in the English version of Bill C-304 to read "Quebec may, *as a party* to the *International Covenant on Economic, Social and Cultural Rights*, participate in the benefits of this Act with respect to its own choices, its own programs and its own approach related to housing on its territory" [emphasis added]. The English translation was corrected in Bill C-400 to

A 2010 report of the Standing Committee on Foreign Affairs and International Development noted that Bill C-304 "directly responds to concerns repeatedly raised by UN treaty bodies."[104] The bill received significant support from communities across Canada and had the support of the majority of members of Parliament but did not come to a vote at third reading before the dissolution of Parliament.[105] Bill C-304 was reintroduced as a private member's bill (C-400) in the subsequent Parliament under a Conservative majority.[106] Despite widespread support from civil society organizations, the bill was defeated on 27 February, though all four opposition parties and two independent members supported it.[107] The extent of support Bill C-304 and Bill C-400 received across the country, within and beyond the

---

read "Quebec may, *having ratified* the *International Convenent on Economic, Social and Cultural Rights*..." [emphasis added]. Quebec has set a unique standard for provincial adherence to international human rights treaties that could be a model for other provinces. It has formally "ratified" key treaties and committed itself to compliance in areas of its jurisdiction. On 21 April 1976, by Order in Council (1438-76), Quebec "ratified" the *ICESCR*, signed it, and transmitted a signed copy of the treaty to the federal government. The Order in Council reads as follows:

> Que le gouvernement du Québec ratifie le Pacte international relatif aux droits économiques, sociaux et culturels, le Pacte international relatif aux droits civils et politiques, le Protocole facultative se rapportant au Pacte international relatif aux droits civils et politiques; Que le texte officiel des modalités et du mécanisme de participation des provinces à la mise en oeuvre de ces instruments internationaux soit signé par le ministre des Affaires intergouvernementales et par le ministre de la Justice; Que le ministre des Affaires intergouvernementales soit chargé de transmettre aux autorités fédérales cette ratification et le texte signé de l'entente; Que cette ratification et cette entente entrent en vigueur à partir du moment où elles auront été communiqués au gouvernement fédéral.

See online (for full text): Social Rights CURA www.socialrightscura.ca.

104 House of Commons, Subcommittee on International Human Rights of the Standing Committee on Foreign Affairs and International Development (Chair: Scott Reid), *Canada's Universal Periodic Review and Beyond — Upholding Canada's International Reputation as a Global Leader in the Field of Human Rights* (November 2010) at 16, online: Parliament of Canada www.parl.gc.ca [House of Commons, *Universal*].

105 Bill C-304, *An Act to Ensure Secure, Adequate, Accessible and Affordable Housing for Canadians*, 3d Sess, 40th Parl, 2011 (Committee report presented in House of Commons 21 March 2011).

106 Bill C-400, *An Act to Ensure Secure, Adequate, Accessible and Affordable Housing for Canadians*, 1st Sess, 41st Parl, 2012 (first reading 16 February 2012).

107 *Ibid*, bill defeated 27 February 2013, 41st Parl, 1st Sess, Sitting No 215, Vote No 619.

housing and anti-poverty communities demonstrates the strength of civil society and public commitment to its underlying rights-based approach.

F. CONCLUSION: EMERGING SITES FOR A MORE INCLUSIVE SOCIAL RIGHTS PRACTICE IN CANADA

Groups advocating for people living in poverty and without adequate housing in Canada have increasingly turned to international human rights for a framework through which to identify and challenge conditions of inequality and socio-economic exclusion. The National Anti-poverty Organization and the *Charter* Committee on Poverty Issues prompted reform of UN treaty body procedures in the early 1990s when they requested and were granted permission to appear before the CESCR in the context of Canada's 1993 periodic review. Until then, stakeholders had no formal voice in the periodic review process before any UN human rights body.[108] Since that time, Canadian NGOs have shown a singular commitment to making the international treaty monitoring processes work more effectively as a framework for domestic human rights practice. Reviews of Canada before human rights bodies are well known within the UN system for the extensive involvement of NGOs, in terms of both the numbers of groups and coalitions engaging with the process and the depth and range of their oral and written submissions. Canadian NGOs have consistently pressed for reform of domestic procedures to ensure more effective follow-up to, and implementation of, treaty body concerns and recommendations and for more effective domestic remedies to violations of social rights.[109]

NGO recommendations for improved domestic implementation have been taken up by and endorsed by parliamentary bodies charged with reviewing the implementation of international human rights. The Senate Committee on Human Rights conducted a review of implementation of Canada's international human rights obligations in 2001, recommending, among other things, the appointment of a human rights ambassador, regular federal/provincial/territorial meetings on human rights, and amend-

108 Bruce Porter, "Using Human Rights Treaty Monitoring Bodies in Domestic Social and Economic Rights Advocacy: Notes from Canada" (1999) 2:1 Economic and Social Rights Review 2.

109 Shelagh Day, "Minding the Gap: Human Rights Commitments and Compliance" in Margot Young et al, eds, above note 6 at 201; Porter, "Claiming," above note 6.

ments to the *Canadian Human Rights Act* to include international human rights.[110] As the senate committee eloquently stated:

> The disjuncture between Canada's international human rights commitments and its domestic law cannot be allowed to go unaddressed. Nor is it fair or proper to sit back and hope that the courts will rescue Canada from the inconsistencies in its approach to its international human rights obligations. A new approach must be found. Otherwise, the continued failure of the government in Canada to systematically address the domestic legal implications of international human rights treaties it has voluntarily ratified could leave this country open to charges of hypocrisy and has the potential to diminish Canada's moral authority as a leading voice for human rights in the international arena.[111]

The senate committee has followed up with reports on Canada's engagement with the UPR process, urging the adoption of "a process that will ensure open and transparent, timely, and substantive engagement with civil society, aboriginal organizations, parliaments, and the Canadian public with respect to implementation of Canada's human rights obligations."[112] The House of Commons Standing Committee on Foreign Affairs and International Development has similarly expressed concern about the lack of consultation with civil society, transparency, and political leadership in implementing international human rights obligations, recommending serious reform of existing federal/provincial/territorial mechanisms for implementation and timely, constructive responses to UN concerns and recommendations.[113]

While provincial governments have taken important steps in engaging with civil society and stakeholders in the design and implementation of housing and anti-poverty strategies, the strategies to date have remained largely within the older paradigm of social rights as moral aspirations. They have failed to engage in any significant way with the notion of social rights as claimable rights or with the need for revitalized human rights

---

110 Senate Human Rights Committee, *Promises to Keep: Implementation of Canada's International Human Rights Obligations* (December 2001), online: Parliament of Canada www.parl.gc.ca.

111 *Ibid.*

112 Standing Senate Committee on Human Rights, *Canada's Universal Periodic Review before the United Nations Human Rights Council. Second Report* (May 2009), online: Parliament of Canada www.parl.gc.ca.

113 House of Commons, *Universal*, above note 104.

institutions and rights claiming mechanisms as have been promoted within the UN system and parliamentary committees.[114]

The model of rights-based approaches to poverty and homelessness that has evolved within international human rights is highly relevant to the ongoing crisis of poverty and homelessness in Canada and to the design of effective policies, programs, and strategies to address it. Sen's early insight about famine and hunger in the development contexts applies *a fortiori* to homelessness and poverty in Canada. Economic deprivation amidst affluence in Canada must be understood as a socially constructed systemic failure of law, policy, and decision making, deriving from the fundamental devaluing of the rights claims of those who have been stigmatized and pushed to the margins of society. It is not simply a problem of unmet needs. This is not to excuse governments from the obligation to reverse cuts to housing and social assistance programs or to ignore the myriad of ways in which programs are failing to meet the needs of those who are most disadvantaged. Rather, it is to situate social program cuts and budgetary decisions within the broader context of the devaluing of the rights and equal dignity and citizenship of those living in poverty and homelessness. Vitriolic attacks and stigmatization of the groups whose needs have been neglected are part of the social context for unmet needs within government programs. Marie-Eve Sylvestre, in her affidavit in support of a *Charter* challenge to governments' inaction on homelessness, notes that "[a]s programmatic responses that addressed the causes of homelessness such as social housing, investment in health care or employment policies, have been reduced or eliminated, governments have adopted unprecedented measures based on the 'stigma' of homelessness as a perceived 'moral' failure and designed to make homeless people disappear from the public sphere."[115] It is no accident that historically unprecedented social program cuts in Canada have been accompanied by withdrawal of funding and support for any rights-based advocacy on behalf of the groups most affected. The attack on programs and the attack on rights are inextricably linked.[116]

What will rights-based strategies look like in Canada? They will require a re-visioning of housing and anti-poverty strategies around the

---

114 For a review of provincial strategies, see Martha Jackman & Bruce Porter, "International Human Rights and Strategies to Address Homelessness and Poverty in Canada: Making the Connection," Ottawa Faculty of Law Working Paper No 2013-09, online: Social Rights CURA www.socialrightscura.ca.

115 Marie-Eve Sylvestre, "Affidavit for *Tanudjaja v Canada*" (Ont Sup Ct File no CV-10-403688) (2011) [Sylvestre, "Affidavit for *Tanudjaja*"].

116 Porter, "Claiming," above note 6.

normative framework of social rights as claimable rights that has emerged internationally. Goals and timelines for the reduction and elimination of homelessness will not simply be targets for governments but will also be articulated as entitlements to reasonable decision making consistent with the obligation of progressive realization and emerging standards of reasonableness internationally as well as with the more robust standard of administrative law reasonableness that has been affirmed by the Supreme Court of Canada, infused with *Charter* and international human rights values. Human rights norms will be written into a range of programs and legislation so as to inform the mandate and guide the decisions of statutory bodies and decision makers that have previously operated outside of any human rights framework. Courts will be required to engage more constructively with positive obligations of governments to implement transformative strategies consistent with the progressive and substantive nature of social rights and to require rights-based housing and anti-poverty strategies as remedies to *Charter* and other claims. The institutional mandate of human rights commissions, landlord and tenant, social benefits, labour, and many other administrative bodies will be reconceived in light of human rights norms and values. All of these changes will begin to ensure that the myriad of entitlement system failures that lie behind poverty and homelessness amidst affluence are brought within a human rights lens and made subject to effective remedies.

Creating a more robust human rights framework for housing and anti-poverty strategies in Canada does not "judicialize" social policy or make policy and programming more litigious. Quite the contrary. Current practices of criminalizing and stigmatizing those who are homeless or living in poverty based on false stereotype and prejudice are an aggressive "judicialization" of homelessness and poverty that has been proven to be fiscally as well as morally irresponsible.[117] A rights-based approach redefines the relationship between justice and socio-economic marginalization in a manner that challenges systemic discrimination rather than reinforces it.

Homelessness and poverty among those with mental health challenges and other disabilities are related to factors beyond scarcity of housing or employment. They call for a multi-dimensional solution, including challenging discrimination and stigmatization, and deconstructing how certain groups are socially constructed as "needy" by exclusionary and discriminatory policies. Clearly, the immediate need for adequate and affordable housing and improved incomes among these groups must be addressed, but the systemic factors and exclusionary systems that create the needs must also be

117 Sylvestre, "Affidavit for *Tanudjaja*," above note 115.

challenged. For example, exclusionary policies based on income, in both the private and not-for-profit housing markets, have resulted in single mothers on social assistance having no choice but to move into the most overpriced apartments, paying significantly higher monthly rent for inadequate apartments than those with higher incomes who are able to secure more affordable and desirable apartments because they are considered more desirable tenants.[118] A rights-based approach to housing and anti-poverty strategies provides the mechanism through which a transformative social rights practice can address and solve structural causes of economic deprivation such as this, while at the same time ensuring that governments' policies and budgetary allocations meet human rights standards of reasonableness.

Recognizing adequate housing and an adequate standard of living as claimable rights in Canada will rely, to some extent, on judicial and quasi-judicial hearings and remedies from courts, administrative tribunals, and on new commitments from institutions such as human rights commissions and tribunals. Emanating from improved legal remedies, however, will be an enhanced community understanding of fundamental rights. This in turn will create new opportunities for rights holders to be heard without the need for formal procedures. Rights-based housing and anti-poverty strategies offer the opportunity to implement, through local initiatives and strategies, the fundamental rights that have been affirmed and clarified at the international level, drawing from a movement that has become global in scope, but which is based on empowering rights holders to affirm and claim rights locally.

Until human rights, including the right to adequate housing and an adequate standard of living, are incorporated into housing and anti-poverty strategies as claimable rights, such strategies will remain, at best, governmental commitments to improved programs. Certainly governmental commitments to eliminate poverty and homelessness through improved programs are critical to any housing and anti-poverty strategy. However, addressing a fundamental human rights crisis must also include human rights as part of the solution and enlist the critical knowledge base and capacity of rights holders to identify systemic problems and devise solutions. Revaluing the rights of those who have been affected by the programmatic failures in the area of housing and income security in Canada remains a critical aspect of any strategic solution.

Provincial/territorial accountability is also critical to rights such as the right to adequate housing and the right to an adequate standard of living.

118 "Human Rights, Access and Equity: CERA's Recommendations for the Homelessness Action Task Force" (November 1998), online: Equality Rights www.equalityrights.org.

Housing and anti-poverty strategies present an ideal opportunity to develop new forms of accountability through municipal/provincial joint strategies with clear goals and timetables for eliminating poverty and homelessness, and providing for effective monitoring, complaints procedures, hearings, and remedies. Institutions such as provincial human rights commissions, law reform commissions, and ombudspersons could play important roles in making international human rights norms meaningful and relevant to rights holders.

Louise Arbour and Fannie Lafontaine have affirmed that "Canada has much to gain and nothing to lose in opening up to international tools for solving its domestic troubles."[119] It is time that governments in Canada responded to the chorus of recommendations, from the UN, parliamentary committees, social policy experts, and community organizations and grassroots movements, to take Canada's international human rights obligations seriously and incorporate them into housing and anti-poverty strategies. Rights-based strategies for the elimination of poverty and homelessness may serve as the next critical frontier through which to reclaim human rights that have been too long ignored.

---

119 Louise Arbour & Fannie Lafontaine, "Beyond Self-Congratulations: The *Charter* at 25 in an International Perspective" (2007) 45:2 Osgoode Hall LJ 239 at 257.

CHAPTER 2

RIGHTS-BASED STRATEGIES TO ADDRESS HOMELESSNESS AND POVERTY IN CANADA

THE *CHARTER* FRAMEWORK*

MARTHA JACKMAN† AND BRUCE PORTER‡

A. INTRODUCTION

The interdependence and overlap between socio-economic rights recognized under international human rights treaties ratified by Canada, including the right to adequate housing and to an adequate standard of living guaranteed by the *International Covenant on Economic, Social and Cultural Rights*,[1] and the rights that are explicitly included in the *Canadian Charter of Rights and Freedoms*,[2] such as the right to life, liberty, and security of the person and the right to equality, are widely acknowledged.[3] As Bruce Porter

---

* This chapter is a revised version of a longer paper written for the Population Health Improvement Research Network. The authors gratefully acknowledge the funding support provided by the Social Sciences and Humanities Research Council of Canada Community-University Research Alliance program.

† Martha Jackman, Professor, Faculty of Law, French Common Law Program, University of Ottawa and Co-Director (Academic) of the SSHRC-CURA Research Project "Reconceiving Human Rights Practice," online: www.socialrightscura.ca.

‡ Bruce Porter, Executive Director, Social Rights Advocacy Centre and Co-Director (Community) of the SSHRC-CURA Research Project "Reconceiving Human Rights Practice," online: www.socialrightscura.ca.

1 16 December 1966, 993 UNTS 3, Can TS 1976 No 46 (entered into force 3 January 1976, accession by Canada 19 May 1976) [*ICESCR*].

2 Part I of the *Constitution Act, 1982*, being Schedule B to the *Canada Act 1982* (UK), 1982, c 11 [*Charter*].

3 Louise Arbour, "'Freedom from Want' — From Charity to Entitlement" (LaFontaine-Baldwin Lecture delivered in Quebec City, 3 March 2005), online: www.ohchr.org

notes in Chapter 1, an enhanced understanding of the indivisibility of these rights was a key factor in overcoming the historic divide between civil and political rights and economic and social rights at the international level.[4] The UN Human Rights Committee has affirmed that positive measures are required to address homelessness in Canada in order to respect right to life guarantees under article 6 of the *International Covenant on Civil and Political Rights* (*ICCPR*).[5] The committee has also pointed out that poverty disproportionately affects women and other disadvantaged groups in Canada and that, as a consequence, social program cuts have had a discriminatory impact on those groups.[6] From an international standpoint, Canadian constitutional guarantees are seen to be directly engaged by Canada's failure to implement effective strategies to address poverty and homelessness. As the UN Committee on Economic, Social and Cultural Rights notes in its *General Comment No 9* on the domestic application of the *ICESCR*, "[t]he existence and further development of international procedures for the pur-

---

[Arbour, "Freedom from Want"]; David Robitaille, *Normativité, interprétation et justification des droits économiques et sociaux : les cas québécois et sud-africain* (Brussels: Éditions Bruylant, 2011); John Currie, "International Human Rights Law in the Supreme Court's *Charter* Jurisprudence: Commitment, Retrenchment and Retreat — In No Particular Order" in Sanda Rodgers & Sheila McIntyre, eds, *The Supreme Court of Canada and Social Justice: Commitment, Retrenchment or Retreat?* (Markham, ON: LexisNexis, 2010) 458 [Rodgers & McIntyre, *The Supreme Court of Canada and Social Justice*]; Margot Young, "Rights, the Homeless, and Social Change: Reflections on *Victoria (City) v. Adams* (BCSC)" (2009–2010) 164 BC Studies 103 [Young, "Rights, the Homeless, and Social Change"]; Malcolm Langford, "Justiciability of Social Rights" in Malcolm Langford, ed, *Social Rights Jurisprudence* (Cambridge: Cambridge University Press, 2008) 3; Gwen Brodsky & Shelagh Day, "Beyond the Social and Economic Rights Debate: Substantive Equality Speaks to Poverty" (2002) 14:1 CJWL 185.

4 See Chapter 1. See also Bruce Porter & Martha Jackman, "International Human Rights and Strategies to Address Homelessness and Poverty in Canada: Making the Connection," Working Paper (Social Rights Advocacy Centre, September 2011), online: CURA http://socialrightscura.ca [Porter & Jackman, "Making the Connection"].

5 United Nations Human Rights Committee, *Consideration of Reports Submitted by States Parties under Article 40 of the Covenant. Concluding Observations of the Human Rights Committee: Canada*, UNHRCOR, 65th Sess, UN Doc CCPR/C/79/Add.105, (1999) at para 12 [UNHRCOR, *Concluding Observations*, 1999].

6 *Ibid* at para 20. See also United Nations Committee on Economic, Social and Cultural Rights, *Consideration of Reports Submitted by States Parties under Articles 16 and 17 of the Covenant. Concluding Observations of the Committee on Economic, Social and Cultural Rights: Canada*, UNCESCROR, 36th Sess, UN Doc E/C.12/CAN/CO/4 & E/C.12/CAN/CO/5, (2006) [UNCESCROR, *Concluding Observations*, 2006].

suit of individual claims is important, but such procedures are ultimately only supplementary to effective national remedies."[7]

In its 2009 report, *In from the Margins: A Call to Action on Poverty, Housing and Homelessness*, the Senate Subcommittee on Cities observes that international human rights continue to be viewed by Canadian governments as "closer to moral obligations than enforceable rights."[8] In this context, the subcommittee points to the use by Canadian courts of international human rights to interpret the provisions of the *Charter* as the primary means through which Canada's international human rights obligations achieve domestic legal enforceability.[9] In his dissenting judgment in *Reference Re Public Service Employee Relations Act (Alberta)*, former Chief Justice Dickson declared that "the *Charter* should generally be presumed to provide protection at least as great as that afforded by similar provisions in international human rights documents which Canada has ratified."[10] In applying this interpretive presumption, which was endorsed by the majority in *Slaight Communications v Davidson*[11] and reaffirmed in *Health Services and*

7 United Nations Committee on Economic, Social and Cultural Rights, *General Comment 9: The Domestic Application of the Covenant*, UNCESCROR, 19th Sess, UN Doc E/C.12/1998/24, (1998) at para 4 [UNCESCROR, *General Comment 9*, 1998].

8 Senate, Subcommittee on Cities of the Standing Senate Committee on Social Affairs, Science, and Technology, *In from the Margins: A Call to Action on Poverty, Housing and Homelessness* (December 2009) (Chair: Hon Art Eggleton, PC) at 69, online: Parliament of Canada www.parl.gc.ca [*In from the Margins*]. See also United Nations Committee on Economic, Social and Cultural Rights, *Consideration of Reports Submitted by States Parties under Articles 16 and 17 of the Covenant. Concluding Observations of the Committee on Economic, Social and Cultural Rights: Canada*, UNCESCROR, 19th Sess, UN Doc E/C.12/1/Add.31, (1998) at paras 14–15; United Nations Committee on Economic, Social and Cultural Rights, *Consideration of Reports Submitted by States Parties under Articles 16 and 17 of the Covenant: Concluding Observations of the Committee on Economic, Social and Cultural Rights: Canada*, UNCESCROR, 36th Sess, UN Doc E/C.12/CAN/CO/5, (2006) at para 11(b); Shelagh Day, "Minding the Gap: Human Rights Commitments and Compliance" [Day, "Minding the Gap"] in Margot Young et al, *Poverty: Rights, Social Citizenship, and Legal Activism* (Vancouver: UBC Press, 2007) 201 [Young et al, *Poverty*]; Gwen Brodsky, "The Subversion of Human Rights by Governments in Canada" in Young et al, *Poverty*, *ibid* at 355.

9 *In from the Margins*, above note 8 at 69.

10 *Reference Re Public Service Employee Relations Act (Alberta)*, [1987] 1 SCR 313 at para 59 [*Alberta Reference*]. See, generally, Ruth Sullivan, *Driedger on the Construction of Statutes*, 3d ed (Markham, ON: Butterworths, 1994) at 330.

11 *Slaight Communications Inc v Davidson*, [1989] 1 SCR 1038 [*Slaight Communications*]. See also *Baker v Canada (Minister of Citizenship and Immigration)*, [1999] 2 SCR 817 at para 70 [*Baker*]; *R v Ewanchuk*, [1999] 1 SCR 330 at para 73 [*Ewanchuk*].

Support — Facilities Subsector Bargaining Assn v British Columbia,[12] the Court has not only considered guarantees with direct counterparts in the *Charter*, such as the right to life or to non-discrimination under the *ICCPR*.[13] It has also made reference to socio-economic rights as part of the unified international human rights landscape within which *Charter* interpretation must be situated. In *Slaight Communications*,[14] the Court pointed to Canada's ratification of the *ICESCR* as evidence that the right to work is a fundamental human right that had to be balanced against the *Charter* guarantee of freedom of expression in that case. In relying on the *ICESCR*, the Court endorsed Dickson CJ's statement in the *Alberta Reference* that

> [t]he various sources of international human rights law — declarations, covenants, conventions, judicial and quasi-judicial decisions of international tribunals, customary norms — must, in my opinion, be relevant and persuasive sources for interpretation of the *Charter*'s provisions.[15]

In the words of McLachlin CJ and Lebel J in *Health Services Assn*, "the *Charter*, as a living document, grows with society and speaks to the current situations and needs of Canadians. Thus Canada's *current* international law commitments and the current state of international thought on human rights provide a persuasive source for interpreting the scope of the *Charter*."[16]

This chapter explores the extent to which a domestic constitutional framework exists in Canada for a rights-based approach to housing and anti-poverty strategies, compatible with and informed by the international human rights law and jurisprudence outlined in Chapter 1.[17] In particular, this chapter will focus on three key *Charter* provisions for the protection of the right to adequate housing and to freedom from poverty: first, the right to life, liberty, and security of the person guaranteed under section 7

12 *Health Services and Support — Facilities Subsector Bargaining Assn v British Columbia*, 2007 SCC 27 at para 70 [*Health Services Assn*].

13 *International Covenant on Civil and Political Rights*, 19 December 1966, 999 UNTS 171, Can TS 1976 No 47 (entered into force 23 March 1976, accession by Canada 19 May 1976) [*ICCPR*].

14 *Slaight Communications*, above note 11 at 1056–57.

15 *Alberta Reference*, above note 10 at para 57. See also Craig Scott, "Reaching Beyond (Without Abandoning) the Category of 'Economic, Social and Cultural Rights'" (1999) 21:3 Hum Rts Q 633 at 648; Martha Jackman & Bruce Porter, "Socio-economic Rights under the Canadian *Charter*" in Malcolm Langford, ed, *Social Rights Jurisprudence: Emerging Trends in International and Comparative Law* (New York: Cambridge University Press, 2008) 209 at 214–15.

16 *Health Services Assn*, above note 12 at para 78.

17 See Chapter 1.

of the *Charter*; second, the right to equal protection and equal benefit of the law under section 15; and third, the obligation to ensure that any limits on *Charter* rights are reasonable and demonstrably justified, pursuant to section 1.[18]

B. SECTION 7: THE RIGHT TO LIFE, LIBERTY, AND SECURITY OF THE PERSON

In a lecture delivered at the outset of her mandate as UN High Commissioner on Human Rights, Louise Arbour pointed to the persistence of poverty and gross inequality in Canada and asked the question: "What is it in Canadian society that prevents the poor and marginalized from claiming equal enjoyment to the full range of their rights recognized under law, including economic, social and cultural rights?"[19] In examining how Canadian courts have applied section 7 of the *Charter*[20] in relation to poverty, she concluded that "[t]he first two decades of Charter litigation testify to a certain timidity — both on the part of litigants and the courts — to tackle head on the claims emerging from the right to be free from want."[21] Almost ten years later, poverty and homelessness cases are still scarce, and judges remain reluctant to impose positive obligations on governments to adopt reasonable measures to ensure access to adequate housing and other necessities, in accordance with the *ICESCR* and other human rights

18 The paper does not address Aboriginal treaty rights under s 35 or the social rights safeguards set out under s 36 of the *Constitution Act, 1982*, being Schedule B to the *Canada Act 1982* (UK), 1982, c 11. For a discussion of social rights issues raised under s 35, see Chapter 9 and see, generally, John Borrows, *Canada's Indigenous Constitution* (Toronto: University of Toronto Press, 2010). For a discussion of s 36, see Martha Jackman & Bruce Porter, "Rights-Based Strategies to Address Homelessness and Poverty in Canada: The Constitutional Framework," Ottawa Faculty of Law Working Paper No 2013-10, online: CURA www.socialscura.ca [Jackman & Porter, "Constitutional Framework"]; Aymen Nader, "Providing Essential Services: Canada's Constitutional Commitment under Section 36" (1996) 19:2 Dal LJ 306.

19 Arbour, "Freedom from Want," above note 3.

20 Section 7 declares that "[e]veryone has the right to life, liberty and security of the person and the right not to be deprived thereof except in accordance with the principles of fundamental justice."

21 Arbour, "Freedom from Want," above note 3. See also Louise Arbour & Fannie Lafontaine, "Beyond Self-Congratulation: The *Charter* at 25 in an International Perspective" (2007) 45 Osgoode Hall LJ 239 [Arbour & Lafontaine, "Beyond Self-Congratulation"].

treaties ratified by Canada.[22] The absence of any clear judicial affirmation of the applicability of the right to life, liberty, and security of the person in this area has led many to dismiss, or to discount, the claim that section 7 requires governments to take positive measures to address poverty and homelessness.[23] However, as outlined below, the Supreme Court continues to affirm its willingness to entertain such *Charter* claims and the possibility that section 7 protects socio-economic rights.

1) Rights to Adequate Housing and Protection from Poverty

In its judgment in *Irwin Toy v Quebec (AG)*, the Supreme Court drew a distinction between "corporate-commercial economic rights," which are excluded from the *Charter*, and "economic rights fundamental to human life or survival,"[24] which may fall within the scope of section 7. As Dickson CJ explained,

> [l]ower courts have found that the rubric of "economic rights" embraces a broad spectrum of interests, ranging from such rights, included in various international covenants, as rights to social security, equal pay for equal work, adequate food, clothing and shelter, to traditional property-contract rights. To exclude all of these at this early moment in the history of *Charter* interpretation seems to us to be precipitous.[25]

In *Gosselin v Quebec (AG)*, the Supreme Court considered a *Charter* challenge to a provincial regulation that reduced the level of social assistance

---

22 Martha Jackman, "Constitutional Castaways: Poverty and the McLachlin Court"; Jennie Abell, "Poverty and Social Justice at the Supreme Court during the McLachlin Years — Slipsliding Away" in Rodgers & McIntyre, *The Supreme Court of Canada and Social Justice*, above note 3, 297 and 257; Kerri Froc, "Is the Rule of Law the Golden Rule? Accessing 'Justice' for Canada's Poor" (2008) 87 Can Bar Rev 459 [Froc, "Golden Rule"]; Margot Young, "Section 7 and the Politics of Social Justice" (2005) 38 UBC L Rev 539 [Young, "Section 7"]; Shelagh Day & Gwen Brodsky, *Women and the Canada Social Transfer: Securing the Social Union* (Ottawa: Status of Women Canada, 2007); David Wiseman, "Methods of Protection of Social and Economic Rights in Canada" in Fons Coomans, ed, *Justiciability of Economic and Social Rights: Experiences from Domestic Systems* (Antwerp-Oxford: Intersentia, 2006) 173 [Wiseman, "Social and Economic Rights"].

23 See, for example, Andrew Petter, "Wealthcare: The Politics of the *Charter* Revisited" in Andrew Petter, *The Politics of the Charter: The Illusive Promise of Constitutional Rights* (Toronto: University of Toronto Press, 2010) 167.

24 *Irwin Toy v Quebec (AG)*, [1989] 1 SCR 927 at 1003–4 [*Irwin Toy*].

25 *Ibid.*

benefits payable to recipients under the age of thirty by two-thirds, unless they were enrolled in education or workfare programs. In her dissenting judgment in the case, Arbour J found that the section 7 right to security of the person places positive obligations on governments to provide those in need with an amount of social assistance adequate to cover basic necessities.[26] Although the majority of the Court viewed the impugned welfare regime as a defensible means of encouraging young people to join the workforce,[27] McLachlin CJ left open the possibility that

> [o]ne day s. 7 may be interpreted to include positive obligations. To evoke Lord Sankey's celebrated phrase in *Edwards v Attorney-General for Canada* . . . the *Canadian Charter* must be viewed as "a living tree capable of growth and expansion within its natural limits . . . ." I leave open the possibility that a positive obligation to sustain life, liberty, or security of the person may be made out in special circumstances.[28]

Security of the person, as defined by the courts, has both physical and psychological dimensions.[29] There is no longer any doubt that section 7 applies well beyond the criminal justice context and that State action that is likely to impair a person's mental and physical health engages the right to security of the person.[30] In *Chaoulli v Quebec (AG)*, the majority of the Court held that the government's failure to ensure access to health care of "reasonable" quality within a "reasonable" time engaged the right to life and security of the person and thus triggered the application of section 7 and the equivalent guarantee under Quebec's *Charter of Rights and Freedoms*.[31] In *Canada (AG) v PHS Community Services Society*, the Court reaffirmed that where a law creates a risk to health, this amounts to a deprivation of the right to security of the person and that "where the law creates a risk not

---

26 *Gosselin v Quebec (AG)*, 2002 SCC 84 at para 332 [*Gosselin*].

27 *Ibid* at paras 74 and 83.

28 *Ibid* at para 82. See also Martha Jackman, "Sommes nous dignes? Légalité et l'arrêt Gosselin" (2006) 17 RFD 161; Gwen Brodsky et al, "*Gosselin v Quebec (Attorney General)*" (2006) 18:1 CJWL 189; Gwen Brodsky, "*Gosselin v Quebec (Attorney General)*: Autonomy with a Vengeance" (2003) 15:1 CJWL 194; Shelagh Day et al, *Human Rights Denied: Single Mothers on Social Assistance* (Vancouver: Poverty and Human Rights Centre, 2005).

29 *Rodriguez v British Columbia (AG)*, [1993] 3 SCR 519 at para 136 [*Rodriguez*]; *Federated Anti-Poverty Groups of BC v Vancouver (City)*, 2002 BCSC 105 at paras 201–2 [*Federated Anti-Poverty Groups*].

30 *Singh v Canada (Minister of Employment and Immigration)*, [1985] 1 SCR 177 [*Singh*]; *New Brunswick (Minister of Health and Community Services) v G(J)*, [1999] 3 SCR 46 [*G(J)*]; *Rodriguez*, above note 29 at para 21.

31 *Chaoulli v Quebec (AG)*, 2005 SCC 35 at para 105 [*Chaoulli*].

just to the health but also to the lives of the claimants, the deprivation is even clearer."[32]

With increased understanding of the significant health consequences of homelessness and poverty, it has become obvious that governments' failure to ensure reasonable access to housing and to an adequate standard of living for disadvantaged groups undermines section 7 interests, certainly as directly as the regulation of private medical insurance at issue in *Chaoulli*.[33] The Mental Health Commission of Canada reported in 2012 that "[p]eople who are homeless more commonly experience serious mental illness, substance abuse, and challenges with stress, coping, and suicidal behavior than the general population [and] mortality among homeless people in Canada is much higher than among the general Canadian population."[34] The commission concludes that governments' reliance on shelters is a "costly and ineffective way to respond to the problem."[35]

In the *Tanudjaja v AG (Canada)* case,[36] a number of individuals who have experienced homelessness and inadequate housing are arguing that the federal and Ontario governments' failure to adopt housing strategies violates their *Charter* rights, including to security of the person under section 7. In her affidavit in support of the *Tanudjaja* claim, Cathy Crowe, a street nurse who has worked with homeless people in Toronto for more than twenty years, describes some of the consequences of homelessness that she has witnessed:

> I saw infections and illnesses devastate the lives of homeless people — frostbite injuries, malnutrition, dehydration, pneumonias, chronic diarrhoea, hepatitis, HIV infection, and skin infections from bedbug bites. For people who live in adequate housing, these conditions are curable or manageable. For homeless people, however, it is much more difficult. The homeless experience greater exposure to upper respiratory disease; more

---

32 *Canada (AG) v PHS Community Services Society*, 2011 SCC 44 at para 93 [*Insite*].

33 *Chaoulli*, above note 31. See, generally, David R Boyd, "No Taps, No Toilets: First Nations and the Constitutional Right to Water in Canada" (2011) 57 McGill LJ 81 at 106–7; Martha Jackman, "*Charter* Review as a Health Care Accountability Mechanism in Canada" (2010) 18 Health LJ 1; Colleen Flood, Kent Roach, & Lorne Sossin, eds, *Access to Care, Access to Justice: The Legal Debate over Private Health Insurance in Canada* (Toronto: University of Toronto Press, 2005).

34 Mental Health Commission of Canada, *At Home/Chez Soi: Interim Report* (Ottawa: Mental Health Commission of Canada, September 2012) at 12 [Mental Health Commission, *At Home/Chez Soi*].

35 *Ibid* at 8.

36 2013 ONSC 5410 [*Tanudjaja*].

> trauma, including violence such as rape; more chronic illness, greater exposure to illness in congregate settings; more exposure to infectious agents and infestations such as lice and bedbugs; suffer more from a greater risk of depression. This is compounded by their reduced access to health care.[37]

Crowe notes that while these physical illnesses and conditions are difficult enough to treat when people lack adequate housing, treating the emotional and mental effects of homelessness is even more difficult. As she explains, "chronic deprivation of privacy, sleep and sense of safety; and living in circumstances of constant stress and violence" leads to "mental and emotional trauma."[38] Crowe goes on to affirm that these negative health outcomes cannot be dealt with effectively "by programs of support for living on the street, emergency shelters, drop-in programs or counselling and referral services despite the critical need for all these services."[39] She argues that they can only be addressed by ensuring access to adequate "permanent housing."[40]

A recent Canadian longitudinal study on the effects of homelessness also found that the negative health outcomes associated with living on the streets or in shelters extend to a much wider segment of the population and also affect those living in inadequate or precarious housing. The results of the study showed that "for every one person sleeping in a shelter there are 23 more people living with housing vulnerability. They are all at risk of devastating health outcomes."[41] People who are vulnerably housed face the same severe health problems as those who are homeless, including reduced life expectancy, increased chronic health conditions, reduced access to health care, and suicide rates that are twice the national average for men and six times the national average for women.[42] As the Mental Health

---

37 Cathy Crowe, "Affidavit for *Tanudjaja v Attorney General (Canada)*," Ont Sup Ct File no CV-10-403688 (2011) at paras 23–24 [Crowe, "Affidavit for *Tanudjaja*"]. See also Emily Holton, Evie Gogosis, & Stephen Hwan, *Housing Vulnerability and Health: Canada's Hidden Emergency* (Toronto: Research Alliance for Canadian Homelessness, Housing, and Health, 2010) [Holton, Gogogis, & Hwan, *Housing Vulnerability and Health*].

38 Crowe, "Affidavit for *Tanudjaja*," above note 37 at para 26.

39 *Ibid* at para 44.

40 *Ibid.*

41 Holton, Gogogis, & Hwan, *Housing Vulnerability and Health*, above note 37 at 4.

42 Mental Health Commission, *At Home/Chez Soi*, above note 34 at 11–12; Michael Shapcott, "Housing" in Dennis Raphael, ed, *Social Determinants of Health*, 2d ed (Toronto: Canadian Scholars' Press, 2008) 221 [Raphael, *Social Determinants*]; Toba Bryant, "Housing and Health: More Than Bricks and Mortar" in Raphael, *Social Determinants*, *ibid*, 235; *In from the Margins*, above note 8 at 69; Senate, Standing Committee on

Commission of Canada concludes, "Living in shelters and on the streets makes it very difficult to take care of one's health, adhere to treatment routines and move forward in one's life."[43]

The damaging effects of poverty on physical and mental health are equally clear. Income-related differences in life expectancy in Canada provide a stark illustration of the importance of poverty as a determinant of health. For men aged twenty-five in 2001, those in the highest income quintile could expect to live 6.9 years longer than those in the poorest; for women, the difference was 4.5 years.[44] Poverty is also associated with higher rates of death and more years of life lost from injury, higher suicide rates, higher rates of strokes and heart attacks, and higher infant mortality rates, among other effects.[45] Beyond its adverse impact on life expectancy, Juha Mikkonen and Dennis Raphael explain why poverty is the single most significant determinant of health in Canada:

> Level of income shapes overall living conditions, affects psychological functioning, and influences health-related behaviour such as quality of diet, extent of physical activity, tobacco use, and excessive alcohol use. In Canada, income determines the quality of other social determinants of health such as food security, housing and other prerequisites of health.[46]

Social Affairs, Science and Technology, *A Healthy, Productive Canada: A Determinant of Health Approach, Final Report of the Senate Subcommittee on Population Health* (June 2009) (Chair: Hon Wilbert Joseph Keon) at 16, online: Parliament of Canada www.parl.gc.ca.

43 Mental Health Commission, *At Home/Chez Soi*, above note 34 at 10.

44 Sheila Leatherman & Kim Sutherland, *Quality of Healthcare in Canada: A Chartbook* (Ottawa: Canadian Health Services Research Foundation, 2010) at 192 [Leatherman & Sutherland, *Chartbook*]. To put this in perspective, it is estimated that eliminating all cancers would increase life expectancy in the US by 2.8 years.

45 See, generally, Health Disparities Task Group of the Federal/Provincial/Territorial Advisory Committee on Population Health and Health Security, *Reducing Health Disparities — Roles of the Health Sector: Discussion Paper* (Ottawa: Public Health Agency of Canada, 2004) at 1–2; Leatherman & Sutherland, *Chartbook*, above note 44 at 192–206; Dennis Raphael, "Social Determinants of Health: An Overview of Concepts and Issues" in Toba Bryant, Dennis Raphael, & Marci Rioux, eds, *Staying Alive: Critical Perspectives on Health, Illness and Health Care*, 2d ed (Toronto: Canadian Scholars' Press, 2010) 145 at 150–52.

46 Juha Mikkonen & Dennis Raphael, *Social Determinants of Health: The Canadian Facts* (Toronto: York University School of Health Policy and Management, 2010) at 12; *In from the Margins*, above note 8; Nathalie Auger & Carolyne Alix, "Income, Income Distribution, and Health in Canada" in Raphael, *Social Determinants*, above note 42 at 61; Chief Public Health Officer, *The Report on the State of Public Health in Canada,*

Raphael concludes that "[p]eople living in poverty experience material and social deprivation, stress, stigma and degradation by others. These experiences are clearly seen as threats to health and quality of life."[47] Given the negative health consequences and adverse impact of poverty and homelessness on physical and psychological integrity, security, dignity, and other interests which the Supreme Court has recognized as falling within the ambit of section 7, it is hard to imagine how these documented effects of government inaction in relation to poverty and homelessness and governments' ongoing failure to implement effective housing and anti-poverty strategies, as recommended by experts and UN bodies, can reasonably be excluded from section 7 of the *Charter.*

2) Principles of Fundamental Justice: Arbitrary Responses to Poverty and Homelessness

Section 7 requires that any deprivation of the right to life, liberty, or security of the person "must be in accordance with the principles of fundamental justice." In his judgment in *Reference Re BC Motor Vehicle Act*, Lamer CJ explained that the concept of fundamental justice "involves more than natural justice (which is largely procedural) and includes as well a substantive element."[48] Factors to be considered include the drafting history of the *Charter*,[49] Canadian identity and values,[50] and Canada's international human

---

2008 — Addressing Health Inequalities (Ottawa: Minister of Health, 2008); Canadian Population Health Initiative, *Reducing Gaps in Health: A Focus on Socio-economic Status in Urban Canada* (Ottawa: Canadian Institute for Health Information, 2008); Federal/Provincial/Territorial Advisory Committee on Population Health and Health Security, Health Disparities Task Group, *Reducing Health Disparities — Roles of the Health Sector: Discussion Paper* (Ottawa: Public Health Agency of Canada, 2004) at 1–3; National Forum on Health, "Determinants of Health Working Group Synthesis Report" in *Canada Health Action: Building on the Legacy — Synthesis Reports and Issues Papers*, vol 2 (Ottawa: Minister of Public Works and Government Services, 1997) at 9.

47 Dennis Raphael, *Poverty in Canada: Implications for Health and Quality of Life*, 2d ed (Toronto: Canadian Scholars' Press, 2011) at 179 [Raphael, *Poverty in Canada*].

48 *Reference Re BC Motor Vehicle Act*, [1985] 2 SCR 486 at para 99; *United States of America v Burns*, 2001 SCC 7 at para 71; *Rodriguez*, above note 29 at 590–91.

49 See Bruce Porter, "Expectations of Equality" (2006) 33 Sup Ct L Rev (2d) 23 [Porter, "Expectations of Equality"]. The drafters and rights holders expected that the *Charter* would impose a new social contract in which new entitlements would be granted to citizens and new (positive) duties imposed on the government to allow for the realization of *Charter* rights.

50 *Rodriguez*, above note 29 at 590–91. See, generally, Martha Jackman, "The Protection of Welfare Rights under the *Charter*" (1988) 20:2 Ottawa L Rev 257 [Jackman, "Welfare

rights commitments.[51] A core principle of fundamental justice under section 7 is the notion that governments cannot arbitrarily limit rights to life, liberty, and security of the person.[52] Prior to the recent *Insite* case,[53] the Supreme Court's consideration of arbitrariness was largely confined to situations where the government had actively interfered with section 7 rights. The Court had not been called upon to consider whether a government's failure to take action or to adopt positive measures to protect life, liberty, or security of the person was arbitrary and therefore fundamentally unjust within the meaning of section 7.

In the *Insite* case, the Supreme Court rejected the claim that the federal *Controlled Drugs and Substances Act*,[54] itself, violated section 7.[55] Instead, the Court considered whether the Minister of Health's failure to grant Insite, a safe injection facility located in Downtown Eastside Vancouver, an exemption from the application of the Act was in accordance with principles of fundamental justice.[56] Acknowledging that "the jurisprudence on arbitrariness is not entirely settled,"[57] the Court considered the alternative approaches it had taken to arbitrariness, including whether the impugned measure is "necessary" to or "inconsistent" with the State objectives underlying the legislation.[58] Reviewing the overwhelming evidence of the benefits of Insite's safe injection and related health services to those in need of them, and the adverse effects of a failure to ensure the continued provision of those services, the Court found that the minister's failure to grant an exemption "qualifies as arbitrary under both definitions."[59] The Court further concluded that "[t]he effect of denying the services of Insite to the population it serves is grossly disproportionate to any benefit that Canada might derive from presenting a uniform stance on the possession of narcotics."[60]

The Court's decision in *Insite* has significant implications for the application of section 7 to governments' failure to act to protect the life and security of the person of those who are homeless or living in poverty. As

---

Rights"].

51 *Canada (Prime Minister) v Khadr*, 2010 SCC 3 at paras 23 and 48.

52 *R v Jones*, [1986] 2 SCR 284 at 303; *Rodriguez*, above note 29 at 203; *R v Malmo-Levine; R v Caine*, 2003 SCC 74 at para 135.

53 *Insite*, above note 32.

54 *Controlled Drugs and Substances Act*, SC 1996, c 19.

55 *Insite*, above note 32 at paras 112–15.

56 *Ibid* at paras 127–36.

57 *Ibid* at para 132.

58 *Ibid* at paras 130–32.

59 *Ibid* at para 131.

60 *Ibid* at para 133.

Bruce Porter outlines in Chapter 1, UN human rights bodies, housing and poverty experts, and a wide spectrum of civil society have called upon Canadian governments to adopt housing and anti-poverty strategies as a matter both of sound, evidence-based social policy and of domestic and international human rights law.[61] And, as Marie-Eve Sylvestre and Céline Bellot document in Chapter 5,[62] there is mounting evidence of the irrationality of governments' inaction in this area, in light of the health outcomes associated with homelessness and poverty, as well as their fiscal consequences. In her affidavit in the *Tanudjaja* case,[63] Sylvestre points to the arbitrary and unreasonable nature of current government responses to homelessness. She argues that

> [a]s programmatic responses that addressed the causes of homelessness such as social housing, investment in health care or employment policies, have been reduced or eliminated, governments have adopted unprecedented measures based on the "stigma" of homelessness as a perceived "moral" failure and designed to make homeless people disappear from the public sphere.[64]

By prohibiting behaviour linked to homelessness in public spaces, such as parks, subway stations, and sidewalks, governments have criminalized homeless people rather than addressing their need for housing.[65] The result of these punitive measures is, as Sylvestre explains, frequently unwarranted incarceration, as well as the imposition of fines on those who are unable to pay them: "homelessness leads to incarceration, and incarceration, in turn, produces homelessness."[66] Janet Mosher also questions

---

61 See Chapter 1.

62 See Chapter 5.

63 *Tanudjaja*, above note 36.

64 Marie-Eve Sylvestre, "Affidavit for *Tanudjaja v Attorney General (Canada)*," Ont Sup Ct File no CV-10-403688 (2011) at para 27 [Sylvestre, "Affidavit for *Tanudjaja*"]. See also Chapter 5.

65 *Ibid* at para 28. See also Commission des droits de la personne et des droits de la Jeunesse, *La judiciarisation des personnes itinérantes à Montréal : Un profilage social* (Montreal: Commission des droits de la personne, 2009); Joe Hermer & Janet Mosher, *Disorderly People: Law and the Politics of Exclusion in Ontario* (Halifax: Fernwood, 2002) [Hermer & Mosher, *Disorderly People*].

66 Sylvestre, "Affidavit for *Tanudjaja*," above note 64 at para 47. Sylvestre's conclusions are reinforced by a recent study conducted by the John Howard Society of Toronto, which found that 69 percent of the respondents experienced residential instability in the two years prior to their incarceration, 24 percent of them had used a shelter during

the rationality of what has, since the mid-nineties, become the dominant approach to poverty in Canada:

> Massive reforms to various federal and provincial social policies . . . have significantly re-shaped both the physical and ideological landscape of poverty. The day-to-day realities of living in poverty have become harsher; . . . welfare benefits have been cut . . . eligibility criteria have been tightened, workfare has been introduced and the discourse . . . of welfare fraud and the practices connected with its detection have led to increased scrutiny and surveillance of recipients. Police have been given new powers to remove from the streets panhandlers and squeegee workers, who, like welfare recipients, have been demonized as a threat to public order and safety.[67]

These arbitrary governmental responses to the needs of a vulnerable population and the failure to take positive steps to better ensure the protection of life and security of the person of people who are living in poverty and who are homeless are clearly not in accordance with section 7 principles of fundamental justice as interpreted by the Supreme Court, particularly in the *Insite* case.

3) Meaningful Participation in Housing and Anti-poverty Strategies

Section 7 of the *Charter* offers important support for the principle of participation in the design, implementation, monitoring, and evaluation of strategies to address poverty and homelessness, in keeping with the recommendations of UN human rights bodies and civil society organizations in Canada, and as Alana Klein argues in relation to health care in Chapter 10.[68] The Supreme Court has ruled that the principles of fundamental justice under section 7 include the procedural safeguards guaranteed under com-

---

that period, and 23 percent were homeless. See Amber Kellen et al, *Homeless and Jailed: Jailed and Homeless* (Toronto: John Howard Society of Toronto, 2010) at 18–20.

67 Janet Mosher, "The Shrinking of the Public and Private Spaces of the Poor" in Hermer & Mosher, *Disorderly People*, above note 65 at 41. See also Raphael, *Poverty in Canada*, above note 47 at 354–67.

68 Porter & Jackman, *Making the Connection*, above note 4 at 7–14; Chapter 10; Martha Jackman, "The Right to Participate in Health Care and Health Resource Allocation Decisions under Section 7 of the Canadian *Charter*" (1995/1996) 4:2 Health L Rev 3 [Jackman, "Health Care"].

mon law principles of natural justice and fairness.[69] Among these are the right to adequate notice of a decision, the right to respond, and the right to be heard by a fair and impartial decision maker.[70] In *New Brunswick (Minister of Health and Community Services) v G(J)*, Lamer CJ held that in order to comply with the requirements of fundamental justice, a person "must be able to participate meaningfully" and "effectively" in a decision making process that engages his section 7 rights.[71] On that basis, the Chief Justice concluded that section 7 imposed a positive obligation on the government to provide legal aid to a mother in receipt of social assistance, who was threatened with the loss of custody of her children and who could not afford a lawyer to represent her.[72]

In addition to participatory rights demanded in individualized decision making, the way in which a program or policy is implemented at a systemic level may also violate section 7 principles of fundamental justice. In *Wareham v Ontario (Ministry of Community and Social Services)*, the Ontario Court of Appeal held that "there is a potential argument to be made that a delay in processing applications for welfare benefits, essential for day-to-day existence and to which the applicants are statutorily entitled, could engage the right to security of the person where that delay has caused serious physical or psychological harm."[73] The court accepted Lorne Sossin's view that bureaucratic disentitlement includes "structural and situational features of the welfare eligibility process which together

---

69 *Charkaoui v Canada (Citizenship and Immigration)*, 2007 SCC 9 at para 29; *Suresh v Canada (Minister of Citizenship and Immigration)*, 2002 SCC 1 at para 113; *Singh*, above note 30 at 212–16.

70 See, generally, Lorne Sossin, "Boldly Going Where No Law Has Gone Before: Call Centres, Intake Scripts, Database Fields, and Discretionary Justice in Social Assistance" (2004) 42:3 Osgoode Hall LJ 363 at 393–94 [Sossin, "Discretionary Justice"]; Martha Jackman, "Section 7 of the *Charter* and Health-Care Spending" in Gregory Marchildon, Tom McIntosh, & Pierre-Gerlier Forest, eds, *The Fiscal Sustainability of Health Care in Canada* (Toronto: University of Toronto Press, 2004) 110; Jackman, "Health Care," above note 68 at 5; John M Evans, "The Principles of Fundamental Justice: The Constitution and the Common Law" (1991) 29:1 Osgoode Hall LJ 51; Jackman, "Welfare Rights," above note 50 at 305–22.

71 *G(J)*, above note 30 at paras 81 and 83.

72 *Ibid* at para 107. For a discussion of the broader issue of access to legal aid, see Melina Buckley, *Moving Forward on Legal Aid: Research on Needs and Innovative Approaches* (Ottawa: Canadian Bar Association, 2010).

73 *Wareham v Ontario (Ministry of Community and Social Services)*, 2008 ONCA 771 at para 17 [*Wareham*].

have the effect of discouraging applicants and demoralizing recipients" and that this amounts to a violation of procedural fairness guarantees.[74]

In the context of housing and anti-poverty strategies, section 7 principles of fundamental justice should be read as requiring participatory rights of the kind called for under international human rights law. In outlining a human rights–based approach to poverty reduction strategies, the UN High Commissioner for Human Rights has called for States to set targets, benchmarks, and priorities in a participatory manner "so that they reflect the concerns and interests of all segments of the society."[75] Former UN special rapporteur on adequate housing Miloon Kothari has also emphasized the importance of using participatory mechanisms for accessing necessary information and for providing accountability to stakeholders in the evaluation of housing programs and strategies.[76] In determining the steps a State must take to meet the "reasonableness standard" set out in the *OP-ICESCR*,[77] the Committee on Economic, Social and Cultural Rights (CESCR) has stated that it will examine whether the decision-making process with regard to the implementation of a policy or program is transparent and participatory.[78]

These types of international human rights law obligations should inform the interpretation and application of the principles of fundamental justice under section 7. Individual dignity, security, and autonomy must be protected through meaningful participation in decision making at both an individual and broader public policy level. Adequate notice should be provided regarding any changes to housing and poverty-related benefits or programs, ensuring that individuals have a right to be heard by decision

74 Sossin, "Discretionary Justice," above note 70 at 399.

75 United Nations Office of the High Commissioner for Human Rights, *Principles and Guidelines for a Human Rights Approach to Poverty Reduction Strategies*, UN Doc HR/PUB/06/12 (Geneva: OHCHR, 2006) at para 55 [OHCHR, *Guidelines*].

76 *Report of the Special Rapporteur on Adequate Housing as a Component of the Right to an Adequate Standard of Living, Miloon Kothari*, UN Human Rights Council, 4th Sess, UN Doc A/HRC/4/18, (2007).

77 *Optional Protocol to the International Covenant on Economic, Social and Cultural Rights*, GA Res 63/117, UNGAOR, 63d Sess, Supp No 49, UN Doc A/RES/63/117, (2008) [*OP-ICESCR*].

78 United Nations Committee on Economic, Social and Cultural Rights, *An Evaluation of the Obligation to Take Steps to the "Maximum of Available Resources" under an Optional Protocol to the Covenant*, UNCESCROR, 38th Sess, UN Doc E/C.12/2007/1, (2007). See Sandra Liebenberg, "Engaging the Paradoxes of the Universal and Particular in Human Rights Adjudication: The Possibilities and Pitfalls of 'Meaningful Engagement'" (2012) 12 African Human Rights Law Journal 1, for a discussion of meaningful participation requirement in the South African context.

makers, a right to appeal decisions, and a right to judicial review.[79] In the broader policy and regulatory setting, participation that meets the requirements of fundamental justice must consist of more than mere consultation and should instead ensure rights-based engagement and access to justice for vulnerable and marginalized groups to ensure that programs and policies respect their rights.

Generalized decisions relating to poverty and homelessness and the allocation of resources and services should be open to hearings and rights-based adjudication and review for compliance with human rights norms, and active steps should be taken to guarantee the inclusion of disadvantaged groups — those whose members are lacking in resources and who do not have an established history of participation or grounds for confidence in its value. Such measures are required to ensure that collective involvement in decision making actually results in a more equitable and efficient distribution of decision-making authority, and does not simply reinforce existing decision-making patterns and structures.[80] As Louise Arbour has affirmed, "the possibility for people themselves to claim their human rights entitlements through legal processes is essential so that human rights have meaning for those most at the margins, a vindication of their equal worth and human agency."[81]

C. SECTION 15: THE RIGHT TO EQUAL PROTECTION AND BENEFIT OF THE LAW

Civil society organizations in Canada, parliamentary committees, and international human rights bodies have emphasized that strategies to address poverty and homelessness should be informed by an equality rights framework.[82] Grounding such a framework in section 15[83] is critical to addressing

---

79 Sossin, "Discretionary Justice," above note 70; Jackman, "Welfare Rights," above note 50.

80 Jackman, "Health Care," above note 68 at 69.

81 Arbour, "Freedom from Want," above note 3.

82 Porter & Jackman, *Making the Connection*, above note 4.

83 *Charter*, above note 2, s 15, which declares that

> (1) Every individual is equal before and under the law and has the right to the equal protection and equal benefit of the law without discrimination and, in particular, without discrimination based on race, national or ethnic origin, colour, religion, sex, age or mental or physical disability.
>
> (2) Subsection (1) does not preclude any law, program or activity that has as its object the amelioration of conditions of disadvantaged individuals or groups including those that are disadvantaged because

the structural and systemic patterns of discrimination and exclusion that underlie these problems, and it assists in understanding poverty and homelessness as more than simply a matter of unmet needs but also, fundamentally, as a denial of dignity and rights.[84] The Senate Subcommittee on Cities notes in its report *In from the Margins*:

> The Charter, while not explicitly recognizing social condition, poverty or homelessness, does guarantee equality rights, with special recognition of the remedial efforts that might be required to ensure the equality of women, visible minorities (people who are not Caucasian), persons with disabilities, and Aboriginal peoples. As the Committee has heard, these groups are all overrepresented among the poor — in terms of both social and economic marginalization.[85]

The Supreme Court's equality rights jurisprudence has been subject to significant criticism for undermining the commitment to substantive equality that has been a unique strength of Canadian human rights law and section 15 of the *Charter*.[86] However, as with section 7, the Court has left the door open to advancing substantive social rights claims under section 15. In light of recent commentary from the Court, there remains a solid conceptual basis for a renewed rights-based approach to poverty and

---

of race, national or ethnic origin, colour, religion, sex, age or mental or physical disability.

84 Amartya Sen, "Property and Hunger" (1988) 4:1 Economics and Philosophy 57, reprinted in Wesley Cragg & Christine Koggel, eds, *Contemporary Moral Issues*, 5th ed (Toronto: McGraw-Hill Ryerson, 2005) 402 at 402–8.

85 *In from the Margins*, above note 8 at 69; House of Commons, Standing Committee on Human Resources, Skills, and Social Development and the Status of Persons with Disabilities, *Federal Poverty Reduction Plan: Working in Partnership towards Reducing Poverty in Canada* (November 2010) (Chair: Candice Hoeppner) at 2, online: Parliament of Canada www.parl.gc.ca.

86 See Sheila McIntyre, "Timely Interventions: MacKinnon's Contribution to Canadian Equality Jurisprudence" (2010) 46 Tulsa L Rev 81; Margot Young, "Unequal to the Task: 'Kapp'ing the Substantive Potential of Section 15" in Rodgers & McIntyre, *The Supreme Court of Canada and Social Justice*, above note 3, 183; Margot Young, "Why Rights Now? Law and Desperation" in Young et al, *Poverty*, above note 8, 317; Sheila McIntyre & Sanda Rodgers, eds, *Diminishing Returns: Inequality and the* Canadian Charter of Rights and Freedoms (Markham, ON: LexisNexis Butterworths, 2006) [McIntyre & Rodgers, *Diminishing Returns*]: for critiques of recent equality jurisprudence from Canadian courts; Fay Faraday, Margaret Denike, & Kate Stephenson, eds, *Making Equality Rights Real: Securing Substantive Equality under the Charter* (Toronto: Irwin Law, 2006).

homelessness in Canada. In *R v Kapp*,[87] the Court reiterated the ideal of substantive equality as it was affirmed in *Andrews v Law Society of British Columbia*,[88] and it acknowledged the formalism of its analytical framework in *Law v Canada (Minister of Employment and Immigration)*.[89] The Court has abandoned the *Law* analysis in favour of the simplified two-step approach from *Andrews*, which asks, first, whether a law, policy, or provision creates a distinction on an enumerated or analogous ground and, second, whether that distinction is discriminatory in a substantive sense.[90]

In *Withler v Canada (AG)*,[91] the Court further clarified that finding a section 15 violation does not depend on identifying a particular comparator group that "mirrors" the claimant's characteristics, as long as the "claimant establishes a distinction based on one or more enumerated or analogous grounds."[92] The Court recognized that a mirror comparator group analysis "may fail to capture substantive inequality . . . — and, indeed, thwart the identification of — the discrimination at which s. 15 is aimed."[93] The Court went on to affirm that consideration of whether a distinction amounts to substantive discrimination should be contextual, rather than rigid, in order to "provide the flexibility required to accommodate claims based on intersecting grounds of discrimination."[94]

As the senate subcommittee notes in its report, *In from the Margins*, governments' failure to implement housing and anti-poverty strategies engages the equality rights of groups protected from discrimination on enumerated grounds under section 15, such as women, people with disabilities, Aboriginal people, and racialized groups because these groups are over-represented among the poor.[95] However, for the purposes of situating housing and anti-poverty strategies within an equality framework, it is im-

87 2008 SCC 41 [*Kapp*].

88 [1989] 1 SCR 143 at para 34 [*Andrews*].

89 [1999] 1 SCR 497 [*Law*].

90 *Kapp*, above note 87 at para 17.

91 2011 SCC 12 [*Withler*].

92 *Ibid* at para 60.

93 *Ibid*. See Dianne Pothier, "Equality as a Comparative Concept: Mirror, Mirror, on the Wall, What's the Fairest of Them All?" in McIntyre & Rodgers, *Diminishing Returns*, above note 86 at 135; Diana Majury & Daphne Gilbert, "Critical Comparisons: The Supreme Court of Canada Dooms Section 15" (2006) 24 Windsor YB Access Just 111.

94 *Withler*, above note 91 at para 63.

95 *In from the Margins*, above note 8 at 69–70.

portant to consider whether poverty and homelessness should, themselves, be recognized as analogous grounds of discrimination under section 15.[96]

1) The "Social Condition" of Poverty and Homelessness

The analogous grounds inquiry must, according to the Supreme Court, be undertaken in a purposive and contextual manner.[97] The "nature and situation of the individual or group at issue, and the social, political, and legal history of Canadian society's treatment of that group" must be considered[98] specifically, whether persons with the characteristics at issue are lacking in political power or vulnerable to having their interests overlooked.[99] In *Miron v Trudel*, the Court identified a number of factors that may be considered in determining whether an analogous ground of discrimination should be recognized under section 15, including whether the proposed ground may "serve as a basis for unequal treatment based on stereotypical attributes"; whether it is a source of historical social, political, and economic disadvantage; whether the group experiencing discrimination constitutes a "discrete and insular minority"; and whether the proposed ground is similar to other prohibited forms of discrimination recognized in domestic and international human rights law.[100] The Court in *Miron* cautioned that "while discriminatory group markers often involve immutable characteristics, they do not necessarily do so."[101]

In *Corbiere v Canada (Minister of Indian and Northern Affairs)*, the Court broadened the concept of immutability, introducing the notion of "constructive immutability," linked to identity and prevailing social attitudes.[102] While reiterating that the analogous grounds inquiry must consider the general purpose of section 15, the majority went on to suggest that analogous grounds must either be "actually immutable, like race, or constructively immutable, like religion" and that other factors to be considered in

96 See Chapter 6; Wayne MacKay & Natasha Kim, *Adding Social Condition to the* Canadian Human Rights Act (Ottawa: Canadian Human Rights Commission, 2009) [MacKay & Kim, *Social Condition*]; Froc, "Golden Rule," above note 22; Martha Jackman, "Constitutional Contact with the Disparities in the World: Poverty as a Prohibited Ground of Discrimination under the Canadian *Charter* and Human Rights Law" (1994) 2 Rev Const Stud 76.

97 *Law*, above note 89 at para 6; *Andrews*, above note 88 at para 46.

98 *Law*, above note 89 at para 93.

99 *Andrews*, above note 88 at para 5.

100 *Miron v Trudel*, [1995] 2 SCR 418 at paras 144–55 [*Miron*].

101 *Ibid* at paras 148–49.

102 [1999] 2 SCR 203 [*Corbiere*].

the analogous grounds analysis "may be seen to flow from the central concept of immutable or constructively immutable personal characteristics."[103] The Court concluded in *Corbiere* that the distinction between on-reserve and off-reserve residential status "goes to a personal characteristic essential to a band member's personal identity, which is no less constructively immutable than religion or citizenship."[104]

There are compelling reasons for recognizing that the socially constructed dimension of homelessness and poverty make these characteristics constructively immutable, in the same way as residential status was found to be in *Corbiere*. A purposive approach must link the economic deprivation associated with homelessness or poverty to the "social condition" or socially constructed characteristics of those who are living in poverty or who are homeless. As Dennis Raphael explains, "[i]n addition to the burdens of living with material and social deprivation — and the stresses associated with these — people living in poverty must deal with the reality that others frequently blame them for their own situation . . . . The experience of stigma adds to the profound issues that people in poverty must live with."[105] Quantifiable measures of income level may accurately identify needs that must be addressed. However, understanding how the group's imputed characteristics are socially constructed, often through stigmatization, stereotyping, and prejudice, brings into focus the social relations and attitudes that accompany and exacerbate physical and material deprivations and that create and legitimate discriminatory governmental responses to poverty and homelessness.

This social dimension of poverty and homelessness has been recognized in domestic human rights legislation under the prohibited ground of "social condition." All provincial and territorial human rights statutes in Canada include protection from discrimination because of "social condition" (New Brunswick, Northwest Territories, and Quebec) or a related ground, such as "social origin" (Newfoundland and Labrador), "source of income" (Alberta, British Columbia, Manitoba, Nova Scotia, Nunavut, and Prince Edward Island), or "receipt of public assistance" (Ontario and Saskatchewan).[106] These grounds have been interpreted broadly to provide protection against discrimination on the basis of poverty, low level of income, reliance on public

---

103 *Ibid* at para 13.

104 *Ibid* at para 14.

105 Raphael, *Poverty in Canada*, above note 47 at 178.

106 Russel Zinn, *The Law of Human Rights in Canada: Practice and Procedure*, loose-leaf (consulted on 2 June 2010), (Aurora, ON: Canada Law Book, 1996) ch 13:30 [Zinn, *The Law of Human Rights*].

housing, and homelessness.[107] The only human rights legislation in Canada that does not prohibit discrimination based on social condition or a similar ground is the *Canadian Human Rights Act*.[108] The Canadian Human Rights Act Review Panel, chaired by former Supreme Court Justice Gerard LaForest, found there was "ample evidence of widespread discrimination based on characteristics related to social conditions, such as poverty, low education, homelessness and illiteracy."[109] The panel recommended "the inclusion of social condition as a prohibited ground of discrimination in all areas covered by the Act in order to provide protection from discrimination because of disadvantaged socio-economic status, including homelessness."[110]

The socially constructed dimensions of poverty and homelessness have also been recognized as analogous grounds of discrimination under international human rights law. In *General Comment No 20* on non-discrimination, the CESCR identifies a number of grounds of discrimination that are comparable to enumerated grounds under the *ICESCR*.[111] Along with grounds such as disability and sexual orientation, the committee lists "economic and social situation," noting that "[a] person's social and economic situation when living in poverty or being homeless may result in pervasive discrimination, stigmatization and negative stereotyping."[112] In a recent report presented to the UN General Assembly, the UN Special Rapporteur on

---

107 See *Shelter Corp v Ontario (Human Rights Commission)* (2001), 143 OAC 54 (Div Ct); *Whittom c Québec (Commission des droits de la personne)*, 1997 CanLII 10666 (CA Qc), aff'g (1994), 20 CHRR D/349 (Tribunal des droits de la personne du Québec); *Quebec (Commission des droits de la personne) v Gauthier* (1994), 19 CHRR D/312, as cited in Zinn, *The Law of Human Rights*, above note 106 at 13–14. See also the Honourable Lynn Smith & William Black, "The Equality Rights" in Gerald Beaudoin & Errol Mendes, eds, *Canadian Charter of Rights and Freedoms*, 4th ed (Markham, ON: LexisNexis Butterworths, 2005) 927 at 1010–111.

108 RSC 1985, c H-6.

109 Canadian Human Rights Act Review Panel, *Promoting Equality: A New Vision* (Ottawa: Department of Justice, 2000) at 107.

110 *Ibid* at 106–12. Although strongly supported by civil society organizations and UN human rights bodies, the LaForest panel's recommendations have yet to be implemented. See also United Nations Committee on Economic, Social and Cultural Rights, *Consideration of Reports Submitted by States Parties under Articles 16 and 17 of the Covenant: Concluding Observations of the Committee on Economic, Social and Cultural Rights: Canada*, UNCESCROR, 19th Sess, UN Doc E/C.12/1/add.31, (1998) at para 51; MacKay & Kim, *Social Condition*, above note 96.

111 United Nations Committee on Economic, Social and Cultural Rights, *General Comment 20: Non-discrimination in economic, social and cultural rights*, UNCESCROR, 42d Sess, UN Doc E/C.12/GC/20, (2009) art 2 para 2 [*General Comment 20*].

112 *Ibid* at para 35.

Extreme Poverty, Magdalena Sepulveda, described patterns of stigmatization and criminalization of poor people as common to both developed and developing countries:

> Penalization measures respond to discriminatory stereotypes that assume that persons living in poverty are lazy, irresponsible, indifferent to their children's health and education, dishonest, undeserving and even criminal. Persons living in poverty are often portrayed as authors of their own misfortune, who can remedy their situation by simply "trying harder." These prejudices and stereotypes are often reinforced by biased and sensationalist media reports that particularly target those living in poverty who are victims of multiple forms of discrimination, such as single mothers, ethnic minorities, indigenous people and migrants.[113]

The special rapporteur points out that "[s]uch attitudes are so deeply entrenched that they inform public policies and prevent policymakers from addressing the systemic factors that prevent persons living in poverty from overcoming their situation," and she recommends that State parties to the *ICESCR*, such as Canada, "ensure that discrimination on the basis of economic and social status is prohibited by law and the law applied by courts."[114]

The Supreme Court has yet to consider the question of whether the social conditions of homelessness and of poverty are analogous grounds of discrimination under section 15 of the *Charter*. Lower-court jurisprudence on the issue is mixed. Where courts have considered evidence of the socially constructed exclusion and devaluation of poor and homeless people, including evidence of stereotyping and stigma, these have been recognized as analogous grounds of discrimination.[115] However, in cases where the courts have focused solely on the characteristic of economic need or income level, analogous grounds claims have been rejected.[116] In some unsuccessful cases the courts have focused on level of income in relation

---

113 *Report of the Special Rapporteur on Extreme Poverty and Human Rights, Magdalena Sepulveda*, UNGAOR, 66th Sess, UN Doc A/66/265, (2011) at para 7.

114 *Ibid* at para 82(b).

115 *Federated Anti-Poverty Groups*, above note 29; *Falkiner v Ontario (Ministry of Community and Social Services)* (1996), 140 DLR (4th) 115 at 130–39 (Ont Ct Gen Div), Rosenberg J, dissenting; *Falkiner v Ontario (Ministry of Community and Social Services)* (2000), 188 DLR (4th) 52 (Ont Div Ct); *Falkiner v Ontario (Ministry of Community and Social Services)* (2002), 59 OR (3d) 481 (CA) [*Falkiner* CA]; *Schaff v Canada* (1993), 18 CRR (2d) 143 at para 52; *Dartmouth/Halifax County Regional Housing Authority v Sparks* (1993), 119 NSR (2d) 91 (CA) [*Sparks*]; *R v Rehberg* (1993), 127 NSR (2d) 331 (SC) [*Rehberg*].

116 Froc, "Golden Rule," above note 22 at 468–70; MacKay & Kim, *Social Condition*, above note 96 at 64–73.

to a generalized poverty line and found that income level may change.[117] In others, the courts have considered economic activities linked to poverty and homelessness, such as "begging" or "panhandling," and have concluded that economic activity is not a personal characteristic that can be protected under section 15.[118] As Fichaud J asserted in *Boulter v Nova Scotia Power Inc* "[p]overty is a clinging web, but financial circumstances may change, and individuals may enter and leave poverty or gain and lose resources . . . . Economic status, poverty or wealth, is not an adopted emblem of identity like religion, citizenship or marital status, that the individual observes peacefully free of government meddling."[119]

The denial of analogous grounds claims on the basis that income level or economic circumstances can change and that people may move in and out of poverty or homelessness represents a misapplication of the concept of immutability and the contextual and purposive assessment called for in *Miron*[120] and *Corbiere*.[121] In considering whether off-reserve status constituted an analogous ground in *Corbiere*, the Court did not consider the question of immutability in relation to residency status in the abstract, nor did it rely on data quantifying the frequency of movement between on-reserve and off-reserve residence. Rather, the immutability analysis was focused on the socially constructed characteristics associated with on-reserve and off-reserve status. The Court considered how residency status was tied to social identity and social relations, such that it may "stand as a constant marker of potential legislative discrimination" and of "suspect distinctions."[122] The majority in *Corbiere* also insisted that the analogous grounds analysis should not be restricted to the facts of a particular case but rather must be conducted in relation to broader historical and systemic patterns of discrimination, in order to develop "a conceptual jurisprudence of the sorts of distinctions that fall under the s. 15 guarantee, without foreclosing new cases of discrimination."[123]

---

117 *Boulter v Nova Scotia Power Incorporated*, 2009 NSCA 17 at para 42 [*Boulter*]; *Guzman v Canada (Minister of Citizenship and Immigration)*, 2006 FC 1134 at para 19.

118 *R v Banks*, 2007 ONCA 19 at para 104, leave to appeal to SCC refused, [2007] SCCA No 139 [*Banks*]; *Thibaudeau v Canada*, [1995] 2 SCR 627; *Donovan v Canada*, [2006] 1 CTC 2041 at para 18 (TCC); *Dunmore v Ontario (AG)* (1997), 37 OR (3d) 287 (Gen Div), aff'd (1999), 182 DLR (4th) 471 (Ont CA), rev'd on other grounds 2001 SCC 94; *Bailey v Canada*, 2005 FCA 25 at para 12.

119 *Boulter*, above note 117 at para 42.

120 *Miron*, above note 100 at para 100.

121 *Corbiere*, above note 102 at para 59.

122 *Ibid* at paras 10–11.

123 *Ibid* at para 11.

Judicial decisions predating *Corbiere* that recognize poverty as an analogous ground are not inconsistent with the focus on socially constructed identity, which the majority in *Corbiere* relied on in developing the concept of "constructive immutability." For instance, in its decision in *Dartmouth/Halifax County Regional Housing Authority v Sparks*, challenging the exclusion of public housing tenants from provincial residential tenancies legislation, the Nova Scotia Court of Appeal found that poverty and reliance on public housing constituted analogous grounds under section 15.[124] The court recognized that while people may move in and out of public housing, social attitudes related to residency in public housing attach to personal identity in a way that attracts stigma and discriminatory treatment. Noting that attitudes toward public housing tenants were linked to the over-representation of racialized households and single mothers among those living in poverty and relying on public housing,[125] Hallett J concluded that "the impugned provisions amount to discrimination on the basis of race, sex and income."[126] The Court of Appeal's reasoning in *Sparks* was later applied by the Nova Scotia Supreme Court in *R v Rehberg*, where the court found that a "spouse in the house" rule that disentitled sole support parents, largely women, from receiving social assistance benefits if they were cohabiting with a man was discriminatory on the ground of poverty.[127]

The *Sparks* and *Rehberg* decisions were cited by the Ontario Court of Appeal in *Falkiner v Ontario (Ministry of Community and Social Services)*, which involved a similar challenge to a "spouse in the house" rule in Ontario social assistance legislation.[128] Referring to the Ontario Divisional Court's earlier decision in *Masse v Ontario (Ministry of Community and Social Services)*,[129] Laskin J acknowledged that recognizing receipt of public assistance as an analogous ground of discrimination has been "controversial primarily because of concerns about singling out the economically disadvantaged for *Charter* protection, about immutability, and about lack of homogeneity."[130] He noted, however, that the inquiry into analogous grounds should be situated in the context of the broader purposes of section 15 and must

---

124 *Sparks*, above note 115.

125 *Ibid* at para 31.

126 *Ibid* at paras 26–27.

127 *Rehberg*, above note 115 at para 83.

128 *Falkiner* CA, above note 115 at para 90.

129 *Masse v Ontario (Ministry of Community and Social Services)* (1996), 134 DLR (4th) 20 (Ont Div Ct), leave to appeal denied without reasons, [1996] OJ No 1526 (CA), leave to appeal to SCC refused, [1996] SCCA No 373.

130 *Falkiner* CA, above note 115 at para 84.

take into account "the nature of the group and Canadian society's treatment of that group."[131] Justice Laskin pointed to the trial court's finding that "[s]ocial assistance recipients face resentment and anger from others in society, who see them as freeloading and lazy" and that the members of the group are "subject to stigma leading to social exclusion,"[132] and he went on to suggest that

> although the receipt of social assistance reflects economic disadvantage, which alone does not justify protection under s. 15, economic disadvantage often co-exists with other forms of disadvantage. That is the case here. The economic disadvantage suffered by social assistance recipients is only one feature of and may in part result from their historical disadvantage and vulnerability. I am comforted in this conclusion by two Nova Scotia decisions: *R. v. Rehberg* (1994), 111 D.L.R. (4th) 336 (S.C.) and *Dartmouth/Halifax County Regional Housing Authority v. Sparks* (1993), 101 D.L.R. (4th) 244 (CA).[133]

Given the significant evidence of historical disadvantage and continuing prejudice experienced by those in receipt of social assistance, including sole support mothers, Laskin J concluded that "recognizing receipt of social assistance as an analogous ground of discrimination under s. 15(1) would further the protection of human dignity."[134]

In *R v Clarke*,[135] the Ontario Superior Court considered whether discriminatory attitudes toward those living in poverty or who are homeless ought to be recognized as a basis for challenges to prospective jurors. Noting the Court of Appeal's findings in *Falkiner*, Ferrier J concluded that "there is widespread prejudice against the poor and the homeless in the widely applied characterization that the poor and homeless are dishonest and irresponsible and that they are responsible for their own plight."[136] He further found that "the prejudice against the poor and homeless is similar to racial prejudice."[137]

131 *Ibid* at para 85.

132 *Ibid* at para 86.

133 *Ibid* at para 88.

134 *Ibid* at paras 86–87.

135 *R v Clarke*, [2003] OJ No 3883 (SCJ).

136 *Ibid* at para 18.

137 *Ibid*.

As Kerri Froc points out in Chapter 6,[138] the analogous grounds analysis outlined by the Supreme Court in *Miron* and *Corbiere*[139] requires an in-depth inquiry into the lived reality — material, political, economic, and social — of the members of the group whose equality rights are at issue. As described above, the material deprivation experienced by people living in poverty and who are homeless directly threatens life, liberty, and security of the person-related interests under section 7 of the *Charter*. Far from justifying exclusion from section 15, these material conditions reinforce the call for equal protection and equal benefit of the *Charter*'s equality guarantees. Above and beyond the economic disadvantage to which they are subject, however, it is evident that people living in poverty and who are homeless are, in the words of Wilson J, "lacking in political power and as such vulnerable to having their interests overlooked and their rights to equal concern and respect violated."[140] This understanding is reflected in both domestic human rights legislation and international human rights laws. In view of the stigma and marginalization which poor people and the homeless experience, individually and as a group, and their effective exclusion from political power and from full participation in social, economic, and political life, judicial recognition of the social condition of poverty and homelessness as prohibited grounds of discrimination under section 15 is long overdue.

Aside from the issue of whether poverty and homelessness constitute analogous grounds in-and-of-themselves, the material reality and social construction of homelessness and poverty must also, as the senate subcommittee observed in *In from the Margins*, be understood as intersecting with other enumerated grounds of discrimination.[141] The CESCR has pointed

138 See Chapter 6.

139 *Miron*, above note 100; *Corbiere*, above note 102.

140 *Andrews*, above note 88 at para 5.

141 *In from the Margins*, above note 8. See also Raphael, *Poverty in Canada*, above note 47 at 62–89; Shelley Gavigan & Dorothy Chunn, eds, *The Legal Tender of Gender: Law, Welfare and the Regulation of Women's Poverty* (Oxford: Hart Publishing, 2010); Human Resources and Skills Development Canada, *Federal Disability Report 2010 — The Government of Canada's Annual Report on Disability Issues* (Ottawa: Human Resources and Skills Development Canada, 2010) at 7–14; Grace-Edward Galabuzi, "Social Exclusion" in Raphael, *Social Determinants*, above note 42 at 252–68; Daniel Wilson & David Macdonald, *The Income Gap between Aboriginal Peoples and the Rest of Canada* (Ottawa: Canadian Centre for Policy Alternatives, 2010); Sharon Donna McIvor, "Aboriginal Women Unmasked: Using Equality Litigation to Advance Women's Rights" in Young et al, *Poverty*, above note 8 at 96; Monica Townson, *Women's Poverty and the Recession* (Ottawa: Canadian Centre for Policy Alternatives, 2009); Hermer & Mosher, *Disorderly People*, above note 65; Grace-Edward Galabuzi, *Canada's Economic Apartheid: The*

out that women, especially single mothers and people with disabilities, racialized groups, Aboriginal people, newcomers, and youth are disproportionately affected by homelessness and poverty in Canada.[142] A purposive equality rights analysis of poverty and homelessness must be informed by an understanding of systemic patterns of discrimination against these groups and must consider, for example, how attitudes toward people with mental health disabilities, youth, or racialized immigrants are manifested in government and public responses to homelessness and poverty. As UN human rights monitoring bodies have underscored,[143] disaggregated data relating to such groups, as well as provisions to ensure their effective representation in decision-making processes, are critical components in any rights-based poverty and housing strategy that is informed by an equality framework consistent with section 15 of the *Charter*.[144]

2) Substantive Discrimination

The second stage of the Supreme Court's equality analysis is to consider whether a law or policy that draws a distinction on a prohibited ground is substantively discriminatory. As the Court explained in *Kapp*, "perpetuation of disadvantage and stereotyping" were identified in *Andrews* "as the primary indicators of discrimination."[145] An understanding of the social construction of poverty and homelessness is therefore critical at this stage of the section 15 analysis as well. This does not mean, as Vincent Greason underscores in Chapter 3, that material deprivation or the adverse effects

---

Social Exclusion of Racialized Groups in the New Century (Toronto: Canadian Scholars' Press, 2006).

142 UNCESCROR, *Concluding Observations*, 2006, above note 6; Day, "Minding the Gap," above note 8.

143 See United Nations Committee on Economic, Social and Cultural Rights, *Guidelines on Treaty-Specific Documents to Be Submitted by States Parties under Articles 16 and 17 of the International Covenant on Economic, Social and Cultural Rights*, UNCESCROR, 2009, UN Doc E/C.12/2008/2, (24 March 2009) at paras 3 and 10 [UNCESCROR, *Treaty-Specific Documents*]; *Report of the Special Rapporteur on Adequate Housing as a Component of the Right to an Adequate Standard of Living, Miloon Kothari*, UN Human Rights Council, 4th Sess, UN Doc A/HRC/4/18, (2007) [UNHRC, *Report of Miloon Kothari*]; *Report of the Special Rapporteur on the Right of Everyone to the Enjoyment of the Highest Attainable Standard of Physical and Mental Health, Paul Hunt*, Commission on Human Rights, 62d Sess, UN Doc E/CN.4/2006/48, (2006).

144 See UNCESCROR, *Treaty-Specific Documents*, above note 143; UNHRC, *Report of Miloon Kothari*, above note 143.

145 *Kapp*, above note 87 at para 23.

of governments' failure to address economic need do not violate equality guarantees.[146] Rather, governments' lack of response to the material needs of those living in poverty should be understood in light of the discrimination, exclusion, and discounting of rights that lie behind the denial of adequate benefits. As Kerri Froc explains:

> Poverty is not easily analyzed under section 15, given its multi-dimensional and relational nature. More than simply an objective economic condition (lack of financial resources), it touches almost every aspect of the lives of those it affects, including the ability to exercise their constitutional rights . . . it is interwoven in various, intersecting relations of oppression, and itself is the basis for subordination (demonstrated by the stereotyping and "victim blaming" of poor people).[147]

An illustration of the link between government failure to address needs and social patterns of stigma and stereotype is provided in Marie-Eve Sylvestre's affidavit in *Tanudjaja*.[148] Sylvestre's research has found that the proliferation of false stereotypes about homeless people and the devaluation of their rights are inextricably linked to government neglect of the needs of this vulnerable group. She points, as one example, to statements by the mayor of Ottawa that the city was attracting the homeless "like seagulls at the dump" by offering too many services. On another occasion, the mayor compared homeless people to pigeons, saying that if Ottawa would stop feeding them, they would stop coming.[149] Sylvestre notes that these attitudes create socially constructed identities, as well as significant barriers to any conception of equal rights to services or programs for members of this stigmatized group. Governments at every level are dissuaded from reasonably addressing the needs of the poor and homeless based on stereotypic views of the groups' moral unworthiness and laziness and prejudicial assumptions that the more their needs are addressed, the more of a "problem" they will become. As Sylvestre explains, "[b]ecause of the prevalence of stereotypes and stigma applied to homeless people, the lived experience of homelessness involves far more than economic deprivation and absence of housing. It becomes an all-encompassing social identity or social label

---

146 See Chapter 3.

147 Froc, "Golden Rule," above note 22 at 468.

148 Sylvestre, "Affidavit for *Tanudjaja*," above note 64. See also Chapter 5.

149 "'Pigeons' Squawk over Mayor's Comments on Homeless" *CBC News* (25 April 2007), online: CBC.ca www.cbc.ca, cited in Sylvestre, "Affidavit for *Tanudjaja*," above note 64 at para 41.

for individuals. It defines one's personhood in a way that is socially constructed and difficult to change." The result is that

> [v]irtually every part of society perceives and treats a person differently once they become homeless. Law enforcement officials treat them as potentially dangerous and disorderly and in need of severe regulation: they apply measures in a discriminatory fashion, on the basis of visible signs of poverty. Politicians tend to treat them as a "problem" to be kept out of a neighbourhood by denying basic sustenance or other services, rather than equal citizens entitled to programs and services to meet their unique needs.[150]

While homelessness is not "immutable" in an absolute sense, Sylvestre describes how this all-encompassing personal identity is difficult to escape:

> Street exit is a long and difficult process which involves considerable movement back and forth from being homeless and being "vulnerably housed." When applying for a job, it is hard to justify the period of time that the individual remained unemployed because he or she was homeless. When applying for an apartment, the homeless person often has difficulties providing references to future landlords and is seen as an undesirable tenant . . . . As noted above, landlords routinely check prospective tenants' credit before renting an apartment, and debt collection on unpaid fines may compromise a tenant's ability to pay rent.[151]

The Supreme Court has recognized that discrimination occurs when a policy fails to take into account "the actual needs, capacity, or circumstances of the claimant and others with similar traits in a manner that respects their value as human beings and members of Canadian society."[152] In *Eaton v Brant County Board of Education*,[153] Sopinka J warned that ignoring the needs and capacities of people with disabilities may be "a case of reverse stereotyping which, by not allowing for the condition of a disabled individual, ignores his or her disability and forces the individual to sink or

---

150 Sylvestre, "Affidavit for *Tanudjaja*," *ibid* at para 51. See also Raphael, *Poverty in Canada*, above note 47 at 153–85 and 356–66.

151 *Ibid* at para 52.

152 *Law*, above note 89 at para 70. The principle was first enunciated in *Andrews*, above note 88 at para 70, where McIntyre J explained that "[i]t will be easier to establish discrimination to the extent that impugned legislation fails to take into account a claimant's actual situation, and more difficult to establish discrimination to the extent that legislation properly accommodates the claimant's needs, capacities, and circumstances."

153 [1997] 1 SCR 241.

swim within the mainstream environment. It is recognition of the actual characteristics, and reasonable accommodation of these characteristics which is the central purpose of s. 15(1) in relation to disability."[154] Housing and anti-poverty strategies must similarly recognize the unique needs, capacities, and circumstances of people who are living in poverty or who are homeless and, in particular, must meet needs that are linked to economic deprivation. At the same time, however, such strategies must remedy the devaluation of rights and capacity that is the underlying cause and fuel for the perpetuation of the inequality being addressed. A rights-based approach, which restores equal citizenship to members of the group, is critical to a remedial, purposive approach to addressing homelessness and poverty amidst affluence.[155] At a fundamental level, such an approach recognizes homelessness and poverty as denials of "a basic aspect of full membership in Canadian society"[156] and demands that government neglect and inaction be addressed as a matter of constitutional right.

D. SECTION 1: THE GUARANTEE OF REASONABLE LIMITS

The Supreme Court has affirmed that section 1 of the *Charter*[157] plays a dual role, both as a limit to rights and a guarantee of rights.[158] As Arbour J observed in *Gosselin*, "[w]e sometimes lose sight of the primary function of s. 1 — to constitutionally guarantee rights — focussed as we are on the section's

---

154 *Ibid* at paras 66–67, as cited in *Eldridge v British Columbia (AG)*, [1997] 3 SCR 624 [*Eldridge*].

155 See, generally, Gwen Brodsky, "Human Rights and Poverty: A Twenty-First Century Tribute to J.S. Woodsworth and Call for Human Rights" in Jane Pulkingham, ed, *Human Welfare, Rights, and Social Activism: Rethinking the Legacy of J.S. Woodsworth* (Toronto: University of Toronto Press, 2010) 136; Lucie Lamarche, "The 'Made in Quebec' Act to Combat Poverty and Social Exclusion: The Complex Relationship between Poverty and Human Rights" in Young et al, *Poverty*, above note 8 at 138.

156 *Law*, above note 89 at para 74; Janine Brodie, "Reforming Social Justice in Neoliberal Times" (2007) 1:2 Studies in Social Justice 93 at 102–3; Janet Mosher, "Welfare Reform and the Re-making of the Model Citizen" in Young et al, *Poverty*, above note 8 at 119; Ken Norman, "The *Charter* as an Impediment to Welfare Rollbacks: A Meditation on 'Justice as Fairness' and as 'Bedrock Value' of the Canadian Democratic Project" in Young et al, *Poverty*, *ibid* at 297.

157 *Charter*, above note 2, s 1: "[t]he *Canadian Charter of Rights and Freedoms* guarantees the rights and freedoms set out in it subject only to such reasonable limits prescribed by law as can be demonstrably justified in a free and democratic society.")

158 *R v Oakes*, [1986] 1 SCR 103 at para 135 [*Oakes*].

limiting function."[159] In interpreting and applying section 1, the Court has underscored governments' obligations to protect the rights of vulnerable groups. In *Irwin Toy*, for example, restrictions on advertising aimed at those under the age of thirteen were found to be a justifiable infringement of section 2(b) rights to freedom of expression because such restrictions were consistent with the important *Charter* value of protecting vulnerable groups, such as children.[160] While evidence in the case suggested that other less restrictive means were available to the government, the Court affirmed it would not "in the name of minimal impairment [of a *Charter* right] . . . require legislatures to choose the least ambitious means to protect vulnerable groups."[161]

In line with similar obligations under human rights legislation, the Supreme Court has situated the assessment of what positive measures are reasonably required to accommodate disability or other characteristics of disadvantaged groups within the section 1 guarantee of reasonable limits.[162] In *Eldridge v British Columbia (AG)*,[163] for example, the Court considered a challenge brought by deaf patients to the government's failure to include sign language interpretation as an insured service within the publicly funded health care system. Having determined that the failure to provide interpretation services violated section 15, the Court examined the cost of providing interpreter services to deaf patients in relation to the overall provincial health care budget. The Court concluded that the government's refusal to fund such services was not reasonable.[164] In the course of his section 1 analysis, LaForest J noted that

> [i]t is also a cornerstone of human rights jurisprudence, of course, that the duty to take positive action to ensure that members of disadvantaged groups benefit equally from services offered to the general public is subject to the principle of reasonable accommodation . . . . In my view, in s. 15(1)

159 *Gosselin*, above note 26 at para 352.

160 *Irwin Toy*, above note 24.

161 *Ibid* at 999; *Dunmore v Ontario (AG)*, 2001 SCC 94 at para 57. See, however, *RJR-MacDonald Inc v Canada (AG)*, [1995] 3 SCR 199 at para 136, where the Supreme Court granted a tobacco manufacturer's s 2(b) challenge to federal tobacco advertising and marketing restrictions, notwithstanding evidence of tobacco related harm to health, and the particular vulnerability of children and youth to tobacco advertising.

162 *Schachter v Canada*, [1992] 2 SCR 679 at 709; *Egan v Canada*, [1995] 2 SCR 513 at para 99; *Nova Scotia (Workers' Compensation Board) v Martin; Nova Scotia (Workers' Compensation Board) v Laseur*, 2003 SCC 54 at para 109.

163 *Eldridge*, above note 154.

164 *Ibid* at para 93.

> cases this principle is best addressed as a component of the s. 1 analysis. Reasonable accommodation, in this context, is generally equivalent to the concept of "reasonable limits."[165]

The "undue hardship" standard was thus found by the unanimous Court in *Eldridge* to fit within the "reasonable limits" requirement of section 1. The majority of the Court reaffirmed this principle more recently in *Multani v Commission Scolaire Marguerite-Bourgeoys*, finding that "correspondence between the legal principles [of reasonable limits and reasonable accommodation] is logical."[166] The standard of undue hardship, as it has been developed under human rights legislation, is a rigorous standard in relation to the allocation of necessary budgetary measures. In *British Columbia (Superintendent of Motor Vehicles) v British Columbia (Council of Human Rights)*,[167] the Court cautioned in regards to financial justifications for rights violations that "it is all too easy to cite increased costs as a reason," that "impressionistic evidence of increased expenses will not generally suffice," and that courts must consider that "there may be ways to reduce costs."[168]

In those *Charter* cases where the Court has approached issues of positive obligations and budgetary measures without reference to the human rights standard of "undue hardship," the standard that has been applied under section 1 has, like in *Eldridge*, been described as a rigorous one. In *New Brunswick v G(J)*, the Court held that the government had a positive obligation under section 7 to provide legal aid to parents who cannot afford a lawyer when the parent's life, liberty, or security is at stake in child custody proceedings.[169] Noting that violations of section 7 rights will only rarely be overridden by competing social interests and, hence, are unlikely to constitute reasonable limits under section 1,[170] the Court found that "a parent's right to a fair hearing when the state seeks to suspend such parent's custody of his or her child outweighs the relatively modest sums, when considered in light of the government's entire budget, at issue in this appeal."[171]

Even in *Newfoundland (Treasury Board) v NAPE*, where the Supreme Court concluded that the province's failure to honour a $24 million pay equity award in favour of female public sector workers was justifiable under

---

165 *Ibid* at para 79.

166 2006 SCC 6 at para 53.

167 [1999] 3 SCR 868.

168 *Ibid* at para 41.

169 *G(J)*, above note 30.

170 *Ibid* at para 99.

171 *Ibid* at para 100.

section 1, the Court claimed to be applying a rigorous standard of review.[172] The province's decision was made as part of an across-the-board reduction of government expenditures in response to a perceived provincial debt crisis that was characterized by the government and accepted by the Supreme Court as amounting to a "financial emergency."[173] While the Court found that a budgetary crisis justified an infringement of section 15 in that case, Binnie J cautioned that courts must remain skeptical of attempts by governments to justify such rights infringements, noting that "there are *always* budgetary constraints and there are *always* other pressing government priorities."[174] At the same time, Binnie J noted the important social values that are engaged in budgetary decision making:

> The weighing exercise has as much to do with social values as it has to do with dollars. In the present case, the "potential impact" is $24 million, amounting to more than 10 percent of the projected budgetary deficit for 1991–92. The delayed implementation of pay equity is an extremely serious matter, but so too (for example) is the layoff of 1,300 permanent, 350 part-time and 350 seasonal employees, and the deprivation to the public of the services they provided.[175]

The Supreme Court has recognized that in these kinds of "weighing" exercises, a certain degree of judicial deference is mandated, since "there may be no obviously correct or obviously wrong solution but, rather, a range of options each with its advantages and disadvantages. Governments act as they think proper within a range of reasonable alternatives."[176] However, as McLachlin CJ underscored in *RJR-MacDonald Inc v Canada (AG)*,[177] acknowledging that there may be a range of policy measures that are reasonable does not justify blanket deference to legislatures in relation to budgetary allocations or socio-economic policy. Section 1 calls for rigorous and independent judicial assessment and oversight of government choices, where these infringe *Charter*-protected rights.[178] Thus, in *NAPE*, Binnie J rejected the Court of Appeal's suggestion that budgetary decisions are inherently

---

172 2004 SCC 66 [*NAPE*].

173 *Ibid* at para 1.

174 *Ibid* at para 72.

175 *Ibid*.

176 *Ibid* at para 83.

177 [1995] 3 SCR 199 at paras 134–38.

178 Douglas Elliott & Jason Tan, "Unequal Benefits or Unequal Persons? Social Benefit Programs and the *Charter*" (2006) 19 NJCL 285 at 308–11; Young, "Section 7," above note 22.

political and should be subject to a unique deferential standard based on the separation of powers.[179] As Binnie J cautioned:

> No doubt Parliament and the legislatures, generally speaking, *do* enact measures that they, representing the majority view, consider to be reasonable limits that have been demonstrated to *their* satisfaction as justifiable. Deference to the legislative choice to the degree proposed by Marshall J.A. would largely circumscribe and render superfluous the independent second look imposed on the courts by s. 1 of the *Charter*.[180]

In light of the rigorous standard of justification imposed under section 1, it is hard to see how governments' refusal to adopt measures to address increasing poverty and homelessness in the midst of affluence in Canada can be characterized as a reasonable limit on the *Charter* rights of those who are harmed and whose rights are infringed by such inaction. In his affidavit in support of the *Tanudjaja* case,[181] former UN special rapporteur on adequate housing Miloon Kothari makes the observation that:

> [t]he most striking feature of my visit to Canada was the contrast between the abundance of resources available and the dire living conditions facing the most vulnerable in society . . . . At the time of my mission, the Federal Government had enjoyed a multi-billion dollar surplus for a decade. Canada Mortgage and Housing Corporation, the federal government's national housing agency, had an increasingly large operating surplus — almost $1 billion in 2007 . . . . And yet, everywhere I visited in Canada, I met people who were homeless and living in inadequate and insecure housing conditions. I received reliable evidence that people had died as a direct result of Canada's nation-wide housing crisis.[182]

There is overwhelming evidence that governments are wasting large amounts of money by failing to adopt anti-poverty and housing strategies called for by international treaty monitoring bodies.[183] A 2009 Alberta government study estimated the cost of supporting each homeless person in that province to be close to $100,000 per year.[184] As Marie-Eve Sylvestre and

---

179 *Newfoundland (Treasury Board) v NAPE*, 2002 NLCA 72.

180 *NAPE*, above note 172 at para 103.

181 *Tanudjaja*, above note 36.

182 Miloon Kothari, "Affidavit for *Tanudjaja v Attorney General (Canada)*," Ont Sup Ct File no CV-10-403688 (2011) at paras 75–77.

183 Porter & Jackman, "Making the Connection," above note 4 at 20–31.

184 Alberta Secretariat for Action on Homelessness, *A Plan for Alberta: Ending Homelessness in 10 Years* (Edmonton: Alberta Secretariat for Action on Homelessness, 2008) at 8.

Céline Bellot note in Chapter 5, the cost of services for homeless people has been estimated at $4,000 per month.[185] Incarceration costs are about the same for adults and significantly higher for youth.[186] In comparison, a program involving rent supplements and support services, which provided access to adequate and stable housing for former homeless residents of Tent City in Toronto, was estimated to have cost about $1,000 per month — a quarter of the cost of incarceration or homelessness services.[187]

Pointing to the estimated $1.4 billion in annual costs of homelessness in Canada, the Mental Health Commission of Canada has recently characterized Canadian governments' response of relying on shelters and emergency and acute health services as "a costly and ineffective way of responding to the problem."[188] In a 2009 report, the Auditor General of British Columbia likewise found that "[a]ccording to a growing body of evidence, the cost to society of not addressing homelessness is significantly higher than the cost of providing housing and intervention services."[189] The Senate Subcommittee on Cities came to a similar conclusion in relation to the cost of poverty and homelessness in its 2009 report, *In from the Margins: A Call to Action on Poverty, Housing and Homelessness*:

> . . . the Committee's testimony clearly underlines that poverty costs us all. Poverty expands healthcare costs, policing burdens and diminished educational outcomes. This in turn depresses productivity, labour force flexibility, life spans and economic expansion and social progress, all of which takes place at huge cost . . . . We believe that eradicating poverty and homelessness is not only the humane and decent priority of a civilized democracy, but absolutely essential to a productive and expanding economy benefitting from the strengths and abilities of all its people.[190]

Governments' refusal to implement effective strategies to address poverty and to ensure access to adequate housing is not only a violation of both domestic constitutional and international human rights. It is also a fiscally irresponsible response to problems that could be better addressed

---

185 See Chapter 5. See also Sylvestre, "Affidavit for *Tanudjaja*," above note 64 at para 50.

186 *Ibid*.

187 Gloria Gallant, Joyce Brown, & Jacques Tremblay, *From Tent City to Housing: An Evaluation of the City of Toronto's Emergency Homelessness Pilot Project* (Toronto: Toronto Shelter, Support and Housing Administration, 2004).

188 Mental Health Commission, *At Home/Chez Soi*, above note 34 at 11.

189 Office of the Auditor General of British Columbia, *Homelessness: Clear Focus Needed* (Victoria: Office of the Auditor General of British Columbia, 2009) at 19.

190 *In from the Margins*, above note 8 at 3; Food Banks Canada, *Hunger Count 2009* (Toronto: Food Banks Canada, 2010) at 3.

in accordance with human rights and values of social inclusion, rather than through the perpetuation of patterns of stigmatization and exclusion. It is precisely in these types of situations that an "independent second look" at government policies through a human rights lens is essential to ensure governmental accountability and the proper functioning of a constitutional democracy.[191]

E. CONCLUSION

The fact that adequate housing and an adequate standard of living are not explicitly recognized as constitutional rights in Canada does not mean that there is no domestic constitutional framework to protect and guarantee these rights. Section 7 of the *Charter* can and should be interpreted as requiring governments not only to refrain from interfering with the survival tactics of people who are homeless or living in poverty in public spaces but to actively address and combat homelessness and poverty through appropriate strategies. Section 7 principles of fundamental justice provide a solid basis for claiming a substantive right to fair and reasonable housing and anti-poverty strategies and procedural rights to meaningful, rights-based participation in the design, implementation, monitoring, and evaluation of such programs. For its part, section 15 not only mandates an effective response to economic and physical needs but also creates an equality framework for challenging structural and systemic injustices and exclusion based on stereotypes, stigma, and marginalization faced by those who are homeless and living in poverty in such a wealthy country as Canada. Section 1, in turn, offers a rights-based approach to assessing the reasonableness of government action and inaction in relation to poverty and homelessness, and for balancing competing needs and budgetary allocations.

Although sections 7, 15, and 1 of the *Charter* have the potential to provide a robust constitutional framework for a rights-based approach to poverty and homelessness, such claims have been resisted by Canadian governments at every level. In the *Tanudjaja* case,[192] for example, the governments of Canada and Ontario have brought a motion to strike the claim, prior to any hearing on the evidence or merits, on the grounds that "the issues raised and the relief sought . . . are not justiciable" and that the applicants' claim "challenges economic and social policies that are essentially political

191 *NAPE*, above note 172 at para 103.

192 *Tanudjaja*, above note 36.

matters, beyond the institutional competence of the Superior Court."[193] Of even greater concern, however, is the prevailing judicial bias in Canada against applying the *Charter* to require governments to act in response to human rights crises of this sort. Although homeless people were successful in their *Charter* challenge in *Victoria (City) v Adams*,[194] this judicial bias is evident even in that case.[195] The *Adams* claim arose from an application by the City of Victoria for an injunction authorizing it to evict a number of homeless people, including the defendants, from a tent city they had created in a public park. In response, the defendants challenged the constitutionality of the municipal bylaw that prohibited the overnight erection of temporary structures, such as tents and tarps attached to trees, in public places. In its intervention in the case, the Attorney General of British Columbia argued against the application of the *Charter* and judicial interference in relation to the problem of homelessness:

> The AGBC says that the solutions to the difficult and challenging circumstances faced by the homeless lie in the hands of the democratically elected legislative and executive arms of government, and not in the courts creating a constitutionally entrenched "right." The courts are not equipped with the resources or the expertise to address the many challenging issues raised by the phenomenon of homelessness, and ought not to extend the reach of the Canadian constitution in an attempt to moderate the effects of homelessness in a manner that inevitably creates more problems than it can resolve.[196]

The attorney general also denied that Canada's international human rights obligations had any bearing on the case, arguing instead that "inter-

---

193 *Ibid* (Notice of Motion of the Attorney General of Canada (on Motion to Strike) at para 15); *ibid* (Factum of the Attorney General of Canada (on Motion to Strike) at paras 3–4, 20–24, 42–46, and 49–57); *ibid* (Factum of the Attorney General of Ontario (on Motion to Strike) at paras 1, 15, 21–25, 30–35, 37–45, and 59–66). The Attorney General's motion to strike was granted in the Ontario Superior Court of Justice in April 2013 (see above note 36). The claimants have appealed the Superior Court decision. The appeal was heard by the Ontario Court of Appeal 26–28 May 2014.

194 *Victoria (City) v Adams*, 2009 BCCA 172 [*Adams* (CA)], aff'g 2008 BCSC 1363 [*Adams* (SC)].

195 See, generally, Young, "Rights, the Homeless, and Social Change," above note 3; Martha Jackman, "*Charter* Remedies for Socio-economic Rights Violations: Sleeping under a Box?" in Kent Roach, ed, *Taking Remedies Seriously* (Montreal: Canadian Institute for the Administration of Justice, 2010).

196 *Adams* (SC), above note 194 (Factum of the Intervenor the Attorney General of British Columbia) at para 3.

national documents to which Canada is a party do not assist the Defendants . . . . They cannot be enforced in Canadian courts."[197]

At trial, Ross J found that the shortage of shelter spaces in Victoria meant that "hundreds of people are left to sleep in public places in the City"[198] and that the government's interference with the ability of homeless people to provide themselves with temporary shelter while sleeping outdoors at night exposed them to a risk of serious harm, including death by hypothermia.[199] On that basis she concluded that the bylaw prohibition on erecting temporary shelter violated section 7 of the *Charter* and could not be justified under section 1.[200] The British Columbia Court of Appeal agreed with this finding.[201] However, like Ross J,[202] the Court of Appeal insisted on interpreting and applying section 7 as a negative "restraint" on government action, rather than as imposing any positive obligations on governments to address the problem of homelessness or the rights of the homeless.[203] While the Court of Appeal recognized that the trial court's ruling would likely require some responsive action by the city to address the inadequate number of shelter beds in Victoria and the lack of housing options available to homeless people, the court declared, "[t]hat kind of responsive action to a finding that a law violates s. 7 does not involve the court in adjudicating positive rights."[204]

As argued above, there is no constitutional basis for courts or governments to draw such distinctions between the "positive" and "negative" rights obligations imposed by the *Charter*, or to focus exclusively on government action that violates rights while ignoring those that result from government inaction. In discussing the application of the *Charter* pursuant to section 32,[205] the Supreme Court has emphasized that the distinction between government action and inaction is "very problematic."[206] Quoting

197 *Ibid* at paras 56–57.

198 *Ibid* at para 58.

199 *Ibid* at para 142.

200 *Ibid* at para 216.

201 *Adams* (CA), above note 194 at para 10.

202 *Adams* (SC), above note 194 at paras 119–20.

203 *Adams* (CA), above note 194 at para 95.

204 *Ibid* at para 96.

205 Section 32 provides that the *Charter*, above note 2, applies "(a) to the Parliament and government of Canada in respect of all matters within the authority of Parliament including all matters relating to the Yukon Territory and Northwest Territories; and (b) to the legislature and government of each province in respect of all matters within the authority of the legislature of each province."

206 *Vriend v Alberta*, [1998] 1 SCR 493 at para 53 [*Vriend*].

from Dianne Pothier, in *Vriend v Alberta*[207] the Court affirmed that section 32 of the *Charter* is "worded broadly enough to cover positive obligations on a legislature such that the *Charter* will be engaged even if the legislature refuses to exercise its authority."[208] The Court went on to state that "[t]he application of the *Charter* is not restricted to situations where the government actively encroaches on rights."[209]

The Supreme Court has also rejected the idea that because such decisions are inherently political in nature, the *Charter* should not apply to executive or legislative choices about what policies or legislation to enact. In *R v Operation Dismantle*, the Court established that "political" questions are not immune from *Charter* review.[210] In *NAPE*, after the Newfoundland and Labrador Court of Appeal invoked the separation of powers as a basis for limiting judicial interference with "policy initiatives within the purview of the political branches of government,"[211] Binnie J responded for the majority:

> The "political branches" of government are the legislature and the executive. Everything that they do by way of legislation and executive action could properly be called "policy initiatives." If the "political branches" are to be the "final arbitrator" of compliance with the *Charter* of their "policy initiatives," it would seem the enactment of the *Charter* affords no real protection at all to the rights holders the *Charter*, according to its text, was intended to benefit. *Charter* rights and freedoms, on this reading, would offer rights without a remedy.[212]

Governmental authority to act, or not, in response to poverty and homelessness must be exercised consistently with the *Charter*, whether through positive measures to ensure equality or to protect life and security or through "negative" obligations to refrain from actively interfering with such rights. Louise Arbour and Fannie Lafontaine make the point that

> [r]ights are not just about protection against abusive or unjustified interference by the state. The role of the state has evolved and it has become central for human dignity and security to be fulfilled through a system of public policy and legislation aimed at protecting the individual and his or

---

207 *Ibid.*

208 Dianne Pothier, "The Sounds of Silence: *Charter* Application When the Legislature Declines to Speak" (1996) 7 Const Forum Const 113 at 115, cited in *Vriend*, *ibid* at para 60.

209 *Vriend*, *ibid.*

210 *R v Operation Dismantle*, [1985] 1 SCR 441 at para 64.

211 *NAPE*, above note 172 at para 110.

212 *Ibid* at para 111.

> her family from want and need . . . . The duality of roles for the state that is mandated by international human rights law needs to be integrated into our understanding of the *Charter.*[213]

As suggested at the outset of the chapter, the Supreme Court has affirmed that "Canada's *current* international commitments and the current state of international thought on human rights provide a persuasive source for interpreting the scope of the *Charter.*"[214] In 2008, the International Commission of Jurists (ICJ) undertook a comprehensive review of socio-economic rights jurisprudence from across Europe, Africa, Asia, and the Americas, including cases from the United States, Germany, Israel, and the United Kingdom among others.[215] The ICJ found that while the constitutions of some of the countries surveyed include explicit protection for socio-economic rights,[216] courts and tribunals in many other jurisdictions rely on more general constitutional guarantees, such as the right to life and to non-discrimination, as a basis for ordering governments to remedy rights violations in the areas of social security, housing, health, education, and other fundamental socio-economic rights.[217] The ICJ report underscores the degree to which Canadian courts stand out in their continuing conservatism in regards to the recognition and enforcement of socio-economic rights. Of the 200-plus trial, appellate, and Supreme Court cases contained in the ICJ's report, only one Canadian case can be found: the 1997 Supreme Court decision in *Eldridge*.[218] The continued reliance by Canadian courts and tribunals on a rights paradigm long abandoned under international law and increasingly rejected in other constitutional democracies undermines Canada's international human rights obligations. For people living in poverty and the homeless, who, unlike affluent Canadians, lack the alternate social, economic, or political means to hold elected governments to account, it

---

213 Arbour & Lafontaine, "Beyond Self-Congratulation," above note 21 at 271.

214 *Health Services Assn*, above note 12 at para 78.

215 International Commission of Jurists, *Courts and the Legal Enforcement of Economic, Social and Cultural Rights: Comparative Experiences of Justiciability* (Geneva: International Commission of Jurists, 2008) [ICJ, *Comparative Experiences*]. See also Malcolm Langford, ed, *Social Rights Jurisprudence: Emerging Trends in International and Comparative Law* (Cambridge: Cambridge University Press, 2009) at 649–76 [Langford, ed, *Social Rights Jurisprudence*].

216 ICJ, *Comparative Experiences*, above note 215 at 4, n 7.

217 *Ibid* at 65–72. See also Langford, ed, *Social Rights Jurisprudence*, above note 215.

218 *Eldridge*, above note 154.

also represents a fundamental failure of constitutionalism and of the rule of law.[219] As Margot Young has observed in relation to the *Adams* decision:

> Ultimately, the tougher and real question is why anyone in Canada should end up sleeping in a park — even with the shelter of a tarp or cardboard box. Governments have failed to respond adequately to this challenge. No wonder that the dispossessed and politically powerless have looked to the *Charter* and the rights it enshrines for just resolution. Whether or not our *Charter* and our Canadian courts are up to this task is still an open question.[220]

219 ICJ, *Comparative Experiences*, above note 215 at 3–4 and 82–83. See also Arbour, "Freedom from Want," above note 3; Froc, "Golden Rule," above note 22; David Wiseman, "Taking Competence Seriously" in Young et al, *Poverty*, above note 8 at 263; Wiseman, "Social and Economic Rights," above note 22; Porter, "Expectations of Equality," above note 49.

220 Young, "Rights, the Homeless, and Social Change," above note 3.

CHAPTER 3
POVERTY AS A HUMAN RIGHTS VIOLATION (EXCEPT IN GOVERNMENTAL ANTI-POVERTY STRATEGIES)

VINCENT GREASON[*1]

A. INTRODUCTION

Poverty is a fundamental violation of the human rights of the poor. To be poor means to have substandard housing or bad teeth, an empty fridge or recurring sickness, or to be afflicted by a myriad of other, often combined, situations that affect one's ability to live as "fully human." A series of human rights that are recognized by States in various international and domestic instruments are ignored, violated, and shunted aside as governments entrench themselves within a "balanced budget" logic. This is the political context in which a majority of Canadian provinces have decided to "fight poverty" — it also frames the new human rights paradigm within which we currently find ourselves.

As of December 2010, Newfoundland and Labrador, Nova Scotia, New Brunswick, Quebec, Ontario, and Manitoba have adopted formal anti-poverty strategies.[2] Five of these are rooted in legislation, whereas Newfoundland

---

* Coordinator, Table ronde des organismes volontaires d'éducation populaire de l'Outaouais (TROVEPO) and Research Partner in the SSHRC-CURA Research Project "Reconceiving Social Rights Practice," online: www.socialrightscura.ca.

1 I wish to acknowledge the financial support of the (now defunct) Community-University Research Alliance (CURA) program of the Social Sciences and Humanities Research Council of Canada. I would also like to acknowledge the invaluable research assistance of Stephanie Chaloult, student at the Faculty of Law, University of Ottawa.

2 Nunavut launched a formal anti-poverty strategy in October 2010. Given the constitutional differences between provinces and territories, we have chosen not to

and Labrador has chosen a non-legislative route. Quebec was first to adopt such a strategy. Between 1995 and 2002, a unique citizens' movement centred on the Collectif pour une loi sur l'élimination de la pauvreté[3] gathered the support of hundreds of thousands of citizens and 1,600 civil society groups who urged the Quebec government to adopt a law to eliminate poverty. Following a massive popular education campaign in the spring of 2002, a citizens' assembly made up of dozens of delegates from civil society groups across Quebec voted for a peoples' law to eliminate poverty, and several months later, 215,316 petitions in support of this demand[4] were presented to Quebec's National Assembly.

In December 2002, the *Act to Combat Poverty*, which contained several of the popular law's recommendations, was unanimously adopted by the National Assembly.[5] Two comprehensive five-year action plans to fight poverty followed in 2004 and 2010.[6]

---

include it in our study.

3 *An Act to Combat Poverty and Social Exclusion*, RSQ c L-7 [*Act to Combat Poverty*]. Following the adoption of Quebec's law, the Collectif pour une loi sur l'élimination de la pauvreté changed its name to Collectif pour un Québec sans pauvreté [Collectif].

4 That is in support of the principle of a law to eliminate poverty, not specifically in support of the content of the popular law. The "popular law" was redacted by progressive jurists and reflected the content that the Collectif would have liked to see in a "law to eliminate poverty."

5 *Act to Combat Poverty*, above note 3. Francois Aubry & Christiane Plamondon, "The Québec *Act to Combat Poverty and Social Exclusion*: How Does it Tackle the Situation of People with Disabilities?" (10 June 2010), online: CCD www.ccdonline.ca [Aubry & Plamondon]. In the foreword to Aubry and Plamondon's article, Lucie Dumais and Yves Vaillancourt make the following statement: ". . . [t]he fact that this law had been democratically co-constructed before its adoption, both in civil and political societies, has allowed it to acquire greater institutional strength and durability than if it had been the work of a single political party and had not been strongly rooted in civil society" (*ibid* at 2). Therefore, they take sides on an issue that has profoundly divided Quebec's anti-poverty movement: Was the *Act to Combat Poverty* co-constructed? Or was it the Quebec government's calculated political response to a politically opportunistic issue? The fact that the Collectif unabashedly welcomed the passage of the *Act to Combat Poverty* certainly painted it into a proverbial corner and limited its role as a critical intervener in the ongoing debates concerning the implementation of the law.

6 Government of Quebec, *Reconciling Freedom and Social Justice: A Challenge for the Future (2004–2010)* (April 2004), online: MESS www.mess.gouv.qc.ca; Government of Quebec, *Combating Poverty and Social Exclusion: A Priority for Québec (2010–2014)* (June 2010), online: MESS www.mess.gouv.qc.ca [Quebec, *Combating Poverty*].

Other Canadian provinces moved quickly to fight poverty. From east to west, several initiatives emerged. *Reducing Poverty: An Action Plan for Newfoundland and Labrador* was tabled in 2006.[7] In Nova Scotia, a private member's bill, adopted by the Provincial Assembly in 2007, obliged the government to form the working group that produced the *Poverty Reduction Strategy* in 2009.[8] Following extensive public consultation, in 2008, New Brunswick released *Overcoming Poverty Together: The New Brunswick Economic and Social Inclusion Plan*[9] and subsequently adopted the *Economic and Social Inclusion Act* in 2010.[10] In 2008, Ontario released *Breaking the Cycle: A Poverty Reduction Strategy*,[11] followed by the *Poverty Reduction Act, 2009*.[12] Finally, Manitoba joined other provinces with *All Aboard: Manitoba's Poverty Reduction Strategy* in 2009,[13] followed by the *Poverty Reduction Strategy Act*,[14] which became law in June 2011. Each of these strategies emerged within the same six- or seven-year period during which the provinces were adjusting to the Canada Social Transfer (2004), a new federal funding formula that dramatically altered the delivery of social programs in Canada.[15] The first decade of the new millennium was also a period when the neo-liberal ascendancy asserted itself on all levels of Canadian government.

Whereas "les trente glorieuses"[16] had given rise to the Keynesian welfare State, with various legislative efforts to redistribute wealth within Canada, the present series of provincial anti-poverty initiatives arrived in a period

7 Government of Newfoundland and Labrador, *Reducing Poverty: An Action Plan for Newfoundland and Labrador* (June 2006), online: Government of Newfoundland and Labrador www.gov.nl.ca.

8 Government of Nova Scotia, *Preventing Poverty. Promoting Prosperity. Nova Scotia's Poverty Reduction Strategy* (April 2009), online: Government of Nova Scotia http://novascotia.ca [Nova Scotia, *Preventing Poverty*].

9 Government of New Brunswick, *Overcoming Poverty Together: The New Brunswick Economic and Social Inclusion Plan* (2008), online: Government of New Brunswick www2.gnb.ca.

10 *Economic and Social Inclusion Act*, SNB 2010, c E-1.105.

11 Government of Ontario, *Breaking the Cycle: Ontario's Poverty Reduction Strategy* (2008), online: Government of Ontario www.ontario.ca [Ontario, *Breaking the Cycle*].

12 *Poverty Reduction Act, 2009*, SO 2009, c 10.

13 Government of Manitoba, *All Aboard: Manitoba's Poverty Reduction Strategy* (2009), online: Government of Manitoba www.gov.mb.ca/fs/misc/pubs/all_aboard_report.pdf.

14 *The Poverty Reduction Strategy Act*, CCSM c P94.7.

15 Barbara Cameron, "Accounting for Rights and Money in the Canadian Social Union" in Margot Young et al, eds, *Poverty: Rights, Social Citizenship, and Legal Activism* (Vancouver: UBC Press, 2007) 162.

16 "Les trente glorieuses" refers to a time of sharp economic growth that began in 1945 and continued until 1973 in the majority of OECD countries including Canada.

of the dismantling of the social State. Provincial anti-poverty strategies have emerged during a period of neo-liberal consolidation — more precisely, they have materialized just as the State is limiting, if not eliminating, its direct role in social program and service delivery. The changed nature of State intervention in the social sphere, coupled with reduced taxation and the offloading of State responsibilities to new social partners (philanthropic, private "for-profit" and private "not-for-profit" organizations), has a direct effect on the nature of these programs and strategies.[17]

B. SEVERAL THREADS, ONE WEB

In this paper, I identify six threads characteristic of Canada's provincial anti-poverty initiatives. Four of these, present and identifiable across the different schemes, form a tightly knit web; two others, conspicuous by their absence, fall outside of the neo-liberal net.

In the first instance, the State is moving away from direct revenue transfer to the poor as a means for fighting poverty. On the other hand, the desire to measure is omnipresent as provincial anti-poverty initiatives give rise to a new "poverty industry" composed of experts in the definition and measurement of poor people and their behaviour. A third common thread can be summed up in the concept of "responsibilization" with its double connotation: the "de-responsabilization" of government as the principal agent for fighting poverty and the "responsabilization" of new social actors, beginning with the poor themselves. Related to the third, a fourth thread posits that social partners must fight poverty with "synergy" — partnerships of stakeholders must be formed and mobilized so that poverty can be attenuated, and the poor can be neutralized as a socio-political threat.[18]

Whereas social commentators from the right and left of the spectrum acknowledge increasing social polarization, with the rich becoming more affluent, the middle class shrinking, and the poor becoming more numerous, none of the provincial strategies include measures, fiscal or otherwise, to limit private wealth accumulation. None acknowledge that a reduction in wealth disparity may hold the key to poverty reduction. This is the absent fifth thread.

---

17 Vincent Greason, "Québec's Community Movement: A Force for Social Change?" (2010), online: TROVEPO www.trovepo.org [Greason, "Québec's Community Movement"].

18 Hélène Thomas, *Les vulnérables : La démocratie contre les pauvres* (Bellecombe-en-Bauges: Éditions du Croquant, 2010) at 256.

Finally, Canada has committed itself to international human rights obligations.[19] Many human rights are directly related to poverty: the right to an adequate standard of living, social protections (pensions, legal aid, workers' compensation, unemployment insurance, etc.), a unionized workforce, adequate housing, food, health care, and free public education. Far from being an occasion for progressively implementing Canada's international human rights commitments, none of the provincial strategies have incorporated a human rights–based approach to fighting poverty. Indeed, apart from Quebec, there is not a single reference to human rights in any of the various provincial strategies.

C. COMMON THREADS IN A NEO-LIBERAL WEB

1) Revenue Transfer to the Poor

Poverty has long been conceptualized as an economic deprivation. The dictionary defines its first sense as "the state or condition of having little or no money, goods, or means of support; condition of being poor; indigence."[20] For the poor person, poverty is an existential fact: "There is no food in my fridge"; "My children will have to make do without a birthday party"; "I can't make the end of the month payments." Poverty is a lack of revenue, a lack of money.[21] In short, for the poor person, poverty is economic want.

---

19 *International Covenant for Economic, Social and Cultural Rights,* 16 December 1966, 993 UNTS 3, Can TS 1976 No 46 (entered into force 3 January 1976, accession by Canada 19 May 1976) [*ICESCR*]. Among the rights guaranteed, article 11 commits the State to ensuring an adequate standard of living for all citizens. In 2006, the UN committee responsible for ensuring compliance of the Convention criticized every province in Canada for having social welfare programs which fell far short of the country's human rights obligations (see Committee on Economic, Social and Cultural Rights, *Canada (Fourth and Fifth Periodic Reports)*, UNESCOR, 36th Sess, UN Doc E/C.12/CAN/CO/4 & E/C.12/CAN/CO/5, (2006) at para 21, online: OHCHR www2.ohchr.org [*ICESCR* Committee]). Apart from this covenant, Canada is signatory to specific treaties enshrining the rights of women, people with disabilities, and children. Each of these agreements contains rights related to specific aspects of poverty experienced by the targeted community.

20 *Canadian Oxford Dictionary*, 2d ed, *sub verbo* "poverty."

21 "It's a little bit more complicated than this," as an ACEF member pointed out to me during a session on the North Shore in Quebec: "It is more a question of the imbalance between revenue and expense." He is absolutely right. However, we both believe that poverty is fundamentally an economic issue, which the neo-liberals deny.

Neo-liberals have repackaged the concept. In their view, poverty is more of a social deprivation than an economic one. Aubry highlights the new approach contained in the Quebec *Act to Combat Poverty*:

> The definition of poverty is broad and inclusive, going far beyond the sole economic situation of an individual. It indeed states that poverty is "the condition of a human being who is deprived of the resources, means, choices and power necessary to acquire and maintain economic self-sufficiency or to facilitate integration and participation in society."[22]

As an object of study, poverty is more complex than only its economic dimension. However, it suits neo-liberals well to repackage the definition of poverty in such a way as to diminish its economic dimension because they promote a vision of government that limits the public role in wealth redistribution. While apparently still important to redistribute wealth towards the private sector in times of economic crisis,[23] the neo-liberal State must be very judicious insofar as the distribution is directed towards individuals. It must not be perceived as a vehicle that subsidizes poor people. Consequently, programs such as welfare, injured workers compensation, and seniors' benefits are at best indexed to the cost of living when they are not completely frozen. Unemployment insurance, while a public program (though no longer publically funded), is now inaccessible to more than 60 percent of the workers who pay into it.[24]

Indeed, most provinces have used their anti-poverty strategy as a pretext for reforming their social welfare programs. Quebec introduced significant welfare reform shortly after the adoption of its *Act to Combat Poverty*. In its 2010 *Progress Report*, New Brunswick announced the creation of a Social Assistance Reform Committee, which is mandated to "move from a rules-based to an outcome based system."[25] Newfoundland

---

22 Aubry & Plamondon, above note 5 at 4. In the same vein, and to cite only one example, another provincial anti-poverty statute states, "Manitoba recognizes that poverty is not only about money; it is about social exclusion." See Government of Manitoba, *All Aboard: Manitoba's Poverty Reduction and Social Inclusion Strategy* (11 June 2011) at 2, online: Government of Manitoba www.gov.mb.ca [Manitoba, *All Aboard*].

23 Think of the billions of public dollars made available by governments to support the Canadian automobile and forestry industries during the economic crisis of 2008.

24 See *ICESCR* Committee, above note 19 at para 22 (observation no 22) "The committee is preoccupied that only 39% of Canadians without work have the right to unemployment benefits in 2001 . . . ." In the intervening years, the Harper government has certainly not reversed this trend.

25 Government of New Brunswick, *Overcoming Poverty Together: The New Brunswick Economic and Social Inclusion Plan* (11 August 2010), online: Government of New

and Labrador, Ontario, and Manitoba have all announced significant welfare reform. Each of these reforms is strikingly similar. While part of an "anti-poverty strategy," they do not significantly increase the benefits paid to the poor.[26] In fact, an evaluation done by the Gatineau's Association for the Defence of Social Rights (ADDS) demonstrates that from 1994 to 2002, the combined effect of a benefit freeze and its non-indexation has actually cost Quebec's welfare recipients the equivalent of one full month of revenue.[27] In real dollars, an employable Quebec welfare recipient is 30 percent poorer in 2011 than she was in 1987, a tendency exacerbated — not corrected — by the provincial "anti-poverty" strategy.

In most provinces, the "anti-poverty strategy" makes or reinforces a clear distinction between poor people based on their ability to work.[28] An ideological distinction, these strategies are not so much conceived to lift people out of poverty as they are to get poor people into the paid labour market. They reinforce the distinction between the deserving and undeserving poor, the meritorious and non-meritorious, for which the tipping point is a person's relationship to paid employment. The distinction between the good and bad poor leads to a subtle reworking of the notion of citizenship and the resurrection of the concept of the "social contract." In the words of Quebec's Conseil de la santé et du bien être, "Employable citizens who refuse to work break their contract with the broader community." [29] Thus,

---

Brunswick www2.gnb.ca [New Brunswick, *Overcoming Poverty Together*].

26 *ICESCR* Committee, above note 19 at paras 20 and 53: The committee on the *ICESCR* having noted "with concern that in most provinces and territories, social assistance benefits are lower than a decade ago" and that "welfare levels are often set at less than half the Low Income Cut-Off" urged the "State party to establish social assistance levels which ensure the realization of an adequate standard of living for all." See also *ICESCR* Committee, *ibid* at para 11ff, which recalls that the committee had made similar demands during the periodic reviews of Canada in 1993 and 1998.

27 ADDS-Gatineau, "Ça suffit! Mémoire présenté à la Commission des affaires sociales à l'occasion de la consultation générale sur le projet de loi n° 57, Loi sur l'aide aux personnes et aux familles" (October 2004) at 9, online: Assemblée Nationale Québec www.assnat.qc.ca.

28 New Brunswick makes a distinction between Transitional Assistance (employable) and Extended Benefits Program (unemployable); Quebec distinguishes between Social Solidarity (unemployable) and Social Assistance (employable) — Quebec also has a separate youth welfare program; Ontario Works is reserved for employable poor people; the Ontario Disability Support Program is for those poor that are unable to work.

29 Conseil de la santé et du bien-être, *L'harmonisation des politiques de lutte contre l'exclusion* (Quebec: Conseil de la santé et du bien-être, 1996) at 55: "un refus de participation [aux activités d'employabilité], en dépit d'offres raisonnables, constitue *une rupture*

the good citizen becomes the responsible citizen who does everything possible to avoid the "regime of last resort"; by extension, the employable citizen who remains on welfare is a bad citizen. Neo-liberal logic holds that by freezing public assistance benefits and making welfare so intolerable that one is prepared to do anything to avoid it, the State actually "helps" people to become good citizens. The strategy is apparently working according to the Government of Quebec:

> Another reason for the improved situation in Quebec is the daily determination of individuals who work together to improve their lot and that of their family. By bettering their own living conditions, these men and women, more than anyone else, contribute to crafting a brighter future for our society in its entirety.[30]

In the neo-liberal world, good, responsible citizens do all that is in their power to avoid "living off the public trough." They find jobs or prepare themselves for the workplace because it is assumed that paid employment is the best, most efficient way to fight poverty — an idea successively relayed by both the Newfoundland and Labrador and Quebec action plans and which finds its way into the terms of reference of Ontario's Commission for the Review of Social Assistance:

- "One of the best ways out of poverty is through a sufficient level of paid employment."[31]
- "Considering that employment constitutes the best means for fighting poverty . . . ."[32]

---

de la relation qui lie ces individus à leur communauté" [emphasis added]. This report is cited several times in Francine Lepage & Chantal Martel, "Mémoire sur le document de consultation intitulé : Un parcours vers l'insertion, la formation et l'emploi — La réforme de la sécurité du revenu" (Québec: Conseil du statut de la femme, 1996) at 27, 30, and 37, online: Conseil du statut de la femme www.csf.gouv.qc.ca.

30 Quebec, *Combating Poverty*, above note 6 at 9.

31 Government of Newfoundland and Labrador, *Empowering People, Engaging Community, Enabling Success, First Progress Report on the Government of Newfoundland and Labrador's Poverty Reduction Strategy* (December 2009), online: Government of Newfoundland and Labrador www.gov.nl.ca [Newfoundland and Labrador, *Empowering People*].

32 Quebec, *Combating Poverty*, above note 6 at 25. The government also restates that employment is the best and most lasting method to improve the poor's living situation and combat poverty (*ibid* at 24).

- "The most promising way to improve outcomes for people receiving social assistance is to substantially improve their employment opportunities . . . ."[33]

Government claiming that paid employment is the best way to fight poverty does not necessarily make it a fact. While it is true that the transition to wage labour is a useful tool for removing citizens from provincial welfare rolls (that is, for meeting the targets that will be discussed in the next section), paid employment does not guarantee that a person will leave poverty. In fact, according to Morris and Gonsalves, in Canada it is not enough to have a job to keep you out of poverty. Most poor people do work full- or part-time. Poverty level wages are a particular problem for women. Women and youth account for 83 percent of Canada's minimum wage workers. Thirty-seven percent of single mothers with paid employment must raise a family on less than $10 per hour.[34] As the historian Jacques Rouillard recently observed, "Depuis trois décennies, les salariés n'augmentent pas leur pouvoir d'achat, même si, en général, la croissance économique est au rendez-vous . . . . La richesse se crée, mais les travailleurs salariés n'en voient pas la couleur."[35] Evidence supporting Rouillard's contention is everywhere: food banks report serving a dramatically increased number of workers and their families; waiting lists for social housing are growing longer as workers are unable to meet market-determined rents; and "good" citizens are working two and three jobs to make ends meet.[36]

From the late 1980s until the middle of the first decade of the new millennium, and across all jurisdictions, Canadian minimum wage levels were frozen. While it is a fact that across the country, anti-poverty strategies are

33 Government of Ontario, *Commission for the Review of Social Assistance in Ontario, A Discussion Paper: Issues and Ideas* (Toronto: Government of Ontario, 2011).

34 Tahira Gonsalves & Marika Morris, *Women and Poverty*, 3d ed (2010), online: Canadian Research Institute for the Advancement of Women http://criaw-icref.ca/WomenAndPoverty#_edn21.

35 "For 3 decades, salaries have not increased purchasing power, even though in general, economic growth is at a head . . . . The wealth has been created but workers' salaries aren't seeing the benefit." Jacques Rouillard, "Les colonnes du temple néolibéral ébranlées" *Le Devoir* (3 October 2008), online: Le Devoir www.ledevoir.com.

36 Quebec Commission of Human Rights and Youth Rights, *Avis au ministre sur le plan d'action en matière de lutte contre la pauvreté* (April 2010) at 3, online: Quebec Commission of Human Rights and Youth Rights www.cdpdj.qc.ca. The working poor have become so prevalent that they make up one in four workers on the market. Single mothers and immigrants are among the highest demographic of the working poor.

credited with increasing minimum wage levels,[37] it is equally true that minimum wage workers are falling deeper into poverty with little likelihood of getting out. This of course begs the question, if paid employment is proposed as the solution to poverty, why is it that the "new poor" are workers?[38]

2) The Urge to Measure

Governments have realized that one of the best ways to fight poverty is to define it and then to adopt specific measures addressing the phenomenon, thus defined. To help them in this endeavour, an entirely new industry of poverty measurement has developed, which goes far beyond traditional university research.[39] The push for measuring poverty is not just domestically generated. Different international bodies, including the UN Committee on Economic, Social and Cultural Rights, criticize Canada for not having an official poverty line. In its 2006 Concluding Observations, "[t]he Committee reiterates its recommendation that the State party establish an official poverty line."[40]

Spurred by different provincial strategies, poverty has become a hot research topic. Both within the academy and within public services inspired by the new public management model, "indicators" are being developed to follow more precisely the evolution of the object of study, and public policy is being fashioned by social modelling.[41] The use of measurement and

37 The following provinces used their anti-poverty initiative to increase the minimum wage in their jurisdictions. The figure between parentheses represents the 2010 provincial rate: Quebec ($9.50), Newfoundland and Labrador ($10), New Brunswick ($10 in 2011), Manitoba ($9).

38 Sylvain Lefèvre, Gérard Boismenu, & Pascale Dufour, *La Pauvreté : Quatre modèles sociaux en perspective* (Montréal: Les Presses de l'Université de Montréal, 2011) at 119.

39 This is a "new poverty industry," which distinguishes itself from the "old poverty industry" rooted in charitable organizations such as the Salvation Army, St Vincent de Paul, and soup kitchens.

40 *ICESCR* Committee, above note 19 at para 60. This follows from the 1998 concluding observations, which read, "The absence of an official poverty line makes it difficult to hold the federal, provincial and territorial governments accountable with respect to their obligations under the Covenant." United Nations Committee on Economic, Social and Cultural Rights, *Consideration of Reports Submitted by States Parties under Articles 16 and 17 of the Covenant: Concluding Observations of the Committee on Economic, Social and Cultural Rights: Canada*, UNCESCR, UN Doc E/C12/1/Add 31, (1998) at para 13.

41 Vincent Greason & Lucie Lamarche, "Indicators and Human Rights — Do We Really Want to Go There, and If So, How Far?" (2011) at 3 & 4, online: TROVEPO www.trovepo.org [Greason & Lamarche].

indicators gives a scientific veneer to the results-based approach to fighting poverty because these tools are characterized as objective and neutral. They are reputed to be detached, non-emotive tools for policy elaboration. Using such a methodology, the Quebec government is confident that its approach "is founded upon a solid scientific base."[42]

Every provincial anti-poverty strategy adopts the measurement approach. In New Brunswick, a public "call for tender" was issued in the summer of 2010 with a clear objective: to develop adequate indicators for the measurement of New Brunswick poverty.[43] Manitoba's *Poverty Reduction Act* legislates the measurement of its anti-poverty strategy's progress.[44] In Ontario, the use and type of indicators are also legislated, requiring "indicators to measure the success of the strategy that are linked to the determinants of poverty, including but not limited to income, education, health, housing and the standard of living."[45]

Quebec's *Act to Combat Poverty* places poverty measurement at the heart of the fight. This legislation commits to "make Quebec, by 2013, one of the industrialized nations having the fewest poor people, *according to internationally recognized methods for making comparisons.*"[46] Itself created by the Quebec Act, the Centre d'étude sur la pauvreté et l'exclusion issued a recent study identifying no fewer than seventy-five different ways of measuring poverty.[47]

While the debate on the "best" measure for calculating poverty is a subject for another paper, it is important to note that the choice of such a measure is eminently political.[48] Since the preferred indicator will be used as a reference point for measuring the success of different government strategies, it stands to reason that the choice of one indicator over another will have political consequences.

---

42 Government of Quebec, *Government Action Plan for Solidarity and Social Inclusion (2010–2015)* (June 2010), online: Emploi et Solidarité Sociale www.mess.gouv.qc.ca. The *Government Action Plan for Solidarity and Social Inclusion* also has a solid scientific foundation thanks to the collaboration of the Centre d'étude sur la pauvreté et l'exclusion (CEPE).

43 New Brunswick, *Overcoming Poverty Together*, above note 25 at 10.

44 Manitoba, *All Aboard*, above note 22 at 6.

45 *Poverty Reduction Act, 2009*, above note 12, s 3(3).

46 *Act to Combat Poverty*, above note 3, s 4 [emphasis added].

47 Government of Quebec, *Inventaire des indicateurs de pauvreté et d'exclusion sociale* (October 2005), online: Centre d'étude sur la pauvreté et l'exclusion www.cepe.gouv.qc.ca.

48 Greason & Lamarche, above note 41 at 5–7.

Similarly, it is politically important to maintain control over the definition of the preferred measure and its application. This is such a sensitive issue that several provinces claim that measures developed by the highly respected Statistics Canada ignore or distort regional particularities. To complement their anti-poverty strategies, both Quebec and Newfoundland and Labrador have chosen to invest time, energy, and resources into developing regional variants of federal data to more accurately measure the progress of their anti-poverty initiatives.[49] As mentioned, the call for tender issued by the New Brunswick government is to develop "adequate" indicators for measuring "New Brunswick poverty." Therefore, "New Brunswick poverty" will fight with "child poverty," "seniors' poverty," and "women's poverty" to claim its "poverty space."

Having accurate provincial data is absolutely essential when one of the measurement outcomes by which anti-poverty strategies are to be judged is comparative. Indeed, these strategies are akin to childish competitive arguments about who has won a contest. Rather than being designed to ensure that the beneficiaries of the strategies are those who have been living in poverty, the purpose of the measurement seems to be to allow one government to say to others, "*We* are better than *you*!"

On this front, Quebec has set the bar very high. Its objective is to be, by 2013, amongst the international jurisdictions with the fewest people living in poverty "measured by internationally recognized standards."[50] Not to be outdone, Newfoundland and Labrador promises to move from the poorest province to the least poor one by 2014.[51] For its part, Ontario's strategy reflects that province's "aspiration to be a leading jurisdiction in reducing poverty."[52] Meanwhile, poor Nova Scotia seems handicapped from the start: "[t]he percentage of Nova Scotians living in low-income circumstances is

---

49 See Newfoundland and Labrador, *Empowering People*, above note 31 at 30. The Newfoundland and Labrador Statistics Agency has developed the Newfoundland and Labrador Market Basket Measure (NLMBM) based on tax data rather than surveys. With this corrected data, it has created a NLMBM of housing affordability and a gender-specific MBM specific to the province. In Quebec, the Institut de la statistique du Québec, together with the Centre d'étude sur la pauvreté et l'exclusion have adjusted federal data to better reflect the Quebec reality. What one measures understandably determines the outcome measured.

50 *Act to Combat Poverty*, above note 3, s 4.

51 Newfoundland and Labrador, *Empowering People*, above note 31 at vii. The goal repeated in Newfoundland and Labrador is audacious: ". . . to realize the Government of Newfoundland and Labrador's commitment to become the province in Canada with the lowest poverty rate in the Country by 2014."

52 *Poverty Reduction Act, 2009*, above note 12, s 2.

the lowest it's been in a decade, and lower than the Canadian average . . . ."[53] The race is on.

The urge to measure has dramatically transformed how poverty is conceptualized. Understood as a human rights violation, poverty is grounded in lived reality. Storytelling gives a voice, and from the perspective of the poor person it is seen as a legitimate method to gain knowledge and understanding. Understood as a neo-liberal construct, poverty becomes a statistical reality, a phenomenon to be measured and compared. Depending upon the measure chosen, a person is poor or not. Poverty becomes an object to be debated amongst those experts who are producing different methods for measuring it. It becomes a contest to see who has the best and most accurate indicator. The poor become dispossessed of their own reality, and their voices are not heard, because they are not important. The poor person is the person deemed poor by the choice of indicator; change the indicator and you change the poor person. Poor people are reduced to statistics on a page, part of an aggregate forming a trend.

Further, when poverty policy decisions are based upon "poverty measurement" criteria, another dislocation occurs. As policy becomes directed to meeting State-identified needs, a hierarchy is established: certain needs are deemed more important than others. Limited resources will be targeted to redress the most urgent needs. The fight against poverty thus becomes the fight to meet targets. In reality, it has little to do with moving poor people out of their situation of poverty. To quote the minister responsible for the Newfoundland and Labrador Poverty Reduction Strategy, "I am proud to report that the indicators point to significant improvement in the fight against poverty in our province."[54] If the indicators say it, it must be true.

Such reliance on measurement and indicators makes it all the more difficult to understand the Harper government's recent decision not to renew the long-form census data collection.[55] As provinces juggle to be able to measure where we are in order to trace and plan to where we want to be, provincial statisticians and planners must be highly frustrated. Except perhaps for Ontario: Munir Sheikh, Canada's former chief statistician and casualty of the Harper government's aforementioned census decision, is

---

53 Nova Scotia, *Preventing Poverty*, above note 8.

54 Newfoundland and Labrador, *Empowering People*, above note 31 at 3.

55 For more, see "Long-Form Census Cancellation Taking Toll on StatsCan Data: Questions Raised over How Data Can Be Used Reliably" *CBC News* (27 October 2012), online: CBC www.cbc.ca.

now the co-chair of the province's Commission for the Review of Social Assistance.[56]

To resume the argument developed to this point: the first two threads linking provincial anti-poverty strategies highlight the emerging nature of the neo-liberal State's intervention in the fight against poverty. Its prime role is to move poor people off the "public purse" towards paid employment, notably by reducing direct public revenue transfers to an absolute minimum. Its role is also to identify indicators in such a way as to accurately measure the evolution of poverty. One further public role needs to be outlined, and that is the State's role in seeking out, convincing, and coordinating those new social actors who must now take up the fight.

3) Responsibilization

The Preamble of Quebec's *Act to Combat Poverty* states, "Whereas persons living in poverty and social exclusion are the first to act to improve their situation and that of their families and whereas such improvement is linked to the social, cultural and economic development of the entire community . . . ."[57] The Act is quite clear: the poor themselves are the principle actors for fighting poverty. This idea is explicitly pursued throughout both Quebec action plans.[58] Other provincial strategies also seem grounded in the idea that good, meritorious, responsible citizens are defined as those who do not make demands upon the State. Responsible citizens learn how to wash and dress themselves and get to work on time. They (when "they" are two parents, rather than single parents) learn to juggle two jobs while looking after young children. Most of all, they are kept so busy surviving that they are unable to become socially or politically involved.[59] While it would be inaccurate to claim that neo-liberalism holds poor people personally responsible for their poverty, the neo-liberal State does hold them responsible for taking "active" measures to escape it.

It is not only the poor themselves who are responsible for fighting poverty. In the words of Manitoba's government, "All aboard!" The neo-liberal loco-

---

56 See *Brighter Prospects: Transforming Social Assistance in Ontario* (2012), online: www.mcss.gov.on.ca/documents/en/mcss/social/publications/social_assistance_review_final_report.pdf.

57 *Act to Combat Poverty*, above note 3, Preamble.

58 Quebec, *Combating Poverty*, above note 6 at 24.

59 See Greason, "Québec's Community Movement," above note 17 at 17–19, for a discussion on how the ideology valorizing "paid" over "militant" labour has had an impact on the depoliticizing of Quebec's community movement.

motive is leaving the station and all passengers must be on the train! Among these paying passengers are the United Way, community organizations, schools, municipalities, and charitable foundations.

In recasting poverty as something other than "economic deprivation," neo-liberalism evokes a form of social determinism. Poverty results from poor schooling, parental incompetence, bad neighbourhoods, violence, unstable family situations, alcoholism, et cetera. Consequently, the fight against poverty shifts from the economic to the social domain. Understood as social deprivation, it follows that "new" (or at least non-traditional, non-State) actors must be brought into the anti-poverty "struggle." Schools must become involved because hungry children do not learn well; social agencies and community organizations need to contribute to building the self-esteem of poor people, making them better parents and preparing them to confront the paid employment market; and municipalities must become involved because poor neighbourhoods are dangerous, dirty, and bad for business. Wealthy people, their trust funds, and companies must contribute (and be recognized for contributing) to the struggle because Canada lags far behind other jurisdictions in its development of a "culture of philanthropy."

Reaching out to the broader community and encouraging it to become actively involved in fighting poverty characterizes every provincial anti-poverty initiative. Newfoundland and Labrador "engages community partners."[60] Nova Scotia uses "a community development model to allow opportunity for public involvement in the fight against poverty. We will also continue to encourage businesses to become actively engaged."[61] Non-State partners are so important to the New Brunswick strategy that their significance is found in the very name of the initiative, *Overcoming Poverty Together*. The strategy continues: The fight against poverty is a " . . . shared responsibility of every citizen."[62] Manitoba's *All Aboard* calls for partnerships with "businesses, non-profit organizations, communities and individuals."[63]

Three provinces, New Brunswick, Quebec, and Ontario, have taken the involvement of new actors a step further by "territorializing" their anti-poverty strategies and delegating specific responsibilities to municipal or local authorities. New Brunswick's Community Economic and Social Inclusion Networks have been established at the local level and are composed of representatives of people living in poverty, non-profit, business,

---

60 Newfoundland and Labrador, *Empowering People*, above note 31.

61 Nova Scotia, *Preventing Poverty*, above note 8 at 7.

62 New Brunswick, *Overcoming Poverty Together*, above note 25 at 1.

63 Manitoba, *All Aboard*, above note 22 at 2.

and government sectors. The province has also developed an "integrated service delivery model" wherein all government departments and service providers are instructed to find ways to work more collaboratively in the fight against poverty.

Quebec has taken this preoccupation a step further with the integrated territorial approach (ITA). This model includes a territorial integration of both actors (governmental, philanthropic, private for-profit, and not-for-profit) and financial resources (public and private) around common projects "determined by the milieu." The ITA is fundamentally an attempt by the public power to "responsibilize" (with money and mandates) municipalities, regions, and non-State actors in the fight against poverty.

Ontario's *Poverty Reduction Act* clearly delineates the role of the third sector, including non-profit and voluntary organizations, as being "integral to a poverty reduction strategy by delivering the programs and services that matter to people, by strengthening communities, and by making a positive contribution to the economy."[64]

4) Use of Philanthropic Organizations

Several of the provincial anti-poverty strategies reserve a role for philanthropic organizations. Given the historical role that organizations such as the Salvation Army and the St Vincent de Paul Society have played in the field of poverty appeasement, this should not be surprising. However, neo-liberals are putting philanthropy to new use. As the State reorganizes service delivery in the social sphere, fiscal policy encourages Canadians to develop a "culture of philanthropy" similar to the one south of the border. Even as income taxes are cut, taxpayers (both individual and corporate) seek new tax shelters. Not-for-profit organizations must become more accountable to real, or potential, donors.[65] Charitable donations increase, private foundations multiply, and the private sector is increasingly called upon to lend its support to fighting poverty.

Within provincial anti-poverty strategies, the role conferred upon the private sector and philanthropic organizations is formalized and institutionalized. In Manitoba, the government contracted the United Way to carry out the public consultation phase of the anti-poverty strategy. In Quebec, private foundations such as the Lucie and André Chagnon Foundation and the Club des petits déjeuners find themselves at the heart of

64 *Poverty Reduction Act, 2009*, above note 12, ss 2 and 8.

65 Georges LeBel, "Quand nos lois encouragent la cupidité" 739 *Revue Relations* (March 2010), online: Centre justice et foi www.cjf.qc.ca.

the public anti-poverty strategy. Also, the Chagnon Foundation is an active partner in three explicit and legislated public-private partnerships to fight poverty, thereby controlling more than $500 million in public funds over ten years.[66] The McCain family has actively committed itself to building a series of child care centres as part of the New Brunswick anti-poverty initiative; in Newfoundland and Labrador, the province has partnered with the Canadian Tire Foundation for Families Jumpstart program.[67] Across the country, community foundations, often controlled by the United Way and local partners, are active in funding anti-poverty projects.

This use of philanthropic interests is another form of privatizing the anti-poverty struggle. Philanthropy relies, to a large extent, on excessive private wealth, which has been poorly redistributed. In another époque, one with greater political courage, such excessive wealth would be the object of fiscal redistribution.

5) Partnerships: Everyone Now Fights Poverty

As the neo-liberal State reduces its role in direct income support and eliminates universal public services and programs, more people become poorer and economic needs increase. Ironically (or tragically), as public services and programs target "the poorest" (thereby statistically reducing the numbers of those in that category, however it is defined), a whole new form of poverty becomes visible.[68] Schools discover poor kids and realize the urgency of becoming involved in anti-poverty measures — in effect, hungry students do not learn well.[69] Immigrant services become involved, because

---

66 Fédération autonome de l'enseignement and TROVEPO, *Mieux comprendre l'affaiblissement des services publics : Quand les fondations privées ébranlent les fondations de l'édifice social* (August 2009), online: ROCFM www.rocfm.org; "Si nous étions la Fondations Chagnon" (5 February 2010), online: Observatoire Fondation Chagnon http://observatoirechagnon.blogspot.ca.

67 Newfoundland and Labrador, *Empowering People*, above note 31 at 6.

68 Collectif pour un Québec sans pauvreté, "Le Crédit pour la solidarité, c'est pour tout le monde!" (2011), online: Collectif pour un Québec sans pauvreté www.pauvrete.qc.ca. It is estimated that fully one-third of Quebec's taxpayers will be eligible to receive the brand new "Solidarity" tax credit, vaunted as an anti-poverty measure. In a rich country, 33 percent is a scandalously high number of citizens who need an anti-poverty measure.

69 Coincidently, students who do not learn well impact very negatively on school graduation rates and related success scores. Newly available anti-poverty funding potentially offers one way of alleviating certain financial stresses which some local schools may be experiencing.

the once-existing public support network has been weakened. Poor health is an indicator of poverty, which costs the health care system. It is apparently not citizens from wealthy neighbourhoods such as Forest Hill or Westmount who are flooding the overextended public health network; therefore initiatives to address the poor health of poor people become "anti-poverty" initiatives. Municipal authorities have no more control over the incomes of poor people than do private foundations, immigrant services, or the local hospital. Yet, these are precisely the actors to whom the State is turning to implement a series of truly baffling anti-poverty programs and initiatives that are being heralded as "success stories" in various provincial government and civil society reports.[70]

A recent study was conducted analyzing Quebec's ITA to fighting poverty.[71] While the anti-poverty model does indeed mobilize local resources and energies, the study concludes that the "anti-poverty" label has become a pretext allowing newly created local elites (school principals, CLSC community organizers, municipal authorities, community organization staffers, employment councillors, representatives from private foundations, and the United Way) to initiate and fund hundreds of projects and measures responding to a variety of needs, but which do very little to reduce poverty understood as the economic deprivation of real people.

D. CONCLUSION: TWO MISSING THREADS

This article has highlighted several of the common themes that characterize the different provincial anti-poverty initiatives. In conclusion, we wish to highlight two common themes that are absent from these initiatives — themes that, coincidentally, are not to be found in the neo-liberal manual of policy directives. Provincial anti-poverty strategies do not address the problem of increasing wealth disparity within their jurisdiction, nor do they adopt a human rights approach to fighting poverty.

---

70 Vincent Greason, "Does Struggling Locally against Poverty Really Produce 'Inspiring Practices'?" (2010) at 9 & 10, online: TROVEPO www.trovepo.org (this is a translation of Vincent Greason, "Lutter localement contre la pauvreté, donne-t-il réellement 'des pratiques inspirantes'?" (2010) 2:4 *Revue vie économique*). In the name of "fighting poverty," dog runs and skate parks have been built in poor neighbourhoods, photo and art exhibits organized, neighbourhood guided tours developed, and community centres and alleyways spruced up.

71 *Ibid.*

1) Clawing from the Bottom, Not Capping the Top

Following decades during which income disparity within industrial societies was reduced, the neo-liberal policies of the past twenty years have reversed the trend and polarized income divisions between the wealthy and the poor. The Canadian Centre for Policy Alternatives,[72] Conference Board of Canada,[73] and Le Monde diplomatique[74] have all documented this tendency within both Canada and the OECD. Obviously the same polarization is occurring between the industrialized world and what used to be called the "developing economies": the rich are becoming richer and the poor, while not necessarily becoming poorer,[75] are becoming more numerous and more confined to a condition from which they cannot escape.

If the middle class is disappearing, if there are more millionaires than ever before, if working people are using food banks and social housing in historic numbers, if both parents are working not because of gender equality but because of economic necessity, one conclusion seems inevitable: wealth distribution has become a serious problem. In this light, it is truly striking that not one provincial anti-poverty strategy addresses the issue of wealth redistribution, or lack thereof, as a potential solution to the problem. The "economic" dimension of poverty has been so ignored that significant fiscal reform has not been envisaged as part of a solution.[76] No province has suggested a cap on wealth.

---

72 See also Errol Black & Jim Silver, "Fast Facts: We Have a Floor, Now We Need a Ceiling. Reducing Canada's Income Inequalities" (4 February 2010), online: Centre for Policy Alternatives www.policyalternatives.ca.

73 Gérard Bérubé, "Les inégalités de revenu progressent plus vite au Canada qu'aux États-Unis" *Le Devoir* (14 September 2011), online: Le Devoir www.ledevoir.com.

74 Till Van Treeck, "Grande crise act II : Victoire à la Pyrrhus pour l'économie allemande" (September 2010), online: Le monde diplomatique www.monde-diplomatique.fr.

75 As with the UN's Millennium Objectives project, provincial anti-poverty strategies target "the poorest clientele," or those "most at risk." By addressing resources and programs for "the neediest," few resources are directed at those who are "needy but not the neediest." The recent "Solidarity tax credit" introduced in Quebec highlights the result of this targeting: no less than 2.7 million households, representing roughly 33 percent of the Quebec population, qualify for this anti-poverty measure. For more, see Revenu Québec, online: Revenu Québec www.revenuquebec.ca. When one-third of the population of a wealthy country qualifies for an anti-poverty measure, alarm bells should be ringing.

76 See, for example, Eve-Lyne Couturier & Bertrand Schepper, "Qui s'enrichit, qui s'appauvrit 1976–2006" (2010), online: IRIS www.iris-recherche.qc.ca. See also Armine Yalnizyan, "The Rise of Canada's Richest 1%" (2010), online: CCPA www.policyalternatives.ca. Within civil society, these groups have put forward very

2) The Idea That "Poverty" Is a Violation of a Person's Human Rights

We do not believe that poverty is primarily a social phenomenon to be measured and counted. We do not believe that urban renewal solves poverty. Poverty is fundamentally a multi-faceted human rights violation of the person who is poor. In this sense, it is highly significant that Canada is signatory to several international human rights treaties guaranteeing all citizens social and economic rights — that is, the progressive realization of their right to an adequate standard of living, decent housing, adequate nutrition, social programs, and the opportunity to join a trade union. Taken seriously, the full realization of these rights would eliminate poverty in this country.

Further, sections 7 and 15 of the *Canadian Charter of Rights and Freedoms* enshrine security of the person and equality rights;[77] the *Charter of Human Rights and Freedoms* has a section on social and economic rights, which guarantees, among others, the right to a decent standard of living.[78]

With the exception of Quebec, not one provincial anti-poverty initiative makes any reference to poverty as a human rights issue. Indeed, only Ontario speaks of the "moral imperative" incumbent upon a rich society to reduce its own poverty.[79] For its part, faced with huge pressure coming from the highly organized human rights movement, Quebec has been forced to recognize its international human rights obligations, which it does most reluctantly in the second action plan.[80]

---

interesting proposals for fiscal reform which address the issue of increasing wealth disparities.

77 Part I of the *Constitution Act, 1982*, being Schedule B to the *Canada Act 1982* (UK), 1982, c 11.

78 RSQ c C-12.

79 Ontario, *Breaking the Cycle*, above note 11 at 5.

80 Referencing the *ICESCR*, above note 19, Quebec's second action plan (Quebec, *Combating Poverty*, above note 6 at 9–10) states, "[t]he government recognizes that in an inclusive society such as ours, everyone has the right to live with dignity and with a sufficient standard of living according to international standards . . . . The Quebec government firmly resolves to continue its action on these fronts because it acknowledges that this action benefits each and every Quebecker, but with a proviso: it must carry out this mission in keeping *with our society's ability to absorb the costs thereof*" [emphasis added]. Two pages later, referencing art 2 of the Convention, the action plan continues, "[i]n 1976, the Quebec government embraced the *International Covenant on Economic, Social, and Cultural Rights*, adopted in 1966 by the General Assembly of the United Nations. This Covenant arises from the *Universal Declaration of Human Rights*. This Action Plan is one of the many ways in which Quebec has pledged to abide by the commitment to progressively provide all citizens with the conditions required for them to live with dignity and with a sufficient standard of living accord-

The challenge to make the discussion of poverty a human rights issue is one that needs to be taken up by the organized civil society. Civil society — organized labour, housing advocates, women's organizations, and anti-poverty groups — must increase their pressure on governments at all levels (federal, provincial, and municipal) so that they respect their freely chosen international and domestic human rights obligations. Strengthening universal public health care is not just an issue for the trade unions and workers who are directly concerned — it is to be supported because it is the means chosen by Canadians to implement their right to health. Reinvesting in social programs such as legal aid, workers' compensation, unemployment insurance, social housing, and publicly funded child care should be supported because they all exemplify a concrete application of a human rights–based approach to fighting poverty.

Our reading of Canadian governments' approaches to fighting poverty indicates that the promotion of human rights is not the motivating factor behind their policies. In sum, poverty is a human rights violation, except in governmental anti-poverty strategies.

---

ing to international standards, while *respecting our society's ability to absorb the costs thereof*" [emphasis added]. Article 2 of the *ICESCR* engages governments to consecrate a maximum of available resources to progressively implementing their international human rights obligations. Tax cuts for the rich, as a means of escaping these obligations, do not fall within our reading of art 2 of the *ICESCR*. Nevertheless, we recognize that the above reference is perhaps the first time that a Canadian provincial or federal government has explicitly recognized its human rights obligations under the *ICESCR* in a domestic policy statement.

CHAPTER 4

ACCOUNTABILITY REGIMES FOR FEDERAL SOCIAL TRANSFERS

AN EXERCISE IN DECONSTRUCTION AND RECONSTRUCTION*

BARBARA CAMERON†

A. INTRODUCTION

Transfers from the federal government to the provinces for social programs within provincial legislative jurisdiction played an important role in both the promotion and the erosion of social citizenship rights in Canada. The constructive use of the transfers was seen in the creation of a Canada-wide system of universal, publicly administered medical insurance (medicare) and national norms for social assistance under the *Canada Assistance Plan*.[1] With the elite retreat from the Keynesian welfare State, the destructive possibilities were apparent in unilateral reductions by the federal

* Research for this chapter was supported by the Social Sciences and Humanities Research Council of Canada (Community-University Research Alliance Program). The analysis in the chapter emerged out of the author's collaboration with the Child Care Advocacy Association of Canada around Bill C-303, *Early Learning and Child Care Act*, a private member's bill introduced by the New Democratic Party in the 39th Parliament, 1st Session, and the 39th Parliament, 2nd Session, where it was debated at third reading. It was reintroduced in the 40th Parliament, 2nd Session as Bill C-373. This text is also published as Chapter 12 in Peter Graefe et al, eds, *Overpromising and Underperforming? Understanding and Evaluating New Intergovernmental Accountability Regimes* (Toronto: University of Toronto Press for the Institute of Public Administration of Canada, 2013) 258.

† Associate Professor, Department of Political Science and Department of Equity Studies, York University and Research Partner in the SSHRC-CURA Research Project "Reconceiving Human Rights Practice," online: www.socialrightscura.ca.

1 *Canada Assistance Plan*, RSC 1985, c 1.

government in the amounts transferred to provinces and the weakening or outright elimination of the conditions attached to the funds. As a consequence, social rights advocates in Canada outside of Quebec became increasingly concerned about accountability in the transfers. They continue to call not only for increases in funding for social transfers but also and very emphatically for the enforcement of existing federal conditions (in the *Canada Health Act*[2]), the reinstatement of federal conditions that were eliminated (for social assistance in the *Canada Assistance Plan*), the introduction of new federal standards (for post-secondary education, housing, poverty), and the creation of new programs with enforceable standards (for child care services). The alternatives proposed to federal social transfers — in the form of the social and economic union provisions of the Charlottetown Agreement, the Social Union Framework, interprovincial cooperation through the Council of the Federation, or devolution to the provinces — have not been seen by these advocates as initiatives to strengthen social rights.

The federal spending power and the social transfers that are based on it are problematic, not least because of the historic opposition to them by Quebec governments supported by social rights advocates in that province.[3] One can imagine alternatives, but these would involve either a major constitutional change that recognizes the multinational character of the country (the preferred option of the author of this chapter) or an unprecedented degree of cooperation of the provinces to create the mechanisms to hold themselves accountable for social rights.[4] As neither of these

---

2 *Canada Health Act*, RSC 1985, c C-6, ss 7–12.

3 For a comprehensive summary, see Quebec, Secrétariat aux affaires intergouvernementales canadiennes, "Quebec's Historical Position on the Federal Spending Power 1944–1998" (1998), online: Secrétariat aux affaires intergouvernementales canadiennes www.saic.gouv.qc.ca.

4 The author's views on the dilemmas of Canadian federalism are elaborated in other publications. See Barbara Cameron, "The Social Union, Executive Power and Social Rights" (2004) 13 Canadian Woman Studies 49; Barbara Cameron, "Federalism and Social Reproduction" in Kate Bezanson & Meg Luxton, eds, *Social Reproduction: Feminist Political Economy Challenges Neo-Liberalism* (Montreal and Kingston: McGill Queen's University Press, 2006) 45; Barbara Cameron, "Accounting for Rights and Money in Canada's Social Union" in Susan Boyd et al, eds, *Poverty: Rights, Social Citizenship and Legal Activism* (Vancouver: UBC Press, 2007) 162; Barbara Cameron, "Harper, Quebec and Canadian Federalism" in Teresa Healy, ed, *The Harper Record* (Ottawa: Canadian Centre for Policy Alternatives, 2008) 419; Barbara Cameron, "Political Will, Child Care, and Canadian Federalism" (Spring 2009) Our Schools, Ourselves 129.

alternatives is likely in the foreseeable future, social rights advocates have to advance their demands to protect and expand social citizenship rights within the constraints of the existing federal division of powers. In recognition of this, this chapter has three objectives: to outline a framework for analyzing (and constructing) accountability regimes for federal social transfers, to use this framework to identify the key elements of the three accountability regimes that have governed federal social transfers, and to apply this framework to the challenge of developing an alternative regime for federal social transfers that is consistent with Canada's constitutional order and with the advancement of social rights and that builds on the experience of previous regimes of accountability.

A fundamental constitutional constraint is that Canada is a federal State with a Westminster system of government. This means that transfers of money from the central to subnational governments require an accountability regime that respects two fundamental constitutional principles: federalism and responsible government. The federal principle requires respect for the constitutional division of powers, which in Canada's case has evolved over time to give the federal government exclusive jurisdiction over unemployment insurance, shared jurisdiction with the provinces over pensions, and a shared responsibility with the provinces under section 36(1) of the *Constitution Act, 1982* for "(*a*) promoting equal opportunities for the well-being of Canadians; (*b*) furthering economic development to reduce disparity in opportunities; and (*c*) providing essential public services of reasonable quality to all Canadians."[5] The provinces have exclusive legislative jurisdiction over social services, but both levels can spend on social benefits and services. Respect for the principle of responsible government requires that the executive branch be accountable to the elected legislature for spending money according to purposes approved by Parliament, even when the money is being spent by another level of government. Successive federal Liberal governments in Canada have attempted to design accountability regimes for federal social transfers that address, in different ways and to different extents, the constraints of these two fundamental constitutional principles.

This chapter identifies three accountability regimes that have governed federal social transfers to the provinces. Identifying these distinct regimes, however, is not sufficient for accomplishing the underlying objective of this chapter, which is to propose a framework for developing an alternative regime of accountability that addresses some of the problems with past regimes and accommodates the objectives of social rights organizations.

---

5 Being Schedule B to the *Canada Act 1982* (UK), 1982, c 11, s 36(1).

For this purpose it is necessary to deconstruct an accountability regime into the relationships and main elements that constitute it. The chapter begins with an outline of a general model of accountability and the elements that are essential to an accountability relationship. Using this model, it is possible to identify the main accountability relationships that underpin Canadian social transfers. The chapter then examines the three regimes of accountability that have governed Canadian social transfers, highlighting the ways each addresses the balance between responsible government and federalism, configures the elements that constitute an accountability relationship, and succeeds or fails to address the central accountability challenges of federal social transfers. The final section of the chapter outlines an alternative regime of accountability that addresses some of the weaknesses and builds on some of the strengths in the regimes studied.

B. A GENERAL MODEL OF ACCOUNTABILITY

The question that underlies even the most basic relationship of accountability is who is accountable to whom and for what. The focus of this chapter is on complex, institutionalized accountability relationships that involve formalized procedures. Such an accountability relationship may be defined as a relationship between parties whereby one party is answerable to the other for the performance of commitments or obligations that are evaluated against criteria or standards known to the parties, and sanctions are applied for failure to meet the commitments. A regime of accountability as the term is used in this chapter involves one or more sets of formal accountability relationships.

In her study of internal contracts in the British National Health System, Anne Davies identifies four key features of an institutionalized accountability relationship (or what she describes as an accountability mechanism): "setting standards against which to judge the account; obtaining the account; judging the account; and deciding what consequences, if any should follow from it."[6] These features are actually processes that she boils down to three activities: standard setting, monitoring (including obtaining and judging the account), and enforcement.[7] This approach is closest to the classical understanding of accountability identified in the introduction to this volume, with the difference that Davies emphasizes the standard-setting process. An advantage of Davies' public law framework is its consistency

6 Anne CL Davies, *Accountability: A Public Law Analysis of Government by Contract* (Oxford: Oxford University Press, 2001) at 81–82.

7 *Ibid* at 89.

with an established approach to accountability for social rights under intergovernmental agreements: the one used by United Nations treaty bodies to monitor country compliance with obligations under international human rights treaties, including those dealing with social rights such as the *International Covenant on Economic, Social and Cultural Rights*,[8] the *Convention on the Elimination of Discrimination against Women*,[9] and the *Convention on the Rights of the Child*.[10]

Slightly modified, Davies' framework may usefully be applied to the study of the accountability relationships inherent in Canadian intergovernmental social transfers. The processes identified by Davies presuppose an instrument that establishes the accountability relationship, such as the internal contract she studies, treaties, a piece of legislation, or an intergovernmental agreement. Other elements necessary to an accountability relationship are parties to the relationship, the obligations or commitments they undertake, standards or criteria against which the performance of the parties is evaluated, monitoring procedures, and sanctions. In the case of federal transfers, the funding mechanism for the transfer (cost-shared or block grant) also needs to be included as an element of an accountability regime. To summarize, using this approach to distinguish different accountability relationships involves identifying for each

1) the parties to the accountability relationship and the nature of the relationship (who is accountable to whom);
2) the obligations undertaken as part of the relationship (what one party is accountable to the other for);
3) the instrument that establishes the accountability relationship;
4) the standards or criteria by which performance in meeting the obligations is to be judged;
5) standard-setting procedures;
6) monitoring mechanisms;
7) sanctions for non-performance and enforcement procedures; and
8) funding mechanism.

---

8 *International Covenant on Economic, Social and Cultural Rights*, GA Res 2200A (XXI), UNGAOR, 21st Sess, Supp No 16, UN Doc A/6316, (1966) 49 (entered into force 3 January 1976).

9 *Convention on the Elimination of All Forms of Discrimination against Women*, GA Res 34/180, UNGAOR, Supp no 46, UN Doc A/34/46, (1981) 193.

10 *Convention on the Rights of the Child*, GA Res 44/25, UNGAOR, 44th Sess, Supp No 49, UN Doc A/44/49, (1989) 167. For a basic overview of UN monitoring, see Shelagh Day, "Minding the Gap: Human Rights Commitments and Compliance" in Boyd et al, eds, above note 4; Barbara J Stark, "Economic, Social, and Cultural Rights" in David P Forsythe, ed, *Encyclopedia of Human Rights* (New York: Oxford University Press, 2009).

This framework allows us to identify three distinct accountability relationships implicated in regimes of accountability for federal social transfers to the provinces. The first of these is the relationship of legislators to citizens for the fulfilment of commitments regarding social entitlements (the social rights relationship). The second is the relationship of the federal executive branch to the House of Commons for spending federal money according to purposes approved by Parliament (the responsible government relationship). The third is the relationship between the executive branches at the federal and provincial levels for the performance of obligations undertaken under the administrative arrangements for the transfer (the federal relationship). The regimes of accountability that have governed the federal social transfer have not clearly distinguished these three relationships of accountability. The result is a confusion of the lines of accountability and, most importantly, obstacles for Canadians attempting to hold governments accountable for promises made regarding social rights.

C. THREE REGIMES OF ACCOUNTABILITY

Three different accountability regimes have governed federal social transfers to the provinces at different times. These differ in terms of the balance established between the principles of responsible government and federalism, the priority given one or other of the three accountability relationships involved in federal social transfers, and the way that the elements identified above are configured. The first accountability regime I describe as the "administrative regime" because the monitoring and enforcement is largely located with federal officials. It is typified by the cost-shared agreements of the post–Second World War era, including the *Canada Assistance Plan*. The second regime I call the "political regime" of accountability to reflect the significant shift of the monitoring and enforcement of standards from officials to the political executive. This regime is exemplified by the *Canada Health Act*, which has been the model for many social rights advocates. The third regime is the "public reporting regime" of accountability characteristic of the child-care and health-care agreements concluded in the era of the Social Union Framework Agreement.[11]

---

11 *A Framework to Improve the Social Union for Canadians. An Agreement between the Government of Canada and the Governments of the Provinces and Territories* (4 February 1999), online: Canadian Intergovernmental Conference Secretariat www.scics.gc.ca [*Social Union Framework Agreement*]. The Government of Quebec was not a party to the agreement.

1) Administrative Accountability Regime

The administrative regime of accountability is typical of the cost-shared, conditional grant programs of the Keynesian era and is found in legislation such as the *Hospital Insurance and Diagnostic Services Act*, 1957,[12] and the *Canada Assistance Plan*, enacted in 1966. In this regime, the monitoring, reporting, and some of the enforcement activities are located substantially in the bureaucracies of the federal and provincial governments. The three accountability relationships identified above — legislators to citizens, executive branch to legislatures, and provincial and federal executive branches to each other — are configured according to the Westminster model, modified to accommodate Canada's federal structure.

The primary instruments of accountability are statutes enacted by federal and provincial legislatures and a bilateral intergovernmental agreement concluded between representatives of their executive branches. The federal legislation delegates authority to the federal minister to enter into an agreement with a province and specifies the mutual obligations of governments in the form of the terms and conditions of that agreement, including the requirement for, and some of the content of, a provincial statute. Through the bilateral agreement, the provincial government commits to enacting legislation that conforms to the criteria in the federal statute and to respect its reporting requirements, and the federal government commits to transferring money once the provincial legislation is in place according to the terms and conditions specified in the federal statute and the bilateral agreement.

Within this model, standards or conditions are set out in the federal statute, repeated in the intergovernmental agreement, and again in the provincial statute. The social programs of the Keynesian era were influenced by the rights discourse of the time, including that found in the *Universal Declaration of Human Rights*, which provides in article 22 that "everyone, as a member of society, has the right to social security and is entitled to realization, through national effort and international co-operation and in accordance with the organization and resources of each State, of the economic, social and cultural rights indispensable for his dignity and the free development of his personality."[13] However, to the extent that rights were recognized in legislation of this period, they were not articulated clearly in the language of rights. Rather, they were expressed as terms of an

12 *Hospital Insurance and Diagnostic Services Act*, RSC 1957, c 28, s 3.

13 *Universal Declaration of Human Rights*, GA Res 217(III), UNGAOR, 3d Sess, Supp No 13, UN Doc A/810, (1948) 71, art 22.

intergovernmental agreement, along with other more administrative provisions, such as record-keeping requirements. Social rights were realized through conditions attached to the federal transfer, such as the *Canada Assistance Plan*'s prohibition on making participation in work activity projects a condition of receipt of welfare or the requirement that provincial social welfare plans provide assistance based on need, taking into account budgetary requirements. The standard-setting process included negotiations with the provinces, but it is the federal government that played the predominant role as a result of its financial clout. The federal Parliament was involved through enactment of dedicated statutes that set out the purposes of the transfers.

Within the administrative accountability regime, two types of monitoring were provided for: monitoring provincial compliance with the terms of the agreements and monitoring the performance of the Cabinet by the House of Commons. Monitoring of the minister was provided for in the requirement that he report annually to Parliament on the operation of the agreements and on the payments made to the provinces. Monitoring of provincial compliance was done through a process whereby provincial programs to be cost-shared had to be approved by federal officials and listed in schedules to the bilateral agreement, which were updated regularly. In addition, federal officials audited provincial records and accounts. The enforcement mechanism related to provincial accountability was a certificate issued by the minister of health and welfare, based on the results of the auditing of provincial records, which would trigger the final payment by the minister of finance. Federal money was both a carrot and a stick, with the refusal to fund a program or transfer money the ultimate sanction. Yet it was federal officials, not Cabinet ministers, who were on the front line of monitoring and enforcement. Federal money was not so much withheld by ministers to punish non-complying provinces as transferred on the authority of these ministers to provinces once federal officials had determined that provincial programs and expenditures complied with standards contained in federal legislation. In the case of the *Canada Assistance Plan*, there was an additional enforcement mechanism in the form of the requirement that the provincial law provide for an appeals mechanism for individuals affected by the decisions of officials administering programs under the authority of the province. The penalty for the failure of an administrator to respect the provincial statute was a reversal of the decision in favour of the individual rights claimant.

The funding mechanism for programs operating within the administrative accountability regime was an open-ended cost-sharing grant, with the federal government contributing 50 percent of whatever the province spent. The link between the amount of the federal transfer and provincial spending meant that a province had to document the amount spent on programs approved and listed in the schedules to the agreement. An audit of provincial records by federal officials was necessary before the minister of health and welfare recommended that the minister of finance release the funds. Cost-sharing can therefore be seen as a part of the accountability regime. There was a wrinkle in these funding arrangements introduced to accommodate the Quebec government's opposition to the exercise of the federal spending power in areas of provincial jurisdiction. In 1965, in anticipation of the coming into effect of the *Canada Assistance Plan*, the federal government offered provinces the choice of receiving the transfer in cash or tax points. The tax point offer included the safeguard of a cash top-up if the tax points turned out to be worth less than a province would have received under the cash formula. The Quebec government expected the tax point arrangement to make the transfer effectively unconditional, because once the tax points were transferred, there would be no way for the federal government to enforce the conditions. While offered to all provinces, only Quebec was expected to take advantage of it and only Quebec did.[14] The administrative accountability regime favoured the executive/legislative accountability relationship over the federal relationship, involving as it did an intrusive role for federal officials in monitoring provincial compliance. It was, however, the federal government's concern with the open-ended nature of the intergovernmental transfers and the requirement that it match provincial spending, more than provincial chafing under the accountability rules, that led to the demise of the regime for health care in 1977 and social assistance in 1995. Some of the conditions attached to the transfers did protect fundamental social rights, such as the obligation to provide assistance based on budgetary requirements. However, these were not clearly expressed in the language of rights but instead appeared as terms of the intergovernmental agreement, along with administrative arrangements.

2) The Political Accountability Regime

The *Canada Health Act*, 1984, is the example of the political regime of accountability, so named because it replaces the administrative monitoring of the previous model with monitoring and enforcement by the political

---

14 Yves Vaillancourt, "Quebec and the Federal Government: The Struggle over Opting Out" in Dan Glenday & Ann Duffy, eds, *Canadian Society: Understanding and Surviving in the 1990s* (Toronto: McClelland and Stewart, 1994) 168.

executive. The effect is that disputes over provincial compliance with standards in federal legislation rapidly become politicized and result in highly public fights between the federal and provincial governments. On paper, the regime seems to correspond closely to that of the Westminster model, with the primary accountability relationship being of the federal executive to the House of Commons for the expenditure of public funds. The principle of responsible government, however, is undermined by the dependence of the monitoring and enforcement provisions on the political will of the federal minister.

The *Canada Health Act* does contain substantive standards in the form of five criteria — public administration, comprehensiveness, universality, portability, and accessibility — set out in federal legislation.[15] The approach adopted by the federal government to the standard-setting process was, in the end, a unilateral one. This was the case in both the substantive (social rights) standards and the operational ones covering provincial reporting requirements. The federal government adopted this approach when achieving a provincial consensus appeared impossible, particularly after the announcement by the Quebec government that it would not sign another agreement.[16] The criteria in the *Canada Health Act* do, however, reflect those set out but not expressed so clearly in earlier legislation and subject to debate and negotiation at that time.

The primary accountability in the *Canada Health Act* is of the federal executive to the federal Parliament for the expenditure of public funds. The main instrument of accountability is the federal statute. It is through the procedures of parliamentary responsibility that the accountability of elected representatives to the public for a social right is to be achieved. The *obligation* of the executive branch to Parliament is to report on the administration and operation of the Act; the implicit obligation of elected representatives to the public is to ensure that the stated objectives of government policy as expressed in the Act are met. These are "to protect, promote and restore the physical and mental well-being of residents of Canada and to facilitate reasonable access to health services without financial or other barriers."[17] In the relationships of the minister to Parliament and of elected representatives to the public, the regime is similar to that of the administrative accountability regime.

---

15 *Canada Health Act*, above note 2.

16 AW Johnson, *Social Policy in Canada: The Past as it Conditions the Present* (Ottawa: Institute for Research on Public Policy, 1984).

17 *Canada Health Act*, above note 2, s 3.

There is no instrument establishing the mutual accountability relationship between the federal and provincial executives. Rather, the terms on which a province may qualify for federal funding are set out only in the federal statute. The requirement of a provincial law reflecting the federal conditions is achieved through the definition section, which defines a provincial health insurance plan as "a plan or plans established by the law of the province to provide for insured health services,"[18] and then specifying in section 7 of the Act the criteria that a provincial health insurance plan must meet. The provincial executive assumes specific obligations, not through an intergovernmental agreement, but through the act of accepting the federal transfer. There is no specific obligation undertaken by a province to introduce a provincial law establishing a system of health insurance that meets the federal criteria. However, if such a system is in place, the province will qualify for federal funding. The implied obligation is then to maintain such a system in exchange for continued federal funding. The other obligation is to "provide the Minister with such information, of a type prescribed by the regulations, as the Minister may reasonably require for the purposes of this Act" and to recognize the federal transfer in public documents and promotional material.[19]

The main monitoring mechanism in the *Canada Health Act* is the annual report by the minister of health to Parliament, supported by a legislated requirement for provincial reporting as a condition of federal funding. Under the Act, the minister of health is to make an annual report to both the House of Commons and the Senate "respecting the administration and operation of this Act for that fiscal year, including all relevant information on the extent to which provincial health care insurance plans have satisfied the criteria, and the extent to which the provinces have satisfied the conditions, for payment under this Act."[20] The Act delegates to the minister the authority to introduce regulations governing the information provinces are required to provide on the operation of their plans, but no other monitoring mechanism is envisaged. In practice, no minister of health has used her authority to issue those regulations, and certainly none has used the authority in the Act to withhold funding if a province does not provide the information necessary for the minister to report adequately to Parliament.

The ultimate sanction for failure to meet the conditions in the Act is the withholding of all or part of the federal transfer. In the absence of effective monitoring procedures, violations of the criteria often come to the

18 *Ibid*, s 2, definition of health care insurance plan.

19 *Ibid*, s 13.

20 *Ibid*, s 23.

minister through complaints of advocacy groups or through the media. The *Canada Health Act* spells out a procedure that the minister of health is to follow in situations where he believes that a province is not respecting the standards set out in the legislation. The minister is to consult with the offending province, and if the province fails to remedy the problem, the minister refers the matter to the Cabinet, which may exercise its discretionary power to withhold all or part of the federal transfer to the provinces. A provincial violation of the extra-billing provisions of the Act triggers a different sanction procedure. The Act makes it mandatory for the minister to withhold payment to a province for services that have been subject to extra billing and directs the minister to deduct from the transfer to the province an amount equal to that billed over the provincial fee schedule by physicians or dentists. While there has been some enforcement of the extra-billing provisions, the Cabinet has not used its discretionary power to punish provinces that do not respect the five criteria of the Act.

The funding mechanism typical of the political accountability regime is the block grant. Indeed, the shift from cost-sharing to the block grant for health care was initially associated with a move away from conditionality. However, public opposition to the removal of conditions and, particularly, to the practice of extra billing by physicians led the federal government to reintroduce conditions through the *Canada Health Act* in 1984.

The strength of the political accountability regime lies in the articulation of substantive standards that in the case of the *Canada Health Act*, amount to a promised guarantee of a universal right to medically necessary services, irrespective of an individual's province or territory of residence. The clear statement of substantive standards (described as "criteria") in the legislation has been helpful to those proponents of universal access to health care services as a right of Canadian social citizenship. The weaknesses of the regime lie in (1) the absence of effective monitoring procedures and the reluctance of the federal minister to make use of the provisions in the legislation regarding provincial reporting and (2) the unwillingness of the federal Cabinet to precipitate public fights with provincial governments by invoking the enforcement mechanisms. In the end, accountability of the federal executive branch to the House of Commons and of the elected legislators to citizens is sacrificed to the goal of maintaining intergovernmental peace.

3) Public Reporting Accountability Regime

The public reporting regime was typified by the multilateral intergovernmental agreements covering health care and programs for children concluded in the era of the *Social Union Framework Agreement*, between 1999 and the coming to office of the Conservative government of Stephen Harper in January 2006.[21] This regime departed significantly from the other two regimes in the balance between the principles of responsible government and federalism. While the administrative accountability regime conformed closely to the Westminster model of the executive–legislature relationship, and the political accountability regime formally conformed to it, the public reporting regime all but abandoned it. For the most part, it bypassed legislatures in favour of accountability relationships between the federal and provincial executive branches and between the executive branch at both levels and the public. The public, however, was positioned more as a consumer of information than an active party to the accountability regime, having no effective institutional avenues of participation. The discussion below focuses on the child-care agreements concluded within the framework of the *Social Union Framework Agreement*, including the 2000 *Early Childhood Development Agreement*[22] and the 2003 *Multilateral Framework on Early Learning and Child Care*.[23]

In the public reporting regime, the primary *instrument* establishing the accountability relationships was the multilateral framework agreement concluded among Cabinet representatives of the federal and provincial

---

21 The *Social Union Framework Agreement*, above note 11, an intergovernmental agreement involving the federal government and the nine provinces in English-speaking Canada, was concluded in 1999, but the public reporting approach contained in it was reflected in the 1997 agreements around the National Children's Agenda by the now defunct federal/provincial/territorial Council on Social Policy Renewal. The *Social Union Framework Agreement* approach was a response to the near loss by federalists of the 1995 Quebec referendum on sovereignty and was designed to prove that Canadian federalism could work, despite the evidence of the spectacular failures of two major initiatives of constitutional reform in the late 1980s and early 1990s.

22 Canadian Intergovernmental Conference Secretariat, News Release, "First Ministers' Meeting Communiqué on Early Childhood Development" (11 September 2000), online: Canadian Intergovernmental Conference Secretariat, www.scics.gc.ca [*Early Childhood Development Agreement*].

23 *Multilateral Framework on Early Learning and Child Care. An Agreement between the Government of Canada and the Governments of the Provinces and Territories* (March 2003), online: Canadian Intergovernmental Conference Secretariat www.scics.gc.ca [*Multilateral Framework on Early Learning and Child Care*]. The Government of Quebec was not party to this agreement.

governments. As a consequence of the Supreme Court 1991 decision in the *Canada Assistance Plan Reference*,[24] parties to the agreements treat them as political accords rather than mutually binding contracts. The statutory basis for the accountability regime is very weak.[25] There were no dedicated statutes setting out Parliament's purposes for the funding under the child-care agreements. Instead, the multilateral framework agreements focused on the mutual obligations of the governments to each other and, to a lesser extent, to their publics.

The multilateral framework agreements contained very weak articulations of standards. Instead, the language of shared visions, objectives, or principles was used. In the case of the Canada Social Transfer, the only substantive standard continues to be the prohibition on provinces imposing a residence requirement for eligibility for social assistance in the *Federal-Provincial Fiscal Arrangements Act*.[26] The *Early Childhood Development Agreement* did not contain any language that could be described as a standard, let alone a condition for a transfer. Instead, it listed two very general objectives (promoting early childhood development and helping families support their children within strong communities) and identified four also very general key areas for action. These are the promotion of healthy pregnancy, birth, and infancy; improving parenting and family supports; strengthening early childhood development, learning, and care; and strengthening community supports. The *Multilateral Framework Agreement on Early Learning and Child Care* was more specific in naming the area of investment as government regulated early learning and child care programs for children under six and identified the principles associated with effective approaches in such settings as accessible, affordable, quality, inclusive, and parental choice. The multilateral agreements also outlined the principles (standards) or criteria to be used to evaluate the progress of a government in meeting its commitments, which were to take the form of indicators developed through intergovernmental negotiations.

---

24 *Reference Re Canada Assistance Plan (BC)*, [1991] 2 SCR 525 [*Canada Assistance Plan Reference*]. The Supreme Court maintained at paras 46 & 47 that an agreement between governments does not have the same binding effect or mutuality as ordinary contracts by virtue of the principle of parliamentary sovereignty. Unlike the "mutually binding reciprocal undertakings" of ordinary contracts, the "parties were content to rely on the perceived political price for non-performance."

25 For more discussion on this point, see Barbara Cameron, "Accounting for Rights and Money in Canada's Social Union" in Boyd et al, eds, above note 4.

26 *Federal-Provincial Fiscal Arrangements Act*, RSC 1985, c F-8, s 24.

The standard-setting process involved intergovernmental negotiations between representatives of the executive branch (first administrative and then ministerial) at the federal and provincial levels of government. These negotiations were conducted, as intergovernmental negotiations generally are, in private, with the results being communicated to the public through the media at the conclusion of first ministers' meetings. Both the *Early Childhood Development Agreement* and *Multilateral Framework Agreement on Early Learning and Child Care* were concluded among all the first ministers, with the exception of the premier of the province of Quebec.

The mechanism for monitoring the performance of governments in meeting their obligations under the agreements was an annual report produced by the governments, organized around the agreed upon criteria or performance measures. There was generally a reference to third-party involvement in monitoring, but this was honoured more in the breach than the observance. The *Early Childhood Development Agreement* committed governments to report annually on their investments and progress in the four key areas and to work together to develop a shared framework that was to include jointly agreed comparable indicators. It gave as an example of indicators the availability and growth of services in each of the areas. The *Multilateral Framework Agreement on Early Learning and Child Care* was more direct about the reporting requirements. It committed governments to release baseline information by the end of November 2003 and to release the first annual report in November 2004. The agreement further specified the kind of descriptive and expenditure information that was to be provided. Both agreements committed governments to ensure that there were unspecified "effective mechanisms" to allow Canadians to participate in reviewing outcomes.

The enforcement mechanism in the public reporting regime was public approval or disapproval of a government's performance based on the information provided in the annual report. Even though the multilateral agreements were occasioned by a federal promise of new funding, the withholding of federal funds as a sanction was explicitly ruled out. Both agreements contained the sentence "the amount of federal funding provided to any jurisdiction will not depend on achieving a given level of performance." Furthermore, funding was not tied in any way to meeting the reporting commitments. Ultimately, the enforcement mechanism was the ballot for both the performance and reporting commitments in the agreements.

The *Social Union Framework Agreement* provided for an enforcement mechanism in the form of a dispute avoidance and resolution procedure that was to replace or modify the role of the federal minister in determining violations of the agreement. The dispute resolution mechanism agreed upon for health care specified an elaborate procedure that was to be followed where violations of the *Canada Health Act* were alleged, but the final decision was still to rest with the Governor in Council at the federal level.[27] Federal Liberal Health Minister Ujjal Dosanjh initiated proceedings under the mechanism around private diagnostic clinics in April 2005, but this approach to enforcement (or to the Social Union more generally) did not survive the defeat of the Liberal Party in the general election of January 2006.[28]

As with the political accountability regime, the funding mechanism for the public reporting model was the block grant, first introduced for social transfers to health and post-secondary education in 1977. In the case of social assistance, the block grant replaced the open-ended shared cost grant after the 1995 federal budget. The government of Prime Minister Paul Martin made use of dedicated transfers, flowed through trusts such as the Medical Equipment Trust or specially named transfers such as the Child Care Transfer, as well as the umbrella Canada Health Transfer and the Canada Social Transfer. The accountability mechanisms were generally too weak to ensure that the funds went to the targeted programs.[29] Under the Canada Social Transfer, the allocation of money between social assistance (income support and welfare services), post-secondary education, child care, and other social services was not specified during the period the Liberals were in office.[30] In 2005, the federal Liberal government moved to a different instrument — bilateral intergovernmental child-care agreements — after failing to gain the support of the provinces to a multilateral framework agreement to govern a promised $5 billion federal transfer over five years. There were two types of bilateral agreements: agreements-in-principle and funding agreements. In the spring and fall of 2005, the federal government reached agreements-in-principle with all the provinces except Quebec, and the more detailed funding agreements were reached with three provinces: Ontario, Manitoba, and Quebec. Like the multilateral framework

27 Health Canada, "*Canada Health Act* Annual Report, 2006–2007" (2007) at Annex C, online: Health Canada www.hc-sc.gc.ca.

28 Odette Madore, *Private Diagnostic Imaging Clinics and the Canada Health Act* (Ottawa: Parliamentary Information and Research Service, Library of Parliament, 2005).

29 Lynell Andersen & Tammy Findlay, *Making the Connections: Using Public Reporting to Track Progress in Child Care Services in Canada* (Ottawa: Child Care Advocacy Association of Canada, 2007); Lynell Andersen & Tammy Findlay, "Does Public Reporting Measure Up? Federalism, Accountability and Child-Care Policy in Canada" (2010) 53 Canadian Public Administration 417.

30 The Conservative government introduced a notional allocation of the CST in the 2007 federal budget, but this is not binding on the provinces.

agreements, these agreements were not enshrined in dedicated statutes, allowing the newly elected Conservative prime minister to unilaterally cancel them immediately after the swearing in of his government. There is, however, some evidence that the governments made an effort to ensure the bilateral agreements were more binding than the earlier agreements under this regime. In contrast to the multilateral agreements, the bilateral agreements-in-principle and the funding agreements were signed by representatives of the two levels of government. The funding agreements were written in contract-like language, although with a clause recognizing that the agreement could be terminated by either party on one year's notice and the caveat that the funding depended on annual approval of the necessary appropriations by Parliament.

The bilateral agreements can be viewed as both an extension of the public reporting model and a departure from it. Like the multilateral framework agreements, they relied heavily on public reporting as a monitoring mechanism, although there was also provision for a dispute resolution mechanism covering disagreements related to finances but not standards. The language around standards was stronger, echoing in some ways the criteria of the *Canada Health Act*, with the principles of quality, universally inclusive, accessible, and developmental being identified and defined. The *standard-setting process* departed from the executive-to-executive process of the multilateral agreements in that the standards are a modified version of the principles announced in the successful 2004 Liberal election campaign.[31] The most significant departures, however, related to accountability instruments: the use of bilateral rather than multilateral agreements and the innovation of a provincial Action Plan.

The bilateral agreements-in-principle required that a province publish an Action Plan as a condition for moving to a funding agreement. This was not a requirement for Quebec, which signed only a funding agreement. Under the agreements-in-principle, the provinces agreed to release an Action Plan covering the five years of new federal money by a specific date. Alberta did not agree to a specific date but instead had inserted in its agreement-in-principle the sentence "Alberta agrees to develop and release as part of its business planning cycle, a strategic plan on early learning and

---

31 The Liberals campaigned on the QUAD principles of quality, universal, affordable, developmental child care services. *Universal* was modified to *universally inclusive* in intergovernmental meetings in the fall of 2004 and appeared in the bilateral agreements-in-principle in this form, with a definition of each reminiscent of the language of the *Canada Health Act*. However, the indicators in the public reporting section of the agreements related only to availability, affordability, and quality.

child care regarding the five years of new federal funding under this initiative."[32] There were slight variations in the wording of the Action Plan section of the bilateral agreements, but all involved identifying priorities for investment, targets, and baseline expenditures against which progress toward meeting the objectives of the agreement may be measured.

The political accountability regime tipped the balance within the Canadian constitutional order very much toward the federal principle. It provided virtually no role for the elected legislature in holding the Cabinet accountable for the expenditure of public funds according to purposes approved by Parliament, as required by the principle of responsible government. To the extent that there was any accountability on social rights, it was between the executive branch and citizens through the annual public reports. Citizens, however, had no effective way to hold the executive branch accountable, either directly or through their elected members of Parliament.

D. TOWARDS AN ALTERNATIVE REGIME

From the perspective of advocates of social rights, the primary purpose of federal social transfers is to expand the social citizenship rights of members of Canadian society. This final section of the chapter draws on lessons of past regimes of accountability to outline an alternative regime consistent with that purpose. It does not attempt to design an ideal system of accountability, which is impossible within the existing Canadian constitutional order. The objective, however, is to address from a social rights perspective the main shortcomings of past regimes and to accommodate as much as possible the inescapable tensions within the Canadian political system. The hope is that the approach here will be of assistance to those social rights advocates committed to ensuring that federal social transfers continue and that effective accountability regimes are put in place to govern them.

Following the approach outlined in this chapter, the first task for anyone designing an alternative regime of accountability for federal social transfers is to be clear about the three distinct accountability relationships that underlie such a regime, each involving different sets of actors. The accountability relationships are of (1) elected legislators to citizens, (2) the federal executive branch to the House of Commons, and (3) the executive branches at the federal and provincial level to each other. Once these are

32 "Moving Forward on Early Learning and Child Care: Agreement in Principle between the Government of Canada and the Government of Alberta" (7 July 2005) at 5–6.

identified, the elements that constitute an accountability relationship need to be considered in turn. As described at the beginning of the chapter, these are the obligations the parties have assumed, instrument(s) establishing the accountability relationship, standards by which performance of obligations is to be assessed, the standard-setting procedure, monitoring mechanisms, sanctions for non-performance, enforcement procedures, and, where appropriate, the funding mechanism.

The obligations undertaken by the parties to the accountability relationship (the "what" of an accountability relationship) differ in each of the accountability relationships. The members of the House of Commons are accountable for fulfilling commitments regarding social entitlements or social rights. The federal Cabinet is accountable to the House of Commons for spending money for purposes approved by Parliament (the responsible government principle). The executive branches at each level are accountable to each other for carrying out the terms of their agreement, which in the case of the federal government means providing the agreed-upon funds, and of the provincial governments, spending that money in the ways agreed upon and then reporting on that spending.

Disentangling the three accountability relationships is an important step to avoid some of the confusion in previous regimes, but from a social rights perspective, it is not sufficient. If the purpose of the transfer is understood to be the realization of social rights, then the relationship between the elected legislators and citizens should be recognized as the primary accountability relationship. For the purposes of the social transfer, the relationship between the federal Cabinet and the members of the House of Commons, and the one between the executive branches at the two levels should be seen as secondary or implementing relationships.

A distinction between primary and secondary accountability relationships permits a further distinction between substantive standards and implementing standards or criteria. The substantive standards relate to the primary purpose of the social transfer, which is the realization of social rights. The implementing criteria relate to the secondary accountability relationships, which are the relationships between the executive branch at the federal level and the House of Commons, and between the executive branches at the federal and provincial levels. The five criteria of the *Canada Health Act* provide an illustration of substantive standards. The reporting requirements of the federal minister to the House of Commons or of the provincial executive to the federal minister are examples of secondary or operational standards. These two types of standards need to be distinguished in legislation and intergovernmental agreements on social programs.

The distinction between substantive and operational or administrative standards is helpful in conceptualizing and locating standard-setting procedures. Intergovernmental forums are a suitable place to determine the standards each level of government is to respect in meeting their mutual obligations. But the fundamental social rights of Canadians should not be determined in negotiations between representatives of the executive branches of the two levels of government. The realization of social rights involves choices about the allocation of society's resources and the regulation of markets that are essentially political. In a democratic society, debates about what priority is to be given to them belong in forums that permit dialogue between elected representatives and the people, including election campaigns, transparent public consultations, and legislatures. Given the shared responsibility for social rights under Canada's Constitution, such debates can occur at the federal or provincial levels or both. The standard-setting procedures for the executive–legislature relationship are the established parliamentary procedures and conventions.

Under the proposed alternative accountability regime, the statute would be the primary instrument for establishing the accountability relationship between legislators and members of society, and between the executive branch and the legislature. At the federal level, these should be dedicated statutes setting out the purposes of the transfer and the accountability regime to govern them, rather than omnibus financial legislation such as the *Federal-Provincial Fiscal Arrangements Act*, which provides little more than spending authorization. The purposes and substantive standards of the transfer should be articulated clearly, using the language of social rights and referencing where appropriate Canada's international human rights commitments.[33]

These should be explicitly linked to the federal Parliament and government's role in promoting a shared, countrywide social citizenship and to their commitment under section 36(1) of the *Constitution Act, 1982*, to pro-

33 An example of this was Bill C-304, *An Act to Ensure Adequate, Accessible and Affordable Housing for Canadians*, 3rd Sess, 40th Parl, 2010 (Committee report presented in House of Commons 21 March 2011), which explicitly referenced the *International Covenant on Economic, Social and Cultural Rights*. This private member's bill would have required that the federal government consult with provinces with a view to establishing "a national housing strategy designed to respect, protect, promote and fulfil the right to adequate housing as guaranteed under international human rights treaties ratified by Canada."

moting equal opportunities for well-being and providing essential public services to all Canadians. The procedures governing the accountability of the minister to the House of Commons should be clearly specified, with details provided on the kind of reporting required. The nature and scope of the authority delegated to the minister to negotiate agreements with the provinces should also be clearly delineated. Intergovernmental agreements would be used to establish the accountability relationship between the executive branches at the two levels of government, as necessary. However, any such agreements should be seen as implementing instruments concluded under authority delegated through the statutes, which is consistent with their status as administrative agreements.

The monitoring and enforcement of standards have been the most problematic elements of previous regimes of accountability. Between elections, which are the ultimate enforcement procedure, citizens are dependent on the legislature to hold the executive branch accountable. They are assisted in this task mainly by non-governmental organizations that monitor the activities of government, usually with very limited resources. The accountability of the federal executive to the House of Commons is governed by the procedures and conventions of Parliament and the often very general statutory delegations of power. Legislative oversight is very weak and could be strengthened by measures such as requiring that intergovernmental agreements be tabled in the House of Commons and automatically referred to a standing committee, which is the current practice regarding regulations — another type of executive instrument. The agreements should also be made publicly available on government websites, as is the case with intergovernmental agreements in Quebec and international treaties at the federal level. Reporting requirements of the minister to the House of Commons could be made more explicit and stricter in legislation. Additional support could be provided to the elected legislature by the creation of a representative advisory council, as recommended below.

It is, however, the monitoring and enforcement procedures involved in the relationship between the executive branches at the two levels of government that have been the most contested and present the greatest challenges. There are two aspects to this. The first is the accountability of the provincial executive for spending federal money according to the terms of the agreement, which effectively means according to purposes approved by Parliament, and reporting on that spending. The second is the accountability of the federal government to deliver on the funding promised to the provinces in exchange for their acceptance of the federal conditions.

The alternative regime would address the tension between federalism and responsible government inherent in the provincial expenditure of federal tax dollars by locating as much of the monitoring and enforcement activity as possible at the provincial level. An innovative approach borrowed from the 2005 bilateral agreements-in-principle around the $5 billion promised by the government of Paul Martin for child-care transfers might help achieve this goal. Instead of tying federal funding to the realization of the substantive objective of the funding, the bilateral agreements made the trigger for the flow of federal money the publication by the province of an Action Plan. This plan was to show how the province intended to use the federal funding to progress toward the realization of objectives. The idea was that the citizens of a province rather than the federal government would hold the province accountable for carrying out its own Action Plan. As discussed earlier, the weakness of the accountability regime in the agreements was that it relied too heavily on public reporting by the provincial executive to the public. Instead, stronger mechanisms for monitoring a province's record in fulfilling its Action Plan need to be created at a provincial level. These mechanisms should provide increased avenues for public engagement linked to and supportive of the legislature's role in holding the executive branch accountable.

An example of a stronger monitoring mechanism was set out in Bill C-303, the private member's bill directed at putting in place an accountability regime for federal social transfers for child-care services.[34] The bill called for an Advisory Council to consist of individuals who support the purposes of the legislation and who would be chosen by a process involving the appropriate House of Commons standing committee. The Advisory Council was to report directly to Parliament, and the minister would be required to mention any advice received from the council in his report to Parliament. An Advisory Committee with similar reporting powers at the provincial level could monitor progress under the province's Action Plan. Another way that monitoring could be located at the provincial level would be to have the provincial auditor general report on the province's use of a federal social transfer. An appeals procedure for individuals with rights under a program funded by the transfer could serve as both a monitoring and enforcement mechanism, as was the case under the *Canada Assistance Plan*.

The federal spending power is a blunt enforcement mechanism and has recently not ensured provincial respect for the criteria in the *Canada Health Act*. Intergovernmental dispute resolution mechanisms may be appropriate for addressing disputes between the executive branches of government

34 See above note * at the beginning of this chapter.

related to federal-provincial implementing arrangements. They are not at all appropriate for enforcing respect for fundamental social rights, which are matters between citizens and legislators. The alternative accountability regime would reserve the sanction of withholding federal money for enforcing provincial reporting (as a necessary condition for the minister's accountability to the House of Commons) and ensuring effective monitoring mechanisms are in place provincially. With respect to substantive standards that express social rights, the emphasis here is on creating mechanisms that facilitate public engagement and encourage enforcement through political means with the province rather than the federal government being the focus of attention. The emphasis should be on political sanctions enforced through public debate, political mobilization, and elections.

The accountability of the federal executive to the provincial executive to deliver on the promised funding is more difficult to resolve. Here, there are two problems: unilateral federal changes in the course of an intergovernmental agreement and the reductions in the federal contribution at the termination of an agreement. The first problem was caused by the 1990 Supreme Court of Canada decision in the reference case on the *Canada Assistance Plan*. While the Court made general statements about the political rather than legal enforceability of intergovernmental agreements, the reasons it gave were more specific, referring to the appearance of the funding formulas only in the federal legislation and not in the funding agreement and other details of the arrangement. Governments appeared to be trying to address these criticisms in the 2005 bilateral child-care funding agreements, which were written in contract-like language. The second problem, sustaining the federal funding commitment over the long term, is essentially a political one, requiring public pressure on the federal government. The provinces could facilitate this by educating Canadians about the shared federal and provincial responsibility for social rights and the role that the social transfers play in this. Instead, the provinces frequently imply that the federal government has virtually no role in social programs and then complain about the inadequacy of federal funding.

The tension between federalism and responsible government needs to be kept in mind in choosing the funding mechanism for the transfer. The federal government can legitimately require that a province report on its expenditure of federal revenue because it must have this information for its accountability to the House of Commons. The province is accountable to its own legislature for the expenditure of revenue raised through provincial taxation. From a practical perspective, a provincial legislature cannot be expected to adopt as its own the purposes of the federal Parliament unless the federal government makes a very significant contribution of money. In those cases, a shared-cost grant might be the appropriate funding mechanism. In cases where the federal contribution does not represent a large, ongoing contribution, then a block grant is more appropriate. Although the cost-shared grants have been associated with the stricter accountability regimes in the past, it is possible to design a regime of accountability consistent with the alternative regime outlined here for a block transfer.

No accountability regime can end the challenge by Quebec governments to the legitimacy of the federal spending power, which is the constitutional basis for federal social transfers. Responding to Quebec concerns ultimately requires constitutional change that recognizes the unique role of the Quebec National Assembly with respect to the presence of a majority French-speaking population in that province. In the meantime, influential social rights advocates in English Canada have learned to accept the special status of Quebec and worked with opposition members of the Canadian Parliament to include a specific Quebec exemption in bills calling for national strategies and national standards. A parallel version of the following paragraph from Bill C-303 appears in Bill C-545, *An Act to Eliminate Poverty in Canada*, which received first reading in the House of Commons on 16 June 2010:[35]

> Recognizing the unique nature of the jurisdiction of the Government of Quebec with regard to the education and development of children in Quebec society, and notwithstanding any other provision of this Act, the Government of Quebec may choose to be exempted from the application of this Act and, notwithstanding any such decision, shall receive the full transfer payment that would otherwise be paid under section 5.[36]

The Quebec exemption allowed Bloc Québécois MPs to join their Liberal and New Democratic colleagues in supporting the child-care and anti-poverty bills. The provision makes explicit and public the recognition of Quebec's special status that political elites have privately accepted in intergovern-

35 Bill C-545, *An Act to Eliminate Poverty in Canada*, 3rd Sess, 40th Parl, 2010 (first reading 16 June 2010). The precise wording of s 4(4) of that bill is

> Recognizing the unique nature of the jurisdiction of the Government of Quebec with regard to poverty elimination in Quebec society, and notwithstanding any other provision of this Act, the Government of Quebec may choose to be exempted from the application of this Act and, notwithstanding any such decision, shall receive the full transfer payment that would otherwise be paid within its territory under this Act.

36 See above note * at the beginning of this chapter.

mental arrangements since the mid-1960s.[37] In the current political context, it offers a path out of an impasse.

The proposed accountability regime outlined in this chapter does not purport to solve all the accountability problems related to federal social transfers. However, it has a number of advantages over the ones that have governed social transfers in the past. It highlights three distinct accountability relationships that underlie federal social transfers and identifies as the primary accountability relationship that of legislators to citizens for the fulfilment of social rights. It provides a reasonable basis for defining and delimiting the federal role by situating it as the promotion of a common social citizenship and emphasizing the social rights content of appropriate federal standards. By locating monitoring at the provincial level, it holds out a greater possibility for an interested public to force governments to deliver on promised social rights. It would allow the conflicts of interest that underlie political struggles around intergovernmental social transfers to play out within a framework in which the democratic issues at stake and the choices being made would be more visible.

37 The author of this chapter was involved in the consultations that led to this provision and supports the approach, although would prefer the wording "Quebec National Assembly" to "Government of Quebec." On elite accommodation in the mid-1960s, see above note 14.

CHAPTER 5

CHALLENGING DISCRIMINATORY AND PUNITIVE RESPONSES TO HOMELESSNESS IN CANADA*

MARIE-EVE SYLVESTRE† AND CÉLINE BELLOT‡

A. INTRODUCTION

State and local governments have long turned to legal norms such as criminal law, anti-panhandling statutes, and land use planning and development bylaws and have relied on policing strategies to control the poor and homeless in Western countries.[1] Since the 1990s, Canadian cities have adopted a new series of local policies that emphasize the enforcement of provincial statutes and bylaws against urban disorder.[2] These strategies

---

* Part of this chapter is based on an expert affidavit filed in support of the applicants in *Tanudjaja v Canada* (Ont Sup Ct File no CV-10-403688) (2011), online: CURA http://socialrightscura.ca. The authors would like to thank Bruce Porter and Martha Jackman for insightful comments on earlier versions of this chapter.

† Marie-Eve Sylvestre, Associate Professor, Civil Law Section, University of Ottawa.

‡ Céline Bellot, Associate Professor, École de service social, Université de Montréal.

1 Michel Foucault, *Discipline and Punish: The Birth of the Prison*, trans Alan Sheridan (New York: Vintage Books, 1977); Katherine Beckett & Steve Herbert, *Banished: The New Social Control in Urban America* (New York: Oxford University Press, 2010); Mary Ann Poutanen, "Images du danger dans les archives judiciaires. Comprendre la violence et le vagabondage dans un centre urbain du début du XIXe siècle, Montréal (1810–1842)" (2002) 55 Revue d'histoire de l'Amérique française 381.

2 Marie-Eve Sylvestre et al, "Le droit est aussi une question de visibilité : occupation des espaces publics et parcours judiciaires des personnes itinérantes à Montréal et à Ottawa" (2011) 26:3 RCDS 531 [Sylvestre et al, "Occupation des espaces publics"]; Catherine Chesnay, Céline Bellot, & Marie-Eve Sylvestre, "Taming the Homeless One Ticket at a Time: The Penalization of Homelessness in Ontario and British Columbia"

have generated much debate and controversy. Scholars, community groups, and lawyers have challenged the legitimacy and the discriminatory aspects of these policies, as they fall disproportionately on homeless people and racial minorities.

In both the historic and modern eras, punitive responses to homelessness were largely based on negative stereotyping, prejudices, and discrimination. Those who are homeless are wrongly portrayed as morally inferior, lazy, and dishonest individuals (the "moral depravation" discourse), blamed for their own misfortunes (the "choice" discourse), and are treated as criminals or potential serious offenders needing to be repressed and confined, rather than as equal citizens worthy of respect and consideration (the "criminality" discourse).

These three sets of beliefs have little to do with homeless individuals' actual circumstances or reality. However, their prevalence has had important legal implications for social rights litigation, preventing a necessary debate about the complexity and the multi-factorial dimension of homelessness — a phenomenon rooted in various social, economic, and political causes. In this chapter, we suggest that a broader discussion of the origins of the moral depravation, choice, and criminality discourses, and the consequences of these three discourses for homeless people and communities, strongly supports the recognition of homelessness as an analogous ground of discrimination under section 15 of the *Canadian Charter of Rights and Freedoms*,[3] as well as claims to social and economic rights, such as access to housing, education, employment, health care, and social services under both section 7 and section 15 of the *Charter*.[4]

(2013) 55:2 Canadian Journal of Criminology and Criminal Justice 161 [Chesnay, Bellot, & Sylvestre, "Taming the Homeless"]; Damian Collins & Nicholas Blomley, "Private Needs and Public Space: Politics, Poverty and Anti-panhandling By-Laws in Canadian Cities" in Law Commission of Canada, ed, *New Perspectives on the Public-Private Divide* (Vancouver: UBC Press, 2003); Joe Hermer & Janet Mosher, *Disorderly People: Law and the Politics of Exclusion in Ontario* (Halifax: Fernwood, 2002) [Hermer & Mosher, *Disorderly People*].

3 Part I of the *Constitution Act, 1982*, being Schedule B of the *Canada Act 1982* (UK), 1982, c 11 [*Charter*].

4 This chapter will focus on section 15. See Margot Young, "Context, Choice and Rights: *PHS Community Services Society v Canada (Attorney General)*" (2011) 44:1 UBC L Rev 221. For more specific arguments on s 7 and the idea of choice, see Marie-Eve Sylvestre, "The Redistributive Potential of Section 7 of the *Charter*: Incorporating Socio-economic Context in Criminal Law Cases and in the Adjudication of Rights" (2012) 42:3 Ottawa L Rev 389.

Since the Supreme Court of Canada's decision in *R v Kapp*,[5] a person claiming that her rights have been violated pursuant to section 15 of the *Charter* has to demonstrate that (1) a law creates a distinction, in purpose or effect, based on an enumerated or analogous ground; and (2) the law is discriminatory within the meaning of the equality guarantee, i.e., that it creates a disadvantage by perpetuating prejudice or stereotyping in a way that does not correspond to the group's actual circumstances or reality.[6] Moreover, the Court has held that an analogous ground of discrimination is often the "basis for stereotypical decisions made not on the basis of merit, but on the basis of a personal characteristic that is immutable or changeable only at unacceptable cost to personal identity."[7] The specific question of whether homelessness is an analogous ground of discrimination under section 15, like the issue of poverty as an analogous ground,[8] has yet to be settled by the courts.[9]

---

5 2008 SCC 41.

6 *Ibid* at para 17.

7 *Corbiere v Canada (Minister of Indian & Northern Affairs)*, [1999] 2 SCR 203 at para 13 [*Corbiere*] (confirmed in *Baier v Alberta*, 2007 SCC 31 at para 64).

8 See *Masse v Ontario (Ministry of Community and Social Services)* (1996), 134 DLR (4th) 20 (Ont Div Ct), leave to appeal to CA refused (1996), Admin LR (2d) 87n, leave to appeal to SCC refused (1996), 39 CRR (2d) 375, in which, at para 71 of the Divisional Court decision, the court refused to recognize welfare recipients as a "discrete and insular minority" where reductions in the level of welfare were challenged; *Polewsky v Home Hardware Stores Ltd* (1999), 68 CRR (2d) 330 (Ont SCJ): Gillese J rejected a challenge under s 15 of the *Charter* because "[t]he poor in Canadian society are not a group in which the members are linked by shared personal or group characteristics" (*ibid* at 346); *Toussaint v Canada (Minister of Citizenship and Immigration)*, 2011 FCA 146 at para 59 and *Boulter v Nova Scotia Power Inc*, 2009 NSCA 17 at paras 42–44, where the courts refused to recognize poverty as an analogous ground. But see *Dunmore v Ontario (AG)*, 2001 SCC 94: L'Heureux-Dubé J, concurring, would have held that the occupational status of agricultural workers constituted an analogous ground; *Falkiner v Ontario (Ministry of Community and Social Services)* (2002), 59 OR (3d) 481 (CA): the court accepted that membership in the group of "sole-support mothers on welfare" could be considered grounds for a claim of discrimination based on the enumerated ground of sex and partly on an analogous ground. Application for leave to appeal to the Supreme Court of Canada was granted on 20 March 2003, but Ontario decided in September 2004 not to pursue its appeal. See, generally, Martha Jackman & Bruce Porter, "Justiciability of Social and Economic Rights in Canada" in Malcolm Langford, ed, *Social Rights Jurisprudence: Emerging Trends in International and Comparative Law* (Cambridge: Cambridge University Press, 2009).

9 *Federated Anti-Poverty Groups of BC v Vancouver (City)*, 2002 BCSC 105. The court upheld a Vancouver bylaw prohibiting aggressive panhandling and solicitation of a captive audience. Justice Taylor was of the opinion that the bylaw did not violate s 15

In the first part of this chapter, we will present homelessness as a complex and multi-factorial phenomenon characterized by a series of important traits related to a lack, or inadequacy, of housing arrangements, as well as by well-defined patterns of social exclusion and discrimination. We will then show how prevalent stereotypes and prejudice faced by homeless persons as they are policed and criminalized, both historically and in the present, are perpetuating disadvantage and have occluded consideration of the broader structural causes of homelessness. Next, we will suggest that homelessness cannot be explained simplistically through narratives of choice, but rather that it is, like several other enumerated or analogous grounds of discrimination, a social construct attached to some individuals that is not immutable, but that is difficult to change. We will argue that when it comes to homelessness or to other enumerated or analogous grounds of discrimination, the courts' consideration of immutability in a section 15 analysis must include consideration of the complexity and embeddedness of the social structures and interactions at play.[10] In particular, we will show how criminalization and penalization[11] of homeless people create further exclusion and homelessness and how such punitive responses make this social condition even more difficult to change. Ultimately, we hope that the reconsideration of the prevailing stereotypes and prejudices applied against homeless individuals will make it possible to address the

---

of the *Charter*, stating that the poor or more specifically "those who panhandle" could not be considered an analogous ground given that the choice to panhandle was not an immutable trait over which they had no effective control (*ibid* at paras 273–76). See also *R v Banks* (2005), 248 DLR (4th) 118 (Ont SCJ) [*Banks*], aff'd 2007 ONCA 19, Juriansz JA, leave to appeal to SCC refused (2007), 376 NR 394, confirming the constitutionality of the Ontario *Safe Streets Act, 1999*, SO 1999, c 8, based on similar reasoning.

10 For an interesting analysis of these issues, see also Sonia Lawrence, "Choice, Equality and Tales of Racial Discrimination: Reading the Supreme Court on Section 15 of the *Charter*" (2006) 33 Sup Ct L Rev (2d) 115; David Robitaille, "La conception judiciaire de la pauvreté au Canada : condition sociale immutable ou simple question de volonté?" (2008), online: Service de lutte contre la pauvreté, la précarité et l'exclusion sociale www.luttepauvrete.be.

11 While this may be an unusual term in English, *penalization* refers to the growing tendency to resort to regulatory criminal law, which includes provincial and federal statutes as well as bylaws rather than criminal law (most notably found in the *Criminal Code* and specific federal statutes), as the primary punitive normative system in the resolution of conflicts related to the use of public spaces. Marie-Eve Sylvestre, "Disorder and Public Spaces in Montreal, Canada: Repression (and Resistance) through Law, Politics and Police Discretion" (2010) 31 Urban Geography 803 [Sylvestre, "Disorder and Public Spaces"].

social, political, and economic causes of homelessness, in order to offer different rights-driven legislative and regulatory responses to homelessness.

B. PERPETUATING DISADVANTAGE: A REVIEW OF PREVAILING STEREOTYPES AND PREJUDICE ABOUT HOMELESS PEOPLE

1) Defining Homelessness as a Multi-factorial Phenomenon

Defining homelessness is a challenging enterprise: social problems are fundamentally constructed by a certain set of social and cultural arrangements and shaped by the intentions and objectives of those committed to such an exercise.[12] Whereas many scholars and policy makers define homelessness more or less restrictively, in terms of lack or inadequacy of housing arrangements, others refer more broadly to complex and multi-dimensional factors embedded in dynamics of rights violation, social exclusion and inclusion, poverty, and discrimination.[13]

In an attempt to come up with an inclusive and comprehensive definition of homelessness in Canada, the Canadian Homelessness Research Network recently developed a typology based on the nature of housing circumstances as well as the duration and frequency of homeless episodes.[14] This typology includes (1) people living on the streets or in places not meant to be permanent living spaces, such as under bridges, in alleys, sidewalks, building doorways, tunnels, and ravines, and in vehicles, shacks, tents, or garages, et cetera ("unsheltered"); (2) people living in emergency shelters, whether on a temporary, occasional, or more permanent basis, including in overnight shelters, violence against women shelters, and emergency

12 John David Hulchanski, "Who Are the Homeless? What Is Homelessness? The Politics of Defining and Emerging Policy" *UBC Planning Papers*, Discussion Paper No 10 (Vancouver: University of British Columbia, 1987); John David Hulchanski et al, "Homelessness, What's in a Word?" in John David Hulchanski et al, eds, *Finding Home: Policy Options for Addressing Homelessness in Canada* (Toronto: Homeless Hub, 2009) 1, online: The Homeless Hub http://homelesshub.ca.

13 See, for example, Le Réseau d'Aide aux Personnes Seules et Itinérantes de Montréal, online: RAPSIM www.rapsim.org. The definition used by RAPSIM "Une personne itinérante, c'est une personne qui n'a pas d'adresse fixe, qui n'a pas l'assurance d'un logement stable, sécuritaire et salubre pour les jours à venir, au revenu très faible, avec une accessibilité souvent discriminatoire à son égard de la part des services publics, pouvant vivre des problèmes occasionnant une désorganisation sociale, notamment, de santé mentale, d'alcoolisme et/ou toxicomanie et/ou de jeux compulsifs, ou dépourvue de groupe d'appartenance stable."

14 Canadian Homelessness Research Network (2012), online: The Homeless Hub www.homelesshub.ca.

shelters for people fleeing disasters ("emergency sheltered"); (3) people who do not have security of tenure or their own home, including people "squatting" in friends', families', or colleagues' living spaces, transitional housing arrangements, people in institutional care, such as prisons or mental health institutions, and in reception centres for newly arrived immigrants ("provisionally accommodated"); and (4) those who are not strictly speaking homeless but who are improperly or vulnerably housed, including those occupying housing that is unsafe, unhealthy, unaffordable, overcrowded, or inappropriate for other reasons, such as lacking in available support services necessary for persons with disabilities or mental health issues, and people living under threat of eviction, unemployment, family breakdowns, or violence and abuse ("at risk of homelessness").[15] This typology also distinguishes between those experiencing transitional, short-term, and chronic homelessness.[16] These groups are not, however, rigid or static. People who are provisionally accommodated or at risk of homelessness are also likely to experience homelessness as described in the first two categories (unsheltered or emergency sheltered) for short periods of time because of housing affordability, poor property maintenance, or other issues.

As a result, the majority of homeless people are not chronically homeless, but rather are temporarily without stable housing for certain periods of time. The length and frequency of these periods will vary according to the person and the circumstances. The most recent study published by the Research Alliance for Canadian Homelessness, Housing and Health (REACH) explains that

> the division between these two groups [those who are vulnerably housed and those who are homeless] is false. The people we identified as "vulnerably housed" were not just at risk of homelessness; in the past 2 years, they had spent almost as much time homeless (just under 5 months per year) as the homeless group did (6.5 months per year). Instead of two distinct groups, this is one large, severely disadvantaged group that transitions between the two housing states.[17]

---

15 *Ibid.*

16 European Federation of National Organizations Working with People Who are Homeless (FEANTSA) (2007), online: FEANTSA www.feantsa.org. This typology largely mirrors ETHOS, the European typology on homelessness and housing exclusion developed by FEANTSA.

17 Emily Holton, Evie Gogosis, & Stephen Hwang, *Housing Vulnerability and Health: Canada's Hidden Emergency* (Toronto: Research Alliance for Canadian Homelessness, Housing, and Health, 2010).

According to this definition, homelessness encompasses different realities and is the result of multiple causes, including economic changes and loss of employment, poverty, domestic violence, land use and planning strategies, neighbourhood gentrification and community displacement, State and institutional failures to address the needs and respect the rights of vulnerable groups such as refugees, youth released from foster homes, ex-prisoners released from correctional facilities, people with mental or intellectual disabilities in need of support, et cetera. There are a myriad of individual circumstances that combine with systemic causes, such as physical and mental health problems, eviction, unemployment, family breakdown, addiction, and migration.[18]

Despite the diversity of the housing arrangements uncovered by this typology, however, homelessness can also be characterized as being the result of massive rights violation, including rights to life, liberty, and security of the person, equality, and various social and economic rights related to housing, decent income, health and access to social services, or education. Homeless people have in common the experience of social exclusion and discrimination, which are both exemplified and exacerbated by the adoption of punitive responses to homelessness.[19] As we shall demonstrate, discrimination and exclusion do not only produce and reproduce homelessness; they are also intrinsically linked to being homeless. Such prejudice and stereotypes obscure the social, economic, and political causes of homelessness and thwart efforts to address these underlying factors by blaming those who are its victims, imputing personal characteristics of moral inferiority, laziness, dishonesty, and criminality, which, in turn, provide an "explanation" for the problem of homelessness. While homelessness in Canada in its current form dates back to policy and economic changes that began to occur in the late 1980s, patterns of discrimination towards homeless people have a much longer history.

2) Historical Patterns of Discrimination

The historical antecedents to modern patterns of discrimination against homeless people can be traced back to at least the thirteenth century, when vagrants, *sans aveux* (without an agreement of loyalty and allegiance to a

---

18 Danielle Laberge, ed, *L'errance urbaine* (Sainte Foy, QC: Les Éditions MultiMondes, 2000).

19 Céline Bellot & Bernard St-Jacques, "La gestion pénale et l'itinérance : un enjeu pour la défense des droits" in Shirley Roy & Roch Hurtubise, eds, *L'itinérance en questions* (Québec: Presses de l'Université du Québec, 2007) 171.

lord) and *gueux* (beggars), were the primary targets of repressive measures of social control in France.[20] Still, in the eighteenth century, the king's agents tirelessly chased homeless people, applied red-hot brands on their bodies, and confined them in *dépôts de mendicité* (workhouses).[21] Historical sources estimate the number of homeless individuals confined in *dépôts* to be more than 230,000 over a period of twenty-two years between 1756 and 1778 with a peak of over 50,000 mendicants arrested in the course of one year in 1767. The mortality rate among those in confinement was extremely high.[22] The first vagrancy ordinance was enacted in France by François 1er in 1534. Subsequently, it appeared under sections 269 and 276 of the *Code pénal* (1810)[23] and was punishable by imprisonment for three to six months. These dispositions were officially abolished in France only in 1992.[24]

Similarly, the first vagrancy statute was passed in England in 1349, making it "a crime to give alms to any who were unemployed while being of sound body and mind."[25] The wording of the statute clearly states that those who "live[d] of begging" did refuse to work and were "giving themselves to idleness and vice, and sometimes to theft and other abominations,"[26] reinforcing the loose associations between homelessness, laziness, and criminality. Yet, for sociologist William Chambliss, there is a close connection between the adoption of the first vagrancy statutes in England and social and economic circumstances of the time. According to Chambliss, there is little doubt that they were enacted for the purpose of "[forcing] laborers (whether personally free or unfree) to accept employment at a low wage in order to insure [landowners] an adequate supply of labour at a price [they] could afford to pay"[27] — this at a time when the Black Death had killed mil-

20 Julien Damon, "Cinq variables historiques caractéristiques de la prise en charge des SDF" (2003) 27:1 Déviance et société 25 at 27; Robert Castel, *Les métamorphoses de la question sociale : une chronique du salariat* (Paris: Gallimard, 1999).

21 David Johnston, *A General, Medical and Statistical History of the Present Condition of Public Charity in France* (Edinburgh: Oliver & Bond, 1829) at 469, online: Open Library http://archive.org/stream/ageneralmedicaloojohngoog#page/n6/mode/2up.

22 *Ibid.*

23 *Code pénal*, arts 269 and 276.

24 *Loi no 92-1336 du 16 décembre 1992*, JO, 23 décembre 1992, 17568. See also Julien Damon, "La prise en charge des vagabonds, des mendiants et des clochards. Le tournant récent de l'histoire" (2007) 43 Revue de droit sanitaire et social 933.

25 William Chambliss, "A Sociological Analysis of the Law of Vagrancy" (1964) 12:1 Social Problems 67 at 68 [Chambliss, "A Sociological Analysis"].

26 35 Ed 1 c 1, cited in Chambliss, "A Sociological Analysis," *ibid* at 68.

27 *Ibid* at 69.

lions of labourers and when landowners were ruined by the price paid for various wars and crusades.

With the abolition of feudalism in England and the subsequent transition to a market economy, vagrancy statutes shifted their focus from labourers to criminals who, "to the great terror of her majesty's *true* subjects,"[28] were attacking merchants transporting goods on the roads or anyone who was likely to engage in criminal activity.[29] In 1824, the United Kingdom adopted *An Act for the Punishment of Idle and Disorderly Persons, and Rogues and Vagabonds*, providing for the commitment of any person wandering in any public place who begged while "being able wholly or in part to maintain himself or herself, or his or her Family, by Work or by other Means, and wilfully refusing or neglecting to do so."[30] Again, references to idleness and disorder as well as explicit distinctions drawn between vagrants and her majesty's "true subjects" have the effect of downplaying the importance of social structures and economic changes, suggesting that homeless people were lazy or morally inferior individuals unworthy of respect or dignity.

The first *Vagrancy Act* was adopted in Canada in 1869, modelled upon English legislation.[31] It was replaced by the Canadian *Criminal Code* in

---

28 *Ibid* at 74, quoting 14 Ed c 17 (1571).

29 *Ibid.* Chambliss's class-based analysis was challenged by some historians who argued that vagrancy statutes evolved throughout history as a response to different concerns unrelated to specific forms of economic organization: from paupers coming from the countryside to the cities, carrying diseases and overburdening poverty-relief aid mechanisms in the city in the sixteenth century, to prostitutes and other wanderers who threatened small-town morality in the nineteenth century, to a catch-all category for any undesirable people in twentieth-century North America: Jeffrey S Alder, "A Historical Analysis of the Law of Vagrancy" (1989) 27 Criminology 209 at 213–16; Paul A Slack, "Vagrants and Vagrancy in England, 1598–1664" (1974) 27 Economic History Review 360. In our view, this historical research adds to Chambliss's analysis but does not discredit it. See also JM Beattie, *Crime and the Courts in England 1660-1800* (Princeton: Princeton University Press, 1986), who suggests that houses of correction were first established in England "to punish and to attempt to reform the able bodied poor who refused to work" (*ibid* at 492). According to Beattie, the detainees held in houses of correction included "the vagrant and disreputable poor, prostitutes, and street urchins, those who refused to work ('wanting more wages than the law allows'), servants and apprentices who disobeyed their masters and unmarried mothers" (*ibid* at 493).

30 *An Act for the Punishment of Idle and Disorderly Persons, and Rogues and Vagabonds*, 1824 (UK), 5 Geo IV, c 83, s 3.

31 Prashan Ranasinghe, "Reconceptualizing Vagrancy and Reconstructing the Vagrant: A Socio-legal Analysis of Criminal Law Reform in Canada, 1953–1972" (2010) 48 Osgoode Hall LJ 55 at 62 [Ranasinghe, "Reconceptualizing Vagrancy"].

1892.[32] Section 207 of the *Criminal Code* created a list of twelve enumerated offences falling within the vagrancy section of the Code and aiming to address a multitude of social problems ranging from labour ("not having any visible means of maintaining himself," "being able to work and refusing to do so," "begging" while not being a "deserving object of charity"), morality ("indecent exhibition," "being a common prostitute," keeping or frequenting a "common bawdy-house," "living off the avails of prostitution"), mischief (breaking windows, roads, walls, or gardens), and other common nuisances ("loitering," causing disturbance while being drunk, "disturbing the peace" by discharging firearms, or rioting). A person convicted of one of these various offences was labelled a "loose, idle, disorderly person or vagrant" within the wording of section 207.[33] According to Ranasinghe, the eclecticism of these offences shows the three different ways in which the vagrant was perceived in nineteenth-century Canada. First, vagrants were thought to be "indolent, lazy and worthless" individuals who did not want to work. Second, they were seen to be "professional" or "habitual criminals," as in the case of prostitutes or tramps, likely to engage in more serious criminality if provided the right opportunity. Lastly, they were considered "morally depraved" or "outcasts," belonging to a "self-perpetuating class of citizens who lived without fixed abode."[34] Furthermore, many of the vagrancy offences listed in section 207 were interpreted by the courts as not applying to "persons of good character" or "respectable citizens,"[35] thereby demonstrating the discriminatory nature of such provisions.[36] These vagrancy provisions remained virtually unchanged until the 1950s, when five offences listed in section 207 of the *Criminal Code*, including offences related to causing disturbance, public

---

32 *Criminal Code*, SC 1892 (55–56 Vict), c 29, ss 207 & 208.

33 Section 207 read as follows: "Everyone is a loose, idle, or disorderly person or vagrant who . . . ."

34 Ranasinghe, "Reconceptualizing Vagrancy," above note 31 at 60–61. See also David Bright, "Loafers Are Not Going to Subsist upon Public Credulence: Vagrancy and the Law in Calgary, 1900–14" (1995) 36 Labour 37 at 41–42. Bright argues that while North American studies have largely emphasized the fact that vagrancy provisions were used by the ruling class to control the lower classes, Canadian studies have rather insisted on promoting respect for values of order and respectability, concealing evident class interests.

35 Ranasinghe, "Reconceptualizing Vagrancy," above note 31 at 74 n87 (referring to *R v Kneeland* (1903), 6 CCC 81 at 87 (Qc KB) and *R v Law* (1924), 42 CCC 123 at 124 (Winnipeg Police Ct)).

36 Jean-Marie Fecteau, *La liberté du pauvre. Crime et pauvreté au XIXe siècle québécois* (Montreal: VLB, 2004); Marcela Aranguiz, *Vagabonds et sans abris à Montréal : perception et prise en charge de l'errance, 1840–1925* (Montréal: RCHTQ, 2000) [Aranguiz].

nuisance, and mischief, were removed and relocated to different sections of the Code, while the other offences were significantly revised.[37]

Section 179 of the current *Criminal Code* still provides that everyone who "(a) supports himself in whole or in part by gaming or crime and has no lawful profession or calling by which to maintain himself" or "(b) having at any time been convicted of an offence under [specific sexual offences involving children], is found loitering in or near a school ground, playground, public park or bathing area"[38] commits vagrancy.[39]

Throughout the Middle Ages and into the contemporary era, homeless people were stereotyped as lazy or morally depraved, or as criminals who were unwilling to work and intentionally chose to remain in such a precarious social condition. Homelessness was explained and addressed as an individual moral failure rather than in relation to its structural causes, so that the victims of economic changes leading to displacement or unemployment were blamed for their predicament, suspected of being a threat to society and likely to engage in serious criminality. As the Supreme Court of Canada acknowledged in *Heywood*,[40] legislative responses to homelessness created "status" offences, related to personal characteristics rather than to prohibited actions. In this respect, Cory J wrote:

> Historically, the essence of the offence of vagrancy was that of *being* a loose, idle or disorderly person or vagrant, rather than the *doing* of any of the specific acts referred to in the vagrancy provisions. In the 1953–54 *Criminal Code* (SC 1953–54, c 51) the vagrancy provisions were restructured so that the focus shifted from being a vagrant to doing the acts prohibited by the section. However, it is significant that the acts prohibited were still primarily related to the status of the accused rather than the nature of the acts themselves.[41]

3) Modern Patterns of Penalization, Social Profiling, and Discrimination against Homeless People

Anti-panhandling statutes and anti-disorder bylaws adopted in Canadian cities in the 1990s are, in many ways, modern substitutes for vagrancy laws.

37 Aranguiz, *ibid* at 67–71; *Criminal Code*, SC 1953–54, c 51, s 164(1).

38 In *R v Heywood*, [1994] 3 SCR 761 [*Heywood*], s 179(b) was held unconstitutional and inoperative by the Supreme Court. Justice Cory, writing for the majority, held that this provision violated s 7 of the *Charter* and was not justified under s 1.

39 *Criminal Code*, RSC 1985, c C-46, s 179.

40 *Heywood*, above note 38.

41 *Ibid*.

Their renewed popularity has been largely attributed to the success and notoriety of the "broken-window" theory. According to this theory, the absence of social and legal responses to petty crime and to the first signs of disorder in a neighbourhood (a broken window, for example) may signal to potential offenders that a neighbourhood is not concerned with preserving order in its public spaces and that crime will be tolerated or accepted. Moreover, according to the theory, disorder causes law-abiding residents to leave because they no longer feel safe in their environment. Thus, informal control mechanisms are relaxed, and a spiral of urban decay and crime begins.[42]

The proponents of this theory have associated homeless individuals with broken windows or signs of disorder. They believe that homeless people are potential criminals and suggest that they should be particularly targeted by police intervention and eliminated from public spaces to prevent subsequent disorder and more serious crime in local communities. They portray homeless people who are deemed responsible for disorderly acts as "disreputable or obstreperous or unpredictable."[43] They distinguish between "regulars" and "strangers" by referring to regulars as "both 'decent folk' and some drunks and derelicts who were always there but 'knew their place,'" while adopting the view that "strangers [are], well, strangers, and viewed suspiciously, sometimes apprehensively."[44] Illustrating the clear moral overtone present in the broken-window theory, proponents suggest that these undesirable people are associated with the threat of having a "stable neighbourhood of families who care for their homes and mind each other's children" transformed into an "inhospitable and frightening jungle," inhabited by "unattached adults."[45] They further compare "respectable people" to "street people," "good citizens" to homeless people, and "good kids" to "criminals or wannabes."[46]

The proponents of broken-window theory also rely heavily on the myth of homelessness by choice, insisting that homeless people should be held responsible and repressed for their choice to live on the streets. They observe that "[c]learly, not all those designated as homeless in these [cases] are in this condition involuntarily. Yet, their choice to live on the streets is disruptive

42 James Wilson & George Kelling, "Broken Windows: The Police and Neighborhood Safety" *Atlantic Monthly* (March 1982) at 29.

43 *Ibid* at 30.

44 *Ibid*.

45 *Ibid* at 31.

46 George Kelling & Catherine Coles, *Fixing Broken Windows: Restoring Order and Reducing Crime in Our Communities* (New York: Martin Kessler Books, 1996).

to others."[47] They adopt Scheidegger's classification of people living in the streets: these individuals fall either in the category of the *have-nots*, who are genuinely poor and will, in time, move back into mainstream society; the *can-nots*, who are seriously mentally ill and/or drug addicts; or the *will-nots*, for whom living in the streets has become a lifestyle (i.e., a choice).[48]

The broken-window theory has been largely discredited in the academic literature. Scholars have demonstrated the lack of conclusive empirical evidence to support the connection between physical disorder and serious criminality or the fact that order-maintenance policing had brought about declines in crime rates.[49] Others have questioned the theory's democratic legitimacy, suggesting that the community on behalf of which policy makers claimed to act was not a homogenous body and that the policing of disorder was actually responsive to specific social, political, and economic interest groups in the neighbourhood, rather than to a general community consensus.[50] Yet others have criticized the discriminatory impact of policies adopted pursuant to the broken-window theory on the poor and racial minorities. For instance, in New York, complaints about police misconduct increased by 68 percent in the first three years of implementation of the recommended programs, and aggressive stop and frisks fell disproportionately on blacks and Hispanics in the city.[51] Finally, some scholars criticized the

---

47 *Ibid* at 66.

48 *Ibid* at 68; Kent Scheidegger, "Brief Amicus Curiae of the Criminal Justice Legal Foundation in Support of Respondents" filed on 25 October 1994 in *Tobe v City of Santa Ana*, 892 P2d 1145 (Cal 1995).

49 Bernard Harcourt, *Illusion of Order: The False Promises of Broken Windows Policing* (Cambridge: Harvard University Press, 2001) [Harcourt, *Illusion of Order*]; Bernard Harcourt & Jens Ludwig, "Broken Windows: New Evidence from New York City and a Five-City Social Experiment" (2006) 73:1 U Chicago L Rev 271; Franklin Zimring, *The Great American Crime Decline* (Oxford: Oxford University Press, 2007); John Eck & Edward Maguire, "Have Changes in Policing Reduced Violent Crime? An Assessment of the Evidence" in Alfred Blumstein & Joel Wallman, eds, *The Crime Drop in America* (Cambridge: Cambridge University Press, 2000) 207; Jock Young, *The Exclusive Society: Social Exclusion, Crime and Difference in Late Modernity* (London: SAGE, 1999).

50 Steve Herbert, *Citizens, Cops and Power* (Chicago: University of Chicago Press, 2006); William Lyons, *The Politics of Community Policing* (Ann Arbor: University of Michigan Press, 1997); Marie-Eve Sylvestre, "Policing the Homeless in Montreal: Is This Really What the Population Wants?" (2010) 20:4 Policing & Society 432.

51 Eliot Spitzer, *The New York City Police Department's "Stop & Frisk" Practices: A Report to the People of the State of New York from the Office of the Attorney General* (New York: Diane Publishing, 1999). Between January 1998 and April 1999, whites, who represent 43.3 percent of the population in New York City, accounted for 12.9 percent of all stops, whereas blacks, who represent 25.6 percent of the population, and Hispanics, who

moralistic aspects of the broken-window theory, suggesting that its proponents made strong normative judgments about what a good life should be and how people should behave in public places.[52]

Despite the raging controversy around this theory, our research has found that public officials and the police in Canada have relied, sometimes heavily, on the practices and on the stereotypes implicit in the broken-window theory (i.e., homeless people are dangerous and potential criminals; homeless people have chosen to live on the streets; and homeless people are morally inferior to other citizens), in order to justify the adoption of punitive responses to homelessness over the last two decades. As programmatic responses that addressed the causes of homelessness such as social housing, investment in health care, or employment policies have been reduced or eliminated, governments have adopted unprecedented measures based on the stigma of homelessness as a perceived moral failure and designed to make homeless people disappear from the public sphere, rendering these social and economic changes invisible.

Throughout Canada, local and provincial authorities have prohibited anti-social behaviour in public spaces, such as parks, subway stations, and sidewalks. Ontario was the first province to adopt this type of legislation with the passage of the *Safe Streets Act, 1999*.[53] British Columbia followed suit, enacting its own province-wide *Safe Streets Act* in 2004.[54] Except for two specific borough bylaws subjecting all public places and squares to curfews, and controlling the presence of dogs and other animals, the City of Montreal and the Province of Quebec did not adopt new legislation. However, local authorities and the police ranked combating anti-social behaviour among the highest concerns in the city and insisted that it should become a priority. The police worked with general, open-ended existing legislation,[55]

---

represent 23.7 percent, accounted respectively for 50.6 percent and 33.3 percent of all stops. See also Paul Eid, Johanne Magloire, & Michèle Turenne, "Profilage racial et discrimination systémique des jeunes racisés" (2011) at 30, online: Commission des droits de la personne et des droits de la jeunesse www.cdpdj.qc.ca, establishing a relation between the adoption of anti-social behaviour policies in Montreal and racial profiling.

52 Harcourt, *Illusion of Order*, above note 49; Sylvestre, "Disorder and Public Spaces," above note 11.

53 SO 1999, c 8 [*Safe Streets Act*].

54 SBC 2004, c 75.

55 Relevant legislation includes City of Montreal, bylaw, RBCM, c B-3, *By-law Concerning Noise*; City of Montreal, bylaw, RBCM, c C-10, *By-law Concerning Dog and Animal Control*; City of Montreal, bylaw, RBCM, c P-1, *By-law Concerning Peace and Order on Public Property*; City of Montreal, bylaw, RBCM, c P-12.2, *By-law Concerning Cleanliness*

while the City of Montreal and its boroughs made regulatory changes to the status of some public places, for instance by transforming them into parks in order for the police to control curfews. Significant architectural changes were also made to the public domain in order to restrict access to public spaces by homeless people. These included erecting walls and fences or adding concrete blocks around vacant lots or abandoned buildings that used to be occupied by the homeless and introducing new public furniture, such as park benches divided into three discrete sections separated by metal armrests, to prevent anyone, including the homeless, from lying down on them.[56]

All these measures have had severe effects on homeless populations and on people who use public space for activities related to their subsistence and survival. Homeless people rely on public spaces, from the moment the shelter requires them to leave in the morning, to the first lineup in front of the community health clinic, food bank, or soup kitchen, to the employment centre or a community organization to get social support, and then back to the final lineup in front of the shelter in the evening. By definition, homeless people are always on the move and always exposed — hence the French word *itinérant*. Their lack of access to private space means that homeless people are forced to meet their most basic needs in public spaces.[57] They are highly dependent on being able to use such spaces, yet at the same time are vulnerable to discriminatory treatment in them.[58]

In a research project on the penalization of homelessness in Canada, we collected data on the number of tickets issued against homeless people for violations related to their use and occupation of public spaces in the last decade in eight Canadian cities, including Vancouver, Winnipeg, Toronto, Ottawa, Gatineau, Montreal, Quebec City, and Halifax.[59] The results provide significant insights on the repressive practices to which homeless people are still subject in Canada, as well as on the patterns of discrimination and social profiling.

---

and Protection of Public Property and Street Furniture; City of Montreal, bylaw, RBCM, c P-3, *By-law Concerning Parks*; City of Montreal, bylaw, RBCM, R-036, *By-law Prescribing Standards of Safety and Conduct to Be Observed by Passengers in the Rolling Stock and Immovables Operated by or for the Société de transport de Montréal*; *Highway Safety Code*, RSQ c C-24.2, ss 444–453.1 and 505.

56 Sylvestre, "Disorder and Public Spaces," above note 11; Service de police de la Ville de Montréal, "Optimization of the Neighborhood Police" (2003).

57 Danielle Laberge & Shirley Roy, "Pour être, il faut être quelque part : la domiciliation comme condition d'accès à l'espace public" (2001) 33 Sociologie et sociétés 115.

58 Hermer & Mosher, *Disorderly People*, above note 2.

59 Sylvestre et al, "Occupation des espaces publics," above note 2.

First, since the adoption of provincial statutes such as the Ontario *Safe Streets Act*[60] or the implementation of policies against anti-social behaviour, there has been a consistent increase in the number of tickets issued against homeless people. For instance, in Toronto, certificates of offences[61] were nine times more frequent in 2006 (6,356 certificates) than they were in 2000 (710 certificates), with an overall increase of 800 percent and with the total number of certificates reaching 16,860 in a period of six years.[62] In Ottawa, certificates of offences were fifteen times more frequent in 2006 (1,527 certificates) than in 2000 (103 certificates), with a total increase of 1,400 percent and a total number of certificates reaching 4,882 in the six years after Ontario's *Safe Street Act* came into force.[63] This finding is echoed by O'Grady et al, who showed that the number of tickets issued to homeless youth had been increasing exponentially over the past decade (2000–10).[64] In British Columbia, 1,370 tickets were issued between 2005 and 2008; 91.7 percent of these were issued within the Metro Vancouver area. The number of tickets has increased six-fold since BC's *Safe Streets Act*[65] came into force in 2005, amounting to an increase of 543 percent over that period.[66] In Montreal, between 1 April 1994 and 31 December 2010, the police issued 64,491 statements of offence to 8,252 homeless people for violations of municipal bylaws or Montreal Transportation Society (STM) regulations. Almost half of those statements (30,551) were issued between 1 January 2006 and 31 December 2010. As a result, there were 6.5 times more tickets issued in 2010 (6,562 statements) than in 1994 (1,035 statements).[67]

In all the above-named cities, including Montreal, these numbers are only the tip of the iceberg since they only include individuals who, at the

---

60 Above note 53.

61 *Provincial Offences Act*, RSO 1990, c P.33, s 3. According to this statute, proceedings may be commenced by filing a "certificate of offence" or a "Provincial Office Notice" in addition to laying an information.

62 Chesnay, Bellot, & Sylvestre, "Taming the Homeless," above note 2.

63 Sylvestre et al, "Occupation des espaces publics," above note 2 at 544.

64 Bill O'Grady, Stephen Gaetz, & Kristi Buccieri, "Can I See Your ID? The Policing of Youth Homelessness in Toronto" (2011), online: The Homeless Hub www.homelesshub.ca. The authors showed that the number of tickets has been exponentially increasing for the past decade (2000–10) in the case of homeless youth.

65 Above note 54.

66 Chesnay, Bellot, & Sylvestre, "Taming the Homeless," above note 2.

67 Céline Bellot & Marie-Eve Sylvestre, "La judiciarisation des personnes itinérantes à Montréal : 15 années de recherche, faits et enjeux" (22 February 2012), online: The Homeless Hub www.homelesshub.ca [Bellot & Sylvestre, "La judiciarisation des personnes itinérantes"].

time of the issuance, gave their address as one of the organizations or shelters working with street youth or the homeless population in the city. Moreover, homeless individuals are also charged with infractions to provincial legislation. For instance, in Ontario, tickets are also routinely issued under the *Highway Traffic Act*,[68] the *Liquor Licence Act*,[69] the *Environmental Protection Act*,[70] and the *Trespass to Property Act*,[71] as well as under municipal bylaws. These non-*Safe Streets Act* infractions are not included in our statistics.

Secondly, in every Canadian city, homeless people are sanctioned either for resorting to street survival strategies (such as practising squeegee or panhandling) or for merely being in public spaces, rather than being punished for causing any particular harm or presenting a specific threat to personal integrity or security. In Ontario, Quebec, and British Columbia, the most common offences for which homeless people are charged include "soliciting a person in a stopped, standing or parked vehicle" (these tickets represent 47.6 percent of the total of tickets issued in Toronto and Ottawa); "soliciting a captive audience — using or waiting to use an automated teller machine, a phone booth, public washroom, bus stop, parking lot"; "soliciting someone who is in a vehicle" (these tickets represent 71 percent of the total of tickets issued in Vancouver);[72] or "public drunkenness" or "public consumption of alcohol" (these tickets represent 61 and 37 percent of all tickets issued pursuant to Montreal and Quebec City bylaws respectively).[73]

Our studies have also found that these repressive measures have had an impact on homeless individuals of all ages. For instance, in Montreal, between 1994 and 2004, 31 percent of statements of offence were issued against individuals below the age of thirty; 36 percent against homeless people between thirty and forty-four years of age; and 33 percent against individuals above forty-five years old. Women received approximately 8 percent of all statements issued during that period, while 92 percent were issued to men.[74] Generally speaking, the more unstable and visible homeless people

---

68 RSO 1990, c H.8.

69 RSO 1990, c L.19.

70 RSO 1990, c E.19.

71 RSO 1990, c T.21.

72 Chesnay, Bellot, & Sylvestre, "Taming the Homeless," above note 2.

73 Bellot & Sylvestre, "La judiciarisation des personnes itinérantes," above note 67; Dominique Bernier et al, "La judiciarisation des personnes en situation d'itinérance à Québec : point de vue des acteurs socio-judiciaires et analyse du phénomène" (November 2011), online: The Homeless Hub www.homelesshub.ca/judiciarisationquebec.

74 Céline Bellot et al, "Judiciarisation et criminalisation des populations itinérantes à Montréal" (2005), online: www.rapsim.org/docs/rapport_Bellot_05_VF.pdf [Bellot et al, "Judiciarisation et criminalisation"].

are, the more likely it is that they will receive statements of offence. Nonetheless, whether individuals are younger or older, male or female, whether they are chronically, episodically, or transitionally homeless, and whether they live on the streets, in shelters, or are transitioning from friends or family housing units, they receive statements of offences simply because they occupy public spaces on a daily basis, to satisfy their most basic needs.

In 2005, the Quebec Human Rights Commission established a taskforce to examine the potentially discriminatory effect of City of Montreal bylaws on homeless people.[75] In November 2009, the commission produced a legal opinion suggesting that the over-penalization of homeless people was a direct consequence of their being targeted and socially profiled by the Montreal police.[76] The commission argued that homeless people were victims of "systemic discrimination" because discrimination ensued from a series of factors including city-wide policies, institutional statements, bylaws, policing practices, and discretion, and was not the result of an isolated factor.[77] Based on our studies, the commission estimated that homeless people had received between 30 percent and 50 percent of all statements of offences issued on the territory served by the Montreal police in 2004 and 2005. For instance, in 2004, at least 3,281 of 10,397 statements of offences were issued to homeless people (31.6 percent). Using the same methodology, we have found that between 2006 and 2010, homeless people received, on average, approximately 25 percent of all statements of offences issued by the Montreal police.[78] In contrast, the most recent estimates establish that homeless people represent between 1 to 2 percent of the population of Montreal.[79]

According to the commission, social profiling is a form of discrimination pursuant to section 10 of the Quebec *Charter of Human Rights and Freedoms*,[80] which prohibits discrimination on a number of grounds, including "social condition." Social condition has been a prohibited ground

---

75 Commission des droits de la personne et des droits de la jeunesse du Québec, "The Judicialization of the Homeless in Montreal: A Case of Social Profiling. Executive Summary of the Opinion of the Commission" (2009) at 1, online: CDPDJ www.cdpdj.qc.ca [CDPDJ, "The Judicialization of the Homeless in Montreal].

76 Christine Campbell & Paul Eid, "La judiciarisation des personnes itinérantes à Montréal : un profilage social" (2009), online: CDPDJ www.cdpdj.qc.ca [Campbell & Eid, "La judiciarisation des personnes itinérantes"].

77 *Ibid.*

78 Bellot & Sylvestre, "La judiciarisation des personnes itinérantes," above note 67.

79 Statistics Canada, *Census 2005*, cited in Campbell & Eid, "La judiciarisation des personnes itinérantes," above note 76 at 43.

80 RSQ c C-12, s 10 [Quebec *Charter*].

of discrimination under the Quebec *Charter* since its adoption in 1975. In a 1994 policy statement on social condition, the Quebec Human Rights Commission describes this ground as referring to a rank, a social position, or class attributed to someone principally because of his or her level of income, occupation, and education, having regard to the objective and subjective components of each.[81] Homelessness has been accepted by human rights tribunals, courts, and the Quebec Human Rights Commission as a form of "social condition."[82] Like racial profiling:

> [s]ocial profiling refers to any action taken by one or several persons in a position of authority with respect to a person or a group of persons, for the purposes of safety, security or public protection, that relies on social condition, whether it is real or presumed, without any reason or reasonable suspicion, with the effect of subjecting that person to differential treatment. This includes any action taken by persons in a position of authority applying a specific measure in a disproportionate manner on one segment of the population because of their social condition, real or presumed.[83]

According to the commission, social profiling is triggered by an action taken against a person based on the fact that the person appears to be a member of an identified group of people. In the case of homelessness, profiling may be based on a person's "sloppy or neglected appearance," "bad bodily odour or personal hygiene," and "used and ill-assorted clothing."[84] Social profiling can be exercised in different ways. It can be the result of a broad interpretation of bylaws in order to criminalize homeless people. For instance, the Montreal police used the general prohibition against using "street furniture for a purpose other than the one for which it is intended"[85] to ticket homeless people who are lying down on a park bench instead of sitting upright on it. It can also be the result of issuing a statement of offence for an offence that would otherwise go unchecked for the

---

81 Commission des droits de la personne et des droits de la jeunesse, *Lignes Directrices sur la Condition Sociale* (Montréal: Commission des droits de la personne et des droits de la jeunesse, 1994).

82 *Ibid* at 45.

83 Campbell & Eid, "La judiciarisation des personnes itinérantes," above note 76 at 89–96 [translated by authors].

84 *Ibid* at 89.

85 City of Montreal, revised bylaw, c P-12.2, *By-law Concerning Cleanliness and Protection of Public Property and Street Furniture*, s 20.

rest of the population, such as jaywalking or throwing a cigarette butt on the sidewalk.[86]

The evidence we collected, as well as the findings of the Quebec Human Rights Commission, is extremely relevant in light of the Canadian *Charter*'s jurisprudence on social and economic rights, because lack of empirical evidence is often used by the courts to reject discrimination claims.[87] For instance, in *R v Banks*, the Ontario Court of Appeal examined the constitutionality of section 3(2) of the Ontario *Safe Streets Act*[88] and found that it did not violate section 15 of the *Charter*. Among other things, the court held that the appellants had failed to establish, as a matter of fact, that there was selective enforcement by the police of the prohibition against soliciting in an aggressive manner while on the roadway against those who beg or squeegee.[89] In coming to this conclusion, Juriansz JA relied on the trial judge, who qualified the evidence in question as "frail."[90]

Our studies also found that authorities frequently adopt abusive, harassing behaviour towards the homeless population, such as issuing a statement of offence to someone who is sleeping or issuing multiple statements of offence for the same behaviour in a very short period of time. The Quebec Human Rights Commission came to the general conclusion that several City of Montreal bylaws had a discriminatory impact on, and that they infringed homeless people's rights to, life, security, integrity, dignity, liberty, and equal access to public spaces.[91] The commission recommended that (1) "the institutional standards and policies of the SPVM [Service de police de la ville de Montréal] be amended to remove any element that targets and stigmatizes the homeless"; (2) "the use of repressive methods by the SPVM against the homeless be based, not on a perception that their presence might be disturbing or threatening, but on neutral behavioural criteria applicable to all citizens, such as the degree of nuisance or danger created by the behaviour"; (3) "each municipality and borough, as well as the provincial government, review all the regulatory and legislative provisions that punish behaviour in public spaces to ensure that they identify

---

86 Campbell & Eid, "La judiciarisation des personnes itinérantes," above note 76 at 90–96.

87 See Martha Jackman, "Reality Checks: Presuming Innocence and Proving Guilt in *Charter* Welfare Cases" in Margot Young et al, eds, *Poverty: Rights, Social Citizenship, Legal Activism* (Vancouver: UBC Press, 2007) 23. The author provides an interesting analysis of the use of empirical evidence.

88 Above note 53.

89 *Banks*, above note 9 at para 95.

90 *Ibid.*

91 CDPDJ, "The Judicialization of the Homeless in Montreal," above note 75 at 5.

a specific nuisance and that the provision is justified"; and (4) "the State strengthens the economic and social rights set out in the Charter at the earliest opportunity to protect the rights of the most vulnerable people in society, and in particular the rights of the homeless."[92] A few days prior to the Human Rights Commission's report, the Commission of Social Affairs of the Quebec National Assembly also released the report of the Parliamentary Commission on Homelessness, recommending the eradication of the judicial records of homeless people who had been convicted of violating municipal bylaws and provincial statutes related to the occupation of public spaces.[93] In doing so, the parliamentary commission recognized the ineffectiveness of punitive strategies aiming at penalizing homeless people in Quebec.

Depending on their personal circumstances, homeless people and vulnerably housed people are a relatively powerless group of individuals in Canadian society. Their voices are largely unheard and their interests tend to be overlooked in the political process. For instance, they are not considered interested parties when cities put forward development or revitalization projects which will have significant impact on homeless communities and on the vulnerably housed, by displacing them, by raising the price of housing or property, or by increasing demands for repression and containment of homeless populations. In the words of a former Montreal city councillor, "they [homeless people] are not welcome anywhere."[94]

Similarly, community organizations and shelters that provide homeless services are not welcome in most neighbourhoods. Local neighbourhood movements informally called "Not in my Backyard" (NIMBY) have been formed in several cities, essentially advocating that while social and community groups working with homeless people should be allowed to exist and continue their activities, they should not be allowed to do so in their neighbourhood. These movements have prevented the operation, centralization, and expansion of community shelters. For instance, there was significant resistance within the community when the *Refuge des jeunes de Montreal*, a drop-in centre and shelter for homeless youth, had to move to the Montreal Gay Village in 2010. Businesses and resident associations expressed their opposition to the move, arguing that there were already too

92 *Ibid* at 5–6.

93 Commission de la santé et des services sociaux sur l'itinérance au Québec, "Itinérance : Agissons ensemble" (2009) at 20, online: Dianova www.dianova.ca.

94 Clairandrée Cauchy, "Les itinérants ne sont bienvenus nulle part, dit le conseiller Peter Yeomans" *Le Devoir* (12 May 2004).

many community organizations serving the homeless population in the area and that it would attract further criminal activity.[95]

The case of the City of Ottawa further illustrates the kinds of stigma and exclusion faced by homeless people and community shelters. In 2005, an Ottawa city councillor called for, and obtained, a moratorium on downtown homeless services. His rationale was that the concentration of social supports in the downtown area had created a ghettoizing effect and had also attracted homeless people to Ottawa. This was a point of view shared by former Mayor O'Brien, who, in 2007, stated that Ottawa was attracting the homeless "like seagulls at the dump" by offering so many services. On another occasion, Mayor O'Brien compared homeless people to pigeons, saying that if we would stop feeding them, they would stop coming.[96] These beliefs reflect general stereotypes about homeless people as inferior, irresponsible, and undesirable inhabitants who will bring about urban decay and disorder. These views are, however, not grounded in empirical evidence: this is not a chicken-and-egg situation, and shelters and community organizations choose to locate near the population they wish to serve. Moreover, if social support for the homeless population were to be stopped, homeless people would not disappear. Their situation would simply become even more critical and precarious.

Attitudes towards homeless people are informed by prejudices and stereotypes that are generally applied to poor people.[97] A recent Angus Reid survey commissioned by the Salvation Army found that, despite widespread concern about poverty as one of the most serious problems facing Canada, a disturbingly high number of respondents viewed people living in poverty as morally inferior, lazy, and responsible for their own circumstances.[98] The survey found that nearly half of all respondents agree with the notion that if poor people really want to work, they can always find a job; 43 percent agree that "a good work ethic is all you need to escape poverty"; 41 percent believe that the poor would "take advantage" of any assistance given and "do nothing"; 28 percent believe the poor have lower

95 Annabelle Nicoud, "Refuge des jeunes : un déménagement controversé" *La Presse* (8 June 2010), online: La Presse www.lapresse.ca.

96 "'Pigeons' Squawk over Mayor's Comments on Homeless" *CBC News* (25 April 2007), online: CBC www.cbc.ca.

97 Martha Jackman, "Constitutional Contact with the Disparities in the World: Poverty as a Prohibited Ground of Discrimination under the Canadian *Charter* and Human Rights Law" (1994) 2:1 Rev Const Stud 76 at 90–95.

98 Salvation Army, "Debunking Myths about Poverty in Canada" (2011), online: Salvation Army www.salvationarmy.ca.

moral values than average; and nearly a quarter believe that "people are poor because they are lazy." The results of this survey reflect the patterns of discrimination and prejudice described in expert evidence considered by Ferrier J in *R v Clarke*, in which it was found that "there is widespread prejudice against the poor and the homeless in the widely applied characterization that the poor and homeless are dishonest and irresponsible and that they are responsible for their own plight."[99]

The prevalence of discriminatory attitudes towards those who are poor or homeless has led most provinces and territories to include some form of protection from discrimination on the ground of social condition, receipt of social assistance, or source of income in their human rights legislation. The *Canadian Human Rights Act*[100] does not however include a ground of discrimination linked to social condition. In 2000, the Act was reviewed by a special panel chaired by former Supreme Court Justice Gérard LaForest at the request of the federal Minister of Justice. The panel was asked to consider whether the ground of "social condition" should be added to the Act. Relying on extensive research and consultations held across Canada, the panel stated:

> Our research papers and the submissions we received provided us with ample evidence of widespread discrimination based on characteristics related to social conditions, such as poverty, low education, homelessness and illiteracy. We believe there is a need to protect people who are poor from discrimination . . . .
>
> We believe it is essential to protect the most destitute in Canadian society against discrimination. At the very least, the addition of this ground would ensure there is a means to challenge stereotypes about the poor in the policies of private and public institutions. We feel that this ground would perform an important educational function.[101]

Nonetheless, these discriminatory attitudes towards people living in poverty still pervade the judicial system. For instance, in rejecting the appellants' section 15 *Charter* claim in *R v Banks*, Juriansz JA held that the proposed analogous ground of "the poor who beg" or "beggars"[102] referred to an activity, rather than to "an immutable or constructively immutable personal quality that [could] only be changed at a 'great personal cost'" to

99 [2003] OJ No 3883 (SCJ).

100 RSC 1985, c H-6.

101 Canadian Human Rights Act Review Panel, "Promoting Equality" at Part One, ch 17(e), online: CURA www.socialrightscura.ca.

102 *Banks*, above note 9 at para 98.

personal identity and dignity.[103] He pointed out that the appellants themselves referred to begging as a "private choice of a means of subsistence."[104]

In light of the prevailing patterns of penalization, social profiling, and discrimination outlined above, we shall now examine the question of immutability as it applies in the context of homeless people. We argue that being homeless cannot be understood merely as a question of personal choice, but rather is a social construct that is difficult to change. We conclude that the use of punitive responses to homelessness by the State aggravates the social condition of homeless individuals.

C. HOMELESSNESS AND THE QUESTION OF IMMUTABILITY AND CHOICE

Understanding homelessness as a choice is a simplistic explanation — one that does not take into consideration how human actions and conditions are socially constructed as well as embedded in social structures, constraints, and interactions.[105] Creating a dichotomy between choice and constraint is misleading, as it does not correspond to lived experience. The challenge, then, becomes to determine how such reality can be effectively translated into our existing legal categories, which tend to be unnecessarily rigid and binary.

In many ways, homeless people are ordinary individuals. They are intelligent, autonomous, and creative. They are rational and capable of elaborating sophisticated strategies. While some of them quietly suffer their fate, others struggle, resist, and fight against injustice. Many homeless people also claim responsibility for their choices, including their decision to become homeless. We could all too easily conclude that homeless people have assimilated and transformed the discourse of their domination into something of their own choosing, but, in doing so, we would be missing something fundamentally important. Choice is indeed crucial for homeless people: it gives them control over their lives, and it allows for resistance against the prevailing social and economic order.

This being said, we should also realize that these affirmations of choice are systematically accompanied by a series of explanations regarding the circumstances surrounding their actual decisions. Ethnographic stud-

---

103 *Ibid* at paras 98–100.

104 *Ibid* at para 101.

105 See Marie-Eve Sylvestre, "Rethinking Criminal Responsibility for Poor Offenders: Choice, Monstrosity and the Logic of Practice" (2010) 55:4 McGill LJ 771: contains a more detailed argument.

ies are replete with stories showing the complexity of homeless people's choices: some relate having been thrown out of their families due to alcohol or drug problems, others report having voluntarily given up on entering the formal economy due to either a lack of cultural capital or skills or simply because of racism, and others admit to having decided to quit a job or a community to preserve their integrity or resist physical, sexual, or institutional violence.[106] This is of particular concern with regards to Aboriginal people who are disproportionately represented in the streets of many Canadian cities. For instance, in Montreal, around 40 percent of children coming from northern communities have been victims of some form of sexual abuse.[107] Distress is also a part of life in these communities: for example, the suicide rate in Nunavik is up to 79 deaths for every 100,000 inhabitants.[108]

Furthermore, recognizing homeless people's freedom and autonomy should not allow us to forget that homelessness and housing precariousness create constraints that have overarching effects on homeless people's options and opportunities, as well as on their immediate everyday life decisions. In his book on the working poor, David Shipler explains how pervasive socio-economic disadvantage can be:

> [E]very problem magnifies the impact of the others, and all are so tightly interlocked that one reversal can produce a chain reaction with results far distant from the original cause. A run-down apartment can exacerbate a child's asthma, which leads to a call for an ambulance, which generates a medical bill that cannot be paid, which ruins a credit record, which hikes the interest rate on an auto loan, which forces the purchase of an unreliable used car, which jeopardizes a mother's punctuality at work, which limits her promotion and earning capacity, which confines her to poor housing.[109]

Choices and options are extremely limited when one experiences homelessness. While the assumption behind criminalization and regulation of homeless people is that governments have an interest in punishing them, and thus "encouraging" them to change their characteristics, social

---

106 See, for example, Mitchell Duneier, *Sidewalk* (New York: Farrar, Straus and Giroux, 1999) [Duneier, *Sidewalk*]; Philippe Bourgois & Jeff Schonberg, *Righteous Dopefiend* (Berkeley: University of California Press, 2010).

107 Brian Myles, "Le tiers-monde au bout de la rue" *Le Devoir* (26 February 2005).

108 *Ibid.*

109 David Shipler, *The Working Poor: Invisible in America* (New York: Vintage Books, 2005) at 7.

science research indicates otherwise. Living in precarious arrangements is not the end of autonomy and agency choice, but rather the context within which personal choices are made. For example, the choice between begging, squeegeeing, selling stolen or lost goods or drugs, singing, or performing is one of limited options among a series of survival strategies. Choosing to sleep on the sidewalk often does not result only from the fact that shelters are full (although this is a stark reality in many cities). Nor is it because the people in question cannot afford to pay for a cheap hotel room for the night (most street people end up making a small sum of money every day) or because they just spend all of their money on drugs (although they may spend some of it that way). Many homeless echoed one of the following sentiments: they feel safer surrounded by friends in the streets; they feel that they can better escape from the police when they are outside; they need to save money for the winter season; they feel more comfortable using drugs in the streets since they disturb fewer people (or so they think); they avoid the risk of becoming sick while alone; they do not want to get used to sleeping in a bed because they are generally unable to afford it; they want to sleep either with their dogs or close to their personal belongings or their place of work (i.e., they need to keep their vending spot on a street), et cetera.[110]

Because of the prevalence of stereotypes and stigma applied to homeless people, the lived experience of homelessness involves far more than economic deprivation and absence of housing. While being homeless cannot be considered as central or essential to one's identity or dignity in the same way as other enumerated grounds of discrimination can,[111] in many ways it becomes an all-encompassing social identity or social label for individuals. Homelessness defines one's personhood in a way that is socially constructed and difficult to change. Virtually every part of society perceives and treats a person differently once she becomes homeless. Law enforcement officials treat homeless people as potentially dangerous, disorderly, and in need of severe regulation, and they apply measures in a discriminatory fashion, on the basis of visible signs of poverty. Politicians tend to treat homeless people as a "problem" to be kept out of a neighbourhood, by denying basic sustenance or other services, rather than as equal citizens entitled to fundamental human rights.

The broader category of homelessness defines a disadvantage that can be difficult for an individual to overcome. Street exit is a long and difficult process, which generally involves considerable movement back and forth from being homeless to being "vulnerably housed." For example, when ap-

---

110 Duneier, *Sidewalk*, above note 106 at 85–87.

111 *Corbiere*, above note 7 at para 13; *Banks*, above note 9 at para 101.

plying for a job, it is hard to justify the period of time that the individual remained unemployed because he was homeless. When applying for an apartment, the homeless person often has difficulties providing references to future landlords and is seen as an undesirable tenant.

Moreover, our research has shown that penalization or criminalization only aggravate this situation, creating further homelessness and social exclusion. In the last decades, homeless people who occupy public spaces in Canada have carried several thousands of dollars in unpaid fines. The vast majority of homeless people are rarely able to pay the fines, and because of this, they frequently end up being incarcerated. For instance, in Ontario, only 0.3 percent of all certificates of offences issued against homeless people (e.g., 51 out of 16,860 in Toronto and 14 out of 4,880 in Ottawa) were actually paid between 2000 and 2006.[112] In Montreal, of the 7,650 statements of offence that reached a complete resolution during the period of the first Bellot study (1994–2004), 72.3 percent were closed after the offender was incarcerated for default of payment of the amount due.[113] Bellot found that offenders in Montreal spent, in total, more than 70,000 days in prison for the non-payment of statements of offence between 1994 and 2004. She further predicted that pending cases would result in an additional 200,000 prison days. According to Statistics Canada, the average daily cost per inmate held in provincial custody is $143.03.[114]

The connections between homelessness and (costly) incarceration in Canada are now well documented. The likelihood of being incarcerated is high among homeless people, and the number of people who are homeless or vulnerably housed when they are arrested, jailed, or released from jail in Canada is steadily increasing. In a 2009–10 study conducted by the John Howard Society of Toronto involving 363 inmates in four provincial correctional facilities in the Toronto area, 69 percent of the respondents experienced residential instability in the two years prior to their incarceration; 24 percent had used a shelter during that period; and 23 percent were homeless (living on the street, in places unfit for habitation, in a shelter, or couch-surfing).[115] Contrary to popular belief, this is not because homeless people are more dangerous and more likely to be criminals than other citizens. In the same study, researchers found that homeless people were

---

112 Sylvestre et al, "Occupation des espaces publics," above note 2 at 550.

113 Bellot et al, "Judiciarisation et criminalisation," above note 74.

114 Laura Landry & Maire Sinha, *Adult Correctional Services in Canada 2005/2006* (Ottawa: Statistics Canada, 2008) at 24. The amount referenced does not include capital costs.

115 Amber Kellen et al, *Homeless and Jailed: Jailed and Homeless* (Toronto: John Howard Society of Toronto, 2010).

significantly less likely to have been incarcerated for a violent offence than other individuals.[116]

High incarceration rates among homeless and vulnerably housed individuals are largely explained by structural factors. First, homeless people are more visible and often targeted by law enforcement because of their occupation of public spaces and may end up incarcerated for these reasons. Second, criminalization has been one of the dominant State responses to homelessness in the last decades, and, accordingly, the number of adults with no fixed address admitted to correctional facilities has increased. Third, studies have shown that homeless people are more likely to be incarcerated for default payment of fines, as well as for being unable to offer guarantees to the criminal justice system upon arrest, but also at the sentencing stage (i.e., their incapacity to provide an address may result in temporary detention, and their incapacity to show employment can prevent the issuance of alternative sentences, such as probation or conditional sentences).[117] Finally, the number of ex-prisoners released onto the streets is very high. Thus, homelessness leads to incarceration, and incarceration, in turn, produces homelessness.

In the same John Howard Society of Toronto study, researchers found that 32.2 percent of respondents expected to be homeless upon discharge from prison. The rate of homelessness among respondents upon discharge was 22.9 percent. That rate had increased to 32.3 percent within days of discharge. Moreover, homeless respondents were more likely to need a full range of services upon discharge. Those surveyed anticipated their service needs within the next six months to include transportation (92 percent), finding affordable housing (90 percent), getting low-cost or free furniture (87 percent), finding low-cost or free clothing (82 percent), replacing identification documents (76 percent), finding low-cost or free food (74 percent), and assistance with finding a job (62 percent). Lack of availability of these services is directly related to rates of homelessness among those discharged from prisons.

Incarceration and criminalization also have long-lasting effects on homeless people, impeding their street exit process and community reintegration. In several studies, including our own, people report losing housing and child custody, as well as their jobs while in jail, increasing the propor-

---

116 This is also confirmed by our studies on the penalization of homelessness in Canada. See above note 74.

117 Danielle Laberge et al, “Le rôle de la prison dans la production de l’itinérance. Rapport de recherche soumis au Conseil québécois de la recherche sociale” (1998), online: UQÀM www.er.uqam.ca.

tion of people relying on income support programs upon discharge. While a warrant of committal will only be issued in Ontario if a Justice is satisfied that the person who has defaulted is able to pay and that the incarceration of the person would not be contrary to the public interest,[118] when a fine has been in default for at least ninety days, the provincial Ministry of the Attorney General may disclose to a consumer reporting agency the name of the defaulter, the amount of the fine, and the date the fine went into default.[119] The fact that a fine remains unpaid will thus affect a person's credit rating. So, a homeless person trying to re-establish herself would be confronted with poor credit and would be unable to get basic services, such as heat, water, or phone. Perhaps even more importantly, landlords routinely check prospective tenants' credit before renting an apartment, and debt collection on unpaid fines may compromise a tenant's ability to pay rent. In the words of an officer for the Collection Services in Ottawa "unless they sort out their unpaid fines, they won't be able to get the rest of their lives in order."[120] Similarly, in British Columbia, having these debts can potentially affect a homeless person's access to a driver's licence or a health card, since the Insurance Corporation of British Columbia, a Crown corporation in charge of collecting fines and fees relating to the BC *Safe Streets Act*,[121] is also responsible for issuing these documents.[122]

In addition to creating homelessness and impeding the street exit process, thereby making homeless people's social condition very difficult to change, punitive measures are very costly for Canadian society. A study conducted in 2006 showed that correctional facilities for adults and young offenders cost $3,720 and $7,917, respectively, on a monthly basis.[123] The monthly costs of homeless services provided by the police, health care system, and other social supports were estimated at $4,583 per capita. The cost of ensuring access to adequate housing and community-based services for homeless people is relatively small in comparison. The Emergency Homelessness Pilot Project (EHPP), initiated by the City of Toronto in 2002, provided rent supplements to former homeless occupants of Tent City and assisted them in finding and maintaining housing. The estimated total

118 *Provincial Offences Act*, above note 61, s 69(14).

119 *Ibid*, s 69.1.

120 Sylvestre et al, "Occupation des espaces publics," above note 2 at 551.

121 Above note 54.

122 Chesnay, Bellot, & Sylvestre, "Taming the Homeless," above note 2.

123 Sylvia Novac et al, *Justice and Injustice: Homelessness, Crime, Victimization and the Criminal Justice System* (Toronto: Centre for Urban & Community Studies, University of Toronto, 2006) at 23 [Novac et al, *Justice and Injustice*].

monthly cost of housing, including the housing component of social assistance, rent supplement, and community worker support, was less than $1,000 per person.[124] The monthly cost of a new social housing unit has been estimated at $1,080.[125] Another study conducted in 2011 analyzed the cost savings associated with the provision of transitional housing and supports for "homeless ex-offenders" relative to the cost of not providing such support.[126] The analysis demonstrated that better outcomes can be achieved at lower costs with transitional housing and supports in place for individuals when they are released from prison. The likelihood of re-offending decreases, and the public funding spent on prisoners is far less than the alternative of continued re-incarceration. The estimated saving was $350,000 per person when services are in place.[127]

D. CONCLUSION

Both historically and in the contemporary era, homeless people have been subject to systemic rights violations, widespread discrimination, and prejudice based on stereotypes and misconceptions. In particular, the false association between homelessness and criminality and the strongly-held beliefs that homelessness is caused by moral failures and personal choices and, therefore, that homelessness can be deterred by regulating homeless people and their use of public spaces have prevented the recognition and enforcement of homeless people's most fundamental human rights. Such ill-founded beliefs in turn supported repressive measures, from the death penalty to banishment in the Middle Ages, to confinement in workhouses and houses of correction in the eighteenth and nineteenth centuries, to the targeted surveillance, profiling, systemic issuance of tickets, and incarceration for default payment of fines of the last decades. Such stereotypes and stereotype-driven public responses do not reflect the complexity of homelessness and do not correspond to the actual circumstances or the reality of homeless people in Canada. On the contrary, these discriminatory and punitive responses simply serve to produce more homelessness by

---

124 Gloria Gallant, Joyce Brown, & Jacques Tremblay, *From Tent City to Housing: An Evaluation of the City of Toronto's Emergency Homelessness Pilot Project* (Toronto: City of Toronto, 2004).

125 Novac et al, *Justice and Injustice*, above note 123 at 23.

126 John Stapleton, Brendon Pooran, & René Doucet, *Making Toronto Safer: A Cost-Benefit Analysis of Transitional Housing Supports for Men Leaving Incarceration* (Toronto: John Howard Society of Toronto, 2011).

127 *Ibid.*

maintaining homeless people under constant surveillance in public spaces, contributing to judicial debts and incarceration and impeding homeless people's street exit processes and their participation in social and political life. Such strategies have also cost significant amounts of money that could have been saved had governments approached the problem of homelessness through more reasonable, cost-effective, and human rights affirming means.

Our analysis challenges the false beliefs and stereotypes that underlie prevailing patterns of penalization, social profiling, and discrimination against homeless people within Canadian society. We argue for a more accurate understanding of homelessness, one which encompasses precarious housing arrangements and multiple transitions from periods of homelessness to periods of being at risk of homelessness and which also accounts for dynamics of rights violations, social exclusion, poverty, and discrimination that constitute the reality of being homeless — making it a condition that is not immutable but is difficult to change. This holistic conception of homelessness, combined with a reconsideration of the various stereotypes and beliefs that surround this condition, provides the basis for recognizing homelessness as an analogous ground of discrimination under section 15 of the *Charter*. When it comes to considering enumerated and analogous grounds of discrimination, we suggest that the courts should follow an analysis of immutability that takes into consideration how personal conditions and identity are socially constructed and embedded in specific economic and political contexts as well as dynamics of power.

In that sense, our analysis highlights the importance of social rights litigation practice which argues for the recognition of human rights for homeless people as well as exposes the discriminatory underpinnings of inadequate programs and of State neglect of the interests of marginalized groups. Our analysis also points to the need for immediate legislative changes to strengthen the human rights claims of people who are homeless. For example, human rights legislation should provide enhanced protection from discrimination based on social condition and against social profiling, including at the federal level, and this should be backed up by solid legal opinions and reports issued by legal organizations. The ground-breaking work produced by the Quebec Human Rights Commission on social and racial profiling provides an example of initiatives that are called for elsewhere.

Although important and necessary, engaging in social rights litigation, combating social profiling, and making legislative changes to human rights legislation alone are not enough to end discriminatory practices and promote homeless people's rights, in particular because of important material and structural barriers to access to justice. Substantive remedies and political changes are also required at both national and local levels. Across Canada governmental responses to homelessness over the past three decades have been marked by a prevailing tendency to neglect programs addressing the social, economic, and political causes of homelessness in favour of punitive responses. As we have argued, programs and policies in this area must be informed by a holistic vision of homelessness and the reality that homelessness is deeply embedded in, and the product of, social structures and interactions rather than the result of individual failure and choice. To effectively tackle the real problems of homelessness and housing insecurity, governments must adopt national and provincial policies on homelessness dealing with income inequality, education, housing, health, employment, and access to justice and to community support and social services.[128] In order to succeed, such policies must be based on the recognition of homeless people as citizens entitled to human rights and must welcome a multiplicity of interventions and actions in order to respond to the diversity of the phenomenon.[129]

---

128 In 2012, in response to longstanding demands from Quebec civil society, the Quebec government announced the establishment of a national policy to help combat homelessness. The Minister for Social Services and Youth Protection, Véronique Hivon, held a forum on 17–18 June 2013 to discuss the preliminary platform and promised to release the policy followed by an intervention plan shortly. See online: Portail Québec http://communiques.gouv.qc.ca. The National Policy on Homelessness was finally adopted on 27 February 2014: Quebec Government, *Politique nationale de lutte à l'itinérance, Ensemble pour éviter la rue et en sortir, 2014*, online: www.msss.gouv.qc.ca/itinerance.

129 In this respect, see the critiques addressed against the adoption of an across-the-board Housing First model in Canada, online: RAPSIM www.rapsim.org.

CHAPTER 6

IMMUTABILITY HAUNTINGS

SOCIO-ECONOMIC STATUS AND WOMEN'S RIGHT TO JUST CONDITIONS OF WORK UNDER SECTION 15 OF THE *CHARTER*

KERRI A FROC*

A. INTRODUCTION

> Haunting is one way in which abusive systems of power make themselves known and their impacts felt in everyday life, especially when they are supposedly over and done with . . . or when their oppressive nature is denied . . . . What's distinctive about haunting is that it is an animated state in which a repressed or unresolved social violence is making itself known, sometimes very directly, sometimes obliquely. I used the term *haunting* to describe those singular yet repetitive instances when . . . the over-and-done with comes alive, when what's been in your blind spot comes into view . . . . The whole essence, if you can use that word, of a ghost is that it has a real presence and demands its due, your attention.[1]

Canadian feminists have been sensitive to the potential of unrecognized grounds of discrimination undermining women's right to equality by shielding government action from searching review, particularly with respect to sexual orientation.[2] However, the dwindling recognition of socio-economic

* PhD (Candidate), Faculty of Law, Queen's University, Trudeau and Vanier Scholar.

1 Avery Gordon, *Ghostly Matters: Haunting and the Sociological Imagination* (Minneapolis: University of Minnesota Press, 2008) at xvi.

2 See, for example, *Vriend v Alberta*, [1998] 1 SCR 493 [*Vriend*]. See also the Supreme Court of Canada "Factum of the Intervenor Women's Legal Education and Action Fund," online: LEAF http://leaf.ca/wordpress/wp-content/uploads/2011/01/1998-vriend.pdf: the Women's Legal Education and Action Fund (LEAF) argued that the failure of the Alberta legislature to include "sexual orientation" as a prohibited ground meant that

status as an analogous ground under section 15(1) of the *Canadian Charter of Rights and Freedoms*[3] seems to have received less sustained analysis in terms of how it might affect women's rights.[4] It is possible that this recognition was not regarded as critical to women's success in constitutional equality litigation, given instances where courts have accepted women's economic disparities as indicia of their sexual inequality.[5]

"some decision-makers have read out lesbians from the protective reach of 'sex,' or erased one element of their identity and their disadvantage to force-fit them into the single ground, sexual orientation" (*ibid* at para 30); Mary Eaton, "Patently Confused: Complex Inequality and *Canada v Mossop*" (1994) 1:2 Rev Const Stud 203.

3 Part I of the *Constitution Act, 1982*, being Schedule B to the *Canada Act 1982* (UK), 1982, c 11 [*Charter*]. Section 15(1) reads, "Every individual is equal before and under the law and has the right to the equal protection and equal benefit of the law without discrimination and, in particular, without discrimination based on race, national or ethnic origin, colour, religion, sex, age or mental or physical disability."

4 But see Martha Jackman, "Constitutional Contact with the Disparities in the World: Poverty as a Prohibited Ground of Discrimination under the Canadian *Charter* and Human Rights Law" (1994) 2:1 Rev Const Stud 76 at 110. The author discusses the lower-court decision in *Thibaudeau v MNR*, [1994] FCJ No 577 (CA), containing "the suggestion that legislation which adversely affects the poor cannot also be challenged by poor women on sex equality grounds unless they suffer some distinct gender-based harm." Citing Bruce Porter, she observes that the result is the reach of sex equality under s 15 being circumscribed "because of the complex and intersecting nature of their claims".

5 See, for example, *Moge v Moge*, [1992] 3 SCR 813: regarding the need for spousal support to take into account women's economic inequality and the feminization of poverty; *Peter v Beblow*, [1993] 1 SCR 980 [*Peter*]; *Kerr v Baranow*, 2011 SCC 10 [*Kerr*]. In both *Peter* and *Kerr*, the Court recognized the non-owning common law spouse's contribution to family property through provision of domestic services because to do otherwise "systematically devalues the contributions which women tend to make to the family economy. It has contributed to the phenomenon of the feminization of poverty . . ." (Peter, *ibid* at 993; Kerr, *ibid* at para 42). See also *Falkiner v Ontario (Minister of Community and Social Services)* (2000), 212 DLR (4th) 633 (Ont CA) [*Falkiner*], one of the few *Charter* cases taking an integrated approach to women's social and economic inequality. It concerned the discriminatory impact of "spouse in the house" regulations on single mothers wherein the Ontario Court of Appeal recognized "receipt of social assistance" as an analogous ground. In part, the court recognized this analogous ground because "the economic disadvantage suffered by social assistance recipients is only one feature of and may in part result from their historical disadvantage and vulnerability" (*ibid* at para 88). Receipt of social assistance, sex, and marital status were all considered pertinent axes of discrimination for the purposes of the *Charter* analysis.

Despite the seeming integration of economic matters into analyses of sex discrimination, the success of women's claims under the *Charter* to just working conditions has been mixed. Some initial positive decisions have been overshadowed by later decisions refusing to recognize discrimination against "women's work"[6] as sex discrimination. I will argue that *Charter* cases involving women's work have been haunted by court findings that socio-economic status is not an analogous ground of discrimination under section 15(1), relying heavily on its purported lack of "immutability."[7] That is, much like the courts' claim that living in poverty or receiving social assistance is not who poor people *are* but what they *do*, similar analytic separations have been used to deny women's claims that unjust treatment of women's work constitutes discrimination, despite the explicit proscriptions in section 15(1) and section 28 of the *Charter* against discrimination on the basis of sex and gender.[8]

---

6 Deanne K Hilfinger Messias et al, "Defining and Redefining Work: Implications for Women's Health" (1997) 11:3 Gender and Society 296. By women's work, I adopt the authors' definition, namely, "domestic work, that is, paid or unpaid housework, child care, and elder care performed in private homes . . . . Women's work also commonly refers to certain occupations and professions such as nursing, teaching, social work, and clerical work" marked by gendered occupational segregation and stratification, which are devalued due to their association with women and the related devaluation of women's unpaid labour in the home (at 298, citations omitted). Women's work could also be considered as the particular way in which women perform paid employment, in light of their role in providing care for children, spouses, and others. That is, there are gaps in their paid employment due to child-bearing and caregiving. Women also have constraints on their abilities to work during certain times during the day and week, and they work part-time as a result of these obligations.

7 The reference to "immutability" in relation to analogous grounds originally appears in the first s 15 case, *Andrews v Law Society of British Columbia*, [1989] 1 SCR 143 [*Andrews*]. Justice LaForest, dissenting in part, agreed that citizenship qualified as an analogous ground, because it was "a personal characteristic which shares many similarities with those enumerated in s. 15. The characteristic of citizenship is one typically not within the control of the individual and, in this sense, is immutable" (*ibid* at para 67).

8 Section 28 states, "Notwithstanding anything in this *Charter*, the rights and freedoms referred to in it are guaranteed equally to male and female persons." Arguably, the reference to "female persons" in s 28 includes their gender, and in any event, the Court on many occasions appears to use sex and gender interchangeably when referencing protection afforded under s 15(1). See, for example, *Benner v Canada (Secretary of State)*, [1997] 1 SCR 358; *Granovsky v Canada (Minister of Employment and Immigration)*, 2000 SCC 28 [*Granovsky*]; *Auton (Guardian ad litem of) v British Columbia (AG)*, 2004 SCC 78; *Sauvé v Canada (Chief Electoral Officer)*, 2002 SCC 68 [*Sauvé*]; *Egan v Canada*, [1995] 2 SCR 513 [*Egan*]; *Canada (AG) v Hislop*, 2007 SCC 10; *Gosselin v Quebec (AG)*, 2002 SCC

I will first outline the contours of this status/conduct dichotomy in Canadian law and the use of immutability to determine the existence of analogous grounds under section 15(1), focusing specifically on grounds related to socio-economic status. I will show that whereas the test for analogous grounds was initially sensitive to social relations of power and the need for a social and historical contextualization, the analysis eventually hardened into a status/conduct binary. Consequently, inclusion as an analogous ground was overdetermined by considerations of "immutability" and membership in a "discrete and insular" minority group. Grounds enumerated and analogous were, instead, naturalized as things that just "are" rather than as constituted by social structures that regulate the performance of identity through their coercive power. Instead, performative behaviour of legal subjects within these regimes was deemed to be extrinsic "conduct" and thus not relevant to the notion of a ground.

Second, I will show how the language of immutability and its group descriptor, "discrete and insular minorities," haunts cases concerning women's right to just conditions of work. I will show that the courts are separating what they see as negative treatment based on the immutable "status" of biological sex (as in *Brooks v Canada Safeway Ltd*,[9] *Janzen v Platy Enterprises Ltd*,[10] and *British Columbia (Public Service Employee Relations Commission) v BCGSEU*[11]) and mutable, gendered, "conduct" (such as having one's paid work influenced by unpaid caregiving responsibilities or being employed in an occupationally segregated workplace, as in *Canada (AG) v Lesiuk*[12] and *Health Services and Support — Facilities Subsector Bargaining Assn v British Columbia*[13]). By recognizing discrimination only in the former circumstance, the courts reproduced what has become the conventional analysis: denying socio-economic status as an analogous ground within

---

84 [*Gosselin*]; *Reference re Same-Sex Marriage*, 2004 SCC 79; *Lavoie v Canada*, 2002 SCC 23. The significance of the distinction between the two concepts is discussed below.

9 [1989] 1 SCR 1219 [*Brooks*].

10 [1989] 1 SCR 1252 [*Janzen*].

11 [1999] 3 SCR 3 [*Meiorin*]. *Brooks*, *Janzen*, and *Meiorin* are not *Charter* cases, but since they represent the few cases in which "adverse effects" discrimination on the basis of sex has been recognized by the Court, I believe it is important to include them in this critical analysis. Further, *Brooks*, in particular, referenced *Charter* jurisprudence, and it was evident that the Court intended the principles it enunciated to apply to the *Charter*.

12 2003 FCA 3 [*Lesiuk*], leave to appeal to SCC refused, [2003] SCCA No 94.

13 2007 SCC 27 [*BC Health Services*].

section 15(1) and depriving section 15(1) of effective application in many of the most critical areas of inequality for women.[14]

David Eng has observed that in the contemporary "colorblind age . . . race appears . . . as only ever disappearing"; it is acknowledged only to dismiss its relevance. He therefore asks, "As race disappears, how will the law ever come to see it?"[15] We might ask in our own country, which also purports to be colourblind (or "multicultural"), "tolerant" of racial, sexual,

---

14 Some of the cases concerning analogous grounds and some of the women's work cases that I will be examining have been the subject of convincing arguments by feminist theorists that the Court is employing the notion of choice to deny women's claims. That is, it has assumed that ability to exercise choice, any choice, is coextensive with equality. See, for example, Sonia Lawrence, "Harsh, Perhaps Even Misguided: Developments in *Law*, 2002" (2003) 20 Sup Ct L Rev (2d) 93; Rebecca Johnson, *Taxing Choices: The Intersection of Class, Gender, Parenthood, and the Law* (Vancouver: UBC Press, 2002); and Diana Majury, "Women are Themselves to Blame" in Fay Faraday, Margaret Denike, & Kate Stephenson, eds, *Making Equality Rights Real: Securing Substantive Equality under the Charter* (Toronto: Irwin Law, 2009) 219. They describe how the Court's decontextualized and formalistic approach to equality elides the various gendered, racial, economic, and other social constraints upon the manner in which choice is exercised and engages in blaming women for any inequality they face rather than acknowledging that true choice is only available in conditions of equality. I believe that these feminist analyses, while complementary to mine, are not exactly the same. First, "choice" as a rhetorical construct does not exclusively map onto conduct, and "no choice" onto status in the Court's framework (see Robert Leckey, "Chosen Discrimination" (2002) 18 Sup Ct L Rev (2d) 445 at 449). With respect to analogous grounds, the Supreme Court in *Corbiere v Canada (Minister of Indian and Northern Affairs)*, [1999] 2 SCR 203 [*Corbiere*], defined the concept of constructive immutability (essentially a "status" designation) as based on fundamental decisions about identity and personhood. In *Corbiere*, as it did earlier in *Miron v Trudel*, [1995] 2 SCR 418 [*Miron*], the majority recognized that choice as to the status represented by the analogous ground (Aboriginality-residence and marital status, respectively) may be constrained, but it did not go so far as to say no choice was involved, nor did it say so with respect to sexual orientation in *Egan*, above note 8. With respect to the cases I will be examining below concerning women's work, "choice" does not completely explain the outcomes. For instance, it was explicitly dismissed as an applicable analytic prism in *Brooks*, above note 9, and not considered at all, even by implication, in *BC Health Services*, *ibid.* Therefore, I see my analysis as a supplement to previous feminist constitutional work done with respect to choice, to provide some thoughts about *why* choice is such an active factor in some women's work cases (namely, that the construction of the issue as "conduct" plays a role), and in other cases it is completely disregarded or minimized.

15 David Eng, *The Feeling of Kinship: Queer Liberalism and the Racialization of Intimacy* (Durham: Duke University Press, 2010) at 33.

and religious difference,[16] and where feminism is "dead" because equal opportunity has triumphed,[17] how will the *Charter* know gender when it sees it? Therefore, in the third part of this paper, I will seek to destabilize the status/conduct dichotomy in order to permit the law to "see gender" in the context of women's work, not only theoretically but as a practical matter. How, when, and where women perform their labour, as well as how they are perceived while working, cannot be disaggregated from their gender, and both are, in fact, mutually constitutive. Recognizing this ineffable reality in *Charter* law would refocus the analysis from stultifying, decontextualized examinations of how closely a legal distinction affecting women's work maps onto sex-based differences (does it affect all women and only women?). It would instead focus on how systems of economic and gender subordination construct women performing gendered work as non-workers, aberrant workers, or "undeserving" workers and how their legal expression thus constitutes a violation of section 15 and section 28. This will necessarily require that immutability be reconsidered as a critical element in analogous grounds analyses and that socio-economic status be given its due.

B. THE STATUS/CONDUCT DICHOTOMY IN LAW

1) Analogous Grounds Generally

An often quoted passage from Professor Peter Hogg encapsulates the Manichaean separation of status, characteristics thought to be fixed (immutable) and "inherent" to individuals, from conduct, expressive and performative behaviour,[18] in identifying analogous grounds:

---

16 See Sunera Thobani, *Exalted Subjects: Studies in the Making of Race and Nation in Canada* (Toronto: University of Toronto Press, 2007) at 148. The author provides a critique of tolerance as reinscribing white supremacy.

17 "Is Feminism Dead?" *Time* (29 June 1998), online: Time www.time.com. This question is a recurring theme in the Canadian media context as well. See, for example, Karen von Hahn, "It's Official: Feminism Is Out of Style" *The Globe and Mail* (26 January 2008), online: The Globe and Mail www.theglobeandmail.com.

18 Diana Meier, "Gender Trouble in the Law: Arguments against the Use of Status/Conduct Binaries in Sexual Orientation Law" (2008) 15 Wash & Lee JCR & Soc Just 147 at 163 [Meier]: explains the correspondence between the immutable/mutable binary and status/conduct, although "[c]ourts have never really explained why they associate immutability with status and mutability with conduct. It seems as if conceptually 'conduct' denotes that which is willed and thus capable of change or proscription; 'Status' denotes that which is innate and acquired.")

> [The enumerated grounds] are not voluntarily chosen by individuals, but are an involuntary inheritance. They describe what a person is rather than what a person does. What is objectionable about using such characteristics as legislative distinctions is that consequences should normally follow *what* people do rather than what they are. It is morally wrong to impose a disadvantage on a person by reason of a characteristic that is outside the person's control.[19]

However, despite Hogg's pronouncement having a seemingly timeless and self-evident quality, this understanding of analogous grounds arose from contested judicial terrain.

Andrews v Law Society of British Columbia[20] first articulated the notion of analogous grounds as a way to limit the potentially expansive scope of section 15(1) so that it did not apply to every possible distinction made under legislation. In *Andrews*, the notion of analogous grounds was only briefly discussed, despite the fact that a non-enumerated ground was the subject of the case. Justice McIntyre, for the majority, pronounced the association of discrimination with

> . . . a distinction, whether intentional or not but based on *grounds relating to personal characteristics of the individual or group*, which has the effect of imposing burdens, obligations, or disadvantages on such individual or group not imposed on others, or which withholds or limits access to opportunities, benefits and advantages available to other members of society.[21]

In finding that citizenship is an analogous ground, he noted that "[n]on-citizens, lawfully permanent residents of Canada, are — in the words of the U.S. Supreme Court in *United States v Carolene Products Co* . . . — a good example of a 'discrete and insular minority' who come within the protection of s. 15."[22] Justice Wilson elaborated in her concurring decision that "discrete and insular minorities" are "those groups in society to whose needs and wishes elected officials have no apparent interest in attending" and, consequently "will continue to change with changing political and social circumstances."[23] This seems to allow for fluidity within the grounds of

19 *Constitutional Law of Canada, 2011 Student Edition* (Toronto: Carswell, 2011) at 55 [emphasis added].

20 *Andrews*, above note 7.

21 *Ibid* at 174 [emphasis added].

22 *Ibid* at 183.

23 *Ibid* at 152, citing JH Ely, *Democracy and Distrust: A Theory of Judicial Review* (Cambridge: Harvard University Press, 1980).

discrimination and for an inquiry into the social relations of power, both historically and in present day, as well as into the relative ability of a subordinated group to marshal the will of the legislature to effect change. In contrast, La Forest J's concurring decision describes an analogous ground "as a characteristic of personhood not alterable by conscious action and in some cases not alterable except on the basis of unacceptable costs," and, thus, a world apart from Wilson and McIntyre JJ's contextual notions of "discrete and insular minorities" that consider social condition.

This division was again present in *Egan v Canada*,[24] wherein L'Heureux-Dubé J, in dissent, rejected the notion of analogous grounds entirely. Instead, she advocated in favour of an approach that would evaluate the discriminatory impact of government action on the social vulnerability of groups, warning that in "looking at the grounds for the distinction instead of at the impact of the distinction on particular groups, we risk undertaking an analysis that is distanced and desensitized from real people's real experiences."[25] Justices Cory and Iacobucci, in dissent, pointed to the (still) flexible concept of "discrete and insular minorities" as one factor to be considered in deciding analogous grounds based on personal characteristics,[26] but LaForest J now held the pen for the majority decision. While not referring to immutability directly, he indicated that sexual orientation met the test for an analogous ground on the basis that it was a "deeply personal characteristic that is either unchangeable or changeable only at unacceptable personal

24 *Egan*, above note 8.

25 *Ibid* at 552. See also *Vriend*, above note 2 at para 186, citing *Miron*, above note 14. Justice L'Heureux-Dubé rejected the necessity of analogous grounds being based on "innate" characteristics and instead supported the "much more varied and comprehensive approach to the determination of whether a particular basis for discrimination is analogous to those grounds enumerated in s. 15(1)."

26 *Egan*, above note 8 at 601. Interestingly, these two judges took the opportunity in their analysis to reject the status/conduct distinction in the determination of analogous grounds:

> Homosexual couples as well as homosexual individuals have suffered greatly as a result of discrimination. Sexual orientation is more than simply a "status" that an individual possesses. It is something that is demonstrated in an individual's conduct by the choice of a partner. The *Charter* protects religious beliefs and religious practice as aspects of religious freedom. So, too, should it be recognized that sexual orientation encompasses aspects of "status" and "conduct" and that both should receive protection. Sexual orientation is demonstrated in a person's choice of a life partner, whether heterosexual or homosexual. It follows that a lawful relationship which flows from sexual orientation should also be protected.

costs."[27] In doing so, he cited his decision in *Canada (AG) v Ward*,[28] in which he based the analogous grounds approach on this distinction: "what one *is* against what one *does*, at a particular time."[29]

The two camps on analogous grounds faced off again in *Miron v Trudel*.[30] Justice McLachlin (as she then was), for the majority, undertook a sensitive, contextual analysis in which the assessment of marital status as an analogous ground appeared to be wrapped into the discussion as to whether the distinction engaged the purpose behind section 15(1). She found that enumerated and analogous grounds were "ready indicators of discrimination" and that they

> . . . serve as a filter to separate trivial inequities from those worthy of constitutional protection. They reflect the overarching purpose of the equality guarantee in the *Charter* — to prevent the violation of human dignity and freedom by imposing limitations, disadvantages or burdens through the stereotypical application of presumed group characteristics rather than on the basis of individual merit, capacity, or circumstance.[31]

Factors such as historical disadvantage, the group's identity as a "discrete and insular minority," distinctions made on the basis of personal characteristics, as well as immutability may all "signal an analogous ground," but McLachlin J was emphatic that none of these were necessary for such a finding. She indicated that immutability ("sometimes" associated with analogous grounds) was present only in an "attenuated" form in relation to the accepted analogous ground of marital status, noting that the "law; the reluctance of one's partner to marry; financial, religious or social constraints" may pose limitations.[32] She also sounded a warning against a discrimination analysis overdetermined by biological status: "if we are not to undermine the promise of equality in s. 15(1) of the *Charter*, we must go beyond biological differences and examine the impact of the impugned distinction in

---

27 *Ibid* at 528.

28 [1993] 2 SCR 689 [*Ward*]. See also Nicole LaViolette, "The Immutable Refugees: Sexual Orientation in *Canada (AG) v Ward*" (1997) 55 UT Fac L Rev 1, an excellent article concerning *Ward*, challenging the appropriateness of immutability determining a refugee's membership in a particular social group. In making this argument, the author relies in part on the lack of consensus about immutability in the Supreme Court s 15(1) *Charter* jurisprudence.

29 *Ward*, *ibid* at 738–39.

30 *Miron*, above note 14.

31 *Ibid* at paras 51–52.

32 *Ibid* at paras 186–73.

its social and economic context . . . ."[33] Nevertheless, Gonthier J, in dissent, advocated for an analysis of analogous grounds that was more discrete and focused on the existence of "personal differences" that were irrelevant to the "fundamental values" underlying the law and "certain biological or physical realities," relying, in part, on La Forest J's decision in *Andrews*.[34]

The focus on immutability/status appeared to solidify in *Corbiere v Canada (Minister of Indian and Northern Affairs)*,[35] now the leading case on analogous grounds. The Court stated:

> It seems to us that what these grounds have in common is the fact that they often serve as the basis for stereotypical decisions made not on the basis of merit but on the basis of a personal characteristic that is immutable or changeable only at unacceptable cost to personal identity. This suggests that the thrust of identification of analogous grounds at the second stage of the *Law* analysis is to reveal grounds based on characteristics that we cannot change or that the government has no legitimate interest in expecting us to change to receive equal treatment under the law. To put it another way, s. 15 targets the denial of equal treatment on grounds that are actually immutable, like race, or constructively immutable, like religion. Other factors identified in the cases as associated with the enumerated and analogous grounds, like the fact that the decision adversely impacts on a discrete and insular minority or a group that has been historically discriminated against, may be seen to flow from the central concept of immutable or constructively immutable personal characteristics, which too often have served as illegitimate and demeaning proxies for merit-based decision making.[36]

While there is new recognition in *Corbiere* that some grounds, both enumerated and analogous, may be only "constructively immutable" (to account for enumerated grounds like religion),[37] this dicta has resulted in an analysis that is intensely focussed on inherent "personal" characteristics, rather than the treatment of groups and the way in which they are per-

---

33 *Ibid* at para 56.

34 *Ibid* at paras 14, 21, and 25.

35 *Corbiere*, above note 14.

36 *Ibid* at 13.

37 See, for example, *Multani v Commission Scolaire Marguerite-Bourgeoys*, 2006 SCC 6. The Supreme Court has largely rejected the status/conduct distinction when it comes to religion. Religious practices that adherents sincerely believe have a nexus with their religion are protected under *Charter* s 2(a), with any variations in practices between adherents having no effect from a constitutional perspective.

ceived in contemporary society. The new analysis also fuses together the (formerly) socially contingent notion of a "discrete and insular minority" with this static notion of immutability.[38]

2) Socio-economic Status (Not Qualifying) as an Analogous Ground

Groups seeking remedies for economic injustices achieved some early success in having grounds based on socio-economic status recognized, due in part to the more flexible notion of analogous grounds contained in the

---

38 See *Corbiere*, above note 14. Nevertheless, taken as a whole, it is arguable that the decision in *Corbiere* does not lead inexorably to such a result. The case concerned the successful claim of off-reserve band members that their lack of eligibility to vote during band council elections violated their s 15(1) right based on the analogous ground of Aboriginality-residence. The majority, in making the above-noted comments, was attempting to foreclose the possible argument that grounds could be considered analogous in some contexts and not others (thereby requiring a case-by-case determination), rather than attempting to constrain the development of new grounds. Justices McLachlin and Bastarache, for the majority, affirmed that once established, analogous grounds are a "constant marker of potential legislative discrimination" (*ibid* at para 10).

It is apparent that the majority regarded an Aboriginality-residence as, essentially, a status-based designation, stating that "the distinction goes to a personal characteristic essential to a band member's personal identity, which is no less constructively immutable than religion or citizenship. Off-reserve Aboriginal band members can change their status to on-reserve band members only at great cost, if at all" (*ibid* at para 14). However, elements of their discrimination analysis suggest possibilities for a more nuanced approach to analogous grounds that need not rigidly adhere to a status-based, immutability standard. First, they were unconcerned about the fact that the claimant group's identity was shaped through conduct in leaving the reserve. They recognized these acts could have been seemingly voluntary or impelled by a combination of social and economic forces, as well as the discriminatory provisions of the *Indian Act* (now repealed) that stripped Aboriginal women of their status for marrying non-status men and expelled them from reserves (*ibid* at para 19). These forces also affected those currently living on reserve, who themselves may have been in the claimant group at another point in their lives. As well, McLachlin and Bastarache JJ appeared to accept that Aboriginal cultural identity, whether an individual is on reserve or not, is performative in that it is maintained through a connection with ancestral lands grounded in "associated ritual, ceremony and traditions, as well as [through contact with] the people who remain there, the sense of belonging, the bond to an ancestral community, and the accessibility of family, community and elders" (*ibid* at para 17, citing the Royal Commission on Aboriginal Peoples, *Report of the Royal Commission on Aboriginal Peoples*, vol 4 (Ottawa: The Commission, 1996) at 521.

Supreme Court's earlier dicta regarding "discrete and insular minorities."[39] However, the hardening of the test of analogous grounds into one focusing exclusively on inherent "personal" characteristics[40] began to move impoverished groups out of constitutional protection.[41]

In *Dunmore v Ontario (AG)*,[42] the Ontario Court (General Division) found that "agricultural workers" who are "poorly paid, face difficult working conditions, have low levels of skill and education, low status and limited

---

39 *Federated Anti-Poverty Groups of British Columbia v British Columbia (AG)* (1991), 70 BCLR (2d) 325 (SC): receipt of public assistance; *Schaff v Canada*, [1993] TCJ No 389 at para 52: poverty; *Dartmouth/Halifax County Regional Housing Authority v Sparks* (1993), 101 DLR (4th) 224 (NSCA) [*Sparks*]: public housing tenants; *R v Rehberg* (1994), 127 NSR (2d) 331 (SC): sex and poverty as an analogous ground "in this instance." Compare *Falkiner*, above note 5 at para 89, wherein receipt of social assistance was recognized as an analogous ground based on what the court viewed as the "expansive and flexible concept of immutability" in *Corbiere*, above note 14, *Granovsky*, above note 8, and *Andrews*, above note 7.

40 See also *Sauvé*, above note 8 at paras 195 and 202. The dissenting judges found that prisoners do not constitute a group protected by an enumerated or analogous ground (the majority declined to pronounce on s 15(1)):

> The status of being a prisoner is brought about by the past commission of serious criminal offences, *acts* committed by the individual himself or herself. The unifying group characteristic is past criminal behaviour . . . . Beyond this, I find any analysis of adverse impact or effect discrimination seems parasitic on finding that prisoner status constitutes an analogous ground, since the adverse effect or impact is allegedly upon Aboriginal prisoners; it is the prisoner status which is alleged to result in the disadvantage, something which is not furthered within the category of Aboriginal prisoner status. [Emphasis in the original.]

41 Outside the context of socio-economic claims, the Court has recognized that there may be some flexibility in the immutability requirement. See *Granovsky*, above note 8 at para 27. The Court acknowledged, referring to temporary disabilities, that not all enumerated grounds are immutable in all circumstances.

42 (1997), 155 DLR (4th) 193 (Ont Ct Gen Div) [*Dunmore* Gen Div], aff'd (1999), 182 DLR (4th) 471 (Ont CA) [*Dunmore* CA], rev'd (*sub nom Dunmore v Ontario*) 2001 SCC 94 [*Dunmore* SCC]. In light of its finding of a s 2(d) *Charter* violation, the majority of the Supreme Court did not find it necessary to entertain the s 15(1) argument and specifically did not adjudicate upon whether "occupational groups" constitute an analogous ground. Justice L'Heureux-Dubé, concurring, supported their inclusion based on the more flexible "discrete and insular minority" assessment that was seemingly discarded by the Court in *Corbiere*, above note 14 at para 166. See also *Guzman v Canada (Minister of Citizenship and Immigration)*, 2006 FC 1134, appeal dismissed as moot 2007 FCA 358, leave to appeal to the SCC refused, [2008] SCCA No 4; *Bailey v Canada*, 2005 FCA 25: indicating that receipt of social assistance and (low) income level, respectively, are not sufficiently immutable to be considered analogous grounds.

employment mobility" did not constitute an analogous ground, in relation to a section 15(1) challenge to legislation excluding them from collective bargaining rights. Justice Sharpe stated, "[T]he evidence before me indicates that agricultural workers are a disparate and heterogeneous group. There is nothing in the evidence to indicate that they are identified as a group by any personal trait or characteristic *other than that they work in the agricultural sector.*"[43]

The case of *R v Banks* relies more explicitly on the sentiment expressed by Professor Hogg regarding the status/conduct binary.[44] This case involves the constitutionality of a provincial "squeegee law" banning solicitation of people on a roadway. The Ontario Court of Appeal refused to find those who beg as a result of extreme poverty ("beggars") as an analogous ground, citing Hogg's passage. The court indicated that while it would not go so far as to find that an "activity could *never* be used to identify a prohibited ground of discrimination," here the activity of begging was not sufficiently immutable or constructively immutable.[45] Even the poor themselves were caught on the horns of the mutable/immutable dichotomy — the court said, "[w]hile it is common to speak of the 'poor' collectively, the group is, in actuality, the statistical aggregation of all individuals who are economically disadvantaged at the time for any reason."[46] In other words, the poor are not the poor; they are individuals who find themselves with no money — an extreme example of inequality becoming so embedded in a subordinated identity that it is rendered invisible.[47]

By way of contrast, see *Pratten v British Columbia (AG)*, 2011 BCSC 656, rev'd 2012 BCCA 480, demonstrating the extent to which s 15(1) socio-economic jurisprudence relies on the immutable (status)/mutable (conduct) distinction to deny claims rather than the results being attributable to findings that the claimants' personal characteristics were too diffuse amongst the population to constitute a "discrete and insular minority." This case was brought by an individual conceived by sperm donation, claiming that the destruction of relevant records regarding the donation was a violation of s 15(1), as compared to adoptees who were entitled to similar records. The court recognized "manner of conception" as an analogous ground, and this was conceded by the Attorney General on appeal. It is difficult to imagine a group that is more diffuse than those conceived by sperm donation.

43 *Dunmore* Gen Div, *ibid* at 216 & 217 [emphasis added].

44 2007 ONCA 19.

45 *Ibid* at para 99 [emphasis added].

46 *Ibid* at para 104.

47 Marcia Rioux, "Towards a Concept of Equality of Well-Being" (1994) 7 Can JL & Juris 127 at 131. The author discusses this phenomenon with respect to persons with intellectual disabilities:

This effort to disappear the poor within section 15(1) analysis continued in *Boulter v Nova Scotia Power Corporation*,[48] deciding the issue of whether power rates that failed to take into account income levels were discriminatory. There, the Nova Scotia Court of Appeal distinguished earlier cases regarding socio-economic status on the basis that they were decided before *Corbiere* and that as a result of that case, it was evident that poverty did not meet the test for immutability or "constructive immutability." Poverty might be a "clinging web, but financial circumstances may change, and individuals may enter and leave poverty or gain and lose resources. Economic status is not an indelible trait like race, national or ethnic origin, color, gender or age. As to the second test . . . [e]conomic status, poverty or wealth, is not an adopted emblem of identity like religion, citizenship or marital status, that the individual observes peacefully free of government meddling."[49]

The reasoning of the court is conduct-based — entering and leaving poverty and losing resources are all seen as mutable conduct. The "web" of poverty appears as a neutral backdrop, rather than representing ongoing conditions of domination and oppression. Following the court's reasoning, for poverty to be considered a constructively immutable ground, it must not be something from which one struggles to free oneself or endures but must be a status that the claimant feels is an "emblem" of identity, implying some sort of visibility and perhaps pride.[50] With respect to the alternate grounds of adverse-effect discrimination on the basis of sex, race, national or ethnic origin, age, disability, or marital status, the court found that the claimant groups and any comparator groups all had "substantial numbers of persons whose power costs add to their unwieldy burden of living expenses."[51] Cit-

---

> When the source of inequality is located in the individual in this way, there is a ready rationale for social inequality and limiting social entitlement. The political and social strategies of such technocratic rationality are then presented as value free . . . and [reinforced] with the principle of "desert," measured by economic and social self-sufficiency and independence, [therefore,] it is possible to formalize inequitable social relations while still maintaining that distributive justice is being upheld and the principle of equality being met.

48 2009 NSCA 17 [*Boulter*].

49 *Ibid* at para 42.

50 See also *Sahyoun (Committee of) v Ho*, 2011 BCSC 567, citing *Boulter*, above note 48. The court found that the requirement of a lawyer to act for a litigation guardian does not violate s 15 of the *Charter*, because poverty is not an analogous ground.

51 *Boulter, ibid* at para 83. Given that the poor are being compared to the poor here, it seems that the court is content to "cancel out" poverty and remove it from the analysis, unlike the earlier case of *Falkiner*, above note 5, in which the court considered both

ing the section 15(1) reasons from *BC Health Services*[52] (discussed below), the court found that there was no adverse effects discrimination on the basis of any enumerated ground.[53]

Most recently, the fused immutability/"discrete and insular minority" criteria was used by the Federal Court of Appeal in *Toussaint v Canada (Citizenship and Immigration)*,[54] to deny a claim that fee waivers for humanitarian and compassionate grounds applications made by poor immigration applicants were required under section 15(1). While the existence of a legislative mechanism for such a claim was found as a matter of statutory interpretation, Sharlow JA denied the *Charter* claim. She stated, "a person's financial condition is not an immutable personal characteristic. People who are poor or who are in need of social assistance are not a discrete and insular group defined by a common or shared personal characteristic."[55] Following this decision, the legislation interpreted as permitting consideration of a fee waiver was subsequently repealed by the federal government.

---

sex and poverty (as an analogous ground) in deciding that the legislation in question discriminated against single mothers on social assistance. See also *PD v British Columbia*, 2010 BCSC 290, further evidence of the courts' hardening their approach towards poverty, in the context of an application to require the government to fund legal aid in a family law case. The claimant attempted to claim s 15(1) discrimination on the basis of sex and poverty as a combined ground, but the attempt to combine grounds in this way was found to be "novel" and not accepted.

52 *BC Health Services*, above note 13.

53 See also *Arias v Canada (Minister of Citizenship and Immigration)*, [1994] FCJ No 1948 (TD), citing Hogg's theory of immutability, then contained in *Constitutional Law of Canada*, 3d ed (Toronto: Carswell, 1992). The court found that income is not an analogous ground in a s 15(1) claim by a single mother on social assistance denied admission into Canada pursuant to s 19(1)(b) of the *Immigration Act*, RSC 1985, c I-2. That provision excluded "persons who there are reasonable grounds to believe are or will be unable or unwilling to support themselves and those persons who are dependent on them for care and support." Justice Nadon indicated that "[t]he applicant, I must assume, deliberately decided to have four children, knowing full well that she did not have an income sufficient to meet their needs" (*ibid* at para 44). See also *Pleau v Nova Scotia (Supreme Court, Prothonotary)* (1998), 186 NSR (2d) 1 (SC), citing the theory of immutability in Peter Hogg, *Constitutional Law of Canada*, loose-leaf, vol 2, and denying a claim that court fees discriminate against indigent persons because the "[p]laintiffs are linked only by the fact they are pursuing remedies or relief in the courts" (*ibid* at para 51); and *Polewsky v Home Hardware Stores Ltd* (2003), 66 OR (3d) 600 (Div Ct), leave to appeal granted, [2004] OJ No 954 (CA), also finding poverty not to be an analogous ground in a constitutional challenge to the lack of a fee waiver for indigent parties in the Small Claims Court rules.

54 2011 FCA 146, leave to appeal to SCC refused, [2011] SCCA No 295.

55 *Ibid* at para 59.

C. SOCIO-ECONOMIC STATUS IN WOMEN'S WORK CASES

Turning now to the cases relating to women's work, it should be noted that these cases are uncommon and the *Charter*'s limitations regarding the discriminatory practices of private actors are felt acutely in this area.[56] Therefore, in my analysis, I have included human rights cases that are *Charter*-like in terms of their influence on *Charter* jurisprudence.[57] As will be shown below, in "women's work" cases where discrimination was found, the court emphasized women's biological sex as the basis for the negative treatment, despite the obvious effects of gendered social structures. In unsuccessful cases, characterization of the issue as involving women's conduct (and in some cases, choice) works to deny the operation of systemic forces that regulate the way in which their labour is performed and perceived. For instance, women's unpaid caregiving work is socially constructed as something "natural," invaluable/valueless, and beyond the purview of the law, whereas paid work is associated with what was historically done by men. This results in the devaluation of "women's work" and women who fail to conform to male patterns of work being penalized. Nevertheless, the courts have refused to see work as both "gendered" and a "gendering practice . . . constrain[ing] and enabling — i.e. construct[ing] — womanhood"[58] as it is performed and regulated within particular social and economic relations of power and inequality. Instead, it is perceived as simply what women do and/or what they choose.

1) Successful Cases Where Biology (Sex-Based Difference) Governs

Brooks v Canada Safeway Ltd[59] concerned a human rights claim challenging the exclusion of women from Safeway's accident and sickness plan based on what the Court characterized as "the mere fact of pregnancy."[60] They were not entitled to access benefits for the period surrounding the birth

---

56 Diana Majury, "The *Charter*, Equality Rights, and Women: Equivocation and Celebration" (2002) 40:4 Osgoode Hall LJ 297 at 326.

57 See the discussion, above note 11, as well as the following *Charter* cases citing *Meiorin*, above note 11: *Gosselin*, above note 8; *Nova Scotia (Workers' Compensation Board) v Martin; Nova Scotia (Workers' Compensation Board) v Laseur*, 2003 SCC 54; *Granovsky*, above note 8.

58 Dorothy Chunn & Dany Lacombe, "Introduction" in Dorothy Chunn & Dany Lacombe, eds, *Law as a Gendering Practice* (Don Mills, ON: Oxford University Press, 2000) 3 at 16: referring to law exclusively but arguably applicable to other social structures and hegemonic discourses.

59 *Brooks*, above note 9.

60 *Ibid* at para 5.

of their children.[61] This landmark decision under Manitoba's *Human Rights Act*[62] recognized that deviation from the male model worker due to physical requirements of pregnancy was not a legitimate demarcation of difference in the workplace, nor should it be considered purely a personal choice. Safeway had argued that pregnancy was a voluntary condition and that it was entitled to provide an insurance plan that was limited to accident and sickness. However, the Supreme Court of Canada found it "indisputable" that pregnancy was a valid reason to be absent from work and was of "fundamental importance" in society; therefore, equating it to voluntary medical conditions (like cosmetic surgery) was "fallacious."[63] It is a "perfectly legitimate health-related reason for not working and, as such, it should be compensated by the Safeway plan."[64] To view it otherwise would run contrary to the purpose of human rights legislation.

As the Court was able to locate the sex difference in the female body itself (the "mere fact of pregnancy"), it was easier for it to find there was discrimination, albeit acknowledging societal imperatives for women to conceive and become pregnant and the social consequences that arise from this physical difference.[65] The Court underscored that this reasoning was status-based, by its reasons overruling the *Bliss* case (finding pregnancy discrimination was not sex discrimination): "They were pregnant because of their sex. Discrimination on the basis of pregnancy is a form of sex discrimination because of the basic biological fact that only women have the capacity to become pregnant."[66] It further quoted, with approval, the appellant's factum, which stated, "The capacity for pregnancy is an immutable characteristic, or incident of gender and a central distinguishing feature between men and women."[67]

---

61 *Ibid.*

62 SM 1974, c 65.

63 *Brooks*, above note 9 at para 28.

64 *Ibid.*

65 *Ibid* at para 29:

> [i]t cannot be disputed that everyone in society benefits from procreation. The Safeway plan, however, places one of the major costs of procreation entirely upon one group in society: pregnant women. Thus in distinguishing pregnancy from all other health-related reasons for not working, the plan imposes unfair disadvantages on pregnant women. In the second part of this judgment I state that this disadvantage can be viewed as a disadvantage suffered by women generally. That argument further emphasizes how a refusal to find the Safeway plan discriminatory would undermine one of the purposes of anti-discrimination legislation.

66 *Ibid* at para 38.

67 *Ibid* at para 40.

The Supreme Court of Canada decision in *Janzen v Platy Enterprises Ltd*[68] was released the same day as *Brooks*, also applying Manitoba's human rights legislation to find that sexual harassment constitutes sex discrimination. It located distinctions made by the harasser in sex difference, indicating that

> in the present sex stratified labour market, those with the power to harass sexually will predominantly be male and those facing the greatest risk of harassment will tend to be female . . . [o]nly a woman can become pregnant; only a woman could be subject to sexual harassment by a heterosexual male . . . . That some women do not become pregnant was no defence in *Brooks*, just as it is no defence in this appeal that not all female employees at the restaurant were subject to sexual harassment. The crucial fact is that it was only female employees who ran the risk of sexual harassment.[69]

Thus, there is some recognition that social enculturation influences the environment where sexual harassment occurs, but nevertheless, the Court, again, locates the source of the discrimination in women's bodies. Sex and its manifestation, "sexual attractiveness to the heterosexual male,"[70] are immutable and, therefore, proscribed bases for differential treatment.[71]

---

68 *Janzen*, above note 10.

69 *Ibid* at para 64.

70 *Ibid* at para 60. The Court in fact associates differential treatment based on "sexual attractiveness" to gender, which is more accurate in that it relates to "discrimination aris[ing] from, belonging to or deviating from a gender stereotype." See Meier, above note 18 at 161–62. However, the distinction does not appear to be intentional. Rather, the Court appears to use sex and gender interchangeably. In fact, sexual harassment has little to do with sexual attractiveness and more to do with the vulnerabilities of the female worker (including those who do not conform to accepted gender roles relating to attractiveness) and unimpeded opportunities in the workplace for men to perform the requirements of hegemonic male masculinity (harassing to demonstrate one's difference from women, for example). See Christopher Uggen & Amy Blackstone, "Sexual Harassment as a Gendered Expression of Power" (2004) 69:1 American Sociological Review 64, and Angela Harris, "Gender, Violence, Race, and Criminal Justice" (2000) 52 Stan L Rev 777.

71 See also *Weatherall v Canada (AG)*, [1993] 2 SCR 872 [Weatherall], a s 15(1) *Charter* case relying primarily on "biological" differences between men's and women's chest areas to find that permitting cross-gender searches of male prisoners and not female prisoners was non-discriminatory; and *Campbell v Canada*, 2004 TCC 460 at para 45, rev'd on other grounds 2005 FCA 420, determining that different rules for men and women to demonstrate parenting roles in order to receive the child tax credit was discriminatory, given that, unlike *Weatherall*, the differential treatment at issue was not focussed on accommodating biological difference but upon "historical sociological patterns or custom . . . ." (*ibid* at para 45).

Similarly, in *Meiorin*, the case of the female British Columbia firefighter who suffered from discrimination due to lung capacity tests based on male physiology, the adverse-effect analysis was squarely in the realm of immutable, biological difference. In her reasons, McLachlin J made an evocative reference to the interaction of social constructions of gender with biology in discussing why the analytic distinction between adverse-effect and direct discrimination was so malleable so as to be unworkable.[72] However, the application of the test to the facts of the case was based exclusively on "scientific data" about the inaccessibility of the aerobic standard to women.[73] While *Meiorin* is a human rights case, it is now the leading case on adverse-effect discrimination in the *Charter* context. The impact of a biological status reference point for adverse-effect sex discrimination is picked up in the caselaw discussed below.[74]

---

72 *Meiorin*, above note 11 at para 42. Justice McLachlin stated generally "the practical result of the conventional analysis [which] is that the complex web of seemingly neutral, systemic barriers to traditionally male-dominated occupations remains beyond the direct reach of the law." This might be thought to extend to social barriers as well as biological ones.

73 *Ibid* at para 80. Justice McLachlin rightly refused to consider the purported negative impact on the morale of the firefighting crew of having someone who did not meet the aerobic standard as an "undue hardship." However, this was rejected only on the basis (assumption) that morale should not be affected if someone is otherwise able to perform her job safely and efficiently. There seems to be no interrogation as to how gendered standards in the workplace themselves might imbue biological difference with negative social meaning, which makes the morale argument tautological and would require a more complete critique of the impact of biological standards on the workplace. I acknowledge other feminist analyses that see *Meiorin* as presenting possibilities for a more contextualized equality analysis. See, for example, Daphne Gilbert & Diana Majury, "Critical Comparisons: The Supreme Court of Canada Dooms Section 15" (2006) 24 Windsor YB Access Just 111 at 140; Melina Buckley, "*Law v Meiorin*: Exploring the Governmental Responsibility to Promote Equality under Section 15 of the *Charter*" in Faraday, Denike, & Stephenson, eds, above note 14 at 179. However *Meiorin*'s legacy of ambivalence in relation to adverse-effect discrimination and socially constructed difference is illustrated by *Canada (AG) v Johnstone*, 2014 FCA 110 (finding, without any gender analysis, that an employer's failure to accommodate parenting responsibilities constituted family status discrimination but only to the extent these responsibilities have "immutable characteristics").

74 Disability scholars and advocates have been successful in resisting adverse effects discrimination being overdetermined by biology/physical capacity. This is reflected in Supreme Court jurisprudence, which has accepted disability as a social construction rather than inherent. Rather than focusing on "accommodation" of difference, these decisions reflect a concept of equality that is dedicated to social inclusion through transformation of dominant norms. Some of this jurisprudence cites *Meiorin* in

2) Unsuccessful Cases — Negative Distinctions against Women's Work Not Discrimination

I would like to compare the above cases to two "women's work" cases, *Lesiuk* and *BC Health Services*, in which the section 15(1) claims were denied. While the claimants in the latter were successful in their action under *Charter* section 2(d) freedom of association due to interference with collective bargaining rights, the Supreme Court nevertheless refused to consider the section 15(1) claim and negated any consideration of sex or gender. In these cases, we see the same issues that arise in the analogous grounds cases concerning socio-economic status — an anxiety about considering identity as constructed through historical as well as contemporary social relations

---

support and potentially lays the groundwork for the case to be used in a progressive way in the context of gender and social rights. See *Granovsky*, above note 8 at paras 30 and 40: "Exclusion and marginalization are generally not created by the individual with disabilities but are created by the economic and social environment and, unfortunately, by the state itself," and in relation to *Meiorin*, "[t]he 'problem' did not lie with the female applicant, but with the state's substitution of a male norm in place of what the appellant was entitled to, namely a fair-minded gender-neutral job analysis"; *British Columbia (Superintendent of Motor Vehicles) v British Columbia (Council of Human Rights)*, [1999] 3 SCR 868 at para 19, citing *Meiorin*, above note 11: "[e]mployers and others governed by human rights legislation are now required *in all cases* to accommodate the characteristics of affected groups within their standards, rather than maintaining discriminatory standards supplemented by accommodation for those who cannot meet them" [emphasis in original].

More recent cases demonstrate the continued tension between social construction of disability and a biologically based framework. In *Auton (Guardian ad litem of) v British Columbia (AG)*, 2004 SCC 78 [*Auton*], the Court rejects the lower court's finding that British Columbia discriminated against children with autism by failing to provide funding for applied behavioural therapy/intensive behavioural therapy, which the British Columbia Court of Appeal found created a "socially constructed handicap." In *Council of Canadians with Disabilities v VIA Rail Canada Inc*, 2007 SCC 15, the majority, citing *Meiorin*, above note 11, found that VIA Rail's purchase of new passenger rail cars with very limited wheelchair accessibility did not satisfactorily accommodate persons with disabilities. This was notwithstanding VIA's defence that it supplied narrow wheelchairs for use in the cars and that the accessibility of VIA services should be assessed over its entire "network," with older, more accessible cars still in operation. Justice Abella for the majority stated, "[i]t is, after all, the 'combined effect of an individual's impairment or disability and the environment constructed by society that determines whether such an individual experiences a handicap'" (*ibid* at para 181). See also *Moore v British Columbia (Education)*, 2012 SCC 61 at para 5, finding special education as the "ramp that provides access to the statutory commitment to education made to *all* children in British Columbia" [emphasis in original].

and performative activities, about taking into account power relations in the *Charter* analysis, and about populations with diffuse, invisible identity markers making economic claims.

In *Lesiuk*, the Federal Court of Appeal considered a critical challenge to systemic discrimination against women in employment insurance benefits.[75] Historically, the employment insurance system has used the male worker and his patterns of employment as the standard for determining strength of attachment to the workforce (and the resulting entitlement to benefits). It has been infused with the implicit philosophy that women worked for "pin money" (which has been reflected at times in explicitly discriminatory provisions), whereas men were breadwinners who supported families. This was moderated in the 1970s when coverage was extended to most paid workers meeting minimum hours and income requirements, and the needs of working women were acknowledged through the provision of maternity benefits.[76] Kelly Lesiuk was a part-time nurse and mother who had applied for Employment Insurance (EI) after her doctor had recommended that she not work. There had been changes to the EI program in 1996, altering the eligibility requirements from a weeks-based model (with a minimum fifteen-hour work week) to one based on annual hours, resulting in a disproportionate drop in the number of women who qualified for EI. This likely had something to do with the disproportionate number of women who made up the ranks of part-time workers (and whose reasons for part-time employment corresponded to certain gendered patterns)[77] and

75 Kerri Froc, "Commentary on *Lesiuk v Attorney General*" (Fall 2003) 22:3 Jurisfemme — Newsletter of the National Association of Women and the Law [Froc]. My discussion of *Lesiuk* is derived, in part, from this brief case comment.

76 *Reference re Employment Insurance Act (Can), ss 22 and 23*, 2005 SCC 56 at paras 19–23 [*EI Reference*]; Gillian Calder, "The Personal *Is* Economic: Unearthing the Rhetoric of Choice in the Canadian Maternity and Parental Leave Debate" in Rosemary Hunter & Sharon Cowan, eds, *Choice and Consent: Feminist Engagements in Law and Subjectivity* (New York: Routledge-Cavendish, 2007) 125 at 132–34; Leah Vosko & Lisa Clark, "Canada: Gendered Precariousness and Social Reproduction" in Leah Vosko, Martha MacDonald, & Iain Campbell, eds, *Gender and the Contours of Precarious Employment* (New York: Routledge, 2009) 26 at 35–36 [Vosko & Clark].

77 *Women in Canada: A Gender-Based Statistical Report*, 6th ed (Ottawa: Statistics Canada, 2011) [*Women in Canada*]. This report provides the links between women and part-time employment, indicating that more women than men are likely to work part-time, and 70 percent of part-time workers are women, a statistic that has remained stable over the last thirty years. Further, more women than men cite child care and other personal or family responsibilities as the reason for their part-time work (17.2 percent versus 2.3 percent, respectively). See also *Lesiuk*, above note 12, where similar contemporary evidence was before the Federal Court of Appeal.

the number of men who worked intensively on a seasonal basis.[78] The latter were, therefore, more likely to benefit from an annual hours-based system. Ms Lesiuk herself would have qualified under the old system, but failed to do so under the new system by thirty-three hours. Indeed, the EI umpire found that the new eligibility requirements constituted adverse-effect discrimination against women, "who predominate in the part-time labour force" and had much less time to devote to the paid work force due to their unpaid labour in the home,[79] valorizing male patterns of employment.

In the discrimination analysis, the Federal Court of Appeal refused to entertain the submissions of the Women's Legal Education and Action Fund (LEAF), as intervener, that all women should be compared to all men.[80] Instead, the court preferred the comparison suggested by the claimant's counsel, "women in a parental status" compared to men, which meant that the court did not have to fully consider the wealth of statistical information comparing women to men in patterns of employment and within the EI system itself. This led to a finding that there was a lack of evidentiary basis for the claim of adverse-effect discrimination, as there was little statistical information on the EI experience of mothers in particular, and therefore "the evidence show[ed] that there [was] no group which [was] uniformly adversely affected."[81] In the court's view, the evidence also showed that the group of those who lost out under the new system was "a very special, small subset" and some actually gained eligibility.[82] In essence, those who lost eligibility as a result of working insufficient hours were too diffuse to even be considered a group for the purposes of section 15(1), similar to the treatment of other socio-economic groups under the analogous grounds test.

Nevertheless, Létourneau JA, writing for the court, went on to accept (for the sake of argument?) differential treatment of the claimant and "others who share the same characteristics," based on her status as a mother.[83] He found that the joint grounds of gender and parental status were sufficient to satisfy the *Corbiere* test because the "period of immutability . . . is suffi-

---

78 Shawn de Raaf, Costa Kapsalis, & Carole Vincent, "Seasonal Work and Employment Insurance Use" (September 2003) 4:9 Perspectives on Labour and Income 5 at 10; Vosko & Clark, above note 76 at 31–32. Women's part-time employment also has certain "gendered patterns" of instability, including lower income and employment in smaller firms with less union coverage.

79 *In the Matter of a Claim by Kelly Lesiuk* (November 1998) CUB 51142 at para 64.

80 In the interests of full disclosure, I was counsel for LEAF in the case.

81 *Lesiuk*, above note 12 at para 32.

82 *Ibid.*

83 *Ibid* at para 33.

ciently long."[84] In discussing the status-based claim, the court addressed the government's contention that the umpire erred in considering women's involvement in part-time work because "employment or occupational status is not an immutable personal characteristic."[85] Justice of Appeal Létourneau characterized this reference by the umpire as merely contextualizing the "circumstances under, or the moment at, which the respondent and members of her group are discriminated,"[86] and as such, it was not an improper embellishment on the analogous grounds already accepted to formulate the claimant group (women in a parental status).

However, this finding reinforces, rather than challenges, the notion of working part-time as conduct extraneous to the equality analysis. In so doing, the court excised working part-time from the claimant's status as a working mother in its analysis as to whether the legislation violated the claimant's human dignity according to the contextual factors outlined in *Law v Canada (Minister of Employment and Immigration)*.[87] With respect to the first factor, pre-existing disadvantage, stereotyping, prejudice, or vulnerability, it quickly mentioned and then discounted the relevance of past discrimination in eligibility under the "old system" and, instead, noted that most women with young children were able to qualify under the new system. Failing to meet the required number of hours and qualify for EI due to part-time work

> . . . do[es] not create or reinforce a stereotype that women should stay home and care for children. Nor do these requirements affect the dignity of women by suggesting that their work is less worthy of recognition. Anyone who works the requisite number of hours in their qualifying period will qualify . . . . Rather, I would imagine that a reasonable person would simply feel that they had narrowly missed qualifying because of an unfortunate confluence of events.[88]

---

84 *Ibid* at para 37.

85 *Ibid* at para 35.

86 *Ibid* at para 6.

87 [1999] 1 SCR 497 [*Law*]. The four factors are (1) pre-existing disadvantage, stereotyping, prejudice, or vulnerability experienced by the individual or group at issue; (2) the correspondence, or lack thereof, between the ground or grounds on which the claim is based and the actual need, capacity, or circumstances of the claimant or others; (3) the ameliorative purpose or effects of the impugned law upon a more disadvantaged person or group in society; and (4) the nature and scope of the interest affected by the impugned law.

88 *Ibid* at para 45. Regarding developments in the *Law* framework, see Margot Young, "Unequal to the Task: 'Kapp'ing the Substantive Potential of Section 15" in Sanda

Thus, negative treatment of part-time work in the legislation was merely unfortunate, not a reflection on Lesiuk's status as a working mother. This would make sense only if part-time work itself was not connected to the claimant's *status* — if it was merely what she did rather than who she was. Negative treatment of part-time work says nothing about the claimant's dignity as a human being because this work is not inherent and can be changed simply by working more hours. This is reinforced by the court's positive references to the "flexibility" afforded to women under the new system, under the contextual factor of "correspondence" between the grounds and the "actual needs, capacity or circumstances of the claimant." Accordingly, it implied that women could simply (re)structure their work over the year to qualify.[89]

The second significant contextual factor in the analysis is the "nature and scope of the interest affected" and, in particular, whether the effects are "severe and localized."[90] This factor from *Law* draws its authority from the *Egan* decision and is meant to gauge the intensity of the infringement on the claimants' human dignity interest.[91] However, in the hands of the Federal Court of Appeal, this contextual factor creates an onus to show that the effect is "localized," in the sense that those working part-time must prove to be a "discrete and insular minority." In that regard, the court found that the group was too diffuse to have "statistical significan[ce] . . .

Rodgers & Sheila McIntyre, eds, *The Supreme Court of Canada and Social Justice: Commitment, Retrenchment or Retreat* (Markham, ON: LexisNexis Canada, 2010) 183. While the Supreme Court has recently disavowed the use of human dignity as a separate hurdle for equality claimants and the use of the contextual factors from *Law* as a legal test, the emphasis on stereotype and prejudice has arguably been strengthened, and, therefore, the reasoning from *Lesiuk* is still just as pernicious.

89 *Lesiuk*, above note 12 at 42.

90 *Law*, above note 87, citing *Egan*, above note 8, decision of L'Heureux-Dubé J.

91 Justice L'Heureux-Dubé's reasoning in *Egan*, *ibid* at 555–56, addressed this contextual factor with reference to the gravity of economic consequences resulting from the differential treatment:

> As I noted earlier, the *Charter* is not a document of economic rights and freedoms. Rather, it only protects "economic rights" when such protection is necessarily incidental to protection of the worth and dignity of the human person (i.e., necessary to the protection of a "human right"). Nonetheless, the nature, quantum, and context of an economic prejudice or denial of such a benefit are important factors in determining whether the distinction from which the differing economic consequences flow is one that is discriminatory. If all other things are equal, the more severe and localized the economic consequences on the affected group, the more likely that the distinction responsible for these consequences is discriminatory within the meaning of s 15 of the *Charter*.

the evidence does not bear witness to much localization at all. The differential treatment is as between those who work at or above the threshold requirement for hours and those who fall short of this threshold."[92] Thus, the eligibility requirement did not perpetuate inequality but was instead a neutral, "administratively necessary tool tailored to correspond to the requirements of a viable contributory insurance scheme,"[93] echoing Canada Safeway's arguments in the *Brooks* case regarding its administrative decision to compensate some health risks and not others.[94] But without a (biological) status-based argument to rely on, Kelly Lesiuk failed to achieve the same result as Susan Brooks, despite the gendered nature of her part-time work.[95]

The status/conduct distinction in the treatment of women's work perhaps reached its nadir in *BC Health Services*, addressing the constitutionality of *The Health and Social Services Delivery Improvement Act* (*Bill 29*).[96] The Bill privatized services, rolled back a number of gains that health care and social services sector workers had made in collective bargaining, and prevented their renegotiation. Members of the affected unions were disproportionately female — 85 to 98 percent depending on the union.[97] They were also disproportionately older and racialized.[98] The Supreme Court's finding under *Charter* section 2(d) was hailed as a significant victory for workers,[99] as it recognized for the first time that "substantial interference"[100] with collective bargaining constitutes a violation of freedom of association. *Bill 29* met this threshold in that many of its provisions, such as those affecting seniority rights and contracting out, were "of central importance to the unions and their ability to carry on collective bargaining," and the government, by interfering with them, "disregarded the fundamental s. 2(d) obligation to preserve the processes of good faith negotiation and consultation with unions."[101]

---

92 *Lesiuk*, above note 12 at para 50.

93 *Ibid* at para 51.

94 Froc, above note 75 at 12.

95 See also *Sollbach v Canada* (1999), 252 NR 137 (FCA); *Canada (AG) v Brown* (2001), 286 NR 395 (FCA); and *Miller v Canada (AG)* (2002), 220 DLR (4th) 149 (FCA), for similar rejections of equality claims regarding EI statutory caps on regular benefits after receipt of maternity benefits.

96 SBC 2002, c 2.

97 *BC Health Services*, above note 13 (Factum of the Appellant at para 6).

98 *Ibid* at para 7.

99 See, for example, Buzz Hargrove, "Striking a Collective Bargain: The Supreme Court Decision in *BC Health Services*" (2009) 59 UNBLJ 41.

100 *BC Health Services*, above note 13 at para 129.

101 *Ibid* at paras 132 and 134.

The appellant unions had also argued that the legislation discriminated against women, contrary to section 15(1). They argued that the provisions had the objective of turning back pay equity gains made by the unions. There was also some evidence that this sector was targeted because pay equity had resulted in higher wages for public sector employees than workers in the private sector and other jurisdictions. Thus, they maintained that the targeting of these workers as having "excessive" wages and benefits was based on the devaluation of women's work and women as workers. It sent a clear message that it was not important to respect their contractual entitlements, thereby perpetuating disadvantage and stereotyping and affecting their human dignity.[102] The Court found that the legislation did not violate section 15(1) in a few scant paragraphs, indicating that the differential, adverse effects related "essentially to the type of work they do, and not to the persons they are"[103] and were not based on stereotyping. The exact use of Hogg's terminology from his passage on analogous grounds is perhaps the clearest example of the reliance on the status/conduct distinction in relation to women's work under section 15(1).[104]

The Court's failure to recognize differential treatment of "women's work" as a sex-based distinction or even to gender its section 2(d) analysis bodes trouble for new litigation arising out of measures passed along with the budget in 2009. One of these measures was the *Public Sector Equit-*

---

102 *Ibid* (Factum of the Appellant at paras 129, 142–50, and 162–68).

103 *Ibid* at para 165.

104 Contra *Newfoundland (Treasury Board) v NAPE*, 2004 SCC 66 [*NAPE*]. In this case, the Court seems to superficially avoid the status/conduct distinction. It found that the legislative deferral of a pay equity increase and the extinguishment of arrears were discriminatory, as it could reasonably be taken by the women, already underpaid, as confirmation that their work was valued less highly than the work of those in male-dominated jobs. This "perpetuated and reinforced the idea that women could be paid less for no reason other than the fact they are women" (*ibid* at para 46). The s 1 justification of the government's decision on the basis of an economic crisis, with little evidence of either the crisis or that other options were considered (such as delaying payment of arrears rather than extinguishing them), is itself a gendered devaluation of women's work. Therefore, the potential transformative impact of this element of the constitutional analysis is extremely attenuated, and later completely eradicated by *BC Health Services* dictum. See Patricia Hughes, "*NAPE*: Women as Sacrificial Lambs" (2004) 11 CLELJ 383, examining the lack of evidence of a fiscal crisis and other options available to the Newfoundland and Labrador government, and Judy Fudge, "Conceptualizing Collective Bargaining under the *Charter*: The Enduring Problem of Substantive Equality" (2008) 42 Sup Ct L Rev (2d) 213 at 241–43 [Fudge], regarding the inconsistency between the treatment of women's work in *NAPE* and that in *BC Health Services*.

able Compensation Act,[105] which applies to federal government workers. For these workers, pay equity complaints are taken out of the *Canadian Human Rights Act*,[106] and "pay equity" is redefined from being concerned with wage discrimination to "equitable compensation" based on market forces. Thus, existing discriminatory pay structures in the private sector are included in this evaluation. "Equitable compensation" is made a matter for collective bargaining, to be negotiated along with the myriad of other collective bargaining issues. It is not treated as a matter of human rights and can be bargained away. Unions will be fined $50,000 if they assist any woman to make a complaint about inequitable compensation to the Public Service Labour Relations Board. Thus, women will be left individually to navigate the highly complex comparisons necessary to found an "equitable compensation" case without necessary data about pay rates or job descriptions.[107]

The *PSECA* is being challenged as a violation of freedom of association and equality under *Charter* sections 2(d) and 15;[108] however, the de-gendered analysis in *BC Health Services* may prove to be a difficult hurdle. It is questionable whether the impact on pay equity will be characterized as being "of central importance to the unions and their ability to carry on collective bargaining,"[109] given the historic devaluation of women's work. Indeed, the Act may be seen as enhancing the collective bargaining relationship by making pay equity an element to be negotiated. As formally applying to federal public sector workers, the section 15(1) claim would face the barrier of the reasoning of *BC Health Services*, possibly causing the legislative distinction to be characterized as based on "kind of work" rather than on sex.

D. FALLACY OF THE CONDUCT/STATUS DICHOTOMY

As I have discussed above, in adjudicating *Charter* claims concerning women's work, courts have attempted to deny the impact of social relations on identity through analyses that are overdetermined by biology, with outright rejection of claims that they perceive as based on performative conduct rather than inherent status. However, the status/conduct distinction is highly malleable and "can thus be used even when framing rights,

---

105 SC 2009, c 2, s 394 [*PSECA*].

106 RSC 1985, c H-6.

107 Public Services Alliance of Canada, "The End of Pay Equity For Women in the Federal Public Service" (February 2009), online: PSAC www.psac-afpc.com.

108 *The Professional Institute v Canada (AG)*, 2012 ONSC 4764; *Gordon et al v Canada (AG)*, Toronto CV-09-377318 (Ont SCJ).

109 *BC Health Services*, above note 13 at para 132.

to define what is at stake as proscribable conduct."[110] So, in the context of enumerated and analogous grounds, religion, for example, is considered "constructively immutable" status, and poverty/socio-economic status is considered mutable and conduct driven, despite the fact that there appears to be little empirical justification for treating religious affiliation[111] as less changeable than poverty.[112] Consequently, in the sex equality context, Kelly Lesiuk is excluded from EI benefits because she needs to spend more time at work, not because the EI system penalizes those who cannot conform to male employment patterns. Those in occupationally segregated workplaces, like health care or social services, who see their pay equity gains eroded through legislative action, have "work issues," not inequality. Decided differently, these cases would have resulted in enhanced recognition of

110 Meier, above note 18 at 156.

111 The Pew Forum on Religion in Public Life, *Faith in Flux: Changes in Religious Affiliation in the US* (Washington: Pew Research Center, 2009). In the US, this recent statistical report has shown that 44 percent of Americans will change their religious affiliation at least once in their lives, and many more than once. There do not appear to be similar statistics compiled for Canada, and there are admittedly differences in religiosity between the two countries. See David Rayside & Clyde Wilcox, "The Difference That a Border Makes: The Political Intersection of Sexuality and Religion in Canada and the United States" in David Rayside & Clyde Wilcox, eds, *Faith, Politics, and Sexual Diversity in Canada and the United States* (Vancouver: UBC Press, 2011) 3 at 11, showing that in comparing Canada to the US, there are fewer evangelical Protestants and more Catholics in Canada, half as many Canadians as Americans that consider religion as important, and church attendance is half as prevalent in Canada as in the US. However, none of these differences necessarily suggest more stability in Canadian religious affiliation over time. Arguably, diversity of religious affiliations and practices amongst residents in two closely connected countries *itself* may illuminate the mutability of religion as dependent on a whole host of social circumstances shaping one's beliefs, including the political culture of the country in which one lives, rather than an inherent status.

112 Ross Finnie & Arthur Sweetman, "Poverty Dynamics: Empirical Evidence for Canada" (2003) 36:2 Canadian Journal of Economics 291 at 316, 322, and 323, finding "[t]he always poor make up 40% of the low-income population in any given year and this rises to 75% if those poor four years out of five are also included." Further, they found that "past low-income status also has a strong predictive impact on current low-income status" and "increases substantially" with the number of years previously spent poor. Even one year spent in poverty in the past five has a dramatic effect on the likelihood that one is currently poor. See also Miles Corak, "Do Poor Children Become Poor Adults? Lessons from a Cross-Country Comparison of Generational Earnings Mobility" in John Creedy & Guyonne Kalb, eds, *Dynamics of Inequality and Poverty* (Oxford: Elsevier, 2006) 143 at 144, finding one-third of low-income Canadian children do not escape low income in adulthood.

the *Charter*'s role in remedying socio-economic injustices, a factor haunting the courts' deliberations.

As Martha McCarthy and Joanna Radbord crisply stated in relation to Canadian equality law:

> Substantive equality demands a recognition that so-called "essential biological differences," like sex and race, are socially constructed, not "natural," and are historically and culturally specific, not universal. The discourses that create "sex" are a major structural support for patriarchy and heterosexism; those that create "race" buttress racism. Accordingly, the language of "biological realities" is not descriptive, but prescriptive; it enforces relations of inequality . . . . In other words, "biological realities" are socially constructed as rationalization for the established power structure, so that what we perceive to be natural and essential differences are in fact historically and culturally rooted.[113]

Thus, within the very structure of the status/conduct dichotomy is the notion that inequality is grounded in biological and inherent differences (and the solution is to root out "irrational" responses thereto), rather than a more pervasive social process in which the very notion of difference is created and regulated by systems of subordination. It ignores decades of academic scholarship that argues that status and conduct are mutually constitutive.[114] We cannot apprehend sex difference and sexuality outside of hegemonic cultural frameworks (including patriarchy, capitalism, racism)

---

113 Martha McCarthy & Joanna Radbord, "Foundations for 15(1): Equality Rights in Canada" (1999) 6 Mich J Gender & L 261 at 280–81.

114 Douglas Kropp, "'Categorical' Failure: Canada's Equality Jurisprudence — Changing Notions of Identity and the Legal Subject" (1997) 23 Queen's LJ 201 at 203. The author makes a similar argument in the Canadian context that the enumerated and analogous grounds framework, with its focus on immutable personal characteristics, is based on an "antiquated notion of the self that is traceable to eighteenth-century 'Enlightenment' thought." He argues that a categorical analysis based on grounds relies on the fallacy of stable identity binaries to determine who falls within the scope of a category, resisting the notion that the binaries are actually dependent on one another for meaning and that "people seldom experience themselves to be fully in or fully out of any particular category" (*ibid* at 218). The result is a focus on whether a claimant can conform to dominant understandings of what "difference" represented by a particular ground "looks like" and complex experiences of subordination failing to be recognized. Instead, much like L'Heureux-Dubé J advocated in *Egan*, above note 8, Kropp's approach would be focused on discrimination, rather than on attaching experiences of subordination to grounds, and "would explore the social construction of [group] identities as well as their relation to background norms" (*ibid* at 228).

that give rise to hierarchical constructions of difference as "natural" and "inherent," and further, in navigating these coercive structures, they regulate our behaviour as we adhere to or resist prescribed identities.

In feminist theory, the concept of gender "gradually came to be understood as referring to the historically specific, socially constructed, subject positions, relationships, and language codes by which biological sex differences are rendered materially, culturally, psychologically, and socially significant."[115] With the recognition of gender as socially constructed came a further recognition that sex could not exist outside this framework, with theorists like Judith Butler maintaining that sex difference is always being observed, perceived, and regulated in a social milieu. In fact, sex/gender are fused, with gender "performatively produced and compelled by the regulatory practices of gender coherence."[116] Thus, despite the fact that gender is constantly being performed, it is not negotiated by individual women completely "free form" — there are coercive normative systems based on socially constructed notions of biological sex difference within which performances of gender are confined. In other words, "conduct creates status; that is, conduct defines who one is in the real world."[117]

Butler's work is supported by other feminist theorists who note the importance of keeping gendered regulation by institutional structures at the forefront of the analysis. To maintain this focus, Iris Marion Young indicates that she prefers to theorize "gender as an attribute of social structures more than of persons"[118] and that these gender structures operate to constrain and direct one's decisions about the extent to which to conform or transgress their conventions. She identifies the sexual division of labour as

---

115 Meg Luxton, "Feminist Political Economy and Social Reproduction" in Kate Bezanson & Meg Luxton, eds, *Social Reproduction: Feminist Political Economy Challenges Neo-Liberalism* (Montreal: McGill-Queen's University Press, 2006) 11 at 30 [Luxton].

116 Judith Butler, *Gender Trouble* (New York: Routledge, 1990) at 24 & 25. The author also addresses inherent constraints on sex/gender despite its social construction (*ibid* at 12):

> This is not to say that any and all gendered possibilities are open, but that the boundaries of analysis suggest the limits of a discursively conditioned experience. These limits are always set within the terms of a hegemonic cultural discourse predicated on binary structures that appear as the language of universal rationality. Constraint is thus built into what that language constitutes as the imaginable domain of gender.

117 Meier, above note 18 at 180.

118 Iris Marion Young, "Lived Body vs. Gender: Reflections on Social Structure and Subjectivity" in Iris Marion Young, *On Female Body Experience: "Throwing Like a Girl" and Other Essays* (New York: Oxford University Press, 2005) at 22.

one "axis" of gender structures along with normative heterosexuality and gendered hierarchies of power.

Meg Luxton recounts how feminist political economy evolved from socialist feminist theory in the 1970s, initially bringing to light how the sexual division of labour and women's reproductive work served the needs of capitalism, and then moved to a contemporary recognition of "social reproduction as a way of conceiving how states, markets, and households all interact in the daily and generational reproduction of an international labour force" as "interdependent processes of production and consumption" of paid and unpaid labour.[119] These processes constitute sex/gender, race, and geopolitical relations of privilege and subordination between the global north and the global south, among others. Sexual divisions of labour, with "feminized" work associated with domestic caregiving carried out in private — socially devalued and unpaid or underpaid — correspond to and reinforce various gendered dichotomies.[120] Law is intimately involved in these relations.[121] For instance, governmental decisions to privatize or to refrain from implementing public programs for family care implicitly rely on the notion that women's unpaid labour is available as a replacement, "exacerbat[ing] the sexual division of labour by shifting more work to women while asserting this is merely a side effect of individual choice."[122] Fudge and Cossman argue that "law plays a central role in the project of privatization,"[123] inscribing

---

119 Luxton, above note 115 at 35.

120 Susan Williams, "Feminist Legal Epistemologies" (1993) 8 Berkeley Women's LJ 63, outlining the various dichotomies of Enlightenment thought, including private/public, emotion/reason, and body/mind, with women and other subordinated groups affiliated with the former in each.

121 See, for example, *Bradwell v Illinois*, 16 Wall 130 at 141 (1872), providing one example from the United States Supreme Court of the naturalization of gender inequalities in law:

> [T]he civil law, as well as nature herself, has always recognized a wide difference in the respective spheres and destinies of man and woman. Man is, or should be, woman's protector and defender. The natural and proper timidity and delicacy which belongs to the female sex evidently unfits it for many of the occupations of civil life. The constitution of the family organization, which is founded in the divine ordinance as well as in the nature of things, indicates the domestic sphere as that which properly belongs to the domain and functions of womanhood.

122 Judy Fudge & Brenda Cossman, "Introduction: Privatization, Law, and the Challenge to Feminism" in Judy Fudge & Brenda Cossman, eds, *Privatization, Law, and the Challenge to Feminism* (Toronto: University of Toronto Press, 2002) 1 at 29–30.

123 *Ibid* at 34. See also Martha McClusky, "Razing the Citizen: Economic Inequality, Gender, and Marriage Tax Reform" in Linda McClain & Joanna Grossman, eds, *Gender Equality: Dimensions of Women's Equal Citizenship* (Cambridge: Cambridge University Press, 2009) 267 at 269.

women's labour as extraneous to the State and the market in a myriad of ways (not only in equality law, labour law, and family law) and, therefore, as both invaluable (as a "labour of love") and without (much) value.

Further, in the contemporary Canadian dual income–earning family, the devalued gender role of women as caregivers is stabilized despite the presence of a female income earner by unequal racial and class divisions and uneven global relations. Female transnational migrant domestic workers are pushed by global disparities and the stringency of domestic immigration laws to leave their own families in the global south and perform private caregiving duties for western families in low paid, poorly regulated employment:

> What makes a female employer appear manlike and "independent" — that is, of family responsibilities — in her own workplace is precisely her dependency on a female worker. Migrant workers are ideally suited to support this labour-market participation, since they can be (made to be) more flexible than citizen-workers . . . . Instead of being transformed, [gender relations in the home and larger society] are merely reproduced with only some changes in the cast.[124]

That the social and legal regulation of women's work is part of the gendering process may be shown by the statistical evidence strongly identifying gender with economic stratification,[125] as manifested by a gender wage gap, occupational segregation by race and sex,[126] and patterns of part-time and other precarious forms of employment.[127] As Fudge points

---

124 Sedef Arat-Koç, "Whose Social Reproduction? Transnational Motherhood and Feminist Political Economy" in Bezanson & Luxton, eds, above note 115, 75 at 88–89. See also Judy Fudge, "Global Care Chains, Employment Agencies, and the Conundrum of Jurisdiction: Decent Work for Domestic Workers in Canada" (2011) 23 CJWL 235.

125 Gwen Brodsky & Shelagh Day, "Beyond the Social and Economic Rights Debate: Substantive Equality Speaks to Poverty" (2002) 14 CJWL 185 at 190–92.

126 *Women in Canada*, above note 77. The report shows that in 2009, 67 percent of all employed women were working in teaching, nursing, and related health occupations, as well as clerical or other administrative positions or sales and service occupations. Only 31 percent of employed men worked in these occupations. As well, 87.1 percent of nurses and health-related therapists, 75.5 percent of clerks and other administrators, 65.9 percent of teachers, and 56.9 percent of sales and service personnel were women. See also Leah Vosko, "Rethinking Feminization: Gendered Precariousness in the Canadian Labour Market and the Crisis in Social Reproduction" (Paper delivered at the Robarts Canada Research Chairholders Series, 11 April 2002) at 14, online: York University www.yorku.ca/robarts/projects/lectures [Vosko, "Rethinking Feminization"], with respect to racial occupational segregation.

127 Vosko & Clark, above note 76 at 32–33.

out, "Since specific kinds of jobs are readily available to specific types of workers, such workers tend to 'choose' these jobs."[128] Further, "the burden of inequality falls greatest on women workers where poverty, the informal economy, weak employment regulation, racial and disability discrimination and subjection to gender-based violence are most pronounced."[129] Women's economic disparity is strongly associated with the sexual division of labour and devaluation of women's work, with women performing two-thirds of unpaid household labour and still unable to access affordable child care.[130] With respect to entrepreneurship, women are less likely to be self-employed than men,[131] and when they are self-employed, they face discrimination and cannot count on the assistance of their spouse in the business to the same extent as men, nor does their unpaid labour in the home change significantly.[132]

Feminist understandings have exposed law as not only "gendered," in that it "insists on a specific version of gender differentiation," but also as a "gendering strategy," in which "[w]oman/women are brought into being."[133] We saw in *Lesiuk* the trope of a mother working for "pin money," attempting to draw on EI benefits without being securely attached to the workforce, for example. This understanding of gender makes the status/conduct dichotomy incoherent, as gender is not located merely in the conduct of a sexed subject, but also in larger social structures that participate in gendering

---

128 Fudge, above note 104 at 236–37.

129 Mary Cornish & Fay Faraday, "Using the *Charter* to Redress Gender Discrimination in Employment" (Presentation to the Summer Law Institute for Secondary School Teachers, 31 August 2005) at 2–3, online: The Ontario Justice Education Network www.ojen.ca.

130 Vosko, "Rethinking Feminization," above note 126 at 20.

131 *Women in Canada*, above note 77, showing 11.9 percent of women are self-employed, versus 35.5 percent of men.

132 Lisa Phillips, "Sketching a Portrait of 'Unpaid Market Labour': Statistical Silences and Narrative Noise" (Paper presented at the Gender & Work: Knowledge Production in Practice Conference, York University, 1–2 October 2004) at 37–38, online: Gender & Work Database www.genderwork.ca; Monica Belcourt, Ronald Burke, & Hélène Lee-Gosselin, *The Glass Box: Women Business Owners in Canada* (Ottawa: The Canadian Advisory Council on the Status of Women, 1991) at 39–42. See also Mary Condon, "Limited by Law? Gender, Corporate Law and the Family Firm" in Chunn & Lacombe, eds, above note 58, 181 at 190 & 191, describing how women's participation in family businesses is governed by the "intractability of traditional familial roles," and that they have little decision making power despite day-to-day involvement in the business and sometimes formal positions in the corporate governance hierarchy.

133 Carol Smart, *Law, Crime and Sexuality: Essays in Feminism* (London: SAGE Publications, 1995) at 191 and 193.

the subject. Deconstructing the status/conduct binary reveals the law itself as unable to stand "outside" of gender to passively observe and adjudicate.[134]

1) Putting the Status/Conduct Binary to Rest

If we accept the fallacy of the status/conduct distinction, how can we work to eradicate it in Canadian law? The first step is to challenge immutability as a critical element in the assessment of analogous grounds. What we know about social constructions of identity reveals the inherent instability of notions of immutability and "constructive immutability" as organizing principles for analogous grounds. The current fusion of immutability with the notion of "discrete and insular minorities" has calcified into a test that starts by examining all those affected by a law, requiring them to have an identifiable and visible status as a group, bound together by their inherent personal characteristics. This removes the focus from the impact of law on groups that suffer under the same relations of subordination and completely eviscerates adverse-effect discrimination. This is so because systemic discrimination is seldom so efficient that it affects an identifiable subordinated group and only that group.

Work, in particular, has long been accepted as a critical constitutive element of identity, to the extent that one author has maintained that "'jobs create people because they shape individuals' behaviour and self-identification."[135] This has also been a consistent theme running through the Supreme Court's jurisprudence outside the section 15(1) *Charter* context,[136] in particular, women's contribution to social reproduction has been singled out for its special social significance and its connection to women's sub-

134 See, for example, Fudge, above note 104 at 241, critiquing *BC Health Services*: "the Court's analysis ignores the extent to which labour legislation reflects and reinforces historical patterns of labour market discrimination and segregation."

135 Joanna Grossman, "Pregnancy and Social Citizenship" in McClain & Grossman, eds, above note 123, 233 at 237, citing Vicki Shultz, "Life's Work" (2001) 100 Columb L Rev 1881 at 1890, and sociological evidence.

136 See, for example, *Reference Re Public Service Employee Relations Act (Alta)*, [1987] 1 SCR 313 at 368: "[w]ork is one of the most fundamental aspects in a person's life, providing the individual with a means of financial support and, as importantly, a contributory role in society. A person's employment is *an essential component of his or her sense of identity*, self-worth and emotional well-being" [emphasis added]. See also *Dunmore* SCC, above note 42 at para 167, L'Heureux-Dubé J, concurring; *Delisle v Canada (Deputy AG)*, [1999] 2 SCR 989 at para 44.

ordinated social identity.[137] However, for an equality analysis to properly address gender and work as mutually constitutive, a different framework may be required that does not focus on identity but rather systems of oppression.

In a previous article, I discussed the difficulty of courts addressing sexual inequality in isolation from other systems of oppression. Attempting to cabin sexual hierarchy from other related hierarchies of race, indigeneity, class, etc in the constitutional analysis often results in courts finding no rights violation at all, thus leading to the "perverse result of rights violations going unrecognized and unremediated, the more complex and intractable the claimant's oppression."[138] As post-intersectionality theory explains, addressing one system of subordination results in the operation of other systems being obscured and, in the absence of critical attention, strengthened. Given gendered and racial patterns of employment and economic disparity, "what one does," whether it be engaging in low-income work[139] or negotiating the intractable social assistance bureaucracy,[140] is critically linked to the operations of patriarchal capitalist white supremacy. Recognizing socio-economic status as an analogous ground would ensure that discriminatory treatment is not shielded from a searching, contextual analysis under section 15 because of the courts' failure to appreciate the intimate connection between systems of economic domination and other forms of oppression (such as sexism or racism).

---

137 See *Brooks*, above note 9 at paras 29 and 40: "That those who bear children and benefit society as a whole thereby should not be economically or socially disadvantaged seems to bespeak the obvious"; *EI Reference*, above note 76 at para 66: "[a] growing portion of the labour force is made up of women, and women have particular needs that are of concern to society as a whole. An interruption of employment due to maternity can no longer be regarded as a matter of individual responsibility"; *NAPE*, above note 104 at paras 45 and 49, recognizing that women's jobs are "chronically underpaid" and that "[l]ow pay often denotes low status jobs, exacting a price in dignity as well as dollars". See also above note 5 and accompanying cases.

138 "Multidimensionality and the Matrix: Identifying *Charter* Violations in Cases of Complex Subordination" (2010) 25 Can J L & Soc 21 at 24.

139 *Kearney v Bramalea Ltd (No 2)* (1998), 34 CHRR D/1 (Ont Bd Inq), aff'd (*sub nom Shelter Corp v Ontario (Human Rights Commission)*) (2001), 39 CHRR D/111 (Ont SCJ). This is one of the few cases having already made this connection in the human rights context. The Board recognized the use of minimum income criteria as a screening mechanism for apartment rentals constituted systemic discrimination on the basis of sex, family status, marital status, race, and citizenship. This was based on exhaustive statistical evidence regarding the incidence of low incomes amongst equality-seeking groups identified by these characteristics.

140 *Falkiner*, above note 5; *Sparks*, above note 39.

Women in particular are affected by economic disparity to a greater extent than men and for reasons highly associated with their gender. Excising these considerations from the equality analysis on the basis that they involve "conduct" is arguably a violation of section 28, which guarantees rights equally to "male and female persons," as this results in substantively unequal access to the section 15(1) right.[141] Similarly, it may be considered a section 28 violation for civil liberties that have traditionally been associated with men's interests, including freedom of thought and religion, to gain protection for practices closely associated with one's social identity, at the same time as the court has insisted on a rigid adherence to "status" in women's equality claims. Until these issues are taken seriously by courts, the injustice will haunt us still.

---

141 As I maintained in my unpublished paper, "Will 'Watertight Compartments' Sink Women's *Charter* Rights? The Need for a New Theoretical Approach to Women's Multiple Rights Claims under the *Canadian Charter of Rights and Freedoms*," complex violations of rights require different analytic tools to reveal them, the same way as intersectional identities require different analyses of discrimination which recognize, for example, that racism and sexism is experienced by black women differently than racism is experienced by black men and sexism is experienced by white women (LLM Thesis, Faculty of Law, University of Ottawa, 2008). Women's lack of equal access to s 15(1) may be seen, in part, by virtue of the fact that they have never had a successful sex discrimination case, under the *Charter* at the Supreme Court of Canada, with several of their cases raising issues of economic injustice. See, for example, *Gosselin*, above note 8; *Hodge v Canada (Minister of Human Resources Development)*, 2004 SCC 65; *Nova Scotia (AG) v Walsh*, 2002 SCC 83. Further, Bruce Ryder and Taufiq Hashmani show that many cases raising these issues have been turned down for leave to appeal. See "Managing *Charter* Equality Rights: The Supreme Court of Canada's Dispositions of Leave to Appeal Applications in Section 15 Cases, 1989–2010" (2010) 51 Sup Ct L Rev (2d) 505, especially their discussion of leave being turned down in *Boulter*, above note 48, despite unresolved issues remaining about poverty as an analogous ground. Fudge, in fact, attributes the finding of a s 15(1) violation in *NAPE* to Binnie J's being able to position the claim as a dignity (identity) claim rather than a claim to economic justice. See above note 104 at para 235.

CHAPTER 7

LITIGATING TO ADVANCE THE SUBSTANTIVE EQUALITY RIGHTS OF PEOPLE WITH DISABILITIES

GWEN BRODSKY,[*] SHELAGH DAY,[†] AND YVONNE PETERS[‡]

A. INTRODUCTION

This chapter analyzes the legal landscape for litigating the substantive equality rights of people with disabilities in Canada since the two landmark human rights decisions of the Supreme Court of Canada, *Meiorin* and *Grismer*.[1]

* Gwen Brodsky, Director of the Poverty and Human Rights Centre; Distinguished Visiting Scholar, Faculty of Law, University of British Columbia and Research Partner in the SSHRC-CURA Project "Reconceiving Human Rights Practice," online: www.socialrightscura.ca.

† Shelagh Day, Chair of the Human Rights Committee, Canadian Feminist Alliance for International Action (FAFIA); Director of the Poverty and Human Rights Centre and Research Partner in the SSHRC-CURA Project "Reconceiving Human Rights Practice," online: www.socialrightscura.ca.

‡ Yvonne Peters, Chairperson, Board of Commissioners, Manitoba Human Rights Commission; Co-Principal Investigator for the SSHRC-CURA Project "Disabling Poverty/Enabling Citizenship" and Research Collaborator in the SSHRC-CURA Project "Reconceiving Human Rights Practice," online: www.socialrightscura.ca.

1 An earlier version of this chapter — "Accommodation in the 21st Century" (March 2012), online: Canadian Human Rights Commission www.chrc-ccdp.gc.ca — was referred to by several interveners in the appeal in the Supreme Court of Canada of *British Columbia (Ministry of Education) v Moore*, 2010 BCCA 478, aff'g 2008 BCSC 264, leave to appeal to SCC granted, 34040 (30 June 2011) [*Moore* BCCA]. It was cited with approval by the Court in its decision in *Moore v British Columbia (Education)*, 2012 SCC 61 at para 28 [*Moore* SCC].

Together, *Meiorin* and *Grismer* offered the promise that human rights legislation would take adverse effects discrimination seriously and that the duty to accommodate would engage with systemic obstacles to equality. However, this promise has been under attack. Post-*Meiorin* and *Grismer* caselaw reveals disturbing trends. Efforts have been made to return us to a minimalist version of accommodation, by narrowing the definition of discrimination and returning to an emphasis on stereotype, applying formalistic versions of comparator group analysis that defeat legitimate claims and distort accommodation analysis, and adopting too narrow definitions of services.

Respondent push back has created new knots in the jurisprudence, which the authors describe and attempt to untangle. The Supreme Court of Canada had an opportunity when it heard the appeal in *Moore v British Columbia (Ministry of Education)* to renew its recognition that the fulfillment of the rights of persons with disabilities requires far-reaching, deliberate, and systemic change to workplaces and services.[2] In the twenty-first century, especially in light of Canada's recent ratification of the *Convention on the Rights of Persons with Disabilities*, adjudicators and governments should be striving to move us, with all speed, towards the goal of full inclusion. In *Moore*, the Supreme Court of Canada took some important steps towards untangling the jurisprudence and provided some much-needed direction for achieving full inclusion.[3]

---

2 At issue in *Moore* SCC, *ibid*, is a claim that the BC Ministry of Education and North Vancouver School District No 44 discriminated against Jeffrey Patrick Moore and other students with severe learning disabilities by failing to accommodate their needs in the public school system. While at elementary school, Jeffrey Moore was diagnosed as having a severe learning disability, in the form of dyslexia, which interfered with his ability to learn to read and to comprehend words. In the wake of funding cuts by the province for education, the school board closed the facility that provided the intensive remediation required by Jeffrey and other students with dyslexia. On the advice of district officials, Jeffrey's parents removed him from the public school system and, at significant personal expense, sent him to private schools that provide special assistance to students with severe learning disabilities. The Moores alleged that the ministry and the district discriminated against Jeffrey Moore individually and that they also discriminated on a systemic basis against students with severe learning disabilities. The claim was successful before the BC Human Rights Tribunal, 2005 BCHRT 580. But the well-reasoned judgment of the tribunal was overturned on judicial review, based on the BC Supreme Court's comparator group analysis and approach to defining the service in issue. On further appeal, a majority of the British Columbia Court of Appeal also ruled against the complainant. Justice Rowles dissented.

3 *Moore* SCC, above note 1.

B. BACKGROUND

The substantive equality rights of people with disabilities in Canada have not yet been realized. People with disabilities are more likely to be poor. Among working age adults, experts estimate that people with disabilities are about twice as likely to live in poverty as their non-disabled counterparts.[4] They have lower education attainment than people without disabilities[5] and are less likely to be employed.[6] When they are employed, they have lower incomes.[7] The many people with disabilities who are not employed are generally reliant on social assistance programs, which are unstable, rule-heavy, and stigmatized.

To improve these basic conditions of disadvantage for people with disabilities in Canada, norms that are based on being able-bodied must be discarded in favour of universal norms that accommodate people with disabilities from the outset in the design of standards, practices, and institutions. In Canada, human rights legislation is a primary means for giving effect to Canada's obligations under international human rights law, including obligations to fulfill the rights to work and education, social security,

---

4 Cam Crawford, "Personally Speaking: Poverty and Disability in Canada," online: Council of Canadians with Disabilities www.ccdonline.ca. Cam Crawford is the Senior Research Advisor to the Canadian Association for Community Living.

5 Cam Crawford, "Trying to 'Make the Grade': Education, Work-Related Training," online: Council of Canadians with Disabilities www.ccdonline.ca. For example, people with disabilities are less likely to have completed high school education than non-disabled people: 27.4 percent vs. 18.3 percent, respectively. They are also less likely to have a university degree or certificate (13.2 percent vs. 20.7 percent). An increase in formal education helps people with disabilities, as it does other groups, to reduce the likelihood of poverty. However, even when they have higher levels of education, people with disabilities have a poverty rate twice as high as non-disabled people.

6 Cam Crawford, "Low Household Income and Disability: Income Sources, Employment and Employment Discrimination," online: Council of Canadians with Disabilities www.ccdonline.ca. For example, in 2006, 51.3 percent of persons with disabilities were employed compared to 75 percent of persons without disabilities.

7 *Ibid.* Crawford describes the employment situation of employed people with disabilities as follows. About 11 percent of people with disabilities who are employed continue to experience low incomes, compared to 7.3 percent of those without disabilities. Compared to people without disabilities living on low incomes, people with disabilities in similar circumstances are twice as likely to work part-time: 14.9 percent and 27 percent respectively. Among those persons with disabilities who are working, the rates of poverty are lowest for the 32.4 percent whose employers have more than one location and 500 or more employees. This is also true for the 32.1 percent who work in a unionized workplace or are covered by a collective agreement. Unfortunately, only 18.1 percent of people with disabilities enjoy this kind of employment.

and an adequate standard of living. Canada's obligations to persons with disabilities are now extended and clarified by the recent ratification of the *Convention on the Rights of Persons with Disabilities*.[8]

If the duty to accommodate embedded in human rights legislation were seriously implemented by governments at all levels and if tribunals and courts adjudicated human rights legislation purposively and substantively to provide clear-sighted direction to public and private actors, much could be done to improve the lives of people with disabilities.

The Supreme Court of Canada's landmark decisions on the duty to accommodate, *Meiorin* and *Grismer*, and the *CRPD*, provide different articulations of the same idea — that accommodation, properly understood, mandates genuine inclusiveness. Our question in this paper is, is the jurisprudence of tribunals and courts helping us to fulfill that promise?

C. THE DUTY TO ACCOMMODATE

The duty to take positive steps to remove barriers to inclusion is a pillar of Canadian human rights law. The duty to accommodate applies to all prohibited grounds of discrimination, but it is of central importance to persons with disabilities. Through more than two decades of statutory human rights decisions dating back to *Huck v Odeon Theatres*, a 1985 decision of the Saskatchewan Court of Appeal,[9] tribunals and courts have developed the principle that the right to non-discrimination encompasses a positive duty, known as the duty to accommodate. It requires employers, service providers, and landlords, including governments, to make such adjustments as are required to remove barriers to access by persons with disabilities to employment, services customarily provided to the public, and housing. There was incremental progress in cases like *Huck*,[10] which clarified that public places, like movie theatres, needed to be modified to make space for people with disabilities. But the decisions in *Meiorin*[11] and *Grismer*,[12] released by

---

8 13 December 2006, 2515 UNTS 3, GA Res 61/106 (entered into force 3 May 2008) [*CRPD*].

9 *Canadian Odeon Theatres Ltd v Human Rights Commission (Sask) and Huck* (1985), 18 DLR (4th) 93 (Sask CA), leave to appeal to SCC refused (1985), 18 DLR (4th) 93n [*Huck*].

10 Some jurisdictions, notably Ontario and British Columbia, recognized adverse effects discrimination in early cases. Ontario named it "constructive discrimination," and remedial orders in some cases required reasonable accommodation.

11 *British Columbia (Public Service Employee Relations Commission) v BCGSEU*, [1999] 3 SCR 3 [*Meiorin*].

12 *British Columbia (Superintendent of Motor Vehicles) v British Columbia (Council of Human Rights)*, [1999] 3 SCR 868 [*Grismer*].

the Supreme Court of Canada in 1999, were especially important victories that ignited a larger aspiration for equality in employment and services and genuine optimism among people with disabilities.

In *Meiorin*, a sex discrimination case, the Court established that the duty to accommodate requires that *standards* be as inclusive as possible, going beyond the idea of accommodation as merely requiring individual exceptions. The Court also untangled some doctrinal knots that had developed because of a failure to take adverse effects discrimination seriously and a conception of accommodation that did not go far enough.[13] Dianne Pothier described *Meiorin* as "a significant turning point in Canadian human rights law," because the Court accepted that "in all types of discrimination, the analysis has to start with scrutinizing general rules or standards claimed to be discriminatory. The Court understood that the particular case was about job definition constructed around traditional male norms, and that had to be directly confronted to advance equality for women."[14] Similarly, Yvonne Peters said:

> The Court's analysis in *Meiorin* represents a significant step forward in that it begins to redefine and reformulate the objectives of reasonable accommodation . . . *Meiorin* shifts the emphasis from the individual to the standard.[15]

In *Grismer*,[16] the Court confirmed that the accommodation analysis articulated in *Meiorin* applies to disability discrimination, and explained:

---

13 See Shelagh Day & Gwen Brodsky, "The Duty to Accommodate: Who Will Benefit?" (1996) 75 Can Bar Rev 433: the authors provide a critique of pre-*Meiorin* problems; Gwen Brodsky, Shelagh Day, & Yvonne Peters, "Accommodation in the 21st Century" (March 2012), online: Canadian Human Rights Commission www.chrc-ccdp.gc.ca, in which the authors provide a fulsome discussion of the Court's decisions in *Meiorin* and *Grismer*.

14 Although Pothier described *Meiorin* as a significant turning point, she also cautioned that the *Meiorin* judgment gives mixed messages about how far anti-discrimination law can go in challenging dominant norms since, in her view, the judgment does not grapple sufficiently with the difference between the two branches of the old bifurcated approach, and suffers from confusion between the idea of accommodation through individual exceptions and the remaking of standards. Dianne Pothier, "*BCGSEU*: Turning a Page in Human Rights Law" (1999) 11:1 Const Forum Const 19 [Pothier].

15 Yvonne Peters, "From Tinkering to Transformation: *Meiorin* Breathes New Hope into Reasonable Accommodation" (Paper delivered at the Transforming Women's Equality: Equality Rights in the New Century Conference, Vancouver, 4–7 November 1999) at 4, as cited in Pothier, above note 14 at 25.

16 *Grismer*, above note 12.

"Accommodation refers to what is required in the circumstances to avoid discrimination. Standards must be as inclusive as possible."[17]

Together, *Meiorin* and *Grismer* raised reasonable expectations in the disability rights community that, going forward, human rights legislation would be interpreted liberally and purposively, to achieve its substantive equality goals, and more particularly, to

- treat adverse effects discrimination as no less serious or less worthy of remediation than direct discrimination;
- avoid reducing the duty to accommodate to only after-the-fact, individual tinkering on the margins rather than challenging discriminatory norms;
- require that disability discrimination embedded in facially neutral standards for services and employment, wherever possible, be tackled systemically and proactively, at the stage of their initial design;
- maintain a strong analytical distinction between proof of discrimination and proof of justificatory criteria;
- ensure that endeavours to justify the maintenance of exclusionary able-bodied norms are subjected to rigorous scrutiny;
- resist formalistic methods of interpretation that do not advance the purpose of human rights legislation; and
- provide meaningful remedies for discrimination, regardless of the form that the discrimination takes.

Meiorin made the first line of inquiry whether the norm can be disregarded altogether without any need to consider exceptions. This decision, followed by *Grismer*, represented the beginnings of a systemic approach to the duty to accommodate.[18]

D. THE PROMISE UNDER ATTACK

The promise that human rights legislation would take adverse effects discrimination seriously, and engage with systemic obstacles to equality, has

---

17 *Ibid* at para 22.

18 Dianne Pothier, "Tackling Disability Discrimination at Work: A Systemic Approach" (2010) 4:1 McGill JL & Health 17 at 22 and 27. A systemic approach to accommodation challenges able-bodied norms by contemplating diversity from the start. Systemic accommodation is founded on "inclusive thought . . . . Such contemplation gives the duty to accommodate the potential to be genuinely transformative in challenging able-bodied norms, instead of limiting it to ad hoc minor modifications."

been under attack. In the post-*Meiorin* and *Grismer* period of human rights litigation, respondents intensified their efforts to prevent complainants from advancing beyond the *prima facie* discrimination stage of a case, in order to avoid the requirement to demonstrate that they could not accommodate complainants without incurring undue hardship. The result has been new conflicts and confusion in the jurisprudence, particularly concerning the meaning of discrimination and where the analytical line should be drawn between *prima facie* discrimination and justification.

1) A Divisive Question: Can Discrimination Exist without Stereotypes?

The most significant question that has emerged in the jurisprudence is whether the complainant must prove stereotyping to establish a *prima facie* case of discrimination. Repeatedly, respondents have sought to recall decision makers to an old paradigm of discrimination that is solely concerned with stereotyping. Despite the fact that this move entails rolling back the right to protection from adverse effects discrimination, well-established in Canadian human rights jurisprudence for over twenty-five years, to pre-*Meiorin* days, decision makers have been divided about how the issue should be resolved.

This can be seen, for example, in the Supreme Court of Canada's decision in *McGill University Health Centre (Montreal General Hospital)*.[19] At issue in *McGill* was whether an automatic termination clause applied to persons absent from work for an extended period. The grievor had been absent from work for thirty-six months, because of health problems, and was unable to return to work for a further indeterminate period. The employer had provided rehabilitation periods more generous than stipulated in the collective agreement.

In the Supreme Court of Canada, the majority addressed the issue as a question of undue hardship. Justice Deschamps explained, "[t]he duty to accommodate in the workplace arises when an employer seeks to apply a standard that is prejudicial to an employee on the basis of specific characteristics that are protected by human rights legislation."[20] This was, then, the majority's version of *prima facie* discrimination. Justice Deschamps then proceeded to apply the three steps established in *Meiorin*, to determine whether the termination was "reasonably necessary," in other words, whether further accommodation would cause undue hardship for the

19 *McGill University Health Centre (Montreal General Hospital) v Syndicat des employés de l'Hôpital général de Montréal*, 2007 SCC 4 [*McGill*].

20 *Ibid* at para 11.

employer. The majority agreed with the arbitrator that the employer had discharged its duty of reasonable accommodation. The majority considered various factors in assessing the question of undue hardship including, among other things, the length of the rehabilitation period negotiated by the parties. The Court viewed the period negotiated by the parties to be one factor when assessing the duty of reasonable accommodation, which, the majority explained, cannot be applied mechanically, but which may be taken into account in the overall assessment of the accommodation granted by the employer.

However, Abella J, with McLachlin CJ and Bastarache J concurring, would have allowed the appeal on the basis that there was no *prima facie* case of discrimination. Justice Abella imported into the definition of *prima facie* case a requirement that the claimant prove that the impugned standard was based on stereotype. For Abella J, the issue in the *McGill* appeal was not whether the employer had accommodated the claimant sufficiently but whether the claimant had satisfied the threshold onus of demonstrating that there was *prima facie* discrimination. According to Abella J, the claimant was required to show that she had been disadvantaged by employer conduct, which was *based on stereotypical or arbitrary assumptions about persons with disabilities.* In Abella J's judgment, the terms stereotypical and arbitrary are apparently interchangeable. On her approach, the employer was not required to justify the termination, even though termination was because of disability-related absence from work. Justice Abella wrote:

> There is no need to justify what is not, *prima facie*, discriminatory. Unlike Deschamps J., then, the issue for me is not whether the employer has made out the justification defence of having reasonably accommodated the claimant, but whether the claimant has satisfied the threshold onus of demonstrating that there is *prima facie* discrimination, namely, that she has been disadvantaged by the employer's conduct *based on stereotypical or arbitrary assumptions about persons with disabilities*, thereby shifting the onus to the employer to justify the conduct.[21]

To explain why automatic termination clauses are not discriminatory, Abella J asserts, "they are not arbitrary in the way we understand arbitrariness in the human rights context, that is, they do not unfairly disadvantage disabled employees because of *stereotypical attributions of their ability*."[22] This singular focus on stereotyping overlooks the possibility that such clauses

---

21 *Ibid* at para 53 [emphasis added].

22 *Ibid* at para 56 [emphasis added].

may have a discriminatory effect on someone who has been required to be absent from work because of disability.

The approach of the majority in *McGill*, regarding what constitutes a *prima facie* case of discrimination, is consistent with *Meiorin* and *Grismer* and with the *O'Malley* framework. In *O'Malley*, the issue was the adverse effects of a scheduling requirement on the religious beliefs of an individual employee, Theresa O'Malley. A commonly stated version of what constitutes a *prima facie* case in a disability case, based on the *O'Malley* framework, is

1) the employee has (or is perceived to have) a disability;
2) the employee received adverse treatment (sometimes stated as "differential treatment" or "adverse effects"); and
3) the employee's disability was a factor in the adverse treatment or adverse effects.

On the other hand, the approach of the minority in *McGill* represents a significant departure from the *O'Malley* framework. The minority approach purports to add a fourth step to what the complainant must prove. It is not enough that disability was a factor in the adverse treatment experienced by a person with a disability. The complainant must go further to show that the adverse treatment and the disability are linked by stereotyping.

The issue of what constitutes a *prima facie* case of discrimination is important because either an insistence on a too-limited conception of discrimination or a misallocation of the burden of proof may mean that the respondent's obligation to rigorously justify systemic obstacles to substantive equality, against the standard of undue hardship, is never reached. More particularly, if the complainant cannot discharge the burden of establishing a *prima facie* case, the respondent is able to avoid having to answer the question, is there a way that the adverse effect could be avoided, without causing undue hardship for the respondent?

2) Adverse Effects Discrimination Must Not Be Rendered Inactionable

There are various reasons why it would be wrong to make stereotyping an essential element of what a claimant must prove to establish a *prima facie* case of discrimination.[23] The central objection to making stereotyping

23 See, for example, *Coast Mountain Bus Company Ltd v National Automobile, Aerospace, Transportation and General Workers of Canada (CAW-Canada), Local 111*, 2010 BCCA 447: some decision makers have declined to apply the minority decision in *McGill*; *National Automobile, Aerospace, Transportation and General Workers of Can-*

an essential element of a *prima facie* case of discrimination is that stereotyping is grounded in an insufficient understanding of discrimination. In particular, discrimination as stereotyping does not work for adverse effects discrimination: it simply misses the mark. Although some disability discrimination arises because of the attribution of inaccurate group-based generalizations (stereotype), a lot of disability discrimination takes the form of facially neutral standards that simply fail to take people with disabilities into account.[24]

---

ada (CAW-Canada) Local 111 v Coast Mountain Bus Company (No 9), 2008 BCHRT 52 at paras 472–73. The decision maker explicitly relied on *Eaton* (see below note 24) and found that stereotype is not the only source of discrimination and that in some cases failing to accommodate the real characteristics of disabled persons may be the source of discrimination. The tribunal thus concluded that the employer's Attendance Monitoring Program was an instance of systemic discrimination against persons with disabilities because it failed to accommodate their needs. On judicial review of the tribunal's decision in *Coast Mountain Bus v CAW Canada*, 2009 BCSC 396 at paras 97–99, the BC Supreme Court found that the tribunal erred in finding systemic discrimination because its reasoning was contrary to the opinion of Abella J in *McGill*, and the program was not based on stereotypical or arbitrary assumptions. The court did, however, uphold some of the individual complaints in the case.

24 *Eaton v Brant County Board of Education*, [1997] 1 SCR 241 [*Eaton*]. This insight is captured by the words of Sopinka J (*ibid* at para 67):

> The principal object of certain of the prohibited grounds is the elimination of discrimination by the attribution of untrue characteristics based on stereotypical attitudes relating to immutable conditions such as race or sex. *In the case of disability, this is one of the objectives. The other equally important objective seeks to take into account the true characteristics of this group which act as headwinds to the enjoyment of society's benefits and to accommodate them.* Exclusion from the mainstream of society results from the construction of a society based solely on "mainstream" attributes to which disabled persons will never be able to gain access. Whether it is the impossibility of success at a written test for a blind person, or the need for ramp access to a library, the discrimination does not lie in the attribution of untrue characteristics to the disabled individual. The blind person cannot see and the person in a wheelchair needs a ramp. Rather, it is the failure to make reasonable accommodation, to fine-tune society so that its structures and assumptions do not result in the relegation and banishment of disabled persons from participation, which results in discrimination against them. *The discrimination inquiry which uses "the attribution of stereotypical characteristics" reasoning as commonly understood is simply inappropriate here.* It may be seen rather as a case of reverse stereotyping which, by not allowing for the condition of a disabled individual, ignores his or her disability and forces the individual to sink or swim within the mainstream environment. It is recognition of the actual characteristics, and rea-

Although the caselaw does not really define stereotype, it can be inferred that what decision makers have in mind, when they refer to stereotyping, is quite often a generalization or misconception about a group or an individual, based on characteristics related to human rights grounds such as disability or sex. The Supreme Court of Canada has said, "[a] stereotype may be described as a misconception whereby a person or, more often, a group is unfairly portrayed as possessing undesirable traits, or traits which the group, or at least some of its members, do not possess."[25]

Although discrimination as stereotyping, so defined, works for cases of direct discrimination, in which a misconception or negative generalization about the group is made explicit, it does not work for the analysis of adverse effects discrimination. In adverse effects discrimination, the group generalization is rendered invisible, or at least less easily visible, by the very facial neutrality of the standard in issue. Thus, an insistence on proof of stereotyping risks rendering adverse effect discrimination inactionable.

Furthermore, discrimination defined as stereotyping does not yield effective remedies for disability discrimination. Typically, the proposed antidote to discrimination through stereotyping (the deployment of inaccurate generalizations) is to ignore group characteristics ostensibly so that individuals may be judged on their merits rather than their group characteristics. There are many circumstances in which liberation from stereotyping, and being treated the same as non-disabled persons, is precisely what persons with disabilities need. However, in other circumstances, it is some form of accommodation that is required, whether it be individual or systemic.

Accommodation, rather than ignoring disability, demands a focus on disability and a quest for the means to achieve inclusion. If we say either that a complainant must prove stereotyping or that the absence of stereotyping can constitute a complete defence to a *prima facie* case of discrimination, this changes the definition of discrimination, taking human rights law backwards to a time long before cases such as *O'Malley* and *Meiorin*, when adverse effects discrimination had not yet been recognized as actionable in law. Introducing stereotyping as part of the definition of discrimination, regardless of who bears the onus of proof, will likely result in defeat of a claim of adverse effects discrimination.

---

sonable accommodation of these characteristics which is the central purpose of s. 15(1) in relation to disability. [emphasis added.]

25 *Law v Canada (Minister of Employment and Immigration)*, [1999] 1 SCR 497 at para 64 [*Law*].

If stereotyping is an essential element of discrimination, many human rights decisions have been silently overruled.[26] Not only was there a complete absence of reference to stereotyping in *Meiorin*, it is clear from the reasons of McLachlin J, as she then was, that the Court was not operating on an understanding that the case was about protection from stereotyping.

Meiorin reveals another understanding of the purpose of human rights legislation, namely the elimination of the "systemic discrimination"[27] which occurs through the application of facially neutral exclusionary *standards* that fail to take into account the real characteristics of a group. The Court explained:

> Employers designing workplaces owe an obligation to be aware of both the differences between individuals, and differences that characterise groups of individuals. Employers designing workplace standards . . . must build conceptions of equality into workplace standards . . . standards governing the performance of work should be *designed to reflect all members of society*, in so far as reasonably possible.[28]

As the Supreme Court understood in *Meiorin*, addressing discrimination is not only about the avoidance of differential treatment based on stereotypes, with possibly a bit of affordable,[29] individual after-the-fact accommodation added on. Addressing discrimination also entails dealing with "the effects of systemic discrimination,"[30] "rigorously assessing" standards that have adverse effects on groups protected by human rights grounds,[31] and challenging "deep seated beliefs about the intrinsic superiority of such characteristics as mobility and sightedness" and the "legitimacy" of standards that systematically privilege certain characteristics over others.[32] It is crucial to people with disabilities, and the project of advancing their substantive equality rights, that these insights about discrimination

---

26 See, for example, *Ontario (Human Rights Commission) v Simpsons Sears*, [1985] 2 SCR 536 [*O'Malley*], and *Eldridge v British Columbia (AG)*, [1997] 3 SCR 624 [*Eldridge*]: to find that the facts of these cases demonstrate any stereotyping would require an incredible stretch. See *Vriend v Alberta*, [1998] 1 SCR 493 at para 72: "it is not *only* through the 'stereotypical application of presumed group or personal characteristics' that discrimination can occur . . . ." See also *Gosselin v Quebec (AG)*, 2002 SCC 84 at paras 115–20.

27 *Meiorin*, above note 11 at para 41.

28 *Ibid* at para 68 [emphasis added].

29 *Ibid* at para 41.

30 *Ibid* at paras 41–42.

31 *Ibid* at para 42.

32 *Ibid* at para 41.

not be shut out by a definition of discrimination that, once again, is too narrowly and exclusively focused on stereotyping.

3) The Analytical Distinction between *Prima Facie* Case and the BFOR Defence Must Be Maintained

Reducing the definition of discrimination to stereotyping transcends the question of where the line should be drawn between *prima facie* discrimination and justification. But *McGill* also raises the issue of reversing the burden of proof for making out a justificatory defence. A requirement for proof of stereotyping can too easily slide into a requirement that the complainant prove, in order to make out a *prima facie* case, that the respondent's conduct was not justified. This can be seen in the minority judgment of Abella J in *McGill*, in that the terms "stereotyping" and "arbitrariness" are used somewhat interchangeably. Arbitrariness is concerned with the reasonableness of the respondent's intention or purpose and the fit or rational connection between means and purpose. It goes to justification and as such is a BFOR issue.[33] If the burden of proof is misallocated, this can be another way of filtering out meritorious claims. The majority in *McGill* respects the analytical distinction between a *prima facie* case of discrimination, putting the respondent to the test of justifying its decision not to provide further accommodation. However, the minority conflates the *prima facie* case and the BFOR defence by adding to the claimant's burden the responsibility of proving that the discrimination is arbitrary. Any erosion of the analytical distinction between *prima facie* case and justificatory considerations risks weakening the scrutiny of the respondent's justificatory arguments and may shield the respondent from the duty of showing that it has accommodated to the point of undue hardship. Ultimately, the danger is that statutory human rights protections are reduced to providing protection only against blatant bigotry.[34]

---

33 See *ibid* at para 54; *Grismer*, above note 12 at para 20. It corresponds to steps one and two of the BFOR analysis.

34 See *British Columbia (Public Service Agency) v BCGSEU*, 2008 BCCA 357 [*Gooding* BCCA], leave to appeal to SCC refused, [2008] SCCA No 460. This is a concrete example of the difference it can make to reverse the onus of proof. The British Columbia Court of Appeal excused the employer from having to justify the termination of an employee whose misconduct was attributable to alcohol dependency. *Gooding* not only erodes the analytical distinction between *prima facie* case and justificatory arguments but revises the definition of discrimination to mean intentional discrimination. This flies in the face of established human rights jurisprudence recognizing that a lack of intention to discriminate does not negate discrimination. Although recent decisions of the

a) Proof of Stereotyping or Arbitrariness Is Not Mandated by the *Charter*

It has been argued by respondents that section 15 *Charter* jurisprudence mandates proof of stereotyping or arbitrariness as an essential element of the definition of discrimination. Respondents have placed particular reliance on the *Law* case to argue that, to establish a *prima facie* case, stereotyping must be proven.[35] This is ironic because *Meiorin* and *Grismer*, which were both decided after *Law*, make no mention of the *Law* framework. *Meiorin* and *Grismer*, as indicated above, applied the *O'Malley* framework for determining what constitutes *prima facie* discrimination. Therefore, it makes no sense to claim that *Law*, a section 15 *Charter* case, altered the jurisprudence

---

Ontario and British Columbia courts of appeal circumvent the minority decision in *McGill*, it is not without influence. See *Honda Canada Inc v Keays*, 2008 SCC 39 at para 71; *International Forest Products Ltd v Sandhu*, 2008 BCCA 204; *Mortillaro v Ontario (Minister of Transportation)*, 2011 HRTO 310; *Dufferin-Peel Catholic District School Board v OECTA* (2008), 177 LAC (4th) 362; *Baum v Calgary (City)*, 2008 ABQB 791; *Goode v Interior Health Authority*, 2010 BCHRT 95; *Boehringer Ingelheim (Canada) Ltd v Kerr*, 2010 BCSC 427, aff'd 2011 BCCA 266; *Cassidy v Emergency Health and Services Commission and others (No 2)*, 2008 BCHRT 125, judicial review allowed, 2011 BCSC 1003; *USW, Local 1-423 v Weyerhaeuser*, 2009 BCHRT 328; *CSWU Local 1611 v SELI Canada and others (No 8)*, 2008 BCHRT 436, judicial review by BCSC requested, Vancouver Registry S-090740. These are numerous cases in which courts and tribunals have referred to the minority decision in *McGill*. Because the cases are quite fact-specific, it is beyond the scope of this paper to analyze each one. However, it is fair to say that in numerous cases respondents have relied heavily on the minority decision in *McGill* and that decision makers have felt it necessary to either apply or distinguish *McGill*. Fortunately, the *Gooding* decision by the British Columbia Court of Appeal is rarely mentioned by decision makers, and in *Weyerhaeuser* it was distinguished as having "turned on its unique facts." It appears to be accepted by both union-side and employer-side lawyers that *Gooding* is not good law.

35 *Law*, above note 25. The caselaw reveals uncertainty and differences of opinion among courts and tribunals about whether and how the *Law* contextual factors apply in the statutory human rights context, particularly in cases decided prior to 2008 when the Supreme Court of Canada issued its decision in *R v Kapp*, 2008 SCC 41 [*Kapp*], discussed below. See *Gwinner v Alberta (Human Resources and Employment)*, 2002 ABQB 685, aff'd 2004 ABCA 210, leave to appeal to SCC refused [2004] SCCA No 342; *BCGSEU v British Columbia (Public Service Employee Relations Commission)*, 2002 BCCA 476; *British Columbia Public School Employers' Assn v British Columbia Teachers' Federation*, 2003 BCCA 323; *Vancouver Rape Relief Society v Nixon (No 2)*, 2005 BCCA 601, leave to appeal to SCC refused, [2006] SCCA No 365 [*Nixon*]; *Health Employers Assn of British Columbia v BCNU*, 2006 BCCA 57, leave to appeal to SCC refused, [2006] SCCA No 139; *Kemess Mines Ltd v IUOE, Local 115*, 2006 BCCA 58, leave to appeal to SCC refused, [2006] SCCA No 140. These are leading pre-*Kapp* cases concerning the application of *Law*.

with regard to interpretation of human rights legislation. Furthermore, a closer look at section 15 *Charter* jurisprudence reveals that this is not an accurate account even of the requirements of a section 15 analysis. Proof of an underlying stereotype is not a requirement imposed by section 15 *Charter* jurisprudence. Understanding where we are on this question requires actually going back to the *Law* case.

In *Law*, the Supreme Court identified contextual factors[36] which, it indicated, could be of assistance in determining whether a law which has adverse effects based on a listed ground discriminates in a substantive sense or, in other words, infringes human dignity. In *Law*, the Court used the concepts substantive discrimination and infringement of human dignity interchangeably.

In statutory human rights cases, respondents have attempted to impose the contextual factors in *Law* as though they amounted to a *legal test*, something to be added on to *prima facie* case.[37] The "correspondence" factor set out in *Law* can be particularly problematic because it is roughly equivalent to the idea of stereotyping. Is the group-based distinction grounded in

---

36 The contextual factors are concerned with (1) pre-existing disadvantage, stereotyping, prejudice, or vulnerability; (2) the correspondence between the ground or grounds on which the claim is based and actual need, capacity, or circumstances; (3) ameliorative purpose or effects of the impugned law on a more disadvantaged person or group in society; (4) the nature and scope of the interest affected.

37 Leslie A Reaume, "Postcards from *O'Malley*: Reinvigorating Statutory Human Rights Jurisprudence in the Age of the *Charter*" in Fay Faraday, Margaret Denike, & Kate Stephenson, eds, *Making Equality Rights Real: Securing Substantive Equality under the Charter* (Toronto: Irwin Law, 2009) 373; Karen Schucher & Judith Keene, *Statutory Human Rights and Substantive Equality — Why and How to Avoid the Injury of the* Law *Approach* (Toronto: LEAF, 2007). Scholars have expressed concerns about the negative implications for complainants of importing the *Law* contextual factors into the analysis of discrimination in the statutory human rights context. Reaume, Schucher, and Keene all agree that the *Law* contextual factors "test" should only be imported into a human rights case when doing so furthers substantive equality — the purpose of human rights statutes. At the same time, both argue that allowing *Law* to dominate the adjudication of complaints is inappropriate for several reasons. Central concerns identified by Reaume, Schucher, and Keene include undermining the codes' purpose of facilitating access to justice by rigidly applying overly complicated tests, elevating the claimant's evidentiary burden, and shifting the evidentiary burden to require complainants to disprove respondent defences at the *prima facie* case stage of a complaint. See Denise Réaume, "Defending the Human Rights Codes from the *Charter*" (2012) 9 JL & Equality 67, in which the author argues against the importation of *Law*'s contextual factors into statutory human rights adjudication.

an inaccurate generalization about need, capacity, or circumstance, or does it, in fact, correspond to need, capacity, or circumstance?

Law, however, did not make stereotyping an essential ingredient of the definition of discrimination. The Court acknowledged in *Law* that substantive discrimination may manifest without regard to any of the contextual factors to which the Court referred.[38] *Law* presents the application of stereotypical characteristics and the "effect of perpetuating or promoting the view that the individual is less capable, or less worthy of recognition" as *alternative* bases for finding discrimination. Support for the proposition that stereotype is not a prerequisite to a finding of discrimination can be found throughout the Court's section 15 equality jurisprudence.[39]

When considering the question of what *Law* means today for the interpretation of human rights legislation, account must also be taken of the fact that a lot has transpired in section 15 jurisprudence since *Law*. In the post-*Law* cases of *Kapp*[40] and *Withler*,[41] the Supreme Court confirmed that the contextual factors in *Law* are not to be rigidly applied as a *legal test*. In *Kapp* and *Withler*, the Court also confirmed that discrimination may result not only from stereotyping but also from the perpetuation of pre-existing group-based disadvantage.[42]

It is to be hoped that the post-*Law* pronouncements by the Supreme Court will diminish respondent claims that there can be no discrimination without proof of stereotyping. Recently, particularly since *Kapp* and *Withler*,

---

38 *Law*, above note 25 at para 62.

39 See above note 26.

40 *Kapp*, above note 35.

41 *Withler v Canada (AG)*, 2011 SCC 12 [*Withler*].

42 *Kapp*, above note 35 at paras 22–24; *Withler*, above note 41 at paras 35–37. In *Kapp*, the Court cites Sophia Reibetanz Moreau, "Equality Rights and the Relevance of Comparator Groups" (2006) 5 JL & Equality 81; Daphne Gilbert & Diana Majury, "Critical Comparisons: The Supreme Court of Canada Dooms Section 15" (2006) 24 Windsor YB Access Just 111 [Gilbert & Majury, "Critical Comparisons"]; Beverley Baines, "Equality, Comparison, Discrimination, Status" in Faraday, Denike, & Stephenson, eds, above note 37, 73; Dianne Pothier, "Equality as a Comparative Concept: Mirror, Mirror, on the Wall, What's the Fairest of Them All?" in Sheila McIntyre & Sanda Rodgers, eds, *Diminishing Returns: Inequality and the Canadian Charter of Rights and Freedoms* (Markham, ON: LexisNexis Butterworths, 2006) 135. See also Dianne Pothier, "Connecting Grounds of Discrimination to Real People's Real Experiences" (2001) 13 CJWL 37; Bruce Ryder, Cidalia Faria, & Emily Lawrence, "What's *Law* Good For? An Empirical Overview of *Charter* Equality Rights Decisions" (2004) 24 Sup Ct L Rev (2d) 103; Mayo Moran, "Protesting Too Much: Rational Basis Review under Canada's Equality Guarantee" in McIntyre & Rodgers, eds, *ibid*, 71; Sheila McIntyre, "Deference and Dominance: Equality without Substance" in McIntyre & Rodgers, eds, *ibid*, 95.

courts and tribunals have begun to demonstrate confidence that, in statutory human rights cases, it is necessary neither to make stereotyping an indispensable element of *prima facie* discrimination nor to apply the contextual factors in *Law* as though they constituted a rigid legal test.[43] In most cases of alleged disability discrimination, it *will* be self-evident that adverse treatment or adverse effects, based on the ground of disability, constitutes substantive discrimination. It is incontestable that people with disabilities are a disadvantaged group. It should not be necessary to prove this in each and every case. Measures that have the effect of disadvantaging persons with disabilities, based on the ground of disability, will as a general rule offend the principle of substantive equality that human rights legislation and section 15 of the *Charter* are intended to promote.

b) The O'Malley Framework Is Adequate

In recent decisions under human rights legislation involving various grounds, courts and tribunals in British Columbia have found the *O'Malley* framework to be adequate. For example, in *Armstrong*, the British Columbia Court of Appeal held that it was not necessary for a complainant to prove stereotyping as a free-standing requirement.[44] Similarly, in *Moore*, the British Columbia Court of Appeal, though divided on other points, was unanimous in its agreement that *O'Malley* is the framework for determining whether there is *prima facie* discrimination.[45] We agree that the *O'Malley* framework is adequate and appropriate for the analysis of statutory human

---

43 *Ontario (Disability Support Program) v Tranchemontagne*, 2010 ONCA 593 [*Tranchemontagne*]. In this regard, the decision of the Ontario Court of Appeal is significant. The challenge in *Tranchemontagne* was to a statutory human rights complaint concerning the exclusion from Ontario's Disability Support Program of people suffering from drug or alcohol dependency as their sole disability. The question of what is required to establish a *prima facie* case of discrimination was hotly contested.

Although the Court of Appeal cited Abella J's minority decision in *McGill* with approval, the court did not actually apply her approach in *McGill*. Rather than adopting an exclusive focus on stereotyping, the court recognized that discrimination consists of a grounds-based distinction that creates disadvantage by perpetuating prejudice, pre-existing disadvantage, *or* stereotyping (*ibid* at paras 84, 85, and 95). Further, instead of holding that the complainant must prove either of these things as a free-standing requirement in the analysis of *prima facie* case, the court found that in most cases an inference of stereotyping, or perpetuating disadvantage or prejudice will arise based on the claimant's evidence showing that a distinction based on a prohibited ground creates a disadvantage (*ibid* at para 90).

44 *Armstrong v British Columbia (Ministry of Health)*, 2010 BCCA 56, leave to appeal to SCC refused, [2010] SCCA No 128 [*Armstrong*].

45 *Moore* BCCA, above note 1.

rights cases. It must be remembered that there are important differences between human rights legislation and the *Charter*. Granted, human rights legislation is intended to address the same general wrong as section 15 of the *Charter*. However, human rights legislation has its own scheme of defences, exceptions, and interpretive provisions. There are also differences between various human rights statutes, which the Supreme Court of Canada has indicated must be taken into account when interpreting them.[46]

c) Context Still Matters

We also agree with the British Columbia Human Rights Tribunal, which observed in *Kelly* that the traditional *O'Malley* framework applies and that it provides enough room to conduct a purposive analysis.[47] The point is not that human rights adjudicators should never consider the social, legal, and historical context for a complaint — that may be part of the richness of what a complainant has to tell and what is necessary to really understand the extent and the nature of the harm that an individual case exemplifies. The *Kelly* case is a good example. Mr Kelly was an Aboriginal inmate who claimed he had been discriminated against because he was not provided with access to an Aboriginal spiritual advisor while in segregation. Mr Kelly argued that historical disadvantage is a factor that is properly considered in assessing treatment on the basis of a prohibited ground, and in particular that historical discrimination against Aboriginal people in the criminal justice system is a factor that should influence a purposive approach to the analysis of discrimination in this case. Against this background, the tribunal agreed to take into account evidence of the historical treatment and experience of Aboriginal people in the Canadian criminal justice system.[48] This evidence helped the tribunal to understand Mr Kelly's vulnerability as an Aboriginal prisoner and, it can be inferred, to reach its conclusion that the denial of access to an Aboriginal spiritual advisor was connected to the complainant's religion and ancestry and was not, as the respondent had contended, based exclusively on his security classification.

The *O'Malley* framework must be understood to permit a contextual analysis so that it can deal with appropriately targeted measures. A recurring issue in the jurisprudence under statutory human rights legislation and section 15 of the *Charter* is whether affirmative action or other initiatives

46 *Andrews v Law Society of British Columbia*, [1989] 1 SCR 143 at para 38 [*Andrews*].

47 *Kelly v British Columbia (Ministry of Public Safety and Solicitor General) (No 3)*, 2011 BCHRT 183 at paras 277–78 [*Kelly*].

48 *Ibid* at para 7. The tribunal accepts that Mr Kelly, as an Aboriginal inmate, was in a particularly vulnerable position.

targeted to disadvantaged groups should be regarded as presumptively discriminatory. There is a valid concern that a decontextualized approach to discrimination analysis in statutory human rights cases may result in such initiatives being struck down.[49] For example, in the wake of section 67 being removed from the *Indian Act*, some worry about the potential for race-based attacks by non-Aboriginal complainants against initiatives targeted to on-reserve Aboriginal people.

d) Problems in *Charter* Jurisprudence Should Not Be Walled Off

Although the *Charter* has section 15(2) as a response to such challenges, human rights legislation provides various, inconsistent, and in some instances incomplete responses, depending on the jurisdiction. To ensure that affirmative action and targeted initiatives are not overly vulnerable to being struck down, it seems appropriate to read human rights legislation as implicitly including the equivalent of a section 15(2) *Charter* provision. Although

---

49 See, for example, *Tomen v OTF (No 3)* (1989), 11 CHRR D/223, cited in *Tomen v OTF (No 4)* (1994), 20 CHRR D/257 (Ont Bd Inq). A successful human rights complaint was brought against the Federation of Women Teachers' Associations of Ontario (FWTAO), ostensibly because female teachers were compelled to be members of the women's teachers' union. The case is complicated in part because the complainants were women. In reality it was a successful union-raiding strategy, in which the female complainants were visible, and behind them, though invisible, was another union that wished to increase its membership. The tribunal found that the complainants had established a *prima facie* case, based on a very low burden of proof and a decontextualized analysis of adverse effects. The FWTAO argued that the FWTAO was an affirmative action program and presented extensive evidence supporting the need for initiatives targeted to women teachers. However, the tribunal found that the FWTAO was unable to qualify as an affirmative action program since it was an organization and not a "program." The result was that FWTAO, an organization very important to women teachers because they had always been disadvantaged in comparison to men, was merged with a "gender neutral" teachers' union that had always been dominated by men. See *Keyes v Pandora Publishing Assn (No 2)* (1992), 16 CHRR D/148 (NS Bd Inq), a challenge to the policy of a newspaper produced by, for, and about women to print letters and articles only from women. The Board of Inquiry decided that Nova Scotia's human rights legislation should be read as though it included a provision analogous to s 15(2) of the *Charter*. See, for example, *Stopps v Just Ladies Fitness (Metrotown) and D (No 3)*, 2006 BCHRT 557: a challenge to a women's only gym and fitness facility; *Nixon*, above note 35: a challenge to a service provided by and for women fleeing male violence; *Armstrong*, above note 44: a challenge to government failure to fund a particular screening test for cancer in men although it provided funding for testing for breast cancer in women. These two cases were ultimately unsuccessful challenges to targeted initiatives.

such a provision could operate as a defence, assigning it the role of interpretive clause is more consistent with treating the prohibition against discrimination as a mandate for substantive, not just formal, equality. In other words, targeted ameliorative initiatives should not be regarded as *prima facie* discriminatory, based on their lack of formal equality.

Complainants' counsel have become wary about the importation of section 15 *Charter* principles into statutory human rights jurisprudence because the Supreme Court has issued numerous section 15 *Charter* decisions that are widely regarded as failing to deliver on the promise of substantive equality. However, problems in section 15 *Charter* jurisprudence must inevitably be confronted. It is not possible for human rights jurisprudence to be walled off from section 15 *Charter* jurisprudence. The two areas of law — statutory human rights law and section 15 constitutional law — have too much in common to be completely separated and compartmentalized.

As Rowles J explained in *Moore*, borrowing from *Charter* jurisprudence can be appropriate, provided that the exercise enriches the substantive equality analysis, is consistent with the limits of statutory interpretation, and advances the purpose and quasi-constitutional status of human rights legislation. However, care must be taken to ensure that meritorious human rights complaints do not get derailed because complainants are being required to contend with an insufficient definition of discrimination or are being required to assume an onus of proof that properly belongs with the respondent. The majority of statutory human rights cases do not involve complaints that affirmative action and targeted initiatives are discriminatory, by definition. In most cases, regardless of the ground of discrimination, it will be self-evident that adverse treatment or adverse effects based on a protected ground amounts to substantive discrimination.

Overall, statutory human rights jurisprudence has more to offer section 15 *Charter* jurisprudence than the other way around. In our view, it is time for the Supreme Court of Canada to be recalled to its commitments to eliminating discrimination, which are reflected in more than three decades of statutory human rights decisions.

E. TWO MORE KNOTS

1) Comparator Group Analysis

Absent from *Meiorin* and *Grismer*, and most statutory human rights decisions, is the highly formalistic comparator group analysis that can be seen in the courts' section 15 *Charter* equality jurisprudence.[50] But since *Meiorin* and *Grismer*, comparator group analysis in human rights jurisprudence has also become a problem, affected by the *Charter* jurisprudence. A glaring example is provided by the lower court decisions in *Moore*,[51] which held that Jeffrey Moore, a student with severe dyslexia, was not entitled to any greater accommodation than that accorded to his comparator group: other students with severe learning disabilities.

Comparator group analysis as understood and applied by the lower courts in *Moore* and the Supreme Court of Canada in *Auton*[52] and *Hodge v Canada (Minister of Human Resources Development)*[53] requires the claimant to establish differential treatment in comparison with a mirror comparator group to whom a sought-after benefit is provided. This model of comparator group analysis is designed to determine whether a benefit scheme treats similarly situated people differently. Such differential treatment is taken to be synonymous with stereotyping.

However, applying a model of comparator group analysis that is intended to determine whether there has been differential treatment of similarly situated groups is antithetical to the duty to accommodate. It is guaranteed to result in defeat for the claimant and to render the duty to accommodate meaningless. Comparator group analysis, with its focus on finding differential treatment, is intended to serve a very particular objective of anti-discrimination and equality guarantees, that of preventing difference, or untrue characteristics, from being taken into account.[54] However, another objective — that of taking difference into account in order to remove barriers to equality — must not be overlooked.[55]

---

50 See Gilbert & Majury, "Critical Comparisons," above note 42 at 138. Over the last decade, the courts have come under intense scholarly criticism because of the way they have applied a form of comparator group analysis to defeat meritorious s 15 claims. See, for example, *Withler*, above note 41, in which the Supreme Court of Canada canvassed concerns that have been raised about the use of comparator group analysis and warned that "care must be taken to avoid converting the inquiry into substantive equality into a formalistic and arbitrary search for the 'proper' comparator group" (*ibid* at para 2).

51 *Moore* BCCA, above note 1.

52 *Auton (Guardian ad litem of) v British Columbia (AG)*, 2004 SCC 78 [*Auton*].

53 2004 SCC 65.

54 Andrea Wright, "Formulaic Comparisons: Stopping the *Charter* at the Statutory Human Rights Gate" in Faraday, Denike, & Stephenson, eds, above note 37, 409 at 410. The author argued that although comparative evidence may, in some cases, assist in illuminating adverse treatment, its use should not be elevated to a conclusory status.

55 See *Eaton*, above note 24 at para 66.

In an accommodation case, it makes no sense to engage in a search for differential treatment. The claim of Jeffrey Moore, and of disability accommodation complainants generally, is not that the complainant was treated differently from members of another group based on disability but rather that there was a failure to take disability into account with the result that the complainant's access to a service (or employment or housing) was compromised. The fact that some other groups may have received similar treatment is irrelevant.

In the *Moore* case, the lower courts rejected the accommodation claim of Jeffrey Moore — a student with a severe learning disability — because there was a lack of evidence that he had been treated any worse than other students with disabilities. Requiring a person seeking an accommodation to compare herself to other persons with disabilities, who, incidentally, may also be suffering from a lack of accommodation, risks reducing the duty to accommodate to a "race to the bottom." It perpetuates the very exclusion from the mainstream that is at the heart of an accommodation claim.

It is wrong-headed and defeating to require a person seeking accommodation because of disability to demonstrate that he has been treated differently from anyone else. Quite simply, the goal of accommodating persons with disabilities is not to address different treatment at all. Rather, it is to render services accessible to persons with disabilities, taking account of disability-related difference, and making such adjustments to norms and practices as are possible, short of undue hardship. As the Supreme Court of Canada explained in *VIA Rail*,[56] the goal of the duty to accommodate is to render services equally accessible to persons with and without disabilities. Significantly, in *VIA Rail*, the Court renewed its commitment to *Meiorin* and *Grismer*. The Court specifically reiterated its adherence to an understanding of accommodation as a positive duty to remove barriers to equal access to services and to implement inclusive standards in the design of services.[57]

It is simply not necessary to apply a detailed comparator group analysis in such a case.[58] This does not mean that accommodation entails no com-

---

56 *Council of Canadians with Disabilities v VIA Rail Canada Inc*, 2007 SCC 15 at para 162 [*VIA Rail*].

57 *Ibid* at paras 118–29.

58 See, for example, Ontario Human Rights Tribunal in *Lane v ADGA Group Consultants Inc* (2008), 64 CHRR D/132 (Ont Div Ct), reviewing 2007 HRTO 34. This has been recognized by some courts and tribunals. The court agreed, *ibid* at para 88, with the commission's submissions that

> . . . the comparator group analysis is inappropriate because a person with a disability who seeks accommodation of his or her needs does not seek to be treated

parison between groups. Underlying the remedial purpose of overcoming a history of exclusion, and making society's structures and services equally accessible to persons with disabilities is an inherent comparison. That comparison is between persons with disabilities and persons without disabilities with regard to the relatively disadvantageous *effects on persons with disabilities of dominant norms designed for persons without disabilities.* The comparison is a constant. It is a defining component of the concept of the duty to accommodate. Because in accommodation cases the comparison is constant, it is unnecessary to discover afresh what the comparator group is on a case-by-case basis.

The appropriate analytical framework for an accommodation case is clearly discernible from a large body of well-established human rights jurisprudence. Typically the complainant must show that a facially neutral rule has adverse effects on her based on a protected ground as compared with others for whom the effects of the rule are not adverse.[59] Accommodation is not about same treatment. It is about inclusion for people with disabilities, who have historically been excluded from full participation in society. In an accommodation case, the issue is not whether the claimant has received formal equality of treatment but whether the actual characteristics of the person have been accommodated so that he can access a benefit that is otherwise unavailable.[60] As McIntyre J explained in *Andrews*, the "accommodation of differences . . . is the true essence of equality."[61]

2) The Definition of a Service

Another significant issue that has emerged in the jurisprudence is how a service is defined.

Human rights legislation in every jurisdiction prohibits discrimination in the provision of "services customarily available to the public."[62] How the service is defined has become an issue of crucial importance. Reflecting the tension between the section 15 decisions of the Supreme Court of Canada

---

the same way that others are treated. Avoiding discrimination on the basis of disability requires distinctions to be made taking into account the actual personal characteristics of people with disabilities.

59 See, for example, *O'Malley v Simpsons-Sears Ltd*, [1985] 2 SCR 536; *Meiorin*, above note 11.

60 *Eaton*, above note 24 at para 66.

61 *Andrews*, above note 46 at para 31.

62 *Human Rights Code*, RSBC 1996, c 210, s 8(1). The language used in British Columbia is "Services customarily available to the public." Human rights legislation in other jurisdictions contains similar language.

in *Eldridge*[63] and *Auton (Guardian ad litem of) v British Columbia (AG)*,[64] statutory human rights decisions now show a conflict between respondents (usually governments) who deny that there is a public service being offered or define the service narrowly and complainants who define the service more broadly, and allege discrimination in access to it.

In *Eldridge*,[65] the plaintiffs claimed that the failure of hospitals in British Columbia and the Medical Services Commission to provide interpreter services for deaf users of health care services violated their right to equality under section 15 of the *Charter*. The Supreme Court of Canada accepted that "effective communication is an indispensable component of the delivery of a medical service" and found that the deaf plaintiffs were adversely affected because the hospitals in British Columbia and the Medical Services Commission, by not providing interpreter services, did not ensure that they received the same benefit from the public health care system as members of the general population.[66] It was held that "[t]he failure of the Medical Services Commission and hospitals to provide sign language interpretation where it is necessary for effective communication constitutes a *prima facie* violation of the s. 15(1) rights of deaf persons. This failure denies them the equal benefit of the law and discriminates against them in comparison with hearing persons."[67] The Court defined the service as the public health care system that is provided to the general population and held that deaf persons were entitled to the sign language interpretation necessary for them to have the equal benefit of that service.[68]

In *Auton*,[69] the plaintiffs alleged that their section 15 right to equality was violated because the British Columbia health care system failed to provide applied behavioural therapy for young autistic children. The Court ruled that the health care system did not provide "funding for all medically required treatment."[70] Rather, it provided core funding for services delivered by medical practitioners and funding, or partial funding, for some non-core services.[71] Applied behavioural therapy for autistic children was not a listed non-core therapy provided by health practitioners. The Court

63 Above note 26.
64 Above note 52.
65 Above note 26.
66 *Ibid* at paras 72 and 78.
67 *Ibid* at para 80.
68 *Ibid* at para 94.
69 *Auton*, above note 52.
70 *Ibid* at para 35.
71 *Ibid* at paras 32–33 and 36.

concluded that the exclusion of a particular non-core service cannot be viewed as an adverse distinction based on disability that amounts to discrimination. In short, applied behavourial therapy was not a part of the service, and there could be no discrimination in the failure to provide it.[72]

The answer given to the question, is this case like *Eldridge* or is it like *Auton*? is now a key determiner of whether a claim of discrimination in a service will be successful. Put differently, that question is, is there discrimination in a service that is already provided because a person with a disability cannot access it or enjoy it fully (*Eldridge*), or is there no service being offered that a disabled person can claim access to (*Auton*)?

A majority of the BC Court of Appeal decided that *Moore*[73] is a case like *Auton*.[74] The service that Jeffrey Moore, who as noted, had a severe learning disability, sought was defined by the majority not as general education, including the opportunity to learn to read, but, more narrowly, as the special education services that were provided by the school district.[75] The majority of the BC Court of Appeal then went on to find that Jeffrey Moore was not discriminated against because he received the special education services that were available at the time, although they did not include the intensive remediation he required in order to become literate.[76] According to this analysis, the service is only what is already provided to other students with disabilities, and the duty to accommodate requires nothing more than providing the same special education services to Jeffrey Moore.

The reasoning of the Court of Appeal in *Moore* illustrates how the definition of the service can be used to artificially narrow the scope and predetermine the outcome of the discrimination analysis. By conflating the "service" with the "accommodation," and circumscribing the type of education that children with disabilities are entitled to, the Province of British Columbia and the North Vancouver School District, the respondents in *Moore*, effectively shielded themselves from a probing consideration of whether their education system allows for equal participation by all children. The respondents were also able to avoid having to show what the undue hardship would have been in providing the sought-after accommodation.

In many post-*Auton* service cases, the judges and adjudicators do not undertake a substantive, contextual analysis of the service in issue that is grounded in the goals of human rights legislation. They simply state that

72 *Ibid* at para 43.

73 *Moore* BCCA, above note 1.

74 *Auton*, above note 52.

75 *Moore* BCCA, above note 1 at para 182.

76 *Ibid* at paras 186–87.

Auton dictates that there is no obligation on the legislature to provide a benefit or a service. Many then go on to assert that the case before them is like *Auton* because claimants are seeking a benefit or service that is not provided by the government. The British Columbia Court of Appeal decision in *Moore*[77] is illustrative.[78]

Although decision makers purport to characterize cases as either more like *Auton* (the service or benefit does not exist) or more like *Eldridge* (the service or benefit does exist), understandably there is confusion about what constitutes an existing service or benefit, particularly in cases where there is an existing program that funds treatment broadly but does not fund a specific treatment or in cases where funding levels for targeted benefits and supports are alleged to be inadequate, even to fulfill the objectives of the scheme.[79]

There is, however, another reason that the eyes of adjudicators and lower-court judges glaze over whenever the *Auton* case is mentioned. If we are honest, we must admit that *Eldridge* and *Auton* are not different, at least not in any way that is convincing. The outcome of *Eldridge* could have been identical to the outcome in *Auton*. One need only observe that the sought-after interpreter services in *Eldridge* were a non-existent benefit, and *Eldridge* becomes *Auton*.

For people with disabilities, the *Auton* analysis can present an absolute wall. If challenges are only permitted to discrimination in services that are already provided, human rights protections cannot be used to compel governments to design or implement different or additional services that may be necessary for persons with disabilities. As Isabel Grant and Judith Mosoff have written:

---

77 *Ibid*.

78 See also *New Brunswick (Social Development) v New Brunswick Human Rights Commission*, 2010 NBCA 40, leave to appeal to SCC refused, [2010] SCCA No 313.

79 See, for example, *Wonnacott v Prince Edward Island (Dept of Social Services and Seniors)* (2007), 61 CHRR D/49 (PEIHRP); *Benson v Saskatchewan (Dept of Health)* (2005), CHRR Doc 05-772 (Sask HRT), and *Benson v Saskatoon School Div No 13* (2006), CHRR Doc 06-212 (Sask HRT); *Cucek v British Columbia (Ministry of Children and Family Development) (No 3)*, 2005 BCHRT 247; *Ehrler v British Columbia (Ministry of Employment and Income Assistance) (No 3)*, 2006 BCHRT 184; *Canada (Human Rights Commission) and First Nations Child and Family Caring Society v Canada (AG)*, 2013 FCA 75, aff'g 2012 FC 445, rev'g (*sub nom First Nations Child and Family Caring Society of Canada v Canada (Minister of Indian Affairs and Northern Development)*) 2011 CHRT 4; *British Columbia (Children and Family Development) v McGrath*, 2009 BCSC 180.

> A true understanding of participation and access to the social world will require some accommodations that are individualized and may make persons with disabilities much like the able-bodied norm, or "like us" [as in *Eldridge*, where the plaintiffs required only a modicum of accommodation to access health services on the same bases as the "able" consumer]. However, other accommodations may require more far reaching modifications to the mainstream physical and social world in order to enable a person with a disability to participate fully . . . .[80]

The enthusiasm of both government respondents and courts for the *Auton* analysis has threatened to gut the meaning of the duty to accommodate because it is a way of relieving governments of any obligation to alter the substance of the services they already provide in order to make a more inclusive, functioning society for people with disabilities.

In the *Moore* case, the Supreme Court of Canada was presented with an opportunity to move away from *Auton* and to clarify that the identification of the service must be made substantively and contextually with a view to ensuring that public services are adapted to create an inclusive society. Fortunately, the Court, in a unanimous decision authored by Abella J, swept away the faulty analysis of the majority of the BC Court of Appeal. The Supreme Court agreed with the dissenter in the lower court, Anne Rowles JA: the service was, in fact, general education, and special education was the accommodation necessary for Jeffrey and other students with learning disabilities to obtain access to the benefits of general education.

F. CONCLUSION: THE WAY FORWARD

In the post-*Meiorin* and *Grismer* caselaw, efforts have been made to return to a minimalist version of accommodation. As we have discussed, this has involved three moves: (1) narrowing the definition of discrimination and returning to an emphasis on stereotype, (2) applying formalistic versions of comparator group analysis that defeat legitimate claims and distort accommodation analysis, and (3) adopting too narrow definitions of services.

In its decision in *Moore*, the Supreme Court provides some relief on two of these issues — comparator group analysis and the definition of services. The Court rejected the findings of the BC Supreme Court and the majority in the BC Court of Appeal that Jeffrey Moore could only be compared to other students with special needs. Justice Abella wrote:

---

80 Isabel Grant & Judith Mosoff, "Hearing Claims of Inequality: *Eldridge v. British Columbia (AG)*" (1998) 10:1 CJWL 229 at 231.

> Comparing Jeffrey only with other special needs students would mean that the District could cut *all* special needs programs and yet be immune from a claim of discrimination. It is not a question of who else is or is not experiencing similar barriers. This formalism was one of the potential dangers of comparator groups identified in *Withler v. Canada (Attorney General)*, [2011] 1 S.C.R. 396. If Jeffrey is compared only to other special needs students, full consideration cannot be given to whether he had *genuine* access to the education that all students in British Columbia are entitled to.[81]

Justice Abella also rejected the finding of the lower courts that the service in question was special education, not general education:

> I agree with Rowles J.A. that for students with learning disabilities like Jeffrey's, special education is not the service, it is the *means* by which those students get meaningful access to the general education services available to all of British Columbia's students . . . .[82]

She also wrote, "Adequate special education . . . is not a dispensable luxury. For those with severe learning disabilities, it is the ramp that provides access to the statutory commitment to education made to *all* children in British Columbia."[83]

For people with disabilities, and especially for the parents of children with learning disabilities, *Moore* is a groundbreaking victory. The Court unanimously swept away the faulty analysis of the lower courts on comparator group analysis and the definition of the service.

However, while the *Moore* decision is an advance, we do not conclude that employers and governments will now relinquish their efforts to move us back to a minimalist version of the duty to accommodate. Especially when what is in issue is the positive obligation of employers and service providers to give life, through human rights law, to the rights to work and education, social security, and an adequate standard of living, resistance is fierce.

Nonetheless, we hope for a shift towards a more inclusive approach. Recently the United Nations General Assembly adopted a new international articulation of the right to equality for people with disabilities in the form of the *Convention on the Rights of Persons with Disabilities*,[84] which Canada

---

81 *Moore* SCC, above note 1 at paras 30–31.

82 *Ibid* at para 28.

83 *Ibid* at para 5.

84 *CRPD*, above note 8.

ratified in 2010.[85] The *CRPD* restates and reinforces the promise of transformation and inclusion that the landmark Supreme Court of Canada decisions in *Meiorin* and *Grismer* hold out.[86]

The *CRPD* establishes the principle of inclusion as the key to equality for people with disabilities and imposes positive obligations on governments to take steps to achieve it. *Meiorin* established the duty to accommodate as a critical component of substantive equality for persons with disabilities. In *Moore*, the Court recognized that the fulfillment of the rights of persons with disabilities requires accommodation that is adequate to achieve genuine inclusion. Both the ratification of the *CRPD* and the Supreme Court's decision in *Moore* should give adjudicators and courts new courage to require employers and service providers to realize the right to substantive equality and to meet the goal of full inclusion for persons with disabilities. Our domestic and international human rights commitments mandate nothing less.

---

85 Council of Canadians with Disabilities, News Release, "Canada Ratifies United Nations Convention on the Rights of Persons with Disabilities" (11 March 2010), online: Council of Canadians with Disabilities www.ccdonline.ca.

86 Ravi Malhotra & Robin Hansen, "The United Nations Convention on the Rights of Persons with Disabilities and Its Implication for the Equality Rights of Canadians with Disabilities: The Case of Education" (2011) 29:1 Windsor YB Access Just 73. Writing about the right to education and art 24 of the *CRPD*, the authors argue that at a time when the Supreme Court of Canada has taken a troubling turn towards more formalistic reasoning, the *CRPD* can provide a new foundation of support for social justice for persons with disabilities.

CHAPTER 8

ACCESS TO ENERGY

HOW FORM OVERTOOK SUBSTANCE AND *DISEMPOWERED* THE POOR IN NOVA SCOTIA

CLAIRE MCNEIL* AND VINCENT CALDERHEAD†

A. INTRODUCTION

Just and equal access to energy has many dimensions — from an underlying regulatory principle to a fundamental component of the right to housing under international human rights law.[1] There is widespread consensus that access to energy is an essential need in today's society. Yet, in the real world, disadvantaged communities are disproportionately denied such access.

Unfortunately, rather than recognizing and addressing this reality, the Canadian judiciary, when given the opportunity, has simply legitimated it. More specifically, through the triumph of formal over substantive equality, the case of *Affordable Energy Coalition* (*Re*) (*Boulter*)[2] has reinforced

* Claire McNeil, Staff Lawyer, Dalhousie Legal Aid Services.

† Vince Calderhead, Senior Staff Counsel, Nova Scotia Legal Aid.

1 The UN Committee on Economic, Social and Cultural Rights has stated that the right to adequate housing under art 11 of the *International Covenant on Economic, Social and Cultural Rights*, 16 December 1966, 993 UNTS 3, includes "energy for cooking, heating and lighting." See *General Comment 4: The Right to Adequate Housing (Art 11(1) of the Covenant)*, UNCESCROR E/1992/23, (1991) at para 8(b).

2 Litigation to defend the equality interests of the poor in accessing electricity in Nova Scotia initially took the form of a conventional statutory interpretation challenge before the Nova Scotia Utilities and Review Board (NSUARB) and ultimately the Nova Scotia Court of Appeal. When that proved futile, low-income electricity consumers looked to the *Canadian Charter of Rights and Freedoms* (see below note 3) to vindicate their claim to equal access to regulated electricity. For clarity, the statutory interpretation cases are *Nova Scotia Power Inc (Re)*, 2005 NSUARB 27 [*DLAS* NSUARB],

and perpetuated this version of systemic discrimination against the poor in Nova Scotia.

Anti-poverty litigation under section 15 of the *Canadian Charter of Rights and Freedoms*[3] has sought to ensure that governments do not discriminate against protected groups by denying them equal access to programs and benefits provided to others. Legal advocacy around this important principle has been built on the foundation put in place by the Supreme Court of Canada over twenty years ago, when the Court rejected the view that "where a government confers a benefit it is entitled to attach whatever conditions it pleases to the receipt of the benefit."[4] Social justice–based equality rights litigation has focused primarily on direct benefits conferred by governments, through transfer payments or social programs, and has mainly targeted the income side of the household account book, seeking to ensure that government income and benefit programs are distributed without discrimination against disadvantaged groups.[5] As we outline in this chapter, litigation in the *Boulter*[6] case took a new approach, shifting the focus from household income levels to the household expenditure side of the ledger.

Under examination in *Boulter* was how the provincial government had, or had not, acted to protect low-income households in their purchase of electricity from monopolistic utilities. Rather than applying concepts of substantive equality to government's obligations to provide direct income benefits through social programs, the concept of substantive equality was applied to the government's duty to ensure that disadvantaged groups had equal financial access to utilities through appropriate regulation of private actors.[7] The focus in *Boulter* shifted from income to expenses and from

---

and, on appeal, *Dalhousie Legal Aid Service v Nova Scotia Power Inc* 2006 NSCA 74 [*DLAS* NSCA]. The subsequent *Charter* litigation produced the following cases: *Affordable Energy Coalition (Re)*, 2008 NSUARB 11 (the name which the case bore at the tribunal level) [*Boulter* NSUARB], and, as upheld by the Nova Scotia Court of Appeal, *Boulter v Nova Scotia Power Inc*, 2009 NSCA 17 [*Boulter* NSCA]. Unless the context specifies otherwise, references to *Boulter* refer to the *Charter* litigation carried out before the NSUARB and, on appeal, the NSCA.

3 Part I of the *Constitution Act, 1982*, being Schedule B to the *Canada Act 1982* (UK), 1982, c 11, s 15 [*Charter*].

4 *Professional Public Service of Canada v Northwest Territories (Commissioner)*, [1990] 2 SCR 367 at para 90, Sopinka J.

5 See Claire Mummé, "At the Crossroads in Discrimination Law: How the Human Rights Codes Overtook the *Charter* in Canadian Government Services Cases" (2012) 9 JL & Equality 103.

6 See above note 2.

7 See the discussion in Section C, below in this chapter.

benefit provision to government regulation of private utility companies providing essential household services. Such a reorientation of perspective was essential in order to capture the full unjust and unequal impact of poverty on low-income families as energy consumers.

During the 1980s in Nova Scotia, as elsewhere, anti-poverty advocates regularly appeared before provincial regulatory tribunals charged with reviewing electricity rate increase applications to seek relief from the credit and collections policies of large monopoly providers against poor customers. Successes were seen in the area of securing due process and in mitigation of collection practices. However, while regulations approved by Nova Scotia's Public Utilities Board,[8] pursuant to the province's *Public Utilities Act*,[9] exhorted providers to take into account "ability to pay" in resolving payment disputes or negotiating arrears settlement agreements, the reality was that there was no relief in sight for low-income customers for whom the cost of power was simply unaffordable.

The affordability problem became critical over the past decade because of a perfect storm of inadequate income assistance rates and fuel cost increases passed on to electricity customers through rate increases. In Nova Scotia, increases in the price of electricity far surpassed the cost of living increases for social assistance recipients. Compounding this problem, social assistance shelter rates in the province had lagged far behind the actual costs of housing for years, even excluding increases in the cost of electricity. The result was that low-income households in Nova Scotia were facing "unsustainable electricity burdens" in terms of the proportion of their income required to purchase electricity. Low-income customers were paying upwards of 20–30 percent of their net income towards heating electricity costs alone in the winter months. This left little for other essential needs, in particular access to adequate housing.

In the United States, similar crises with respect to unsustainable energy burdens resulted in a range of innovative low-income programs and other multi-faceted "universal service programs" that provided rate assistance, crisis relief, and access to energy efficiency measures to poor households, all approved and funded through regulated utility rates rather than by tax dollars.[10] Such programs were paid for by utility customers, using a sliding

---

8 The Public Utilities Board was the predecessor to the current statutory body known as the "Utility and Review Board" responsible for electricity regulation in Nova Scotia.

9 *Public Utilities Act*, RSNS 1989, c 380 [*PUA*].

10 For an overview of utility-funded, low-income programs in the US, see the overview of "rate assistance" programs outlined online: http://liheap.ncat.org/Supplements/2012/supplement12.htm. For background on the development of

scale, through mechanisms such as "systems benefit charges." These programs were thus "revenue/cost neutral" to the utilities and government. And, importantly, they ensured at least some equality in access to energy, independent of income.

The objective of the *Boulter* litigation was to challenge the Nova Scotia government's approaches to energy regulation that further marginalized the poor and their ability to access energy. In the *Boulter* case,[11] we attempted to force government implementation of rate-funded, low-income electricity programs, approved and adopted through the Nova Scotia Utility and Review Board (NSUARB), using the application of constitutional equality rights protections to the provincial regulatory price-setting mechanism. In order to achieve this objective, we targeted a provision in the provincial *PUA* that required the same price be charged for all residential electricity customers and that simultaneously prohibited any accommodative pricing regime.[12] The premise of the approach taken in *Boulter* was that when governments intervene in the market to regulate corporate actors — in this case private sector utilities — they must do so in a way that takes into account the needs and economic circumstances of the most vulnerable consumers.

The *Boulter* case raised the question of whether public utility legislation that fails this test adequately protects the socially marginalized in their dealings with private sector actors, given government obligations to substantive equality under section 15(1) of the *Charter.* The litigation sought to ensure that, in discharging its duty to protect Nova Scotians in their access to basic services, governing legislation must actually accommodate the needs of the most vulnerable. While the Nova Scotia courts ultimately dismissed the *Boulter* challenge, our work has raised important questions about the nature and scope of the duty imposed on government, as a regulator, in situations where its legislation and practices result in barriers (in this instance, pricing barriers) affecting the poor in their access to energy.

---

utility-funded, low-income programs in the US, see Chapter 7 ("Utility Affordability Programs Description and Implementation") in Charles Harak et al, *Access to Utility Service*, 5th ed (Boston: National Consumer Law Centre, 2011) 159, including *Low-Income Rate Discount Programs* (ch 7.2.2), *Percentage of Income Payment Plans* (ch 7.2.3), *Arrearage Forgiveness* (ch 7.2.5), and *Systems Benefits Charges in Restructured States* (ch 7.2.7).

11 See above note 2.

12 *PUA*, above note 9, s 67(1). See the discussion below at note 21 and following.

B. THE CONTEXT OF THE *BOULTER* CHALLENGE

1) Electricity Regulation — An Overview

At the turn of the nineteenth and early twentieth centuries, public utility regulation of electricity in the United States and Canada followed a similar pattern based on comparable market forces. Both were regulated at the State or provincial level through the introduction of legislation to protect the consumer, to promote economic efficiency, and to support the expansion of what was a new form of energy and a unique industry. Public utilities were, and continue to be, regarded as a business that is a natural monopoly (typically due to large demands for capital and other barriers to entry) and one which has public interest implications for public health, welfare, or the economy.[13]

The rapid early growth in the electricity industry was marked by instability, as small producers and suppliers of electricity found it difficult to compete and were swallowed up by large corporations. Regulation of the transmission, supply, and distribution of the electricity industry in Nova Scotia, as in most jurisdictions, resulted in a single, multi-tasking, publicly owned and regulated body. In the absence of meaningful market-based competition, public utility regulation was also intended to mitigate the potential for unfair and predatory practices against consumers, who found themselves at the mercy of large corporate monopolies. Regulation in this area further recognized the failure of market-driven competition to achieve affordable prices through "the magic" of supply and demand, creating an exception to the *laissez-faire* economic principles of the industrial revolution.

In addition to furthering economic development, the push towards universal electrification was also associated with social benefits. One commentator wrote in 1936 that "[i]t is now generally recognized through the civilized world that no other single factor is so conducive to the material and social welfare of any community as to have at its disposal a cheap supply of electrical power."[14] From the beginning, the concern for consumer protection and for encouraging economic growth extended beyond procedural safeguards to price regulation and affordability. Finding the balance between public and corporate interests came to be expressed in legislation

---

13 Charles Harak et al, *Access to Utility Service*, 3d ed (Boston: National Consumer Law Centre, 2004) Appendix B.1.3.1 at 2.

14 Donald F MacDonald, *Light in the East: Rural Electrification* (1936) (unpublished, archived at St Francis Xavier University, Department of Extension), online: St Francis Xavier University Digital Collections http://collections.stfx.ca/cdm/compoundobject/collection/stfx_coady/id/1073/rec/2.

as the duty to regulate prices to ensure that they remained "just and reasonable."[15]

The development of economic principles of utility regulation included a "cost of service" approach, which restricted profit margins and demanded that electricity utilities be publicly accountable and capable of justifying rate increase demands by demonstrating economic efficiency, prudence, and sound management of costs. Interpreting a provision in the *PUA* dating from the original statute passed in 1909, the Nova Scotia Supreme Court elaborated on the basis for the reasonableness standard:

> Customers expect a utility to supply good services at a reasonable rate. The concept of a reasonable rate is a heritage from the common law when it was called a "reasonable price" (*pro mercede rationabili*) or "whatever is deserving" (*quantum meruit*). The statutory element of "just" complements the "reasonable" test of the common law, so it can now be said that the Board must determine rates that are "just and reasonable." In determining a just and reasonable rate, the objective of the Board is to protect both the customer and utility, and to safeguard the overall public interest.[16]

Public utility regulation also contained principles such as "non-discrimination" in the administrative law sense. In exchange for a monopoly over production, transmission, and distribution of electricity, the regulated utility was not permitted to simply cherry-pick the low-cost, easy-to-serve customer but was required to establish access to service for all customers — that is, by offering similar terms to customers in similar circumstances.[17]

In Nova Scotia, the courts interpreted the powers of the public utility regulatory authority broadly. In a 1976 case, the Nova Scotia Supreme Court stated:

> The Nova Scotia Act, somewhat broader in scope and more intensive in its controls than the Acts of most other provinces, was the first Canadian statute of its type. It was closely similar to those of some American states, such as New Jersey, which have been described as giving an "extensive measure of control . . . amounting to a complete system for the full control of all public utilities as far as it can be given by legislation."[18]

---

15 See *PUA*, above note 9, references to "just," "reasonable," and "unreasonable" rates include the board's duty to investigate (s 19), to determine rates (ss 44 & 45), and to maintain oversight of the public utility (ss 83 and 87).

16 *Re City of Dartmouth*, [1976] NSJ No 457 at paras 10–11 (SCAD) [*City of Dartmouth*].

17 See *PUA*, above note 9, ss 52 and 67(1), discussed at length below.

18 *City of Dartmouth*, above note 16 at para 8.

This expansive approach to the regulatory authority, reaffirmed in Nova Scotia in the 1970s based on legislation dating from the turn of the century, has continued largely uninterrupted to the present day.

2) The Failure of the Statutory Interpretation Approach to Rate Affordability

In the wake of the 1970s oil crisis, public utility regulation in the United States took a new turn. Increasing demands by vulnerable consumer groups for added protection in the form of affordability led to new initiatives, including regulated lifeline rate programs, low-income energy efficiency measures, and modified credit and collections policies.[19] Deregulation in the 1990s led to a further push for greater protection of low-income consumers through the regulatory process as a kind of safety net to the new world of competition in the arena of utility pricing in the United States. New legislative reforms were introduced to bolster low-income affordability programs in many states. As a result, over thirty-five states currently boast regulated utility-rate funded low-income programs providing rate assistance, crisis relief, and/or energy efficiency measures.[20]

Two interrelated principles underlay the pressure for rate accommodation for low-income consumers. The first is the inelasticity of the demand. Because a certain amount of electricity is a basic need, it is not susceptible to price signals: i.e., even if the cost is unaffordable, consumers cannot reduce their expenditures below a minimum amount because electricity is essential to cooking, lighting, refrigeration, and, in some cases, heating. The second is energy burden, calculated as the proportion of net income required to meet electricity costs. Sustainable electricity burdens have been calculated at 3–4 percent of net household income for non-heating households or 6 percent of income for customers who use electricity to heat their homes.[21]

---

19 Lifeline rates provide minimum basic service, often for vulnerable groups or for those living in poverty.

20 LIHEAP Clearinghouse, "2010 State-by-State Supplements to Energy Assistance and Energy Efficiency," online: LIHEAP Clearinghouse http://liheap.ncat.org.

21 See, for example, the expert evidence of Roger Colton referred to by the NSUARB at para 102 of the *Charter* decision (*Boulter* NSUARB, above note 2) and also Roger Colton, "Home Energy Affordability in Manitoba: A Low-Income Affordability Program for Manitoba Hydro," online: Fisher, Sheehan, & Colton www.fsconline.com; "Impact Evaluation and Concurrent Process Evaluation of the New Jersey Universal Service Fund" (April 2006), online: APPRISE Inc www.appriseinc.org.

In contrast to the United States, the field of public utility regulation in Canada saw fewer innovations and changes. While deregulation was tried in Alberta and Ontario for relatively short time periods, in the 1990s and 2000s, it was not embraced as it had been in California and other American jurisdictions. Credit and collections policies in Canada were modified in response to consumer protection concerns, but largely in order to ensure procedural fairness in the delivery of disconnection notices and in providing a process for resolution of billing disputes, without substantive write-offs or reduction in arrears. In the mid-2000s, energy efficiency programs also began to form part of regulatory measures as a means of averting the additional capital investment costs of expanding production.

Thus, energy rate affordability was an area that had been largely untouched and unchallenged in Canada, until a group of Nova Scotia low-income advocates and consumers, represented by Dalhousie Legal Aid Service (DLAS), intervened in a 2004 application by Nova Scotia Power Inc for a rate increase.[22] A first approach in advancing affordability claims on behalf of low-income consumers — the one adopted by DLAS in that case — was to ask that utility regulators interpret their role in imposing "just and reasonable" rates[23] as requiring the accommodation of low-income consumers in order to ensure that rates for these customers were in fact manageable and "just." Interpretive reference was made to the equality rights provision of the *Charter* as mandating the public value of substantive equality central to statutory interpretation. It was argued that such an approach was necessary in order to ensure an "equality-consistent" interpretation and application of the statute. As DLAS formulated this submission before the Nova Scotia Utility and Review Board:

22 *DLAS* NSUARB, above note 2. Since then in Nova Scotia, Ontario, and Manitoba, boards and courts have been asked to interpret the scope of the existing regulatory framework to set utility prices or rates based on affordability for low-income consumers; see *Advocacy Centre for Tenants-Ontario v Ontario Energy Board* (2008), 293 DLR (4th) 684 (Ont Div Ct); *Boulter* NSCA, above note 2.

23 The NSUARB's remedial authority under the *PUA*, above note 9, is broad. Under "Orders by Board respecting rates and charges of utility," s 44 states, "The Board may make from time to time such orders as it deems just in respect to the tolls, rates and charges to be paid to any public utility for services rendered or facilities provided, and amend or rescind such orders or make new orders in substitution therefor." A similar statutory provision does not exist in the public utility legislation of Ontario or Manitoba, where jurisdictional impediments to the consideration of low-income programs have not been a factor.

> Accordingly, it is incumbent on the Board, when exercising its discretion under s. 44 of the *PUA* to make an order that is "just," to do so in a manner which is consistent with the value of Equality. It is now well settled in law that when determining the interpretive scope of inherently open-ended terms in an *Act* (such as "just"), especially in a context where access to an essential "service" is being considered, a tribunal or court should construe the term in a way which best promotes *Charter* values. Similarly, the Board's discretion in s. 44 of the PUA to make remedial orders must be informed by and consistent with *Charter* values. The open-ended discretion in that section is to be exercised in a manner which is compliant with *Charter* values.[24]

This statutory interpretation claim was rebuffed by both the NSUARB[25] and the court,[26] as requiring powers outside the scope of the board's statutory jurisdiction. Relying on section 67 of the *PUA*,[27] the NSUARB and, ultimately, the Nova Scotia Court of Appeal concluded that the board lacked the jurisdiction to consider either accommodation of the poor or rate affordability as a factor in the rate-making exercise. In the Court of Appeal's view:

> The statute does not endow the Board with discretion to consider the social justice of reduced rates for low income customers. It is not for the Board or this court to read into s. 67(1) the words: ". . . similar circumstances and conditions in respect of *the income level of customers and* service of the same description." It is for the Legislature to decide whether to expand the Board's purview with the italicized words.[28]

This initial foray to establish equality in energy affordability was thus unsuccessful.

C. THE CONSTITUTIONAL APPROACH TO RATE AFFORDABILITY: FRAMING THE *CHARTER* CLAIM IN *BOULTER*

1) The Equality Claim in *Boulter*

With the door to an equality-consistent application of the statute closed to low-income electricity consumers in Nova Scotia, one litigation option remained: a full section 15 *Charter* challenge to a regime which stipulated a

24 *DLAS* NSUARB, above note 2 at 251.

25 *Ibid.*

26 *DLAS* NSCA, above note 2 at paras 25, 33, and 39.

27 *PUA*, above note 9, s 67(1).

28 *DLAS* NSCA, above note 2 at para 25.

single price for all consumers of electrical energy, with no accommodation for the poor. There seemed little doubt as to the applicability of the *Charter* to a regulated price-setting regime (even where the entity being regulated was a private corporation) in light of the Supreme Court of Canada's conclusion in *Vriend v Alberta*: "The respondents' submission has failed to distinguish between 'private activity' and 'laws that regulate private activity.' The former is not subject to the *Charter*, while the latter obviously is."[29]

In framing the substantive claim in *Boulter*, we first had to consider what the focal point of the section 15 challenge should be. Given that the NSUARB and the court had interpreted the legislative provision at issue to require that all residential customers pay identical rates for electricity, the question about how to frame the discrimination argument was critical. The applicable provision of the Nova Scotia *PUA* read as follows:

> 67 (1) All tolls, rates and charges shall always, under substantially similar circumstances and conditions in respect of service of the same description, be charged equally to all persons and at the same rate, and the Board may by regulation declare what shall constitute substantially similar circumstances and conditions.[30]

Was the appropriate equality claim that the "one price/no accommodation" rule, embedded in section 67 of the *PUA*, resulted in the poor having to spend a larger percentage of their income on electricity than others? Was it that section 67 increased their poverty? Or was it a claim that section 67 imposed a disproportionate burden on the poor, on women and children, and on people with disabilities?

In the end, the focus of our equality argument was informed by advice from a colleague in the United States: "Remember, the hook has got to be about equal *access* to electricity." What our colleague was referring to was the fact that in most utility regimes in North America, there is a provision that assures everyone *access* to the utility service. In Nova Scotia, the provision in question, section 52 of the *PUA*, states that "[e]very public utility is required to furnish service and facilities reasonably safe and adequate and in all respects just and reasonable."[31] In common with other regulatory regimes throughout Canada, the Nova Scotia *PUA* has created "an economic and social arrangement dubbed the 'regulatory compact,' which ensures

---

29 *Vriend v Alberta*, [1998] 1 SCR 493 at para 65, Cory and Iacobucci JJ.

30 *PUA*, above note 9.

31 *Ibid*, s 52.

that all customers have access to the utility at a fair price — nothing more."[32] A focus on "access" would provide the foothold for the equality argument.

The promise of regulated utilities access is that a monopoly utility such as Nova Scotia Power Inc has a legal obligation to furnish service "to all members of the public in Nova Scotia."[33] This is not a trivial benefit of the *PUA*. The Nova Scotia Court of Appeal characterized the "duty to serve all members of the public as one of the 'two great objects' of the Act."[34] This takes on added importance in the context of an essential service that is solely available from a monopoly provider. The protective features of public utilities law, acting sometimes as a proxy for market competition and other times as a protection from the adverse consequences of profit-based provisions of essential services, are well understood within that field, but have not been examined from the perspective of the equality rights guarantees enshrined in the *Charter*.

With this as a departure point, the section 15 argument became relatively simple. The requirement of section 67 of the *PUA* that everyone pay the same for electrical energy effectively deprives protected groups of the right to equal access to electricity. By requiring everyone (including the poorest of the poor) to pay identical rates for electricity, section 67 has the effect of preventing the poor — including, disproportionately, members of other equality-seeking groups — from enjoying equal access to electricity. All others, excepting the poor, realize the section 52 guarantee of access. Therein lies the *Charter* breach. Put simply, the government had partially discharged its duty to protect consumers in their interactions with a powerful utility but, in doing so, had failed to adequately accommodate the unique needs of the poor in accessing electricity. As a consequence, the poor were effectively deprived of the legislation's promise of access to service by all members of the public in Nova Scotia.

Thus, the objective of the *Boulter* claim was to challenge the Nova Scotia government's failure to comply with its statutorily recognized duty to regulate essential utility services — especially when a utility is provided

---

32 *ATCO Gas and Pipelines Ltd v Alberta (Energy and Utilities Board)*, 2006 SCC 4 at paras 62–63 [*ATCO*]; *Nova Scotia (Public Utilities Board) v Nova Scotia Power Corp* (1976), 18 NSR (2d) 692 at para 17 (SCAD), MacKeigan CJ [*Nova Scotia (Public Utilities Board)*].

33 Section 52 of the *PUA*, above note 9, and *Montreal Trust Co of Canada v Nova Scotia Power Inc*, [1994] NSJ No 382 at para 10 (SC), Palmeter ACJ [*Montreal Trust Co*].

34 *Nova Scotia (Public Utilities Board)*, above note 32 at para 17. See also *ATCO*, above note 32 at paras 62–63: "Rate regulation serves several aims — sustainability, equity and efficiency . . . . In return for this right of exclusivity, utilities assume a *duty to adequately and reliably serve all customers*" [emphasis added].

by a monopoly.[35] In *Boulter*, we affirmed that while the existing regulatory regime worked fairly for most, it let down the poor inasmuch as the "one price/no accommodation" rule in section 67 created a barrier to the equal enjoyment of the access rights created by section 52 of the *PUA*. We argued that the systemic effects of section 67, and the failure to address them, constituted adverse effects or indirect discrimination on the analogous ground of "poverty," contrary to section 15 of the *Charter*.

The *Boulter* claim crystallized the experience of our clients. Living in poverty, they faced substandard housing, were unable to meet their nutritional needs, and often experienced the dilemma to "heat or eat." Evidence presented in earlier phases of the electricity litigation had demonstrated that the effect of unaffordable electricity rates is to curtail access to electricity for those living in poverty or subject them to unacceptable choices. Accessing electricity meant — and means — many other compromises, but especially compromised nutritional health.[36] Low-income mothers are known, for example, to compromise their own nutritional intake in an attempt to feed their children.[37]

In this respect, public utilities law is analogous to consumer protection, human rights, or residential tenancies legislation, all of which seek to redress critical power imbalances. By stipulating many of the terms of the relationship between two private entities, in this case, the monopoly private electrical utility and the residential consumer, these forms of government intervention in the market protect the vulnerable and advance equality. Further, when government imposes such protective controls on the activities of either State or non-State actors (including private corporations) in their dealings with the vulnerable public, such legislation must not effectively burden and, thus, indirectly discriminate against members of disadvantaged groups. To emphasize, whether such burdening or dis-

35 In its judgment, *Boulter* NSCA, above note 2 at para 5, the NSCA articulated a commonly held understanding of the underlying rationale for regulatory schemes: "the policy reason for regulation of prices and terms is that the utility as a virtual monopoly, would otherwise have an unacceptable degree of market power."

36 See Nova Scotia Food Security Network, *Can Nova Scotians Afford to Eat Healthy: Report on 2010 Participatory Food Costing* (May 2011) at 23–26, online: Nova Scotia Department of Health and Wellness www.foodsecurityresearchcentre.ca.

37 See Lynn McIntyre et al, *Hungry Mothers of Barely Fed Children: A Study of the Diets and Food Experiences of Low-Income Lone Mothers in Atlantic Canada* (Nova Scotia: Public Health Services, Capital District Health Authority, 2001).

crimination is intentional or simply an effect is immaterial to the legally recognized harm.[38]

However, as described below, it was precisely the interface of constitutional equality rights with market pricing that appears to have been at the heart of the extraordinary judicial resistance we confronted in the *Boulter* case. While statutory human rights protections have been successfully used for decades to intervene in the labour market or in the area of consumer services, in order to ensure non-discrimination in the provision of employment or accommodation, the strictures of equality rights protections had, to this point, not been engaged against the archetype of regulated market pricing.

2) The International Lens: The Duty to Protect

There is an interesting and intriguing link between the undoubted applicability of the *Charter*'s equality guarantees to public utilities law — in particular the "right to equal protection" (referred to by Bertha Wilson J as one of the "four equalities" in section 15) — and the "duty to protect" in international human rights law.[39] This connection brings into clearer focus the principle underlying our litigation in the *Boulter* case: that within the protective context of public utilities regulation, governments in Canada have a particular duty to protect vulnerable groups when government regulates in areas impacting social and economic interests and that this duty has constitutional status located within section 15 of the *Charter*.

---

38 An important statement from the Supreme Court of Canada concerning the significance of carrying out an effects-based assessment is found in *CN v Canada (Human Rights Commission)*, [1987] 1 SCR 1114 [*Action Travail*], in which the Court affirmed at para 27 that ". . . the imputation of a requirement of 'intent,' even if unrelated to moral fault, failed to respond adequately to the many instances where the effect of policies and practices is discriminatory even if that effect is unintended and unforeseen." Shortly after *Action Travail*, in its decision in *Robichaud v The Queen*, [1987] 2 SCR 84 at paras 10–11, the Court felt the need to, yet again, indicate that in the consideration of equality rights claims, it must be remembered that ". . . the Act is directed to redressing socially undesirable conditions quite apart from the reason for their existence . . . [and] . . . the central purpose of a human rights Act is remedial — to eradicate anti-social conditions without regard to the motives or intention of those who cause them."

39 *R v Turpin*, [1989] 1 SCR 1296 at para 43.

The prevailing paradigm[40] in international human rights law is that all human rights impose a three-fold obligation on State parties: the duties to respect, protect, and fulfill, referred to colloquially as "the typology of obligations." As one commentator explains:

> The obligation to respect requires the State, and thereby all its organs and agents, to abstain from doing anything that violates the integrity of the individual or infringes on her or his freedom, including the freedom to use the material resources available to that individual in the way she or he finds to satisfy basic need. The obligation to protect requires from the State and its agents the measures necessary to prevent other individuals or groups from violating the integrity, freedom of action or other human rights of the individual including the prevention of infringements of his or her material resources. The obligation to fulfil requires the State to take the measures necessary to ensure for each person within its jurisdiction opportunities to obtain satisfaction of those needs, recognized in the human rights instruments, which cannot be secured by personal efforts.[41]

Thus, if we look at the right to health under international human rights law, the UN Committee on Economic, Social and Cultural Rights (CESCR) has stated that the State's duties to protect are extensive. For example, in the area of health policy the CESCR has affirmed:

> Obligations to protect include, *inter alia*, the duties of States to adopt legislation or to take other measures ensuring equal access to health care and health-related services provided by third parties; to ensure that privatization of the health sector does not constitute a threat to the availability, accessibility and quality of health facilities, goods and services; to control the marketing of medical equipment and medicines by third parties; and

---

40 This approach, while still dominant, is undergoing erosion at the margins, as well as internal elaboration. See, for example, Ida Elisabeth Koch, "Dichotomies, Trichotomies or Waves of Duties?" (2005) 5:1 Human Rights Law Review 81. The UN Committee on Economic, Social and Cultural Rights has explained that the third element of the "respect, protect, fulfill" typology should actually be understood as incorporating "both an obligation to facilitate and an obligation to provide." Office of the High Commissioner for Human Rights, *General Comment No. 12: The Right to Adequate Food (Art 11 of the Covenant)*, UNCESCOR, UN Doc E/C.12/1999/5, (1999) at 15 [*General Comment No 12*].

41 Asbjørn Eide, "Realization of Social and Economic Rights and the Minimum Threshold Approach" (1989) 10 HRLJ 35 at 37; Henry Shue, *Basic Rights: Subsistence, Affluence and U.S. Foreign Policy*, 2d ed (Princeton: Princeton University Press, 1996) at 160; *General Comment No 12*, above note 40.

> to ensure that medical practitioners and other health professionals meet appropriate standards of education, skill and ethical codes of conduct.[42]

The UN Human Rights Committee has also commented on the duty to protect arising under the *International Covenant on Civil and Political Rights*[43] and, in particular, the *ICCPR*'s own equality rights provision:

> [T]he positive obligations on States Parties to ensure Covenant rights will only be fully discharged if individuals are protected by the State, not just against violations of Covenant rights by its agents, but also against acts committed by private persons or entities that would impair the enjoyment of Covenant rights in so far as they are amenable to application between private persons or entities . . . . The Covenant itself envisages in some articles certain areas where there are positive obligations on States Parties to address the activities of private persons or entities . . . . In fields affecting basic aspects of ordinary life such as work or housing, individuals are to be protected from discrimination within the meaning of article 26.[44]

The equality rights argument we adopted in *Boulter* reflected this key international principle. We argued, in challenging section 67 of the *PUA*, that the concept of substantive equality in Canadian equality rights jurisprudence provides guarantees analogous to the "duty to protect" under international human rights law.[45] We argued that the century-old provision of the *PUA*, which had been enacted to ensure equality of treatment, failed to adequately protect the equality of enumerated and analogous groups under section 15. This was indirect discrimination on the basis of poverty in the enjoyment of access to electricity as guaranteed under section 52 of the *PUA*. By enacting a rule that essentially says, "unless you can pay the same as everyone else, you will not be entitled to electricity in Nova Scotia," the legislature granted access to all except those living in poverty.[46] The legislature discriminatorily permitted income-sorted access to electricity, forcing low-income households into unacceptable choices as to whether to

---

42 Committee on Economic, Social and Cultural Rights, UNCESCR, *General Comment 14: The Right to the Highest Attainable Standard of Health (Art 12 of the Covenant)*, UNCESCROR, 22nd Sess, UN Doc E/C.12/2000/4, (2000) at para 35 [*General Comment 14*].

43 *International Covenant on Civil and Political Rights*, 19 December 1966, 999 UNTS 171, Can TS 1976 No 47 [*ICCPR*].

44 Human Rights Committee, *General Comment 31: The Nature of the General Legal Obligation Imposed on States Parties to the Covenant*, UNHRCOR, 2004, CCPR/C/21/Rev.1/Add.13, (2004) at para 8.

45 *PUA*, above note 9.

46 *Ibid.*

eat or heat. And the right to access set out in the legislation is in effect discriminatorily granted to some and denied to others.

One of the ironies of this case is that, from a historical perspective, section 67 of the *PUA* was always understood as a standard anti-discrimination provision — a principle contained in all public utilities statutes. It provides that all "tolls, rates and charges" will "be charged equally to all persons and at the same rate."[47] The principle codified in section 67 of the *PUA* has its origins in provincial legislation dating from 1913.[48] Seen in this way, the *Boulter* litigation presented a clash between two distinct conceptions of *discrimination*: the traditional administrative law notion of identical treatment crystallized in section 67 of the *PUA*, on the one hand, and the substantive conception of equality enshrined in section 15 of the *Charter*, on the other.[49] Thus, the court was being asked to decide whether section 67's insistence on identical treatment for members of the residential rate class was in conflict with and, if so, would be trumped by the requirement of substantive equality under section 15.

3) "Poverty" and Alternative Grounds of Discrimination in *Boulter*

An important hurdle had to be crossed in this litigation. Continuing uncertainty around judicial recognition of "poverty" as an analogous, standalone ground of discrimination meant that our pleadings in *Boulter* claimed, first, that poverty qualifies as an analogous ground of discrimination. But we also included an alternative adverse effect discrimination claim arguing that, despite being facially neutral, the impugned provision of the *PUA* resulted, and results, in many vulnerable Nova Scotians being unable to access electricity. Section 67 thus disproportionately affects members of groups possessing, in many cases, several intersecting personal characteris-

---

47 *Ibid*, s 67(1).

48 *Public Utilities Act*, SNS 1913, c 1, s 19: "All tolls, rates and charges shall always, under substantially similar circumstances and conditions in respect to service of the same description, be charged equally to all persons and at the same rate, and the Board may by regulation declare what shall constitute substantially similar circumstances and conditions. The taking of tolls, rates and charges contrary to the provisions of this section and the regulations made pursuant thereto is prohibited and declared unlawful."

49 The Supreme Court of Canada has drawn attention to the conceptual distinction between administrative law and human rights understandings of "discrimination." See *Shell Canada Products Ltd v Vancouver* (*City*), [1994] 1 SCR 231 at para 58. See also *Greater Vancouver Sewerage and Drainage District v Ecowaste Industries Ltd*, 2006 BCSC 859 at paras 287–88.

tics expressly protected by section 15 of the *Charter*. To support these claims, considerable evidence was introduced before the regulatory tribunal.

All of the claimants told their stories: their lives in poverty, the struggles they faced in trying to obtain electricity, the desperation they felt in their attempts to make ends meet, and the systemic indifference they encountered. They identified themselves as women with disabilities, single parents, racialized women, and seniors.[50] The claimants' personal testimony was supplemented by the evidence of nine experts, who established, *inter alia*, that poverty is similar to other grounds of discrimination prohibited by section 15, as poverty has served as an historical basis of disadvantage, is accompanied by pervasive stereotyping,[51] and people living below the poverty line (including those in receipt of social assistance) cannot afford a nutritious diet while also paying for shelter and other basics.[52] Significantly, much of this latter evidence came from the provincial government's own sources. In addition, an expert in social policy statistics provided evidence of the overrepresentation — dramatically in some cases — of members of equality-seeking groups, such as single mothers, people with disabilities, and visible minorities, among the poor.

Finally, two experts gave evidence on the experience in the United States of regulated utilities pricing designed to accommodate low-income people. A United States–based consultant (retained by the Nova Scotia Utility and Review Board–appointed "Consumer Advocate") gave evidence in the area of "regulatory policy, rate design and low-income rates."[53] This witness established that accommodative, income-based rate regimes are commonplace in the United States, where most states have rate structures

---

50 The evidence of one of the claimants (Carvery) and many of the experts is on the NSUARB web page. Go to the NSUARB's web page for its "Cases & Evidence," online: http://uarb.novascotia.ca/fmi/iwp/cgi?-db=UARBv12&-loadframes, and enter the case number "M05474" into the "Find Cases by Case Number" field. A link to the case appears, which will lead you to the pleadings, decisions, orders, and the evidence, which are available for download.

51 See the expert evidence by Bruce Porter filed with the NSUARB in *Boulter* NSUARB, above note 2, which served as an important part of the evidentiary foundation for the contention that "poverty" is an analogous ground of discrimination. Porter's evidence can be found online: Social Rights CURA www.socialrightscura.ca.

52 The expert evidence of Dr Patricia Williams relied on her published work for these conclusions. See *Working Together to Build Food Security in Nova Scotia* (2007), online: Nova Scotia Canada www.novascotia.ca, and *Healthy Eating Nova Scotia* (2005), online: Nova Scotia Canada www.novascotia.ca.

53 See the expert evidence of Nancy Brockway in *Boulter* NSUARB, above note 2, referred to at paras 79–80.

designed to ensure substantive access to utilities by the poor.[54] The *Charter* claimants' own expert was personally involved in the design of many accommodative programs in the United States and spoke to the various ways in which the income-based rates can operate.[55]

This evidence, which was neither seriously challenged nor rebutted in any way, established two significant points. First, Nova Scotians who are living in poverty[56] simply do not have sufficient incomes to obtain minimally adequate food, clothing, and housing (including utilities). Second, the poor in Nova Scotia are disproportionately made up of members of groups protected under section 15 of the *Charter*. Expert statistical evidence from Dr Richard Shillington showed that women, single parents (and especially single mothers), people with disabilities, black Nova Scotians, children, and the elderly are overrepresented among the poor in Nova Scotia.

In contrast to the claimants' extensive record, there was only a single sentence of evidence[57] adduced by the Province of Nova Scotia — to the effect that the province was unaware of any income-based utility rates in Canada.[58] As indicated earlier, the claimants' experiences of either going without electricity for lights or heating or having to make unacceptable choices to either heat or eat were not rebutted. This claimant evidence, along with that of the experts, was in fact accepted by the tribunal.[59] Indeed, the claimants' evidence of the inadequacy of social assistance rates, founded on government supported research, was buttressed by statements from a former premier admitting that social assistance rates were inadequate.[60] Consequently, it seemed that the evidentiary basis, as well as

---

54 *Ibid.*

55 See the expert evidence of Roger Colton in *ibid* at paras 57ff.

56 Using the generally accepted (including by the Respondent Province of Nova Scotia) Statistics Canada Low Income Cut-Off (LICO) criteria for measuring poverty. A 2007 provincial government background study on poverty reduction calls the LICOs the "yardstick" in the measurement of poverty.

57 As with all regulatory hearings in Nova Scotia, stakeholders and members of the public received standing to make submissions. Although all electricity customers opposed Nova Scotia Power Inc's application for a rate increase, none opposed our cross application for a *Charter* remedy, a universal service program to assist the poor. However, the role of opposition was taken, not by the power utility, but by the Province of Nova Scotia, also an intervener, which took the sole lead in opposing our application.

58 Respondent's evidence of Scott McCoombs referred to by the NSUARB in *Boulter* NSUARB, above note 2 at para 109.

59 *Ibid* at para 160.

60 See "Welfare Rates Likely to Get Boost in Next Budget" *Chronicle Herald* (29 December 2005) B4, attached as Exhibit "H" to the expert evidence of Paul O'Hara in *Boulter*

the legal argument, for a finding of unconstitutional discrimination were strongly established.

D. THE OUTCOME OF THE CONSTITUTIONAL CHALLENGE IN *BOULTER*

1) The Nova Scotia Utility and Review Board Decision

In its decision in *Boulter*, the NSUARB expressly accepted the evidence of the *Charter* claimants with respect to their inadequate incomes and the struggles they face in attempting to obtain and maintain electricity and/or having to choose between heating and eating.[61] However, the NSUARB dismissed the claim that section 67(1) of the *PUA* violated the equality rights provisions in section 15 of the *Charter*. The board held that, on its face, section 52 of the *PUA*, which mandated access to service for all, did not provide a "right to affordable electricity" to anyone, and, therefore, there was no distinction in the enjoyment of the accessibility protections in section 52 of the Act between the affluent and the poorest of the poor. In the view of the NSUARB, both enjoyed equal treatment.[62] As the board put it:

> [Section] 67(1) does not confer affordable electricity rates or rates based on ability to pay on any group, including the comparator group. It cannot be said that affordable electric service or service in accordance with ability to pay is provided to either comparator group. The position of the Claimants seems to assume that either or both of these benefits is a benefit of law, that one comparator group receives and that the benefit has been denied the Claimants based on their personal characteristics. The Board does not accept this argument.[63]

In short, the NSUARB considered that the facial neutrality of the *PUA* and, in particular, section 67's "non-discrimination" provision — with its rigid prohibition of accommodation — was not problematic under section 15

NSUARB, above note 2.

61 *Boulter* NSUARB, *ibid* at para 160.

62 *Ibid* at paras 157–58. Of course, the *Charter* claimants had at no point assumed or claimed that the *PUA* provides that electricity rates would be set based on ability to pay. Had there been any doubt on this point, the matter was made clear after the Court of Appeal's earlier decision in *DLAS* NSCA, above note 2. Indeed, had affordability in accessing service been a feature of the existing *PUA*, there would obviously have been no need to file an elaborate *Charter* challenge to the rate-setting regime in the Act; the claimants could simply have asked the board to set affordable rates.

63 *Boulter* NSUARB, above note 2 at para 158.

of the *Charter*. The board found section 67 to be in perfect compliance with the *Charter*.

The board's error lay in its failure to drill down past the textual identical treatment required by section 67 of the *PUA* in order to assess whether despite such a guarantee substantive inequality resulted. The NSUARB failed to conduct any adverse effects analysis in order to ascertain whether governmental regulatory intervention effectively resulted in unequal access to regulated electricity. As McLachlin J underscored in *Meiorin*, in the context of a statutory human rights case (but no less apt here), "Interpreting human rights legislation primarily in terms of formal equality undermines its promise of substantive equality and prevents consideration of the effects of systemic discrimination."[64] As the Supreme Court also underscored in *Andrews v Law Society of British Columbia*, "It must be recognized at once . . . that every difference in treatment between individuals under the law will not necessarily result in inequality and, as well, that identical treatment may frequently produce serious inequality."[65]

2) The Nova Scotia Court of Appeal Judgment in *Boulter*

On appeal before the Nova Scotia Court of Appeal, we again argued that the insistence in section 67 of the *PUA* that everyone must pay the same rate, along with the rigid prohibition of any accommodation in the setting of electricity rates, effectively created unequal access to electricity. This, we argued, constituted adverse effect discrimination on the analogous ground of "poverty," contrary to section 15 of the *Charter*. In the alternative, the appellants claimed that the "one price/no accommodation rule" disproportionately affected members of equality-seeking groups with multiple identification under enumerated and analogous grounds under section 15(1) in their access to electricity in Nova Scotia.

The Court of Appeal decision[66] began by refusing to follow earlier rulings from Nova Scotia courts that discrimination on the analogous ground of "income" or "poverty" fell within the scope of section 15.[67] Precedents

64 *British Columbia (Public Service Employee Relations Commission) v British Columbia Government and Service Employees' Union (BCGSEU) (Meiorin Grievance)*, [1999] 3 SCR 3 at para 41 [*Meiorin*].

65 [1989] 1 SCR 143 at 164 [*Andrews*].

66 *Boulter* NSCA, above note 2.

67 See *Dartmouth/Halifax County Regional Housing Authority v Sparks* (1993), 101 DLR (4th) 224 at 232–34 (NSCA); *R v Rehberg* (1993), 111 DLR (4th) 336 at para 83 (NSSC); *Tupper v Nova Scotia (AG)*, [2007] NSJ No 341 at para 27 (SC):

from elsewhere in Canada were equally rejected.[68] Instead, the court relied on the Supreme Court of Canada's reasoning in *Corbiere v Canada (Minister of Indian and Northern Affairs)*[69] as a basis for deciding that "poverty" is not an analogous ground of discrimination within the meaning of section 15 of the *Charter*.[70] In the court's analysis:

> Poverty is a clinging web, but financial circumstances may change, and individuals may enter and leave poverty or gain and lose resources. Economic status is not an indelible trait like race, national or ethnic origin, color, gender or age. As to the second test, the government has a legitimate interest, not just to promote affirmative action that would ameliorate the circumstances attending an immutable characteristic, but to eradicate that mutable characteristic of poverty itself. That objective is shared by those living in poverty . . . . Economic status, poverty or wealth, is not an adopted emblem of identity like religion, citizenship or marital status, that the individual observes peacefully free of government meddling. Poverty *per se* does not suit the legal pattern for an analogous ground under *Corbiere*'s formulation.[71]

Having dismissed "poverty" as an analogous ground of discrimination, the Court of Appeal went on to address the alternative equality claim in *Boulter*, which focused on the adverse impact of section 67 of the *PUA* on groups identified by either analogous or enumerated grounds of discrimination in section 15. The court started by examining the question

---

> In cases of well-defined and serious poverty, some courts have found an analogous ground and substantive discrimination. Social assistance recipients were recognized as an analogous class in *Falkiner v Ontario (Minister of Community and Social Services)*, [2002] O.J. No. 1771 (C.A.) at para. 73 and in Justice Kelly's decision in *R v Rehberg*, [1994] N.S.J. No. 35 (S.C.). In *Sparks v Dartmouth/Halifax County Regional Housing Authority*, [1993] N.S.J. No. 97 (C.A.) our Court of Appeal, constituted by a panel of five, overturned a previous holding and, in doing so, found the legislation in question discriminated 'on the basis of race, sex and income' (para 21). On the third ground, the court found that eligibility for public housing was a sufficient indication of poverty.

68 *Falkiner*, mentioned above in note 67 at paras 84–93. See also *Federated Anti-Poverty Groups of British Columbia v British Columbia* (*AG*) (1991), 70 BCLR (2d) 325 at 354 (SC), finding that "persons receiving income assistance" constitute a group protected by s 15; Martha Jackman, "Constitutional Contact with the Disparities of the World: Poverty as a Prohibited Ground of Discrimination under the Canadian *Charter* and Human Rights Law" (1994) 2:1 Rev Const Stud 76 at 77–101 [Jackman].

69 *Corbiere v Canada* (*Minister of Indian and Northern Affairs*), [1999] 2 SCR 203.

70 *Boulter* NSCA, above note 2 at paras 32–34.

71 *Ibid* at para 42.

of "comparator groups." In the process, it rejected the comparator groups proposed by the claimants, notwithstanding they had been accepted by all parties during the *Charter* hearing before the NSUARB, by the board itself in its decision, and, once again, by all parties in their written submissions to the Court of Appeal. Throughout the earlier proceedings, the accepted axis of comparison in terms of access to electricity had been "residential consumers of electricity in Nova Scotia who are living in poverty compared with those who are not living in poverty." This comparator group flowed intuitively from a claim by poor people that while the requirement in section 67 of the *PUA* that everyone pay the same rate worked for many Nova Scotians, it had the effect of excluding the poor in accessing electricity.

Based on its rejection of "poverty" as an analogous ground of discrimination, the Court of Appeal went on to insist that the proper axis of comparison in *Boulter* could not be defined on a basis that it had rejected. Instead the court held that the comparator group analysis ought properly to focus on comparing the financial difficulties in accessing electricity of different groups of poor people *with each other*.[72] The court repeatedly[73] stated that it was required to apply the "mirror comparator group" analysis adopted by the Supreme Court of Canada in *Hodge v Canada*.[74] Under that approach, the comparator group should "mirror the characteristics of the claimant or claimant group relevant to the benefit or advantage sought, except for the personal characteristic related to the enumerated or analogous ground listed as the basis of the discrimination."[75] Thus the Court of Appeal affirmed:

> [In the context of] the claimants' submission based on sex, one would compare a female claimant under LICO[76] to male consumers of residential power also under LICO. To consider the disability claim, one would compare a disabled claimant under LICO with non-disabled consumers

72 The Court of Appeal applied *Hodge* to require that the comparator group must itself be based on an enumerated or analogous ground of discrimination in s 15. See *Hodge v Canada (Minister of Human Resources Development)*, 2004 SCC 65 [*Hodge*]; *Boulter* NSCA, above note 2 at paras 57–67.

73 *Boulter* NSCA, *ibid* at paras 56, 61, and 67.

74 *Hodge*, above note 72.

75 *Ibid* at para 67.

76 The court's reference to LICO is to the Statistics Canada "Low Income Cut-Offs," a statistical tool widely used by governments and others in Canada as a poverty line. As used here, "under LICO" would refer to living on an income below the poverty line; *ibid* at para 46.

of residential power under LICO. And so on, for the other claimant categories in this s. 15(1) claim.[77]

It is readily apparent that this kind of *intra-poverty* comparison would lead to the predictable result that all poor people, whether men or women, able-bodied or disabled, face similar obstacles in paying for electricity. In short, *all* people in poverty must decide whether to heat or eat. Such circular reasoning, illustrated by the following quote, doomed the claim:

> Both the complainant and comparator groups have substantial numbers of persons whose power costs add to their unwieldy burden of living expenses, forcing prioritization among basic needs. The *PUA* does not treat the complainants differently than it treats the comparator groups, either directly or by adverse effect, based on sex, race, ethnic or national origin, age, disability or marital status.[78]

Because of the presence of "substantial numbers" of people *among the poor* who were not members of the disadvantaged groups identified by the claimants, but who also faced severe barriers in their ability to access electricity, the adverse impact claim in *Boulter* was rejected by the court.[79] However, the observation that substantial numbers of poor people outside the claimant group were similarly disadvantaged is irrelevant in the determination of an adverse effects claim. The court not only avoided addressing the systemic discrimination claim entirely, it also failed to recognize that indirect discrimination can occur even though not all members of the claimant group are disadvantaged within the meaning of section 15.

The court's reasoning in *Boulter* erased the stark realities of income inequality and income inadequacy from view in three ways. First, its rejection of "poverty" as a ground of discrimination permitted the court to strip aching income inadequacy from the 6,000 pages of evidence before it. Second, the court conducted a de-contextualized and pointless comparison of, for example, the position of men and women living in poverty vis-à-vis each other's difficulties in accessing electricity. Finally, the court's reasoning failed entirely to come to grips with adverse effect discrimination.[80]

---

77 *Boulter* NSCA, above note 2 at para 67.

78 *Ibid* at para 83.

79 *Ibid* at paras 68 and 83.

80 This test was first enunciated by the Supreme Court of Canada in *Ontario (Human Rights Commission) v Simpsons Sears Ltd*, [1985] 2 SCR 536 [*O'Malley*]. In *O'Malley*, the Court cited the seminal US case of *Griggs v Duke Power Co*, 401 US 424 (1971), involving a screening test for job applicants that served to eliminate a disproportionate number of black job applicants, while also eliminating some white job applicants.

Insofar as the court even referred to the statistical evidence showing that poverty is not experienced randomly in our society, it dismissed this with its observation that a "substantial number" of poor men or able-bodied people in poverty face similar obstacles to accessing electricity. The court failed to appreciate that the relevant question was whether members of equality-seeking groups are disproportionately represented among the poor struggling with heat or eat problems. It is irrelevant whether or not some able-bodied men also live in poverty in Nova Scotia.

Dianne Pothier has pointed out that if the presence of "significant numbers" of members from the comparison group is sufficient to defeat an adverse effects claim, then section 15 violations will turn solely on whether direct, rather than systemic, discrimination has occurred. Pothier helpfully distinguishes between two kinds of adverse effect claims:

> Although they are both instances of adverse effects discrimination, there is a difference between *O'Malley* as a *categorical exclusion* case (all observant Seventh Day Adventists were unable to work on Saturdays) and *Meiorin* as a *disproportionate impact* case (although women disproportionately failed the test compared to men, some women passed the test). In the disproportionate impact cases, it cannot be that the comparison is with those who face the same consequences as the claimant(s) — in *Meiorin* men who failed the aerobic fitness test — because that would preclude ever finding discrimination in disproportionate impact cases.[81]

Pothier then points to the flaw in the Court of Appeal's reasoning in *Boulter* more specifically:

> On [the NSCA's *Boulter*] analysis, only in adverse effects cases of categorical exclusion (where *only* the claimants faced the consequences) could a comparator be identified so as to successfully claim discrimination . . . . However, in a disproportionate impact case, there are, by definition, some outside the claimants' category who face the same consequences as the claimants. If, in *Boulter*, there is no discrimination because both disabled and non-disabled persons face inability to pay because of poverty, then *Meiorin* was wrongly decided; both men and women who failed the aerobic fitness test were subject to termination of employment, meaning no discrimination.[82]

81 Dianne Pothier, "Tackling Disability Discrimination at Work: Towards a Systemic Approach" (2010) 4 McGill JL & Health 17 at 35 [emphasis added].

82 *Ibid* at 36.

Having stripped "poverty" from the primary section 15 claim in *Boulter*, the Court of Appeal's "see no evil, hear no evil" approach to issues of poverty means that barriers to accessing electricity disproportionately experienced by women, by people with disabilities, by newcomers to Canada, and by black Nova Scotians remain untouchable. Instead of seeing the fact that single mothers are almost four times more likely to live in poverty than one would expect if poverty occurred randomly, the court's comparisons led it to the innocuous conclusion that everyone who is poor experiences similar barriers accessing electricity, including men who are poor.

An application for leave to appeal the Court of Appeal's decision was denied by the Supreme Court of Canada, thus ending the *Boulter* claim.[83] It is important to note, however, that since the Court of Appeal's ruling in *Boulter*, the Supreme Court of Canada has rethought the doctrinal elements so critical to the unfortunate findings of the Court of Appeal. The *Withler*[84] decision critiques "mirror" comparator group analysis from *Hodge*. This is an important development as that analysis has frequently been used by government lawyers and lower courts to defeat substantive equality claims of the kind advanced in *Boulter*.[85] In *Withler*, the Supreme Court states bluntly that "use of mirror comparator groups as an analytical tool may mean that the definition of the comparator group determines the analysis and the outcome."[86] The Court warned that short-circuiting section 15 claims at a preliminary stage had the effect of marginalizing or eliminating full consideration of the discrimination issues raised.[87] This seems highly appropriate as a criticism of *Boulter*.

The Supreme Court of Canada accepted the criticisms of numerous scholars in the course of addressing and explaining, at length, why the now-discredited mirror comparator group approach undermined substantive equality and ought not to be applied. The Court summarized the flaws in the *Hodge* "mirror comparator" groups approach in the following terms:

> . . . a mirror comparator group analysis may fail to capture substantive inequality, may become a search for sameness, may shortcut the second stage of the substantive equality analysis, and may be difficult to apply. In all these ways, such an approach may fail to identify — and, indeed, thwart the identification of — the discrimination at which s. 15 is aimed.[88]

83 *Boulter v Nova Scotia Power Inc*, leave to appeal to SCC refused, [2009] SCCA No 172.

84 *Withler v Canada (AG)*, 2011 SCC 12 [*Withler*].

85 See the cases discussed in Daphne Gilbert & Diana Majury, "Critical Comparisons: The Supreme Court of Canada Dooms Section 15" (2006) 24 Windsor YB Access Just 111.

86 *Withler*, above note 84 at para 56.

87 *Ibid*.

88 *Ibid* at paras 55–60.

While comparison remains an element of a section 15 claim, the Supreme Court of Canada has rejected the formality and rigidity of the mirror comparator approach.[89] It has refreshed the principles that are to guide a court's comparison analysis in the determination of equality claims. As the Court explained in *Withler*:

> It is unnecessary to pinpoint a particular group that precisely corresponds to the claimant group except for the personal characteristic or characteristics alleged to ground the discrimination. Provided that the claimant establishes a distinction based on one or more enumerated or analogous grounds, the claim should proceed to the second step of the analysis. This provides the flexibility required to accommodate claims based on intersecting grounds of discrimination. It also avoids the problem of eliminating claims at the outset because no precisely corresponding group can be posited.[90]

E. CONCLUSION

In the wake of the Nova Scotia Court of Appeal's judgment in *Boulter*, one is left to ponder, what went so wrong in this claim, and how could things have turned out differently? Clearly, a key factor in the *Boulter* case was the court's negative view of "poverty" as an analogous ground of discrimination. The court's approach to this issue foreshadowed its resistance to the broader equality rights claim, based on the recognized grounds of discrimination under section 15. There is support from Nova Scotian and other Canadian courts, law reform bodies, and scholars[91] for the recognition of

89 For a critical assessment of *Withler*, see Jennifer Koshan & Jonnette Watson Hamilton, "Meaningless Mantra: Substantive Equality after *Withler*" (2011) 16:1 Rev Const Stud 31.

90 *Withler*, above note 84 at para 63.

91 Jackman, above note 68; Canadian Human Rights Act Review Panel, *Promoting Equality: A New Vision* (Ottawa: Department of Justice, 2000) at 106 [CHRA Review Panel]. Compare *R v Banks*, 2007 ONCA 19; *Federated Anti-Poverty Groups of BC v Vancouver (City)*, 2002 BCSC 105; *Dunmore v Ontario (AG)* (1997), 155 DLR (4th) 193 at para 217 (Ont Ct Gen Div), aff'd (1999), 182 DLR (4th) 471 (Ont CA), rev'd 2001 SCC 94 (on s 2(b) grounds, not on s 15(1)); *Masse v Ontario (Ministry of Community and Social Services)* (1996), 134 DLR (4th) 20 at 45 (Ont Div Ct); *Polewsky v Home Hardware Stores*, [2003] OJ No 2908 at para 24 (Div Ct). Since *Boulter*, additional courts have cited it for the principle that poverty is not an analogous ground of discrimination: *Sahyoun (Committee of) v Ho*, 2011 BCSC 567 at para 56; *Mackie v Toronto (City)*, 2010 ONSC 3801 at para 69; *PD v British Columbia*, 2010 BCSC 290 at para 155; and *Toussaint v Canada (Minister of Citizenship and Immigration)*, 2009 FC 873 at para 76.

"poverty" as a prohibited ground of discrimination under the *Charter*. All provinces and territories in Canada have provided protection, under their human rights legislation, from discrimination because of either "source of income," "receipt of public assistance," or "social condition."[92] At a statutory level, this then is a national consensus that discrimination against poor people is endemic and requires remediation through fundamental human rights legislation.[93] In addition, United Nations bodies have explicitly recognized "poverty" as a basis of discrimination under international human rights law,[94] which, as the Supreme Court of Canada has repeatedly affirmed, bears directly on the interpretation of the Canadian *Charter*.[95] The Nova Scotia Court of Appeal's complete failure to address these domestic and international sources, all of which support acceptance of "poverty" as a prohibited ground of discrimination, is a further problematic aspect of the *Boulter* decision.

From the experience in *Boulter*, it would also appear that courts involved in determining poverty-focused claims are still reluctant to embrace adverse effects discrimination — especially the sort proven by disproportionate impact. The Court of Appeal's section 15 analysis in *Boulter* certainly marks what can be seen as a historic low point in the use of comparator group analysis to trump substantive equality claims. On the other hand, it is tempting to speculate, in light of the Supreme Court of Canada's abandonment

---

92 In *Andrews*, above note 65 at para 38; *Egan v Canada*, [1995] 2 SCR 513 at para 176; and *Miron v Trudel*, [1995] 2 SCR 418 at paras 148–49, the Supreme Court of Canada has stated that the interpretation of s 15 builds on the body of legislation and jurisprudence from the human rights field. Thus, recognition of a ground as analogous will be informed by whether that ground, or a similar ground, has been included in human rights legislation.

93 Only the *Canadian Human Rights Act*, RSC 1985, c H-6, lacks a poverty/social condition ground of discrimination; see CHRA Review Panel, above note 91 at 106.

94 See the general comment issued by the UN Committee on Economic, Social and Cultural Rights regarding discrimination, especially as it relates to discrimination on the basis of "social and economic situation": "Individuals and groups of individuals must not be arbitrarily treated on account of belonging to a certain economic or social group or strata within society. A person's social and economic situation when living in poverty or being homeless may result in pervasive discrimination, stigmatization and negative stereotyping which can lead to the refusal of, or unequal access to, the same quality of education and health care as others, as well as the denial of or unequal access to public places," UNCESCR, *General Comment 20: Non-discrimination in Economic, Social, and Cultural Rights (Art 2 of the Covenant)*, UN Doc E/C12/GC/20, 2 July 2009 at para 35.

95 See, for example, *Divito v Canada (Public Safety and Emergency Preparedness)*, 2013 SCC 47 at paras 22–23, and also Chapter 1.

of formalistic comparator group analysis in *Withler*, whether a similar claim would be decided differently now.

It is worth noting that it was the provincial government, rather than the utility Nova Scotia Power Inc, which opposed the equality rights claim in *Boulter*, vigorously resisting the application of adverse effects analysis generally and the analogous ground of poverty in particular. Yet the proposal for a rate-funded electricity program imposed no additional financial burdens on government or taxpayers, so the motive for the government's position must be found elsewhere. Indeed, to the extent that a rate-funded program would have limited pressure on government to improve social assistance rates, one could argue that it was actually against government's immediate pecuniary interests to oppose such a program.

This leaves the substantive equality rights claim and, in particular, the inclusion of "poverty" as an analogous ground under section 15 of the *Charter* as the most likely target of the Nova Scotia government's opposition in *Boulter*.[96] Despite the fact that a universal service program would have cost the government nothing, and actually provided a non-tax-funded approach to "poverty reduction," the ideological and jurisprudential opposition to such an expansion in the field of equality rights proved more powerful than the achievement of fiscal and social policy goals. As to the provincial government's role in opposing the rights claim, as Sujit Choudhry commented in relation to the Supreme Court of Canada's decision in *Chaoulli v Quebec (AG)*, "It is impossible to say whether a class bias, unconscious or otherwise is at work. But, as they say in politics, the optics are bad."[97] In the end, governments' duty to effectively protect those within their borders, especially the most vulnerable, must comply with the requirements of substantive equality. Contrary to the problematic reasoning and the disappointing outcome in *Boulter*, equality must trump ideology if Canada is to meet its domestic and international human rights obligations towards people living in poverty, and, most especially, towards low-income electricity consumers in Nova Scotia.

---

96 See the comments of counsel for the utility cited in the *Lawyers Weekly* coverage of the NSCA's *Boulter* decision: ". . . the point that is of national significance is that the court has firmly rejected the argument that poverty itself is a characteristic that has constitutional protection from discrimination, analogous to the characteristics which are named in the *Charter of Rights*." *Lawyers Weekly* (6 March 2009) at 5.

97 Sujit Choudhry, "Worse than Lochner?" in Colleen M Flood, Kent Roach, & Lorne Sossin, eds, *Access to Care, Access to Justice: The Legal Debate over Private Health Insurance in Canada* (Toronto: University of Toronto Press, 2005) 75 at 95.

CHAPTER 9

THE RIGHT TO SAFE WATER AND CROWN-ABORIGINAL FIDUCIARY LAW

LITIGATING A RESOLUTION TO THE PUBLIC HEALTH HAZARDS OF ON-RESERVE WATER PROBLEMS ▶▶▶▶

CONSTANCE MACINTOSH*

A. INTRODUCTION

The focus of this chapter is relations of injustice and finding a route for realizing a core social right that many Indigenous peoples live without: access to safe drinking water. This chapter explores whether fiduciary law could be the enabling instrument for Indigenous peoples residing on reserves to gain consistent access to safe drinking water. The context driving this work can be summarized with reference to three key facts.

First, there is growing international consensus that access to safe water in adequate quantities is a human right simply because it is foundational for human well-being and, thus, a precondition for enjoying many other recognized rights. Fundamentally, this right is defined as entitling everyone "to sufficient, safe, acceptable, physically accessible and affordable water for personal and domestic uses."[1] When elements of this right are not realized, there is a high risk for outbreak and spread of communicable diseases, and

---

* Associate Professor of Law and Director, Health Law Institute, Schulich School of Law, Dalhousie University.

The author thanks Martha Jackman and Bruce Porter for their encouragement to explore the issues raised in this chapter, as well as all the participants of the 2011 CURA symposium for their collegiality and scholarly generosity. The author also thanks Zeynep Hursevoglu for her meticulous research assistance.

1 UN Committee on Economic, Social and Cultural Rights, *General Comment No 15: The Right to Water (Arts 11 and 12 of the International Covenant on Economic, Social and Cultural Rights)*, UNESCOR, 29th Sess, UN Doc E/C.12/2002/11, (2002) at 1 & 2.

basic hygiene practices essential to good health are undermined. Second, for decades we have known that Indigenous Canadians residing on reserves often live with risky water and have been denied the fundamental human right to safe drinking water on an intergenerational level. This is obviously part of the matrix that has resulted in Indigenous peoples bearing a disproportionate burden of ill health compared to other Canadians.[2] This situation, where Indigenous peoples are often denied access to safe water, has garnered considerable international criticism for several decades and has been identified as inconsistent with Canada's obligations under key international human rights instruments, which implicitly recognize a right to safe water.[3] The final fact in this triumvirate is that Canada has become a leader in resisting the international trend of explicitly recognizing water rights as human rights.[4] This bodes poorly vis-à-vis Canada having a meaningful political commitment to remedying its domestic situation.

Canada's resistance was exemplified in 2008 when the United Nations Human Rights Council put forward a resolution to recognize access to safe water in adequate quantities as a human right and, importantly, to create a body to monitor State compliance with this resolution. Canada front lined the opposition, which ultimately led to the resolution's being defeated.[5] In a similar vein, Canada was one of forty-three States that abstained when a General Assembly resolution recognizing access to water as a human right was passed in 2010.[6] The abstaining States objected on several bases, including arguments that the General Assembly was the wrong forum and

---

2 See Constance MacIntosh, "Indigenous Peoples and Health Laws and Policies: Responsibilities and Obligations" in Jocelyn Downie, Timothy Caulfield, & Colleen Flood, eds, *Canadian Health Law and Policy*, 4th ed (Markham, ON: LexisNexis Canada, 2011) at 581–84.

3 See, for example, Economic and Social Council, *Concluding Observations of the Committee on Economic, Social and Cultural Rights: Canada*, CESCR, 36th Sess, UN Doc E/C.12/CAN/CO/4, (2006) at paras 11(d) and 64.

4 David Boyd, "No Taps, No Toilets: First Nations and the Constitutional Right to Water in Canada" (2011) 57:1 McGill LJ 81 at 126.

5 See Lynda Collins, "Environmental Rights on the Wrong Side of History: Revisiting Canada's Position on the Human Right to Water" (2010) 19:3 RECIEL 351 at 351. The author provides a fulsome discussion of international law in this area.

6 *The Human Right to Water and Sanitation*, GA Res A/RES/64/292, UNGAOR, 64th Sess, A/64/L.63/Rev.1, (2010); UN-Water Decade Programme on Advocacy and Communication and Water Supply and Sanitation Collaborative Council, Media Brief, "The Human Right to Water and Sanitation," online: UN www.un.org/waterforlifedecade/pdf/human_right_to_water_and_sanitation_media_brief.pdf. This document provides an overview of the resolution.

that the meaning of the right was uncertain.[7] Canada specifically criticized the resolution as premature because the vote arose "without allowing states the benefit of full deliberation based on the Independent Expert's findings, their own internal processes and the agreement of states."[8] However, Canada has also had other motivations ascribed to its objections to the two resolutions, including its intention to avoid being found in violation of these resolutions vis-à-vis its Indigenous reserve-based population.[9]

The facts outlined above risk creating the impression that Canada has utterly ignored the crisis of on-reserve water quality or tried to pretend that the problem does not exist; however, this is not the case. For decades, Canada has been investing in policies, protocols, and spending practices directed to remedying the on-reserve water situation. Unfortunately, these political commitments have failed to afford satisfactory improvements in aligning on-reserve living standards with other Canadian rural communities. Rather, as of 2008, Indigenous communities continue to compose the majority of the 1 percent of Canada's rural population that lives with inadequate drinking water and sanitation.[10] The persistence of this problem substantiates a practical need to identify the circumstances under which water rights may be justiciable, since relying merely on political will has proven inadequate to resolve the water rights deficit. In this chapter I propose that the social right of having access to safe drinking water in adequate quantities could found or form part of an action in Canadian courts. The chapter opens with a quick overview of the current water quality situation on First Nation reserves before turning to legal argument.

B. INDIGENOUS PEOPLES LIVE WITH RISKY WATER

Many Indigenous Canadians residing in reserve communities live with water that places their health and well-being at risk. An arm's-length and comprehensive engineering assessment of on-reserve water systems was

7 See Bruce Pardy, "The Dark Irony of International Water Rights" (2011) 28 Pace Envtl L Rev 907. Pardy provides a discussion of the vote, as well as an argument as to potential risks arising from recognizing a right to water.

8 UNGAOR, 64th sess, 108th plenary meeting, UN Doc A/64/PV.108 (2010) at 17. Explanation of the vote after the vote: UNGA-64 A/64/L.63/Rev.1, resolution "The Human Right to Water and Sanitation" by His Excellency Henry-Paul Normandin, for Canada, online: www.un.org/en/ga/search/view_doc.asp?symbol=A/64/PV.108.

9 See, for example, James Harnum, "Deriving the Right to Water from the Right to Life, Liberty and Security of the Person: Section 7 of the *Canadian Charter of Rights and Freedoms* and Aboriginal Communities in Canada" (2010) 19:3 RECEIL 306 at 306.

10 Boyd, above note 4 at 83.

released in April 2011, identifying 73 percent of the systems as being either medium or high risk[11] (34 percent and 39 percent, respectively). Medium risk means that the system has deficiencies such that there is a "medium probability that any problem could result in unsafe water."[12] High risk is defined as "major deficiencies in most of the components" such that there is a "high probability that any problem could result in unsafe water,"[13] which "may lead to potential health and safety or environmental concerns" and requires "immediate corrective action."[14] The risk levels associated with water systems are presently considerably worse than they were a decade ago, when "only" 22 percent of water systems garnered a "high-risk" rating.[15] At that time, such a level of risk was considered significant enough for the federal government to conclude that urgent action was required.[16] The current figures clearly demonstrate the fact that existing protocols, policies, and practices need to be carefully assessed to determine why and how they fall short and to consider whether an entirely new approach is warranted. According to the report's definitions, the 39 percent of water systems that

---

11 Indian and Northern Affairs Canada, *National Assessment of First Nations Water and Wastewater Systems: National Roll-Up Report Final* (2011) at 16, online: AANDC www.aadnc-aandc.gc.ca/DAM/DAM-INTER-HQ/STAGING/texte-text/enr_wtr_nawws_rurnat_rurnat_1313761126676_eng.pdf [INAC, *2011 National Assessment*]. A total of 571 out of the 587 reserve-based First Nations participated in the study, so its figures can be considered representative (*ibid* at i). It is important to note that these water systems serve different-sized communities. Although 39 percent of water systems are high risk, they serve 25 percent — not 39 percent — of the reserve-based population in Canada (*ibid* at 16).

12 *Ibid* at Appendix A: Glossary.

13 *Ibid*.

14 *Ibid* at 15 & 16.

15 See Treasury Board of Canada Secretariat, *First Nations Water Management Strategy: Plans, Spending and Results for 2003/2004* (2004) [Treasury Board of Canada, *First Nations 2003/2004*]. This document reports the 2002 figure. See, for example, Indian and Northern Affairs Canada, *Plan of Action for Drinking Water in First Nations Communities: Progress Report — December 7, 2006* (Ottawa: INAC, 2006) at 1 [INAC, *Plan of Action*]. This government report describes 29 percent of systems as having been at high risk in 2001 and 2002. Reported figures on risk levels are often slightly in variance due to overlapping (but slightly different) time periods being scanned, and due to the fact that different reports/studies seem to use slightly different definitions of risk.

16 Indian and Northern Affairs Canada & Health Canada, *Summative Evaluation of the First Nations Water Management Strategy: Project 06/13* (2007) at 3, online: AANDC www.aadnc-aandc.gc.ca/DAM/DAM-INTER-HQ/STAGING/texte-text/efnw08_1100100012017_eng.pdf [INAC, *Summative Evaluation*].

received the high-risk rating are in need of "immediate corrective action."[17] Aboriginal Affairs and Northern Development Canada (AANDC)'s[18] response to the *2011 National Assessment*, however, downplays the significance of the data. One of its key comments on the figures, which it repeats twice in its official statement released with the report, is that "risk rating is a measure of overall system management risk, not necessarily of water safety or quality."[19]

In fact, a high-risk rating can be triggered through the cumulative effect of factors other than immediate water safety risks, such as lacking plans for maintenance, source protection, or for responding to emergencies, as well as not having a certified systems operator. However, the *2011 National Assessment* makes it clear that water safety concerns did drive many of the high-risk designations. Of the 314 water systems that were rated as high risk, 192 (61 percent) received that designation because they failed to meet a health-related parameter. For example, 150 of these systems were high-risk due to bacteriological risk levels. A further 120 systems also failed to meet health parameters, but because of the manner in which those parameters were weighed, they were not assessed as high risk.[20] It is worth noting that the risk evaluation system that AANDC required the independent assessors to use did not meet the assessors' approval in a number of ways. One of their critiques was that the system failed to weigh the risk from contaminants, including lead, arsenic, antimony, and uranium, on par with bacteriological contaminants, despite the fact that these contaminants "may be just as harmful with prolonged exposure."[21] As a result, it is important to consider whether more systems would have received poorer ratings if contaminant health risks were weighed in accordance with the standards that the independent assessors felt were appropriate. Although the actual level of risk from unsafe water is therefore not entirely clear, the baseline figures support the conclusion that an unacceptable number of water systems place the health and well-being of reserve residents at risk.

---

17 INAC, *2011 National Assessment*, above note 11 at 15–16.

18 The Ministry of Indian and Northern Affairs Canada (INAC) was recently renamed. It is now called Aboriginal Affairs and Northern Development Canada (AANDC). This chapter will refer to AANDC, except in situations where INAC is used in a direct quote.

19 Aboriginal Affairs and Northern Development Canada, *Department's Response to the National Assessment of First Nations Water and Wastewater Systems* (2011), online: AANDC www.aadnc-AANDC.gc.ca/eng/ 1314383237592/1314383364994.

20 INAC, *2011 National Assessment*, above note 11 at 23.

21 *Ibid* at 42.

AANDC's quieted description of the relevance of this data is striking given the fact that in 2003 AANDC had committed to addressing all high-risk water systems by 2006 as a key plank of its First Nations Water Management Strategy (FNWMS). In fact, under the FNWMS the number of systems rated as high risk decreased rather incrementally, going from 22 percent in 2002 to 20 percent in 2004–05.[22] By 2006, the federal government had shifted its deadline to 2008, while remaining clear that "the main objective of the First Nations Water Management Strategy is to address all of the high risk systems by the end of March of 2008."[23] By January 2008, AANDC reported that the number of communities with high-risk systems had decreased to eighty-five.[24] It seems reasonable to assume that a contributing factor[25] to the failure in bringing all systems to low- (or even medium-) risk status is AANDC's policy to fund only 80 percent of estimated operations and maintenance costs for reserve-based capital infrastructure once administrative responsibility for that infrastructure is transferred to communities, regardless of the reserve community's actual costs and ability to find alternate funding.[26] The *2011 National Assessment* reported "a general feeling" within communities that the transferred operations and maintenance budgets were too low to retain certified facility operators, to replace components as needed, and to engage in the required level of monitoring.[27] This feeling was substantiated in part by assessment

---

22 Treasury Board of Canada Secretariat, *First Nations Water Management Strategy: Plans, Spending and Results for 2004/2005* (2005); Treasury Board of Canada, *First Nations 2003/2004*, above note 15. This commitment was part of the 2003 to 2008 First Nations Water Management Strategy.

23 INAC, *Plan of Action*, above note 15 at 2.

24 Indian and Northern Affairs Canada, *First Nations Water and Wastewater Action Plan: Progress Report January 2008–March 2009* (Ottawa: INAC, 2009) at 6. It is unclear whether this figure refers to the number of high-risk systems (and some reserves have two or more systems on their land) or to the number of reserve communities which are served by one or more high-risk systems. In the latter case, a figure of eighty-five would correlate with approximately 14 percent of communities having high-risk systems.

25 Constance MacIntosh, "Testing the Waters: Jurisdictional and Policy Aspects of the Continuing Failure to Remedy Drinking Water Quality on First Nations Reserves" (2007) 39:1 Ottawa L Rev 63 at 80–84 [MacIntosh, "Testing the Waters"]. The author provides a more detailed discussion of the complexities involved in addressing on-reserve water, which include jurisdiction complications.

26 See Constance MacIntosh, "Envisioning the Future of Aboriginal Health under the Health Transfer Process" (2008) Health LJ (Special Edition) 67 at 73–84 [MacIntosh, "Envisioning the Future"].

27 INAC, *2011 National Assessment*, above note 11 at 37.

inspectors who found equipment in disrepair due to "a [reported] lack of funding."[28] It was also identified as a fact in the scathing 2005 Auditor General report, which found that "INAC ignores whether First Nations have other resources to meet this requirement" of covering the outstanding 20 percent of the costs.[29]

However, when mandated by law, safe water has been provided to reserve residents. The federal labour code requires federal employees to have access to safe drinking water.[30] As a result, many nursing stations on reserves (when staffed by federal employees) have had their own water filtration system installed when reserve water has been deemed to be potentially unsafe.[31] There is a troubling irony in this situation: although the federal government will take the necessary steps to actually provide safe water in the face of clearly legislated liability, the reserve population served by these health care professionals must boil and disinfect or import their water, or else drink and use unsafe water. This speaks both to the questions of political will and to the force of the threat of liability.

C. FIDUCIARY LAW AS A ROUTE TO REALIZING WATER RIGHTS

The question of whether the ongoing failure to provide safe water to on-reserve residents is justiciable in a Canadian courtroom has never been litigated,[32] although it is beginning to attract some scholarly attention.[33] The remainder of this chapter explores the possibility that on-reserve Indigenous people may have an actionable right to safe water that arises under the operation of fiduciary law.

---

28 *Ibid.*

29 Office of the Auditor General of Canada, *Report of the Commissioner of the Environment and Sustainable Development to the House of Commons* (2005) at 19 & 20, online: OAG www.oag-bvg.gc.ca/internet/docs/c20050905ce.pdf [OAG, *2005 Report*].

30 *Canada Labour Code*, RSC 1985, c L-2, s 125(1)(j); *Occupational Health and Safety Regulations*, SOR/86-304, s 9.24.

31 OAG, *2005 Report*, above note 29 at 10.

32 See MacIntosh, "Testing the Waters," above note 25 at 85–87. The author briefly considers the potential for fiduciary law in this previous article but does not, in any way, properly canvass its potential.

33 See, for example, Boyd, above note 4. The author identifies how ss 7 and 15 of the *Canadian Charter of Rights and Freedoms* support an argument that Indigenous peoples have an enforceable constitutional right to safe and adequate water.

1) Fiduciary Law in the Aboriginal-Crown Context

Fiduciary law is developing in a unique fashion within the Crown-Aboriginal context.[34] In general, Canadian courts only impose fiduciary duties "with regard to obligations originating in a private law context."[35] They seldom impose enforceable fiduciary obligations on the Crown when it is acting on its public responsibilities; rather, courts are typically limited to only scrutinizing Crown action for lawfulness.[36] This limitation is rationalized on the basis that the Crown is considered to be politically accountable when acting on its discretion. Furthermore, because the Crown must manage "the public's property for the common good," it normally ought not to have its discretion restrained by fiduciary obligations to singular groups or segments of the public.[37]

Although "the Crown is not normally viewed as a fiduciary in the exercise of its legislative or administrative function[s],"[38] the Supreme Court of Canada has determined that in specific circumstances, the Crown owes fiduciary obligations to Indigenous peoples that are "in the nature of a private law duty."[39] As a result, they are directly actionable.[40] If the required criteria are met, courts have the authority to scrutinize the quality or character of Crown laws, policies, decisions, and actions affecting Indigenous

---

34 Lynda Collins & Meghan Murtha, "Indigenous Environmental Rights in Canada: The Right to Conservation Implicit in Treaty and Aboriginal Rights to Hunt, Fish, and Trap" (2010) 47:4 Alta L Rev 959 at 965. The authors describe the "free-standing fiduciary duty" as being "relatively undeveloped in the Aboriginal law jurisprudence" and, therefore, "fertile ground."

35 *Guerin v The Queen*, [1984] 2 SCR 335 at para 104 [*Guerin*].

36 See, for example, *Reference Re ss 193 and 195.1(1)(c) of the Criminal Code (Manitoba)*, [1990] 1 SCR 1123 at 1142, Dickson CJC [*Reference*]: "[t]he issue is not whether the legislative scheme is frustrating or unwise but whether the scheme offends the basic tenets of our legal system."

37 David Elliot, "Much Ado about Dittos: *Wewaykum* and the Fiduciary Obligation of the Crown" (2003) 29:1 Queen's LJ 1 at 9.

38 *Guerin*, above note 35 at para 104.

39 *Ibid.*

40 *Ibid.* See also Leonard Rotman, "*Wewaykum*: A New Spin on the Crown's Fiduciary Obligations to Aboriginal Peoples?" (2004) 37:1 UBC L Rev 219 at 220–26: overview of Supreme Court of Canada jurisprudence regarding the development of the Crown-Aboriginal fiduciary relationship; Elliot, above note 37 at 7–17. See, generally, James Reynolds, *A Breach of Duty: Fiduciary Obligations and Aboriginal People* (Saskatoon: Purich Publishing, 2005).

peoples against fiduciary standards,[41] rather than merely their compliance with, for example, an underlying statutory process. Given the nature of fiduciary law, courts are also able to impose remedies that are informed by principles of equity shaped towards restitution[42] and reconciliation,[43] instead of simply awarding damages.

This variation from the general law has been determined to be a unique and necessary feature of Crown-Aboriginal law. The justiciable character of Crown decisions, practices, and policies has emerged as a practical restraint on how the Crown has and continues to assume or assert the right to control aspects of Indigenous people's lives and communities. In his decision for the Supreme Court of Canada in *Wewaykum Indian Band v Canada*, Binnie J explained that "the degree of economic, social and proprietary control and discretion" that the Crown has asserted or assumed over Indigenous peoples' land, lives, and interests may leave "aboriginal populations vulnerable to the risks of government misconduct or ineptitude."[44] Given this vulnerability, these assumed powers must be constrained and their exercise subjected to external and independent scrutiny: "[t]he fiduciary duty, where it exists, is called into existence to facilitate supervision of the high degree of discretionary control gradually assumed by the Crown over the lives of aboriginal peoples."[45]

The Supreme Court of Canada further clarified the law in *Manitoba Metis Federation Inc v Canada (Attorney General)*.[46] For fiduciary obligations to arise, the majority found that one of two tests must be made out. The first test asks whether the Crown has undertaken discretionary control over a "specific or cognizable Aboriginal interest" in "land or property," where the interest is "a communal Aboriginal interest in the land that is integral to the nature of the [Aboriginal] distinctive community and their relationship to the land."[47] The interest does not, however, need to be one which attracts constitutional protection as an Aboriginal or treaty right,

41 See, for example, *Guerin*, above note 35; *Blueberry River Indian Band v Canada (Department of Indian Affairs and Northern Development)*, [1995] 4 SCR 344 [*Blueberry River*]; *Wewaykum Indian Band v Canada*, 2002 SCC 79 [*Wewaykum*].

42 Rotman, above note 40 at 227, n 36.

43 Constance MacIntosh, "The Reconciliation Doctrine in Chief Justice McLachlin's Court: From a 'Final Legal Remedy' to a 'Just and Lasting' Process" in David Wright & Adam Dodek, eds, *Public Law at the McLachlin Court: The First Decade* (Toronto: Irwin Law, 2011) 201.

44 *Wewaykum*, above note 41 at para 80.

45 *Ibid* at para 79.

46 2013 SCC 14 [*Manitoba Metis*].

47 *Ibid* at para 53 [emphasis added].

nor does it need to be one where the fiduciary obligation has been codified through legislation.[48] The second test has some similar features. It is made out where there is:

> (1) an undertaking by the alleged fiduciary to act in the best interests of the alleged beneficiary or beneficiaries; (2) a defined person or class of persons vulnerable to a fiduciary's control . . . ; and (3) a legal or substantial practical interest of the beneficiary or beneficiaries that stands to be adversely affected by the alleged fiduciary's exercise of discretion or control.[49]

The application of these tests is considered in the next section.

2) Evidence that Fiduciary Duties Arise

As is discussed below, in the case of on-reserve water, a *prima facie* case can be made out for each of the two tests. That is, *vis-à-vis* the first test, it can be argued on the public record that the Crown took discretionary control over communal Aboriginal interests in land and thus water. As well, the interest in safe drinking water, like harvesting trees for shelter,[50] is a matter of survival and *prima facie* integral to Aboriginal community well-being. As to the second test, it can similarly be argued on the public record that the Crown undertook to act on behalf of Aboriginal peoples through the creation of reserves, leaving Aboriginal peoples' water safety interests vulnerable to the Crown's control.

It is evident that the British Crown and then Canada historically left Indigenous peoples with little choice but to reside on reserves.[51] The Crown asserted authority over those lands and communities through no less than the constitutional division of powers, under which the federal government claimed jurisdiction over "Indians, and Lands Reserved for the Indians."[52] Acting under this assumed power and among other measures, Canada

---

48 *Weywaykum*, above note 41 at para 79.

49 *Manitoba Metis*, above note 46 at para 50.

50 *R v Sappier*; *R v Gray*, 2006 SCC 54.

51 See Constance MacIntosh, "From Judging Culture to Taxing 'Indians': Tracing the Legal Discourse of the 'Indian Mode of Life'" (2009) 47:3 Osgoode Hall LJ 399. Indeed, both historically and recently, one's status and statutory rights as an "Indian" turned on living an Indian "mode of life," a conceptualization that centrally turned on residing on reserved land. Although the situation has, over time, become less rigid, in the recent taxation case of *Bastien Estate v Canada*, 2011 SCC 38, the Supreme Court of Canada affirmed that the tax exemption provisions of the *Indian Act* are tied to owning personal property that is situated on reserves.

52 *Constitution Act, 1867* (UK), 30 & 31 Vict, c 3, s 91(24), reprinted in RSC 1985, App II, No 5.

enacted legislation under various incarnations of the *Indian Act* that purported to dictate the nature of band governments and to define and thus restrain the scope of authority of these governments over matters including reserve land, capital infrastructure, and water systems.[53]

Under the current *Indian Act*, as under previous versions, the federal government delegated insignificant powers to statutorily created band councils to actually create a water protection regime.[54] Having failed to delegate such powers, the federal government presumed to preserve for itself the authority to control matters such as reserve capital infrastructure and the design and delivery of core services, like water.[55] Thus the Crown has unilaterally asserted or claimed discretionary authority through both constitutional and legislative instruments.

Alongside creating this legislative regime, under which reserve-based Indigenous communities are legally precluded from effectively self-regulating their water regimes, the Crown has acted upon its assumed powers through enacting various policies and practices; as a result, an argument can be made on the basis of conduct. For example, the Auditor General of Canada provided this overview of federal practices in 2005:

> Federal programs and funding related to drinking water on reserves are based on government policy adopted in the 1960s and 1970s, and parliamentary appropriations. The objective of the government policy is to ensure that people living on reserves attain a comparable level of health and have access to water facilities comparable with other Canadians living in communities of a similar size and location.[56]

---

53 See, for example, *Indian Act*, RSC 1985, c I-5, s 8.

54 See, for example, *ibid*, ss 81(1)(f) and 81(1)(l). See also MacIntosh, "Testing the Waters," above note 25 at 69.

55 See Office of the Auditor General of Canada, *Report of the Auditor General of Canada* (Ottawa: Public Works and Services Canada, 1995) ch 23 at para 23.45 [OAG, *1995 Report*]. The specific date when Canada assumed control over drinking water is not relevant for the purposes of this analysis. It is sufficient to note that throughout the 1970s, Indian and Northern Affairs Canada assigned project managers to oversee all on-reserve capital projects and infrastructure, including water and sewage treatment facilities. The Auditor General's assessment is that the Indigenous inhabitants of the reserves had essentially no role. As a result, their interests were in practice entirely at the mercy of the federal government.

56 OAG, *2005 Report*, above note 29 at 3. See also Nicolas Auclair & Tonina Simeone, "Legislative Summary of Bill S-11: *The Safe Drinking Water for First Nations Act*" (Ottawa: Library of Parliament, 2010) at 2 [Auclair & Simeone, "Bill S-11"].

Specific examples of policies and protocols that demonstrate Canada's assertion of discretionary control over this interest, and a promise to act in the best interests of reserve communities, are readily available. In 1991, Indian and Northern Affairs Canada (INAC) affirmed its commitment to a policy dictating that reserve communities would live in conditions comparable to non-Aboriginal communities by 2001,[57] a commitment that obviously embraces water quality. Then, in 1995, INAC asserted it would remedy all deficient on-reserve water systems by 2004.[58] In 2003, Canada introduced the First Nations Water Management Strategy, which was to address all high-risk facilities, address infrastructure deficits to bring them up to industry standards, design and implement multi-barrier quality standards, and ensure all water operators were certified by 2008.

It is evident that, long ago, Canada undertook or assumed discretionary control over reserve lands, which included supervising the on-reserve water regime and, given the terms of the Constitution and the *Indian Act*, decided that First Nations had no independent authority to do so themselves. Given the crucial character of the interest in safe drinking water, it must be assumed that the Crown sought to act in the best interests of reserve residents in asserting and exercising its control. Any other proposition would be monstrous. It is not relevant whether this control was asserted unilaterally, or if it arose in a different fashion — the conduct alone is sufficient to found the fiduciary relationship.[59]

3) Fiduciary Standards Have Not Been Met

The standards that are required of a fiduciary are high. In the pivotal case of *Wewaykum*, Binnie J confirmed that the nature and scope of the Crown's fiduciary duties align with those that are usually imposed on persons who assume private law fiduciary relationships:

> [T]he imposition of a fiduciary duty attaches to the Crown's intervention the additional obligations of loyalty, good faith, full disclosure appropriate to the matter at hand and acting in what it reasonably and with diligence regards as the best interest of the beneficiary.[60]

57 See OAG, *1995 Report*, above note 55 at para 23.21.

58 See *Report of the Royal Commission on Aboriginal Peoples: Gathering Strength*, vol 3 (Ottawa: Supply and Services Canada, 1996) at 380-81 [*RCAP*, vol 3].

59 See *M(K) v M(H)*, [1992] 3 SCR 6 at 61:"fiduciary obligations are imposed in some situations even in the absence of any unilateral undertaking by the fiduciary."

60 *Wewaykum*, above note 41 at para 94.

"Good faith" efforts that are informed by "diligence" are adequately supported and funded and are reasonably responsive to objective assessments of why existing efforts are failing. However, Crown efforts to date have failed: although all federal initiatives have resulted in some level of improvement, none have met their goals.[61] In both designing and implementing plans, federal policies and practices have consistently been selectively responsive to concerns and observations regarding why they have failed (or are going to fail). It is this selective responsiveness to evidence and, in particular, a failure to modify approaches based on that evidence, that largely grounds the breach.

For example, federal policy has aimed to attempt to require reserve-based Indigenous communities to take responsibility for operating and maintaining existing water treatment facilities that AANDC constructed and has or had been operating. This is despite AANDC's knowledge, gained from multiple reports, that many of the facilities are already not producing safe water and are not capable of meeting health and safety guidelines or protocols. AANDC has strong-armed this offloading onto its "beneficiary" via various transfer and contribution agreements, a practice that, in this instance, has been criticized as being primarily "a deficit-fighting measure,"[62] instead of a measure designed to address water quality or safety. A slight digression is in order, to explain how this policy has been operationalized. As noted above, the federal Crown has long assumed control over reserve-based communities. Given the federal-provincial division of powers, this means that it has claimed fields that are usually deemed to fall under provincial jurisdiction, such as education and social services programming.

Transfer or contribution agreements are the route by which AANDC offers reserve-based Indigenous communities the opportunity to administer the programming which has been designed, administered, funded, and delivered by federal government offices,[63] purportedly as part of supporting

---

61 Office of the Auditor General of Canada, *Status Report of the Auditor General of Canada to the House of Commons* (Ottawa: Public Works and Government Services, 2011) ch 4 [OAG, *2011 Report*].

62 Assembly of First Nations, *Federal Government Funding to First Nations: The Facts, the Myths, and the Way Forward* (Ottawa: Assembly of First Nations, 2004) at 11.

63 See MacIntosh, "Envisioning the Future," above note 26, in which the author provides a detailed discussion of these agreements in the context of health transfers; Judith Rae, "Program Delivery Devolution: A Stepping Stone or Quagmire for First Nations?" (2009) 7:2 Indigenous LJ 1 at 14–17, in which the author discusses how communities are typically deeply dissatisfied with these agreements in the context of education and child protection services, but enter into them nonetheless.

Indigenous self-government. Programs offered include considerable aspects of public health and social services programming, and so are of great interest to many communities. However, any community that wishes to enter into an agreement where it has any level of discretionary control over public health, for example, must agree to deliver certain programs, including environmental/occupational health and safety.[64] The Environmental Health Program includes, in turn, drinking water monitoring and sewage infrastructure.[65] While responsibility is allegedly transferred, adequate funding to fulfill responsibilities is not. This is because it is AANDC's policy that transfer agreements are to limit funding to 80 percent of the estimated operations and maintenance costs of water infrastructure.[66] Given that systems have been identified as not operating safely when run by AANDC (and, therefore, with allegedly full funding), this practice has been identified by the Auditor General and by the Royal Commission on Aboriginal Peoples as likely setting communities up to fail.[67] Calls for reform to AANDC's policy, however, remain unanswered.

Coupled with this policy, starting around 2007, the standard transfer agreement to design and administer such programs as education and housing was modified to impose the following mandatory obligation:

> [Band] Council shall:
>
> a. provide for the preservation of public health, safety and the environment (e.g. address drinking water advisories in a timely manner); and
>
> b. at a minimum, *adhere to all the applicable codes, protocols and guidelines standards for design, construction, operation, maintenance and monitoring of facilities*. This includes the *Protocol for Safe Drinking Water in First Nations Communities*.[68]

The required commitment for Indigenous communities to shoulder these responsibilities is a draconian imposition that Indigenous communities are extremely unlikely to meet. The federal government itself has, in many instances, been unable to comply with these codes and protocols. For

---

64 Health Canada, *Transfer of Health Programs to First Nations and Inuit Communities: Handbook 2 — The Health Services Transfer* (Ottawa: Health Canada, 2004) at 9.

65 *Ibid* at 10 & 11.

66 OAG, *2005 Report*, above note 29 at 4.

67 See, for example, OAG, *1995 Report*, above note 55 at paras 23.45–46; OAG, *2005 Report*, above note 29; *RCAP*, vol 3, above note 58 at 379.

68 Indian and Northern Affairs Canada, *Comprehensive Funding Arrangement National Model for Use with First Nations and Tribal Councils for 2010–2011* (2010) s 10.1.1 [emphasis added], online: AANDC www.aadnc-aandc.gc.ca/eng/1100100010071.

example, despite the promise of the federal government's 2003 First Nations Water Management Strategy that it would have all water treatment plants on reserves overseen by certified operators by 2008,[69] thus bringing practice in line with one of the elements of the Safe Drinking Water Protocol — by 2011 only 54 percent of operators were certified.[70] According to the Safe Drinking Water Foundation, reserve communities who tried to refuse to commit to meeting these standards and resisted signing the contribution agreement "had funds withheld for housing, education, health services or for water projects."[71]

This coercive alleged offloading of responsibility to meet standards which AANDC has failed to meet, and which AANDC knows in many instances the First Nation will not be able to meet because the facilities that AANDC designed and constructed are already not compliant,[72] is clearly inconsistent with the responsibilities of acting as a fiduciary. Such policies do not align with what one can "reasonably and with diligence regard . . . as the best interest of the beneficiary."[73]

Assuming the legitimacy of the constitutional division of powers and the assignment of the head of power over "Indians and lands reserved to the Indians" to the federal government under section 91(24) of the *Constitution Act, 1867*, such a divesting of responsibility is also not possible in law as constitutional obligations cannot be contracted out of.[74] In its assessment of the transfer agreements, the Auditor General has determined that regardless of the wording of such agreements, INAC "continues to be responsible and accountable" for on-reserve water systems,[75] a conclusion that was also reached by Health Canada's Interdepartmental Working Group on Drinking Water in 2005.[76] This point is taken up again, below, where an argument

---

69 MacIntosh, "Envisioning the Future," above note 26 at 76 & 77; INAC, *Summative Evaluation*, above note 16.

70 INAC, *2011 National Assessment*, above note 11 at 24.

71 Safe Drinking Water Foundation, *A Review of the Engagement Sessions for the Federal Action Plan on Safe Drinking Water for First Nations: Position Statement* (Saskatoon: Safe Drinking Water Foundation, 2009) at 2.

72 Constance MacIntosh, "Public Health Protection and Drinking Water Quality on First Nation Reserves: Considering the New Federal Regulatory Proposal" (2009) 18:1 Health L Rev 5 at 6 [MacIntosh, "Public Health Protection"], regarding how facilities have not been built to meet provincial or other building and design codes.

73 *Wewaykum*, above note 41 at para 94.

74 See, for example, *Eldridge v British Columbia (AG)*, [1997] 3 SCR 624 at para 40.

75 OAG, *1995 Report*, above note 55 at paras 23.45–46.

76 Health Canada, *Guidance for Providing Safe Drinking Water in Areas of Federal Jurisdiction: Version 1* (Ottawa: Health Canada, 2005) at 25. The group concluded that

is presented that the Crown, as a fiduciary, is responsible for remedying the situation that it has enabled.

Similarly, despite the fact that Canada invests money into reserve water systems and claims it is committed to providing "comparable" living standards, the federally appointed Expert Panel on Safe Drinking Water for First Nations concluded in 2006 that "the federal government has never provided enough funding to First Nations to ensure that the quantity and quality of their water systems was comparable to that of off-reserve communities."[77]

The federal government received a detailed engineering analysis in 2011 from an arm's-length source, complete with a cost figure for the investment that is actually required to realize the various commitments and standards that are allegedly supported by political will and recommended under protocols. The *2011 National Assessment* reported that "[t]he total cost (both construction and non-construction) associated with upgrading water systems to comply with applicable guidelines, protocols and legislation is estimated to be $846 million."[78] As noted above, the federal government seeks to make the Indigenous beneficiary responsible, under transfer agreements, for addressing the compliance gap that Indigenous communities are allegedly inheriting. Consistent with holding its course, the federal government's response to the *2011 National Assessment* cost estimate was to assert that the figures were inflated and to state that any funds to improve water-quality infrastructure will come from the existing funding base.[79] This statement is quite troubling. In examining the federal government's capital plan for 2002–2007, the expert panel reported that "the federal government's initial estimates of the capital needed to invest in First Nations water and wastewater systems turned out to be one-third of what was actually needed."[80] The expert panel found that the programs were underfunded, in part because the figures were not based on a detailed engineering analysis.[81] To plan without data once is surprising enough, but to choose to not invest the

---

INAC can contract out specific duties to First Nations, but remains responsible for actually meeting drinking water objectives.

77 Harry Swain, Stan Louttit, & Steve Hrudey, *Report of the Expert Panel on Safe Drinking Water for First Nations*, vol 1 (Ottawa: Indian Affairs and Northern Development, 2006) at 22 [Swain, Louttit, & Hrudey, *Report of the Expert Panel 2006*, vol 1].

78 INAC, *2011 National Assessment*, above note 11 at 35.

79 "First Nations' Drinking Water 'High Risk': Report" (19 July 2011), online: The Canadian Press www.thecanadianpress.com. In this article, these statements were attributed to Michelle Yao, spokesperson for Aboriginal Affairs Minister John Duncan.

80 *Ibid.*

81 *Ibid.*

funds that independent engineers have determined are necessary to bring facilities and practices up to standard seems counterintuitive and certainly inconsistent with acting reasonably and with due diligence.

The government's stance also seems to suggest that a decision has already been made that the findings from the *2011 National Assessment* do not signal a crisis situation. Once again, in the face of 73 percent of water systems operating at medium- or high-risk levels, such action and inaction are hard to reconcile with the Crown "acting in what it reasonably and with diligence" could suggest is in "the best interest of the beneficiary."[82]

Just as the federal government has never provided the funding that its own panels, working groups, and other studies have concluded is necessary, there are examples of AANDC not fulfilling even some of its basic commitments. One such instance is AANDC's lack of compliance with its policy that on-reserve water systems undergo annual inspections. When the Auditor General's office conducted a "spot test" in regions where a drinking water advisory had been issued between January 2009 and March 2010, the office found that from 2006 to 2010 "INAC had conducted only 25 of 80 required annual inspections and 47 of 80 risk evaluations."[83] Given these facts, it is hard to imagine how one could find that AANDC has acted with loyalty and in good faith.

Fiduciary standards may also not have been met in the federal government's most recent initiative, which is to bring in a legislative framework to regulate on-reserve water quality. This initiative can be seen as a partial response to the consistent findings of arm's-length government-based or other assessors, since at least 2005, that a regulatory regime is necessary if reserve residents are to experience safe water. In particular, such assessors have identified a need for justiciable quality standards.[84] For example, the 2005 Auditor General report stated:

> When it comes to the safety of drinking water, residents of First Nations communities do not benefit from a level of protection comparable to that of people who live off reserves. This is partly because there are no laws and regulations governing the provision of drinking water in First Nations communities, unlike other communities.

82 *Wewaykum*, above note 41 at para 94.

83 OAG, *2011 Report*, above note 61 at 17.

84 OAG, *2005 Report*, above note 29; Swain, Louttit, & Hrudey, *Report of the Expert Panel 2006*, vol 1, above note 77.

The federal government did table a bill to regulate on-reserve water in May 2010. On 19 June 2013, the *Safe Drinking Water for First Nations Act*[85] received royal assent, and came into force 1 November 2013.

Although legislation is clearly required, it is not at all certain that the statute will remedy the situation. Indeed, there is reason to believe that it may actually enhance risk. This is because the statute selectively addresses the issues that were identified as pressing.[86] In particular, although the statute grants the federal government considerable power to pass regulations to do things such as make provincial quality standards apply on reserves, it fails to create a structure under which such standards can, in fact, be achieved. This is because it does not contemplate mandating the necessary funding obligations. The expert panel on Safe Drinking Water for First Nations, whose primary role was to identify key features of an adequate legislative regime, concluded that "[g]iven the resource concerns of First Nations, it would be useful, almost necessary for INAC's funding role to be mandated in legislation."[87] This legislative element complemented the expert panel's conclusion that "adequate resources — for plants and piping, training and monitoring, and operations and maintenance — are more critical to ensuring safe drinking water than is regulation alone."[88]

In its 2011 audit, the Office of the Auditor General commended the federal government for its commitment to developing a regulatory regime, while noting that "even after the bill is passed into law, however, it may still take years to develop and implement related regulations,"[89] and indeed, regulations have still not surfaced. Regardless of when the yet-to-be drafted regulations come into force, the Auditor General was clear that more is required if safe water is to become a reality. The Auditor General wrote:

> Broader concerns that we believe have inhibited progress include the lack of clarity about service levels on First Nation reserves, *lack of a legislative base to fund service delivery on reserves, a lack of an appropriate funding mechanism*, and a lack of organizations that could support local service delivery.[90]

---

85 SC 2013, c 21.

86 See MacIntosh, "Public Health Protection," above note 72. The author provides a discussion of the legislation's general approach and an assessment of which factors may improve under the legislation, as well as where it may fail.

87 Harry Swain, Stan Louttit, & Steve Hrudey, *Report of the Expert Panel on Safe Drinking Water for First Nations: Legal Analysis*, vol 2 (Ottawa: Indian Affairs and Northern Development, 2006) at 30.

88 Swain, Louttit, & Hrudey, *Report of the Expert Panel 2006*, vol 1, above note 77 at 22.

89 OAG, *2011 Report*, above note 61 at 16.

90 *Ibid* at 8 [emphasis added].

The Auditor General cautioned that unless these concerns are addressed, there is a "risk that living conditions on many First Nation reserves will remain significantly below national averages, with little prospect of a brighter future . . . ."[91]

The Expert Panel on Safe Drinking Water for First Nations similarly highlighted the need for adequate funding, while cautioning that enacting a regulatory regime without the necessary investment could create heightened risk as resources go towards meeting regulatory requirements (such as filing reports so as to avoid being fined), instead of building and maintaining the actual infrastructure. It concluded:

> It is no coincidence that the report of the Walkerton Inquiry . . . put regulation at the end of the list of elements needed for a comprehensive framework. Regulation alone will not be effective in ensuring safe drinking water unless the other requirements — a multiple-barrier approach, cautious decision-making and effective management systems — are met. These other requirements depend on adequate investment in both human resources and physical assets. *Regulation without the investment needed to build capacity may even put drinking water safety at risk* by diverting badly needed resources into regulatory frameworks and compliance costs.[92]

The federal government has this information but resists incorporating it into its plans, policies, and proposed legislation; this criticism was even pointed out in the parliamentary library's legislative summary of the bill:

> Several First Nations participating in the engagement sessions on the government's proposed legislative approach have expressed concern that the introduction of water standards legislation, *without adequate investment* to build capacity, could place First Nations drinking water *at further risk* by increasing costs associated with monitoring, reporting and compliance, as well as potential financial penalties associated with enforcement.[93]

The summary also notes the Assembly of First Nations' assessment that "regulations without the capacity and financial resources to support them will only set up First Nations to fail."[94]

---

91 *Ibid.*

92 Swain, Louttit, & Hrudey, *Report of the Expert Panel 2006*, vol 1, above note 77 at 18 [emphasis added].

93 Auclair & Simeone, "Bill S-11," above note 56 at 9 [emphasis added].

94 *Ibid* at 10, citing Assembly of First Nations, News Release, "AFN National Chief Calls for Real Action on Safe Drinking Water for First Nations: Need Action to Address the 'Capacity Gap as well as the Regulatory Gap'" (27 May 2010).

There is, therefore, a rich body of evidence to support a claim that Canada has assumed roles and responsibilities over an identified Indigenous interest, with resulting fiduciary obligations, and that Canada has not acted consistently with fiduciary standards on a number of levels. The mere fact that Canada is operating in a context where it can "invoke competing interests" does not permit it to "shirk its fiduciary duty."[95]

D. INTERNATIONAL LAW AND CANADIAN OBLIGATIONS

If a claim based on fiduciary law were brought forward, Indigenous litigants would, no doubt, frame their claimed right to safe water within the overarching context of international law, which clearly supports the realization of these rights. Central to such submissions may be the fact that Canada's recent positions at the United Nations, referred to above, do not undo Canada's existing commitments.

Canada has freely chosen to accede to a number of international instruments that either explicitly or implicitly recognize a right to safe water. For example, Canada ratified the *International Covenant on Economic, Social and Cultural Rights* in 1976, which requires that parties "recognize the right of everyone to the enjoyment of the highest attainable standard of physical and mental health."[96] The *ICESCR* specifically calls on States to address hygiene, as well as the prevention, treatment, and control of epidemic and endemic diseases.[97] The committee that oversees the *ICESCR* confirmed in *General Comment No 14* that these health rights require States to "ensure access to basic shelter, housing and sanitation, and an adequate supply of safe and potable water."[98]

In their *General Comment No 15*, the committee considered the human right to safe drinking water.[99] The comment explains that the right "entitles

---

95 *Wewaykum*, above note 41 at para 104. See also *Osoyoos Indian Band v Oliver (Town)*, 2001 SCC 85 at para 51 [*Osoyoos Indian Band*].

96 *International Covenant on Economic, Social and Cultural Rights*, 16 December 1966, 993 UNTS 3, art 12, 6 ILM 368 [*ICESCR*]. Canada acceded to the *ICESCR* on 19 May 1976. These rights are not absolute, but are intended to be realized gradually in accordance with the resources of member States (*ibid*, art 2).

97 *Ibid*, art 12.

98 Economic and Social Council, *Substantive Issues Arising in the Implementation of the International Covenant on Economic, Social and Cultural Rights General Comment No 14. The Right to the Highest Attainable Standard of Health*, UNESCOR, 22d Sess, UN Doc E/C/12/2000/4, (2000) at para 43 [*General Comment No 14*].

99 Economic and Social Council, *Substantive Issues Arising in the Implementation of the International Covenant on Economic, Social and Cultural Rights General Comment No*

everyone to sufficient, safe, acceptable, physically accessible and affordable water for personal and domestic uses."[100] The comment also indicates that States are required to "give special attention" to those who have faced difficulty "in exercising this right" and identifies Indigenous peoples as one such group.[101] While the general comments do not create independent rights,[102] they are authoritative interpretations of the existing obligations under the *ICESCR*[103] and support the conclusion that the right to water is part of international customary law, to which Canada is already bound.[104]

It is also clear that Canada knows it cannot meet its *ICESCR* obligations unless it addresses drinking water concerns. Canada has consistently included descriptions of the state of on-reserve water and of its efforts to improve drinking water quality on reserves in its reports to the committee which oversees the *ICESCR*.[105] In response, the committee has repeatedly found that Canada has failed to address the lack of access to safe water for its Indigenous peoples.[106]

The committee has been particularly frustrated with Canada's failure to develop legislation that recognizes "the right to water as a legal entitlement."[107] In 2006, it urged Canada to act upon these and other outstanding obligations. In particular, the committee requested that Canada take the required steps to make Covenant rights directly enforceable and to establish "effective" mechanisms to oversee the implementation of the *ICESCR*.[108] It was concerned by:

15: The Right to Water, UNESCOR, 29th Sess, UN Doc E/C 12/2002/11, (2002) [*General Comment No 15*].

100 *Ibid*, principle 2.

101 *Ibid*, principle 16.

102 See Rebecca Bates, "The Road to the Well: An Evaluation of the Customary Right to Water" (2010) 19:3 RECIEL 282 at 287.

103 Lynda Collins, "Environmental Rights on the Wrong Side of History: Revisiting Canada's Position on the Human Right to Water" (2010) 19:3 RECIEL 351 at 354; Salman Salman & Siobhán McInerney-Lankford, *The Human Right to Water: Legal and Policy Dimensions* (Washington: The World Bank, 2004) at 5.

104 Bates, above note 102 at 287.

105 See, for example, *International Covenant on Economic, Social and Cultural Rights: Fourth Report of Canada* (Ottawa: Public Works and Government Services Canada, 2004) at paras 383–85.

106 See, for example, Committee on Economic, Social and Cultural Rights, *Reports of States: Canada*, 36th Sess (Geneva, 1–19 May 2006) at 2, online: ISHR http://olddoc.ishr.ch/hrm/tmb/treaty/cescr/reports/cescr_36/Canada_CESCR_36.pdf.

107 Economic and Social Council, *Concluding Observations of the Committee on Economic, Social and Cultural Rights*, UNESCOR, 36th Sess, UN Doc E/C.12/CAN/CO/4, (2006) at para 11(d).

108 *Ibid* at para 35.

> The State party's restrictive interpretation of its obligations under the Covenant, in particular its position that it may implement the legal obligations set forth in the Covenant by adopting specific measures and policies rather than by enacting legislation specifically recognizing economic, social and cultural rights, and the consequent lack of awareness, in the provinces and territories, of the State party's legal obligations under the Covenant; [and] . . . . The lack of legal redress available to individuals when governments fail to implement the Covenant, resulting from the insufficient coverage in domestic legislation of economic, social and cultural rights, as spelled out in the Covenant; the lack of effective enforcement mechanisms for these rights; the practice of governments of urging upon their courts an interpretation of the Canadian Charter of Rights and Freedoms denying protection of Covenant rights, and the inadequate availability of civil legal aid, particularly for economic, social and cultural rights.[109]

These comments are from the committee's response to Canada in 2006. Canada was scheduled to deliver its next report on implementation in 2010, which presumably would have had to respond to these requests for action. However, at press time, this report appears to still be outstanding. Given the calibre of criticisms that the Canadian situation has engendered due to failings under the *ICESCR*, it is hardly surprising that Canada resists treaties that include overseeing bodies that would specifically monitor Canada's compliance with the right to water.

Canada has also ratified or acceded to several international instruments that directly recognize a general right to water. These include the *Convention on the Rights of the Child*, which requires State parties to "take appropriate measures" to "combat disease . . . through . . . the provision of . . . clean drinking water,"[110] and the United Nations *Convention on the Elimination of All Forms of Discrimination against Women*, which requires State parties to ensure "women in rural areas . . . enjoy adequate living conditions, particularly in relation to housing, sanitation, electricity and water supply . . . ."[111]

Perhaps more pointedly, Canada has also ratified the *United Nations Declaration on the Rights of Indigenous Peoples*. This instrument recognizes both the right of Indigenous people to the improvement of their "social

---

109 *Ibid* at para 11.

110 *Convention on the Rights of the Child*, 20 November 1989, 1577 UNTS 3, art 24(2)(c), 28 ILM 1456.

111 *Convention on the Elimination of All Forms of Discrimination against Women*, 18 December 1979, 1249 UNTS 13, art 14(2)(h), 19 ILM 33. Canada ratified this treaty on 10 December 1981.

conditions," including sanitation and health, as well as a positive obligation on States "to ensure continuing improvement" of these conditions.[112] Both sanitation and health depend upon, among other factors, safe drinking water in sufficient quantities. Given that this term is framed as a positive obligation, it is explicit that signatory countries must take steps to enable the realization of *UNDRIP* rights instead of merely not interfering with matters that may affect rights.

Additionally, article 38 of *UNDRIP* explicitly requires States to take action to implement the Declaration, including enacting legislation.[113] Some domestic courts have found that even absent domestic implementation, the Declaration directly constrains domestic action. A case in point is the 2007 decision of the Supreme Court of Belize in *Aurelio Cal et al v Belize*.[114] In this case, in "elaborating on his finding of a violation of customary international law, [the Chief Justice] stated his view that the 2007 Declaration 'embodying as it does, general principles of international law relating to indigenous peoples and their lands and resources, is of such force that the defendants, representing the Government of Belize, will not disregard it.'"[115]

These international instruments result in more than the creation of an adjudicative space.[116] They also crystalize the legitimacy of rights claims by giving the rights form and recognition, while creating public expectations that the terms of treaties will be honoured by governments. Canada's ratification of the above instruments results in their having interpretive force as courts will assume that Canada intends not to act in violation of international legal instruments. For example, courts will strive to interpret legislation to be consistent with obligations shouldered under international law[117] and will interpret the *Charter* "to provide protection at least as great as that afforded by similar provisions in international

---

112 *United Nations Declaration on the Rights of Indigenous Peoples*, UNGAOR, 61st Sess, UN Doc A/61/L.67, (2007), arts 1, 20, 23, and 29 [*UNDRIP*].

113 See Siegfried Wiessner, "United Nations Declaration on the Rights of Indigenous Peoples: Introduction," online: Audiovisual Library of International Law http://legal.un.org/avl/pdf/ha/ga_61-295/ga_61-295_e.pdf [Wiessner]. Several States have complied with this requirement.

114 This judgment is reproduced online: www.elaw.org/node/1620.

115 Wiessner, above note 113.

116 Bruce Porter, "Claiming Adjudicative Space: Social Rights, Equality and Citizenship" in Margot Young et al, eds, *Poverty: Rights, Social Citizenship, and Legal Activism* (Vancouver: UBC Press, 2007) 77 at 80.

117 *Baker v Canada (Minister of Citizenship and Immigration)*, [1999] 2 SCR 817 at para 67.

human rights documents that Canada has ratified."[118] It is consistent with these understandings to posit that courts will similarly expect Canada to respect its freely assumed international obligations, especially those articulated in *UNDRIP*, as informing the meaning of fulfilling its fiduciary obligations to Indigenous peoples.

E. FINDING A REMEDY, RIGHTING THE WRONG

An action based on a breach of fiduciary duties may be successful, but what would the remedy actually be?[119] In the cases where fiduciary breaches have been made out, the courts have been concerned with ensuring justice is achieved. For example, in the germinal decision of *R v Guerin*,[120] the Supreme Court found that the following principles ought to guide considerations of remedies where the Crown has breached its fiduciary obligations to Indigenous peoples:

> [I]f a breach has been committed then the trustee is liable to place the trust estate in the same position as it would have been in if no breach had

118 *Slaight Communications Inc v Davidson*, [1989] 1 SCR 1038 at 1056–57. See Martha Jackman & Bruce Porter, "Canada: Socio-Economic Rights under the Canadian Charter" in Malcolm Langford, ed, *Social Rights Jurisprudence: Emerging Trends in International and Comparative Law* (New York: Cambridge University Press, 2008) 209 at 214–15. The authors provide a discussion of this presumption and the jurisprudence that supports it.

119 See *Wewaykum*, above note 41 at para 135. Limitation periods concerns may also arise. However, limitation periods are not likely to be a barrier as there are copious instances of new breaches. This contrasts with the situation of a singular historic breach with continuing consequences, which would indeed be statute barred. Pursuant to the *Federal Courts Act*, RSC 1985, c F-7, s 39(1), claims based on fiduciary law against the federal government are subject to provincial limitation period legislation. See also *Wewaykum*, above in this note at 114; *Blueberry River*, above note 41 at 107. There is also evidence of recent instances where the Crown knew of the negative consequences of older federal policies and practices and received that knowledge at a time when it held the ability to effectively act to remedy the situation. There is an analogy here to *Blueberry River*, where acting on a specific breach was barred by limitation periods, but the Crown was still liable because it had a continuing power to act that extended into a period which was not statute barred. The Supreme Court of Canada found that "[s]o long as the [federal department] has the power . . . the [federal department] was under a fiduciary duty to exercise this power" (*ibid* at 365); Reynolds, above note 40 at 202. Thus an actionable breach based on fiduciary law was found in the Crown's failure to remedy the situation once it became aware of it.

120 *Guerin*, above note 35.

> been committed. Considerations of causation, foreseeability and remoteness do not readily enter into the matter . . . . The principles embodied in this approach do not appear to involve any inquiry as to whether the loss was caused by or flowed from the breach. Rather the inquiry in each instance would appear to be whether the loss would have happened if there had been no breach.[121]

Thus the remedy award in *Guerin* was crafted to reflect a lost best opportunity. Similarly, in *Blueberry River*,[122] the damages award reflected the current value of an interest that the Crown had transferred in a manner inconsistent with its fiduciary obligations to the First Nation. In *Osoyoos Indian Band*, in the face of uncertainty over which interests in reserve land had been expropriated by the Crown several decades before, the Court read the expropriation action to be consistent with the fiduciary duty, thereby limiting the expropriation to the minimal interests necessary to fulfill the Crown's purposes. This, in turn, left sufficient interest in the land such that it was available to be taxed by the First Nation in question.

In some respects water is an easy issue to address. The technology for making water safe is known, and we already have a national and arm's-length engineering analysis in hand that provides much of the required baseline information. A short-term step is to make the financial commitments that are required to address pressing concerns about basic infrastructure and operations. The question of how to maintain that infrastructure and sustain water safety is more complex: it necessarily involves developing just approaches to governance relationships between the Crown and Indigenous peoples that recognize the impact of intergenerational poverty and social marginalization on capacity. Such approaches must therefore be informed by a decolonizing and empowering ethic, not just the imposition of, for example, a municipal model on a First Nation community.

Scholars assessing fiduciary claims in other contexts have proposed approaches that may be helpful here. For example, Kent McNeil has assessed how the fiduciary doctrine plays out in terms of the facts surrounding Canada's assertion of control over Indigenous governments. He concludes that given past and continuing interferences and the current state of Indigenous communities due to those interferences, there is a "positive fiduciary obligation to provide Aboriginal nations with assistance to rebuild their

121 *Ibid* at para 50, citing *Re Dawson; Union Fidelity Trustee Co v Perpetual Trustee Co* (1966), 84 WN (Pt 1) (NSW) 399 at 404–6.

122 *Blueberry River*, above note 41.

capacity to govern themselves autonomously."[123] This approach is consistent with both the jurisprudence and the scholarship of others. Writing on the general topic of transferring control over areas from the Crown's hands to Indigenous communities, Leonard Rotman observes that given the principles of fiduciary law, "it is insufficient for the Crown to attempt to dispose of its obligations by dumping them unceremoniously on the Native people without providing for their harmonious transition . . . ."[124] Such reasoning is clearly applicable to the case of water as well. Having asserted control over water and created a dysfunctional and risky status quo, fiduciary law dictates that Canada is required to provide the specific assistance that will remedy the situation. The sort of remedy required could not be dictated in any detail from the bench, especially since planning and implementation is most likely to succeed where it is aligned with remediating the underlying conditions of political marginalization, alienation, and poverty that are experienced by many Indigenous individuals and communities.[125] Nevertheless, a judge could set some basic parameters as dictated by fiduciary law and remain seized of the matter while the parties negotiate an appropriate process or framework for realizing the Crown's obligations and the transition into a situation where on-reserve water is no longer inordinately risky.

F. CONCLUDING COMMENTS

It is depressing to consider that the water woes of on-reserve Indigenous peoples in Canada may only be effectively addressed as a result of litigation, instead of as a product of dedicated political will. This is especially the case given Canada's relative wealth and the growing international recognition that access to safe and sufficient water is a human right that plays a foundational role in enabling the realization of other rights.

There is ample evidence of the failure to realize this right and of the fact that this failure is not a new phenomenon, but rather a persistent one

---

123 Kent McNeil, *The Inherent Right of Self-Government: Emerging Directions for Legal Research* (Chilliwack, BC: First Nations Governance Centre, 2004) at 31.

124 Leonard Rotman, *Parallel Paths: Fiduciary Doctrine and the Crown-Native Relationship in Canada* (Toronto: University of Toronto Press, 1996) at 259–60.

125 Janet Smylie & Paul Adomako, eds, *Indigenous Children's Health Report: Health Assessment in Action* (Toronto: Centre for Research on Inner City Health, 2009) at 4. See also Gerald Taiaiake Alfred, "Colonialism and State Dependency" (2009) 5:2 Journal of Aboriginal Health 42 at 44: "[i]t is evidence to anyone who has experience living or working within First Nation communities that conventional approaches to health promotion and community development are not showing strong signs of success."

with a considerable pedigree. While fiduciary claims are seldom possible against the federal government, the unique facts of this situation, coupled with the distinct constitutional relationship between Indigenous peoples and the State, make such claims legally possible. In particular, there seems to be a *prima facie* case, as the requirements identified under developing law for establishing Crown-Indigenous fiduciary obligations are likely present in this situation.

First, the Crown asserted discretionary control over Aboriginal peoples' land and water interests, including on-reserve water systems. This control was asserted in a variety of forms, pursuant to both legislation and policy, as well as through practice, resulting in fiduciary obligations. Second, evidence from the public record illustrates, on a *prima facie* basis, that the Crown has not met the standards to which fiduciaries are held. To support this claim, I note the acknowledged underfunded approach Canada has taken to overseeing water, its neglect in following through explicitly assumed responsibilities, and its recent introduction of legislation that has been flagged as potentially increasing the risk of unsafe water, largely due to its approach to the funding base. The case for a breach is further bolstered by the understanding of water rights and the rights of Indigenous peoples, which have been recognized under international law. International law inflects the content of the fiduciary obligations that Canada has assumed and, therefore, informs the standards that ought to be met. It also likely informs the nature of the remedy that is in order, requiring that it engage Indigenous capacity building and that it be sensitive to sustainability.

Given the public record and the jurisprudence, a claim based on fiduciary law is one route that may reasonably be pursued to enable on-reserve Indigenous peoples to realize the core social right of access to safe water in sufficient quantities.

CHAPTER 10
PARTICIPATION AND ACCOUNTABILITY
NEW AVENUES FOR HUMAN RIGHTS ENGAGEMENT WITH THE DISTRIBUTION OF HEALTH RESOURCES IN CANADA

ALANA KLEIN*

A. INTRODUCTION

Concern about the fair distribution of health resources in Canada is growing. International human rights norms appear to require Canada to move progressively towards a more equitable distribution of health-affecting resources. However, despite Canada's celebrated tradition of public health insurance promising comprehensive, universal, and accessible health care, Canada seems to be moving towards *less* equitable health resource distribution.

There are many challenges to undertaking human rights scrutiny of the distribution of health care resources in Canada. For years, opaque, disaggregated, and overlapping spheres of authority determined the funding, administration, and delivery of health care services, rendering any kind of meaningful analysis difficult.[1] In addition, human rights methodologies in Canada and internationally continue to wrestle with the content of social and economic rights (including the right to health) and the appropriate tools for enforcement. At the domestic level, judicial decisions under the

---

* Assistant Professor, Faculty of Law, McGill University.

1 See Colleen Flood, Duncan Sinclair, & Joanna Erdman, "Steering and Rowing in Health Care: The Devolution Option?" (2004) 30 Queens' LJ 156 at 176 [Flood, Sinclair, & Erdman].

Canadian Charter of Rights and Freedoms[2] suggest room for novel, collaborative approaches towards more meaningful constitutional social and economic rights enforcement, but these approaches are still in their infancy. At the international level, actors enforcing the human right to the highest attainable standard of health have, until recently, focused on universal minimum standards,[3] resulting in little discussion about the distribution of resources in a developed country like Canada. Despite these challenges, recent developments in health care governance in Canada, dovetailing with an emergent focus on governance and a social-determinants-of-health approach to the human right to health, may, together, open new possibilities for human rights analysis of the distribution of health-related goods and services in Canada.

In this chapter, I briefly analyze three interrelated trends in health and human rights and suggest the ways in which they might open new avenues for human rights scrutiny of the distribution of health resources in Canada. First, I note that courts may be more open to enforcing social and economic rights claims where legislative frameworks exist to facilitate meaningful scrutiny. Moreover, judicial actors may be willing to encourage and shape the development of such frameworks, even where they express — as they have from time to time — anxiety surrounding their institutional capacity to direct resource allocation. Second, at the international level, institutional and scholarly conceptions of the right to health are, likewise, expanding their gaze beyond monitoring States' health policies in search of violations and towards supporting processes designed to enhance democratic self-governance in relation to health. Finally, Canadian provinces have, over the last twenty years or so, moved towards allocating health care resources at the sub-provincial regional level, relying on participation- and accountability-enhancing governance features to drive more responsive resource allocation.

However, the turn towards participatory, accountable governance processes to ensure fairer distribution of health resources may not be entirely positive. For domestic and international human rights, as well as in health care governance itself, the development presents promise but also risks. The chapter concludes with a brief discussion of the ways by which the agendas of scholars and activists might be affected by the turn towards governance as a means for driving the progressive realization of the right to health.

---

2 Part 1 of the *Constitution Act, 1982* being Schedule B to the *Canada Act 1982* (UK), 1982, c 11 [*Charter*].

3 See Katharine Young, "The Minimum Core of Economic and Social Rights: A Concept in Search of Content" (2008) 33 Yale J Int'l L 113 at 130–31.

B. HUMAN RIGHTS AND DISTRIBUTION OF HEALTH RESOURCES IN CANADA

The international human right to health has a clear distributive dimension. The *International Covenant on Economic, Social and Cultural Rights*, to which Canada is a signatory, recognizes "the right of *everyone* to the enjoyment of the highest attainable standard of physical and mental health."[4] Article 12(2)(d) of the *ICESCR* requires that States take all steps necessary for the "creation of conditions which would assure to *all* medical service and medical attention in the event of sickness."[5] Article 2(2) of the *ICESCR* adds that the right to health is to be enjoyed "without discrimination," and, in particular, without discrimination based on "social origin, property, birth or other status."[6] The United Nations Committee on Economic, Social and Cultural Rights (CESCR) adds, in its non-binding but influential *General Comment No 14* on the right to the highest attainable standard of mental and physical health, that States have a "core obligation" to, *inter alia*, "ensure rights of access to health facilities, goods and services on a non-discriminatory basis, especially for vulnerable and marginalized groups," and "to ensure *equitable* distribution of all health facilities, goods and services."[7]

Concern over fairness in the distribution of health care resources in Canada is high. The *Canada Health Act* promises provinces funding for medically necessary hospital and physician services on the condition that provinces do not charge people for those covered services, effectively guaranteeing a core of free health care.[8] But the content of this core is contestable. Colleen Flood and colleagues, for example, have questioned the opaque and physician-interest-driven processes for determining procedures that qualify as medically necessary.[9] The set of services that ultimately

4 *International Covenant on Economic, Social and Cultural Rights*, 16 December 1966, 993 UNTS 3, art 12(1), Can TS 1976 No 46 (entered into force 3 January 1976, accession by Canada 19 May 1976) [*ICESCR*] [emphasis added].

5 *Ibid*, art 12(2d) [emphasis added].

6 *Ibid*, art 2(2).

7 Economic and Social Council, *Substantive Issues Arising in the Implementation of the International Covenant on Economic, Social and Cultural Rights. General Comment No. 14 (2000) The Right to the Highest Attainable Standard of Health*, UNCESCROR, 22nd Session, 2000, UN Doc E/C/12/2000/4, (2000) at para 43 [*General Comment No 14*] [emphasis added].

8 *Canada Health Act*, RSC 1985, c C-6, ss 7–12 [*CHA*].

9 Colleen Flood, Carolyn Tuohy, & Mark Stabile, "What's In and Out of Medicare? Who Decides?" in Colleen Flood, ed, *Just Medicare: What's In, What's Out, How We Decide* (Toronto: University of Toronto Press, 2006) at 15 [Flood, Tuohy, & Stabile, "What's In and Out of Medicare?"].

qualify as medically necessary have been the subject of litigation and other critical attention.[10]

Further, as suggested by both scholars and a succession of reports that investigated the state of millennium-era publicly funded health care in Canada,[11] overall distribution of health care resources in Canada may be slowly growing *less* equitable as a greater proportion of health services used by Canadians falls outside the ambit of the *Canada Health Act*'s user fee ban. For example, mental health care, palliative care, post-acute care, home care, and pharmaceuticals, among numerous other services, are increasingly relied upon, yet their accessibility is not assured by the *Canada Health Act*'s user fee ban.[12] These non-*CHA*-covered health services are funded (or not) at provincial discretion. The related question about the relationship between health care services and social determinants of health raises similar difficulties, as the *CHA* generally addresses curative and not preventative care.[13] In addition, wait times and other non-financial barriers to access

10 Martha Jackman, "*Charter* Review as a Health Care Accountability Mechanism in Canada" (2010) 18 Health LJ 1; Cathy Fooks & Steven Lewis, "Romanow and Beyond: A Primer on Health Reform Issues in Canada" (Ottawa: Canadian Policy Research Networks, November 2002) at 14ff and 17ff, online: Canadian Policy Research Networks www.rcrpp.org [Fooks & Lewis, "Romanow and Beyond"]; Government of Saskatchewan Commission on Medicare, *Caring for Medicare: Sustaining a Quality System* (Regina: Policy and Planning Branch Saskatchewan Health, 2001) at 55, online: Government of Saskatchewan www.health.gov.sk.ca [The Fyke Commission]; National Forum on Health, *Canada Health Action: Building on the Legacy. Vol. I: Final Report* (Ottawa: Minister of Public Works and Government Services, 1997) at 7 and 13, online: Health Canada www.hc-sc.gc.ca [*Canada Health Action*]. See also *Hogan v Ontario (Minister of Health and Long-Term Care)* (2006), 58 CHRR D/317 at paras 104–5, 130, 152, and 182 (HRTO) [*Hogan*]; *Auton (Guardian ad litem of) v British Columbia (AG)*, 2004 SCC 78 at paras 13, 30, and 32 [*Auton*].

11 See, for example, Vandna Bhatia, "Social Rights, Civil Rights, and Health Reform in Canada" (2010) 23 Gov 37 at 44, 49, 53, & 54. This user fee ban under the CHA effectively prohibits service providers from charging fees for government-insured services.

12 See, for example, The Fyke Commission, above note 10 at 34, discussing palliative care in the Canadian health care system; *Canada Health Action*, above note 10 at 8 and 14, discussing post-acute care in the Canadian health care system; Carol Donovan, "Overview of Policy Issues in Finding and Financing Home and Community Care" (Presentation delivered at the Home and Community Care Policy Meeting, Health Canada, Toronto, 2000), discussing home care in the Canadian health care system; Fooks & Lewis, "Romanow and Beyond," above note 10 at 9, discussing pharmaceuticals and mental health care in the Canadian health care system.

13 See Carolyn Hughes Tuohy, "The Hedgehog and the Fox: Glouberman and Marmor on 'Healthy Public Policy'" (2007) 2:1 Health Economics, Policy and Law 107 at 107 and 110, defining social determinants of health as "that broad set of socio-economic

have received increasing attention, particularly following the wave of reports on publicly funded health care in Canada.[14]

In this context, it is fair to conclude that the introduction of the single-payer model only initially moved towards equalizing the distribution of health care resources in Canada. When the *CHA* was introduced, health care resources were understood as being composed almost entirely of hospital and physician services, and all such services were provided at no cost to the user. But over time, a greater proportion of health-related expenditures have come from supplementary insurance plans or out-of-pocket payments for services that fall outside the *CHA*, particularly for those with chronic illness and disabilities. Vandna Bhatia calls this failure of governments to expand medicare to include the large and growing number of services that fall outside its ambit a "passive policy drift," arguing persuasively that it has called into question the solidarity claims of medicare's advocates.[15] Certainly, it has become increasingly difficult to claim that health care distribution is driven by need rather than ability to pay.

Finally, an overarching concern in each of these areas is accountability: overlapping and unclear lines of responsibility for decisions affecting the provision of health services have made it difficult to identify the goals of health-related spending, whether decisions are achieving desired goals, and

---

factors well beyond the purview of health care systems, strikingly correlated with socio-economic status, that influence the health of populations."

14 Commission d'étude sur les services de santé et les services sociaux, *Emerging Solutions. Report and Recommendations* (Québec: Government of Quebec, 2000) at 2 and 6, online: CPRN www.cprn.org [The Clair Commission Report]; Fooks & Lewis, "Romanow and Beyond," above note 10 at 18; The Fyke Commission, above note 10 at 35; *Canada Health Action*, above note 10 at 5; Ontario Health Services Restructuring Commission, *Looking Back, Looking Forward. A Legacy Report* (Toronto: The Ontario Health Services Restructuring Commission, March 2000) at 2ff; Premier's Advisory Council on Health, *A Framework for Reform* (Edmonton: Premier's Advisory Council on Health, Government of Alberta, December 2001) at 4, online: Legislative Assembly of Alberta www.assembly.ab.ca [The Mazankowski Report]; Premier's Health Quality Council, *Health Renewal* (Saint John, NB: The Premier's Health Quality Council, Government of New Brunswick, 2002); Senate, Standing Committee on Social Affairs, Science and Technology, *The Health of Canadians: The Federal Role, Volume Six: Recommendations for Reform* (Ottawa: Government of Canada, 2002) at 10 & 11, ch 5, online: Parliament of Canada www.parl.gc.ca [The Kirby Report].

15 See Bhatia, above note 11 at 46, observing that "the burden [of the growing private component of health care] is heaviest for those who were the most vulnerable: the very sick or those with chronic illnesses, many of who are on fixed incomes and lack supplementary insurance."

who is responsible where they do not.[16] Meanwhile, the internationally recognized human right to health demands progress towards needs-based health resource distribution. Neither the Canadian and provincial/territorial governments nor the bodies charged with human rights monitoring and enforcement — judges, UN bodies, human rights commissions — have adequately addressed the requirements of equitable distribution in terms of human rights.

1) Domestic-Level Judicial Scrutiny of Health Care Allocation

At the domestic level, judges have been somewhat cautious about intervening in what they may consider to be legislative and policy decisions about health care allocation challenged under the *Charter* or provincial human rights legislation. In challenges to health care distribution decisions under section 15(1) guarantee of equality and section 7 guarantees of life and security of the person, the Supreme Court has affirmed the constitutional guarantee of non-discriminatory access to publicly funded health services.[17] The Court has also affirmed a right against State interference with individual health-seeking behaviour.[18] The reasonableness of government decisions in relation to allocation, however, has not yet been subjected to meaningful *Charter* scrutiny.

The high-water mark in challenges to health allocation under section 15 (1) of the *Charter* is the decision in *Eldridge v British Columbia (AG).* In that case, the Supreme Court held that a provincial government's failure to provide sign language interpretation where necessary to ensure equal access to health care violated the constitutional equality guarantee enshrined in section 15(1) of the *Charter.*[19]

By 2004, the Supreme Court appeared to circumscribe somewhat the reach of *Eldridge* in the context of health care priority setting. In *Auton (Guardian ad litem of) v British Columbia*, a unanimous Court held that failure to provide a particular behavioural treatment to children with autism did not violate the *Charter*'s equality guarantee.[20] The Court reasoned that

---

16 See, for example, Timothy Caulfield & Nola Ries, *Accountability in Health Care and Legal Approaches* (Ottawa: Canadian Policy Research Network, 2004) at 7, online: CPRN www.rcrpp.ca.

17 *Eldridge v British Columbia (AG)*, [1997] 3 SCR 624 [*Eldridge*].

18 *Auton*, above note 10 at para 46; *Chaoulli v Quebec (AG)*, 2005 SCC 35 [*Chaoulli*]; *Canada (AG) v PHS Community Services Society*, 2011 SCC 44.

19 *Eldridge*, above note 17.

20 *Auton*, above note 10.

section 15(1) protected only equal access to benefits "provided by law"; since the province had decided not to fund the service sought by the appellants, there could be no discrimination.[21] The Supreme Court in *Auton* did go on to preclude funding decisions with a "discriminatory purpose, policy or effect."[22] This decision set a high threshold for discrimination in health care funding allocation decisions, however; absent a "readily identifiable" discriminatory purpose or policy, an allocation decision could generally only be considered discriminatory where it failed to comport with the overall scheme of its own governing legislation.[23] Since the federal and provincial laws establishing public health care in Canada create only a partial-coverage scheme, the exclusion of some treatments from coverage would not engage the equality right. The decision appears, at first blush, to narrow the scope for scrutiny of discriminatory impact in health care allocation.[24]

However, the insistence in *Auton* that section 15 is not engaged by health service funding allocation decisions because such funding is discretionary seems somewhat at odds with section 15 jurisprudence. In *Gosselin v Quebec*, for example, the Court scrutinized a legislative exclusion from benefits more closely than it did in *Auton*.[25] *Gosselin* was a challenge to a law that denied full welfare benefits to people under thirty who failed to participate in a workfare program. The Court did not follow the *Auton* logic that the choice to exclude people under thirty who failed to participate in workfare meant that there was no benefit provided to them by law and, thus, no basis for a claim of discrimination. Instead, the analysis progressed further to consider whether the scheme was discriminatory in substance. Ultimately, the Court held that there was no discrimination on the basis that the denial affirmed the dignity of those under thirty by underscoring the legislature's confidence in their ability to work for a living. Perhaps the *Auton* Court's refusal to engage in substantive consideration of effects-based discrimination in the context of health care allocation decisions reflects a generalized anxiety around judicial review of health care allocation.

Moreover, and perhaps more importantly for the purposes of this discussion, *Auton* might have been understood with reference to the dialogical relationship between *Charter* and legislative norms. Commenting on *Auton*,

---

21 *Ibid* at para 46.

22 *Ibid* at para 41.

23 *Ibid* at para 42.

24 See Mel Cousins, "Health Care and Human Rights after *Auton* and *Chaoulli*" (2009) 54:4 McGill LJ 717; Martha Jackman, "Health Care and Equality: Is There a Cure?" (2007) 15 Health LJ 87 [Jackman, "Health and Equality"].

25 *Gosselin v Quebec (AG)*, 2002 SCC 84 [*Gosselin*].

Greschner and Lewis suggest that courts can play a role in encouraging more evidence-based allocation and in signalling problems with governmental decision making. Specifically, they suggest that courts should demand that governments consider the nature of the condition, the effectiveness of treatment, and cost in making allocation decisions in order to encourage better transparency and rationality in health care allocation decisions.[26]

The dynamism that Greschner and Lewis call for is reflected somewhat in the judicial scrutiny of health resource allocation under section 7 of the *Charter*. Although, at first glance, recent section 7 jurisprudence might appear to support a move towards a free market rather than a redistributive agenda, it also reflects judicial willingness to demand government accountability in relation to health policy and finance. For example, in *Chaoulli v Quebec (AG)*,[27] the Supreme Court accepted, by a 4:3 majority, that a provincial prohibition on obtaining private health insurance for publicly insured services violated the Quebec *Charter of Human Rights and Freedoms*' "right to life, and to personal security, inviolability, and freedom."[28] Three of the majority judges also ruled that the prohibition violated the similar life and security of the person guarantee enshrined in section 7 of the Canadian *Charter*. The government had defended the legislation as a means of protecting the public system. The majority reasoned that the insurance ban, in conjunction with excessive wait times for covered services in the public system, forced Quebeckers onto unduly long wait-lists, thus compromising their ability to attend to their own health needs. While *Chaoulli* can be criticized for unjustifiably supporting a negative rights vision of the Constitution,[29] it might also be understood as a call for better accountability.[30] The majority of the Court relied on the notion that the private insurance ban was unnecessary because some jurisdictions managed to have thriving

26 Donna Greschner & Steven Lewis, "*Auton* and Evidence-Based Decision-Making: Medicare in the Courts" (2003) 82 Can Bar Rev 501 at 523 and 525.

27 *Chaoulli*, above note 18.

28 *Charter of Human Rights and Freedoms*, RSQ c C-12, s 1.

29 See Sujit Choudhry, "Worse than Lockner?" in Colleen Flood, Kent Roach, & Lorne Sossin, eds, *Access to Care, Access to Justice: The Legal Debate over Private Health Insurance in Canada* (Toronto: University of Toronto Press, 2005) at 75.

30 See, for example, David Hadorn, "The *Chaoulli* Challenge: Getting a Grip on Waiting Lists" (2005) 173:3 Can Med Assoc J 271. The author suggests that *Chaoulli* be viewed as an encouragement to develop objective criteria for the limits of what public health care might guarantee.

public health systems without it. Many scholars, however, disagreed with the Court's appreciation of the facts on this point.[31]

This paper proposes that a legislative framework geared towards providing more meaningful accountability in relation to legislatively set goals might generate judicial forbearance where policies are demonstrably moving towards those goals and may, indeed, help justify a discrimination claim where policies are failing to achieve them. For example, a legislative requirement to assess whether the exclusion of under-thirties from welfare, in fact, resulted in better integration into the workforce might have prevented courts from accepting the government's bare assertion in *Gosselin*. Similarly, a legislative framework providing for accountability between measures like the private insurance ban and the government's ability to provide a universal, accessible health care system might have made it more difficult for the court to consider the ban as arbitrary.

Distribution-related questions have been more squarely addressed under human rights legislation, where legislation has supported a requirement of government accountability.[32] For example, in *Ontario Human Rights Commission & Hogan et al v Ontario*, claimants argued that the removal of sex reassignment surgery (SRS) from the list of medical services covered under the province's health insurance scheme discriminated on the basis of both sex and disability.[33] The Ontario Cabinet, in the late 1990s, was engaged in a "tightening and modernization" process designed to save the province $50 million a year in health care. Although the service cost the government only $123,891.81 per year, the Ontario Cabinet removed SRS and a number of other services from the schedule of publicly insured benefits. A number of SRS recipients challenged the removal.

Ontario human rights legislation shifts the burden to the respondent to justify any actions that create effects-based discrimination on prohibited grounds of "race, ancestry, place of origin, colour, ethnic origin, citizenship, creed, sex, sexual orientation, age, marital status, family

31 See Martha Jackman, "The Last Line of Defence for [Which?] Citizens: Accountability, Equality and the Right to Health in *Chaoulli*" (2006) 44 Osgoode Hall LJ 349 at 357; Hamish Stewart, "Implications of *Chaoulli* for Fact-Finding in Constitutional Cases" in *Access to Care, Access to Justice*, above note 29 at 211; Charles G Wright, "Different Interpretations of 'Evidence' and Implications for the Canadian Healthcare System" in *Access to Care, Access to Justice*, *ibid* at 223, all criticizing the Supreme Court's failure to attend to expert evidence justifying the insurance ban, Wright calling it "utterly inexplicable."

32 Cousins, above note 24 at 732.

33 *Hogan*, above note 10 at para 3.

status or disability."[34] An alleged discriminator must thus explain why a rule or measure with discriminatory effects is reasonable and *bona fide* in the circumstances and show that the respondent cannot accommodate the claimant without incurring undue hardship.[35] This arguably represents a broader equality protection than is available under section 15(1) of the *Charter.* Finally, the State action requirement that was used as the basis for denying the applicability of equality analysis under the *Charter* in *Auton* is absent here: the equality guarantee applies to all "services, goods and facilities," publicly or privately delivered.[36] The result is that the analysis under the Ontario *Human Rights Code* proceeds quickly to an examination of the reasonableness and *bona fides* of the rule or decision.

What is interesting about the *Hogan* decision is that both the majority and the dissenting judges went on to examine, and disagree on, whether the processes of delisting rendered that decision reasonable and *bona fide* in the circumstances. The majority held that since delisting was a cabinet decision, no justification was required,[37] effectively undermining the impact of the shift of the justificatory burden to the government. In any event, it held, there was sufficient evidence to suggest that sex reassignment surgery was not "money well-spent."[38] The majority supported this view mainly with reference to the statements of Dr Dickey, who, ironically, was an expert witness for the claimants and one of the primary supporters of maintaining SRS on the schedule of insured services.[39] Dr Dickey had conceded that not everyone was always satisfied with the results of SRS and that some people with gender identity disorder "go away and learn to live with it."[40] The majority declined to attribute any weight to the "turbulent political wrangling" that surrounded the delisting.[41] It also rejected the contention that the delisting had taken place without sufficient consultation with the Ontario Medical Association, gender identity disorder specialists, and the transsexual community.

The dissent had a different appreciation of the facts. It found little reason to question the effectiveness of SRS for people with the most profound

34 *Human Rights Code*, RSO 1990, c H.19, ss 1 and 11 [*Human Rights Code*].

35 *British Columbia (Public Service Employee Relations Commission) v British Columbia Government and Service Employees' Union (BCGSEU)*, [1999] 3 SCR 3 at para 22.

36 *Human Rights Code*, above note 34.

37 *Hogan*, above note 10 at para 109.

38 *Ibid* at para 105.

39 *Ibid* at para 62.

40 *Ibid* at para 105.

41 *Ibid* at para 108.

gender identity disorder.[42] More important for the present purposes, however, was the dissenting judge's attention to processes of delisting. At the time the decision to delist was made, the dissenting judge determined that there was no evidence that the government had any medical, policy, or budgetary rationale, or any other non-discriminatory reason for this decision.[43] She also placed heavy emphasis on the fact that while other delisting decisions were made pursuant to a "tightening and modernization review" process that included extensive consultation with medical experts and publicity on the Ministry of Health's website, delisting of SRS was undertaken without any meaningful consultation.[44] In her view, the "way in which sex reassignment surgery was delisted was so reckless, particularly when compared to the way in which other services were reviewed and delisted at the same time, that it constituted an abuse of power."[45] The decision was taken in bad faith and, as a result, constituted direct discrimination.

The *Hogan* story, and most notably the dissent's attention to processes surrounding allocation decisions, suggests that legislative or judicial demands for better transparency and consultation may helpfully play a role in addressing power relations in determination of health policy and particularly decisions affecting the distribution of resources.[46] In a context where governments are required to justify health care decisions with reference to standards for participation and accountability, these power relations might be more open to judicial scrutiny than when the focus is on the substance of the decision alone.

---

42 *Ibid* at para 260: ". . . it is a legitimate, international, medically-recognized, effective, non-cosmetic treatment of longstanding for transsexuals who have the most profound [gender identity disorder]."

43 *Ibid.*

44 *Ibid*, indicating that the delisting of SRS was not accompanied by the same level of consultation as other delisting of services, due to a discriminatory and arbitrary decision making process; in light of the seriousness of this disability, there was "no medical, policy or budgetary rationale, or any other non-discriminatory reason for this decision."

45 *Ibid* at para 444.

46 See Martha Jackman, Commission on the Future of Health Care in Canada, *The Implications of Section 7 of the* Charter *for Health Care Spending in Canada, Discussion Paper No 31* (Ottawa: Health Canada, 2002) at 13, arguing that s 7 of the *Charter* demands, *inter alia*, that policy and regulatory decision making regarding allocation of health care resources must be made with adequate involvement of those whose fundamental interests are affected, and with particular attention to those lacking in resources and influence.

Take, for example, the decision to delist hearing aid evaluations in Ontario, which was considered by the Ontario Superior Court in *Shulman v College of Audiologists and Speech Language Pathologists of Ontario*.[47] In that case, Perdu J determined that the delisting did not violate section 15 of the *Charter*, reasoning in much the same way as the Chief Justice in *Auton* that the ambit of the equality guarantee was limited to equal access to existing services and could not affect the scope of those services.[48] Justice Perdu stated that "in delisting hearing aid evaluations and re-evaluations, the hearing impaired are treated no differently from others who must pay for medications, maintenance of their prosthetic devices, wheelchairs, and or eyeglasses."[49]

This decision has been criticized, like *Auton*, for relying on formal, decontextualized conceptions of equality.[50] As Jackman has pointed out, the delisting of hearing aid evaluations would clearly have a disproportionately adverse effect on the health and well-being of people with impaired hearing,[51] who are also more likely to be poor.[52] One solution to this problem is to urge, as Jackman and others rightfully have, a return to a meaningful application of substantive equality standards in judicial interpretations in section 15 analyses.[53] Another way to address the delisting process and its failures is to ensure that the groups most affected by delisting decisions are better represented, accounted for, and responded to. As suggested below, the seeds for such a legislative context are emerging in relation to health resource distribution in Canada.

2) International-Level Monitoring of Health Care Allocation

Distributional features of Canada's health care system have received little mention in international-level human rights monitoring. Non-governmental organizations (NGOs) have certainly raised concerns about coverage in their submissions to the Committee on Economic, Social and Cultural

---

47 [2001] OJ No 5057 (SCJ).

48 *Ibid* at para 106.

49 *Ibid* at para 34.

50 See, for example, Jackman, "Health and Equality," above note 24 at 111.

51 *Ibid* at 110.

52 Council of Canadians with Disabilities, *Disabling Poverty and Enabling Citizenship: Understanding the Poverty and Exclusion of Canadians with Disabilities* (June 2010), online: CCD www.ccdonline.ca.

53 Jackman, "Health and Equality," above note 24 at 132; Daphne Gilbert & Diana Majury, "Critical Comparisons: The Supreme Court of Canada Dooms Section 15" (2006) Windsor YB Access Just 111.

Rights.[54] One NGO shadow report has noted that the exclusion of prescription drugs, dental, and vision benefits from coverage under the public plan and provincial delisting of hospital and physician services, together, make health services unaffordable for those who lack the means to pay.[55] Another has argued that the increasing reliance on private insurance and the lack of coverage of prescription drugs and physiotherapy have a disproportionate impact on First Nations people and people with disabilities.[56] Another report has expressed concerns about increasingly long wait-lists in the public system.[57] These distributional features have also been well documented in Canadian scholarship. Lahey, for example, has pointed out that Canada's health care system is primarily designed to meet the acute health care needs of otherwise healthy Canadians,[58] rather than the mental health care needs, home care needs, and pharmaceutical needs that are more prevalent among those who may be more politically, socially, or economically marginalized.

The CESCR, however, has yet to take up these concerns in any depth. In its 1993 concluding observations, the CESCR praised Canada's high standard of health care, as well as accountability created by the *Canada Health Act*.[59] In 1998, it recommended in general terms that "federal and provincial agreements . . . be adjusted so as to ensure, in whatever ways are

---

54 See The Canadian Council for Refugees, The Canadian Council for Churches, & The Inter-Church Committee for Refugees, *Draft Statement to the UN Committee on Economic, Social and Cultural Rights* (1998), online: Equality Rights www.equalityrights.org. The report notes "severe cutbacks" in health care for Canadians or permanent residents.

55 See African Canadian Legal Clinic, *The Hidden Side of Paradise: Violations of the Economic and Social Rights of African Canadians*, Submission to the United Nations Committee on Economic, Social and Cultural Rights on the Occasion of the Review of Canada's Fourth and Fifth Periodic Reports under the *International Covenant on Economic, Social and Cultural Rights* (May 2006) at 23, online: OHCHR www2.ohchr.org.

56 Kairos: Canadian Ecumenical Justice Initiatives, *Report on Cross-Canadian Citizen Dialogues on Social, Economic and Cultural Rights*, Submission to the United Nations Committee on Economic, Social and Cultural Rights 36th session (May 2006) at 16, online: http://socialrightscura.ca/documents/CESCR-Submissions/kairos.pdfOHCHR www2.ohchr.org.

57 The St James Town LEAD Project (Local Empowerment and Access to Democracy) & Residents of St James Town, *Community Report on Economic Social and Cultural Human Rights in St. James Town, Toronto*, Draft UN Report for Residents/Community Review (2007) at 9, 11, and 14, online: OHCHR www2.ohchr.org.

58 William Lahey, "Medicare and the Law: Contours of an Evolving Relationship" in Jocelyn Downie, Timothy Caulfield, & Colleen Flood, eds, *Canadian Health Law and Policy*, 4th ed (Markham, ON: LexisNexis Canada, 2011) 1 at 79–80.

59 United Nations Committee on Economic, Social and Cultural Rights, *Consideration of Reports Submitted by States Parties under Articles 16 and 17 of the Covenant: Concluding*

appropriate, that services such as mental health care [and] home care . . . are available."[60] In 2006, the committee expressed general concerns about health outcomes and access barriers faced by Aboriginal people, African Canadians, and homeless girls[61] but had nothing but praise (however brief in length) for Canada's health care system as a whole.[62]

The CESCR's relative silence on the growing inequities in health resource distribution in Canada may result from a number of factors. At a time when federal actors were abandoning their role in steering social welfare policies via conditional funding to the provinces, which were in turn slashing programs, the CESCR might have wisely chosen to focus its normative energies elsewhere.[63] Other obstacles to the CESCR's addressing human rights dimensions of health resource distribution may relate to the theoretical quandaries pertaining to the right to health. One such obstacle is the unwieldiness of the principle of non-retrogression, particularly in the context of a relatively well-developed, single-payer health care system like Canada's. The concept of non-retrogression, which represents an effort to concretize the duty of progressive realization, has been variously defined[64]

Observations of the Committee on Economic, Social and Cultural Rights: Canada, UNCESCROR, 1993, Supp No 3, UN Doc E/C.12/1993/5 at para 19.

60 United Nations Committee on Economic, Social and Cultural Rights, *Consideration of Reports Submitted by States Parties under Articles 16 and 17 of the Covenant: Concluding Observations of the Committee on Economic, Social and Cultural Rights: Canada*, UNCESCROR, 19th Sess, Supp No 2, UN Doc E/C.12/1/Add.31, (1998) at para 42.

61 United Nations Committee on Economic, Social and Cultural Rights, *Consideration of Reports Submitted by States Parties under Articles 16 and 17 of the Covenant: Concluding Observations of the Committee on Economic, Social and Cultural Rights: Canada*, UNCESCROR, 36th Sess, Supp No 2, UN Doc E/C.12/CAN/CO/4 & E/C.12/CAN/CO/5, (2006) at paras 15 and 57.

62 *Ibid* at para 8: "[t]he Committee notes with satisfaction the numerous health programmes conducted by the State Party, such as the 10-year Plan to Strengthen Health Care and the launch of the Public Health Agency."

63 See Shelagh Day & Gwen Brodsky, *Women and the Canada Social Transfer: Securing the Social Union* (Ottawa: Status of Women Canada, 2007), for an account of the massive social welfare retrenchment that began in the 1990s.

64 The principle is rarely carefully explored and has been defined in numerous ways. See United Nations Committee on Economic, Social and Cultural Rights, *General Comment No. 3: The Nature of States Parties Obligations (art 2, para 1 of the Covenant)*, UNCESCROR, 5th Sess, UN Doc E/1991/23, (1990), at para 9 [*General Comment No 3*], which suggests that it imposes a strong justificatory burden on States that would take any "deliberately retrogressive measures"; Maastricht Guidelines on Violations of Economic, Social and Cultural Rights (1998) 20:3 Hum Rts Q 691 at para 14(e), going somewhat further and declaring it a violation for States to "adopt any deliberately retrogressive

and criticized as an "extremely crude and unsatisfactory yardstick"[65] for measuring compliance with progressive realization. The principle notably fails to address what it means to move backward and obscures the need for old strategies to be abandoned and new strategies to be adopted in light of changing socio-economic circumstances.[66] In the case of health care in a well-developed country like Canada, retrogression and progression cannot easily be disentangled.[67] Indeed, critics of health care governance in Canada have complained that entrenched interests have blocked the abandonment of costly, antiquated treatments in favour of more cost-efficient ones.[68]

In addition, the continued influence of early "minimum core content" conceptions of economic, social, and cultural rights may suggest, spuriously, that when it comes to distributional questions, the right to health has greater application in developing countries or countries with very rudimentary health care infrastructure.[69] In its early work, the CESCR, reflecting prevailing academic views at the time,[70] sought to cabin and clarify

---

measure that reduces the extent to which any right is guaranteed"; Siddiqur Osmani, "Globalization and the Human Rights Approach to Development" in Bård A Andreassen & Stephen P Marks, eds, *Development as a Human Right* (Cambridge, MA: Harvard University Press, 2007) 265 at 278. Osmani understands the principle to mean that "nobody should be allowed to suffer an absolute decline in the enjoyment of any right at any time" and that the principle "does not permit the level of enjoyment of any right to decline in comparison with the past."

65 Mary Dowell-Jones, *Contextualising the International Covenant on Economic, Social and Cultural Rights: Assessing the Economic Deficit* (Leiden, The Netherlands: Nijhoff Publishers, 2004).

66 *Ibid* at 52–54.

67 See, for example, Gunilla Backman et al, "Health Systems and the Right to Health: An Assessment of 194 Countries" (2008) 372:9655 The Lancet 2047 at 2049, suggesting that the right to health is violated by an absolute lack of mental health facilities and asserting, without reference to a standard, that few countries devote adequate resources to mental health.

68 Flood, Tuohy, & Stabile, "What's In and Out of Medicare?" above note 9. See also Lauchlan T Munro, "The Human-Rights Based Approach to Programming — A Contradiction in Terms?" (Paper delivered at Conference on Winners and Losers from Rights-Based Approaches to Development, University of Manchester, England, 21–22 February 2005), online: School of Environment and Development www.sed.man.ac.uk. Munro called non-retrogression a profoundly conservative concept for this reason.

69 See, for example, Matthew Craven, *The International Covenant on Economic, Social, and Cultural Rights: A Perspective on its Development* (Oxford: Clarendon Press, 1998) at 143–44.

70 See Karin Lehmann, "In Defense of the Constitutional Court: Litigating Economic and Social Rights and the Myth of the Minimum Core" (2006) 22 Am U Int'l L Rev 163

obligations in the *ICESCR* not only through the principle of non-retrogression but also through a concept of minimum core obligation linked primarily to subsistence-level needs.[71] Some theorists have doubted that anyone can properly define basic survival level needs or that human dignity should be situated primarily at the level of what it takes to survive.[72] Others have suggested a more flexible minimum core that would place different obligations on countries of different levels of development.[73] In addition, the CESCR's concept of the minimum core has evolved to include largely procedural obligations, alongside a substantive mainly survival-level minimum.[74] Nonetheless, the idea that the primary role of economic, social, and cultural rights is to protect against the most severe cases of material deprivation has retained a persistent influence.[75] Whether the concept of minimum core, the difficulties of progressive realization, or political fac-

---

at 180. See also Young, above note 3 at 172, noting that "most human rights scholars are minimum core campaigners."

71 See *General Comment No 3*, above note 64 at para 10: "[t]he Committee is of the view that a minimum core obligation to ensure the satisfaction of, at the very least, minimum essential levels of each of the rights is incumbent upon each State party. Thus, for example, a State party in which any significant number of individuals is deprived of essential foodstuffs, of essential primary health care, of basic shelter and housing, or the most basic forms of education is, *prima facie*, failing to discharge its obligations under the Covenant."

72 See Young, above note 3 at 130 & 131.

73 See *ibid* at 114, citing Asbjørn Eide, "Economic, Social and Cultural Rights as Human Rights" in Asbjørn Eide, Catarina Krause, & Allen Rosas, eds, *Economic, Social and Cultural Rights: A Textbook* (Dordrecht: Martinus Nijhoff Publishers, 2001) 27, and Craig Scott & Philip Alston, "Adjudicating Constitutional Priorities in a Transnational Context: A Comment on Soobramoney's Legacy and Grootboom's Promise" (2000) 16:2 SAJHR 206 at 250. Young cites these authors, who argue for and against a core content that would vary depending on resource availability. These authors indicate that countries with more resources have a higher level of minimum core obligation. See also Fons Coomans, "In Search of the Core Content of the Right to Education" in Danie Brand & Sage Russell, eds, *Exploring the Core Content of Economic and Social Rights: South African and International Perspectives* (Pretoria: Protea Book House, 2002) at 159, in which the author suggests that a country-specific concept of the minimum core would undermine the universality of human rights.

74 See *General Comment No 14*, above note 7.

75 See, for example, David Bilchitz, *Poverty and Fundamental Rights: The Justification and Enforcement of Socio-Economic Rights* (Oxford: Oxford University Press, 2007) at 179–80. Bilchitz prefers a universal survival-based definition of the minimum core. See also Young, above note 3 at 128–29, citing Henry Shue, *Basic Rights: Subsistence, Affluence, and U.S. Foreign Policy*, 2d ed (Princeton, NJ: Princeton University Press, 1996) at 19, discussing how the focus on survival-level need helps bridge the divide between

tors are to blame, the fact remains that while developing countries have attracted significant international human rights scrutiny in relation to the right to health, the human rights dimensions of policies in developed countries have received less attention.

C. AN EMPHASIS ON PROCESSES FOR ENSURING ACCOUNTABLE POLICY

Recently, however, strategies, methodologies, and rhetoric employed to identify and remedy exclusions of marginalized groups and individuals from social and State institutions have shifted. Traditional methodologies seek to identify explicit State violations of fixed rules against individual rights claimants. These have not been abandoned. However, as Bruce Porter describes in Chapter 1, a recent dynamism has emerged around new tools geared towards enhancing people's (especially marginalized people's) input into policies that affect human rights, broadly understood.[76] Rights, therefore, become more concerned with ensuring — beyond the basic democratic processes and beyond international-level monitoring — transparency, accountability, and stakeholder participation in policies affecting human rights.

These newer interventions, advanced by human rights scholars and reflected in international institutions, emphasize the need to address, rather than avoid, the problems of progressive realization and gaps in information. They do so by requiring States to identify and attend to obstacles to assessing progressive realization within their States as part of their international

---

the better-established CPRs and ESCRs through a focus on the right to life and on the necessity of meeting basic needs if other rights are to be meaningfully enjoyed.

76 See Chapter 1; *Report of the Special Rapporteur on the Right of Everyone to the Enjoyment of the Highest Attainable Standard of Physical and Mental Health, Paul Hunt,* UNGAOR, 4th Sess, UN Doc A/HRC/4/28, (January 2007) at paras 26 and 87 [*Report of the Special Rapporteur, 2007*], stating that "traditional" human rights tools like "naming and shaming, letter writing campaigns, test cases, sloganizing and so on" may have "served the human rights community well" for a time but, recognizing the breadth of areas that affect the right to health, the need for the right to be operationalized through all of those areas, and recognizing the potential fluidity that lies beneath a concept like progressive realization, recommending "additional methods, techniques, and skills" including benchmarks, indicators, and impact assessments. See also Jonathan Klaaren, "A Second Look at the South African Human Rights Commission, Access to Information, and the Promotion of Socioeconomic Rights" (2005) 27:2 Hum Rts Q 539, suggesting a national model of socio-economic rights protection based on participation, transparency, and a constitutional right of access to information.

human rights obligations.[77] This approach has been described as a move beyond substantive monitoring of human rights fulfillment within States, to include, in addition, an appraisal of how well States monitor and account for their own human rights fulfillment. This has been termed "monitoring-of-monitoring"[78] or "managing accountability."[79] According to these approaches, States are expected to self-monitor using tools and processes which are themselves grounded in human rights principles and which themselves aim to render rights meaningful even when the rights' substantive content might vary over time and context.

Procedurally grounded human rights measures — such as human rights indicators, benchmarks, and impact assessments — are being developed so as to enhance somewhat less substantive human rights principles like accountability, transparency, non-discrimination, democratic participation, and individual self-determination.[80] They do not purport to give conclusive

---

77 See AnnJanette Rosga & Margaret Satterthwaite, "The Trust Indicators: Measuring Human Rights" (2009) 27:2 Berkeley J Int'l L 253 at 275 [Rosga & Satterthwaite]. See also *Report of the Special Rapporteur, 2007*, above note 76 at para 87: "[w]ithout accountability, a State could use progressive realization and the scarcity of resources as an excuse to do virtually nothing — or to respond to whichever interest group has the loudest voice. Independent, effective and accessible mechanisms of accountability compel a State to explain what it is doing and why and how it is moving, as expeditiously and effectively as possible, towards the realization of the right to health for all"; *General Comment No 14*, above note 7 at para 43(f), requiring that States, as part of their minimum core obligations, set up and implement a national health plan, devise it using "participatory and transparent processes," and include methods such as indicators and benchmarks for measuring progress. It also requires that the content of the plan and the processes by which it is created "give particular attention to all vulnerable or marginalized groups"; Young, above note 3 at 116–18, suggesting that theorists of economic and social rights should move away from substantive definition of the content of core rights and obligations and towards "concepts that facilitate rights' content, operating as law," including benchmarks, indicators, participatory processes, and justification requirements.

78 Rosga & Satterthwaite, *ibid* at 259.

79 Tara Melish, "Maximum Feasible Participation of the Poor: New Governance, New Accountability, and a 21st Century War on the Sources of Poverty" (2010) 13:1 Yale Human Rts & Dev LJ 1 at 75 [Melish].

80 See Joseph Raz, "Human Rights in the Emerging World Order" (2010) 1 Transnational Legal Theory 31 at 47, describing a threefold role of human rights in the post-Cold War period as, "first . . . expressing the worth of all human beings; second . . . placing on the agenda concerns other than those of inter-governmental relations or big business profit; and third . . . empowering individuals and voluntary associations in creating an additional channel for exerting influence and affecting the international order," while expressing concerns about institutional capacity and legitimacy of

answers to questions about how priorities should be set among competing objectives.[81] Rather, in addition to being valued norms in themselves, these principles are expected to drive progressive realization[82] by seeking to ensure that decisions about priority setting are reasonable, transparent, informed by evidence, and take into account the needs of the most marginalized as understood by the most marginalized.[83] The growing popularity of these tools, which are applicable to economic, social, and cultural rights (ESCR) and also to civil and political rights (CPR),[84] suggests that

---

international institutions for enforcement of rights to health and education. See also Brigitte I Hamm, "A Human Rights Approach to Development" (2001) 23:4 Hum Rts Q 1005 at 1019–23; Mac Darrow & Amparo Thomas, "Power, Capture and Conflict: A Call for Human Rights Accountability in Development Cooperation" (2005) 27:2 Hum Rts Q 471 at 493, noting that there can be normative or instrumental rationales for adopting human rights-based approaches to programming and development, but that instrumental conceptions "seem to be the most compelling"; stating also that "this rationale harnesses human rights ideas and energies in order to reach the excluded, or reinforces participatory approaches to situation assessment, empowering people as actors for their own development, strengthening institutions of governance and accountability, and so on."

81 *Report of the Special Rapporteur, 2007*, above note 76 at paras 26, 29, and 87.

82 *Ibid* at para 27. See also Alicia Ely Yamin, "Defining Questions: Situating Issues of Power in the Formulation of a Right to Health under International Law" (1996) 18:2 Hum Rts Q 398 at 407 [Yamin, "Defining Questions"], suggesting that the "distinction between instrumental and normative value of defining health as a human right collapses" when rights are understood to advance empowerment as both a goal and strategy.

83 See Paul Hunt & Gillian MacNaughton, *Impact Assessments, Poverty and Human Rights: A Case Study Using the Right to the Highest Attainable Standard of Health* (31 May 2006) at 30, citing *General Comment No 14*, above note 7 at para 11, online: www.who.int/hhr/Series_6_Impact%20Assessments_Hunt_MacNaughton1.pdf, noting, for example, that "a further important aspect of the right to health 'is the participation of the population in all health-related decision-making at the community, national, and international levels.' Participation implicates, among other factors, the rights to seek and impart health-related information, the right to express views freely, and the right to basic health education, as well as transparency in policymaking processes. Full participation on a non-discriminatory basis also requires special attention to sharing information with and seeking the views of women and men, as well as the views of vulnerable and marginalized people." See also Paul Hunt & Gunilla Backman, "Health Systems and the Right to the Highest Attainable Standard of Health" (2008) 10:1 Health & Hum Rts 81 at 83.

84 Rosga & Satterthwaite, above note 77 at 266, citing Charles Humana, *World Human Rights Guide* (London: Hutchison, 1983); Charles Humana, *World Human Rights Guide* (London: Hodder & Stoughton, 1986), explaining how social scientists interested in applying statistical tools to civil and political rights began using indicators to assess

human rights are relied upon increasingly for their values-driven, governance-enhancing function over any fixed, detailed substantive normative content they might prescribe.[85] That is, deliberation-enhancing, accountability-oriented processes are used to create spaces of contestation — and to suggest values that might inform that contestation.

For example, the work of the former UN special rapporteur on the right to health Paul Hunt has come to place heavy emphasis on right-to-health indicators.[86] These indicators reflect processes, structures, and institutions linked to health, in addition to health itself. For example, *General Comment No 14*[87] requires that indicators measure whether States have adopted a national public health strategy that includes the right to health, whether the plan is formulated and monitored through the participation of "the most vulnerable and disadvantaged" individuals and groups, and whether there are effective internal monitoring and accountability mechanisms.[88] Emphasis is placed on States' duties to generate data in relation to health indicators that are disaggregated to reflect contextual vulnerability and discrimination[89] and on States' duties to monitor their own progress internally through indicator-based benchmarking.[90] The depth of mon-

---

States' overall human rights performance. Humana assigns percentage ratings to countries based on scores concerning forty CPRs, and ranking them "good, fair, poor or bad".

85 Scott Cummings & Louise Trubek, "Globalizing Public Interest Law" (2009) 13 UCLA J Int'l L and Foreign Aff 1, describing a "rule of law" movement relying on the language of human rights to "temper excesses of open markets with appropriate regulation and democratic rights."

86 See *Report of the Special Rapporteur on the Right to the Highest Attainable Standard of Health to the Commissioner on Human Rights — Paul Hunt*, UNESCOR, 62nd Sess, UN Doc E/CN.4/2006/48, (2006). A recent effort to operationalize this model to evaluate the health systems of the full range of States sets out some seventy-two indicators. Many of these can be understood as outcome indicators, such as infant mortality rates and life expectancy, but many are better understood as requirements for domestic monitoring designed to leverage local political processes: the existence of a health plan, whether there is legal protection for participation of the marginalized within that health plan, and even transparency in national financing. See Backman et al, above note 67 at 2057–58.

87 *General Comment No 14*, above note 7 at para 43.

88 *Ibid* at para 49(c).

89 *Ibid* at para 49(b).

90 *Ibid* at paras 35 and 58. See, especially, *ibid* at para 34, which emphasizes the key role indicators play in driving internal accountability and participation:

> . . . [i]ndicators and benchmarks fulfill two important functions that underpin much of the discussion in this chapter. *First*, they can help the State to monitor

itoring-of-monitoring is vividly reflected in the fact that right-to-health indicators even measure the extent to which States undertake health or right-to-health impact assessments prior to adopting national health plans. The result is that indicators move from being a tool for committee-level assessment of States' progressive realization to driving internal processes likely to improve right-to-health outcomes by bringing to light discriminatory, arbitrary, or ineffective policies.[91] Indicator-based monitoring is relied upon for opening up spaces for civil society participation in generating systemic human rights–based reform at national and sub-national levels.[92] Hunt and MacNaughton, although they admit the novelty of the concept,[93] argue that human rights impact assessment is "highly recommended, *if not required*, [for States] to comply with [their] international human rights obligations to progressively realize human rights."[94]

This shift in emphasis towards participation and accountability as a driver of progressive realization is not limited to the UN institutional actors or those who explicitly adopt their frameworks. For example, as Vincent Greason notes in Chapter 3, there has been increasing reliance on measurement rather than values of social solidarity in anti-poverty policies in Canada.[95]

---

its progress over time, enabling the authorities to recognize when policy adjustments are required. *Second*, they can help to hold the State to account in relation to the discharge of its responsibilities arising from the right to health, although deteriorating indicators do not necessarily mean that the State is in breach of its international right to health obligations, an important point which is discussed further below. Of course, indicators also have other important roles. For example, by highlighting issues such as disaggregation, participation and accountability, indicators can enhance the effectiveness of policies and programmes [emphasis in original].

91 See also Hunt & MacNaughton, above note 83 at 57, defining the right to health as the "right to enjoy a variety of goods, facilities and services that are necessary to realize the highest attainable standard of health."

92 See, for example, Alicia Ely Yamin, "The Future in the Mirror: Incorporating Strategies for the Defense and Promotion of Economic, Social and Cultural Rights into the Mainstream Human Rights Agenda" (2005) 27:4 Hum Rts Q 1200 at 1207 and 1212 [Yamin, "Future in the Mirror"], arguing that human rights organizations should move beyond identifying individual-level violations and instead collaborate with other disciplines, such as public health, to use indicators, such as rates of access to emergency obstetric care, in order to advocate in relation to structural and institutional factors in human rights and to create a "starting place for defining appropriate measures for governments to take towards progressive realization."

93 Hunt & MacNaughton, above note 83 at 9.

94 *Ibid* at 7 [emphasis added].

95 See Chapter 3.

Greason remains profoundly skeptical of indicators, viewing them as open to manipulation by governments seeking to set the terms of progress so that they can claim to have achieved it, all the while distracting from neo-liberal moves away from redistribution.[96] Other human rights scholars, and right-to-health scholars in particular, have expressed similar skepticism.[97] Some, however, have elaborated upon and refined how indicators can contribute to a human right to health understood in terms of locating responsibility and opening spaces for meaningful participation in determining health-affecting State policies through monitoring processes.

Alicia Ely Yamin, for example, emphasizes empowerment as an underlying theme in human rights and suggests re-framing the right to health as "the highest attainable standard of *control over* health."[98] She notes that poor health is "the product not only of human beings' incomplete domination of nature, but of the domination of some people by others."[99] The central task of human rights and right-to-health activists is redefined as an exploratory one "to discern the societal relations, combinations, and alignments of power that both produce and distribute disease . . . ."[100] Yamin would seek to shift the dialogue in the right to health to "reveal the human role in constructing health and illness."[101] In doing so, she would reject (perhaps provisionally) any normative account of an ideal health care regime and focus instead on fleshing out the meaning of empowerment in context and through collaboration with affected communities themselves.[102] In 1996, Yamin was skeptical of indicators as a process for achieving empowerment as she worried they might render human rights monitoring too technocratic.[103] By 2005, Yamin advocated that progressive realization could be driven by indicators, so long as those indicators remain contestable, not overly technocratic in that they include the qualitative, and defined through the

96 *Ibid.*

97 See, for example, Sally Engle Merry, "Measuring the World: Indicators, Human Rights, and Global Governance" (2011) 52:3 Current Anthropology at S83.

98 Yamin, "Defining Questions," above note 82 at 400 [emphasis in original].

99 *Ibid* at 402.

100 *Ibid.*

101 *Ibid* at 412.

102 *Ibid* at 436 and 438.

103 *Ibid* at 410–11, expressing the concern that indicators will render health status "an objective, quantitative quality . . . one more output to be produced . . . to be measured according to standardized morbidity and mortality indicators . . . [turning] human beings (and their behaviors) into one more input and thus the targets of incentive changes and objects of surveillance."

collaboration of human rights NGOs with other stakeholders including public health actors.[104]

AnnJanette Rosga and Margaret Satterthwaite likewise respond to concerns over the risks of indicators by emphasizing the role of meaningful participation in creating a contestable set of indicators. They suggest that "indicators must be created that will measure the participation of the populace in decisions affecting both institutional design and policy priorities in the field of human rights" and that "participation should . . . extend to the process of designing and implementing indicators themselves."[105]

This new accountability-centred focus, whereby public goods are scrutinized not (primarily) for their substantive distribution but for whether processes for distribution comply with foundational human rights principles, does hold some theoretical promise for human rights–based assessments of health systems in Canada. By recognizing that all rights have components whose contents are in evolution and which can be better enforced through participation, accountability, and monitoring, it diminishes the argument that CPRs and ESCRs are of fundamentally different natures, with ESCRs occupying the lower rung.[106] Likewise, where States' duties to self-monitor, disaggregate data, benchmark, and open up participation in human rights–related policy making occupy a more central place among their human rights obligations, the differences between "violations" and "minimum core" approaches on the one hand and progressive realization on the other, diminish.[107] Free of the need for universal substantive normativity, "immediately enforceable" ESCRs need not be restricted to the level of basic survival and can have greater resonance in a well-developed health care system. Unjustifiable choices rooted in power, ignorance, or stereotype — what some might consider systemic discrimination, which traditional approaches have failed to address — cannot hide as easily behind privatized and disaggregated lines of responsibility and authority when they are brought into the public sphere through accountability and participation requirements. Concerns about transparency, accountability, and substantive distribution in Canadian health care — well voiced in the political sphere — may be structured in concrete human rights terms.

---

104 Yamin, "Future in the Mirror," above note 92 at 1210: "[i]f human rights groups are willing to work with other disciplines . . . [indicators] can form the basis for the standard-setting work the human rights movement has successfully engaged in for years with respect to many civil and political rights issues, including prison conditions."

105 Rosga & Satterthwaite, above note 77 at 313–14.

106 See also Yamin, "Defining Questions," above note 82.

107 See Young, above note 3 at 166; Rosga & Satterthwaite, above note 77 at 265.

Although the new emphasis on processes in human rights implementation is relatively recent, its set of core themes is not. A number of authors have noted common intellectual underpinnings and features of the new conceptions of accountability and responsibility in human rights and new ideas about governance in the public sector (including health policy).[108] That is, the driving themes here — enhancing democratic governance through flexible norm-setting that responds to community-level needs, reliance on transparent, deliberative processes, evidence-based decision making, and citizen participation — are closely paralleled in public (including health) policy literature in Canada and internationally.[109] The emphasis on these core themes has increased as resource constraints have put pressure on the Canadian health care system and raised concerns about accountability in the scope and distribution of publicly funded services. The next section will examine the evolution of health governance in Canada along such lines, with a view to exploring how Canada might respond to the demands of the procedural dimensions of the human rights to health and to expose contextual challenges to the procedural project in the human right to health.

D. PARTICIPATORY GOVERNANCE IN CANADIAN HEALTH CARE PRIORITY SETTING

Government did not always play an active role in determining the distribution of health care in Canada. In the early days of public insurance, government simply underwrote the hospital and physician services that already existed, and distribution was effectively left to the clinical judgment of individual physicians. From medicare's inception in the 1960s until significant cuts in the 1990s, costs were kept in check largely without resort to restricting services available under the public plan.

The passage of time, however, brought new challenges and conceptions around health, medical care, and insurance that fundamentally tested the conception of medicare rooted in the 1960s. New technologies made costlier interventions possible. The importance of health interventions outside of covered hospital and physician services became clearer. Governments experimented with hospital restructuring and delisting of services as ways

108 Lisa Alexander, "Stakeholder Participation in New Governance: Lessons from Chicago's Public Housing Reform Experiment" (2009) 16:1 Geo J on Poverty L & Pol'y 117; Melish, above note 79.

109 See Norman Daniels & James Sabin, "The Ethics of Accountability in Managed Care Reform" (1998) 17:5 Health Affairs 50.

of controlling escalating costs.[110] However, the major change in management of health care distribution came through regionalization.

In the late 1980s and early 1990s, each province established a task force or commission of inquiry to deal with health care costs in times of economic restraint.[111] All reflected a similar set of general goals. Many were about efficiency: better health outcomes with less overall spending. Others addressed broader political concerns like increasing accountability of decision makers and enhancing citizen participation. Suggested directions for achieving those goals included a shift from institutionally-based to community-based care, a focus on a broader range of health determinants beyond the health care delivery system, making room for the representation of a variety of interests in the health field in health policy planning, and the integration of services across the continuum of care.[112] Regionalization of health care was the favoured structural approach for achieving these reforms and was adopted from the late 1980s through the 1990s in every province[113] except Ontario, which finally adopted a form of regionalization in the mid-2000s.[114]

---

110 Carolyn Hughes Tuohy, *Accidental Logics: The Dynamics of Change in the Health Care Arena in the United States, Britain, and Canada* (New York: Oxford University Press, 1999) at 180 [Tuohy, *Accidental Logics*].

111 For a summary, see Sharmila L Mhatre & Raisa B Deber, "From Equal Access to Health Care to Equitable Access to Health: A Review of Canadian Provincial Health Commissions and Reports" (1992) 22:4 International Journal of Health Services 645; Gregory Marchildon, *Health Systems in Transition: Canada* (Toronto: University of Toronto Press, 2006). These sources provide a summary.

112 Tuohy, *Accidental Logics*, above note 110 at 97.

113 Marchildon, above note 111 at 108–9. There has since been some retreat from regionalization: Prince Edward Island, Canada's smallest province with a population of 140,000, eliminated regional boards in 2005. See Donald J Philippon & Jeffrey Braithwaite, "Health System Organization and Governance in Canada and Australia: A Comparison of Historical Developments, Recent Policy Changes and Future Implications" (2008) 4:1 Healthcare Policy 168 at 178. In 2008, Alberta announced that it would create a single "super-region," but one that would maintain the consolidation of authority and the accountability requirements under the *Regional Health Authorities Act*; Tom McIntosh et al, "Population Health and Health Reform: Needs-Based Funding in Five Provinces" (2010) 4:1 Canadian Political Science Review 42 at 48.

114 For a description of the Ontario experience, see Robert Bardner, *Local Health Integration Networks: Potential, Challenges and Policy Directions*, online: The Wellesley Institute http://wellesleyinstitute.com. See also Brent Moloughney, *A Discussion Paper on Public Health, Local Health Integration Networks, and Regional Health Authorities*, online: OPHA www.opha.on.ca, criticizing the Ontario regional structure for failing to include authority over public health and for failing to eliminate hospital boards.

Regionalization was expected to help in a number of ways. It was expected to allow resources to move more fluidly in response to local needs, as regions would be required to assess the health care needs of their populations and craft plans setting out how they anticipate meeting those needs.[115] It was envisioned that increased reporting of spending, projected and actual health outcomes, and wait times — as would be necessary for re-distributing funding within regions — would result in more direct accountability to local citizens and make funding less conventionally politicized and less dominated by professional interests.[116] Other ostensible benefits included increased service quality and reliance on evidence-based practice, as well as increased spaces for public participation.[117] Less optimistically, regionalization can be understood as a way to contain discontent and conflict as service expectations seem increasingly to exceed what governments are prepared to pay for.[118]

The most significant accountability-related achievement resulting from regionalization is the improved transparency achieved through bottom-up reporting mechanisms. Working within broad provincially set parameters,[119] Regional Health Authorities (RHAs) must typically develop and publicize a regional plan setting out how they will meet statutory obligations to provide for the health needs of the population.[120] As for reporting

---

115 Marchildon, above note 111 at 107; Flood, Sinclair, & Erdman, above note 1 at 176.

116 Steven Lewis & Denise Kouri, "Regionalization: Making Sense of the Canadian Experience" (2004) 5:1 Healthcare Papers 12 at 15–20.

117 See Jonathan Lomas, "Devolving Authority for Health Care in Canada's Provinces: 4 Emerging Issues and Prospects" (1997) 156 Can Med Assoc J 817 at 819; Flood, Sinclair, & Erdman, above note 1; Lewis & Kouri, above note 116 at 16.

118 Lomas, above note 117 at 818.

119 See, for example, *Regional Health Authorities Act*, SNB 2002, c R-5.05, s 6(1) [New Brunswick Act], which sets out guidelines for the development of the provincial health plan; *Regional Health Services Act*, SS 2002, c R-8.2, s 4 [Saskatchewan Act], which affirmed that the minister (i.e., the provincial government) is responsible for overall strategic direction, including, *inter alia*, the establishment of goals, objectives, performance measures and targets, and development of methodologies for resource allocation.

120 See, for example, New Brunswick Act, above note 119, s 32(1); *Health and Community Services Act*, SNL 1995, c P-37.1, ss 16 and 21(1) [Newfoundland and Labrador Act]; *Regional Health Authorities Act*, CCSM c R34, ss 24(1) and 34(3) [Manitoba Act]; Saskatchewan Act, above note 119; *Regional Health Authorities Act*, RSA 2000, c R-10, s 9(1) [Alberta Act]; *Health Authorities Act*, RSBC 1996, c 180, s 5(1)(a) [British Columbia Act]; *Act Respecting Health Services and Social Services*, RSQ, c S-4.2, ss 346(1), 350, and 385(1)–(3) [Quebec Act]. Quebec's legislation requires RHAs to set out multi-year strategic plans supplemented by an annual "management and accountability

requirements themselves, each RHA is statutorily required to report publicly on the extent to which its plans are met through some combination of financial reports, audited statements, and, most novel in this context, indicators of the health status of the population and the efficacy of the RHA basket of services.[121] In addition, most RHA legislation places a premium on the flexibility of objectives and modes of assessment,[122] and RHAs increasingly negotiate the addition of accountability mechanisms through "performance agreements" with the provinces and incorporate these into their mandate beyond what is explicitly set out in statutes.[123] RHAs are

---

agreement" negotiated between the provincial government and the RHA. Statutory duties of RHAs vary from province to province. The Quebec Act, s 340, lists RHA duties including allocating budgets, ensuring public participation, ensuring efficient distribution of resources, assessing the results of the implementation of its strategic plan, and carrying out any other mandate entrusted to it by the minister. See the New Brunswick Act, above note 119, s 30. Responsibilities of RHAs in the New Brunswick Act are simpler: determining needs, setting priorities, and allocating resources. See also *Health Authorities Act*, SNS 2000 c 6, ss 19–20 [Nova Scotia Act].

121 The detail with which legislation prescribes the content of reports varies. See, for example, Alberta Act, above note 120, ss 9(4)(a) and 14(2)(b): in Alberta, for example, annual reports must contain audited financial information, senior management and board remuneration, and "other performance information required by regulation"; Manitoba Act, above note 120, s 38(2): Manitoba legislation specifies that annual reports shall contain, in addition to financial statements, the health services provided, their costs, and a "report respecting the health status of the population and the effectiveness of the health services provided or funded by the regional health authority"; Nova Scotia Act, above note 120, s 21(1)(c): in Nova Scotia, the legislation is more open-ended: district health authorities are required to provide financial statements and "such information as is required by the Minister for the purpose of monitoring and evaluation of the quality, accessibility and comprehensiveness of health services."

122 Saskatchewan Act, above note 119, s 54(2); British Columbia Act, above note 120, s 7(2); Newfoundland and Labrador Act, above note 120, s 24.

123 See Mark Considine, "The End of the Line? Accountable Governance in the Age of Networks, Partnerships, and Joined-Up Services" (2002) 15:1 Governance 21 at 22. Performance agreements are becoming an increasingly common tool in the public sector for governments to set the course for agencies without micromanaging their work. These are most prominently used in British Columbia and Quebec, where they are becoming increasingly elaborate. See Quebec Act, above note 120, s 387.5. This section explicitly requires the use of performance agreements and consequent reporting. Section 385.7 requires that the annual report measure results against the plan in the management and accountability agreement. In addition, legislation requires each RHA to report on the reliability of the data and the monitoring mechanisms. British Columbia consolidates its RHA reports and publishes them on the Ministry of Health website, online: www.health.gov.bc.ca.

also required to ensure the release of reports on progress towards achievement.[124] The combined result has been a massive shift towards the use of targets or benchmarks, followed by the collection of statistical indicators of population health, service usage, wait times, and other aspects of system effectiveness.[125] Flood and Archibald have described this new indicator-based system as a "significant improvement on what provincial governments were historically prepared to divulge to citizens."[126]

Nonetheless, regionalization has not fully lived up to its promise. The most oft-cited obstacle is the failure of most regions to situate full fiscal responsibility for all services within a given region.[127] A broad conception of the social determinants of health would suggest a very wide range of community services be included within a RHA's budget.[128] However, both physician remuneration[129] and drug plans outside hospitals[130] have been left out of RHA budgets, undermining their capacity to redirect funding where participatory processes reveal that it is most needed. In Ontario, regional distribution has allegedly been captured by the interests of policy makers and private medical practitioners whose financial interests are at odds with the promotion of investment in "upstream" factors like social determinants of health.[131] In other words, curative approaches are being unjustifiably preferred, even where preventative approaches that address the social inequities and inequalities that drive poor health might result in better health outcomes. Capture and politicization may explain why, despite legislation demanding responsive planning, in most cases "this year's plan is last year's

---

124 British Columbia Ministry of Health Services, *Report on Health Authority Performance Agreements 2002/2003* at 6, online: Ministry of Health www.health.gov.bc.ca. The British Columbia Ministry of Health Services describes the purpose of reports pursuant to performance agreements as "an opportunity to compare the performance of health authorities relative to each other, Ministry expectations, and to provide the public with ongoing information on the impact of redesign on patient services."

125 Colleen Flood & Tom Archibald, *Hamstrung and Hogtied: Cascading Constraints on Citizen Governors in Medicare* (2005), online: CPRN www.cprn.org.

126 *Ibid* at 25. See Manitoba Act, above note 120, s 38(2); Quebec Act, above note 120, s 346.

127 Flood, Sinclair, & Erdman, above note 1 at 193; Lomas, above note 117 at 823–24; Lewis & Kouri, above note 116 at 20–23; Moloughney, above note 114.

128 See Michael Marmot, "Social Determinants of Health Inequalities" (2005) 365 The Lancet 1099, setting out the potential breadth of the concept of social determinants of health.

129 Lewis & Kouri, above note 116 at 25.

130 *Ibid*.

131 McIntosh et al, above note 113.

plan slightly twigged to reflect updated information."[132] Part of the problem may lie in the technical challenge of drawing up formulas for determining relative need that extend beyond age- and gender-adjusted population counts[133] and the fear that such formulas might become so complex that they shut out stakeholder participation.[134] The difficulties associated with implementing needs-based funding also suggest that it may be impossible to depoliticize allocation decisions within regions.[135]

Instead, the goals of regionalization and rationalization might be better understood not as de-politicizing but modifying the political environment in which the decisions are made. Regionalization and needs-based assessment should not be understood to offer a technocratic solution to moving away from hospital- and physician-based care and towards prevention, health promotion, and other upstream investments, or to be the solution to the broader problem of spending wisely and fairly. Instead, their promise lies in setting the stage for more transparent allocation and, much like the new emphasis in human rights approaches set out above, opening up new kinds of spaces for democratic accountability and participation beyond the ordinary political process. Understanding whether the ostensible shifts towards evidence-based distribution through regional consolidation have indeed opened up new spaces for determining the distribution of health care resources, particularly for marginalized groups, requires an examination of the accountability frameworks that have accompanied the move towards regionalized governance. This presents a new challenge to social and economic rights advocates, monitors, and judges: to attend to the ways in which transparent, accountable governance can reveal and provide space to address illegitimate exercises of power as part of the human rights project.

E. CONCLUSION: NEW AGENDAS IN HUMAN RIGHTS MONITORING, ADVOCACY, AND SCHOLARSHIP

In this paper I have argued that human rights actors might usefully take advantage of this shift towards participatory and accountable governance

---

132 Jeremiah Hurley, "Regionalization and the Allocation of Healthcare Resources to Meet Population Health Needs" (2004) 5:1 Healthcare Papers 34 at 36.

133 See, for example, McIntosh et al, above note 113.

134 Hurley, above note 132.

135 *Ibid*, stating that in retrospect the optimism around needs-based funding coupled with regionalization was unfounded and that this "perhaps should have been obvious when one reflects how difficult reallocation is within fully integrated, hierarchical organizations, much less a regional health authority with far more muted power."

both in right to health and in health resource allocation. The move towards regionalization, accompanied as it has been by preoccupations over ensuring accountability, participation, and evidence-based policy, appears notably apt to incorporating new conceptions of human rights and the right to health, as described above. Like the human rights approaches, such an approach begins by recognizing the disproportionate emphasis on curative provisos over social and structural determinants of health. It seeks to dis-entrench structures that support an anachronistic reliance on curative models and move away from arbitrary, inefficient, and ineffective allocation decisions by coordinating services[136] and the opening up of priority-setting mechanisms to flexible, transparent, accountable, and participatory local-level decision making. Participation is sought; transparency and accountability are, likewise, pursued through public planning and reporting. Through orchestration, including comparison of targets and means of achieving progress towards those targets, it might promote continual improvement by revealing progress over time.

At the same time, context is important. Canada's new institutions for managing health care distribution were not designed as, nor do they fully reflect, a participation-oriented human rights–based approach to determining distribution of health care resources in Canada. Politically, these changes were motivated by concerns about service integration, cost containment, and communicating accountability to an increasingly dissatisfied public. The changes were also justified publicly with reference to their value for citizen engagement.[137] Unfortunately, in practice the programs are not primarily designed to ensure genuinely responsive, human rights–oriented health care allocation decisions. Nonetheless, the ostensible reliance on participatory, transparent, accountable governance to ensure fair and reasonable allocation both in the right to health and in health governance offers new opportunities for advocacy, as well as new questions with which to struggle.

As to the judicial challenges noted above, the existence of such accountability and participation requirements might bolster traditional human rights claims. For example, had human rights–based obligations of participatory accountability guided the process for determining the delisting of sex reassignment surgery in *Hogan*, the result might have been very differ-

---

136 Hunt & Backman, above note 83 at 47–48.

137 Lomas, above note 117, noting the empowerment rhetoric that came along with regionalization, but doubting whether community participation was ever necessary to the central vision of regionalization, and suggesting that empowerment was bound to take a backseat to cost-cutting goals.

ent. The *Auton* Court, for its part, might have been less fearful of examining the *bona fides* of the claim to services if the choice of which services to provide had been grounded in a more robust and transparent participatory accountability framework.

In terms of policy advocacy, human rights lend credence to the suggestion that if participation, transparency, and accountability form the basis of more responsive decision making, such governance should be extended to *all* health-affecting services.[138] There is, of course, a risk of overextending the scope of what health authorities are required to consider. This potential overextension is a key criticism of the human rights focus on social determinants of health. The more factors that go into reports, indicators, and benchmarks, the greater the risk that spaces opened up for democratic participation will be too complex for stakeholders to navigate. In this particular context, however, this difficulty is largely outweighed by the concerns noted by those committed to a fair distribution of health resources based on need rather than ability to pay. They argue that the historic focus on funding hospital and physician services operates at the expense of social determinants — the social and political exclusion and inequality that drives poor health. Placing social determinants on a level, deliberative playing field may be the best way to ensure the process of identifying and ranking determinants (even as they remain potentially boundless) against traditional health services becomes possible in the context of ossified health care allocation structures.

Finally, given the increasing importance placed on participation and accountability at the international level, human rights monitors, scholars, and advocates should carefully monitor the practice of participatory governance in the Canadian health care context, with a view to evaluating whether, when, and how meaningful participation can be assured in these kinds of contexts. Human rights can provide important justification for insisting on real rather than "sham" opportunities for participation. In practice, most RHA legislation in Canada provides only modestly for citizen involvement.[139] Processes themselves may not create room for meaningful participation, for example, when unidirectional flows of information (typically from professionals to citizens) have stood in place of real deliberative

---

138 See Martha Jackman, "The Right to Participate in Health Care and Health Resource Allocation Decisions under Section 7 of the Canadian *Charter*" (1995/1996) 4:2 Health L Rev 3.

139 See Flood & Archibald, above note 125 at 23–25.

exchange,[140] or information presented was too technical or rushed through for participants to understand.[141] Moreover, there is little evidence that citizen deliberators are actually listened to.[142] A more troubling problem is addressing power differences among participants. Left unassisted, those with the fewest resources are likely to be least able to participate. Unstructured participation might result in certain citizen voices being disproportionately heard. Expensive autism treatment[143] may generate more support than inexpensive but equally effective needle-exchange programs.[144] At the same time, there is a risk that deliberative processes will become bare cost-benefit analyses along axes of measurement set and controlled by those in power.[145] Some health services may be important but resistant to measurement in terms of health outcomes, such as palliative care. Scholars and activists contending with the move towards human rights–based governance processes will need to contend with these difficulties if the move towards justificatory, participatory processes persists.

It is always possible that the turn towards participatory processes in international law is a misguided one. Canada's experiences will help determine whether traditional methods of locating violations based on set substantive norms remain preferable. However, it is important to remember where we started. These approaches may provide novel avenues for addressing ossified, substantively discriminatory, and, arguably, retrogressive distributions of health resources in Canada that have proved difficult to address adequately under traditional human rights scrutiny. In turning towards the procedural considerations, the right to health makes a modest step and a bold one. Modestly, it gives traction to (without deciding) concepts like "progressive realization" and the ultimately indeterminate "core obligations." More boldly, it locates the denial of the right to health squarely

---

140 Julia Abelson et al, "Deliberations about Deliberative Methods: Issues in the Design and Evaluation of Public Participation Processes" (2003) 57:2 Social Science & Medicine 239 at 246.

141 *Ibid.*

142 *Ibid* at 247.

143 Eric Fombonne, "The Prevalence of Autism" (2003) 289:1 Journal of the American Medical Assocation 87 at 89: ". . . ironically, what has triggered substantial social policy changes in autism appears to have little connection with the state of the evidence . . . . [F]urther consideration should be given to how and to why the least evidence-based claims have achieved impressive changes in funding policy."

144 Franklin Laufer, "Cost-Effectiveness of Syringe Exchange as an HIV Prevention Strategy" (2001) 28:3 Journal of Acquired Immune Deficiency Syndromes 273 at 277.

145 See Kevin Davis, Benedict Kingsbury, & Sally Engle Merry, "Indicators as a Technology of Global Governance" (2012) 46:1 Law & Soc'y Rev 71.

in the disenfranchisement and disempowerment of citizens from control over what affects their body. In doing so, the human right to health both delegitimizes professional and market capture and renews its own fundamental challenge of guaranteeing dignity-based self-realization.

CHAPTER 11

SOCIAL RIGHTS AND ADMINISTRATIVE JUSTICE

LORNE SOSSIN* AND ANDREA HILL†

A. INTRODUCTION

When the topic of social rights arises, people rarely think of administrative tribunals. Yet more people have their rights relating to housing, social benefits, employment, and other human rights determined in tribunals than in courts. While administrative decisions are subject to the oversight of judicial review, the barriers of cost and complexity mean that for the overwhelming majority of people, an administrative tribunal will be their first and final recourse to protect their social rights.

Administrative justice is defined by its diversity. While courts in every part of the country look remarkably similar, few people can close their eyes and picture what a landlord tenant board, immigration and refugee board, or social benefits tribunal looks like. Yet that is where a vulnerable tenant goes to stave off eviction, where a refugee claimant goes to avoid deportation, and where a person whose benefits have been curtailed goes for recourse. There are hundreds of tribunals, at the federal, provincial, and municipal levels, involving thousands of full- and part-time adjudicators applying a myriad of statutory schemes and regulatory regimes.

The diversity of administrative justice extends beyond the appearance and jurisdiction of tribunals. Tribunals also vary with respect to procedure — some are as adversarial as courts while others adopt a more activist approach to adjudication, and some involve inquisitorial processes which

* Lorne Sossin, Dean, Osgoode Hall Law School, York University.

† Andrea Hill, Lawyer at Wildeboer Dellelce LLP, Toronto.

place the decision maker in the position of eliciting the necessary information from the parties. Hearings may occur electronically, over the phone, in person, or in writing. Appearances before the Human Rights Tribunal may stretch into weeks of complex evidentiary testimony while some hearings before the Landlord and Tenant Board take less than thirty minutes. Fundamental human rights may be at stake in both.

Thus, any discussion of social rights in administrative justice must confront the realities and implications of this diversity. For example, to say that the Health Professions Appeal and Review Board has jurisdiction over the *Canadian Charter of Rights and Freedoms*[1] does not address the question of how a self-represented patient might identify or develop submissions on a *Charter* issue. To say that international human rights norms should constrain the decisions of the Social Benefits Tribunal raises obvious problems of how those norms are communicated to decision makers, who may or may not be legally trained, or to parties coming before those decision makers. Complicating a rights-based approach to administrative justice is the fact that those decision makers are not protected by judicial independence,[2] and there is a long history of partisan and patronage appointments to tribunals expected to act in an impartial fashion. The assumption in cases such as *Nova Scotia v Martin* (2003),[3] *Tranchemontagne v Ontario* (2006),[4] and *R v Conway* (2010)[5] — which affirm the jurisdiction of administrative tribunals over human rights legislation and the *Charter* — is that it is up to the legislature to determine the mandate of these adjudicative bodies, up to government to decide their budget and appointments, and up to the courts to correct serious errors when and if a party seeks judicial review.

It is striking how out of touch with reality the Court's analyses in those cases appear to be — the majority judgment in each case simply finds "practical considerations" such as a tribunal's capacity to undertake the hearing and adjudication of rights, to be irrelevant. While it may be irrelevant to the question of jurisdiction, practical capacity is the defining set of considerations as to whether the rights in question will be meaningful and accessible.

1 Part I of the *Constitution Act, 1982*, being Schedule B to the *Canada Act 1982* (UK), 1982, c 11 [*Charter*].

2 See *Ocean Port Hotel Ltd v British Columbia (General Manager, Liquor Control and Licensing Branch)*, 2001 SCC 52, for discussion of the doctrinal distinction.

3 *Nova Scotia (Workers' Compensation Board) v Martin; Nova Scotia (Workers' Compensation Board) v Laseur*, 2003 SCC 54 [*Martin*].

4 *Tranchemontagne v Ontario (Director, Disability Support Program)*, 2006 SCC 14 [*Tranchemontagne*].

5 2010 SCC 22 [*Conway*].

Put differently, is it open to the government to create administrative bodies with jurisdiction over social rights and then fail to provide the necessary resources to permit those bodies to discharge that jurisdiction? Because administrative decision makers in Canada are part of the executive and not the judicial branch, however, they also are subject to additional constraints in relation to social rights, which flow from the *Charter*, and arguably from the international commitments to which Canada is subject. While such commitments may not have the force of law until incorporated into domestic legislation, these commitments create a meaningful framework that shapes the discretion of administrative bodies (until and unless such a framework is inconsistent with a domestic act).

We consider tribunals and administrative justice from this dual perspective: as adjudicative bodies with jurisdiction over decisions on social rights and as executive bodies subject to rights-protecting constitutional and international law instruments. We argue that a rights-based culture can, and should, be developed within the sphere of administrative justice. This paper is divided into three parts. In the first part, we canvass the social rights literature and its relevance to the realities of administrative justice. In the second part, we consider the *Charter* and international human rights obligations and the ways in which they may enhance a rights-based culture within administrative justice. In the third and concluding part, we argue that only a vantage point that is firmly rooted in constitutional and international human rights commitments, in the lived realities of the boards and tribunals that comprise the administrative justice community, and in the parties who come before these adjudicative bodies can lead to a meaningful and accessible system of establishing and protecting social rights.

B. PART ONE: ADMINISTRATIVE TRIBUNALS AS ADJUDICATIVE SPACE FOR SOCIAL RIGHTS

Social rights have been described as rights relating to the meeting of basic needs that are essential for human welfare, such as the right to adequate housing, freedom from poverty, and access to opportunities for social and economic advancement.[6] Margot Young has observed that social rights are "necessary correctives" to classic liberal rights; the rights to life, liberty, and expression are not meaningful absent adequate standards of living, edu-

6 See, for example, Conor Gearty & Virginia Mantouvalou, *Debating Social Rights* (Portland, OR: Hart Publishing, 2011) at 90.

cation, and other standards of material and social well-being.[7] As Virginia Mantouvalou[8] has observed, "[W]e realize that living a life deprived of fundamental necessities like shelter, food and basic healthcare . . . is a terrible plight."[9] Redressing social deprivation is not simply a "moral yardstick" for government but also the foundation of the commitment of States, ultimately tracing their heritage back to the *Universal Declaration of Human Rights*.[10]

This correlation of social rights with human rights was weakened, however, in 1961 when the rights recognized in the *UDHR* were split[11] between two United Nations covenants: the *International Covenant on Civil and Political Rights*[12] and the *International Covenant on Economic, Social and Cultural Rights*.[13] Many civil and political rights, such as freedom of religion and the prohibition of torture, were incorporated into the former, and a number of positive material entitlements, including social rights, were addressed by the latter.[14] The *ICESCR*, which was ratified by Canada in 1976,[15] recognizes a number of specific socially oriented rights, including

- the right to work, and to freely choose one's work;[16]
- the right to just and favourable conditions of work;[17]
- the right to social security, including social insurance;[18]
- the right to the broadest possible support for families as they are established and as they grow;[19]
- the right to an adequate standard of living, including adequate food, clothing, and housing;[20]

---

7 Margot Young, "Introduction" in Margot Young et al, eds, *Poverty: Rights, Social Citizenship, Legal Activism* (Vancouver: UBC Press, 2007) at 4.

8 Gearty & Mantouvalou, above note 6.

9 *Ibid* at 86.

10 *Ibid* at 91. *Universal Declaration of Human Rights*, GA Res 217(III), UNGAOR, 3d Sess, Supp No 13, UN Doc A/810, (1948) 71 [*UDHR*].

11 Gearty & Mantouvalou, above note 6 at 92.

12 *International Covenant on Civil and Political Rights*, 16 December 1966, 999 UNTS 171, 6 ILM 368 (entered into force 23 March 1976) [*ICCPR*].

13 *International Covenant on Economic, Social and Cultural Rights*, 16 December 1966, 993 UNTS 3, 6 ILM 368 (entered into force 3 January 1976) [*ICESCR*].

14 *Ibid*.

15 United Nations Treaty Collection, *International Covenant on Economic, Social, and Cultural Rights. Ratifications and Reservations*, online: UNTS http://treaties.un.org.

16 *ICESCR*, above note 13.

17 *Ibid*, art 7.

18 *Ibid*, art 9.

19 *Ibid*, art 10.

20 *Ibid*, art 11.

- the right to the highest attainable standard of physical and mental health; and[21]
- the right to education.[22]

The nature, content, and evolution of social rights in international and domestic law are discussed in greater detail elsewhere in this volume. The focus of social rights, however, includes not only direct legal challenges to deprivation and discrimination against those in need but also challenges to government for failing to develop plans, policies, and infrastructure to address such deprivation and discrimination. As Martha Jackman and Bruce Porter have argued:

> The new conception of rights creates the foundation for a more principled and strategic approach to rights-based policy development, bringing future-oriented, strategic aspects of policy and program development and planning, that were previously beyond the lens of human rights, squarely into an expanded human rights framework. A failure to adopt appropriate strategies and plans to realize rights to adequate housing or adequate income within a reasonable period of time can now be seen as actionable violations, subject to rights claims and to adjudication in the present.[23]

Patrick Macklem[24] has suggested that Canada's domestic implementation of its commitment to social rights and the *ICESCR* has occurred on two "planes": a legislative plane, where the government establishes and administers social policy programs associated with social rights, and a juridical plane, where courts implement social rights by interpreting statutory and constitutional provisions in light of Canada's international legal obligations.[25] In our view, while these areas deserve attention, the most meaningful activity in the field of social rights in Canada may happen neither in the legislature nor in the courts. Rather, it occurs in the sphere of administrative justice, where decisions are made and discretion is exercised. Too often this is a sphere of rights protection that is overlooked or discounted in the social rights literature. If the focus of social rights is shifting to the plans and policies of the State, then the scrutiny of the agencies, boards,

21 *Ibid*, art 12.

22 *Ibid*, art 13.

23 Martha Jackman & Bruce Porter, "International Human Rights and Strategies to Address Homelessness and Poverty in Canada: Making the Connection" at 5, online: CURA http://socialrightscura.ca [Jackman & Porter, "Making the Connection"].

24 Patrick Macklem, "Social Rights in Canada" in Daphne Barak-Erez & Aeyal M Gross, eds, *Exploring Social Rights* (Portland, OR: Hart Publishing, 2007).

25 *Ibid* at 213–14.

and commissions of the State charged with implementing those plans and policies should be enhanced.

The dilemma in the context of administrative justice is that adjudicators do not have inherent jurisdiction or authority (in contrast to the judiciary); rather, they derive all of their powers from statutory or other delegated authority. In other words, if administrative adjudicators are to interpret and implement social rights, they must be given a mandate to do so in their governing statute. This mandate is sometimes clear, as in the case of human rights tribunals, immigration and refugee boards, or labour boards, but other times may be oblique. An energy board regulator or import and trade tribunal member may not at first glance be understood as presiding over dispute resolution involving social rights, but a rights-based approach to their jurisdiction may have profound consequences for vulnerable communities. Therefore, there is a crucial role for advocacy organizations and activists to also focus on administrative justice.

Bruce Porter proposes understanding and evaluating access to justice in relation to access to adjudicative forums and engagement with decision makers, even where there is little prospect of success.[26] He illustrates this proposal by reference to a Poor People's Conference held in Ottawa in October of 1993, during which "claims to adjudicative space for social rights in Canada were . . . affirmed as victories, although neither legal remedies nor policy changes had been obtained."[27]

Many of those seeking to advance social rights recognize the potential paradigm shift simply in approaching administrative justice from a rights-based perspective. For example, the Income Security Advocacy Clinic (ISAC) has litigated dozens of "special diet" cases before the Ontario Human Rights Tribunal, claiming that the province of Ontario systemically underfunds or fails to fund certain medical conditions in this program.[28] By so doing, ISAC is transforming a benefit-funding discourse based on scarce resources into a rights-based discourse based on minimum guarantees of equality and fairness.

If we think about the "adjudicative spaces" most relevant to people in need, tribunals matter far more than courts. For example, in 2009 and 2010, the Landlord and Tenant Board of Ontario alone received a total of

---

26 Bruce Porter, "Claiming Adjudicative Space: Social Rights, Equality, and Citizenship" in Young et al, eds, above note 7 at 77.

27 *Ibid.*

28 See Income Security Advocacy Center, "Current Legal Challenges," online: ISAC www.incomesecurity.org.

78,072 applications and resolved 82,464 applications.[29] By contrast, the Ontario Small Claims Court, historically referred to as the "people's court" as it promotes broad public access to justice by providing a simple and cost-effective forum for dispute resolution,[30] saw 64,254 small claims proceedings during the same period across all ninety provincial locations.[31] While the courts rarely hear social rights cases involving people in need, courts have been instrumental in broadening the jurisdiction of tribunals to do so. In *Tranchemontagne*, the Supreme Court of Canada expanded the jurisdiction of administrative tribunals to encompass consideration of the *Human Rights Code*[32] in the course of its determinations regarding eligibility for disability support. In other words, it is not simply the Human Rights Tribunal with jurisdiction over rights cases. Rather, these cases now may be brought in any tribunal whose legislation has not expressly precluded such cases.

Chief Justice McLachlin seemed to anticipate this state of affairs more than a decade ago when she wrote in dissent in *Cooper v Canada*,[33] a case which, like *Tranchemontagne*, probed the extent to which tribunals had jurisdiction to consider the constitutionality of their enabling legislation. The majority in *Cooper* held that a human rights commission lacked the authority to decide *Charter* questions because its purpose and structure were not aligned with the adjudication of *Charter* rights. Chief Justice McLachlin's dissent in *Cooper* included the following memorable reference to the "holy grail," which has underscored the debate about how vulnerable parties gain access to legal processes through which to assert their rights:

> The Charter is not some holy grail which only judicial initiates of the superior courts may touch. The Charter belongs to the people. All law and law-makers that touch the people must conform to it. Tribunals and commissions charged with deciding legal issues are no exception. Many more citizens have their rights determined by these tribunals than by the courts. If the Charter is to be meaningful to ordinary people, then it must find its expression in the decisions of these tribunals.[34]

---

29 Government of Ontario, Landlord and Tenant Board, *Annual Report 2009–2010* (2010) at 20, online: Landlord Tenant Board www.ltb.gov.on.ca.

30 Ontario Superior Court of Justice, *Report 2008–2010: 20th Anniversary Edition* at 15, online: Ontario Courts www.ontariocourts.on.ca.

31 *Ibid.*

32 RSO 1990, c H.19.

33 *Cooper v Canada (Canadian Human Rights Commission)*, [1996] 3 SCR 854 [*Cooper*].

34 *Ibid* at para 70.

This passage was later adopted by a majority in *Martin*, where the Court reversed *Cooper* and confirmed that tribunals that have the power to decide any question of law will presumptively have the power to hear and adjudicate the *Charter*.[35]

In *Conway*,[36] the Supreme Court extended administrative jurisdiction even further by establishing that tribunals that are competent to decide questions of law also have jurisdiction not only to consider *Charter* issues but also to grant *Charter* remedies to the extent those remedies are consistent with their enabling legislation. Tribunals can therefore be understood as adjudicative spaces that enjoy both full access to the *Charter* and a broad capacity for public engagement. While opening up tribunals for claimants seeking to advance human rights and *Charter* rights appears at first glance as a victory for proponents of social rights, it may be a hollow victory (at best) so long as government can circumscribe the jurisdiction and curtail the resources available in such settings. We return to this concern in the third part of this paper.

Tribunals have not only been accorded jurisdiction to adjudicate and apply rights but also have been made subject to those rights as decision makers who form part of the executive branch of government. As we explore in the next section, a promising (if not always clear) line of jurisprudence has evolved which elaborates on the constraints applicable to such bodies based on the *Charter* and international human rights obligations.

C. PART TWO: TRIBUNAL DISCRETION, THE *CHARTER*, AND INTERNATIONAL HUMAN RIGHTS NORMS

To the extent parties seek to assert social rights in the context of administrative justice, one of two kinds of decisions will follow. The first kind is where the statutory jurisdiction of the board or tribunal dictates a result. If the criteria are met, then eligibility for the benefit will follow, and if they are not, then the benefit cannot be granted. Most rights, however, depend on the second kind of decision — the exercise of administrative discretion — where either a positive or negative outcome is possible, and the decision maker must apply a set of principles to the circumstances and determine the appropriate outcome. This is particularly relevant in the administrative justice context, where tribunals, boards, and other decision makers usually have discretion to fashion a remedy appropriate for the circumstances.

35 *Martin*, above note 3.

36 *Conway*, above note 5.

The exercise of discretion is subject to administrative law guarantees of procedural fairness and substantive reasonableness. For example, in *Baker v Canada*,[37] the Supreme Court of Canada found that an immigration officer's decision that a woman did not have humanitarian and compassionate grounds to exempt her from deportation notwithstanding that she had four Canadian-born children was an unfair exercise of discretion (since the reasons offered by the decision maker disclosed a reasonable apprehension of bias), as well as unreasonable (since the decision maker ignored the ministry's own guidelines, the applicable international human rights norms, and the relevant criterion of the best interests of the children affected by the decision). Beyond the common law requirements that administrative decision makers, whether immigration officers, tribunals, or boards, act fairly and reasonably, those decision makers when exercising discretion are also subject to the *Charter*. In this sense, even highly adjudicative tribunals are distinct from courts, whose exercises of judicial discretion are not subject to the *Charter*.[38]

In the early days of *Charter* jurisprudence, the Supreme Court explored the possibility of reconciling *Charter* and administrative law principles.[39] The *Charter* may justify intervention in administrative decisions in several different circumstances involving different degrees of discretion.[40] First, a law granting discretion may be unconstitutional by its very terms. For example, a law authorizing a tribunal to grant a benefit to a defined group creates a discretion that, by its very terms, might violate section 15 of the *Charter* if it necessarily excludes another group from the benefit based on race, religion, or one of the other enumerated or analogous grounds. For example, in *M v H*, a provision of Ontario's *Family Law Act* was held to be discriminatory since it granted courts the discretion to award spousal support only to heterosexual spouses and not to same-sex couples.[41]

---

37 *Baker v Canada (Minister of Citizenship and Immigration)*, [1999] 2 SCR 817 [*Baker*].

38 *RWDSU, Local 580 v Dolphin Delivery Ltd*, [1986] 2 SCR 573.

39 See, especially, *Slaight Communications Inc v Davidson*, [1989] 1 SCR 1038 [*Slaight*]; *Ross v New Brunswick School District No 15*, [1996] 1 SCR 825 [*Ross*]. Portions of this analysis are drawn from Lorne Sossin, "Discretion Unbound: Reconciling the *Charter* and Soft Law" (2002) 45 Canadian Public Administration 465. Portions of the analysis to follow are drawn from Susan Gratton & Lorne Sossin, "In Search of Coherence: The *Charter* and Administrative Law under the McLachlin Court" in David Wright & Adam Dodek, eds, *Public Law at the McLachlin Court: The First Decade* (Toronto: Irwin Law, 2011) 145.

40 In most cases, the grounds for a *Charter* challenge in administrative discretion cases are based on violations of ss 2, 7, or 15, but the unconstitutional exercise of discretion might also be located elsewhere under the *Charter*.

41 *M v H*, [1999] 2 SCR 3.

The second circumstance involves a law that grants discretion to a tribunal that is not unconstitutional on its face but such that it might nevertheless be applied in an unconstitutional manner. For example, in *Eldridge v British Columbia (AG)*, a law authorizing the British Columbia Medical Services Commission to fund certain health services was found not to violate the *Charter*, but the exercise of discretion by that commission deciding not to fund interpreters for deaf patients was found to be unconstitutional.[42] Similarly, in *PHS Community Services Society*,[43] a federal minister's discretion not to provide a statutory exemption to a safe injection site that satisfied all of the factual criteria was held to violate the *Charter*. The Court held, "The discretion vested in the Minister of Health is not absolute: as with all exercises of discretion, the Minister's decisions must conform to the Charter."[44]

In the third circumstance, a law granting wide discretionary authority without sufficient guidance as to its application or without safeguards against arbitrary conduct might violate the procedural component of section 7 of the *Charter*. This basis for challenging discretion was relied upon by the majority of the Supreme Court in *R v Morgantaler*.[45] In *Morgentaler*, the impugned provision was a law prohibiting abortion unless a physician determined that the life or health of a woman was endangered. The procedures that therapeutic abortion committees established in hospitals to decide whether this threshold was met in individual cases were found by the majority to lack coherence, predictability, and fairness.

Fourth, a law granting a discretion that is too vague to provide sufficient notice to those who might infringe it might violate the substantive component of section 7.[46] For example, in *R v Morales*, the Court held that a provision granting pre-trial detention where it was justified in "the public interest" was unconstitutionally vague.[47] The Supreme Court's first detailed examination of the relationship between the *Charter* and administrative discretion was in *Slaight*.[48] At issue in that case was a remedial discretion in the *Canada Labour Code* that allowed adjudicators to resolve grievances

42 *Eldridge v British Columbia (AG)*, [1997] 3 SCR 624.

43 *Canada (AG) v PHS Community Services Society*, 2011 SCC 44.

44 *Ibid* at para 117.

45 *R v Morgentaler*, [1988] 1 SCR 30.

46 See, generally, *R v Nova Scotia Pharmaceutical Society*, [1992] 2 SCR 606.

47 *R v Morales*, [1992] 3 SCR 711.

48 *Slaight*, above note 39. See June Ross, "Applying the *Charter* to Discretionary Authority" (1991) 29:2 Alta L Rev 382, on the significance of *Slaight*.

under collective agreements.[49] The grievance in *Slaight* concerned an allegation of wrongful dismissal. The adjudicator found that the dismissal had been wrongful and ordered the company, first, to provide the employee with a factual reference and, second, to refrain from expressing any other views about the employee. Chief Justice Dickson for the majority chose to conduct a *Charter* analysis and held that neither aspect of the adjudicator's order violated the *Charter*. Justice Lamer dissented in part and would have resolved the dispute on administrative law grounds. However, Lamer J wrote for the Court on the issue of the proper approach to discretionary decision making under the *Charter*. He identified two kinds of discretion, each of which led to different remedies under the *Charter*:

> 1. The exercise of discretion was made pursuant to legislation which confers, either expressly or by necessary implication, the power to infringe a protected *Charter* right.
>
> — It is then necessary to subject the legislation to the test set out in s. 1 by ascertaining whether it constitutes a reasonable limit that can be demonstrably justified in a free and democratic society.
>
> 2. The legislation pursuant to which the exercise of administrative discretion was made confers an imprecise discretion and does not confer, either expressly or by necessary implication, the power to limit the rights guaranteed by the *Charter*.
>
> — It is then necessary to subject the order made to the test set out in s. 1 by ascertaining whether it constitutes a reasonable limit that can be demonstrably justified in a free and democratic society; . . . .[50]

In the circumstances of *Slaight*, the Court found that the Code did not require expressly, or by necessary implication, that a *Charter* right be infringed, since the arbitrator could have remedied the wrongful dismissal through other means; and therefore the Code created an imprecise discretion

49 *Canada Labour Code*, RSC 1970, c L-1, as amended by SC 1977–78, c 27, ss 21 and 61.5(9): "[w]here an adjudicator decides pursuant to subsection (8) that a person has been unjustly dismissed, he may, by order, require the employer who dismissed him to (a) pay the person compensation not exceeding the amount of money that is equivalent to the remuneration that would, but for the dismissal, have been paid by the employer to the person; (b) reinstate the person in his employ; and (c) do any other like thing that it is equitable to require the employer to do in order to remedy or counteract any consequence of the dismissal" [Code].

50 *Slaight*, above note 39 at 1080.

that permitted a *Charter* right to be limited. Thus, it was the order and not the legislation that was subjected to *Charter* scrutiny.[51]

The central holding of *Slaight* was that no public official could be authorized by a statute to breach the *Charter*, and, therefore, all discretionary authority had to be read down to authorize only decision making that is consistent with *Charter* rights and guarantees. Justice Lamer explained this reasoning in the following terms:

> Although this court must not add anything to legislation or delete anything from it, in order to make it consistent with the Charter, there is no doubt in my mind that it should also not interpret legislation that is open to more than one interpretation so as to make it inconsistent with the Charter and hence of no force or effect. Legislation conferring an imprecise discretion must therefore be interpreted as not allowing the Charter rights to be infringed. Accordingly, an adjudicator exercising delegated powers does not have the power to make an order that would result in an infringement of the Charter and he exceeds his jurisdiction if he does so.[52]

Thus, discretionary authority always comes with an implied condition, which is that it be exercised in a manner consistent with all applicable *Charter* rights. The principle in *Slaight* was applied in subsequent cases,[53] where the Court highlighted the overlapping nature of the *Charter* and administrative law analysis, observing that it was difficult to conceive of a case that a court would conclude was unconstitutional where it would not also conclude that it was unreasonable.

The Court confronted the dilemma of administrative discretion again in the context of *Little Sisters Books and Art Emporium v Canada (Minister of Justice)*.[54] At issue was the discretionary authority of customs officials to seize imported goods that met the obscenity test under section 163 of the *Criminal Code*. Justice Binnie, writing for the majority, characterized the administration of the *Customs Act* by customs officers as oppressive and dismissive of the appellants' freedom of expression. He concluded that the effect — whether intended or not — was to isolate and disparage the appellants on the basis of their sexual orientation.

---

51 The majority found that while both the positive and the negative order violated the freedom of expression under s 2(b) of the *Charter*, each was a reasonable limit under s 1 and therefore the orders were upheld.

52 *Slaight*, above note 39 at 1077–78.

53 See *Ross*, above note 39, and *Eaton v Brant County Board of Education*, [1997] 1 SCR 241.

54 2000 SCC 69 [*Little Sisters*].

The Court also held that although the exercise of discretion by customs officers violated the *Charter*, the *Customs Act* provision authorizing this conduct did not. Following the *Slaight* approach, the majority of the Court characterized the discretion contained in the customs legislation as capable of being applied in a fashion consistent with the *Charter*. Therefore, the majority saw no basis to strike down the authority of customs officials to seize material on the grounds of obscenity.[55]

Sometimes, the Court may apply a *Charter* and administrative law analysis to the same exercise of discretion. *Suresh v Canada*,[56] for example, dealt with the discretionary authority of the minister to deport refugees in circumstances where they faced the possibility of torture.[57] Suresh challenged the minister's deportation order on both *Charter* and administrative law grounds. A unanimous Court conducted both a *Charter* review of the enabling provision and an administrative review of the minister's decision pursuant to that provision, eventually determining that the process by which Suresh was ordered deported violated his *Charter* rights.

With its decision in *Multani v Commission scolaire Marguerite-Bourgeoys*,[58] the Court made its first effort to develop a more comprehensive approach to the dilemma of whether a *Charter* or administrative law analysis should apply to administrative action. *Multani* involved the discretionary decision of a school board to prohibit a Sikh student from wearing his kirpan, a ceremonial dagger, to school. The student and his family challenged the decision as an infringement of his freedom of religion. The Supreme Court was unanimous in allowing the challenge and striking down the board's decision, but it split 6:2 on whether a *Charter* or administrative law analysis should be applied in reaching this result.

Madame Justice Charron, for the majority, adopted a *Charter* analysis, since the central issue in the case was whether or not the board's decision

55 See *ibid* at para 204. Justice Iacobucci, writing for himself and two other members of the Court, dissented on this point. He held that the legislation itself was unconstitutional since it did not contain sufficient safeguards against unconstitutional enforcement. For the minority, simply trusting the customs bureaucracy to improve its administration of the Act was not enough, and they would have imposed a different decision making structure to remedy the *Charter* breach.

56 *Suresh v Canada (Minister of Citizenship and Immigration)*, 2002 SCC 1 [*Suresh*].

57 *Ibid*. Section 53(1)(b) of the *Immigration Act*, RSC 1985, c I-2, gave the minister limited discretion to deport where the refugee's "life or freedom would be threatened" if she were returned to her country and the minister believed that the refugee constituted "a danger to the security of Canada" (*ibid* at para 24).

58 2006 SCC 6 [*Multani*].

complied with the requirements of the *Charter*.[59] In contrast, Deschamps and Abella JJ for the minority argued that an administrative law analysis should be conducted instead of a *Charter* analysis, because the instrument being assessed by the Court was an administrative decision rather than a "norm of general application" such as "a law, regulation, or other similar rule of general application."[60]

The majority defined the role of administrative law solely in terms of jurisdiction and warned against allowing the fundamental values protected by the *Charter* to be dissolved into mere administrative law principles.[61] The majority position appears either to be unaware of or to discount the significant substantive role of administrative law in supervising the exercise of discretion and the exercise of public authority more broadly. It is difficult to reconcile the *Multani* majority's thin and one-dimensional view of administrative law with the robust view of administrative law animating earlier Supreme Court judgments, such as *Baker*.

The Court returned to this issue in an attempt to reconcile *Charter* and administrative law principles in *Doré v Barreau du Québec*.[62] In that case, the Court reviewed the decision of a provincial law society that imposed a disciplinary penalty on a lawyer for inappropriate criticism of a judge. The Court of Appeal approached *Doré* as a *Charter* case, much like *Slaight*, but the Supreme Court took a different approach. Justice Abella, writing for the Court, adopts an administrative law analysis to the review of the Quebec Barreau's decision and asserts that there is nothing in such an approach inconsistent with strong *Charter* protections. This approach is set out in the following terms:

> The alternative is for the Court to embrace a richer conception of administrative law, under which discretion is exercised "in light of constitutional guarantees and the values they reflect" (*Multani* at para. 152, per LeBel J.). Under this approach, it is unnecessary to retreat to a s. 1

59 *Ibid* at para 2. The majority (McLachlin CJ, Charron, Bastarache, Binnie, and Fish JJ) held that the board's decision infringed the student's freedom of religion under s 2(a) of the *Charter* and that the infringement could not be justified under s 1. Justice LeBel wrote a separate opinion agreeing with the majority that a *Charter* analysis was appropriate but proposing that the s 1 analysis should be modified in cases involving administrative discretion (*ibid* at paras 140–55).

60 *Ibid* at paras 103 and 85. The minority would have reviewed the board's decision on a standard of reasonableness and would have concluded that the decision was unreasonable in disregarding the student's freedom of religion.

61 *Ibid* at para 16.

62 2012 SCC 12 [*Doré*].

> *Oakes* analysis in order to protect *Charter* values. Rather, administrative decisions are always required to consider fundamental values . . . . These cases emphasize that administrative bodies are empowered, and indeed required, to consider *Charter* values within their scope of expertise. Integrating *Charter* values into the administrative approach, and recognizing the expertise of these decision-makers, opens "an institutional dialogue about the appropriate use and control of discretion, rather than the older command-and-control relationship" (Liston at p 100).[63]

While the Court's decision in *Doré* may have the potential to infuse *Charter* values throughout administrative justice and to develop a more "robust" approach to administrative law principles,[64] there remain important ambiguities. For example, while the onus clearly shifts from the claimant to the government in a *Charter* section 1 analysis, the onus always remains on the party challenging a decision on administrative law grounds. The real potential of *Doré* may lie less in the realm of administrative law theory and more in the day-to-day decision making of administrative justice.

If the principle that discretion should be exercised in a manner consistent with *Charter* values is incorporated into the guidelines, directives, and practices of tribunals, this could have a profound effect on the opportunity for these adjudicative spaces to advance social rights. By contrast, if such values turn out to be irrelevant in the everyday decision making of such bodies, then the Court's rhetoric in *Doré* will suggest a rights orientated framework that is illusory.

D. INTERNATIONAL HUMAN RIGHTS NORMS

While the constraints imposed by the *Charter* have been examined in the series of Supreme Court cases discussed above, the constraints imposed by international human rights instruments such as the *ICESCR* are far less clear. In *Baker*, the Court has affirmed that such instruments do not have the force of law unless enacted through a domestic statute but has similarly suggested that such instruments ought not to be ignored (that case considered the application of the *Convention on the Rights of the Child*.)[65] The Court held that international human rights norms from unimplemented treaties may be considered as persuasive and contextual factors in inter-

---

63 *Ibid* at para 35.

64 *Ibid* at para 34.

65 *Convention on the Rights of the Child*, 20 November 1989, 1577 UNTS 3, 28 ILM 1456 (entered into force 2 September 1990) [*CRC*].

preting and applying statutory provisions.[66] The inconsistency between the immigration officer's exercise of discretion and the requirements of the Convention was cited as one of the grounds for quashing the decision as unreasonable.

Other common law jurisdictions have also considered the same dilemma. In *R v Secretary of State for the Home Department, ex parte Brind*,[67] the House of Lords held that while international agreements could be used as an aid in the construction of ambiguous statutes, they could not be used to fetter the exercise of discretionary powers granted to a minister by statute. To do so would be to "incorporate" the Convention through the back door. In *Brind*, the House of Lords held that administrative discretion could not be read down by reference to the demands of the unimplemented *European Convention on Human Rights*.[68] Lord Bridge of Harwich wrote:

> [W]here Parliament has conferred on the executive an administrative discretion without indicating the precise limits within which it must be exercised, to presume that it must be exercised within Convention limits would be to go far beyond the resolution of an ambiguity.[69]

Similarly, in *Ashby*, Richardson J rejected arguments that the minister's discretion could only be exercised in conformity with New Zealand's obligations under the Convention.[70] Rather, the courts were bound to give effect to domestic legislation whether or not it was consistent with New Zealand's international obligations.[71]

The idea that the presumption of conformity should be extended to encompass administrative discretion received its most emphatic support from the Court in *Minister of State for Immigration and Ethnic Affairs v Ah Hin Teoh*,[72] where Mason and Deane JJ stated that

66 *Baker*, above note 37 at para 70.

67 [1991] 1 AC 696 (HL) [*Brind*].

68 *Convention for the Protection of Human Rights and Fundamental Freedoms*, 4 November 1950, ETS 5, 213 UNTS 221 (entered into force 3 September 1953).

69 *Brind*, above note 67 at para 2. Explained in *Tavita v Minister of Immigration*, [1994] 2 NZLR 257 at 266. In *Tavita*, however, the Court of Appeal referred to *Brind* as "in some respects a controversial decision" and invoked the *CRC* and the *ICCPR* to influence the exercise of a statutory discretion. As mentioned above, while not directly addressing the issue, it indicated that in exercising discretionary powers, the executive is not free to ignore international human rights norms.

70 *Ashby v Minister of Immigration*, [1981] 1 NZLR 222 at para 228 (CA) [*Ashby*].

71 *Ibid*.

72 (1995), 128 ALR 353 (HCA) [*Teoh*].

> ratification by Australia of an international convention is not to be dismissed as a merely platitudinous or ineffectual act, particularly when the instrument evidences internationally accepted standards to be applied by courts and administrative authorities in dealing with basic human rights affecting family and children. Rather, ratification of a convention is a positive statement by the executive government of this country to the world and to the Australian people that the executive government and its agencies will act in accordance with the Convention. That positive statement is an adequate foundation for a legitimate expectation, absent statutory or executive indications to the contrary, that administrative decision-makers will act in conformity with the Convention and treat the best interests of the children as "a primary consideration."[73]

Gerald Heckman has argued that Canadian courts should recognize this presumption, writing in the context of the *Ahani* case, where the Ontario Court of Appeal found that the Government of Canada could deport an individual who had exhausted his appeals (including an unsuccessful appeal to the Supreme Court of Canada)[74] notwithstanding that an application had been filed with the UN Human Rights Committee alleging a breach of the optional protocol to the *ICCPR*, to which Canada is a signatory.[75] He concludes that Canadian judges would be justified to intervene on judicial review where an administrative decision maker fails to apply the presumption of conformity and interprets statutory powers in a manner inconsistent with international human rights obligations set out in a binding but unimplemented treaty.[76]

Applying this reasoning to the Supreme Court's judgment in *Suresh*, Heckman observes that "[a]pplying the presumption of conformity, the Court could have read down the Minister's statutory discretion consistently with the international customary prohibition on torture."[77] Similarly,

---

73 *Ibid* at para 34.

74 *Ahani v Canada (Minister of Citizenship and Immigration)*, 2002 SCC 2 [*Ahani*], which was released as a companion case to *Suresh*, above note 56.

75 UN Human Rights Committee, "Communication No 1051/2002: Canada" (15 June 2004), online: United Nations Office of the High Commissioner for Human Rights http://tbinternet.ohchr.org/_layouts/treatybodyexternal/Download.aspx?symbolno=CCPR%2FC%2F80%2FD%2F1051%2F2002&Lang=en. The UN committee ultimately found Canada's deportation of Ahani to be "deficient."

76 Gerald Heckman, "International Human Rights Law Norms and Discretionary Powers: Recent Developments" (2003) 16 Can J Admin L & Prac 31.

77 *Ibid*. See also Gerald Heckman, "The Role of International Human Rights Norms in Administrative Law" (2007) (unpublished, on file with the authors) at 31–32.

Brunnée and Toope, in their analysis of the *Baker* decision, add that it was fully open to the Court to hold that Canada's immigration decision makers were bound to consider the best interests of the child because to do so would bring the interpretation of the Act in conformity with international obligations binding on Canada.[78]

A corollary of the presumption of conformity is the principle of legitimate expectations. In other words, the legitimate expectations of a person subject to the discretion of an administrative decision maker would include that the decision will conform to the international human rights obligations to which Canada is subject. This reasoning has guided the Australian High Court in reconciling international obligations and domestic law.[79] The question of whether international agreements that are signed and ratified by the executive, but not implemented by the legislature, can give rise to legitimate expectations in domestic decision making was most comprehensively dealt with in *Teoh*, which also dealt with the exercise of discretion and consideration of the best interests of the child. Mr Ah Hin Teoh argued that Australia's ratification of the *CRC* resulted in "an expectation that those making administrative decisions under the aegis of the executive government of the Commonwealth [would] act in accordance with the Convention wherever it [was] relevant to the decision to be made."[80] A majority of both the Federal and High Court agreed with Teoh. Justice Toohey stated that while ratification of an international treaty does not make the obligation enforceable in court, "the assumption of such an obligation may give rise to legitimate expectations in the minds of those who are affected by administrative decisions."[81] Melissa Poole suggests another reason for compliance. She compares New Zealand's international human rights commitments to its dealings with the Maori and argues that, in both instances, the Crown is bound by a fiduciary-like responsibility.[82]

Canada has adopted a different approach. The doctrine of legitimate expectations has been held to augment existing procedural rights rather

---

78 Jutta Brunnée & Stephen Toope, "A Hesitant Embrace: The Application of International Law by Canadian Courts" in David Dyzenhaus, ed, *The Unity of Public Law* (Oxford: Hart Publishing, 2004) 357.

79 See Margaret Allars, "International Law and Administrative Discretion" in Brian Opeskin & Donald Rothwell, eds, *International Law and Australian Federalism* (Melbourne: Melbourne University Press, 1997) 232.

80 *Teoh*, above note 72 at 23.

81 *Ibid* at 29.

82 Melissa Poole, "International Instruments in Administrative Decisions: Mainstreaming International Law" (1999) 30 VUWLR 91.

than serve as a basis for the right.[83] Canada also has a well recognized fiduciary obligation toward Aboriginal peoples, now captured in the concept of the "Honour of the Crown," which has in some circumstances been generalized to other government decision making settings, but which has not been extended to general obligations to adhere to international human rights standards.[84] The Canadian approach after *Baker* has been to treat international human rights standards as non-binding. That said, *Baker* also serves as a precedent that ignoring such standards may justify a court finding a discretionary decision to be unreasonable. Building upon this middle-ground approach to international human rights standards as a guiding constraint on administrative discretion, and further elaborating upon the Court's approach to *Charter* values in *Doré,* holds out the promise of infusing a rights-based culture within administrative justice in Canada.

E. PART THREE: THE FUTURE OF SOCIAL RIGHTS AND ADMINISTRATIVE JUSTICE

The goal of a rights-based culture in Canadian administrative justice is part of a broader focus on the apparatus of government as a means of developing systemic solutions to poverty, the lack of adequate housing, and social deprivation. Jackman and Porter assert that the new understanding of social rights has inspired the emergence of innovative approaches to addressing poverty and homelessness in a rights-based framework, focused on the design of strategies and programs to realize rights within identified time frames and with measurable goals and targets, to recognize the central role that must be played by rights claimants, and to strengthen governmental accountability through complaints procedures, monitoring, and evaluation.[85] Their argument suggests that social rights should move from the judicial to the administrative sphere. This paper has explored that administrative sphere and its potential for advancing social rights.

---

83 *Baker*, above note 37 at para 26. See Grant Huscroft, "The Duty of Fairness" in Colleen Flood & Lorne Sossin, eds, *Administrative Law in Context*, 2d ed (Toronto: Emond Montgomery, 2012), for discussion of this topic.

84 See Brian Slattery, "Aboriginal Rights and Honour of the Crown" (2005) 29 Sup Ct L Rev (2d) 433, for a discussion on the Honour of the Crown. See also Lorne Sossin, "Public Fiduciary Obligations, Political Trusts and the Evolving Duty of Reasonableness in Administrative Law" (2003) 66 Sask L Rev 129, for a discussion of the circumstances where this obligation has been extended beyond the Crown-Aboriginal setting, and an argument for doing so.

85 Jackman & Porter, *Making the Connection*, above note 23.

First, as suggested above in the context of *Doré*, administrative justice should be seen as advancing *Charter* values. So, for example, where two interpretations are open to a tribunal member, and one will advance equality or fairness or dignity more than the other, that is the interpretation to be preferred. Similarly, we argue that the presumption that statutory discretion will be exercised in compliance with international human rights norms should also apply to adjudicative tribunals as much as immigration decision makers. How these values and norms interact with particular statutory mandates of particular tribunals and boards, however, remains to be worked out in a contextual fashion. It will take a participatory process involving affected communities, advocacy organizations, tribunal adjudicators, public officials, and courts to articulate them further.

As part of taking their social rights jurisdiction seriously, administrative tribunals need to further develop models of "active adjudication," which may allow for meaningful adjudication of social rights. This form of more flexible adjudication may be particularly important in contexts where one or more parties often will have no legal representation and where adjudicators often will not have legal training. Tribunals are less constrained by an adversarial model of adjudication and have developed methods to accommodate the challenges that vulnerable parties coming before the tribunal may experience. In the social rights context, this more effective and efficient model may involve the adjudicators identifying rights issues where the parties do not have the background or capacity to do so, and taking steps to obtain the information or submissions necessary to adjudicate rights issues, which may involve mechanisms that range from retaining amicus counsel to engaging in inquisitorial questioning or developing interpretive guidelines upon which parties and decision makers can rely.[86]

While creating adjudicative space matters, resources may ultimately matter more if those spaces are to be accessible to those in need. While it is open to government to create a tribunal, to determine its jurisdiction, and to decide on the budget of a tribunal, it is not acceptable to create such bodies and then starve them of the capacity needed to carry out their mandate.[87] This question has particular relevance for the shift in social

---

86 See Samantha Green & Lorne Sossin, "Administrative Justice and Innovation: Beyond the Adversary/Inquisitorial Dichotomy" (Presented at The Nature of Inquisitorial Processes in Administrative Regimes: Global Perspectives Conference, University of Windsor, May 2011), for further discussion of this range of mechanisms.

87 See Lorne Sossin & Zimra Yetnikoff, "I Can See Clearly Now: Videoconference Hearings and the Legal Limit on How Tribunals Allocate Resources" (2007) Windsor YB Access Just 247.

rights to a more systemic approach. Justice Abella raised this concern in *Tranchemontagne*, in dissent, confirming that all tribunals in the province have the jurisdiction to apply the Ontario *Human Rights Code* unless expressly precluded by legislation. For Abella J, the issue was, not how best to value rights, but rather how to ensure access to a forum where those rights could be protected. With respect to the Social Benefits Tribunal, she observed:

> The [Social Benefits Tribunal] is meant to be an efficient, effective, and quick process. Yet it seems to be having difficulty meeting this mandate. In 2004–2005, the SBT had a backlog of 9,042 cases and received 11,127 new appeals under the [*Ontario Works Act*] and the ODSPA. This Court recognized in Tétreault-Gadoury . . . that administrative bodies responsible for ensuring the payment of monetary benefits to eligible applicants would undoubtedly be impeded from this important and time-sensitive undertaking if they were asked to decide constitutional challenges.
>
> Imposing Code compliance hearings on the SBT will similarly and inevitably impact its ability to assist the disabled community it was established to benefit in a timely way. It will be difficult to explain to the thousands of disabled individuals waiting for their appeals to be heard — many without any interim support — that there is any public benefit in the SBT hearing a complex, lengthy, and inevitably delaying jurisprudential issue with no precedential value. That is the real access issue in this case.[88]

Indeed, the year following *Tranchemontagne*, the Social Benefits Tribunal received over 560 human rights–based complaints, including many of the "special diet" challenges discussed above, which represented a 37 percent increase over the prior year. More rights-based challenges can be a positive sign. For organizations like the Social Benefits Tribunal (now part of Ontario's Social Justice Cluster) to fulfill a rights-based mandate, a number of practical considerations must be addressed, from the appointments process, to training and education of members and staff, to guidelines and shared interpretive practices. Such tribunals must also be accessible.[89] If administrative justice is to be an adjudicative space capable of advancing social rights, it must be apparent in the lived experience of decision makers and those affected by their decisions.

---

88 Above note 4 at paras 90–91.

89 For discussion, see Lorne Sossin, "Access to Administrative Justice and Other Worries" in Flood & Sossin, eds, above note 83 at 211.

F. CONCLUSION

We have argued in this chapter that advancing social rights requires a greater focus on administrative justice. We have explored two perspectives on administrative justice and social rights: first, the jurisdiction of tribunals to adjudicate and remedy human rights and *Charter* claims and second, the ways in which tribunals are subject to *Charter* and international human rights norms. We suggest that administrative justice needs a rights jurisdiction tailored to its contexts, challenges, and realities — one that assumes the diversity of practice, capacity, and parties that defines administrative justice. We look forward to new ideas and innovative strategies to develop a rights protection framework for the adjudicative space of administrative justice, keeping in mind that in many cases, improving the social rights of vulnerable members of society was precisely the purpose in establishing these administrative bodies in the first place.

CHAPTER 12

ENVIRONMENTAL CONCERNS AND THE INTERDEPENDENCE OF HUMAN RIGHTS

A PATH TO POLITICAL RESPONSIBILITY?

SYLVIE PAQUEROT*

TRANSLATED FROM THE ORIGINAL FRENCH BY SADIE SCAPILLATO

A. INTRODUCTION

Our development practices have led us to a state of global systemic crisis.[1] The pace of economic globalization is only increasing, with far-reaching and sometimes devastating effects upon the environment. The environmental consequences of development must be understood in order to develop new theories and practices that are relevant in this increasingly global context. Environmental issues in turn frequently involve a wide range of human rights issues, from civil and political to economic, social, and cultural. Rights do not exist in a vacuum, isolated and independent of one another; rather, all rights are inherently interrelated, each dependent upon the others for its existence and free exercise. Indeed, this principle — the interdependence of rights — was formally recognized by the international community during the 1993 World Conference on Human Rights in Vienna: "All human rights are universal, indivisible and interdependent and interrelated."[2]

The goal of this paper is to illustrate the significance and scope of the interdependence of rights by drawing upon the example of the Ligue des

---

* Associate Professor, Faculty of Social Sciences, University of Ottawa.

1 The expression "global systemic crisis" is often used to convey the structural dimension of the situation and its systemic and multidimensional nature. See, among several others, online: LEAP www.leap2020.eu.

2 World Conference on Human Rights, *Vienna Declaration and Programme of Action*, 1993, UN Doc A/CONF.157/23, 32 ILM 1661 at 24 [World Conference, *Vienna Declaration*].

droits et libertés du Québec's gradual incorporation of environmental issues into its mandate. This is followed by a reflection upon the strategic advantage that an understanding of the interdependence of environmental issues and human rights can bring to citizen-led political initiatives. The paper concludes with a discussion of the notion of public responsibility that is implicit in article 28 of the *Universal Declaration of Human Rights*, which states, "Everyone is entitled to a social and international order in which the rights and freedoms set forth in this *Declaration* can be fully realized."[3]

The current global crisis presents a crucial opportunity to discuss the broad spectrum of interrelated rights issues and how they may be understood and reconciled. If we accomplish this, we will have fulfilled the necessary conditions for all rights to be exercised, and in so doing we will make important strides towards overcoming our sense of powerlessness as citizens.

B. ENVIRONMENTAL ISSUES AS HUMAN RIGHTS ISSUES: A HISTORICAL OVERVIEW

There is nothing particularly groundbreaking about linking human rights and environmental issues. Indeed, this link was explicitly recognized by the international community in 1972 at the UN Conference on the Human Environment in Stockholm.[4] It was proclaimed that "both aspects of man's environment, the natural and the man-made, are essential to his well-being and to the enjoyment of basic human rights [and] the right to life itself."[5] The right to a healthy environment was recognized as the first principle in the *Stockholm Declaration*: "Man has the fundamental right to freedom, equality and adequate conditions of life, in an environment of a quality that permits a life of dignity and well-being."[6] Since 1972, a number of steps have been taken in the international system and in several national legal systems to implement this principle. Retracing those steps shows that the path from general principle to legal formulation and effective implementation has been long and winding indeed.

---

3 *Universal Declaration of Human Rights*, GA Res 217 (III), UNGAOR, 3d Sess, Supp No 13, UN Doc A/810, (1948) 71 [*Declaration*].

4 *Declaration of the United Nations Conference on the Human Environment*, GA Res 2994 (XXVII), UNGAOR, 1972, UN Doc A/CONF. 48/14/Rev. 1 (1973); 11 ILM 1416, (1972) [*Stockholm Declaration*].

5 *Ibid*, art 1.

6 *Ibid*, principle 1.

1) Procedural Protections Following the Rio Conference

Twenty years after Stockholm, at the 1992 UN Conference on Environment and Development in Rio de Janeiro (the Rio Conference),[7] the international community revisited the link between human rights and the right to a healthy environment with a new focus: the participation of all citizens.[8] This was an early step toward establishing a strong procedural dimension of the right to the environment, and it helped clarify the civil and political rights linked to environmental issues:

> PRINCIPLE 10: Environmental issues are best handled with the participation of all concerned citizens, at the relevant level. At the national level, each individual shall have appropriate access to information concerning the environment that is held by public authorities, including information on hazardous materials and activities in their communities, and the opportunity to participate in decision-making processes. States shall facilitate and encourage public awareness and participation by making information widely available. Effective access to judicial and administrative proceedings, including redress and remedy, shall be provided.

Concrete mechanisms for public participation were gradually introduced in the years following Rio, not only by local governments but also within various national legal systems.[9] Quebec introduced the option of legal recourse through the *Environment Quality Act*,[10] and the Bureau des audiences publiques sur l'environnement (BAPE)[11] became the primary body for implementing the Act's requirements for public participation in, and consultation on, environmental issues.

---

7 *Rio Declaration on Environment and Development*, UNCEDOR, 1992, UN Doc A/CONF. 151/5/Rev.1, (vol I); 31 ILM 874, (1992) [*Rio Declaration*].

8 In contrast to the *Stockholm Declaration*, humans are now only "entitled to a healthy and productive life in harmony with nature" (*ibid* at principle 1).

9 An expanded discussion of these mechanisms is beyond the scope of this paper. For further reading on the effectiveness and limitations of some of these instruments (particularly the Espoo and Aarhus Conventions in Europe), we recommend Maguelonne Déjeant-Pons & Marc Pallemaerts with the collaboration of Sara Fioravanti, *Human Rights and the Environment* (Strasbourg: Council of Europe Publishing, 2002).

10 *Environment Quality Act*, RSQ c Q-2, division III.1.

11 *Ibid*, division II.1. See Mario Gauthier & Louis Simard, "Le BAPE et l'institutionnalisation du débat public au Québec : mise en œuvre et effets" in Martine Revel et al, eds, *Le débat public : une expérience française de démocratie participative* (Paris: La Découverte, 2007) 78.

Following the implementation of a formal procedure for public participation under Quebec's *Environment Quality Act*[12] and similar legislation elsewhere, the number of citizen-led environmental groups multiplied and public expertise on current issues improved, significantly enriching public debate. In response, however, developers attempted to circumvent the consultation process entirely whenever possible and limit the length of any consultations that could not be avoided. They also employed tactics intended to silence dissenting voices, in particular by means of SLAPPs (Strategic Lawsuits Against Public Participation).[13] The result was a power struggle between the competing interests surrounding environmental issues, and it quickly became clear that the enormous advantage in resources enjoyed by the proponents of development left the contest woefully unbalanced, despite the mechanisms put in place to ensure equal participation. Several of the rights stipulated in the *International Covenant on Civil and Political Rights*[14] were arguably violated, in particular freedom of expression and freedom of association, effectively serving as proof and a cautionary tale of the need for robust and effective procedural protections of civil liberties in order to exercise the right to the environment.

2) Socio-economic and Cultural Rights Violations: Expanding the Discussion of Interdependence

Around the world, clear violations of many economic, social, and cultural rights were increasingly being exposed in relation to environmental issues. Indeed, the link between protection of the environment and human health had been recognized in 1966. Article 12 of the *International Covenant on Economic, Social and Cultural Rights* explicitly included environmental quality as an essential condition for the right to health: "The steps to be taken by the States Parties to the present Covenant to achieve the full realization of

12 Above note 10.

13 See, for example, Uniform Law Conference on Canada, *Strategic Lawsuits Against Public Participation (SLAPPs). Report 2008*, online: ULCC www.ulcc.ca; Mayo Moran, Brian MacLeod Rogers, & Peter Downard, *Anti-SLAPP Advisory Panel Report to the Attorney General* (28 October 2010), online: Ontario Ministry of the Attorney General www.attorneygeneral.jus.gov.on.ca.

14 *International Covenant on Civil and Political Rights*, 19 December 1966, 999 UNTS 171, Can TS 1976 No 47 (entered into force 23 March 1976, accession by Canada 19 May 1976) [*ICCPR*].

this right shall include those necessary for . . . (b) The improvement of all aspects of environmental and industrial hygiene."[15]

Certainly, the right to health is necessarily linked to the condition of the environment. Infamous cases have dramatically illustrated the multidimensional nature of the rights violations caused by environmental abuses. Examples include the 1978 Love Canal disaster,[16] when it was discovered that a neighbourhood had been built on a toxic-waste dumping ground, thereby violating the entire population's right to housing and education, in addition to their right to health. Other examples include major dam construction projects that led to the forced displacement of millions,[17] violating their cultural rights in many instances as well as their right to choose their place of residence.[18] Finally, headline-grabbing cases have documented instances of pollution and disaster that directly endangered the lives of many, of which Bhopal, Chernobyl, and the Exxon Valdez are only the most well known.

On the topic of socio-economic and cultural rights, the right to equal enjoyment of economic, social, and cultural rights as stipulated in article 2(2) of the *ICESCR* and in *General Comment No 20: Non-Discrimination in Economic, Social and Cultural Rights*[19] has certainly attracted particular attention. Research has shown that disadvantaged groups and communities are at far higher risk of exposure to contamination that adversely affects their health and quality of life: "Disadvantaged or minority groups (racial minorities, individuals of low socio-economic status, Aboriginal peoples, local farmers, etc.) bear a disproportionate share of the risks resulting from pollution."[20] This environmental inequality can also be observed on a global scale, notably in the practice of shipping mass amounts

---

15 *International Covenant on Economic, Social and Cultural Rights*, 16 December 1966, 993 UNTS 3, 6 ILM 360, art 12(2) on the right to health (entered into force 3 January 1976, accession by Canada 19 May 1976) [*ICESCR*].

16 Pierre Rainelli, "Pollution des sols : problèmes économiques" (1996) 3:4 Études et gestion des sols 307 at 310.

17 See, among others, University of Oxford, Forced Migration Online, "Types of Development Projects Causing Displacement," online: FMO www.forcedmigration.org.

18 Article 13(1) of the *Universal Declaration of Human Rights*, GA Res 217(III), UNGAOR, 3d Sess, UN Doc A/810, (1948) 71 [*UDHR*], and art 12(1) of the *ICCPR*, above note 14.

19 Economic and Social Council, *Non-discrimination in Economic, Social and Cultural Rights (art. 2, para. 2, of the International Covenant on Economic, Social and Cultural Rights). General Comment No. 20*, UNESCOR, 42d Sess, E/C.12/GC/20, (2009) [*General Comment No 20*].

20 Jean-Paul Deléage, "Des inégalités écologiques parmi les hommes" (2008) 35:1 *Écologie & Politique* 11 at 13 [translated from the original French].

of waste from developed countries to the developing world for storage, treatment, and recycling, usually without safety measures in place to protect local workers.[21]

3) Global Environmental Issues, Depletion of Natural Resources, and the Right to Self-Determination

Even before the Rio Conference, another step in the growing awareness of the relationship between human rights and environmental issues prompted further refinement of the principle of the interdependence of rights. It had become apparent that the relationship between human rights and environmental issues extends beyond individual impacts to include collective implications and effects. This can be observed in a number of different cases, particularly in the above example of large dams and in pollution resulting from the exploitation of natural resources. Closer to home, it can be seen in development decisions that are either unsustainable or are incompatible with certain populations' cultures and ways of life, or that monopolize basic resources such as land and water.

The collective nature of the relationship between human rights and environmental issues is addressed mainly through article 1 of the two covenants (*ICCPR* and *ICESCR*): "All peoples may, for their own ends, freely dispose of their natural wealth and resources without prejudice to any obligations arising out of international economic co-operation, based upon the principle of mutual benefit, and international law. In no case may a people be deprived of its own means of subsistence."[22]

Addressing this collective dimension meant acknowledging two important implications. First, because of its strong connection to development choices and political decisions, the collective component of the relationship between human rights and environmental issues called for the scope of the right of peoples to self-determination to be clarified. Second, in

---

21 "L'équité environnementale : clef du développement durable" (17 April 2009), online: Université Laval www.ihqeds.ulaval.ca. This deplorable practice has led to the adoption of both an international treaty and regional instruments. For the treaty, see *Basel Convention on the Control of Transboundary Movements of Hazardous Wastes and Their Disposal*, 22 March 1989, 1673 UNTS 126, 28 ILM 657 (entered into force 5 May 1992). For the regional instruments, see *Bamako Convention on the Ban of the Import into Africa and the Control of Transboundary Movement and Management of Hazardous Wastes within Africa*, 30 January 1991, Organization of African Unity (entered into force 22 April 1998), online: African Union www.au.int/en/content/bamako-convention-ban-import-africa-and-control-transboundary-movement-and-management-hazard.

22 *ICCPR*, above note 14; *ICESCR*, above note 15, art 1, para 2.

terms of future impact, it drew attention to the intergenerational nature of rights.[23] The World Commission on Environment and Development was thinking in similar terms: "every human being — those here and those who are to come — has the right to life, and to a decent life."[24] This prompted deeper consideration of our obligations toward future generations, gradually expanding the field of international human rights law.[25]

Discussion and work around the world focusing on defining the influence of environmental issues on human rights has thus progressed beyond the right to a healthy environment and the procedural dimension, diverging in at least three directions. The first focuses on the present, direct effects of environmental damage on recognized rights, such as the rights to life, health, and housing. The second concerns the temporal aspect and our obligations to the future, brilliantly expressed by the United States Supreme Court as our responsibility to consider "answers to questions that we have not yet learned to ask."[26] The third relates to our duty to make

---

23 Edith Brown Weiss, "The Planetary Trust: Conservation and Intergenerational Equity" (1984) 11 Ecology LQ 495 (a leading researcher on this subject through her work beginning in the mid-1980s); Edith Brown Weiss, "Conservation and Equity between Generations" in Thomas Buergenthal, ed, *Contemporary Issues in International Law* (Kehl: Engel, 1984) 245; Edith Brown Weiss, "International Law, Common Patrimony and Intergenerational Equity: Research in Progress" in René-Jean Dupuy, ed, *L'Avenir du droit international de l'environnement* (Dordrecht: Martinus Nijhoff Publishers, 1985) 445; Edith Brown Weiss, *In Fairness to Future Generations: International Law, Common Patrimony, and Intergenerational Equity* (Tokyo: UN University Press, 1989) at 385 (her subsequent work at the United Nations University); Edith Brown Weiss, *Environmental Change and International Law: New Challenges and Dimensions* (Tokyo: UN University Press, 1992) at 493. The author assigns responsibility to future generations on the basis of three principles: conservation of options [diversity], conservation of quality, and conservation of access.

24 *Report of the World Commission on Environment and Development: Our Common Future*, UNGAOR, 42d Sess, Annex, UN Doc A/42/427, (1987) at para 54 [*Report of the World Commission*].

25 Anthony D'Amato, "Agora: What Obligation Does Our Generation Owe to the Next? An Approach to Global Environmental Responsibility" (1990) 84 AJIL 190.

26 US, House of Representatives, 93d Cong, *Report of the House Committee on Merchant Marine and Fisheries on HR 37* (HR Doc No 93-412) (1973), cited in *TVA v Hill*, 437 US 153 at 153 (1978); Joseph Sax, "Le petit poisson contre le grand barrage devant la Cour suprême des États-Unis" (1978) 4 RJE 368. See also Edith Brown Weiss, above note 23: the author assigns responsibility to future generations on the basis of three principles: conservation of options [diversity], conservation of quality, and conservation of access.

sustainable use of the planet's limited natural resources in the present and for the future.

C. INTERDEPENDENCE IN ACTION: THE QUEBEC SHALE GAS DEBATE

The entire range of interdependent dimensions — environmental and human rights — can be observed in the Quebec shale gas debate. This case includes an attempt to restrict procedural rights and its effects on other recognized rights, in particular the right of peoples to freely determine their development. It also illustrates our responsibilities to future generations with respect to an energy source that we do not actually need in the present and the risk of irreversible depletion of groundwater resources. These rights issues were what drew the attention of the Ligue des droits et libertés du Québec.

Since its inception in 1963, the Ligue has been involved in many cases concerning rights violations, including cases that could be linked, directly or indirectly, to environmental issues. However, the Ligue was not officially involved in environmental issues per se until relatively recently. Instead the Ligue focused on Aboriginal rights, the right to adequate housing, freedom of expression, and even the right to water to a certain extent, without placing these issues squarely within any kind of environmental justice framework. It was the Ligue's participation in the fight against SLAPPs that forged a link between the two major branches of citizen initiatives: human rights struggles and eco-citizenship.

1) The Fight against SLAPPs: Early Procedural Protections in relation to Environmental Issues

SLAPPs are lawsuits filed by companies or institutions against individuals or lobby groups in an attempt to neutralize or censor them when they speak out against corporate activities. This is a well-known tactic in Canada that has been the subject of a number of studies.[27] SLAPPs come in a variety of forms and are used in a number of disputes involving larger issues including, but not limited to, environmental issues.[28] In Quebec, though, the

27 Susan Lott, "Corporate Retaliation against Consumers: The Status of Strategic Lawsuits Against Public Participation (SLAPPs) in Canada" (September 2004), online: PIAC www.piac.ca.

28 Comité au ministre de la Justice, "Les poursuites stratégiques contre la mobilisation publique : les poursuites-bâillons (SLAPP). Rapport du comité au ministre de la

SLAPP tactic made its first appearance as a result of environmental disputes, and environmental activist groups were the first to react, launching a public awareness campaign in 2006 called *Citoyens, taisez-vous!*[29]

As a result of this campaign, the Quebec Ministry of Justice commissioned a report and public hearings were held, in which the Ligue participated.[30] The Ligue's strong interest in this process was unsurprising considering the many civil rights issues involved, in particular the rights to participate in public affairs, to freedom of expression, to access to justice, and to a fair and equitable hearing.

The Ligue joined forces, in its interventions on the SLAPP issue, with the Réseau québécois des groupes écologistes (RQGE), the Association québécoise de lutte contre la pollution atmosphérique (AQLPA), and Éditions Écosociété to push for legislation. A new law, the *Loi modifiant le Code de procédure civile pour prévenir l'utilisation abusive des tribunaux et favoriser le respect de la liberté d'expression et la participation des citoyens aux débats publics*, was finally enacted in June 2009.[31] Upon the adoption of the *Projet de loi 9*, the president of the AQLPA stated that "this law is the result of the effective mobilization of united citizens. Together, we can move mountains."[32] The Ligue had thus successfully made its first foray into environmental affairs, and in so doing it had discovered the substantial range of civil rights issues underlying environmental concerns. The Ligue quickly recognized the need for alliances with and among groups working in the areas of both human rights and environmental conservation.

Justice" (15 March 2007), online: Justice Québec www.justice.gouv.qc.ca.

29 [Translation: Citizens, Be Quiet!] This campaign was launched by the AQLPA (Association québécoise de lutte contre la pollution atmosphérique) and the Comité de restauration de la rivière Etchemin.

30 Ligue des droits et libertés, "Les poursuites stratégiques contre la mobilisation publique — les poursuites — *bâillons (SLAPP)*" (1 February 2008), online: Ligue des droits http://liguedesdroits.ca.

31 SQ 2009, c 12 [*Projet de loi 9*].

32 "Adoption du projet de loi 9 : fruit d'une mobilisation citoyenne efficace" (3 June 2009), online: AQLPA www.aqlpa.com [translated from the original French].

2) You Can't Make an Omelette without Breaking a Few Eggs: Socio-economic Rights at Risk

Public opposition had already been expressed in response to earlier large-scale development projects, such as Suroît,[33] Mont-Orford Park,[34] and the Rabaska initiative.[35] In addition to these cases, the shale gas debate gave the Ligue an opportunity to gauge the potential rights violations in many development projects, and especially the rights impact of the prevailing practice of exploiting resources without restraint. Development, it was discovered, often took the form of an attack on communities. The development of the shale gas industry in Quebec, which relies on the controversial process of hydraulic fracturing (fracking), met passionate opposition from environmental groups who claimed that it put groundwater and drinking water resources at risk.[36] In previous projects, citizens' strategies had emphasized environmental concerns rather than direct violations of the rights of affected communities.[37] The shale gas debate, however, was an entirely different story.

Indeed, as soon as shale gas exploration and development began, it became apparent that civil and political rights as well as socio-economic and cultural rights were being directly threatened, if not violated outright, in the process. Bolstered by the two international rights Covenants as well as the *Aarhus Convention*[38] — generally considered the leading legal framework

---

33 Opposition movement launched in 2004 against construction of a thermal power station based on climate change concerns. See, in particular (in French only), Denis Lessard, "Le Suroît définitivement liquidé avant la commission parlementaire" *La Presse* (17 November 2004), online: Vigile http://archives.vigile.net.

34 Opposition movement launched in 2006 to save a natural park from privatization (in French only): "SOS Parc Orford appelle la population à se mobiliser de nouveau, le 3 juin à Québec" (11 May 2006), online: SOS Parc Orford www.sosparcorford.org.

35 Opposition movement from 2006 to 2008 against construction of a liquefied natural gas terminal on the south shore of the St Lawrence River (in French only): "L'échec d'une mobilisation" (5 December 2008), online: Radio-Canada www.radio-canada.ca.

36 See, among others, "Quebec Seeks Fracking Moratorium in Shale Gas Rich Area" (15 May 2013), online: Reuters www.reuters.com.

37 This is not to say that violations were not a concern. For example, in the Rabaska case, the Agence de la santé et des services sociaux de la Capitale-Nationale and the Agence de la santé et des services sociaux de Chaudière-Appalaches spoke out against the project because of concerns for public health: Martin Pelchat, "Rabaska: inquiétudes à la Santé publique" *Le Soleil* (13 April 2008), online: gouvernement.QC.ca http://forum.gouvernement.qc.ca.

38 *Convention on Access to Information, Public Participation in Decision-Making and Access to Justice in Environmental Matters*, 28 June 1998, 2161 UNTS 447, 38 ILM 517 (1999)

reflecting best practices for applying procedural rights to environmental issues — the Ligue identified several violations of civil and political rights in relation to the BAPE's mandate, geographical restrictions, duration of the mandate, access to information, and inequality of means.[39]

Among other provisions, the Ligue relied upon paragraph 51 of the *ICESCR*'s *General Comment No 14: The Right to the Highest Attainable Standard of Health* on the right to health[40] to challenge the decision to develop the shale gas sector "without first collecting all the information required for ensuring its safety,"[41] which the government is obligated to do as part of its international human rights obligations. *General Comment No 14*, issued by the Committee on Economic, Social and Cultural Rights (the UN body responsible for monitoring the implementation of the *ICESCR*), placed particular emphasis on access to information. By invoking the *ICESCR* and *General Comment No 14*, the Ligue clearly underscored the relationship between procedural and substantive rights and the interdependence of all rights.

Regarding substantive rights, the Ligue cited in its report, *Le droit de dire NON*, that "some of the features of shale gas exploration and development methods used in Québec to date pose a threat to[. . .]the right to peaceful enjoyment of one's property, particularly in the form of challenges some nearby residents face in insuring their properties and in refusing exploration on their properties, as well as problems relating to the presence of nearby wells and access roads."[42] The Ligue focused on two rights that were especially at risk in this situation — the right to health and the right to water:[43]

(entered into force 30 October 2001) [*Aarhus Convention*].

39 Ligue des droits et libertés, *Le droit de dire NON* [translation: The Right to Say NO]. Report presented to the Bureau des audiences publiques sur l'environnement (BAPE) as part of a consultation process entitled "Développement durable de l'industrie des gaz de schiste au Québec" [Sustainable Development of the Shale Gas Industry in Québec] (November 2010) (in French only), online: Ligue des droits http://liguedesdroits.ca [Ligue, *Le droit de dire NON*].

40 United Nations Economic and Social Council, *The Right to the Highest Attainable Standard of Health. General Comment No 14*, UNESCOR, 22d Sess E/C.12/2000/4, (2000) [*General Comment No 14*].

41 Ligue, *Le droit de dire NON*, above note 39 at 13 [translated from the original French].

42 *Ibid* at 15 [translated from the original French].

43 The right to water, though notably omitted from the *ICESCR*, was considered a right in the *ICESCR* Committee's *General Comment No 15* in 2002, by the General Assembly of the United Nations on 28 July 2010, and by the United Nations Human Rights Council on 30 September 2010.

> The available studies clearly demonstrate that shale gas exploration and development carry risks to public health, especially with respect to the numerous chemicals — some with known carcinogenic effects — used in the so-called fracking process.[44] The greatest risk factor for significant rights violations is potential water contamination, since the processes involved in shale gas exploration and development require large quantities of water. We have therefore chosen to focus on these two rights, which are strongly interdependent.[45]

The Ligue broke new ground in its approach to linking environmental issues and human rights by suggesting a complex, interdependent connection between the two. The Ligue argued that the Quebec government's own laws required it to protect its water resources and, therefore, to study the impacts of development projects that affect these resources in advance of any decision being made in relation to shale gas development. The Ligue also insisted that the government must provide citizens with all essential information pertaining to their health. It argued that environmental impact studies, which are mandatory, must also assess the human rights component of projects and not limit their focus solely to environmental effects. This led the Ligue to make the following specific recommendation:

> . . . from now on, respect for human rights should be an integral component of the project evaluation criteria used in all environmental consultations. In addition, regarding the impact of projects on all interdependent rights, the results of these evaluations should be made public. Respect for the rights and liberties of all citizens is a fundamental prerequisite for a project to be considered "socially acceptable."[46]

This interdependence-based analysis also led the Ligue to highlight the need to apply the precautionary principle[47] in any decision relating to shale gas development, even though this principle is not explicitly includ-

---

44 See Environmental Protection Agency, *Hydraulic Fracturing Research Study*, US Environmental Protection Agency, Office of Research and Development, EP-A/600/F-10/002, June 2010, online: EPA www2.epa.gov; Environmental Protection Agency, *Evaluation of Impacts to Underground Sources of Drinking Water by Hydraulic Fracturing of Coalbed Methane Reservoirs: Executive Summary*, EPA 816-R-04-003 (June 2004), online: EPA www2.epa.gov; Environmental Protection Agency, "Natural Gas Extraction - Hydraulic Fracturing" (2014), online: EPA www2.epa.gov.

45 Ligue, *Le droit de dire NON*, above note 39 at 15 [translated from the original French].

46 *Ibid* at 20 [translated from the original French].

47 According to principle 15 of the *Rio Declaration*, above note 7, the precautionary principle states the following: "Where there are threats of serious or irreversible damage,

ed in Canadian or Quebec legislation.[48] The Ligue affirmed in this regard that "given the dangerous nature of the substances involved and the glaring lack of information, the Ligue is of the opinion that protecting the Québec population's right to health and water necessitates a *strict application of the precautionary principle in the present case*."[49]

Though traditionally a rights-advocacy organization, the Ligue justified its appearance before a consultative body on environmental matters by citing a specific article that the Quebec government had included in the Quebec *Charter of Human Rights and Freedoms* in 2006. Article 46.1 states, "Every person has a right to live in a healthful environment in which biodiversity is preserved, to the extent and according to the standards provided by law."[50] The Ligue inferred that "the legislator's clear intent in adding article 46.1 to the *Charter* was to provide enhanced protection of the right to live in a healthy environment."[51] The Ligue's interdependence-based analysis provided a much more precise understanding of the impact that the environmental aspects of development decisions have on rights.

3) The Right to Say NO: Report by the Ligue des droits et libertés du Québec

When it appeared before the BAPE, the Ligue outlined its involvement in terms of the rights potentially violated by shale gas development. On a more fundamental level, the Ligue also focused on the right of peoples to self-determination, set out in the first article of the two Covenants. This explains the title of the Ligue's report: *Le droit de dire NON* [The Right to Say NO]. The Ligue chose this particular focus because, throughout the many environmental cases that have sparked controversy in Quebec in the past decade, the ability of affected communities to make their own development choices has been the fundamental issue at stake. The result has been "an increasing breakdown in trust between the population and its government in matters of resource exploitation, development projects, and

---

lack of full scientific certainty shall not be used as a reason for postponing cost-effective measures to prevent environmental degradation."

48 Although this principle is mentioned at several points throughout Canadian environmental law, it is, in practice, a general provision. See *114957 Canada Ltée (Spraytech, Société d'arrosage) v Hudson (Town)*, 2001 SCC 40.

49 Ligue, *Le droit de dire NON*, above note 39 at 18 [translated from the original French, emphasis in original].

50 RSQ, c C-12, s 46.1.

51 Ligue, *Le droit de dire NON*, above note 39 at 5 [translated from the original French].

the protection of the environment and of their communities."[52] The Ligue stressed in its report that "the fresh perspective we bring to these proceedings is that of respect for all human rights, be they civil and political rights that call for collective decision-making processes or the economic, social, and cultural rights that are affected by the decisions made."[53]

The Ligue also highlighted Quebec society's collective responsibilities to future generations:

> Recall that rights are inherent, interdependent and universal, as emphasized at the 1993 Vienna Conference.[54] In other words, they apply to all human beings in the present and to those not yet born.
>
> To that effect, Québec society must consider *two specific obligations* in its decision on shale gas exploration and development.
>
> First, we are obligated to *safeguard options* for future generations. This means that Québec's genuine energy needs must be taken into account in decisions on whether or not to develop shale gas resources. If we do not have such a need, it is our duty to leave this non-renewable resource for generations to come.
>
> Second, it is our collective duty to *protect the basic life-sustaining ecosystem* so that future generations can also enjoy conditions conducive to living with dignity. Our first task is to protect potential sources of potable water, and *not only those that are known and currently in use*. Indeed, we are aware that there are water resources underground, some at great depth, whose characteristics and properties are still unknown. Given our current level of knowledge, the precautionary principle must prevail if we are to protect our resources, especially those that are most vital to life.[55]

Through its involvement in the Quebec shale gas debate, the Ligue fostered a new way of thinking about development by suggesting that citizens have the right to oppose development projects that are proposed to them. This opened the door to new alliances not only with environmental groups but also with groups focused on economic issues, and provided a fresh perspective that needed to be expanded upon and circulated as widely as possible.

---

52 *Ibid* [translated from the original French].

53 *Ibid* at 6 [translated from the original French].

54 World Conference, *Vienna Declaration*, above note 2, art 5: "All human rights are universal, indivisible and interdependent and interrelated."

55 Ligue, *Le droit de dire NON*, above note 39 at 18 [translated from the original French, emphasis in original].

The Ligue's work certainly appears to have staying power. As a result of its participation in the SLAPP issue and then in the shale gas debate, long-lasting partnerships seem to have been forged. The Ligue's joint work with the RQGE now extends to procedural protections — with significant investments from both organizations into SLAPP-related awareness campaigns. It also extends to democratic rights more broadly, and includes developing a deeper understanding of environmental issues as human rights issues. In particular, the two organizations held a colloquium on the latter topic in February 2012 to broaden their alliances with other sectors. Indeed, if all rights are interdependent, then this interdependence must also encompass socio-economic and ecological issues, and the strategies needed to address them.

The Ligue's strategy in the shale gas debate was not entirely new: it had already generated and fuelled discussion in Quebec on social issues in terms of rights and rights interdependence. Extending this strategy to environmental issues, however, was unprecedented in Quebec, and may in future foster new alliances with other sectors by providing a common analytical framework, despite the breadth and diversity of their respective objectives.

D. A BROADER UNDERSTANDING OF RIGHTS INTERDEPENDENCE: FUTURE DIRECTIONS?

The final brief discussion is intended to suggest avenues that might be worth exploring to deepen our understanding of the interdependence of rights and the implications of that interdependence, and thereby advance political struggles.

1) Defending Civil and Political Rights instead of Balancing Competing Interests

As a general rule, all social issues inherently create power struggles in which the parties involved make use of all the resources available to them. As suggested above, SLAPPs are no exception. Framing such issues within the context of rights and freedoms, however, would allow us to understand and present them not as conflicts between competing interests, but rather as violations of common standards, and therefore as violations of the foundations of our social order. This change in perspective would provide citizens with a legitimate platform that would make it more difficult for the government to ignore them. Opinions may differ as to whether it is acceptable, within a democratic society, for different individuals or groups to have an unequal ability to defend their interests, based on their financial or other means. But one thing is clear: the use of court proceedings to silence dissent and to prevent a right from being exercised is an abuse of justice. When this tactic is assessed in light of its impact on rights and freedoms, rather than as an issue of competing interests, it inevitably loses some of its legal force and legitimacy.

Applying an interdependence analysis to the strategies used by economic interests or other powerful players allows us to identify and illustrate the consequences of neglecting to consider rights as interdependent — the alternative is an inherently restrictive perspective on rights. Viewing rights as interdependent also enables us to bring the focus back to the central and cross-disciplinary nature of the principle of equality. Interdependence concerns not only the fulfillment of rights but also their violation, and only public participation can offset the inequality of means and restore the conditions needed for all rights to be fulfilled.

2) Environmental Issues and the Right of Peoples to Freely Determine Their Own Development

As with social issues, environmental issues are often understood merely as competing interests and conflicting priorities. Compromises must be made, sides must be chosen, and pros and cons must be weighed. Sometimes the solution presented is a simple cost-benefit analysis. Adopting the perspective of rights interdependence constitutes a departure from utilitarian philosophy. It becomes a question of abiding by societal norms. And so, as in the shale gas case discussed above, integrating a rights-impact component into environmental impact studies could make it possible, in the future, to give more weight and validity to non-economic criteria. It could also help the BAPE to escape from the rut in which it has been trapped for several years because of its strict focus on balancing interests, which has gradually led it to exclude the option of rejecting proposed projects.[56] What is more, this interdependence approach could potentially form the basis for a renewed understanding of the links between rights and democracy.

In light of the foregoing analysis, both the right of peoples to self-determination and the right of peoples to freely determine their own development take on a new dimension that paves the way for developing clear standards for our fundamental social principles. Phrases such as "self-

---

56 Nicole Desroches, "Plus insidieux que la corruption et la collusion : la mainmise sur les prises de décisions" (7 January 2013) (in French only), online: GaïaPresse www.gaiapresse.ca.

determination" and "freely determine" presuppose the ability to freely exercise all civil and political rights. For that reason, development directions cannot be predetermined and set in stone. Respect for economic, social, and cultural rights thus becomes a deciding factor in development choices and provides a common standard for guiding debate on the topic.

Reinterpreting the right of peoples to self-determination would provide an alternative perspective on the infamous "democratic deficit" and would allow us to rethink democratic requirements in ways that are more compatible than traditional approaches with how our society is developing. This, in turn, could bring a new, deeper meaning to "the right to participate in public affairs," which is an essential component of implementing article 28 of the *Universal Declaration of Human Rights.*

E. IN CLOSING: RIGHTS INTERDEPENDENCE IN A GLOBALIZED WORLD

At the beginning of this paper, the term "global systemic crisis" was chosen deliberately, because the label applied to a situation has a significant influence on how it will be addressed. Despite the strategic advantage of a global outlook, it must be noted that the dominant tendency in the past few decades has been for different groups and movements to focus on their own sector-specific issues. The Ligue's approach in the shale gas debate shows the strategic advantage of a more comprehensive perspective, one that takes into account the many layers of complexity present.

The strategy discussed herein will not necessarily generate significant legal change; at the end of the day, however, political choices and decisions, as well as the implementation of public policies, are indeed the forces that enable rights to be exercised effectively. This political dimension will be a key factor in our collective ability to address global environmental issues in order to achieve a greater measure of justice for both environmental and human rights.

Linking social and human rights issues to environmental concerns creates the possibility of moving beyond a restrictive and individualistic interpretation and broadening our understanding of the interdependence of all rights. As previously stated, this link is implicit in article 28 of the *Universal Declaration of Human Rights*; making it explicit will force those in political power to take this connection into account if they wish to retain their legitimacy.

Furthermore, establishing this link allows environmentalists to operate from a social choice perspective within a broader political framework, enabling them to reach a much broader audience, significantly raise their credibility, and maximize their impact. Interpreting environmental issues within a rights interdependence framework allows the foundations of environmental responsibility to be reinforced both politically and judicially. This may allow society to transcend the prevalent and narrow views of sustainable development and restore social growth[57] to its rightful place as a priority in our development choices.

57 Recall that, originally, sustainable development rested upon three pillars: development, environmental protection, and equality. See *Report of the World Commission*, above note 24 at paras 27–29.

CHAPTER 13

HAS PUBLIC PROTEST GONE TO THE DOGS? A SOCIAL RIGHTS APPROACH TO SOCIAL PROTEST LAW IN CANADA

GRAHAM MAYEDA*

A. INTRODUCTION

How should the law react to social protest? Should it facilitate it? Should it limit it? This question is particularly poignant today, when protests such as the Occupy movement, the Quebec student tuition protests, and the Idle No More movement demonstrate the continued importance of protest as a form of social action. In this chapter, I argue that the social rights approach to resolving social conflict can be applied to develop a progressive legal framework for dealing with social protest.

To determine the proper role of law in regard to social protest, I begin by examining what "legal rights" are.[1] The traditional approach to rights treats them as having determinate content — each right can be given a legal meaning. For instance, the right to privacy is the right to be free from

---

* Associate Professor, Faculty of Law, Common Law Section, University of Ottawa.

1 I do not think that law can be reduced to an understanding of the meaning of legal rights. Elsewhere, I have examined the law from the point of view of our experience of judgment (see Graham Mayeda, "Uncommonly Common: The Nature of Common Law Judgment" (2006) 19:1 Can JL & Jur 107 [Mayeda, "Uncommonly Common"]) and as the nexus of principle and pragmatism (Graham Mayeda, "Between Principle and Pragmatism: The Decline of Principled Reasoning in the Jurisprudence of the McLachlin Court" in Sheila McIntyre & Sanda Rodgers, eds, *The Supreme Court of Canada and the Achievement of Social Justice: Commitment, Retrenchment or Retreat* (Markham, ON: LexisNexis Canada, 2010) 41 [Mayeda, "Between Principle and Pragmatism"]. But a reflection on the role of social rights in social protest naturally leads to a consideration of the nature and meaning of legal rights.

unreasonable intrusion into personal life by the State.[2] Moreover, in the traditional approach, rights holders can come into conflict. When they do, the role of law is to resolve their competing rights claims. The essential paradigm of the law that animates the traditional view is one of *conflict* and *confrontation*. Two or more rights holders enter into conflict, and the conflict must be resolved through a *theoretical confrontation* between competing rights holders undertaken in the abstract by legal tribunals.

In this paper, I compare this traditional approach to a *social rights* approach. The *social rights* movement, which expands the panoply of rights from traditional political rights to socio-economic rights, is marked not just by its broader conception of rights but by its understanding of what rights are, how social conflicts arise, and how they should be resolved. The fundamental approach adopted by the social rights movement is that social justice is not just about balancing rights but about creating the conditions for a truly deliberative form of democracy in which the law both reflects and plays an integral part in social transformation. The social rights movement considers rights discourse as an essential part of the achievement of social justice.

For the social rights movement, conflict need not be approached as a competition between competing rights holders. First, rights have shifting meanings — they mean different things to different people depending on who they are and the social conditions in which they live.[3] Second, when social conflict arises, rather than framing it as a conflict between individuals or between an individual and the State, a social rights approach sees the conflict as a *transformative moment* — i.e., an opportunity to reassess past interpretations of a right in light of newly emergent social circumstances and to engage the public in the process of articulating the meaning of rights in a particular social context. In this way, a social rights approach to law sees conflict as contributing to the strengthening of the social fabric by engaging us in democratic deliberation.

The purpose of this paper is to consider how these different paradigms frame the issue of social protest and to develop a legal framework for the

---

2 *Hunter et al v Southam Inc*, [1984] 2 SCR 145 at 159.

3 Nancy Fraser explains the varied understandings of the substance of justice claims: "'. . . class-accented appeals for economic redistribution are routinely pitted against minority recognition,' while feminist claims for gender justice often collide with demands for supposedly traditional forms of religious or communal justice. The result is a radical heterogeneity of justice discourse . . . ." (Nancy Fraser, *Scales of Justice: Reimagining Political Space in a Globalizing World* (New York: Columbia University Press, 2009) at 2).

social rights model of social protest. I will not deal with the criminal law response to social protest except in a general way. However, I will discuss civil law approaches, including injunctions, contempt of court proceedings, and various legislative approaches to public protest such as anti-SLAPP suit legislation.[4] As we will see, a social rights approach to social protest advocates for legal rules that facilitate peaceful protest, which is an important part of democratic deliberation. It also advocates inclusiveness to ensure that all social groups are able to use protest as a means of testing the legitimacy of our existing legal and social order.

B. WHAT IS SOCIAL PROTEST?

1) The Goals of Social Protest

Social protest is a form of social action that aims at making the public aware of the interests of a group or, more rarely, of an individual. It is at once an appeal for awareness, an appeal for engaged deliberation, and an appeal for action.[5] For example, the Occupy movement seeks to bring public attention to systemic injustice that arises from our global financial system and the disproportionate impact of this injustice on marginalized groups.[6] Its goal of engaging public deliberation is expressed in one of its principal driving forces, which is "[e]ngaging in direct and transparent participatory

---

4 A SLAPP suit is a Strategic Lawsuit Against Public Participation. The lawsuit is not necessarily initiated with the prospect of winning it, but rather as an intimidation tactic to prevent public participation in debate.

5 Social protest does not necessarily have all of these goals at once, nor does it necessarily pursue all of them with the same energy. As Herbert Blumer points out, social movements, of which social protest often forms a part, can be general, in which case they "take the form of groping and uncoordinated efforts. They have only a general direction, toward which they move in a slow, halting, yet persistent fashion" (Herbert Blumer, "Social Movements" in Vincenzo Ruggiero & Nicola Montagna, eds, *Social Movements. A Reader* (London: Routledge, 2008) 64 at 65 [Ruggiero & Montagna, eds]). However, specific social movements can also develop. In these movements, "agitation" plays a role, which Blumer describes as "arousing people" (informing them) (*ibid* at 67), "jar[ring them] loose from their customary ways of thinking and believing" (*ibid*) (public deliberation), and finally "liberat[ing] them for movement in new directions" (*ibid* at 68) (action).

6 See, for example, Matt Taibbi, "Wall Street Isn't Winning — It's Cheating" *Rolling Stone* (25 October 2011), online: Rolling Stone www.rollingstone.com. On its website, Occupy Wall Street states that it "aims to expose how the richest 1% of people are writing the rules of an unfair global economy that is foreclosing on our future," online: http://occupywallst.org/about/.

democracy."[7] Similarly, the Idle No More movement has focused on raising awareness among Indigenous peoples and others in order to empower them to engage with issues of Indigenous sovereignty and the protection of the environment and to bring about change through this engagement.[8] Protest is a call for a further deliberative process. The legal institutions that structure social protest ought to reflect this by recognizing the marginalized interests given voice at the protest and creating a forum for public deliberation that can lead to cooperative action to resolve the issues being raised.

One of the many concerns about the Occupy protests was that they create a forum for other forms of illegality such as violence, drug use, and alcohol abuse. In the traditional competing rights model, this is an excuse for placing the "public interest" in the balance against the interests of individual protestors seeking to exercise their right to free speech. However, a better way of understanding these inter-linked phenomena is to see the message of peaceful protestors and violence, drug, and alcohol abuse as part of the phenomenon of marginalization that motivates most social protests.[9] This marginalization — often as a result of state suppression — has the effect of attracting to the protest those who are marginalized in diverse ways, and at the same time motivating suppressors to corral other marginalized groups together with protestors.[10] The violence, the manifestation of petty illegality, and expressions of indigence and poverty are

---

7 New York City General Assembly, "About," online: NYC General Assembly www.nycga.net.

8 Idle No More, Press Release (10 January 2013), online: Idle No More http://idlenomore.ca.

9 While marginalization is often at the root of social protest, I am not arguing that marginalization and reaction against it is the primary impetus for social mobilization. Indeed, the success of mobilization depends in large part on the availability of forms of organization such as social networks that lower the costs of building coalitions and hence the costs of group mobilization (in this regard, see Sidney Tarrow, *Power in Movement: Social Movements and Contentious Politics*, 2d ed (Cambridge: Cambridge University Press, 1998) at 23; see also Marco Giugni's discussion of resource mobilization theory in *Social Protest and Policy Change. Ecology, Antinuclear, and Peace Movements in Comparative Perspective* (Oxford: Rowman & Littlefield, 2004) at 148–50).

10 By "attracting," I mean that those marginalized by poverty, substance abuse, mental disorder, and so on are attracted, be it ideologically or psychologically, to participate in a social protest. By "corralled," I mean that the process of state suppression is over-inclusive, capturing within the boundaries of its suppressive force groups that may not naturally have coalesced at the protest. For instance, at the Occupy Wall Street protest, police officers tended to corral the homeless and other marginalized groups into the occupation site, either accidentally or as a means of disrupting the protest.

not good reasons to increase state suppression. Indeed, they are often the result of such suppression.

For instance, the Occupy protests express the economic marginalization of a large group of people, and it is no surprise that complaints about employment, economic stability, and so on are intermixed with the manifestation of actual poverty and marginalization. Those who are marginalized for other reasons find themselves attracted to the location of public protest — occupied spaces attract the homeless, the criminalized, and so on, in the hope that they will be able to capture some of the power that comes from the visibility of peaceful protestors who have attracted the public eye. If the movement is perceived as efficacious, people will be drawn to it.[11]

Another way of understanding the intermixing of these phenomena of exclusion is as different manifestations of the State's power to exclude. When the State wishes to hide certain kinds of marginalization, it often resorts to burying them within other forms of marginalization that it can more successfully control. For example, the marginalization of which Occupy protestors complain is vilified, labelled, and thereby controlled by associating it with violence and morally reprehensible behaviour. In practical terms, this means police corralling the poor, the criminalized, and so on into territories occupied by peaceful protestors to elicit public condemnation of the protest itself.

Some may argue that explaining the reason for the nexus between social protest and anti-social behaviour (or, at least, behaviour perceived as anti-social by particular social groups) does not provide a justification for allowing this behaviour. However, the result of suppressing the anti-social behaviour is generally to suppress the legitimate ends of social protest. This is not an incidental result of state suppression. While the state may claim that its goal in dealing with anti-social behaviour is to channel protest into alternate, more acceptable public fora, such a rationalization is not legitimate if no such forum exists. The effect of state suppression is usually to deny *any* forum to social protest of the marginalized. As political scientist Doug McAdam points out in his work on the political causes of social protest, social mobilization is a form of resistance to institutionalized political power. It is a response to the "enormous obstacles [that excluded groups face] in their efforts to advance group interests. Challengers are excluded from routine decision-making processes precisely because their bargaining

11 Gerald Marwell & Pamela Oliver, *The Critical Mass in Collective Action: A Micro-Social Theory* (Cambridge: Cambridge University Press, 1993), reprinted in part in Ruggiero & Montagna, eds, above note 5, 128 at 131.

position, relative to established polity members, is so weak."[12] Social protest is in part the result of the inaccessibility of other "legitimate" public fora, and so state suppression cannot hope to shift social protest into them.

2) Social Protest as a Social Phenomenon

I have described social protest in terms of its social and political roles as a mechanism for initiating or continuing a process of deliberative democracy and as a way of challenging and hence ensuring the continued validity of the state monopoly on force. But to understand the appropriate role of law in regulating social protest, we must identify the source of the normative meaning underlying it. This requires us to understand what social protest expresses as a *social phenomenon*, which means understanding how we experience social protest in order to comprehend what it tells us about our collective social life. To do this, we must acknowledge that we experience injustices of individuals and groups — even of those from radically different cultures, religious, classes, etc. — *as a society*. From the point of view of social experience, protest is a way to communicate to others the experience of injustice of the protestors. Through this experience emerges the normative force of public protest, which arises from the recognition of a tear in the social fabric and the need to respond to and take responsibility for it.

There is a large phenomenological literature on how we experience the intersubjective or social dimensions of human experience. In East Asian philosophy, phenomenologists such as Watsuji Tetsurō have adumbrated the ways in which we directly experience the suffering of others. For instance, in a famous passage from his *Ethics*, Watsuji describes that we have direct experience of the suffering of those cut off from us by a natural disaster. When the disaster occurs, lines of communication are damaged, and this can be felt as a physical wound by society as a whole:

> [I]f a certain area [of a country] were to be cut off from the services of communication, news reports, transportation, and so forth, then the people in this region would be cut off from the wider public. In this case, so far as physical space is concerned, however, there is no change. As extended, the greater public suffers damage. No matter how distant this region is, whether a remote place in the mountains or a secluded island, it is usually quite removed from the intense contact of communication, transporta-

12 Doug McAdam, *Political Process and the Development of Black Insurgency 1930–1970* (Chicago and London: University of Chicago Press, 1982), excerpted in Ruggiero & Montagna, eds, above note 5, 177 at 179.

tion, and the like. If this contact is interrupted against the will of the local people, then this event itself comes to emerge as an event of the gravest public concern. The interruption of contact is felt as physical damage by that society, so to speak.[13]

Here, Watsuji refers to communication as a phenomenon of everyday life that manifests our capacity for experiencing the life of others as part of our society. I suggest that a truly *social* theory of social rights should likewise be able to account for protest as a social phenomenon involving damage to intersubjective life. Such a theory takes into account our direct experience of others.

If this experience of the social is to inform the theory of social rights, then it must have some normative force. After all, the law is a normative institution. In the East Asian tradition, Confucianism has long held that the normative force of another's distress is experienced directly. The story of the child falling into the well that we find in *Mencius* is a famous example.[14] There, Mencius explains that when we observe a child falling into a well, regardless of our life experience, our first instinct is to save it. As we reflect on what we have witnessed, we may well hesitate or justify non-action to ourselves, but the initial normative force of witnessing a tragedy is experienced the same by all.

In Western philosophy, Emmanuel Levinas explains in many of his writings the different ways in which we are confronted by others and brought to acknowledge the responsibility that these encounters engender. He highlights the normative force of our experience of the suffering of another and describes how when we come face-to-face with this suffering — say a panhandler on the street — we directly experience the accusation that that person makes against us, and simultaneously, acknowledge the responsibility we bear for alleviating that person's suffering. Indeed, the very act of justifying to ourselves why we should not help — because the panhandler will just spend the money on alcohol or drugs or because she should just get a job and help herself, etc. — attests to the initial experience of accusation (we feel accused by the person in need) and the presumption of responsibility. The encounter with another in need puts my self-identity and my abundance of resources in question. Whether rich or poor, everything I have becomes surplus in the face of the needs of the other.[15]

---

13 Tetsurō Watsuji, *Tetsurō Watsuji's* Rinrigaku (Albany: State University of New York Press, 1996) at 158–59.

14 *Mencius*, trans David Hinton (Washington, DC: Counterpoint, 1998).

15 Robert Bernasconi, "Strangers and Slaves in the Land of Egypt: Levinas and the Politics of Otherness" in Asher Horowitz & Gad Horowitz, eds, *Difficult Justice: Commentaries on*

In addition to explaining that our experience of responsibility is universal, Levinas adds to this experience the dimension of justice. Whether the panhandler, the child falling into the well, or the effects of a natural disaster, we are called to responsibility, which means called to respond, not just to ourselves, not just to our conscience, but to a third party.[16] This is the meaning of justice — to be called to explain to a third party how our response to the need of another can be justified. How is our treatment of a particular person in need a just treatment of all who need?

From a phenomenological point of view, we experience social protest as a wound to the social fabric. When others protest, they and we feel unease, as the protest communicates dissatisfaction with the social *status quo*. Indeed, we may even feel accused if we are targeted for criticism by protestors. Moreover, our immediate normative experience of this tearing of the social fabric is always one of responsibility — we are responsible for the suffering of others — indeed, we are accused by their suffering. And while we may then follow this experience with *ex post* rationalizations and justifications of our behaviour and condemn the protestors, this merely reinforces the underlying unease that we experience when encountering protest. The unease is an indication that we recognize our responsibility to them and for the issues they raise, and our evasion is unjust if it avoids justifying to them and others why our inaction is reasonable. I shall make the link between this experience of social protest and legal responses in a subsequent section. For now, I turn to how the law interacts with social protest and how it may better respect the normative force of protest by moving beyond the prevailing competing rights paradigm.

C. LEGAL PARADIGMS FOR DEALING WITH SOCIAL PROTEST — THE COMPETING RIGHTS PARADIGM AND THE SOCIAL JUSTICE PARADIGM

1) Introduction

The "competing rights" paradigm has been the most prevalent legal paradigm for addressing marginalization and oppression, of which social protest is a manifestation. When this paradigm is applied to social protest, those using it first seek to find a right of the protestor that is infringed — common choices include rights to free speech, association, freedom, or security of

---

Levinas and Politics (Toronto: University of Toronto Press, 2006) 246 at 249.

16 Gad Horowitz, "Aporia and Messiah in Derrida and Levinas" in Horowitz & Horowitz, eds, *ibid*, 307 at 310.

the person. Once this right is identified, using a competing rights approach to the *Charter* framework, the State may justify the infringement by proposing and defending an important social goal that it achieves. Outside the *Charter* context, which applies only to conflicts involving the rights enumerated in constitutional documents, legal actors resolve conflicts by determining if the protest affects other public or private legal interests not protected by the Constitution, and weighing these competing interests in a balance or bringing them into "dialogue" with each other.

The competing rights approach has been used in protest cases, most recently, in cases dealing with the various Occupy movements in cities such as Toronto and Vancouver, to which I now turn as examples.

2) The Competing Rights Paradigm in the *Charter* Context

In *Batty v Toronto (City)*,[17] DM Brown J of the Superior Court of Justice for Ontario dealt with Occupy Toronto protestors' challenge of the City of Toronto's trespass notice issued to occupiers of St James Park, part of which is public property. In rejecting their challenge, he appeals to the need to balance competing rights under the *Charter*. In response to the protestors' views that they were free to occupy St James Park, he explained:

> The *Charter* offers no justification for the Protesters' act of appropriating to their own use — without asking their fellow citizens — a large portion of common public space for an indefinite period of time.
>
> The *Charter* does not remove the need to apply common sense and balance to the way we deal with each other in our civic relationships. The *Charter* does not remove common sense from the process of trying to figure out how to balance the competing rights which now characterize our contemporary Canadian policy. On the contrary, the *Charter* speaks of "reasonable limits" on guaranteed freedoms, thereby signalling that common sense still must play a role — indeed, a very important role — in that balancing exercise.[18]

Having set out the general competing rights framework, Brown J then reviewed the nature of the encampment at St James Park and the goals of the Occupy Toronto protestors in occupying it in order to identify the right they asserted. The occupiers claimed that the occupation represented an open, democratic process and was a manifestation of their rights of freedom

---

17 2011 ONSC 6862 [*Batty*].

18 *Ibid* at paras 12–13.

of speech and association. Moreover, they argued that the occupation of the park was essential to the exercise of these rights.[19]

Accepting that the protestors were invoking section 2 rights,[20] Brown J sought to identify the competing right that would be balanced against speech interests. He found that the protestors' use of the park had "materially altered the traditional use of the Park and has prevented traditional Park users from using and enjoying the Park . . . ."[21] The right of the occupiers to exercise free speech was thus in competition with the right of local residents to access a public space without impediment and with a feeling of safety and enjoyment, as well as a right to use their private property without nuisance. The State — in this case, the City of Toronto — likewise identified interests that were infringed by the protestors' occupation. It quoted numerous bylaw infringements[22] in support of the claim by non-protestors that access and use of the park was limited by the protest.

In his section 1 analysis under the *Charter*, Brown J assessed the protestors' claim as a competition between the protestors' rights under section 2 of the *Charter* and the public interest of "all to share a common resource and ensuring that the uses of the parks will have a minimal adverse impact on the quiet enjoyment of surrounding residential lands."[23] In Brown J's view, the government objective of ensuring that public resources are shared was a pressing and substantial objective.[24] Having so found, it then followed that the trespass notice and parks bylaws were rational means of achieving these objectives, as they "ask one group of the public to let go of their monopoly over the use of the Park and share the Park with other people in Toronto . . . ."[25] The measures minimally impaired the protestors' section 2 rights, because the protestors could continue to exercise their section 2 rights by other means — just not by occupying St James Park and erecting structures in it.[26]

The judge rejected the protestors' contention that the occupation was an important part of their message that could not be communicated by other means. He explained, "If I were to accept the applicants' argument, then any protest group could come along, assert that monopolizing a particular piece of public space was an important part of their political message,

---

19 *Ibid* at para 64.
20 *Ibid* at paras 70–72.
21 *Ibid* at para 41.
22 *Ibid* at para 48.
23 *Ibid* at para 95.
24 *Ibid* at para 96.
25 *Ibid* at para 97.
26 *Ibid* at para 104.

and the City would be powerless to object."[27] The judge seemed particularly offended by the suggestion of protestors that those unwilling to use St James Park during the occupation use other parks.[28] He felt that the logic of the protestors would lead to an eventual occupation of all Toronto parks, to the entire exclusion of local residents.[29] Finally, Brown J explained that it is entirely impractical to impose on the city the constitutional requirement to consult with protestors before issuing a trespass notice. Such consultation might be a matter of political prudence, but it cannot be a constitutional obligation.[30]

In regard to the last part of the *Oakes* test, the assessment of the proportionality of the salutary and deleterious effects of the measure, Brown J concluded that the test was met:

> I have no hesitation in concluding that the evidence shows that there is proportionality. In seeking compliance with two provisions of the Parks By-law, the Trespass Notice would have the effect of ending the Protesters monopoly of a public park in downtown Toronto and requiring them to share it with the rest of the public. The Protesters have ample means left to express their message, including continued use of the Park (but no structures or "midnight hours"), and other Torontonians can resume their use of the Park. In my view such a result would more than meet the test for proportionality of deleterious and salutary effects.[31]

In the Superior Court's judgment, we see a clear example of the competing rights approach to a protest case. The case is framed as one of competition between protestors, who are asserting the right of freedom of expression under the *Charter*, and local residents, who wish to have access to a public space and to use and enjoy their own private space without nuisance.

The drawbacks of this approach are first, the court balances a constitutionally protected *right* — freedom of expression — against a collective *interest* in using public property. We are not given a criterion for measuring the appropriate balance between a right and a collective interest. The Supreme Court of Canada in *R v Oakes* required the government objective to be "pressing and substantial."[32] As Peter Hogg points out after a review of that seminal case, its language "indicate[s] that a reviewing court

27 *Ibid* at para 105.

28 *Ibid* at para 112.

29 *Ibid* at para 113.

30 *Ibid* at para 115.

31 *Ibid* at para 123.

32 *R v Oakes*, [1986] 1 SCR 103 [*Oakes*].

should engage in a rigorous scrutiny of the legislative objective."[33] However, Brown J does not conduct such a review, and one is justifiably left wondering how an essential right such as freedom of expression must yield to those who wish to walk their dog in St James Park.[34] To mimic Brown J's alarmist concerns, this certainly gives dogs a very high place in our constitutional order — or at least a place far above that of social activists with an important democratic message.

Also troubling is the court's failure to deal with the importance of the competing rights and interests being asserted to the identity of the parties. Clearly, the protestors felt that the occupation of the park was an essential part of their goal of communicating an alternative form of social and democratic organization, whereas the local users of the park did not express any close relationship between their identities, either as individuals or as a group, and their use of the park. The rights of association, assembly, and speech are at the core of a protestor's identity — they are essential to the purpose of protest. However, the interest in using a public park is only a peripheral aspect of most local residents' interests and identities. The court failed to take into account the social context in which rights and interests were being asserted in the process of dialogical balancing. The judge did not directly question whether local residents could or should exercise their interest in accessing a public space at a different park. Instead of assessing the constitutional rights claimed in the specific context in which they were claimed and with proper regard for the power relationships that exist between protestors and residents, he awoke the spectre of a rabid spread of occupations to every Toronto park, as if the Occupy Toronto protest threatened the use of every public space, and so genuinely threatened the residents' interest in access to public space generally. At paragraph 13 of his judgment, Brown J wrote:

> . . . if the Protesters possess a constitutional right to occupy the Park and appropriate it to their use, then the next protest group espousing a political message would have the right to so occupy another park, say, Moss Park; and the next group the next park, and so on, and so forth. So would result a "tragedy of the commons," another ironic consequence of a movement advocating greater popular empowerment.

---

33 Peter Hogg, *Constitutional Law of Canada*, 5th ed (Toronto: Thomson Carswell, 2007) at 38.9(b). I expand on this point in Mayeda, "Between Principle and Pragmatism," above note 1 at 54–55.

34 Most of the residents quoted in the judgment encountered protestors while walking their dogs.

At a more fundamental level, there is something troubling about the balancing approach used in the application of the competing rights paradigm. Protestors and local residents all acknowledged the experience of unease caused by the demonstration. Protestors were uneasy about many important social issues, but primarily about the lack of a public forum where they could voice them. Residents felt this unease and experienced it directly in their confrontations with protestors. Isn't this experience of a common communal life a signal that there is a real issue to be dealt with? Is it effective to deal with this issue by subordinating marginalized views (those of protestors) to those of the majority (the convenience of local residents) as the competing rights paradigm forces us to do? Are there more productive ways of transforming a situation of tension into one of problem solving rather than confrontation? In my view, pitting dog walkers against protestors is not a productive way of using a protest as a catalyst for democratic discourse. A different approach to the proportionality analysis under *Oakes* should be adopted. Such an approach would recognize that the interests of an individual or group should not be given the same weight as legally protected rights. It would take into account the centrality of a given right or interest to the identity of the group asserting it, and it would recognize social protest as an essential part of the deliberative democratic process rather than as a competition between groups. In such a competition, marginalized groups inevitably lose out to majoritarian values.

3) Applying the Competing Rights Paradigm in Civil Law: Injunctions as an Equitable and Statutory Remedy

Public protest is not only dealt with in the *Charter* context; indeed, it is more often dealt with by civil law outside of a constitutional framework. In most cases, protestors are not challenging the constitutionality of State action. Rather, they become subject to State action because the State or a private party initiates a civil action against them, in the context of which they can obtain an interlocutory injunction to restrain protestors pending resolution of the civil action. Such injunctions are backed by the threat of State force should they be disobeyed. Often, the party challenging protestors has no actual intention of continuing with the civil action — the action is begun strategically in order to make injunctive relief possible. In such cases, this party hopes that having put an end to a protest temporarily, she will in effect prevent it from continuing at all. Such civil suits, brought strategically to prevent public protest, are often called SLAPP suits (Strategic Lawsuit Against Public Participation).

Two cases illustrate the application of the competing rights paradigm in the civil law context. The first continues the theme of Occupy protests, this time in Vancouver. The second is illustrated by non-Aboriginal protestors at Sharbot Lake, who were protesting uranium exploration on Crown land near their residences and the failure of the Crown and Frontenac Ventures Corporation, a mining company, to fulfill their legal obligation to consult with local First Nations in regard to their exploration activities.

a) *Vancouver (City) v O'Flynn-Magee* — The Occupy Vancouver Protest

In *Vancouver (City) v O'Flynn-Magee*,[35] we observe an indirect application of the competing rights paradigm. The case involved the issuing of an injunction against protestors to require them to remove the structures they had built on occupied lands. As we will see, the test for issuing an injunction to enforce a law presumes that once the city has demonstrated breach of a law, unless there are strong countervailing factors, the injunction should issue. This presumption is based on the presupposition that the protestors' rights to free speech and association (not to mention their right to housing, to adequate financial security, and other rights that motivated the protest) are outweighed by the public interest in state regulation of public space, barring exceptional circumstances. The courts assume that in passing by-laws about the use of public space, public officials have already balanced the interests of various sectors of the public, and so there is little balancing for them to do. This approach is an indirect application of the competing rights paradigm — the court proceeds on the basis that lawmakers are best situated to balance competing rights, and it does not question whether the balance itself violates constitutional norms.[36]

The judge in this case, the Associate Chief Justice of the BC Supreme Court, was uncertain about the appropriate legal test to apply in assessing the

35 2011 BCSC 1647 [*Vancouver v O'Flynn-Magee*].

36 One might argue, as the judge did in *Vancouver v O'Flynn-Magee*, *ibid*, that it is up to the parties to challenge the constitutionality of laws if they disagree with the constitutionality of the balance these laws strike between competing rights. This overlooks the fact that the law for issuing injunctions may itself violate the Constitution. In the administrative law context, the Supreme Court of Canada has acknowledged that an administrative decision making process ought to take into account *Charter* values (*Doré v Barreau du Québec*, 2012 SCC 12). Likewise, I believe that the process used by judges to render their decisions can be more or less supportive of democracy, a fundamental value underlying not only our written Constitution but our unwritten common law constitution (on the norms informing this common law constitution, see David Dyzenhaus, "The Deep Structure of *Roncarelli v Duplessis*" (2004) 53 UNBLJ 111).

suitability of an injunction. An injunction can be an equitable remedy, in which case the test across Canada is contained in the case *RJR-MacDonald Inc v Canada (AG)*.[37] Alternatively, it can be a statutory remedy, used when the State seeks to enforce its laws. In the latter case, the British Columbia precedent is *Maple Ridge (District) v Thornhill Aggregates Ltd*.[38] The test for the statutory remedy is relatively straightforward. First, it places the onus on the public authority to demonstrate a breach of legislation. Once this has been demonstrated, the injunction will be issued unless there are exceptional circumstances, which can include

> . . . the willingness of the defendants to refrain from the unlawful act, the fact there may not be a clear case of "flouting" the law because the defendant has ceased the primary unlawful activity, or the absence of proof that the activity carried on was related to the mischief the statute was designed to address.[39]

In contrast, the test for the equitable remedy has three steps:

> First, a preliminary assessment must be made of the merits of the case to ensure that there is a serious question to be tried. Secondly, it must be determined whether the applicant would suffer irreparable harm if the application were refused. Finally, an assessment must be made as to which of the parties would suffer greater harm from the granting or refusal of the remedy pending a decision on the merits.[40]

It is easier for the State to obtain the statutory remedy because it is presumed that the State, in enforcing its laws, is acting in the public interest. In consequence, when seeking a statutory remedy, there is no need for the court to consider the balance of convenience or the existence of irreparable harm as is the case with the equitable remedy.[41] Justice MacKenzie concluded that in the case of the Occupy Vancouver protestors, it was not necessary to decide on the appropriate test; regardless of which was applied, she found that an injunction should be ordered.

---

37 [1994] 1 SCR 311 [*RJR-MacDonald*].

38 (1998), 162 DLR (4th) 203 (BCCA) [*Maple Ridge*]. A similar case in Ontario is *Newcastle Recycling Limited v Clarington (Municipality)* (2005), 204 OAC 389 at para 32.

39 *Vancouver v O'Flynn-Magee*, above note 35 at para 47, referring to *British Columbia (Minister of Environment, Lands & Parks) v Alpha Manufacturing Inc et al* (1997), 150 DLR (4th) 193 at para 32 (BCCA).

40 *RJR-MacDonald*, above note 37 at 334.

41 *Vancouver v O'Flynn-Magee*, above note 35 at paras 27–28.

The equitable remedy leaves more of the balancing to courts, which must determine if the city would suffer irreparable harm and balance this harm against the inconvenience to the protestors. The application of the competing rights paradigm is more overt in such a case than when a party seeks a statutory remedy. In either case, what is being placed in the balance are the rights of a minority — the protestors — and the rights of the majority, as expressed by the public interest embodied in the city's bylaw.

As we can see, when the State applies for an equitable injunction or an injunction to enforce a statutory regime, balancing is involved. While this is not a balancing of competing constitutional rights and/or important public interests as occurs in the *Charter* context, courts nonetheless balance the protestors' interest in continuing the occupation to assert their constitutional rights against the rights and interests of the applicant seeking the injunction. It is thus a clear application of the competing rights paradigm. Moreover, it is a problematic application of that doctrine, as it overlooks the social significance of protest as part of a dialogical process of deliberative democracy.

b) *Frontenac Ventures Corporation v Ardoch Algonquin First Nation —* The Sharbot Lake Protests

In the previous cases, the interests of a public authority and private individuals are placed in the balance. However, sometimes the competing rights of two private parties are in competition, as is the case with the Sharbot Lake protests. In the cases that emerged from this protest, Frontenac Ventures Corporation (Frontenac), a mining exploration company, had obtained provincial permission to conduct mining exploration activities on Crown land near Sharbot Lake, just north of Kingston, Ontario. Two local First Nations groups, the Ardoch and the Shabot, which had historic land claims to this Crown land, objected to these activities. They combined with local non-Aboriginal environmental activists to conduct a protest at one of the exploration sites.

Frontenac began a civil suit against the Ardoch and Shabot, part of the Algonquin First Nation, seeking $77 million in damages. It then used this suit to bring an application for an interlocutory injunction to put an end to the protest. The Superior Court heard the application *ex parte*, as the Ardoch and Shabot refused to participate in the proceedings until the Crown had fully discharged its obligation to consult in good faith with them in regard to their land claim. Justice Thomson issued the order enjoining the protest, which was subsequently enforced by the Ontario Provincial Police and through contempt of court proceedings, as a result of which a number of local Aboriginal residents were sentenced to prison. The order took the form of what is called a "John Doe and Jane Doe" injunction, which applies to all unnamed parties found in violation of it.[42]

A John Doe and Jane Doe injunction is an equitable remedy. As we have seen, the appropriateness of such a remedy depends in part on weighing the rights and interests of protestors against those of a private party such as a natural resource extraction company. While not directly a party, the State is not wholly irrelevant, as it is responsible for enforcing the injunction through sheriffs, local police forces, and contempt of court proceedings. Quasi-criminal penalties are also possible, including fines and imprisonment.[43] Moreover, in the case of natural resource extraction companies, the private party is benefitting from a public resource, be it plants, animals, minerals, and so on, to which it has been granted a right of extraction or exploitation by the State.[44] Thus, the State — representing the public interest — is also implicated in this way.

The balancing of competing rights and interests typical of the competing rights paradigm is evident in the Sharbot Lake case. Indeed, in overturning the prison sentences imposed on some of the Ardoch and Shabot, the Ontario Court of Appeal made it clear that courts are involved in balancing private interests against opposing private and public interests. It criticized the Superior Court for issuing the injunction *ex parte* without taking proper account of the Aboriginal rights of the Algonquin. Writing for the court, Laskin J stated:

> I am quick to point out that in this case, the AAFN [Ardoch Algonquin First Nation] did not appeal either the interim or the interlocutory injunctions granted by Thomson J. and Cunningham A.S.C.J.C. It is thus not for this court to address the merits of either order. However, I think it is important to give judicial guidance on the role to be played by the nuanced rule of law described in *Henco* when courts are asked to grant injunctions, the violation of which will result in aboriginal protestors facing civil or criminal contempt proceedings.
>
> Where a requested injunction is intended to create "a protest-free zone" for contentious private activity that affects asserted aboriginal or

---

42 For an overview of this kind of order and problems with it, see Julia Lawn, "The John Doe Injunction in Mass Protest Cases" (1998) 56:1 UT Fac L Rev 101.

43 Graham Mayeda, "Access to Justice: The Impact of Injunctions, Contempt of Court Proceedings, and Costs Awards on Environmental Protestors and First Nations" (2010) 6:2 JSDLP 143.

44 Chris Tollefson, "When the 'Public Interest' Loses: The Liability of Public Interest Litigants for Adverse Costs Awards" (1995) 29 UBC L Rev 303 at 316.

> treaty rights, the court must be very careful to ensure that, in the context of the dispute before it, the Crown has fully and faithfully discharged its duty to consult with the affected First Nations. The court must further be satisfied that every effort has been exhausted to obtain a negotiated or legislated solution to the dispute before it. Good faith on both sides is required in this process.[45]

This is a clear statement that courts issuing injunctions in such cases should be responsive to the competing rights at issue — in this case, Aboriginal rights protected under section 35 of the *Constitution Act, 1982*,[46] the public interest in developing its natural resources, and the private interest in exploiting them. Indeed, one of the criticisms brought against John and Jane Doe injunctions issued *ex parte* is that they do not properly allow the specific rights and interests of defendants to be represented in court for consideration by it when issuing the injunction.[47] Even in the case of a dispute between private parties, courts frame the issue using the competing rights paradigm.

D. THE SOCIAL RIGHTS PARADIGM — TRANSFORMATIVE CONSTITUTIONALISM AND DELIBERATIVE DEMOCRACY

I wish to contrast the traditional competing rights model used in the cases discussed in the previous section with the social rights approach. The social rights paradigm is often construed narrowly to refer to an expansion of human rights from civil and political rights such as the right to freedom of expression and assembly to include socio-economic rights such as the right to an adequate standard of living, to housing, to access to adequate health care, and the right to education, among others. However, a broader interpretation of social rights sees the whole panoply of human rights as essential elements in the pursuit of a healthy and inclusive society — what I have called a healthy "social fabric."

A very comprehensive consideration of the principled justification of a social rights approach has been undertaken by Sandra Liebenberg.[48] She

45 *Frontenac Ventures Corporation v Ardoch Algonquin First Nation*, 2008 ONCA 534 at paras 47–48 [citations removed].

46 Being Schedule B to the *Canada Act 1982* (UK), 1982, c 11.

47 For these criticisms, see Lawn, above note 42 at 124–25.

48 Sandra Liebenberg, *Socio-economic Rights: Adjudication under a Transformative Constitution* (Claremont: Juta, 2010). For other articulations, see David Robertson, "Thick Constitutional Readings: When Classic Distinctions Are Irrelevant" (2007) 35 Ga J Int'l & Comp L 277; Dikgang Moseneke, "The Fourth Bram Fischer Memorial

locates the social rights movement within an approach to constitutional rights that she identifies as "transformative constitutionalism,"[49] and which is based on the jurisprudence of the Constitutional Court of South Africa.[50] In her view, the underlying norms of this approach are dictated by the need to ensure the full participation of all members of a society in the process of transforming it. These norms can be identified with a broad conception of human rights, which includes socio-economic rights. These rights, she asserts, are essential for ensuring that everyone has a voice in the articulation of social goals and the way to achieve them.

In addition to identifying the rights that must be in place in order for everyone to have access to the democratic deliberation regarding the process of social transformation, Liebenberg identifies a procedure for judgment that legal actors — especially judges — must employ in order to ensure that legal norms reflect the constantly changing composition of society and its evolving goals. In Liebenberg's words, legal reasoning must reflect the fact that the law is an "open-ended process of ongoing dialogue and contestation in the quest for a more just society."[51] To do so, legal rights must be

---

Lecture: Transformative Adjudication" (2002) 18 SAJHR 309; Heinz Klug, "Five Years On: How Relevant Is the Constitution to the New South Africa?" (2001–2002) 26 Vt L Rev 803; Cathi Albertyn & Beth Goldblatt, "Facing the Challenge of Transformation: Difficulties in the Development of an Indigenous Jurisprudence of Equality" (1998) 14 SAJHR 248.

49 This idea is articulated in the work of Karl Klare, who describes transformative constitutionalism as follows:

> [Transformative constitutionalism is a] long-term project of constitutional enactment, interpretation and enforcement committed (not in isolation, of course, but in a historical context of conducive political developments) to transforming a country's political and social institutions and power relationships in a democratic, participatory, and egalitarian direction. Transformative constitutionalism connotes an enterprise of inducing large-scale social change through nonviolent political processes grounded in law.

Karl Klare, "Legal Culture and Transformative Constitutionalism" (1998) 14 SAJHR 146 at 150.

50 For example, in *S v Makwanyane*, [1995] ZACC 3 at para 262; *Du Plessis v De Klerk*, [1996] ZACC 10 at para 157; *Bato Star Fishing (Pty) Ltd v Minister of Environmental Affairs and Tourism*, [2004] ZACC 15 at paras 73–74; *Minister of Finance v Van Heerden*, [2004] ZACC 3 at para 142; *City of Johannesburg v Rand Properties (Pty) Ltd*, [2006] (6) BCLR 728 (W) at paras 51–52; *Rates Action Group v City of Cape Town*, [2004] (12) BCLR 1328 (C) at para 100; *Treatment Action Campaign (TAC) v Minister of Health*, [2002] (4) BCLR 356 (T); *Government of the Republic of South Africa v Grootboom*, [2000] (11) BCLR 1169 (CC). Many of these are cited in Liebenberg, above note 48 at 25.

51 Liebenberg, *ibid* at 29.

interpreted differently than in the traditional competing rights approach. First, these rights are not static — through democratic deliberation, society is constantly interpreting and reinterpreting them to reflect current social conditions. Second, the process of giving meaning to legal rights is responsive both to the context in which social conflict arises and to the identity of those in conflict.[52] In other words, legal rights are truly social rights — rights defined in and through a dynamic process of social change and social locatedness.

To reflect this concept of legal rights, the process of legal reasoning must be reconceived. Legal reasoning and legal judgment must be seen as part of the process of transformative constitutionalism — i.e., part of a deliberative democratic process.[53] As such, legal judgment must be open to and permeated by the broader democratic deliberation that exists in a healthy democratic society.

This process of deliberation reflects the complexity and diversity of the social fabric. There are no readily identifiable universal social goals. Instead, as Iris Marion Young points out, democratic deliberation must reflect the differences redolent in society. Liebenberg relies on Young's view, which she explains as follows:

> Young points out that an emphasis on reasoned, dispassionate deliberation, and the assumption of a unity of ends, values and interests among participants, particularly under circumstances of social inequality, "sometimes excludes the expression of some needs, interests, and suffering of injustice, because these cannot be voiced within the operative premises and frameworks" (Young, *Inclusion and Democracy*, 37). She thus argues for a model of deliberative democracy which does not assume, or even aim at, a commonality of ends or interests, but seeks the more modest goal of reaching "situation-specific agreements" which are always "provisional and renewable" (ibid 43).[54]

From this perspective, courts must reflect the complex patterns of the social fabric by being responsive to the various sources of marginalization in society. As such they must adopt an "open-textured" approach to inter-

---

52 *Ibid* at 47–48.

53 On the compatibility of social rights with democracy, see Malcolm Langford, "The Justiciability of Social Rights: From Practice to Theory" in Malcolm Langford, ed, *Social Rights Jurisprudence: Emerging Trends in International and Comparative Law* (Cambridge: Cambridge University Press, 2008) 3 at 32–33.

54 Liebenberg, above note 48 at 31, n 37.

preting rights that is receptive to social inequality.[55] Liebenberg identifies the role of the court as follows:

> First, it (*sic*) can provide a forum where the impact of legislation and policies on the lives of the poor receives serious and reasoned consideration in the light of the values and commitments of the Constitution. Second, it can facilitate meaningful participation by civil society and communities in the formulation and implementation of social programmes by requiring such participation as a component of the relevant rights, and by requiring transparency in the formulation of social policies and programmes. Third, it can develop the normative basis of those parts of our legal system that regulate traditionally private relations in ways that protect and facilitate poor people's access to socio-economic resources. Finally, it can prod our polity as a whole to be more responsive to systemic socio-economic inequalities and deprivations.[56]

What can litigants hope for from courts? According to Liebenberg, they can expect remedies that will align legal norms with the concrete reality of their lived experience: "The significance of the courts' remedial jurisdiction is that successful litigants can expect some concrete measures aimed at aligning social realities with constitutional rights and values."[57]

The social rights approach as articulated by Liebenberg identifies legal conflicts as contributing to an ongoing process of articulating social norms through democratic deliberation. A constitution provides certain basic rights, but to take advantage of these rights, the full panoply of socio-economic rights must be recognized and realized as the preconditions of meaningful participation in transformative democratic deliberation.

1) Applying the Social Rights Paradigm to Social Protest

The social rights approach can be extremely useful in reimagining the law's response to social action. However, I suggest that Liebenberg's articulation of the social rights paradigm within the context of transformative

---

55 Liebenberg, *ibid* at 34, explains the importance of this "open-textured approach":

> The interpretation of open-textured human rights norms provides particular scope for developing interpretations of rights which are as responsive as possible to the disjuncture between lived experiences of poverty and deep power imbalances and the constitutional ideal of social justice.

56 *Ibid* at 37–38.

57 *Ibid* at 66.

constitutionalism must be adapted in order to apply to a different form for democratic deliberation — social protest.

According to the competing rights model, social conflict is conceived as a conflict between individual rights holders (or holders of group rights), and it can be resolved through a dialogue between rights holders, which often takes the form of a balancing of competing rights and interests. According to the social rights model, on the other hand, the law should contextualize conflicts and not be bound by formalistic interpretation of rights. Moreover, the law must facilitate full participation in society by guaranteeing and actualizing a full range of socio-economic rights.[58] To achieve this goal, rights must be interpreted to recognize the social reality of the marginalized, which is constantly changing, and legal remedies should be aimed at aligning these realities with an interpretation of constitutional norms based on the inclusion of previously marginalized voices in the process of deliberative democracy.

For the social rights approach to be useful in creating the legal norms and institutions for dealing with social protest, it must recognize what the social phenomenon of a protest is. In Section B, I examined the sociological and political role of social protest as an expression of democratic dialogue. This concept of social protest was in turn analyzed as a *social phenomenon* in order to understand its underlying normative content, which in turn can inform the framework of legal norms that should apply to structure it.

A truly social approach to law must integrate the social fully — i.e., acknowledge that the social is a dimension of our experience of togetherness with others. This experience demands that we take responsibility for the suffering of others, seek to understand this suffering in the context in which it arises, and evaluate it in social context. When making a decision about how to react to the situation, a social rights approach should demand that we act in a way that is responsive to the experience of the other and to all those who are in similar situations. Liebenberg has admirably articulated the role of courts in resolving conflicts of rights when participants in the conflict have chosen the courts as their deliberative democratic forum. However, to understand how the law should deal with social protest, in which participants have chosen a different public forum than the courts, one must integrate what social protest expresses more deeply into the social rights approach. As I have explained, social protest expresses a tear in

58 For a good overview of the role of social rights as tools for challenging "structural disadvantage and social exclusion," see Martha Jackman & Bruce Porter, "International Human Rights and Strategies to Address Homelessness and Poverty in Canada: Making the Connection" at 4, online: CURA http://socialrightscura.ca.

the social fabric, and the normative response is a recognition of the need to take responsibility for this tear.

To truly take responsibility for what is expressed in social protest, we must use our social experience as the touchstone of our acts. Because experience is necessarily circumstantial and situational, just outcomes cannot be determined beforehand by a legal principle alone. Instead, a social rights approach to social protest must take into account the situational factors that have brought about the dissatisfaction expressed in the protest, consider the probable effects of a proposed solution on all those likely to be affected by it, and choose a solution that can be justified to those affected based on the circumstances observed.

2) A New Social Rights Approach to the Law of Social Protest

I have articulated from a theoretical perspective what the social phenomenon of protest represents and how a phenomenological approach can enrich Liebenberg's social rights approach by enabling it to respond to this phenomenon. I now wish to turn to the concrete ways in which the social rights paradigm will change the practice of law. In doing so, I hope to reflect the benefits of the phenomenological approach to social rights.

In the previous section and in Section B, I explained that a phenomenological approach to social rights recognizes the way that we experience others in society. Most of us immediately jump from news about the marginalization or oppression of others into pre-determined assessments of whether these claims are right or wrong. Indeed, this is the approach on which the competing rights model is based — the presumption of an opposition between competing claims and the presumption of a need to accept one side and reject the other. When we examine media reports, public protest often elicits this kind of polarizing response.

However, underlying these ideological responses are other experiences that are more fundamental. When we witness public protest first- or second-hand, we immediately understand that what is being expressed is dissatisfaction with social conditions. We might have different views about whether this dissatisfaction is warranted. We might have different views about its source. But we all experience the expression of dissatisfaction. In my interpretation of the social rights approach to law, one must begin with what is communicated by social phenomena such as public protest. Such an approach resists immediately jumping to an assessment of whether those communicating are right or wrong. It delays judgment in an effort to give voice to what is being expressed. It facilitates transmission of expressions of marginalization and oppression into a system of democratic deliberation. It is for this reason that those advocating social rights promote access to justice, as access to the legal system is a major conduit for ideas to enter into the public forum. It is also for this reason that the conduct of justice must treat all with equal respect, even if this requires differential treatment. Only in this way can those who are expressing marginalization and oppression be truly given the voice they need to give their input and allow a public discussion about the merits of their claims.

a) How to Balance Rights and Interests within the Social Rights Paradigm

In practice, a social rights approach in law requires a shift away from the traditional competing rights approach, instead adopting a contextualized process of decision making that recognizes the social function of conflict that openly acknowledges competing positions as part of an integrated process of democratic decision making. Courts should try as much as possible to understand rights-based challenges as contributions to improving and creating a just society, rather than as claims that are opposed to State and public interests. Rights-based challenges are part of the democratic process of ensuring the legitimacy of the law; they are not necessarily corrosive to the public interest.

In regard to the constitutional evaluation of the enforcement of bylaws to suppress free speech, as occurred in the *Batty* case, the approach to social rights that I have articulated recommends a different approach from that taken by the trial judge. The potential contribution of social protest to democratic decision making must be taken seriously. In consequence, when applying the *Oakes* test to establish whether the rights-infringing law is justifiable in a free and democratic society, the search for a pressing and substantial objective must involve a probing inquiry. In the *Batty* case, the court found that the objective of the City of Toronto in passing its bylaws was to "enabl[e] all to share a common resource and ensur[e] that the uses of the parks will have a minimal adverse impact on the quiet enjoyment of surrounding residential lands." This goal was found to be pressing and substantial. In my view, it should be a rare case in which a State interest such as this will be considered pressing and substantial enough to warrant overriding a constitutional right in a situation such as a public protest that not only expresses a social injustice but contributes to the democratic debate about government and private sector policies.[59]

---

59 For an elaboration of this view, see Mayeda, "Between Principle and Pragmatism," above note 1.

b) A New Approach to Judgment: Sensitivity to Context and a Principled Approach

Courts should take an approach to adjudication that is more sensitive to the context in which a dispute arises and that is more responsive to those affected by the judgment. To do so, they may have to alter some legal rules. For instance, the rules of evidence must facilitate rather than hinder the introduction of social science evidence and other kinds of evidence that illustrate the social context in which a decision is to be rendered.[60] Courts have already greatly expanded the role of social context evidence in adjudication, so further developments in this regard are not radical.

As well, judges may need to adopt a different approach to judgment. The role of the judge will be less formalistic, instead requiring the judge to place herself in the position of those who will be affected by her decision in order to render a just decision.[61] Moreover, reasons for judgment will have to be based on principle rather than formalism, meaning that they will have to be responsive to the arguments that parties and those affected by the judgment would consider reasonable and coherent.[62]

c) Adapting the Civil Law of Injunctions and Contempt of Court to Reflect a Social Justice Approach

In addition to changes in the rules of evidence and a more principled and context-sensitive approach to judgment, there must also be changes in the way that the legal system deploys State-sponsored force. I will not address this in the context of the criminal law response to social protest, but instead return to the issue of civil law approaches to resolving disputes arising from social protest. The legal framework for social protest should have the following characteristics:

1) Take protests seriously as part of the democratic process and create public mechanisms that foster and promote them as important contributions to the democratic process
2) Adopt laws that enhance democratic process by
   a) creating a legislative framework for negotiating responses to social protest;
   b) modifying the law of injunctions to discourage SLAPP suits and limit John/Jane Doe injunctions; and

---

60 See Graham Mayeda, "Taking Notice of Equality: Judicial Notice and Expert Evidence in Trials Involving Equality-Seeking Groups" (2009) 6:2 JL & Equality 201.

61 Mayeda, "Uncommonly Common," above note 1.

62 Mayeda, "Between Principle and Pragmatism," above note 1.

c) changing the law of contempt of court, which is an outdated remedy in the context of public protest

A social rights approach to social protest would include *democratic* methods for determining whether certain uses of public space are in the public interest. At the very least, there should be some formalized way for the public to meaningfully influence the State's decisions to enforce bylaws that restrict public protest. Perhaps an ombudsperson would be useful as an intermediary between protestors and the State. Maybe certain public spaces can be arranged to facilitate peaceful public protest rather than to hamper it. At any rate, more creative legislative schemes are possible that facilitate dialogue and negotiations between the State and the public seeking to use a public space for democratic purposes. We must recognize that public protest is evidence of a dynamic and engaged public.

Injunctions are an unwieldy tool for brokering democratic deliberation, as their enforcement necessarily involves the use of State force or the threat of it. A different approach could be taken. Perhaps courts should be able to require the State to devote resources to mediating disputes, working together with protestors to find meaningful solutions to ongoing problems. Anti-SLAPP suit legislation — legislation that would prevent the strategic use of litigation by private and public bodies to prevent democratic public protest — would also be useful in order to prevent private interests from seeking injunctions that quell public democratic deliberation for private ends. The existence of such legislation would give protestors some comfort that when they arrive in court, they have a legal basis for challenging the legitimacy of lawsuits begun against them.

Courts can also play a role in fostering a social rights approach by modifying the law of injunctions and contempt of court in order to adapt it to the modern realities of democratic public protest. Some appellate courts are already supportive of such a move, as demonstrated by their criticism of and hesitation in applying the law on injunctions in cases of public protest.

For instance, in *R v Bridges*,[63] Southin J of the British Columbia Court of Appeal points out that it may be inappropriate to apply the law of injunctions, developed in the context of labour disputes in a time when courts were decidedly anti-union, to modern social protests, which are increasingly recognized today as an important contribution to the democratic process. She says of the order issued by the lower court in *Bridges*:

> It is obvious to me that the terms of this order were taken from precedents developed during the course of labour disputes. There is much to be

63 *R v Bridges* (1990), 78 DLR (4th) 529 at 541–42 (BCCA) [*Bridges*].

> said for the proposition that such precedents should be put permanently away and the court should give, in these cases where the citizens take to the streets and an injunction is sought, a fresh consideration to the extent to which the court should go. That consideration should, in every case, depend on the precise nature of the dispute, the precise conduct in issue and so on.[64]

This contextual approach to equitable remedies such as injunctions is supported by *dicta* from the Supreme Court of Canada. In *Pro Swing Inc v Elta Golf Inc*,[65] Deschamps J, writing for the majority, emphasized that equitable remedies must be adapted to social realities.[66]

The overall approach to equitable remedies must be flexible and responsive to context. It is for this reason that I think that the *RJR-MacDonald* test for equitable injunctions applied in the *Vancouver v O'Flynn-Magee* case is not well suited to the context of most public protest. In particular, it does not take into account the role of public protest in democratic debate, and more specifically, it does not require the court issuing the injunction to consider whether the parties have sought to negotiate a solution that respects the contribution of the protest to democracy. There are precedents for such a contextual approach in cases dealing with protests by Canada's Indigenous peoples. These cases require courts to take a contextual approach to the rule of law and to ensure that the government is respecting its constitutional obligation to consult Indigenous people in good faith.[67] I suggest that a similar approach should be taken in all public protests — the State should be required to negotiate with protestors to find a solution that enhances democratic participation and takes into account other interests engaged by the protest such as access to public space. Indeed, the requirement of consultation in Aboriginal law may be a good model for public protests generally. On this approach, governments would be obliged to consult with protestors, accommodate them where they are contributing to the public good, and implement the outcome of these consultations. The fulfillment of this duty to consult would in turn be an important element in the assessment of whether an equitable injunction ought to be issued to stop the protest.

Some changes could also be made to the rules on injunctions when the latter are used to enforce bylaws. As discussed above, the presumption

---

64 *Ibid* at 542.

65 2006 SCC 52.

66 *Ibid* at para 22.

67 *Ibid* at paras 140–42.

of the courts is that lawmakers have already balanced competing interests when creating bylaws for access to public spaces. This overlooks the iterative nature of democratic dialogue. As Seyla Benhabib has explained in many of her writings, democratic participation involves constantly revisiting norms as society and social context change.[68] A law is made that is thought to cover all relevant contingencies, but then a situation arises that was not foreseen or not adequately debated, and views differ about how to apply the law to that situation.

To apply this idea in context, while it might be true that municipal councils have considered many of the competing interests in establishing bylaws relating to public spaces, emerging circumstances such as the Occupy protests may not have been considered — or may not have been adequately considered, with full consultation of affected parties. In recognition of the fact that a public protest might be a democratic iteration — a demand for democratic discussion about the application of a law in an emergent social context — courts should not automatically grant injunctions to enforce bylaws in cases of social protest. In consequence, the presumption that exists in cases such as *Maple Ridge*[69] that an injunction should be granted absent exigent circumstances should be re-examined by courts in cases of legitimate public protest.

E. CONCLUSION — RECONCILING DOG WALKERS AND PROTESTORS BY MEANS OF THE SOCIAL RIGHTS PARADIGM

Public protest is not anti-social behaviour. It is not aimed at preventing dog owners from enjoying parks. Rather, it is an important social phenomenon by means of which individuals and groups seek a response to social harms such as marginalization and exclusion. An application of the phenomenological approach to social rights that I have articulated can help us to recognize this and give this recognition legal effect. Indeed, the recognition is inherent in our very social existence. When we read about public protests, watch recordings of protestors' activities, and listen to reports of their doings, our natural response is one of unease. This unease is a sort of responsibility — we understand that the actions of our fellow community members

68 Benhabib defines democratic iterations as "linguistic, legal, cultural, and political repetitions-in-transformation, invocations that are also revocations. They not only change established understandings but also transform what passes as the valid or established view of an authoritative precedent" (Seyla Benhabib, *Another Cosmopolitanism* (Oxford: Oxford University Press, 2006) at 48).

69 *Maple Ridge*, above note 38.

are asking us to respond to what they are expressing. Naturally, each one of us, based on his or her past experiences and tendencies, will wish to respond in different ways — anger and resentment, anger and sympathy, and so on. Each of us will assess the legitimacy of the claim that protestors make. But none of us ignores what is being expressed.

A legal system that is true to the nature of our social existence would facilitate peaceful public protest because it is part of the process of democratic deliberation and decision making. A social rights approach must not exclude protestors or cast them in opposition to the rest of the public. To do so would be to fail to acknowledge the claim others are making against the justice of our social order. Rather, a social rights approach to law must be inclusive — it should seek to promote democratic input and present it to the public to assess as a means of testing the legitimacy of the existing order. Such a legal system requires legal norms and institutions that adequately distribute justice — i.e., institutions that ensure access to legal means of dispute resolution and the process of lawmaking. It also requires substantive justice — the law must recognize the substantive claims to exclusion being brought to light by protestors and create legal mechanisms for taking responsibility for them rather than creating legally justifiable excuses for ignoring our responsibilities. In other words, the law must be just in the sense of responsive to claims of need of all kinds.

The returns of a social rights approach to the law of social protest would be real. The competing rights paradigm that seeks to place different social groups or individuals in opposition to each other can be exchanged for a paradigm that gives voice to both sides, calls on lawmakers and judges to place themselves in the positions of all the parties when making law or enforcing it, and requires these decision makers to render their decisions in language that is responsive to all parties, even if it must ultimately vindicate one against another. With an eye to practice, I have explained how the proportionality analysis conducted under section 1 of the *Charter* can be modified when dealing with public protest in the constitutional context. I have also explored ways in which civil law rules such as the law of injunctions and contempt of court can be changed to channel public protest — an important democratic process — into the broader process of public deliberation that involves both lawmakers and courts.

The social rights approach to law may well give the appearance of a less stable society. But in essence, it recognizes the transformative role of public protest in a democratic state. In the long run, by acknowledging marginalization and oppression and confronting it head on, the social rights approach will help us all to understand each other better and encourage us to engage in the iterative processes of a democratic society. By renewing faith in democracy, we can avoid the divisive approaches that have become so common in our political culture and that are exacerbated by our legal culture.

CHAPTER 14

SLEEPING ROUGH AND SHOOTING UP

TAKING BRITISH COLUMBIA'S URBAN JUSTICE ISSUES TO COURT[*]

MARGOT YOUNG[†]

A. INTRODUCTION

Canada sits in a different spot than thirty years ago when the *Canadian Charter of Rights and Freedoms*[1] was proclaimed amid grand hopes for a society marked by the key liberal values enshrined in that document. Today, Canadians are no longer a people with appropriate confidence in a "kinder, gentler" national soul. Poverty is more than ever a critical issue,[2] highlighting desperation and deprivation surrounded by privilege and excess.[3]

---

* Thanks are due to Kenda Shupe, Ted Murray, Brad Por, Kate Mulherin, and Alexander Makoff for research assistance. Martha Jackman and Bruce Porter proved patient editors. Funding assistance was provided by SSHRC and by the UBC Peter Wall Solutions Initiative.

† Professor, Faculty of Law, University of British Columbia and Research Partner in the SSHRC-CURA Project, "Reconceiving Human Rights Practice," online: www.socialrightscura.ca.

1 Part I of the *Constitution Act, 1982*, being Schedule B to the *Canada Act 1982* (UK), 1982, c 11 [*Charter*].

2 In 2010, three million people, about 9 percent of Canadians, were below the after-tax Low Income Cut-Off — Canada's unofficial low income measurement. Included in this figure are 546,000 children. Statistics Canada, "Incomes of Canadians, 2010" at 1, online: The Daily www.statcan.gc.ca.

3 For example, food security is a real issue across Canada, and particularly for Indigenous peoples. The United Nations Special Rapporteur on the Right to Food made the following statement in May 2012: "A growing number of people across Canada remain unable to meet their basic food needs. In 2007/2008, approximately 7.7 per cent of

Homelessness has emerged as a seemingly intractable urban blight.[4] Our nation ranks as one of the more unequal among Western countries.[5] This inequality grows and the chasm between the "haves" and the "have-nots" yawns, increasingly evident in indicators of social dysfunction, injustice, and anomie.[6] The triumph of neo-liberalism, and its attendant vision of the sturdy, calculating individual, ground many of these developments. Theorists chart both the "hollowing out" and, then, the "filling in" of the State as part of neo-liberal policies.[7] The role of government is both reduced and expanded to serve the "rational, entrepreneurial, economic individual."[8] The idea of "social" citizenship is eviscerated: social issues are viewed as essentially economic problems, and the economic order reaches to include all human activities within its logic. The State is no longer offered by our political elite as a resource for social justice and a facilitator of substantive equality and freedoms. The citizen stands alone, free to succeed or fail on his own.

---

households in Canada reported experiencing moderate or severe food insecurity. Approximately 1.92 million people in Canada, aged 12 or older, lived in food insecure households in 2007/2008 and a staggering 1 in 10 families, 10.8 per cent, with at least one child under the age of six were food insecure during the same period." Olivier De Schutter, Special Rapporteur on the Right to Food, "Visit to Canada from 6 to 16 May 2012 — End-of-Mission Statement," online: Office of the High Commissioner for Human Rights www.ohchr.org.

4 A 2007 report issued by the then United Nations Special Rapporteur on Adequate Housing, Miloon Kothari, stated, "The Special Rapporteur remains concerned about the significant number of homeless in all parts of the country . . . . It has been stated that the widespread and rapid growth of homelessness in Canada since the mid-1990s is unprecedented since World War II." Human Rights Council, *Promotion and Protection of all Human Rights, Civil, Political, Economic, Social and Cultural Rights, Including the Right to Development: Report of the Special Rapporteur on Adequate Housing as a Component of the Right to an Adequate Standard of Living, and on the Right to Non-discrimination in This Context, Miloon Kothari*, UNGAOR, 10th sess, UN Doc A/HRC/10/7/Add.3, (2009) at paras 53–54.

5 Armine Yalnizyan, *The Rise of Canada's Richest 1%* (Ottawa: Canadian Centre for Policy Alternatives, 2010), online: Canadian Centre for Policy Alternatives www.policyalternatives.ca; "Canadian Income Inequality: Is Canada Becoming More Unequal?," online: Conference Board of Canada www.conferenceboard.ca.

6 See, for example, Richard G Wilkinson & Kate Pickett, *The Spirit Level: Why More Equal Societies Almost Always Do Better* (London: Allen Lane, 2009).

7 Luke Desforges, Rhys Jones, & Mike Woods, "New Geographies of Citizenship" (2005) 9:5 Citizenship Studies 439 at 440.

8 Leslie Kern, *Sex and the Revitalized City: Gender, Condominium Development, and Urban Citizenship* (Vancouver: UBC Press, 2010) at 6.

Yet, against this backdrop and, in fact, because of it, collective social and political resistance surges. This is despite funding cuts and political disparagement of civil society organization and voice. The *Charter* has been the focus of much of this activism, with particular attention paid to sections 15 and 7 of the *Charter*. As things have worsened, as governments have backtracked on social responsibilities and promises, the courts have been used in the attempt to soften or moderate this harsher Canada.

British Columbia is no stranger to such *Charter* cases. Indeed, some of the most notable *Charter* cases of the past thirty years have their origin in British Columbia.[9] This is no wonder: British Columbia is a province in which the major social justice challenges of Canada are clearly apparent — particularly in that province's two major cities. Both Vancouver and Victoria are marked by disparities of income and wealth, issues of inadequate and unaffordable housing, the impact of colonization on Indigenous peoples, and the presence of ill-health, poverty, homelessness, and marginalization in a country of tremendous affluence. These cities have active communities of civil society groups strategizing about how to make use of the Constitution to achieve social justice.

This piece takes up two relatively recent cases shaping the current constitutional social justice landscape in British Columbia. One of these cases — *Victoria (City) v Adams*[10] — sits stopped at the level of the Court of Appeal.[11] The other — *PHS Community Services Society v Canada (AG) (Insite)*[12] — concluded with a judgment from the Supreme Court of Canada. This chapter makes a familiar observation: the cases of *Adams* and *Insite* highlight and reinforce the importance of context to effective *Charter* analysis. However, my argument has a twist: it urges a larger and spatially situated context for these cases. I emphasize the importance of both the urban context of many modern social justice struggles and the acknowledgement that rights have spatial dimension and influence.

---

9 *Andrews v Law Society of British Columbia*, [1989] 1 SCR 143; *Eldridge v British Columbia (AG)*, [1997] 3 SCR 624; *Auton (Guardian ad litem of) v British Columbia (AG)*, 2004 SCC 78; *Rodriguez v British Columbia (AG)*, [1993] 3 SCR 519; *Withler v Canada (AG)*, 2011 SCC 12.

10 *Victoria (City) v Adams*, 2009 BCCA 563 [*Adams* (BCCA)], on appeal from *Victoria (City) v Adams*, 2008 BCSC 1363 [*Adams* (BCSC)].

11 The Court of Appeal decision was not appealed.

12 *Canada (AG) v PHS Community Services Society*, 2011 SCC 44 [*Insite* (SCC)], on appeal from *PHS Community Services Society v Canada (AG)*, 2010 BCCA 15 [*Insite* (BCCA)], on appeal from *PHS Community Services Society v Attorney General of Canada*, 2008 BCSC 661 [*Insite* (BCSC)].

Contextualization of the claimants' circumstances is a key prerequisite to recognition of social justice claims in *Charter* litigation. At its fullest, contextualization allows revelation of the systemic factors central to shaping the course of individual opportunity and experience. Contextualization is necessary to capture the dense interpellation of social facts and relations, and the significance of this connection for comprehending the harm at issue. *Adams* and *Insite* make this clear. But, the clarion call to contextualization, a constant refrain from progressive scholars and activists, needs geographic enrichment.[13] By so elaborating, one can apprehend more fully the fundamental lessons of substantive equality and justice that must underpin every right in the Constitution.

B. THE CASES

The parallels between *Adams* and *Insite* are many and provocative. Both cases present a legal moment in a more complex social and political struggle over the rights and life chances of groups significantly marginalized and disadvantaged in Canadian society, generally, and in the urban life of the cities at issue, in particular. In this sense, then, both *Adams* and *Insite* are importantly part of larger, and longer, political strategies. The cases neither begin nor end political struggle, but are a piece and interact with other tactics, of different duration.

Argument in *Adams* and *Insite* raised constitutional issues around section 7 of the *Charter*. This section of the *Charter* sets out constitutional guarantees for the rights of life, liberty, and security of the person.[14] Similar argumentative structure was accepted in relation to this section in each of the cases by the courts. And, ultimately, in both cases, the rights claimants were successful — a noticeable departure from the usual fate of low-income claimants under our *Charter*.[15]

Of course, there are also differences between the cases. The *Insite* case pits levels of Canadian government against each other, engaging constitutional judgments about federalism as well as about individual rights. The

13 See, for example, Dianne Pothier, "But It's for Your Own Good" in Margot Young et al, eds, *Poverty: Rights, Social Citizenship, and Legal Activism* (Vancouver: UBC Press, 2007) 40 at 40–56; Martha Jackman, "Reality Checks: Presuming Innocence and Proving Guilt in *Charter* Welfare Cases" in Young et al, eds, *ibid*, 23 at 23–39.

14 Section 7 reads, "Everyone has the right to life, liberty and security of the person and the right not to be deprived thereof except in accordance with the principles of fundamental justice" (*Charter*, above note 1, s 7).

15 See, for example, *Gosselin v Québec (AG)*, 2002 SCC 84.

Adams case is structured more formally as a claim of individual rights, with no federalism issues involved. As well, *Insite* focuses on criminal law prohibitions, while the State action at issue in *Adams* is simply a municipal bylaw injunction. But the similarities, I argue, are stronger than these factual disparities. Both cases situate a very marginalized and dispossessed group in the urban environment in key relation to fundamental rights under the *Charter*.

1) *Victoria (City) v Adams*

Canada faces a homelessness crisis. The only member of the G8 without an ongoing national housing strategy,[16] Canada has more than a million people facing housing insecurity, with an estimated 150,000–200,000 homeless.[17] This is despite the fact that Canada has signed onto the United Nation's *International Covenant on Social, Economic and Culture Rights*, which recognizes the "right of everyone to an adequate standard of living . . . including adequate . . . housing."[18] In particular, British Columbia faces its

---

16 The federal House of Commons recently defeated on second reading Bill C-400, *An Act to Ensure Secure, Adequate, Accessible and Affordable Housing for Canadians*, 1st Sess, 41st Parl, 2012. This was the second private member's bill of the same name on this subject before the house. The first, Bill C-304, elapsed upon dissolution of the house for the 2011 election (*An Act to Ensure Secure, Adequate, Accessible and Affordable Housing for Canadians*, 2nd Sess, 40th Parl, 2009). The Centre for Equality Rights in Accommodation has an application before the Ontario Superior Court claiming that federal and provincial failures "to implement effective national and provincial strategies to reduce and eventually eliminate homelessness and inadequate housing" violate ss 7 and 15 of the *Charter* (*Tanudjaja et al v AG (Canada)*, Court File No CV-10-403688 (Ont SCJ) (Notice of Application, filed 26 May 2010), online: The Social Rights Advocacy Centre www.socialrights.ca).

17 Wellesley Institute, *Precarious Housing in Canada* (Toronto: Wellesley Institute, 2010) at 4, online: Wellesley Institute www.wellesleyinstitute.com; John Irwin, *Home Insecurity: The State of Social Housing Funding in BC* (Ottawa: Canadian Centre for Policy Alternatives, 2004) at 7, online: Canadian Centre for Policy Alternatives & Tenant's Rights Action Coalition www.policyalternatives.ca. See also Toba Bryant, "The Current State of Housing in Canada as a Social Determinant of Health" (2003) 24:3 Policy Options 52; Ontario Human Rights Commission, *Right at Home: Report on the Consultation on Human Rights and Rental Housing in Ontario* (Toronto: Ontario Human Rights Commission, 2008) at 7 [*Right at Home*].

18 *International Covenant on Economic, Social and Cultural Rights*, 16 December 1966, 993 UNTS 3, art 11.

own housing emergency, with provincial government neglect of the creation of new social housing stock.[19]

The *Adams* case involved a constitutional challenge under section 7 of the *Charter* to two City of Victoria bylaws: the *Parks Regulation Bylaw No 07-05*[20] and the *Streets and Traffic Bylaw No 92-84*.[21] These bylaws, at the time of the trial, prohibited taking up temporary abode in a public space.[22] In practice, this meant a ban on erecting any form of overhead protection while sleeping outside on public property, even on a temporary basis, at all times.[23] Thus, putting up tents, tarps, or even sheltering under cardboard boxes for only a few hours on public property while sleeping was forbidden.

The municipal bylaws at issue in *Adams* were an example of "roll-out neo-liberalism." This term is used to refer to "the purposeful construction and consolidation of neoliberalized state forms, modes of governance, and regulatory relations."[24] It captures the positive actions of neo-liberal governance that span the neo-liberal State, as opposed to privatization or "roll-back neo-liberalism."[25] Across the continent, cities have, as part of this new form of governance, proactively targeted the ways in which low-income or homeless people necessarily use public spaces. Protest response to these forms of municipal street legislation is also politically pointed and prevalent. Nick Blomley, a Canadian geographer, reminds us that the squatting at issue in *Adams* and in other situations is a form of "personal empowerment and democratization."[26]

The *Adams* case arose in October 2005 when the City of Victoria commenced an action to obtain a civil injunction to enforce these two bylaws in relation to a tent city consisting of seventy people and twenty tents in Victoria's Cridge Park. The defendants — nine of the homeless people living

---

19 Irwin, above note 17 at 7.

20 City of Victoria, Bylaw No 07-059, *Parks Regulation Bylaw*, ss 13(1) & (2), 14(1) & (2), and 16(1) [*Parks Regulation Bylaw*]. City of Victoria, Bylaw No 92-84, *Streets and Traffic Bylaw*, ss 73(1) and 74(1) [*Streets and Traffic Bylaw*].

21 *Streets and Traffic Bylaw*, *ibid*, ss 73(1) and 74(1).

22 In August 2007, the *Parks Regulation Bylaw* was amended by the city so that it "no longer prohibited 'loitering' in public parks" (*Adams* (BCSC), above note 10 at para 24). Prior to the hearing, at the defendants' request, the city clarified that the "operational policy of the Victoria Police" for enforcement of the bylaws allowed for sleeping in public in some circumstances but did not allow the use of any tents, tarps, boxes, or other structures (*ibid* at para 26).

23 *Ibid* at para 4.

24 Jamie Peck & Adam Tickell, "Neoliberalizing Space" (2002) 34:3 Antipode 380 at 384.

25 *Ibid* at 399.

26 Nicholas K Blomley, *Unsettling the City: Urban Land and the Politics of Property* (New York: Routledge, 2004) at 20.

in the tent city — opposed the application, raising the *Charter* in defence. After significant procedural and interim wrangling (including the city's attempt to have the action discontinued),[27] the case came to trial in June 2008.

The result at the trial level was a finding that the bylaws at issue "to the extent to which they prohibit the erection of overhead protection"[28] were contrary to section 7 and not justifiable under section 1 of the *Charter*. The court issued a declaration of invalidity, stating that the bylaws "are of no force and effect insofar as they apply to prevent homeless people from erecting temporary shelter."[29] Critical to this result was the framing of the issue as one about temporary, not permanent, shelter.

The provincial Supreme Court judgment was upheld, on appeal by the city, at the British Columbia Court of Appeal (BCCA). The Court of Appeal framed the issue at stake more narrowly:

> [W]hen homeless people are not prohibited from sleeping in public parks, and the number of homeless people exceeds the number of available shelter beds, does a bylaw that prohibits homeless people from erecting any form of temporary overhead shelter at night — including tents, tarps attached to trees, boxes or other structure — violate their constitutional rights to life, liberty and security of the person under s. 7 of the *Canadian Charter of Rights and Freedoms*?[30]

As this quote illustrates, the appeal judges linked the holding of unconstitutionality expressly to the factual finding that the number of homeless people exceeded the number of available shelter beds. Consequently, the Court of Appeal judgment elaborated, were there sufficient shelter places to accommodate the homeless population in Victoria, a blanket prohibition of overhead protection in public parks might be constitutional.[31] Similarly, constitutional acceptability might exist if there were "appropriate designated areas outside of parks to accommodate the homeless."[32]

The order that issued from the Court of Appeal reflected this more specific, narrower parsing:

---

27 For a description of this, see *Adams* (BCSC), above note 10 at paras 6–30.

28 *Ibid* at para 217.

29 *Ibid* at para 239.

30 *Adams* (BCCA), above note 10 at para 1.

31 *Ibid* at para 74.

32 *Ibid* at para 162. The Court of Appeal judgment also limits the legal finding to a smaller number of the provisions of only one of the two originally impugned bylaws, the *Parks Regulation Bylaw*. The court found that the other provisions and bylaw need not have been mentioned in the declaration.

> Sections 14(1)(d) and 16(1) of the *Parks Regulation Bylaw* No. 07-059 are inoperative insofar and only insofar as they apply to prevent homeless people from erecting temporary overnight shelter in parks when the number of homeless people exceeds the number of available shelter beds in the City of Victoria.[33]

This Court of Appeal conclusion rests on finding that the bylaw failed to meet the principles of fundamental justice referenced in section 7 because of overbreadth. Thus, the judges did not find that the provisions of the bylaw were generally void. Rather, the provisions were selectively void. Should shelter conditions change, the bylaw could survive constitutional scrutiny.[34] The result? Under certain conditions pertaining to availability (or lack) of alternative shelter, homeless residents of Victoria can erect temporary overnight shelter in public parks. In response, municipal bylaws have been amended to now allow overhead outdoor shelter between the stipulated hours of 7 p.m. and 7 a.m.[35] Anecdotal reports are that these time limits are strictly enforced by local police.[36]

---

33 *Adams* (BCCA), above note 10 at para 166.

34 James Hendry, "Section 7 and Social Justice" (2009) 27 NJCL 93 at 100.

35 The exception is during daylight saving time, and then the time limit is 8 p.m. and 7 a.m. The full text of the relevant section of the amendment to the bylaw stipulates:

> **Overnight Shelter**
>
> 16A (1) Sub-section (2) applies despite the general prohibitions under section 14(1)(d) and section 16(1) of this Bylaw.
>
> (2) A homeless person must not place, secure, erect, use, or maintain in place, in a park, a structure, improvement or overhead shelter, including a tent, lean-to, or other form of overhead shelter constructed from a tarpaulin, plastic, cardboard or other rigid or non-rigid material:
>
> (a) subject to sub-section (b), except between the hours of:
>
> (i) 7:00 o'clock p.m. of one day and 7:00 o'clock a.m. of the next day when Daylight Saving time is not in effect; and
>
> (ii) 8:00 o'clock p.m. of one day and 7:00 o'clock a.m. of the next day when Daylight Saving time is in effect,
>
> (b) at any time, in a playground, sports field, footpath, a road within a park, Bastion Square, environmentally sensitive area, or any area within a park that has been designated for an event or activity under a valid and subsisting permit issued under the authority of this Bylaw.

City of Victoria, Bylaw No 10-021, *Parks Regulation Bylaw, Amendment Bylaw (No 6)*, s 3.

36 In a subsequent case, *Johnston v Victoria (City)*, a claim that s 7 was breached when a homeless person was prevented from erecting daytime shelter in a park was defeated at the BC Court of Appeal. The court found no evidence of a shortage of adequate daytime shelter for homeless persons in Victoria. Thus, the condition for the finding

This outcome is, of course, a victory — on the terms set by the rights claimants themselves. Broader rights to, say, actual housing, or even shelter beds, are not part of this success.

2) *PHS Community Services Society v Canada (AG)*

The *Insite* case concerns North America's first legally sanctioned supervised injection site (SIS).[37] While there are today over seventy-five SISs operating around the world, Vancouver is the only municipality on the continent with a sanctioned SIS.[38] The Vancouver SIS was set up as a research pilot project, is located in Vancouver's Downtown Eastside (DTES), and operates under the name of Insite. Insite was opened on 12 September 2003 by Vancouver Coastal Health, in partnership with the Portland Hotel Society.[39] The facility responds to injection drug-related issues in Vancouver's Downtown Eastside[40] and provides a range of services to injection drug users, including

---

of the breach in *Adams* was not met (*Johnston v Victoria (City)*, 2011 BCCA 400, aff'g 2010 BCSC 1707 [*Johnston v Victoria*]).

37 The Dr Peter AIDS Foundation, an HIV/AIDS health care facility in Vancouver, has for some time allowed its registered nurses to provide supervised injection services without a ministerial exemption. The foundation argues that these supervised injection services are part of the primary health care its nurses provide to clients. The Dr Peter AIDS Foundation is a non-profit registered charity, funded through various government health and housing agencies, with the purpose of assisting and caring for persons who are poor or needy and who suffer from HIV/AIDS.

38 Brandon DL Marshall et al, "Reduction in Overdose Mortality after the Opening of North America's First Medically Supervised Safer Injecting Facility: A Retrospective Population-Based Study" (2011) 377 The Lancet 1429, online: Insite www.communityinsite.ca/injfacility.pdf; Public Health Physicians of Canada, "Support for Supervised Injection Sites (SIS) Proposed Federal Bill C-65 *Respect for Communities Act, 2013* Public Health Physicians of Canada Position Statement" (10 July 2013), online: Public Health Physicians of Canada http://nsscm.ca/Resources/Documents/ECAC%20Docs/PHPC%20SIS%20Position%20Statement_Final.pdf. The Netherlands, for example, opened several sites in the 1970s (Lawrence Campbell, Neil Boyd, & Lori Culbert, *A Thousand Dreams: Vancouver's Downtown Eastside and the Fight for Its Future* (Vancouver: Greystone Books, 2009) at 177). A site in Zurich in 2003 also had a restaurant that employed addicts, a laundromat, public computers, and a medical team to attend to clients. As well, it had an inhalation room for addicts who smoked drugs (*ibid* at 178).

39 The program was supported by the Vancouver Police Department, City of Vancouver, Province of British Columbia, injection drug users, community groups, academic institutions, and others.

40 Insite provides a number of services. Specifically, it is staffed by a combination of clinical and non-clinical staff, including peers, program assistants, RNs, alcohol and

clean needles and a safe and supervised place to inject drugs.[41] It is also associated with Onsite, a detox unit located in the same building, on the floor above Insite. Insite runs on a model of harm reduction: "decreasing the adverse health, social and economic consequences of drug use without requiring abstinence from drug use."[42] The substances injected at Insite are prohibited, have been obtained illegally, and are in the possession of the users before entry into the facility. About 60 percent of the drugs are opioids, two-thirds of which are heroin and one-third of which are morphine or hydromorphone. The remainder, roughly 40 percent of injected drugs, consists of stimulants such as cocaine and methamphetamine.[43]

The legal regime under which Insite operates is both federal and provincial in origin and at its most functional was a good example of federal/provincial cooperative federalism.[44] The safe injection facility was opened as an initial exercise of provincial jurisdiction over health and hospitals.[45] Key institutional, local leadership is provided by Vancouver Coastal Health, the regional health authority funded and empowered under the BC Ministry of Health Services. Portland Hotel Community Services Society (PHS),[46] a local private, non-profit agency, administers the facility. The

---

drug counsellors, and coordinators. It is open eighteen hours a day, seven days a week: 10 a.m. to 4 a.m. Its injection room has twelve booths with a daily capacity of roughly 850 injections. Drugs are not provided and injections are supervised with emergency response to overdoses available. The staff offers immunization and wound care, and injection-related first aid. Referrals to addiction treatment and other health services are available, accompanied by harm-reduction services and access to sterile injection equipment. Insite provides a post-injection space for observation and peer interaction. Vancouver Coastal Health, Brochure, "Saving Lives: Vancouver's Supervised Injection Site" at 2.

41 *Ibid* at 3.

42 Vancouver Coastal Health, "Insite — Supervised Injection Site," online: Supervised Injection http://supervisedinjection.vch.ca.

43 See *Insite* (BCSC), above note 12 at para 72.

44 The Supreme Court of Canada notes this (*Insite* (SCC), above note 12 at para 19). For a discussion of cooperative federalism generally, see Gerald Baier, *Courts and Federalism: Judicial Doctrine in the United States, Australia, and Canada* (Vancouver: UBC Press, 2006) at 146–52.

45 *Constitution Act, 1867* (UK), 30 & 31 Vict, c 3, ss 92(7), (13), and (16), reprinted in RSC 1985, App II, No 5.

46 The Portland Hotel Community Services Society is a non-profit and registered charity whose purpose is to provide housing and support to individuals in Vancouver's Downtown Eastside. The individuals on whom its services are focused are those with the general description of "hard to house, hard to reach or hard to treat" (*Insite* (BCSC), above note 12 at para 4). For more information about this organization, see Raising

City of Vancouver supported the site both politically and financially. However, the facility also engages aspects of federal jurisdiction and law. More specifically, federal jurisdiction over illicit drugs exists under the federal government power to enact criminal laws.[47] Broadly speaking, possession and trafficking in a controlled substance is contrary to federal criminal law: sections 4 and 5 of the federal *Controlled Drugs and Substances Act* criminalize possession and trafficking in controlled substances. (Appendices I–IV of the *CDSA* set out what substances are "controlled," and include such drugs as heroin and cocaine, two drugs commonly in use at Insite.[48]) The federal statutory regime allows for some exceptions to such wide criminalization. Section 56 of the *CDSA* provides for the federal Minister of Health to grant exemptions from application of any provision of the *CDSA*. According to this section, an exemption can be granted if "in the opinion of the Minister, the exemption is necessary for a medical or scientific purpose or is otherwise in the public interest."[49] Importantly, absent such a ministerial granted exemption, users and staff of Insite would be liable to prosecution under the *CDSA*. So, federal government involvement in sanctioning Insite, through the grant of an exemption, is legally necessary.

Insite received an initial three-year ministerial exemption under section 56 of the *CDSA* from the ambits of sections 4 and 5, commencing 12 September 2003.[50] The two-section exemption was extended to 31 December 2007 and then to 30 June 2008. At some point, after the election of the Conservative government under Stephen Harper, extension of the exemption became unlikely. This apparent political unwillingness to further extend

---

the Roof, "Initiatives Profiles: Portland Hotel Society," online: Shared Learnings on Homelessness Project www.sharedlearnings.org.

47 *Constitution Act, 1867*, above note 45, s 91(27).

48 *Controlled Drugs and Substances Act*, SC 1996, c 19, ss 4 & 5, Schedules I–IV [*CDSA*]. The relevant sections state:

> 4. (1) Except as authorized under the regulations, no person shall possess a substance included in Schedule I, II or III . . . .
>
> 5. (1) No person shall traffic in a substance included in Schedule I, II, III or IV or in any substance represented or held out by that person to be such a substance.

49 The full section reads, "The Minister may, on such terms and conditions as the Minister deems necessary, exempt any person or class of persons or any controlled substance or precursor or any class thereof from the application of all or any of the provisions of this Act or the regulations if, in the opinion of the Minister, the exemption is necessary for a medical or scientific purpose or is otherwise in the public interest" (*ibid*, s 56).

50 *Ibid.*

the exemption led a number of supporters of Insite to seek judicial remedy to the threat of illegality under the federal statute.

More specifically, the uncertainty resulted in the initiation of two actions before the British Columbia Supreme Court. One was brought by the PHS and another by individuals representing the Vancouver Area Network of Drug Users (VANDU).[51] Together, these plaintiffs asked for a number of declaratory remedies with the shared goal of ensuring that Insite could continue its activities immune from potential criminalization under the *CDSA*. Most importantly, the court was asked to declare two things. First, it was argued that the criminalization of Insite activities was an unjustified violation of section 7 of the *Charter*, and, second, it was argued that provincial jurisdiction over Insite as an instance of provincial health care provision was constitutionally immunized from being affected by the federal statute. The trial court accepted the section 7 argument suspending the declaration of invalidity for one year but granting Insite, during that period, constitutional immunity from application of the *CDSA*. The trial court rejected the interjurisdictional immunity argument. At the BCCA, two judges found for the claimants in terms of both the section 7 and the interjurisdictional argument, with the interjurisdictional immunity finding taking precedence.[52] This argument references the rather obtuse doctrine of interjurisdictional immunity. One judge was in dissent on both points.

The Supreme Court of Canada (SCC) decision was issued in the form of a unanimous judgment written by the Chief Justice. Ultimately, the judgment reached a conclusion that let Insite continue legally, but the decision was narrow and Insite-specific. The Court considered both the interjurisdictional immunity and the section 7 claims — rejecting the first and significantly altering the focus of the second. The judgment is interesting for its development of doctrine in the area of interjurisdictional immunity, for the section 7 result specific to Insite, and for the relevance of that result for plans other Canadian cities might have for their own supervised

51 The Vancouver Area Network of Drug Users is a non-profit society with the primary purpose of advocating on the behalf of drug users in order to increase the ability of addicts to live healthy lives. For more information, see Vancouver Area Network of Drug Users, "About VANDU," online: VANDU www.vandu.org.

52 It was unclear on the basis of the BCCA judgment which finding took precedence: interjurisdictional immunity or the *Charter* infringement. A later order from the court clarified the situation (Order of the Court, 15 January 2010).

injection sites. It is the section 7 considerations that concern and are the focus of this chapter.[53]

With respect to section 7, the SCC relied on the contextual findings of the trial judge, discussed in the next section, to hold that the rights to life, liberty, and security of the person were infringed by section 4(1) of the *CDSA*, for both drug users and the staff supervising injections at Insite.[54] Having reached this conclusion, the Court then examined whether or not such infringement was, as section 7 requires, "in accordance with the principles of fundamental justice." The Court concluded that the statute, because of section 56 — the exemption clause discussed earlier, was not contrary to any principle of fundamental justice. Section 56 was described as "a safety valve" that "prevents the CDSA from applying where such application would be arbitrary, overbroad or grossly disproportionate in its effects."[55] Thus, concerns about the offence provisions of the statute were met by the availability of the minister's exemption. There was, therefore, the Court asserted, no *Charter* problem with the statute itself.[56]

However, the Court continued on to find a *Charter* issue with the minister's decision to refuse an exemption to Insite. Disputing the (somewhat ingenuous, perhaps) assertion by the Attorney General of Canada that the minister had yet to reject the application for renewal of the exemption, the Court found that an exemption for Insite had been denied and that such a denial was unconstitutional. More specifically, the Court held that the minister's refusal to grant the exemption was "arbitrary and grossly disproportionate in its effects, and hence not in accordance with the principles of fundamental justice."[57] Key to this result was the Court's insistence that the *Charter* applied to the minister's decisions. Then, in an unusual move, the Court ordered the minister to grant the exemption for Insite under section 56 of the *CDSA*.[58] There was, the Court maintained, "nothing to be gained (and much to be risked)" in sending the matter back to the

53 Continuing the trend of recognition but also constraint of the doctrine of interjurisdictional immunity, the Supreme Court of Canada declined to apply it in this case, stating that the area of provincial jurisdiction involved was too "broad and extensive" to be appropriately protected by way of the doctrine (*Insite* (SCC), above note 12 at para 68).

54 Unlike the lower courts, the SCC did not consider s 5(1) — the trafficking provision of the *CDSA* — a constitutional problem (*ibid* at para 95).

55 *Ibid* at para 113.

56 The federal statute is not only *Charter*-proof but also valid, applicable, and paramount should conflict with provincial action continue.

57 *Insite* (SCC), above note 12 at para 127.

58 *Ibid* at para 156.

minister for reconsideration.[59] So the victory goes, by a thin thread, to the rights claimants in this case as well.

C. ONE LAYER OF CONTEXT

Contextualization of the issues at stake and of the circumstances of the groups affected by the government action was instrumental in each case. It is this paper's argument that comprehending the rich and dense circumstances out of which rights claims emerge is a necessary part of effective rights analysis. More precisely, the specific social and economic context of the claimants will shape the harm experienced, as well as structure understandings of State responsibility in relation to that harm.[60] But context must be recognized on a number of levels in order to fully grasp the import of modern rights claims. In this section, I point out one dimension of context, as it was captured by the judgments in *Adams* and *Insite*. The section that follows further complicates this understanding of context by adding spacial and geographic dimensions.

The trial court in *Adams* examined wide ranging evidence elucidating the histories and circumstances of the claimants. Wide ranging evidence considered by the court centred on the homeless population in Victoria, the availability of services for the homeless, the causes of homelessness, and the effects of sleeping outside without shelter. The court considered evidence from homeless individuals themselves, from surveys and studies conducted by non-profit organizations, from government reports, and from a medical practitioner and a wilderness expert.[61] Four sets of foundational factual findings emerged. First, the trial judge found that homelessness is the result of complex social, economic, and personal factors. It is not simply a matter of personal choice:

> While there may be some people for whom urban camping is a lifestyle choice, it is clear that this is not the situation of the majority of the population of Victoria's homeless. Rather, these are people who do not have practicable alternatives.[62]

---

59 *Ibid* at para 150.

60 As I have argued elsewhere, contextually dense legal analysis must be careful not to assign undue importance to the issue of individual choice as the fulcrum for assigning (or not) State responsibility for the harm claimed. See Margot Young, "Social Justice and the *Charter*: Comparison and Choice" (2013) 50:3 Osgoode Hall LJ 669.

61 Catherine Boies Parker, "Update on Section 7: How the Other Half Is Fighting to Stay Warm" (2010) 23:2 Can J Admin L & Prac 165 at 172 [Parker, "Update on Section 7"].

62 *Adams* (BCSC), above note 10 at para 66.

Second, evidence was accepted that "the number of homeless people exceeds the available supply of *shelter beds*."[63] Third, the trial judge accepted medical expertise that

> (d) exposure to the elements without adequate shelter such as a tent tarpaulin or cardboard box is associated with a number of substantial risks to health including the risk of hypothermia, a potentially fatal condition.[64]

And, finally, fourth, it was accepted that

> (e) adequate shelter for those sleeping outside in the West Coast climate requires both ground insulation and appropriate overhead protection in the form of a tent or tent-like shelter.[65]

Cumulatively, these findings allowed the court to find that "compliance with the Bylaws exposes homeless people to a risk of serious harm, including death from hypothermia."[66] These findings and their cumulative import were not disturbed by the Court of Appeal.

Insite, similarly, had key factual findings based on contextual evidence on which, equally, the case turned. Justice Pitfield was attentive to the social context surrounding issues particular to Insite: he began his judgment by noting that such factors are "central" to an understanding of the issues raised.[67] Here, the court relied on "numerous government reports and action plans, individual affidavits regarding the development and operation of Insite, affidavits about the experiences of the individual parties, expert affidavits relating to the nature of addiction and expert evidence relating to the outcomes of Insite."[68] Considerable discussion was taken up by the social and medical context surrounding the circumstances of Insite's creation and its geographic location and focus of service.[69] The court noted the thick

---

63 Specifically, the judge wrote that "(a) there are at present more than 1,000 homeless people living in the City; (b) there are at present 141 permanent shelter beds in the City, expanded to 326 when the Extreme Weather Protocol is in effect; (c) the number of homeless people exceeds the available supply of shelter beds" (*ibid* at para 69).

64 *Ibid.*

65 *Ibid.*

66 *Ibid* at para 142.

67 *Insite* (BCSC), above note 12 at para 13.

68 Parker, "Update on Section 7," above note 61 at 173.

69 Extensive affidavit evidence was put before the courts. The Attorney General of Canada initially objected to a summary trial on affidavits, arguing instead for in-court testimony, based on the complexity of evidence, appearance of material conflict in affidavits, and importance of issues. The court decided to consider the affidavit evidence first, and then, if Canada renewed its objections, at that point the court would

political and policy history around issues of drug use in the DTES,[70] highlighting, first, a series of reports and policies on health issues of injection drug use in the area,[71] second, *The Vancouver Agreement*,[72] and, third, the report *A Framework for Action — A Four Pillars Approach to Drug Problems in Vancouver: Prevention, Treatment, Enforcement and Harm Reduction*.[73] The DTES was described as a place where "[e]xistence is bleak."[74] The discussion of these factors — collectively termed the "Historical and Operating Context" — was lengthy. Conclusions from this evidence established a clear link between injection drug use and multiple health issues, indeed public health emergencies, in the DTES of some variety. As one expert affidavit stated "[the DTES] [was] the perfect storm for a continued public health crisis."[75]

Five findings emerged. First, the government lawyer, John Hunter QC, made a significant concession during oral argument allowing Pitfield J to conclude as a fact that "Addiction is an illness."[76] Second, the judge found

---

consider the application. After eight days of hearings, counsel for Canada withdrew objections to a summary trial, provided that the court not make findings of fact on matters of science on which evidence was in conflict (*Insite* (BCSC), above note 12 at paras 9–12).

70 This section considers, for example, the level of HIV/AIDS in the area, noting that by 1997, 27 percent of injection drug users were infected, an epidemic level of infection and public health emergency (*ibid* at paras 24 and 26).

71 See British Columbia Task Force into Illicit Narcotic Overdose Deaths in British Columbia, *Report of the Task Force into Illicit Narcotic Overdose Deaths in British Columbia* (Victoria: Office of the Chief Coroner, 1994); Vancouver/Richmond Health Board, *Action Plan to Combat HIV/AIDS in the Downtown Eastside* (Vancouver: Vancouver/Richmond Health Board, 1997); Dr John S Miller, Provincial Health Officer, *HIV, Hepatitis, and Injection Drug Use in British Columbia — Pay Now or Pay Later?* (Victoria: Ministry of Health, 1998).

72 *The Vancouver Agreement* originated in March 2000 and involved the provincial and federal governments in an agreement dealing with co-operation and funding for the city's critical needs. This agreement had a focus on the DTES and proposed a string of strategic objectives for that area. *A Framework for Action* followed in April 2001 (Canada, British Columbia, & City of Vancouver, *The Vancouver Agreement* (2000)).

73 This was released in April 2001 and adopted by the city on 15 May 2001 (*Insite* (BCSC), above note 12 at paras 33 and 40).

74 *Ibid* at para 8. There is an important and equally valid story to be told about the DTES — that it is also a community of hope, creativity, optimism, and belonging. This strong sense of solidarity and acceptance is noted, for example, in Susan C Boyd, Donald MacPherson, & Bud Osborne, *Raise Shit!: Social Action Saving Lives* (Halifax: Fernwood Publishing, 2009) at 12. The DTES is a complicated and complex neighbourhood with significantly different tropes and narratives invoked in its description.

75 *Insite* (BCSC), above note 12 at para 28.

76 *Ibid* at para 87.

that communicable diseases such as hepatitis C or HIV/AIDS are caused not by the introduction into the bloodstream by injection of controlled substances such as heroin and cocaine. Rather, use of unsanitary equipment, techniques, and procedures for injection allows transmission of such infections, illnesses, diseases from one individual to another. Third, risks of morbidity and mortality associated with addiction and injection are lessened by injection supervised by qualified health professionals.[77] Fourth, Insite is a health care facility.[78] And, fifth, addiction is the result of a range of "personal, governmental and legal factors."[79] Injection drug addiction is not equatable to recreational drug use, nor is addiction a question of individual choice. Thus, the trial judge accepted a complicated understanding of addiction, one in which addict choice or control is a minor factor only. Health issues were central; individual volition was downplayed. The parallels with the *Adams* decision are obvious.

Certainly, many of the facts found by these courts about homelessness and injection drug use are not controversial. As Catherine Boies Parker (one of the claimants' counsel in the *Adams* case) elaborates about the findings in *Adams*, "while there was dispute about whether certain shelters were fully utilized, there could be no question that the number of homeless greatly exceeded the number of shelter beds."[80] Nor was the expert evidence that significant detrimental health effects attached to sleeping outside without shelter of any great dispute. The *Insite* case similarly invoked broad consensus about a number of key facts: that Insite provided critical and harm reducing health services to injection drug users and that the facility had not increased crime and disorder in its neighborhood.[81] More contested are the understandings of homelessness and addiction — that neither are simply reducible to lifestyle or recreational choices — that the courts accept. In the context of drug addiction, several addiction researchers see the shift to viewing addiction as a health rather than moral or criminal issue as "culturally momentous."[82]

---

77 *Ibid.*

78 *Ibid* at para 136.

79 *Ibid* at para 89.

80 Parker, "Update on Section 7," above note 61 at 175.

81 I maintain this despite the fact that these understandings were all repeatedly challenged by the federal government. However, the governmental assertions had thin credibility and were remarkable for their dismissal and manipulation of scientific evidence.

82 Dan Small, Anita Palepu, & Mark W Tyndall, "The Establishment of North America's First State Sanctioned Supervised Injection Facility: A Case Study in Culture Change" (2006) 17:2 Int'l J Drug Pol'y 73 at 73.

Thus, the analytical results in these cases — the trail of which is adumbrated above — depended upon judicial acceptance of subaltern stories about the activities involved. And such judicial acceptance relied upon the key relevance of context to constitutional claims.[83] Judicial analysis of each challenge employed recognition of a complex and socially evolving set of conceptions about the activities — sleeping rough and shooting up — at issue in the cases. Judicial framing allowed non-mainstream experiences to emerge as authoritative. The judges at the trial level gave a less orthodox narrative about, in one instance, homelessness and, in the other, drug injection. Each alternative narrative comes out of the community's struggle against negative hegemonic understandings of the marginalized groups.

It is worth emphasizing that the contextual understandings accepted by the judges tell stories starkly in contrast to those asserted by governments in each case.[84] The governments defending against the rights claims argued that the activities at centre of each case were the result of claimants' free choice or will. Thus, in *Adams* at the Court of Appeal level, the municipal government argued that the circumstances of the homeless claimants resulted from "lifestyle choice."[85] Therefore, harm that follows from such homelessness was the responsibility of the claimants, not the government.[86] In *Insite*, at the Supreme Court of Canada level, McLachlin CJ distilled Canada's argument as asserting that "from a factual perspective, personal choice, not the law, is the cause of the death and disease Insite prevents."[87] Written argument by the federal government at the trial level of *Insite* referred repeatedly to "unbridled injection of illegal drugs."[88] At the stage of the Court of Appeal in the same case, Canada's factum argued, "[u]nsafe injection or, for that matter, consumption by injection at all, is a choice made by the consumer."[89] The Supreme Court of Canada factum submitted by this Attorney General also described the clients at Insite as "hard-core addicts, the mildly addicted, frequent users or occasional users."[90] A specific picture is conveyed — a sliding scale of necessity for supervised

83 Hendry, "Section 7 and Social Justice," above note 34 at 100.

84 This reference is to the federal attorney general in the *Insite* case and the municipal government in *Adams*.

85 *Adams* (BCCA), above note 10 (Factum of the Appellant).

86 Hendry, "Section 7 and Social Justice," above note 34 at 98.

87 *Insite* (SCC), above note 12 at para 99.

88 *Insite* (BCSC), above note 12 (Memorandum of Argument of the Attorney General of Canada at paras 9 and 76).

89 *Insite* (BCCA), above note 12 (Factum of the Appellants at para 63) [Factum of the Appellants].

90 *Insite* (SCC), above note 12 (Factum of the Appellants at para 90).

injection needs and an implied reduced sense of urgency for users at Insite.[91] The heading of the written argument at the SCC level charges "The deprivation is not the result of the possession law, but, individual choice."[92] These governmental assertions of choice and lifestyle paint the injection drug users at Insite and the homeless needing overhead shelter as authors of their own misfortune and harm. Thus, the Attorney General of Canada critiques the BCCA and BCSC *Insite* decisions as "absolv[ing] drug users of responsibility for the choices they make."[93] However, these arguments were defeated by the factual record laid down at trial in each case.

There is no doubt that attentiveness to this first layer of context thickened judicial assessment of the harms the claimants suffered in *Adams* and *Insite*. Without such consideration and elaboration, it is unlikely that the claimants would have succeeded. That is, once these findings were accepted by the courts in each case, it was a simple step to see that fundamental interests protected under section 7 were at stake.[94] The contextual underpinnings of the trial judges' holdings ensured that the courts' understanding of each of the interests protected under section 7 was given a deeper understanding, one that extends the notions of life, liberty, and security of the person into territory more responsive to the circumstances of the vulnerable individuals in each case. This is simply to say that

> [f]or many persons in other circumstances, the ability to erect overnight shelter in a public park, or to inject dangerous drugs in a certain setting, would not trigger the liberty interest. But once the circumstances of the claimants are understood, it is clear that these are important choices which go to the dignity, autonomy and independence of those living without shelter or under the heavy burden of addiction.[95]

It is also the case that absent this contextual shaping of the experiences and circumstances of the rights claimants and their treatment by the State, the second stage of the claimants' section 7 challenges would also have failed. Section 7 requires a showing that not only had one of the rights the section protects been breached but also that such a breach is contrary to the principles of fundamental justice. Factual findings determine this possibility. Thus, breach by the government of the fundamental principles of

---

91 For elaboration of this point, see Margot Young, "Insite: Site and Sight" (2010–2011) 19 Const Forum Const 87.

92 Factum of the Appellants, above note 89 at para 97 [emphasis omitted].

93 *Ibid.*

94 Parker, "Update on Section 7," above note 61 at 175.

95 *Ibid* at 176.

justice about overbreadth, arbitrariness, and gross disproportionality could not have been made out without the factual findings. So, these cases demonstrate the importance of contextual narrative to claims by marginalized and disadvantaged individuals. As Dianne Pothier has written about other constitutional rights, "the ultimate question is whether the court 'gets' the context of the claimant in order to be able to make a sensible judgment."[96] The stories and experiences of the marginalized do not easily make their way into law and legal judgment.[97] Context is the primary vector for carrying the reality of lives lived at the margin of society into the centre of the judicial arena.

D. ANOTHER LAYER: SPACE AND THE CITY

I have promised to complicate the discussion of context: the *Adams* and *Insite* cases point to a different kind of context to the claiming of rights. These cases involve claims that target allocation of urban property and invoke consideration of how that allocation shapes the social relations of the city. So questions about both the relationship of rights to physical space and the claiming of rights within *urban* space present themselves clearly in *Adams* and *Insite*.

1) Spatialization of Rights

The *Adams* and the *Insite* cases illustrate a more general point about the rights that many specific and traditionally formulated rights exist in and are recognized through spatial, geographic ordering.[98] Resolution of the issues faced by the rights claimants in these cases involves thinking "spatially about questions of citizenship, democracy, politics, and (in)justice."[99]

This is an interesting amplification of the idea of context relative to these cases. Geographic spaces are the sites for articulation and struggle over "identity politics, citizenship, and alternative political agendas."[100] Al-

96 Pothier, "But It's for Your Own Good," above note 13 at 40–56.

97 *Ibid* at 42.

98 Eugene J McCann, "Space, Citizenship, and the Right to the City: A Brief Overview" (2002) 58:2 GeoJournal 77 at 78 [McCann, "Space, Citizenship"]. See, generally, Benjamin Davy, "Centenary Paper: The Poor and the Land: Poverty, Property, Planning" (2009) 80:3 Town Planning Review 227.

99 Mustafa Dikeç, "Police, Politics, and the Right to the City" (2002) 58:2 GeoJournal 91 at 95 [Dikeç, "Police, Politics"].

100 McCann, "Space, Citizenship," above note 98 at 77.

location of space communicates moral and political judgments[101] and thus sets the terms or conditions for the social interactions that occur in and around space. Spatial dynamics, like social dynamics, produce and reproduce injustices.[102]

Interesting parallels stand between how social theorists think about the construction of social differences and how one might understand the shaping of geographies. Melissa Gilbert, for instance, argues that just as race and gender, as categories of identity, must be understood through the lens of non-essentialist epistemology — "we can most usefully understand 'race' and 'gender' as processes whereby people become racialized and gendered"[103] — so too must "space and place" be seen as produced by political, social, and economic processes.[104] Space is constituted through social structures and, in turn, itself constitutes social structures: "places [result] as processes of social relations rather than as bounded enclosures, and [have] multiple meanings and identities."[105] So reads a "social constructivist" approach to space.[106] Thus, to understand the inequality and the hierarchies of power manifest in Canadian society, it is important to think about the pattern of our built structures, the organization of public and private spaces, and the distribution of people among buildings and spaces.[107]

Rights claims thus can entail a claim not only for metaphorical political space but also, often, for physical space. Rights open up space — clearly a kind of metaphorical room for assertion and attentiveness to interests and claims, but many rights demand access to and create, if successful, real space.[108] Rights, in these cases at least, represent a "moment in the production of space — especially material, physical space."[109] Demanding rights can encode a "critique of human geography."[110] The human practices at

101 Blomley, above note 26 at 76.

102 *Ibid* at 93.

103 Melissa R Gilbert, "Identity, Space, and Politics: A Critique of the Poverty Debates" in John Paul Jones, Heidi J Nast, & Susan M Roberts, eds, *Thresholds in Feminist Geography: Difference, Methodology, Representation* (Lanham, MD: Rowman & Littlefield Publishers, 1997) 29 at 30 [Gilbert, "Identity, Space, and Politics"].

104 *Ibid.*

105 *Ibid.*

106 Dikeç, "Police, Politics," above note 99 at 95.

107 Gilbert, "Identity, Space, and Politics," above note 103 at 42.

108 Don Mitchell, *The Right to the City: Social Justice and the Fight for Public Space* (New York: Guilford Press, 2003) at 29.

109 *Ibid* at 28.

110 *Ibid* at 19 and 29, quoting Guy Debord, *The Society of the Spectacle*, trans Donald Nicholson-Smith (New York: Zone Books, 1994) at 126.

issue change what the meaning of the space at issue is and how that space folds into community narratives, associations, and understandings.

2) Urban Spaces

Moreover, the cases are about the larger political contexts of urban justice, of urban space and its uses. The political or social movements out of which each of these cases emerged involve attempts to "reshape the city in a different image,"[111] to rethink the "ideals of urban identity, citizenship and belonging."[112] In this manner, then, both cases, albeit in more specific terms, represent claims to urban citizenship — to inclusion, justice, and respected identity as part of a civic population. Discourses of citizenship, in the words of two feminist theorists, "constitute horizons of possibilities."[113] The issues around citizenship of these two cases pinpoint the very immediate and local scale of the city and its politics, a scale where "state, civil society and individual particularity intersect."[114]

City spaces are the sites for articulation and struggle over "identity politics, citizenship, and alternative political agendas."[115] Thus, "citizenship rights and urban space are produced in relation to each other."[116]

Urban justice studies are of increasing importance. Since 2007, the majority of the world's population lives in urban centres.[117] Eighty-one percent of Canadians live in urban areas.[118] Consequently, the city has emerged as a site for research across a range of scholarly disciplines. It is correspondingly argued that cities occupy a place of recent, resurgent importance. For example, the large or global city locates possibilities of new forms of power and politics at the subnational level, creating new transnationality

111 David Harvey, "The Right to the City" (2008) 53 New Left Review 23 at 33.

112 *Ibid* at 32.

113 Pnina Werbner & Nira Yuval-Davis, "Introduction: Women and the New Discourse of Citizenship" in Nira Yuval-Davis & Pnina Werbner, eds, *Women, Citizenship and Difference* (London: Zed Books, 1999) 1 at 3.

114 *Ibid* at 8.

115 McCann, "Space, Citizenship," above note 98 at 77.

116 *Ibid*. See Eve Darian-Smith, *Laws and Societies in Global Contexts: Contemporary Approaches* (Cambridge: Cambridge University Press 2013) at 78.

117 Margaret Shaw et al, "Introduction" in Carolyn Whitzman et al, eds, *Building Inclusive Cities: Women's Safety and the Right to the City* (New York: Routledge, 2013) 1 at 8 [Shaw et al, "Introduction"].

118 These are areas of 1,000 people and more with a density of 400 people per square kilometre. Statistics Canada, "Population, Urban and Rural, by Province and Territory," online: Statistics Canada www.statcan.gc.ca.

and translocality. Cities are "key geographical sites" for the playing out of neo-liberal policies and programs.[119] The new modes of neo-liberal governance bear directly and powerfully on the shape of large cities. As cities reach for global city status, physical arrangements of public and private space and notions of citizen and citizenship are enlisted in this goal.[120] The city is a physical manifestation of the social relations and norms that reflect and sustain this extension.

Moreover, a focus on cities emphasizes the immediate everyday environment in which citizenship is experienced. Urban citizenship reveals localized sets of social relations and practices core to our daily experiences. Here, for some feminist theorists, the focus is on the "ordinary," a concept that encompasses both social and legal orders, and the standard, routine, or average experience.[121] Urban citizen literature thus looks to the prosaic, not extraordinary, instances and experiences of citizenship: the "humdrum" of daily life containing the unfolding of "acts of citizenship."[122] The approach has been characterized as "bottom-up," signalling that it is this local context, the sites of people's everyday experiences and exchanges, that grounds the possibilities and actualities of law and of politics.[123]

By way of illustration of this point, Leslie Kern, in a study of condominium development in Toronto, sees urban development in the cities of Western democracies as a significant force in the neo-liberal reconstitution of urban citizenship. She argues, more specifically, that the marketing of condominiums to women, with its combination of urban space construction and consumerism, has reconfigured gendered urban citizenship in a restrictive and constrained manner. Women are enticed by the image of consumer agency into patterns of consumption that short-sheet and sideline effective political agency.[124]

Most relevant, perhaps, to this discussion is the additional claim that cities provide concentrated illustrations of inequality and of citizens' responses to injustices as everyday practices of power.[125] The destabilization

---

119 Kern, above note 8 at 7.

120 *Ibid.*

121 Lynn A Staeheli et al, "Dreaming the Ordinary: Daily Life and the Complex Geographies of Citizenship" (2012) 36:5 Progress in Human Geography 628 at 630 [Staeheli et al, "Dreaming the Ordinary"].

122 Engin F Isin & Bryan S Turner, "Investigating Citizenship: An Agenda for Citizenship Studies" (2007) 11:1 Citizenship Studies 5 at 16.

123 Darian-Smith, above note 116 at 167.

124 Kern, above note 8.

125 Saskia Sassen, "The City: Its Return as a Lens for Social Theory" (2010) 1:1 City, Culture and Society 3 [Sassen, "The City"].

of categories and identities of citizens catalyzed by recent changes plays out most pointedly in cities. Cities are "strategic terrain"[126] for the conflicts, contradictions, and openings of global capitalism, new transportation and telecommunication technologies, and the fracturing and multiplying of identity.

It is no surprise then that theorists see the development of new progressive citizenship practices in the spaces of cities. Cities locate institutional innovation and creative individual and group agency.[127] New political actors emerge[128] with fresh public practices. Cities thus are important spaces of inclusion and exclusion, of centrality and marginalization.[129] They are "strategic arena[s] for the development of citizenship because they engage the tumult of citizenship through the concentration of difference and the availability of public space."[130] Thus, how cities contemplate, order, and recognize diversity in their built environments ground and make concrete, and pragmatic, more abstract discussions of the politics of difference.[131]

After all, "cities are part of a larger society . . . their spatial form is inter-related with the economic, social, cultural, and political structures of the society within which they exist."[132] These broader power relations manifest in urban space:[133] "[S]ystems and structures of inequality become entrenched and reproduced in the actually existing world."[134] Saska Sassen argues that the global city has a dynamic that reflects direct interaction with other levels of community — the national, regional, and global. The urban experience casts a uniquely distinct formation of social relations and political structures.[135] Cities provide terrain where new political, economic, cultural, and subjective processes emerge, particularly in light of the transformation and diminishment of the national level.[136]

---

126 *Ibid* at 19.

127 *Ibid.*

128 *Ibid.*

129 Kern, above note 8 at 7.

130 *Ibid* at 11.

131 Lynn A Staeheli, "Introduction: Cities and Citizenship" (2003) 24:2 Urban Geography 97 at 98.

132 Peter Marcuse & Ronald van Kempen, "Introduction" in Peter Marcuse & Ronald van Kempen, eds, *Globalizing Cities: A New Spatial Order?* (Oxford: Blackwell Publishers Ltd, 2000) 1 at 5 [Marcuse & van Kempen, "Introduction"].

133 Peter Marcuse & Ronald van Kempen, "Conclusion: A Changed Spatial Order" in Marcuse & van Kempen, eds, *Globalizing Cities: A New Spatial Order?*, *ibid*, 249 at 273 [Marcuse & van Kempen, "Conclusion"].

134 Mitchell, above note 108 at 30. See also Susan S Fainstein, *The Just City* (Ithaca: Cornell University Press, 2010).

135 Sassen, "The City," above note 125.

136 Saskia Sassen, "The Repositioning of Citizenship: Emergent Subjects and Spaces for Politics" (2002) 46 Berkeley J Sociology 4.

The material shaping of the city, through the built environment and its articulation of public and private spaces, is crucial to political processes and outcome. "Capitalist cities are not only sites for strategies of capital accumulation; they are also areas in which the conflict and contradictions associated with historically and geographically specific accumulation strategies are expressed and fought out."[137] City spaces are where the articulation and struggle over "identity politics, citizenship, and alternative political agendas"[138] are fought out.

The city emerges as an important cite of social analysis. It is, in the words of Peter Marcuse, "the point at which the rubber of the personal hits the ground of the societal, the intersection of everyday life with the socially created systemic world about us."[139] The routinized and intimate personal interactions of local sites forge the substratum of citizenship.[140]

The cases of *Insite* and *Adams* arise from a particular urban form, what some academics have described as "a spatial concentration within cities of a new urban poverty."[141] Polarization of income, wealth, quality of life in cities has increased.[142] The downtown cores in Vancouver and in Victoria are marked by a density of homelessness and social affliction. And, the geography of the two cities — Vancouver and Victoria — is affected by the outcome of each of these cases.[143]

3) The Right to the City

The section 7 rights requested by each set of claimants invoke the larger and evocative politics of what commentators refer to as the "right to the city," the entitlement to form and occupy the city in ways reflective of diverse needs and circumstances. David Harvey in an influential New Left Review article describes this as "the right to change ourselves by changing

---

137 Neil Brenner, Peter Marcuse, & Margit Mayer, "Cities for People, Not for Profit: An Introduction" in Neil Brenner, Peter Marcuse, & Margit Mayer, eds, *Cities for People, Not for Profit: Critical Urban Theory and the Right to the City* (New York: Routledge, 2012) 1 at 1.

138 McCann, "Space, Citizenship," above note 98 at 77.

139 Peter Marcuse, "From Critical Urban Theory to the Right of the City" (2009) 13:2 City 185 at 185.

140 *Ibid.*

141 Marcuse & van Kempen, "Introduction," above note 132 at 3.

142 Shaw et al, "Introduction," above note 117 at 8.

143 By "geography," I mean "the physical pattern of development of a city" (Marcuse & van Kempen, "Conclusion," above note 133 at 266).

the city."[144] Formulation of such a collective right rests on the understanding that it is through the city — the process and outcomes of urbanization — that we "make . . . ourselves."[145] The concept imagines rights to access of essential services, to housing security, to livability, to mobility, and to participation.[146] The city, "its special forms, social practices, and power relationships, is integral to the construction of citizenship and of the public."[147]

French urbanist Henri Lefebvre's essay "The Right to the City"[148] serves as inspiration for this idea of civic struggle. The city is an *oeuvre*, or a work, reflective of practices of inclusion and exclusion, and of legitimized and illegitimated actors. It is a "production" — of spaces and a public.[149] And the notion of the right to the city, in the words of Isin, is "the right to claim presence in the city, to wrest the use of the city from privileged new masters and democratize its spaces."[150] It is, simply, the right not to be marginalized in the city's governance structures and in relation to the development and use of the spaces of the city.[151] It is a claim to a "city of centrality" — where diverse groups are included in core processes and structures, recognized as central to the city's constitution.[152]

This idea of a right to the city runs the risk of meaning everything and thus nothing. The claim has not been sufficiently articulated by theorists, but the notion of the right to the city offers "promise as a way of responding to the problem of urban disenfranchisement."[153] It has potential as a conceptual device for thinking about the importance of the urban environment to the justice on our lives. Indeed, the concept of the "right to the city" has considerable circulation internationally. The *World Charter for the Right to the City* was enacted in 2004 and has been endorsed by a

---

144 Harvey, "The Right to the City," above note 111 at 23.

145 *Ibid.*

146 Shaw et al, "Introduction," above note 117 at 8.

147 Staeheli et al, "Dreaming the Ordinary," above note 121 at 73.

148 "The Right to the City" in Henri Lefebvre, *Writings on Cities*, trans Eleonore Kofman & Elizabeth Lebas (Cambridge, MA: Blackwell, 1996) 147.

149 Staeheli et al, "Dreaming the Ordinary," above note 121 at 75.

150 Engin F Isin, "Introduction: Democracy, Citizenship and the City" in Engin F Isin, ed, *Democracy, Citizenship and the Global City* (London: Routledge, 2000) 1 at 14.

151 McCann, "Space, Citizenship," above note 98 at 78.

152 *Ibid.*

153 Mark Purcell, "Excavating Lefebvre: The Right to the City and Its Urban Politics of the Inhabitant" (2002) 58:2 GeoJournal 99 at 106.

number of cities and countries.[154] In Canada, the City of Montreal's *Charter of Rights and Responsibilities* endorses the underlying notion.[155]

So, attention to space — to urban space — is an important amplification of the idea of context relative to these cases. And, *Adams* and *Insite* thus urge a particular "spatial turn" to understanding rights.[156] This insight links the *Adams* and *Insight* cases to the larger political struggles taking place in their cities and makes sense of why these cases involve access in particular ways to particular spaces within the urban environment. Both cases invoke the larger political context of urban justice, of urban space and its uses.

E. CONCLUSION: SOCIAL JUSTICE AND THE CITY

My discussion of these two cases is essentially a discussion about social justice in the city. The notion of social justice reminds us that the struggle for justice must be configured by social context and necessary reference to social conceptions of citizenship, group membership, and institutional structures. A concern with social justice has particular political content. It is a call for the alleviation of social and political exclusion, and the reduction of inequalities as a matter of justice, not merely charity, and as a matter of State, not individual, responsibility.[157]

What I hope this chapter adds to the legal conversation is that, as geographer Don Mitchell argues, there is an inherently geographical character to the normative notion of social justice.[158] Social justice is not merely a political concept but also a practice that requires a space of representation and struggle. Most Canadians live in cities, and discussions of social justice necessarily, therefore, invoke a focus on the city — its politics and the "crucial importance of public space, action, and connection; and a sense of order that is progressive and democratic rather than repressive and oppressive."[159] Thus, as I have already discussed, we are reminded by these cases that the city is "a terrain of spatially informed politics."[160]

---

154 Shaw et al, "Introduction," above note 117 at 5.

155 *Montréal Charter of Rights and Responsibilities*, online: Ville de Montréal http://ville.montreal.qc.ca.

156 The quoted term is Darian-Smith's. Darian-Smith, above note 116 at 167.

157 Janine Brodie, "Reforming Social Justice in Neoliberal Times" (2007) 1:2 Studies in Social Justice 93 at 97.

158 Mitchell, above note 108.

159 Kern, above note 8 at 12.

160 Dikeç, "Police, Politics," above note 99 at 96.

These cases mark two of the few occasions when the poor, homeless, and marginalized have been able to advance their specific interests in the area of social and economic rights under the *Charter*. The cases involve moral disturbances that render the spatial landscape uncertain, up for grabs.[161] The contested property and its uses instantiates localized agency working to shape the material and symbolic landscapes of the relevant cities.[162] Opposed to these efforts are the politics of neo-liberalism, argued by many to demand the redistribution of the resources of the city to a small political and economic elite.[163] This makes the city a preeminent site for the struggles of the dispossessed. The disbursement of and access to public and private spaces is central. Both groups of claimants in these cases seek access to property for their needs. This is a result of, in different ways, being consigned to playing out private needs — sleeping or injecting — in public spaces. The homeless in *Adams* want private use of public space, and the users in *Insite* need a private space for their private needs but one that has a significant public profile and that is open to the public. In *Adams*, it is public property that is advanced upon; in *Insite*, it is private property that is enlisted.

The results of these two cases stand in complicated relationship to larger struggles for social justice.[164] The *Adams* decision grants some comfort to those left sleeping outside in our parks — the cover of a tarp or a cardboard box is better than nothing on a cold, rainy Victoria night. And, most definitely, keeping Insite open is tremendously crucial to the life opportunities of the injection drug users in Vancouver's Downtown Eastside. Oppos-

---

161 Blomley, above note 26 at 76.

162 *Ibid* at 59.

163 Harvey, "The Right to the City," above note 111 at 38.

164 Apart from the specific points that follow in the text, the following legal developments after each of the cases are important and poignant reminders of the often limited and unpredictable catalytic effects of rights litigation. The *Adams* decision did not convince the municipal government of Vancouver to amend bylaws closely resembling those found unconstitutional in Victoria. A local advocacy organization has subsequently launched a challenge specific to this nearly identical Vancouver legislation. For a discussion of this Vancouver court action, see online: PIVOT www.pivotlegal.org. The *Insite* case has engendered a legislative response by the federal Conservative government. Legislation was introduced into the House of Commons that would dramatically increase the difficulty of obtaining a ministerial exemption from the operation of the *CDSA* for a supervised safe injection site. The legislation may indeed impede further extension of the exemption for the Insite facility ordered by the Supreme Court of Canada. Bill C-65, *An Act to Amend the Controlled Drugs and Substances Act*, 1st Sess, 41st Parl, 60-61-62 Elizabeth II, 2011-2012-2013.

ite results in these cases would have profoundly deepened the harshness of the social and political landscape in Canada evoked in the opening paragraph of this chapter. Indeed, it is shameful that the claimants had to go to court to assert these rights against a government. But these are narrow victories. The right to housing, writ large, is left unattended still. And, the Supreme Court's judgment in *Insite* leaves everything except one specific governmental decision intact. Other safe injection sites face hurdles to legality that remain significantly unaltered.

But these cases mark an important moment in understanding social justice struggles under the *Charter.* With the downsizing, downloading, and downscaling typical of neo-liberalism in full bloom across Canada, we can expect to see prominent rights issues emerging from the streets, lanes, parks, and structures of Canadian cities. It would be unfortunate if this dynamic local struggle, so richly evocative of the lived contexts of injustice and inequality in Canadian society, is stymied at the level of constitutional analysis by too narrow a focus on the abstract character of rights. We need to think about social and economic rights as often deeply located in local politics and as requiring a re-ordering and re-allocation, and thus a re-production, of spaces and civic geography. A socially just Canada calls for no less.

Printed and bound by CPI Group (UK) Ltd, Croydon, CR0 4YY

15/09/2026

14962401-0005